# PURPOSES OF ART

Albert E. Elsen
*Stanford University*

HOLT, RINEHART AND WINSTON, INC.
*New York Chicago San Francisco Atlanta*
*Dallas Montreal Toronto London Sydney*

# PURPOSES OF ART

*third edition*

## An Introduction to the History and Appreciation of Art

To Matthew, Nancy, and Katherine

**Acknowledgments** The bibliography at the end of the book suggests the many historians to whom I am indebted for ideas and information. Not always thus acknowledged but deserving of gratitude are the teachers at Columbia University under whom I studied many years ago, among them Professors Meyer Schapiro, William Bell Dinsmoor, Julius Held, Emerson Swift, Millard Meiss, and Howard Davis. Former colleagues at Indiana University, Henry R. Hope, Roy Sieber, Bertrand Davezac, Diether Thimme, and John Jacobus, were generous in helping me reduce errors of fact and in supplying sources for information in the second edition. Present colleagues at Stanford, Lorenz Eitner, Isabelle Raubitschek, and Kurt Forster, have been of great assistance in bringing me up to date in their respective fields. Creighton Gilbert, of Queens College in New York, was kind enough to correct an error in the section on Masaccio. The constructive criticisms of Professors Alfred Moir and Corlette Walker of the art history faculty at the University of California, Santa Barbara, strongly influenced the second edition. For the third edition, I have been the beneficiary of the critiques of the manuscript prepared by Professors Don Murray at the University of Florida, Gainesville, and John Paoletti of Dartmouth College. Annually the development of *Purposes of Art* has received considerable impetus from the many good art history graduate students with whom I have worked, formerly at Indiana University and more recently at Stanford University, and who have taught from it. Among those from Indiana whose contributions I am able to recall are Peggy Gilfoy, Mazelle Kirkpatrick, Jan and Gerald C. Maddox at the Smithsonian Institution, Ellen and George Bauer at the University of Minnesota, Millard Hearn and Rheinhold Heller, both on the faculty of the University of Pittsburgh, David Rogers, Wilma Stern, now teaching at Pennsylvania State University, Bradley Nickels, associated with the University of Florida at Tampa, Arthur Stevens, on the faculty at Scripps College, and Harry Gaugh of Skidmore College. From my Stanford association go my thanks to Lou Anne Culley, now teaching at Kansas State University, Paula Harper, member of the faculty at the California Institute of Arts, and Kirk Varnedoe, currently Finley Fellow of the National Gallery of Art.

A.E.E.

*Editor* Dan W. Wheeler
*Production editors* Jane Mayo Roos and Rita Gilbert
*Picture editor* Joan Curtis
*Designer* Marlene Rothkin Vine
*Associate designer* Ronald Gilbert
*Proofreader* Susan Horowitz
89 071 9876543

Library of Congress Catalogue Card Number: 77-171524
**College ISBN: 0-03-089708-8**

*Composition* Les Presses Centrales, Lausanne, Switzerland
*Black-and-white printing* Kingsport Press, Tenn.
*Color separations* Les Imprimeries Réunies, Lausanne, Switzerland
*Color printing* Lehigh Press, Pennsauken, N.J.
*Binding* Kingsport Press, Tenn.
First printing of third edition, 1972.

# Preface

"How will we know it's us without our past?"
John Steinbeck, *The Grapes of Wrath*

To the younger generation, *relevance* is a word that implies criticism and challenge to teachers and writers like myself. We are criticized for not giving our students and readers a vision of a better life than the one our technologically oriented society now offers. In addition, we are challenged to transform our subjects and methods so as to make learning more interesting. Often this implies that we should focus our attention more narrowly on the present and the immediate past. As teachers, we are expected to help the young to discover and preserve their identities, to live full rather than "successful" lives, and it is the pursuit of self-realization that has motivated many young people to turn to art and artists. The questions of who we are and how we shall live are the urgent issues raised by the depersonalization and regimentation that unparalleled velocity of change has brought to all aspects of our lives. The value of experiencing art in the light of such questions was summed up by John Steinbeck in *The Grapes of Wrath*, when he movingly wrote about the Oklahoma farm wives who were loading their worldly goods into a small truck in preparation to leave for California. Having discarded many old, personal objects, one of the women lamented, "How can we live without our lives? How will we know it's us without our past?" Although posed during the Great Depression of the 1930s, these questions are valid today. No teacher or writer worth his salt can help others face the present by discarding the past.

The instincts that lead to criticism and challenge are good, and I respect them, but the charge of "relevance" is double-edged. Those who would be educated to a fuller life have an obligation to make themselves open and relevant to culture. To the blacks in America, who are deeply concerned to establish their cultural identity in world history, the past is relevant. But to understand the meaning of African tribal art, they must learn about the societies that produced their artistic heritage. Those of any color or age who scorn Michelangelo, Rembrandt, and Picasso for giving them nothing relevant might also consider what they have brought to the experience of the visions of life expressed in the art of these men. Who can savor a triple play during his only visit to a ballpark or grow ecstatic over a 100-yard kickoff return at his first football game? What parent does not merit his children's disgust if his first experience of their music, as performed by The Who, is to cover his ears? More charitably, that parent is irrelevant to rock music. Unlike sports and popular music, art is marginal to the experience and interests of most Americans today, and it benefits from instruction.

One purpose of this book is to help its readers become more relevant to art by increasing their awareness, understanding, and tolerance. The full enjoyment of art presupposes these conditions of mind. Historically, in terms of the artist's intentions and the interests of his audience, art is not for everyman. This is not a book that tries to bring art to the public by oversimplifying its complexity, ignoring its mysteries, or selecting from older art only what seems topical for today's interests. The concern here has been with making complexity intelligible and with interesting those who enjoy the study of the past for itself. The public that cares should be encouraged to come to art seriously and openly, and it is for such readers that *Purposes of Art* was first written and has now been revised a second time.

*Purposes of Art* is a book that seeks to evade chronarchy, the tyranny of time. At the expense of strict linear chronology, it follows important themes and ideas separately by unabashedly doubling back into history so as to avoid encountering them scattered throughout a text whose structure is dictated by a timetable and a map. It is an approach promising the delight and intellectual satisfaction possible in analogy and juxtaposition. The plan is also an antidote to the art appreciation survey that, like a cookbook or anatomy text, "objectively" dissects works of art into "elements" and "principles," thereby giving a piecemeal exposure to what was intended by the artist to be a unified expression of a complete experience. Each work of art is here treated as an integrated whole and given a historical or topical context. In scope, *Purposes of Art* is a fragmentary history, a mosaic of themes, sometimes arranged within themselves or, where natural, as a group, so as to follow a chronological and geographic evolution. The art history we carry in our heads is in fragments, a condition which no teacher or writer can hope seriously to change, but which, once developed, can make the thematic approach more memorable and useful to the reader. When, for example, we look at a city square, a church, or a still life, we tend to associate and compare each with others of the same genre. It is instinctive to make analogies and comparisons, to telescope time and in a museum enjoy simultaneously an African and modern sculpture, a Baroque or Oriental landscape. A thematic inquiry allows writer and reader to reconsider the art of a period or painter several times instead of just once, a process that is true to our life experience of art. However, in developing the themes, I have used chronology as the main principal of organization not only in the internal composition of chapters but also in the sequential relationships of chapter to chapter. In the third edition, this feature is supplemented by time charts placed at the end of each chapter.

The nature of the title makes it important for this book to have a premise: *Along with providing immeasurable joy to its creators, art's great purposes have been to assist men to come to terms with their environments and to realize self-reproduction and self-liberation.* Art takes its place along with science, for example, in the civilizing of humanity. The various chapters or themes include many environments that overlap each other and influence, as Ernst Gombrich phrased it, "what we bundle together under the name of art...": the religious and spiritual, the political and economic, the natural and man-made, the intellectual and aesthetic. No less than sex, art expresses the timeless drive and Pygmalion dream of man to reproduce himself, to guarantee his presence in nature and to resist oblivion. The "liberation" to which the book's premise refers is from those restrictions on the individual's right to choose and pursue purposes—in short, freedom as defined by Herbert Muller in *Issues of Freedom.* Obviously this implies intellectual as well as political and social freedom, and the victories achieved by artists in the former are older and more significant for art and civilization than the latter two. When it comes to defining art, the historian has as much difficulty as the biologist who must define life. As John Ciardi points out in *How a Poem Means,* or as one might be told by many painters and sculptors asked to explain what art is, the language of experience is not that of classification. When trying to define his subject the art historian recognizes that he is concerned with images in caves and the structure of cathedrals, saltcellars and ceiling paintings, the large and small, the ephemeral and durable in staggering ranges. He must concern himself both with cultures that did not have the word "art" in their language and more recently with many young artists throughout the world who want to redefine it totally. For the last century art has been viewed as something exclusively made by man, but in earlier ages, dating back to the Renaissance, art was also thought to reside in nature where the artist had to discover it. To satisfy readers who insist that an author begin by defining his terms, and until the next revision of *Purposes of Art,* this formulation is offered as functional for most of the works to be discussed: *Art is a skillful and imaginative process of expression that historically has led to the creation of objects capable of producing an aesthetic response.* These "objects," in the broadest sense, may have originally been practical or simply useless, except as things to view with pleasure. In recent years many artists have stressed the *work* of art, the process of making as art, and denied its exclusive residence in or necessity for a physical object, as well as the imperative of appealing to taste.

Historians seek to answer the questions of what, where, when, how, and why. The *why*, or purpose of art, is the issue that I have wanted to develop, in the hope of answering the questions most asked by the public concerned about works of art. In the process, I have made no attempt to give equal space to painting, sculpture, and architecture, or to Eastern and Western art. The final imbalance continues to reflect my ideas about appropriateness for an introductory book of this type as well as my own competence in these areas. In a real sense, art history is the record of how individual historians, influenced by their time and teachers, react to their subject.

The late critic and connoisseur Bernard Berenson reportedly was once asked if he had changed his views about a Renaissance artist expressed in a book written fifty years earlier. Berenson is supposed to have replied (in a paraphrase of Oscar Wilde), "No! One does not tamper with a classic." As in the preface to the second edition of *Purposes of Art*, I should again like to reassure the reader of my continuing modest estimate of the book, which enables me to tamper with its original, unclassical plan. Principal changes have been the enlargement and updating of the chapters, both in text and in illustrations, of which there are now many more and more of them in color. There are also new topics, notably in the chapter entitled "Life and Death of the City Square," which reflects our concern with making modern cities livable. The chapter on the human figure in sculpture has been recast entirely, and the final chapter is now a rather substantial overview of developments in contemporary art, which, with its focus on the artist, provides a balance for Chapter 1, a survey of the training and social condition of the artist in history. Other new features are a glossary of technical terminology, placed along with the bibliography and index at the end of the text, and a system of cross references among illustrations in the book. The former begins with an essay that briefly takes up in discursive fashion certain fundamental considerations of form in the visual arts. The latter is intended to serve better than could an index the interest of readers who may wish to see at the point where, for instance, Matisse has been cited other works by the same artist reproduced in different sections of the book. These references are intended to be conveniences, not commands, and, knowing this, the reader should feel free to pass them over in the event they seem to impede involvement with the local passage.

In 1967, I wrote that "today it appears harder than five years ago to interest students and the general reader in art before this century." Now I would say, "before 1960." This is still due partly to the greater familiarity with modern art, made possible by the mass media and countless exhibitions in museums and galleries throughout the country, and to the work of many young artists that seems to ignore all tradition. While I have made additions to the modern material in the third edition, I have also expanded the passages on older art. The motive for this and other changes is one that I still hope to share with readers. Mary Renault expressed it in *The Bull from the Sea* : "It is the mark of little men that they like what they know." The quality and productive research by colleagues in art history are always reminders of that irritating but wonderful discontent that advances knowledge and makes imperative the rewriting of what has been written.

A.E.E.

*March 1972*
*Stanford, California*

# Contents

# PURPOSES OF ART

# 1

A true and thorough study of art and its historical development necessarily calls for an examination of the artist and his work from many points of view. Beginning with the work itself and taking account of all the available relevant information, the student of art should recognize that an intelligent appreciation of creative activity must proceed from a variety of sources: biographical data, knowledge of the historical situation and social context, philosophical and aesthetic premises of the time, and such particular considerations as working methods, patronage systems, and immediate purposes. The history of art is also a process of research and discovery in the myriad ways that man, in response to his eye, mind, and feelings, has caused his hands to endow the raw, uninformed materials of nature with aesthetic significance by imposing on them an order that, for the artist and his fellowmen, is expressive. It is a history of the symbols that man has devised to give form to his vision of himself in relation to time, place, and eternity. The human hand has been both a symbol and a source of art for millenniums, but despite our familiarity with this most visible and accessible component of the human anatomy, a close examination of a mica hand made in a prehistoric age by an American Indian (Fig. 1) reveals that our modern experience, with its accumulation of cultural richness, does not prepare us to understand all that potentially visual language can communicate. Great and interesting as the challenge of art history may be, the very fascination we feel for this evidence of an ancient culture reinforces the hard truth that in fact we in art history are without information in many areas of our discipline.

The image reproduced in Figure 1 confronts the viewer like a stop sign. This object is a many-sided sign, however, for it directs one to the past, to a distinctive culture and possibly to religious beliefs, to an excellent craft tradition that allowed beautiful work in such unlikely material, and to a creator of considerable artistic intelligence. Although the hand was found in a burial mound in Ohio, experience with similar burial finds in other cultures, such as those in the southeastern United States, does not allow us to say with certainty whether this object was identified with a funerary cult, a god, or simply the deceased, or whether it was a ritual object or talisman, a sign of prestige or an occupational symbol. There is no suggestion that the hand was broken off from a wrist, so that it has a curious and mysterious look of completeness and self-sufficiency. Yet, without a convincing explanation of the actual burial, social, or religious context, can we even be sure of this impression? The hand may have been traced from that of the artist. The fingers, long and tapered, do not testify to hard manual exercise; but is this perhaps a convention of style

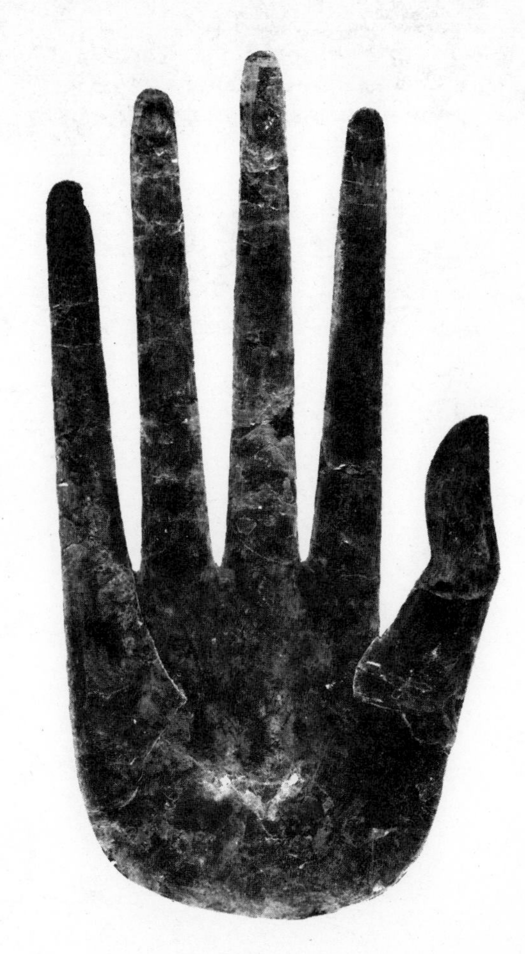

# INTRODUCTION
# The Artist's Profession

rather than a symbol of elevated rank? We cannot be certain whether the hand was intended to be seen from a given direction only or whether it portrays some symbolic gesture. What *is* sure is its existence, and the reminder it provides that such a presentation of the human hand by itself still has the power to move us, to provoke thought and wonder. Whatever the motive behind its creation, we can assume that the hand was important to its maker and his patron, living or deceased.

Of all the professions, the visual arts are most closely identified with the human hand. Certainly, writers and composers also execute their work "by hand," but we do not place the same value on their manuscripts. The most fragmentary sketch by Rembrandt or Michelangelo is self-sufficient and complete; a manuscript, by contrast, is eventually transposed into type by a mechanical process that does nothing to damage its contents. It is the form of an artist's notation or statement that is thus indispensible and immutable.

In the preface to this book, it was mentioned that the purpose of art includes self-reproduction—the artist's wish to perpetuate himself. Some of the oldest wall paintings known give abundant testimony that leaving a visible trace of one's hand had great importance for prehistoric men. Older than the fingerprint, the hand has long been a surrogate for personal identity. On the walls of the northern Spanish caves of Altamira, for example, Stone Age men are presumed to have blown colored pigments through a hollow bone, like a rudimentary spray gun, on and around their hands placed against the wall so that the outlines would thus be traced on the surface (Fig. 2). There is no evidence that the handprints were arranged in any kind of sequence; nor is there any discernible relation to the bison depicted with them. Moreover, they are not always found in conjunction with painted animals, so that one becomes cautious about their identification as the artist's "signature." We must also be guarded in attributing the fre-

*opposite:* 1. *Hand,* from Ross County, Ohio. Hopewell Culture, 300 B.C.–A.D. 500. Mica, $11^{1}/_{5} \times 6''$. Ohio Historical Society, Columbus.

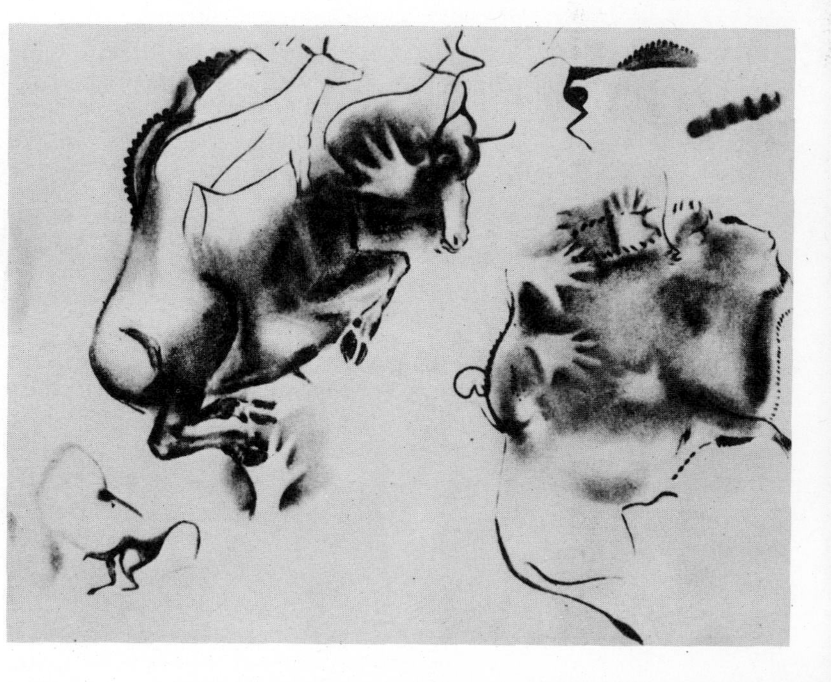

*right:* 2. *Polychrome Bison,* with hands superimposed. Magdalenian period, c. 15,000–9000 B.C. Cave painting. Length of bison c. 36″. Altamira, Spain.

quency of such handprints merely to a childlike delight in discovering how to leave marks of one's presence, for these animal paintings show signs of a certain sophistication.

The most obvious form of self-reproduction by means of sculpture is to have a cast made of one's hand, as was done by Auguste Rodin shortly before his death in 1917. But Rodin placed one of his own sculptures in the resulting cast (Fig. 3), both to identify the hand as that which made art and to permit us to contrast mechanical and artistic reproduction of life. Despite its fidelity to the skin and bone of the artist's hand, the life cast gives us an accumulation of details that by contrast with the modeled torso add up to something lifeless. As a result of more than sixty years of studying art and life, Rodin's hands figuratively carried in them the history of sculpture, which the cast alone does not tell us. His gift was to be able to create in a tiny torso a surface that conveyed what a life cast could not, the animation of life. The mystery of his art was that he knew when to withhold anatomical information and could treat the surface by inspired touches of his fingers so that it seemed responsive to the subject's inner life. This is an example of the language of the experience of the hand defying classification or paraphrase in words. It is also a demonstration of how the artist more meaningfully reproduced himself when interpreting the bodies of *others*. We look at the small torso and say not just, "That is a woman's body," but, "That is a sculpture by Rodin." What is valuable to the historian is that while Rodin may have made the small torso in minutes, this short period of creativity presupposed half a century of thought and work in which he had modeled thousands of other bodies. This same cast and sculpture help us to understand how one of art's purposes has been self-liberation. The headless, armless, legless torso was offered by Rodin to future artists as a last will and testament. Roughly translated, he was saying that a complete work of art need not presuppose the whole human figure intact. Beauty need not depend upon the ancient Greek ideal of relating the part to other parts and to the whole. Beauty and mystery could exist in the fragment. This, Rodin's discovery, became a vital premise or option from which most major modern figure sculptors have worked, a liberation of the artist's imagination and sensibility from the convention or prejudice that, to have finish and perfection, the sculptor must produce a whole figure. Much of the history of art evolves from the establishment of new options, new ways of working by which the artist may then impose his will. The art historian Ernst Gombrich correctly observed that in art it is not a matter of where there is a will there is a way, but, rather, where there is a way there is a will.

That a man's individuality could be expressed through his hand has been known for centuries; even in ancient times, it was customary to refer to a work of art as "coming from the hand of" some artist. To our knowledge, not until the twentieth century did an artist actually affirm his identity in his work by means of his handprint. The American abstract painter Jackson Pollock not only applied his paint-covered hand to the upper right corner of his canvas, but he also repeated the gesture several times—perhaps in view of the absence of any other single readily comparable shape in his entire painting (Fig. 4). Rarely used by Pollock, the handprint is, needless to say, the best possible guarantee against forgery of his abstractions.

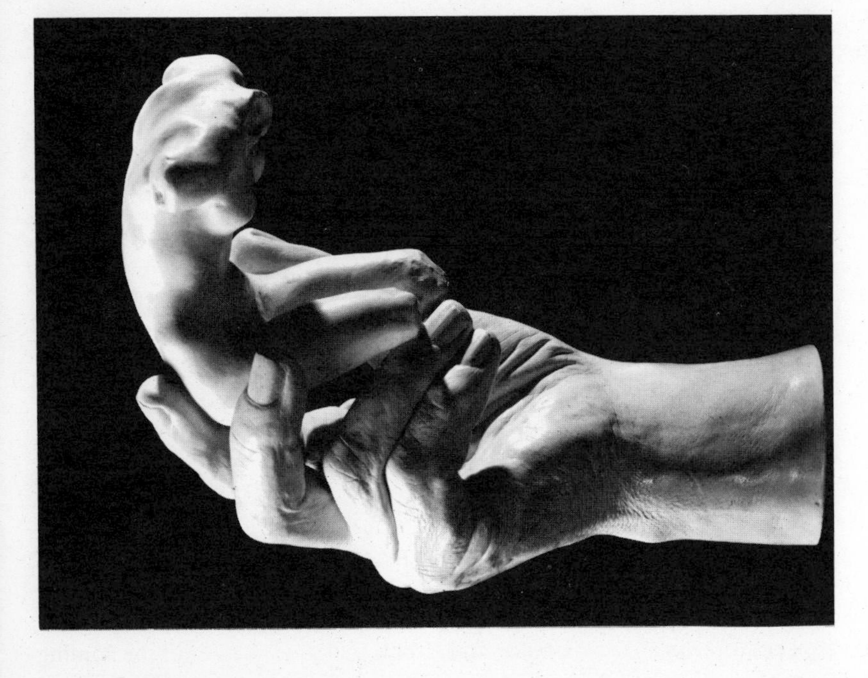

*left:* 3. AUGUSTE RODIN. *The Artist's Hand Holding a Torso*. 1917. Plaster, $6^1/_4 \times 9 \times 3^3/_4$". Philadelphia Museum of Art (given by Jules Mastbaum).

*opposite:* 4. JACKSON POLLOCK. *Number 1*. 1948. Oil on canvas, 5′8″ × 8′8″. Museum of Modern Art, New York (purchase).

Even more than in the instance of the cave artists or Rodin, Pollock's use of his hand directly influences the form of his work, serving both as self-reproduction and self-liberation. By introducing his own handprint, Pollock was winning a new right for the artist to choose and pursue purposes, to intervene meaningfully in the making of art with whatever was at hand—in this case the hand itself.

The absence of evidence beyond the works themselves confounds us when we try to discover why the Indian and Altamira artists made their objects and chose their motifs. Despite the fact that Rodin and Pollock had many friends and made personal statements about their art, modern research methods still cannot disentangle and decide the psychological motives or the purposes that impelled their response to life through the art they created. Every serious artist has, in a sense, been the pupil and rival of artists who came before him, and the twin motives of continuing and surpassing art of the past were certainly not unknown to Rodin or Pollock. More surprisingly, perhaps, present-day studies of Stone Age peoples suggest that these same incentives, though associated with religion, magic, and other purposes, may have obtained from the earliest periods in which art was made.

Despite the similar inclusion of the handprint in both the Paleolithic and the Pollock paintings, there is a difference between them that, in order to be accounted for, involves citing the whole history of Western and, to some extent, Eastern art. Not only the character and location of their paintings, their styles and media, but also the differences in the very relationship of the artists to their societies and the occasion for making their paintings are factors that required thousands of years to evolve. Rather than write in generalities about art in this introduction, the author feels that it may be more helpful for the reader to learn something of the history of the Western artist's profession.

**The Artist in Antiquity** Throughout much of history, the manual effort required for the creation of art was the principal reason for the artist's low social status. Physical labor of any sort was looked down upon by the ruling classes in the Ancient Near East, Greece, and Rome, and it was not until the coming

5. *Egyptian Craftsmen at Work*. c. 1400 B.C. Wall painting. Tomb of the Sculptors Nebamun and Ipuki, Thebes.

of Christianity and the making of religious art by monks —many of whom had been noblemen—that there was a significant change in attitude toward the manual activity required by art. There is circumstantial evidence that some form of art training existed even in prehistoric times, if one is to judge on the basis of cave drawings that appear to have been done by apprentices and then corrected by more skilled hands. There is abundant evidence that art schools existed in Egypt over 5,000 years ago. Many models of sculpture and painting from which students were trained to imitate have survived. Egyptian wall paintings show craftsmen, artists' assistants, and master artists at work on projects for the royal palaces, temples, and tombs (Fig. 5). Since "high" art, as distinguished from village handcrafts, was the prerogative of the pharaohs and priests of Egypt, the best artists were in their service. With some few exceptions, basic formulas and styles of Egyptian art hardened at an early date and persisted for almost three millenniums. Artists were enjoined to repeat the art that already existed, and originality was unheard of and uncalled for as a quality of art. The perpetuation of a relatively constant art was intimately linked with the preservation of the pharaoh's political authority and the power of the priests; the art schools ensured this continuity. While certain Egyptian architects achieved distinction, and even divinity (not being required to use their hands), there

was no such official or social recognition for painters and sculptors.

In Classical Greece, well before the time of Alexander the Great (4th century B.C.), painters and sculptors of distinction were known by name. From scenes on Greek vases we obtain an idea of what the activity in a sculptor's shop was like: assistants are shown working at various tasks amid the tools and products of their craft (Figs. 6, 7). Classical Greek literature before the 4th century B.C., however, tells us nothing about important artists and their training, a fact which suggests that although great visual art was appreciated, its makers were either scorned or considered unworthy of mention in poetry and drama. A 6th-century Greek sculptor named Theodorus of Samos is known to have cast a bronze sculpture of himself holding a file, and the 5th-century sculptor Polyclitus wrote a celebrated "canon" of ideal proportions in sculpture, both of which works are lost. The activity of these men indicates that some artists were interested in recognition and were concerned with passing on their ideas and work to later generations. It is thus from the 5th century B.C. that we have the first record of writing by artists on art. Manual labor in ancient Greece was reserved for slaves, and although painters and sculptors were mostly freemen, their engaging in work with their hands and for monetary reward combined to keep their social status down in pre-Classical and Classical times. From the age of Alexander the Great, there arose in Greek literature the celebration of the godlike attributes of great painters such as Apelles. For centuries after, even into the Renaissance, stories were told of the favors that Alexander bestowed upon his favorite painters, such as that of his giving one of his mistresses to Apelles. During and after Alexander's time, famous artists were known to have dressed well, lived in luxury, and made magnanimous civic gestures: Polygnotus, for instance, painted public walls without recompense. Working for money was a social stigma in Greece and Rome. In the late 4th century B.C., Douris of Samos wrote the first biographical book on artists, composed largely of traditional stories or anecdotes concerning artists who had died long before. Although this book survives only in a fragment, it is important historically for inaugurating the biographical literature on artists. One does not find in Greek literature, however, any appreciation of or commentary on the imaginative or aesthetic aspect of art, simply references to its technical aspects.

Roman writers such as Seneca and Plutarch were repeating Greek prejudices when they commented that works of art might be enjoyed but their makers were to be disdained. What drew the ire of Roman writers upon their artist contemporaries was, more usually, the high prices affixed to their works. Roman emperors, such as Nero, were dilettante painters (none was a sculptor, probably explainable by the physical effort demanded of the sculptor), but even this circumstance did not elevate the painters socially. Despite the great importance of artists for the Romans—their use by generals to record military campaigns, by emperors to establish their authoritative image throughout the Empire and to decorate whole cities, and by the priests to give tangible form to the gods—Roman literature shows no interest in the personalities or life histories of Rome's artists. In consequence of the great interest the Romans had in Classical Greek art of the 5th century B.C., as expressed in their avid collecting and their commissioning of copies, Roman artists were unfavorably compared with their Greek predecessors in the quality of sincerity. It is not surprising that, other than a few painted vases, there has not come down to us from Greece and Rome any significant body of painting or sculpture having artists and their work as the subject matter (Fig. 8). When it was suspected that the great Greek sculptor Phidias had carved his own portrait on the shield of the *Athena Parthenos,* housed in the illustrious temple on the Acropolis, he was publicly criticized for his vanity. This overall absence of self-portraits or other visual evidence of the making of art should not be construed as proof that important ancient artists were but anonymous, or humble workmen; yet the nature of their paid physical work did link them with the craftsmen assigned a low rung on the social ladder despite the flamboyant and zealous efforts of a few great Greek artists. Not until the

*opposite left:* 6. THE FOUNDRY PAINTER. *Bronze Foundry* (detail of an Attic kylix). c. 470 B.C. Pottery, height 4³/₄″. Staatliche Museen, West Berlin.

*opposite right:* 7. Opposite side of the kylix in Fig. 6.

*right:* 8. Tombstone of Philonicus and Demetrius, Greek freedmen of Publius Licinius. Fasces and sculptor's tools at the sides, coining implements above. Early 1st century A.D. Marble, 26³/₄″ high. British Museum, London.

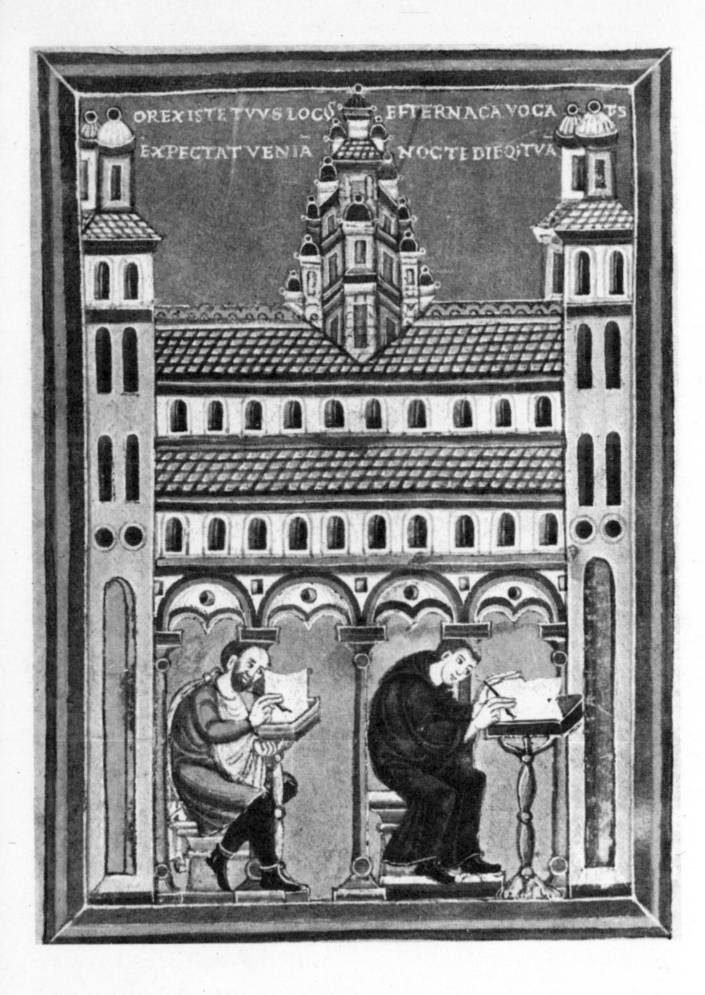

*left* and *right:* 9. *Two Scribes at Work* and *Presentation of the Manuscript to the Emperor,* from *The Book of Pericopes of Henry III.* 1039–40. Manuscript illumination. Staatsbibliothek, Bremen.

15th century, when certain Italian artists began to concern themselves with theoretical knowledge, was art ranked with the liberal arts and thus given greater dignity than mere craft or artisanship.

**The Monastic Artist** From the 4th to the 12th century, Christian monasteries in Western Europe were the great schools and production centers of art. In the early Middle Ages the chief task of the monastic libraries was the preservation and duplication of books, many of which had come down from antiquity. In the monastic writing rooms, where there was often a division of artistic labor, scribes and illuminators reproduced and decorated Christian texts and, to a lesser extent, ancient secular books. As part of the monastic routine, the artistic work of the monks was viewed as the proper service of God and the Church, and some of the social stigma attached to the physical labor involved was removed. From the time of Charlemagne, at the end of the 7th and the beginning of the 8th century, many monasteries had imperial support and undertook important royal commissions for making sumptuous books. An 11th century German manuscript illustrates such officially sponsored monastic activity (Fig. 9). Book adornment was not the only artistic form engaged in by the monasteries, however; sculpture, goldsmithing, enamel work, weaving, and building also enlisted the talents of the monks and lay brethren who were brought into the monasteries because of their special skills. Secular artists and architects so employed were often itinerant, and they formed a mobile labor supply that journeyed about Europe, working in various monasteries on painting, sculpture, or architectural projects. Until the rise of the large cities of Western Europe in the 11th and 12th centuries, monasteries were unrivaled in the training of artists and in their artistic production. Through the centuries many monasteries had accumulated great wealth along with their religious and artistic prestige. By the 11th and 12th centuries, in the large monastic centers much of the actual art was made by laymen, inside and outside the walls, and the monks were often cast in the role of organizers or overseers of secular artistic labor. All through the Middle Ages, the monasteries provided the artistic schooling for those employed in the manors, courts, and gradually in the cities, until by the 12th and 13th centuries, the cities themselves began to rival and then surpass the monasteries in the training of artists and in the production of art.

**Lodge, Guild, and Workshop** Of great importance in the history of art is the transition, during the 12th and 13th centuries, from the making of art by monks in monasteries to secular artists working in cities. During this period the *lodge* form of artist's organization and artisan's cooperative came into being in conjunction with the building and decorating of the great cathedrals. The lodge hierarchy consisted of the supervising master architect, who directed the general artistic program, other master artists, and journeymen masons and carvers. Members were free to come and go, but usually a nucleus of lodge members remained to finish an assignment and then often moved on as a group to a new project. The activities of the lodge were all coordinated by one supervisor, who in turn followed specifications set down by the Church. The organization was thus intended to facilitate and harmonize the various special tasks of these great undertakings.

In the 11th and 12th centuries, the decorative carving and painting were actually executed directly on the building, with artists working from scaffolds. Gradually, in the 12th and 13th centuries, the painters and sculptors quite literally "detached" themselves from the architecture and began to make the sculpture and paintings in workshops located near the site or elsewhere in the town (Fig. 10). This was reflected in and eventually changed the character of the relationship of painting and sculpture to the architecture (with the first two becoming more independent). The craftsmen who worked in the lodge proper, which was usually a building attached to or near the cathedral, were committed to live on the premises as well and were subject to strict regulations regarding their pay and standards of workmanship.

It was not until the 14th and 15th centuries, when a broad middle class first had enough money and the incentive to commission painting and sculpture on its own, that it became economically feasible for an artist to set up his own workshop in a city. With the growing wealth and the increasing demand of the urban populace for both religious and secular art, the lodge organization gave way to the guilds of painters and sculptors. Other professions had, in general, organized into guilds even earlier than the artists. In Italy, one finds artists associated in guilds as early as the 13th century. In northern Europe, the artist guilds became numerous in the 14th and 15th centuries, with some of the earlier ones being formed in Ghent (1339), Tournai (1341), and Bruges (1351).

The purposes of the guilds were to protect members from outside competition and to instill and ensure pride, respectability, skill, and loyalty by providing and enforcing standards for the professional and personal welfare of the members. With the exception of royal commissions, which were outside such regulation, in many cities only guild members were allowed to work at painting and sculpture. The organization of the

10. *Sculptors Carving Statues for Chartres Cathedral,* detail of north apse window, Chartres Cathedral. c. 1225.

guild was hierarchical, consisting of a board of overseers responsible for the observance of rules, the master artists, journeymen (or paid assistants), and apprentices, and each group had its own spokesmen. Regulations for training, for performance, and for promotion to the different grades were set forth in writing. The guild often solicited customers, determined the just price of a finished work, and decided whether or not its quality met required standards. Defective work could be confiscated, and delinquent members fined or expelled. Prices were largely determined on the basis of the cost of materials and the time involved. Artists were expected to be able to do an accepted amount in a given period of time, and they could be paid on the basis of the size of the area painted.

The guilds' emphasis was placed not on artistic theory but on the more matter-of-fact technical considerations, such as the making of tools and the employment of high-quality materials. The guilds also occupied themselves with providing codes of morality for members and ensuring fair labor practices, such as the proper housing of apprentices. In addition, they were responsible for burial insurance, widows' pensions, and the saying of Masses for deceased members. Organized artists also participated effectively in local political affairs and were found in civic posts such as town councilmen or tax-collecting officials. Both in Italy and the Netherlands, guilds were themselves important patrons of art and commissioned paintings and sculpture for their guild halls and chapels. As an attempt by artists to achieve some measure of collective security, the medieval guilds had no counterpart in antiquity.

The guilds were not always confined to painters and sculptors, but often included other professionals and artisans such as saddle makers, pharmacists, and glass blowers. Artists were also called upon to decorate banners, armor, ships, furniture, and other household objects. Such alliance with the crafts did not help to raise the social status of artists as a whole, but there were outstanding individual painters and sculptors who did achieve public recognition and played important roles in their city's history. At the height of the guild system, nonetheless, it was held that the honor of the guild was to be placed above all by its members.

The patron saint of many artists' guilds throughout Europe was St. Luke the Evangelist, who it was believed had been an artist and had actually drawn the Virgin and Christ. A 15th-century panel painting by the Flemish artist Rogier van der Weyden (Pl. 1, p. 25) depicts the Evangelist sketching the Virgin and the Christ child; in the light of its subject, this painting may have been a guild commission. Of particular interest to the history of the artist himself is the fact that there is a strong likelihood that Van der Weyden painted himself as St. Luke. Since the 14th century, artists and their secular patrons have left their own image in religious works of art, whereas formerly a monk or abbot would have at most signed a work as being by his hand or through his commission.

Van der Weyden's painting, and conceivably even his likeness, would have passed guild inspection and approval primarily in these respects: the preparation and quality of the wood of the panel; the priming coat of a plasterlike substance; the quality of the pigments purchased and then ground either by the artist himself or by an apprentice; the clarity and purity of the glazes laid over the paint; the appropriateness and decorum of his symbols and figure types, as well as their setting. From the guild, an artist would learn of the lives of the saints and their symbols—in other words, all the suitable elements for a religious painting. When an artist inherited his profession, as was often the case, the guild served to school him from childhood in many areas directly and indirectly connected with his profession.

**Artistic Genius and Official Patronage** During the Middle Ages a few artists, such as Giotto, enjoyed the status of cultural heroes and were acclaimed for their individuality. Generally, however, medieval artists were thought of as producers, and not until the Renaissance did the image of the artist as creator

11. NANNI DI BANCO. *Sculptor's Workshop,* detail of *The Tabernacle of the Four Saints.* c.1410–14. Marble. Or San Michele, Florence.

*left* and *right:* 12. LORENZO GHIBERTI. *Self-Portraits.* Detail from *The Gates of Paradise,* Baptistery, Florence. c. 1435. Detail from the North Doors, Baptistery, Florence. 1403–24. Gilded bronze.

gain currency. It was during the 15th century in Italy that the most important steps were taken to elevate art from the lower, craft status of the mechanical arts to that of the liberal and theoretical arts. What impeded a general improvement of the artists' social condition in Italy during this century were the age-old considerations of their low birth—with the exception of a very few artists such as Alberti and Leonardo—and their training in a workshop as craftsmen. For until the end of the century, with the advent of the art of Michelangelo, large painting and sculpture commissions were expected to be collaborative efforts (Fig. 11). This does not mean that individual artists failed to gain handsome financial reward and great civic admiration; but when this was the case, it was often because the artist had been able to resist the guild monopoly by undertaking important commissions for the Church or official court circles, enterprises that permitted artists to move more or less freely from town to town and at least temporary exemption from guild membership and regulations. (It was not until 1571 that Italian artists could legitimize their independence from the guild as legally recognized supported individual professionals.)

In 1455, the sculptor Lorenzo Ghiberti published the first artist's autobiography. It appeared after the successful completion of his second pair of bronze doors for the Baptistery of Florence, *The Gates of Paradise*, on which Ghiberti had the temerity to include his own portrait (Fig. 12, *left*), not as an artisan, which he had done on his first set of baptistery doors (Fig. 12, *right*), but as a well-dressed citizen and man of property. This change is described in his autobiography; not only does Ghiberti proudly proclaim all that he has accomplished and that he is an inventive rather than an imitative artist, but he also writes what he feels the education of the new artist of his day should include. His insistence upon the liberal arts, still acquired in the context of a workshop such as he himself operated, is symptomatic of the changing status of the artist. Ghiberti wrote: "The sculptor—and the painter also—should be trained in all these liberal arts: Grammar, Geometry, Philosophy, Medicine, Astronomy, Perspective, History, Anatomy, Theory of Design, Arithmetic." Ghiberti was thus equating the artist with the scholar, and the idea of the artist as a man of learning was taking shape. It was the High Renaissance masters Leonardo, Michelangelo, and Raphael who were most responsible for putting Ghiberti's admonition into practice, and by working independently, they achieved great respect for themselves and new recognition for their profession in the early 16th century. Leonardo established nature, rather than a workshop master, as the true source and guide of artistic inspiration.

*above:* 13. ALBRECHT DÜRER. *Melencolia I.* 1514. Engraving, $9\frac{1}{4} \times 6\frac{5}{8}$". National Gallery of Art, Washington, D.C. (Rosenwald Collection).

*above right:* 14. PIETER BRUEGEL THE ELDER. *The Painter and the Connoisseur.* c. 1565. Brown ink on paper, $9\frac{5}{8} \times 8\frac{1}{2}$". Albertina, Vienna.

Albrecht Dürer's engraving of 1514 entitled *Melencolia I* (Fig. 13) is a spiritual self-portrait that illustrates, in an appropriately esoteric way, the new concept of the artist as a genius, albeit a melancholy one. By means of symbol and allegory, in keeping with the practice and intellectual taste of his time, Dürer shows genius or the creative gift in terms of a superior feminine winged being who is reduced to a state of inaction amid the symbols of the arts and sciences. In Dürer's time, people of melancholy disposition (hence of unpleasant and unstable nature) were considered superior to other men. Born under Saturn, they were though to have the gift of imagination, but to be limited in attainment in such higher fields as metaphysics. Dürer used the inactive, despondent pose and the varied array of objects to indicate that, although inspired by transcendent visions, his own limitations as a human prevented him from realizing his hopes. Having mastered the skills and the geometry required in his art, he was in turn trapped by their very inadequacies. It was in the 16th century that the concept of artistic "genius" achieved widespread acceptance, when important artists such as Dürer, Michelangelo, and Titian gained intellectual recognition and helped substantially to upgrade their profession. It was also from the time of Albrecht Dürer that collectors came to value drawings as finished and significant works of art in themselves, important especially in that they intimately reflect the hand of the artist who made them.

In the annals of the 16th century it is not uncommon to read of the great artists accepted in the ambiance of intellectuals as well as royalty. Pieter Bruegel the Elder, for example, kept company with some of the most learned men in Europe. His drawing of the 1560s (Fig. 14), in which he had the self-confidence and courage to satirize those who purchase art, may have been a spiritual self-portrait in the manner of the Dürer engraving. Bruegel shows an artist intent upon his work, as a bespectacled buyer fumbles for the money to buy the painting. The drawing is a calculated contrast in human types and in vision. The artist frowns at that which clearly pleases the foolish patron. (The Flemish word for spectacles also signified "fool.") The strong, sure hand of the artist emphasizes the awkward gesture of the patron. Both Bruegel and Dürer tell us that the artist's vision is inaccessible to us, and that the making of art involves problems the layman cannot recognize.

The homely dress of Bruegel's artist is deceptive in regard to the way the successful artist of his century and thereafter might be expected to appear in public. From the 16th and 17th centuries innumerable prints and paintings have survived in which artists pay homage to other artists and affirm that in dress and manners they could be gentlemen. Upon the death of the Flemish artist Hans Bol, his friend Hendrik Goltzius did an engraving (Fig. 15) in which the dead man was accorded symbolic funerary honors of an important person. Bol is shown as a well-groomed and handsomely attired gentleman, his effigy surrounded by attributes of his profession as well as those of death.

During the 17th century, Peter Paul Rubens attained not only great artistic fame in northern Europe but also renown as a diplomat in the service of the Spanish king. Amassing great wealth as a consequence of the quality and productivity of his large workshop (run not unlike that of a medieval artist), he acquired a palatial house in Antwerp, filled it with works of art and antiquities, and on their wedding day painted himself and his bride in their beautiful rose garden (Fig. 16). Rubens and his wife are seen dressed in the height of fashion, and their good looks and personal bearing help to create what might well be an aristocratic image.

Artists had served kings since the time of the pharaohs, usually being attached to the court but assigned an inferior status. By the 16th century, however, famous artists who had made their reputations as independent figures were often honored by kings and given titles and special prerogatives. One of the great paintings in the history of art involving the work of the artist at court was done by Diego Velázquez, who in the 17th century held the office of chamberlain to Philip IV, King of Spain. Originally titled *The Royal Family*, the painting reproduced as Figure 17 later came to be called *Las Meninas* because of the young ladies-in-waiting grouped around the Infanta Marguerita, the king's blond daughter. The scene is in a high-ceilinged, sparsely furnished room of the royal palace, with paintings from the King's collection filling the walls. A mirror on the far wall reflects the images of the King and Queen as if they are in the position of a viewer looking at the scene. Velázquez, standing at the left before a tall canvas seen from the back, is attired in court dress and wears at his belt the key of his office. The foreground focus is shared by the Infanta, her attendants, a dwarf, and a dog. Mindful of his station and prerogatives, Velázquez discreetly portrays himself in a position that is logical both in the context of the painting and for the courtly world of rank. The ingenuity and brilliance

*below:* 15. HENDRIK GOLTZIUS. *Portrait of Hans Bol.* c. 1593. Engraving, 10¼ × 7″. Private collection.

*right:* 16. PETER PAUL RUBENS. *Self-Portrait with Isabella Brandt.* 1609–10. Oil on canvas, 5′9½″ × 4′5½″. Alte Pinakothek, Munich.

17. DIEGO VELÁZQUEZ. *The Maids of Honor (Las Meninas)*. 1651. Oil on canvas, 10′5″ × 9′. Prado, Madrid.

of the conception of this painting, as well as its virtuoso execution, help us to understand why such exceptional painters were favored by 17th-century rulers for projecting their official public image and for capturing the more private scenes of court life.

**From Art Clubs to the Academies** Leonardo protested in his writings against the guild method of education, in which children would begin at about twelve years of age as apprentices, learning their craft by cleaning and repairing brushes, grinding pigments, preparing the canvas, and then imitating the drawing and painting of the master until the novice could complete a work from a sketch given to him. During this period, which might last for as long as six years, the apprentice would perform a variety of other, nonartistic services for the master. His journeyman period involved working for other artists in various locations, until he could show by his proficiency that he was ready to join a guild or company in some city, where he then settled down. Leonardo wanted aspiring artists to study science, especially perspective, so that by such theoretical learning, painting as a creative effort might be divorced from mere craft. Michelangelo avoided the rigors and regimentations of the guild system, since he was given the opportunity instead to study ancient works of art under the guidance of an old sculptor in the court of Lorenzo de' Medici. Michelangelo's subsequent refusal to accept pupils or to employ assistants for his important work exemplified a new ideal of individuality.

In the first half of the 16th century, several artists' clubs were formed in Italy. An engraving by Eneas Vico from a drawing by Baccio Bandinelli, a sculptor and rival of Michelangelo, shows a group of artists of various ages gathered in a room, where they have come to draw or watch others draw and to discuss theories and the work being done (Fig. 18). Not an art school in the sense of students executing a problem under the direction of a teacher, this group was rather an informal gathering or apprentices and artists, in order to practice drawing in a room of the Vatican provided for Bandinelli by the Pope.

One of the earliest art academies was founded in Florence in 1561 by the artist Giorgio Vasari, celebrated for his *Lives of the Artists*, which is the foundation of art historical writing. His Accademia del Disegno, which brought together outstanding artists in an organization under the patronage of the Grand Duke of Florence, Cosimo I de' Medici, provided an alternative to the guilds. Vasari's academy planned a more enlightened education of young artists, which was to include lectures on such subjects as geometry. Students were encouraged to learn from studying artists such as Michelangelo by imitating his figures or whole compositions. In reality, however, Vasari's academy did little more than create a new artists' guild, and it made some contribution to elevating the social status of the profession.

*left:* 18. Eneas Vico (after Baccio Bandinelli). *Artist and Apprentices*. c. 1550. Engraving, $12^1/_4 \times 19''$. Private collection.

*above:* 19. Sebastien Leclerc. *Academy of the Fine Arts and Sciences*. 1700. Engraving, $9^1/_2 \times 14^7/_8''$. Private collection.

The most important and influential of the early academies was that called the Accademia di San Luca, founded in Rome in 1593. It received papal encouragement because of concern over the poor quality of art produced for the Church by inadequately trained young artists. Although there seems to have been a substantial emphasis on abstract theory, guided by the artist Federigo Zuccari, a definite educational program was outlined whereby students would be taught to draw from plaster casts of ancient sculpture and from life. Their work was to be corrected by instructors and prizes occasionally awarded. While the academy was not a great success—and, in fact, did not finally rival the guilds or sustain a system of course instruction—its ideas, like those of Leonardo and Vasari, were to influence the future training of artists. At the beginning of the 17th century, small groups of artists in various Italian cities such as Genoa and Bologna often assembled in one of their own studios or a room provided by a patron for purposes of studying together and drawing from a live model. It was from Italy that this idea was exported to northern Europe, at first on a small scale in the Netherlands at the end of the 16th and into the 17th century. Rembrandt, for example, taught his pupils to draw from life; he also urged them as to study older art for its lessons.

The most famous and influential of all art academies was that founded in France in 1648, which under Louis XIV came to be known as the Académie Royale. In the preceding century, the idea of an academy had been developed to allow artists greater freedom from the guilds; but under the King and his prime minister Colbert, the royal academy of painting and sculpture was closely tied to the absolutist centralization of government and culture in France. As a consequence, while the artists or academicians attained greater social security and prestige, they sacrified their independence. The leading French artists were obliged to become members, and a definite schedule of teaching and courses was established—even to a timetable for each week's instruction held in a wing of the Louvre. An elaborate hierarchy of graded membership was established, and assigned duties included attending workship services and

20. MASSÉ. *The Studio of Baron Gros.* 1830. Oil on canvas, 33½ × 39¼″. Musée Marmottan, Paris.

business meetings, selecting and posing the model, providing examples of art to be drawn from, and correcting student work. The chief aim of the Académie Royale was to teach students to draw, model, and paint in the officially approved court style. Drawing from a live model was a right reserved for the royal academy, and its artistic monopoly extended even to the area of printmaking, so that engravings had to carry the notice *cum privilège du roi*. This inscription is found in Sebastien Leclerc's engraving of 1700 (Fig. 19), in which he shows an ideal academy of fine arts and sciences. Colbert had seen that through such officially sponsored academies all forms of culture could be harnessed to the aims of the King. The Leclerc vision is an enactment of the ideals of Leonardo, Alberti, Ghiberti, and other earlier artists who were concerned with joining visual arts with the liberal arts. In the engraving, small groups of teachers and students are disposed throughout a courtyard and arcades of an academically approved style of architecture based upon precepts of the Renaissance and antiquity. In this splendid setting, students are being instructed in natural science, perspective, astronomy, geography, palm reading, heraldry, architecture, painting, drawing from ancient sculpture, measuring, building, mechanics, and theology. The students and instructors are shown in ancient costume, as if Leclerc were reconstructing some mythical academy from antiquity, but very likely he was also showing an academician's distaste for contemporary costume. The art of antiquity set the norm for subjects, postures, figure type, and dress.

In actuality, students at the Académie Royale did listen to lectures on art theory, particularly with regard to perspective, anatomy, proportion, decorum (the proper appearance and conduct of painted figures), drawing, and composition. Canons, or definite rules, of art were established and taught. Often the lectures were based upon analysis of officially approved paintings and sculpture, thereby anticipating the modern teaching of art history. After four years of schooling in the academy and successful passage of examinations, the more promising students were allowed to work in Rome for four years and to send back to France copies of Roman art. When by satisfactorily completing various tests a student finally achieved the rank of academician, he could still choose to ally himself with some company of painters in a town, and he was assured of royal patronage. Art continued in the 17th and 18th centuries to be a hereditary profession, and the sons of academicians were given preferential treatment of various kinds when they entered upon their formal schooling.

In the 18th century the authoritarian rule of the Académie Royale by the king was relaxed. Despite a subsequent decline in power, after 1750 the French academy became the basis for similar academies sponsored by royalty throughout Europe, as a means of bringing art into its service and improving the economy. Craftsmen as well as artists could benefit from the same artistic training, based on the French model of drawing from other drawings, then from casts, and finally from the live model. Business interests saw a greater accessibility of art education as a means of improving their products and stimulating trade. Free-tuition art schools and other schools dedicated only to the crafts emerged in the 18th century. The French royal academy did not undergo serious alteration in its makeup until the time of the Revolution, when its concept of art in the service of the state was challenged. From the time of the academy's founding and in its subsequent history, artists continued, after the fashion of the Middle Ages, to learn much of their profession under master artists, from whom a letter was required as part of the imperatives of academic admission.

As had taken place in 16th-century Italy, English art academies were started from private artists' studios in the 18th century. In contrast to the official auspices of the European royal academies, those in England were private schools, with studies centered upon drawing from the live model. Artists in Holland, though allied to the old guilds, had the greatest independence—and the least financial security—of any European artists. Unlike French academicians who worked for lucrative and often grandiose, but circumscribed, commissions issuing from a narrow patronage base in the court, Dutch painters sold small-scale easel paintings either out of their studios or to dealers who served a broad middle-class clientele. (The first art dealers appeared in the 16th century, but as a profession they became more numerous and international in the 17th century.) Thus, the precedent for—that is, conditions encouraging the rise of—the modern artist who works on an independent basis is to be found in the wider sources of patronage in 17th-century Holland.

The 19th century saw the greatest proliferation and enrollment in art academies throughout Europe; yet this was also the century of their decline in importance. There were many reasons for this change: the large size of many academies, such as the Ecole des Beaux-Arts in Paris (which continues today, as successor to the Académie Royale); the routine and methods of instruction, which were felt to be too impersonal, too old-fashioned, or inimical to the development of young artists with talent and originality. Moreover, the alliance of the academies, be it formal or indirect, with conservative political forces aroused the antipathy of many artists. Academic training and its apparatus for exhibiting and selling works of art did not change with the new ideals of individualism that were sweeping Europe in 19th-century art, nor did it make effective provision for exhibition and sale of works by thousands of painters and sculptors to the newly expanding middle-class market.

**Independence** In a series of 19th-century French paintings, one can see some of the significant changes in the history and status of the artist. The first, by an artist named Massé (Fig. 20), depicts a scene in the private art school of Baron Gros, in which a group of students are shown drawing from a female model posed in the manner of an ancient sculpture or drawing of Venus. On the wall are displayed the palette and a profile portrait in plaster relief of the painter Jacques-Louis David, whose school Gros had taken over when David was forced to flee France for political reasons. During the French Revolution David, though a product of the Académie, had attacked its leadership, drastically curbed its powers, and liberalized the opportunities for artists to exhibit under its auspices. David and Gros, like other important 19th-century artist-teachers, in reality continued the long-established master-pupil relationship but introduced into their studio schools teaching methods they derived from the academies, such as courses in drawing from master drawings, casts, and the live model. Instead of a faculty of several instructors, as found in the academies, the artist himself guided his pupils. The private art school was the source of many important 19th- and early-20th-century painters, such as Manet, Degas, Toulouse-Lautrec, and Matisse.

A possible self-portrait by the French painter Théodore Géricault (Fig. 21) shows the artist alone in his studio, flanked by a plaster model of a figure used for studying anatomy, his palette, and a skull. The inactive, reflective pose of the artist suggests, like Dürer's *Melencolia*, the dilemma of the artist who must work alone, guided by his own genius, achieving freedom but also suffering from indecision, doubt, or unattainable

*right:* 21. THÉODORE GÉRICAULT (?). *Portrait of an Artist in His Studio (Self-Portrait?)*. c. 1810–12. Oil on canvas, 4′9 1/8″ × 3′8 1/8″. Louvre, Paris.

visions. In France as well as Germany, the new Romantic concept of artistic genius and the need for its free expression meant that the artist had to work outside the academic tradition, whereas for Dürer the artist of genius could still work effectively within the guild system.

In 1855, Gustave Courbet painted a large picture entitled *The Studio, A Real Allegory of the Last Seven Years of My Life* (Fig. 22). Because this work was not accepted by the official jury that determined who would show in the great annual exhibitions, or Salons, Courbet borrowed money to present the first one-man exhibit in art history. His painting is not only a manifesto of the type of art he had given up and of how he worked, but it also conveyed an attitude toward the artist's place in society. Unlike Velázquez, Courbet does not show himself at court or even in the home of a patron; representatives of society come to his studio, to seek out the artist and his work. He divides them into two groups—at the left, those who are mercenary or gain from others, often through their suffering, and at the right, those who support the artist, including writers such as the poet Baudelaire, his patron, and other friends. Literally and symbolically, the artist situates himself in the middle of his world; he is the fulcrum, the heart and creative center of modern society. As a young student, he had studied at a provincial branch of the academy, and in the background of the studio can be seen hanging a figure of St. Sebastian, indicative of the art-school milieu and problems. For several years he had worked under the inspiration of literature and from his imagination, in the tradition of older artists. But in this painting he shows himself painting a landscape from memory, with nature, like the nude model standing behind him, serving as his inspiration. In a letter to some prospective students, Courbet voiced the feelings of many artists.

> I cannot teach my art, nor the art of any school, since I deny that art can be taught... art is completely individual, and that talent of each artist is but the result of his own inspiration and his own study of past tradition... [1861].

For many of the important independent 19th-century artists, personal study in the museum, where they freely chose the works they would copy, replaced the academic insistence upon a steadfast focus on the antique. They could not accept the definitions, laws, or regulations of the academy but insisted instead upon personal empirical experience in art. Some older independent artists, such as Delacroix and Ingres, had large groups of formal students; others, such as Corot and Pissarro,

*below:* 22. GUSTAVE COURBET. *The Studio, A Real Allegory of the Last Seven Years of My Life.* 1855. Oil on canvas, 11′9¾″ × 19′6⅝″. Louvre, Paris.

*right:* 23. Pierre-Auguste Renoir. *Monet Painting in His Garden at Argenteuil.* 1873. Oil on canvas, $19^3/_4 \times 42''$. Wadsworth Atheneum, Hartford, Conn.

had quite informal but intimate teaching relationships with younger painters. (Pissarro learned from Corot, and Cézanne from Pissarro, for example.) In France the old guild or master-apprentice instruction in craft had died out with the Revolution and with the dissolution of the Compagnie de St-Luc. Thereafter, artists had to learn craft techniques from each other or by themselves, and Degas spent a lifetime regretting the absence of this older tradition yet constantly experimenting with various media on his own. With the Impressionists, mutual stimulation by the artists in the form of informal café discussions, studio visits, and joint painting outings served to further the artist's education and were, in fact, continuations of practices among artists that go back at least to the time of Baccio Bandinelli and his evening drawing sessions. Renoir's picture of Monet painting in a garden (Fig. 23) is but one record of how serious independent artists worked together and directly from nature, rather than through the intermediary of academic theories and plaster casts.

In the 19th century, especially in France, the art critic and the art dealer did much to fill the breach caused by the separation of the serious artist from the academy and from state patronage. Writers such as Baudelaire and Zola not only commented on exhibitions of academic work but they also criticized or praised the younger and independent artists. The critic's role has continued and increased in the 20th century, as an influence not only on the buying public but on the work of the artists themselves. The great market for paintings that developed with the prosperity of the middle class in 19th-century France, England, Germany, and the United States led to a revival of art dealing in the late 1850s, and through this development artists such as the Impressionists were able to reach the public and eventually support themselves. The emergence of nonacademically trained artists who supported themselves and achieved personal freedom through their art is related to another modern phenomenon, that of young men relinquishing their training or practice in law, medicine, and business professions to convert themselves into artists, with Manet, Degas, Gauguin, and Van Gogh as notable examples.

The art dealer, museum official, and critic have replaced the old guilds in determining the market, quality, and price of a work of art in modern times. The public's recognition that paintings and sculpture by good artists can increase in monetary value and the example of artists such as Van Gogh who were neglected in their own lifetime by the general public have led to speculation and to avid purchasing of the works of both known and unknown artists. Acquisition of art today constitutes a large-scale international business and presents a great lure for both the young artist and the neophyte collector.

It was in the late 18th and early 19th century that writers and artists began to proclaim the sovereignty of the artist over his art, the absence of any obligation to create his work for the public welfare. Down to the time of the French Revolution and David, it was taken for granted that artists would work on commission and serve the Church or the state, a prince or a cardinal, when called upon. In the Renaissance, only those on the craftsmen level produced or reproduced their work for the general public; even the greatest figures such as Michelangelo and Raphael worked solely on commission. In the 17th century only the Neapolitan painter Salvator Rosa declared for artistic independence in Italy. Dutch artists produced paintings in large quantity for unknown or potential buyers, but they geared to the market by specializing in portraits, still lifes, landscapes, genre, or animal pictures. The last great artist who willingly devoted his talents to the service of his government on a large scale was Delacroix, who died in 1863.

The artist's own life experiences have always been one of the principal resources of his art; equally influential are the means and materials available to him for creating form out of concept. Readers who believe they could begin their study of art and its history by having some initial familiarity with the essentials of form in the visual arts and with the language that identifies them may wish to turn first to the glossary, which begins on page 474, and read the opening essay. The artist, his means, and his materials—these resources have even greater significance for artistic production in the modern period. Thus, a coda, prepared as Chapter 23, concludes the book with a survey of the condition of the artist in the 20th century.

# 2

Throughout the world, from the beginnings of civilization to the present, men have made art for many social and religious purposes, but it has always satisfied some need and desire for beauty as well. Magical and symbolic purposes of art have not, however, required beauty for their efficacy. Nonliterate peoples as well as those with rudimentary written languages may not have had specific words for *beauty* and *art,* but both are virtually universal as concepts. Recent research among nonliterate Stone Age peoples in Africa and the South Pacific has shown that, contrary to long-standing Western views, these societies do have a strong appreciation of artistic quality and of the importance of the artist. Even in cultures of which only the art survives, such as pre-Columbian Mexico and Latin America, the practical purposes for which sculpture was made, for example, cannot alone explain the rich variety and sophisticated form of the works. Contemporary views of creativity—which for many has come to mean individuality and originality—make it difficult to understand the making of art in the societies discussed in this chapter. In these cultures the artist was recognized and esteemed as a creator, despite the absence of such a word or of a wide range of style and subject matter in a particular region, social group, and period. In societies strongly committed to tradition, adherence to the conventions of ritual or of previous forms of art was not felt as a restriction on creativity by the artists. While we cannot fully re-create the cultural context that brought these works of art to life, the fact that we are moved by their quality and beauty links us, if only superficially, with the past and with the peoples from whom they came. Thus the timeless purpose of unification is in some ways still served by art.

What distinguishes the art in this chapter from that of our own culture is that it was seriously involved with life and death, closely interwoven with all phases of human existence. Whether magical or symbolic, this art was intended to secure for men well-being in this life and hereafter. In early as well as late phases of many societies, art performed the vital function of assisting men to control their environment, whether human or natural, and to intervene in the course of events. Magical art was and is primitive man's science. Anthropologists and art historians have found in African and Oceanic cultures that this type of art was an agent of control over those things men could not govern fully by themselves—rain, the growth of crops, the fecundity of animal supply, health, childbirth, or what might broadly be termed "success" in life.

In general, art gives us a history of how men have interacted with their environments, and from this we learn that there are no absolutes for beauty and reality—both are man-made and susceptible to change. To approach sympathetically an art derived from religious beliefs or social customs different from one's own involves a willing suspension of disbelief, a setting aside of one's own cultural frame of reference. The initial confrontation of African, Oceanic, Aztec, or Chinese art can be a shock. But, in the words of the late distinguished anthropologist Melville Herskovits, "In art, familiarity breeds appreciation, which is to say that it takes time and experience to perceive, internalize and respond to the aesthetic values of peoples whose culture differs from one's own."

## FERTILITY ART

The known art of the prehistoric period was created between 30,000 and 10,000 B.C. The paintings in the French cave at Lascaux (Pl. 2, p. 26; Fig. 24), for instance, are estimated to be about 15,000 years old. The difficulties in providing exact dates for cave paintings are matched by the problems of interpreting the art itself. Because there are no written records to assist the archaeologist, he must rely to some extent upon cautious study of those primitive tribes of today among whom art has a religious or magical basis. More direct data are supplied by archaeological investigations of the floor strata near the cave paintings, of the location of art within underground chambers, of what the paintings themselves depict, and of whether or not anything had been done to the images as part of tribal rituals. The poor ventilation, absence of light, and dampness of the deepest caves in which art such as that at Lascaux is found are all factors that immediately suggest

# ART AS A MATTER OF LIFE AND DEATH

a prehistoric purpose as sanctuaries devoted not to daily human habitation but to special rites and perhaps to worship.

Even a casual glance at the walls of Lascaux indicates that aesthetic ornamentation was not the primary intent of their artists. Many of the painted animals, such as the bison, deer, horses, and cows that constituted the principal staple of the artist's repertory and of his tribe's food supply, are to be found in both accessible and nearly inaccessible places within the caves. Some locations are remote from the entrance and require arduous climbing, crawling, and squeezing through narrow apertures to obtain uncomfortable glimpses of the paintings and rock engravings. On some of the ceilings of these subterranean grottoes, hundreds of painted and engraved images have been superimposed in the same area—a practice suggesting that there were privileged or sacred spots in which to locate art.

There is general agreement that the purpose of prehistoric art was magical, in that the representation of the animals in some way partook of the reality of the beasts themselves. Further definition of the type of magic or the use of the images remains a matter of controversy among archaeologists. Found in sites other than Lascaux are images that show unmistakable signs of having been defaced by pointed instruments, as if by sympathetic magic the hunters' rituals in the sacred cave were meant to ensure their power over the quarry. Most of the animals, however, are intact and healthy, and all the females are gravid. Pregnant animals may have been depicted to assure the tribe's food supply.

It is impossible to look at these cave paintings without being impressed by their intrinsic aesthetic value and by the skill of the hands that realized them on the rough living rock of the cave walls. They suggest a mature artistic tradition in which the artist gained part of his training from his experience as a hunter, an activity in which he had to rely upon keenness of eye and hand to provide his food. Many of the polychrome paintings at Lascaux reflect a great sensitivity not only to the configuration of the animals but also to their color and modeling. The paint, made from ground minerals and charcoal and bound with gummy

24. Paleolithic cave painting, Lascaux (Dordogne), France, c. 30,000–10,000 B.C.

substances, may have been either scraped on with shredded bone or blown on through a hollow bone. Animals were repainted from time to time, and in certain epochs the prevailing taste was for red or brown. A characteristic of the cave paintings is the predominance of the side view of the animals. Foreshortening was a difficult concept for the artist, and the frontal view would also have meant the visual, and perhaps magical, loss of the main body and hind legs of the animal. It was from the side that the most distinctive features of the animal—so important for magical purposes—were to be seen and rendered.

A wall from Lascaux may at first seem to have been painted with no plan or consistency, but a closer examination brings into focus several series, such as those of the reindeer and horses, which suggest that the artist may have been attempting to show more than one animal in the same area

*right:* 25. *Venus of Willendorf.* Paleolithic, c. 30,000–10,000 B.C. Limestone, height 4³/₈″. Naturhistorisches Museum, Vienna.

*below:* 26. Idol, from the Cyclades Islands. Helladic, c. 2600–1100 B.C. Marble, height 15⁵/₁₆″. City Art Museum, St. Louis.

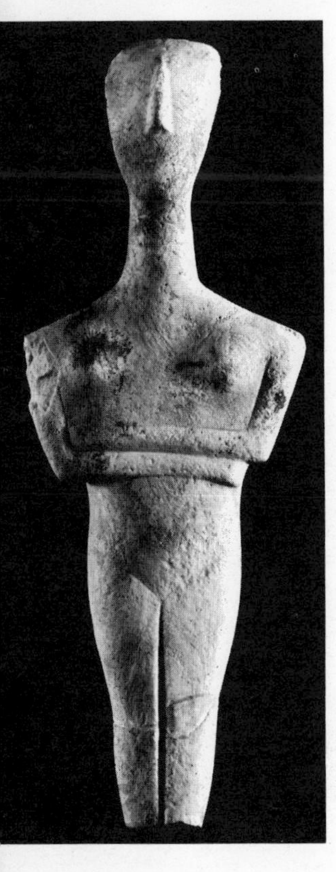

*below:* 27. *Tlazoltéotl,* Aztec goddess of childbirth. c. A.D. 1500. Aplite with garnets, height 8¹/₈″. Dumbarton Oaks, Washington, D.C.

simultaneously. The confrontation of large bulls or the back-to-back arrangement of different animals seemingly painted in the same style and at the same time suggests that prehistoric painting may have known, at least in rudimentary form, devices such as groupings and episodes, even if the latter were emblematic or ritualistic in character. The location of each animal and the overall dispersal of groups depended to some extent upon the surface quality of the wall. Ground lines were never drawn. It is possible that a certain rock formation evoked an animal image in the mind of the artist which he then drew, or that an outcrop or shelf served as a natural base for the figures. Again, it should be stressed, we may only conjecture about the presence of aesthetic intent at Lascaux and other caves.

Stone Age figure sculpture is rare. The famous *Venus of Willendorf* (Fig. 25), an object less than 5 inches in height, is probably one of the oldest sculptures made to promote fertility. Support for this conjecture comes wholly from the suggestive proportions of the feminine figure; the reproductive areas of the body are exaggerated, and the face and the thin arms resting across the breasts are minimized. Judged against anthropological reconstructions of what women may have looked like anywhere from 12,000 to 15,000 years ago, the sculptor's bodily exaggeration may not have been too great, and the natural configuration of the small stone may have aided or suggested the final shaping of the figure. The small scale allows it to be held in the hand; but this is about all that can be said concerning its original use.

The making of fertility images has been a global phenomenon, which should not be surprising in view of the fundamental importance of reproduction to all peoples. In some civilizations lacking written records, we must rely upon the location in which the art object is found to give us some clue to its use. On the Cyclades Islands, north of Crete in the Mediterranean Sea, all that survives of their inhabitants from 2600 to 1100 B.C. are stone tombs, from which archaeologists have obtained marble sculptures varying in height from a few inches to several feet (Fig. 26). The Cyclades finds provide the oldest known life-size nudes. The female figures, usually represented with arms folded across the abdomen, are possibly to be identified with a fertility and mother goddess known throughout the eastern Mediterranean world at this time. As many as a dozen such sculptures were found in a single grave. The placing of a fertility image in a grave is not surprising or uncommon in many parts of the world.

Cycladic figures, usually referred to as *idols,* are uniformly frontal presentations of the body, and their surfaces show sophisticated shaping by scraping and rubbing, probably by hand as well as with tools. Portions of the body which protrude, such as the nose, breasts, and abdomen, were shaped in relief, and a knife blade was used to etch the outlines of other parts of the body. On the basis of certain of the finds,

it is evident that at least some of these white-marble figure sculptures were painted in various colors on both the face and the body, thus supplying certain features omitted by the sculptor in his modeling. The fact that the sculptures cannot stand by themselves probably means that they were laid on their backs like the dead, a pose that makes the folded arms appropriate.

One of the most powerful sculptures of birth, probably made in the great Valley of Mexico about A.D. 1500, served the Aztec religion (Fig. 27). Tlazoltéotl, the goddess of childbirth and "Mother of God," squats in the manner of Aztec Indian women as she brings forth the god of maize. The sculptor of this small green-stone figure has chosen to show the goddess as baring her teeth at the moment the male child emerges, so that the pain or violence of birth is not concealed. The Aztecs were a particularly violent people, whose priests wore the skins of sacrificial victims to perform the rites of this mother goddess. The sculpture may also have signified a calendar change, indicating the birth of a special time period that the emerging male figure perhaps personified.

The concept of an all-powerful creator god or spirit arose long before the Judeo-Christian God was first worshiped. Some religions forbade the making of an image of their most important god; this proscription has been generally true in African cults and, variously, according to Jewish, Moslem, and Christian religious beliefs. One of the most unusual works of art giving form to a supreme deity is also a unique sculpture from its geographical area. Carved sometime in the 18th or 19th century on one of the Austral Islands in the South Pacific was the pale hardwood figure of Tangaroa, a Polynesian sea god (Fig. 28). According to tradition, at the time when the world was in chaos, Tangaroa created gods and men. Although committed to a human figure for his god, the unknown artist made of the head a great flat circular form, which like the smooth expanses of the rest of the body may have evoked associations with the sea. The god is shown giving birth to creatures that seem to rise out of his body through its surface. Just as they take their form from Tangaroa, by their own placement they seem to define his features, being located where the god's eyes, nose, and mouth would be. The sculpture is hollow, and not only are there figures carved on its back, but other small figures are found inside. The male genitals are attributes of the Polynesian supreme god's creative power. What is amazing about this sculpture is that it was made in a geographical area where the figural tradition was not strong. Until some precedent for it is discovered, this work apparently contradicts the generalization in primitive art that the sculptor invariably worked from some prototype.

Along the Atlantic west coast of Africa in French Guinea, the Baga peoples employ a large shoulder mask, known as a *nimba,* as protection for pregnant women (Fig. 29). When the mask is being worn, the body of the wearer is covered by a raffia dress, and the carved headpiece itself rests on the shoulders. Members of a secret society known as the *Simo Society* are entrusted with carrying the mask in ceremonies

*top:* 28. *Tangaroa,* Polynesian god of the ocean. 18th or 19th century. Hollow wood closed at back with lid, height 44$^1/_8$". British Museum, London.

*right:* 29. *Nimba* dance headdress with carrying yoke, from Guinea (Baga, Simo Society). 19th century (?). Wood, height 46$^1/_2$". Museum of Primitive Art, New York.

while the women dance around it. The raised ridge on the head probably relates to the tribal hairdress. The large, protruding nose is a fertility symbol. When not being worn on ceremonial occasions, the *nimba* is placed in a hut at a crossroads and set off by trees, where it serves as protection for the village. It is possible that the *nimba* represents the wife of Simo, the great spirit from whom the cult takes its name. Along with the nose, the swelling profile of the *nimba* in general may also allude to ripeness and fecundity.

As protection for the pregnant mother, to ensure a good birth and a perfect child, the Ashanti peoples of Ghana use a small wooden figure that is constant in type but variable in details (Fig. 30). The lower part of the sculpture is formed like a hand grip, and it was carried as a charm. The face is in the form of a disk, with stylized hair rendered around the edge and on the back, and indications of the eyes and nose are carved in relief. The mouth is marked by a thin incision, and below there may be a nob for the chin. The ringed neck is attached to the back of the head so that the disk of the face is allowed to slant slightly forward. The body, reduced to minimal indications of the breasts and torso, ends just below the navel. Studies of the Ashanti peoples help us to account for the rings of the neck, which are schematizations of the rolls of fat considered desirable among them. The Ashanti also shape the heads of their newborn children artificially to develop broad receding foreheads, thereby enhancing, in their eyes, beauty.

30. *Akua'ba,* Ashanti-style doll. Wood, height 10″. Pepease Village, Kwanu, Ghana.

## THE MASK

Masks and disguises link modern man with his tribal counterpart. Role-playing is universal; all cultures in various ways employ the mask, either the actual object or in the form of facial decoration ranging from tattoos to cosmetics. Masks thus give the face an importance, dignity, and status, and they are an important example of nature transformed into culture. But masks also gratify the dualistic nature of man, enabling him to dramatize his repressions and his play instinct. Halloween parties and other masquerades remind us of the effects of wearing a face mask: It permits us to assume a new identity emanating from the character of the mask itself, and for some wearers, it is the occasion for casting off inhibitions and social responsibility.

These possibilities of having fun, of becoming another being and playing a new role, are in some ways related to the various purposes served by the mask throughout the world in Stone Age cultures. Among tribal societies in Africa, the Northwest Coast Indians, and peoples of the South Pacific, the mask has a tradition as the symbol or locus of supernatural forces. The acts performed by the mask or directives attributed to it carry the authority of a particular spirit or power. That a face mask alone can embody supernatural power, without presenting the entire figure, is explainable because of the widespread belief that the head is the prime residence of such power. When movement is necessary for the mask to fulfill its proper function, it is worn by a dancer as part of a ritual. Therefore, to see masks hanging on museum walls is a distortion of their original purpose. In most societies important masks, when not in use, were enshrined as cult objects, kept out of sight, or often destroyed. Although we tend to think of the variety possible in human features as depending upon individual differences evident in living persons, primitive masks that are not likenesses of the living manifest a comparable rich variety. In addition, they demonstrate the strong emotion and imagination called upon to make these supernatural forces tangible and impressive in the eyes of their tribes.

More so than in our society of today, masks have had long and notable histories of fulfilling serious and varied functions for the living. Besides dealing specifically with religious life, they have been regarded as important agents for good by helping to guarantee social order, fertility of crops and herds, health, victory in battle, and desirable solutions to various other crises in life; they have helped as well to maintain a general equilibrium among the living and the dead and the spirit world. Despite the great number of masks in museums and private collections and the appreciable study and writing done on their purposes, there is still a great deal that we do not know about their important and complex usages. Research in the field, among groups where masks are still being made and put to genuine ritual use, depends on the memories and interpretations of tribe members and on how much information they do not have to keep.

In *Homo Ludens: A Study of the Play Element in Culture*, Johan Huizinga observed that the mask is the result of an

Plate 1. ROGIER VAN DER WEYDEN. *St. Luke Drawing the Virgin.* c. 1435. Oil on panel, $4'6^{1}/_{4}'' \times 3'7^{7}/_{8}''$. Museum of Fine Arts, Boston (gift of Mr. and Mrs. Henry Lee Higginson).

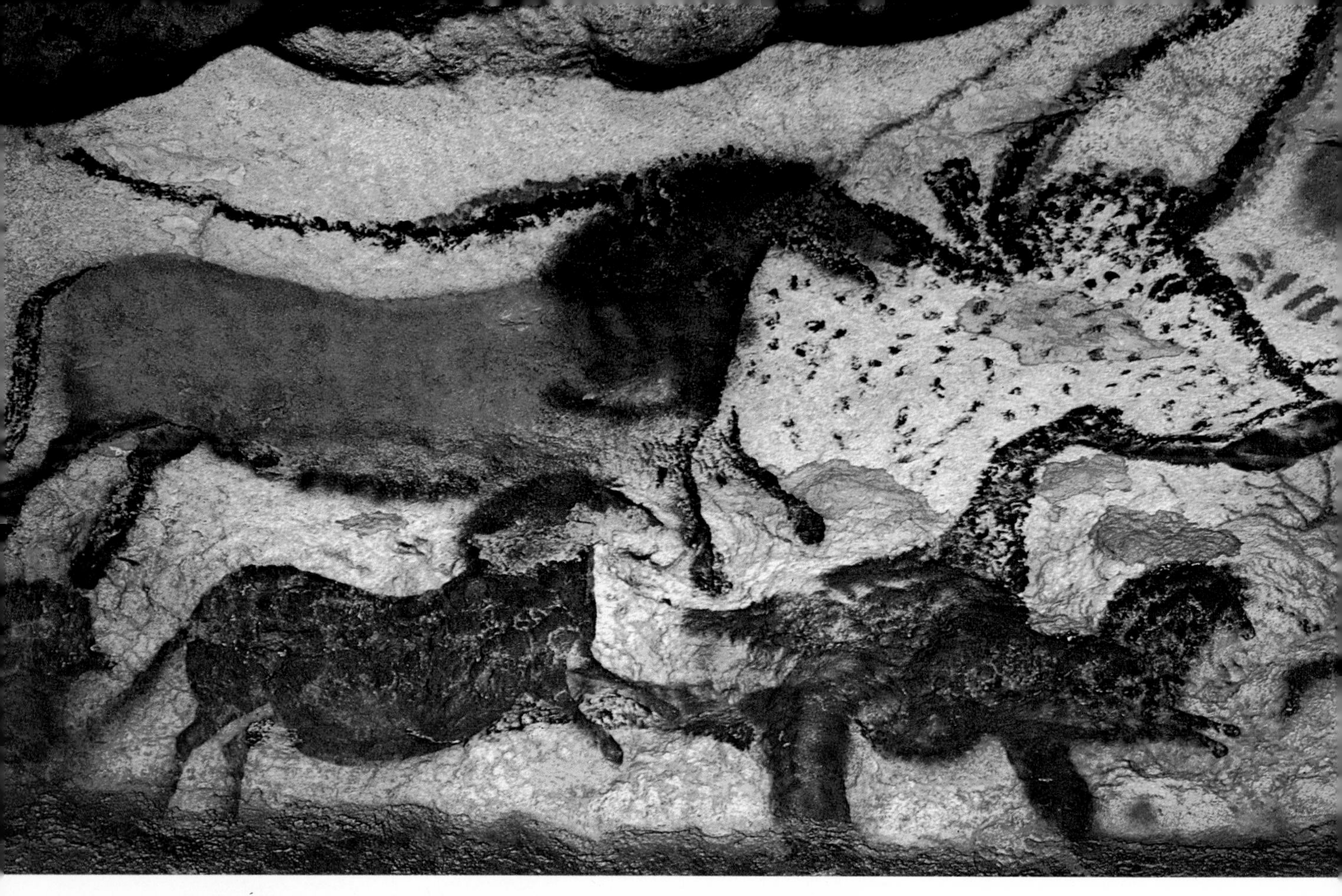

*above:* Plate 2. Cave paintings, Lascaux (Dordogne), France. c. 15,000–9000 B.C. (See p. 20.)

*left:* Plate 3. Movable mask, from Cape Mudge, British Columbia. 1850–75. Painted wood, height 21 1/2″. Museum of the American Indian (Heye Foundation), New York. (See p. 29.)

31. Owl mask, from Baining, New Britain. Collected 1922. Cane and bark cloth, height $31^{1}/_{4}$″. Museum für Völkerkunde, Basel.

imagination which is poetic and playful and that it is crucial to the community's interpreting, grasping, and representing the purposes of rituals, which themselves are indispensable for the well-being of any community, for its social development and its understanding of the world. Tribal man's rites are closely associated with serious play, and they involve a unity of belief and disbelief, being in "sacred earnest" but also in the spirit of make-believe or fun.

Tribal peoples know full well that masks are paid for, made of familiar materials, carved, and worn by members of their own groups, but this knowledge does not weaken the drama or potency of the masks. Masks usually are made in secret and the rituals attended with respect. Although generally considered to have cast off his previous identity, the mask wearer does not have license to shed social responsibility, and dancers or other performers in the rites are trained to observe conventions governing their movements and general mien. To wear a mask is to assume a different and more important social responsibility, and the mask wearer shares magically in the power of the spirit or force he represents. Masks still play a vital religious and social role in many parts of the world, but any further generalization about masks would be difficult to make. The selection offered here is a meager sampling of the manifold purposes masks serve and of the infinite ways in which they have been made and decorated.

Many types of masks have a protective function. On New Britain, off the coast of New Guinea, an owl mask made of cane and bark cloth is used to give supernatural protection to children (Fig. 31). The eyes alone relate to our experience of an owl, and only by learning the formal (visual) language of this tribal society, as we would master its verbal language, could we come to recognize all that is meaningful in such art. Because the owl of the natural world has been assimilated into, or transmuted by, certain artistic conventions compounded of symbols and decoration, the children of the tribe must be *taught* that this is an owl. Our acquaintance with any type of head makes the radically asymmetrical structure of the face most disturbing. Too, we are not accustomed to art in which a minimal resemblance to physical reality is sufficient to conjure effectively the presence of an animal or a human.

The "Fire Spitter" helmet masks made by the Senufo tribes of the Ivory Coast have several animal derivations, none of which relates to their actual purpose. The long-horned, open-jawed head with tusks (Fig. 32) comes from the water buffalo, the wart hog, the antelope, and the crocodile. Hornbill birds symbolizing fertility perch between the horns. The open jaws generously fitted with teeth create a ferocious apparition, for the mask is meant to inspire fear. The "Fire Spitter" performs the function of driving off or destroying "soul-eating" spirits. Its sacred character is enforced by the scrupulous treatment given it by the secret-society member who wears it and who is hidden behind a sacklike garment (Fig. 33). Brought forth at night, the mask is worn horizon-

*above:* 32. Senufo "Fire Spitter" helmet mask, from the Ivory Coast. 19th–20th centuries. Wood, length $35^{5}/_{8}$″. Museum of Primitive Art, New York.

*right:* 33. Man wearing double helmet mask with costume, from central Senufo region (Nebunyonkaa Village), Ivory Coast. 1930–39(?). Ethnographic Museum, Antwerp.

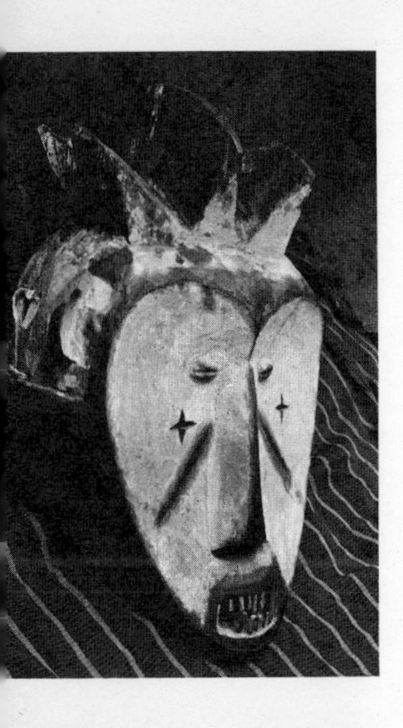

*above left:* 34. Egu Orumamu mask, from Nigeria (eastern Igala Tribe). Carved c. 1940. Wood, height 23″. Museum Jos, Nigeria.

*above:* 35. Bambara ancestor figure, from Mali. 19th–20th centuries. Wood, height $4^{15}/_{8}$″. Museum of Primitive Art, New York.

*left:* 36. Ibibio mask (worn by the Ekpo secret society), from Nigeria. Wood, height 12″. Linden-Museum, Stuttgart.

tally on top of the head so that the jaws and horns are parallel to the ground. Sacrifices are made to it by the villagers to ensure its good will. The mask wearer calls out incantations and also blows sparks through the jaws of the mask, or brandishes them about his person. Believed to have superhuman powers, because he has fused his being with the demon of the mask, the mask wearer can also walk or sit on burning coals. As in many other areas of Africa, the "Fire Spitter" is used for varied functions, such as initiation rites for secret societies, funerals, and agricultural ceremonies.

The widespread conversion of African tribes to the religions and legal systems of the modern Western world has created serious problems, some of which arise from loss of the power previously invested in sculpture. This transition can be understood more easily from an example of a mask that had played a dominant role in the civil procedures of a Nigerian tribe presently undergoing Westernization. On one of many field trips to Nigeria, the art historian Roy Sieber studied the purposes of Egu Orumamu, or the "chief of masks," among the eastern Igala peoples (Fig. 34). In his studies showing its extensive use as an agent of social control, he wrote:

> Its power apparently is derived from the ancestors and it oversees the general well-being of the village. Certain of its appearances, for instance, are related to agriculture. More pertinent . . . is its judicial role in cases of murder and petty civil offenses. . . . Orumamu (hidden in a hut) arbitrated complaints and arguments of the women . . . usually of a financial nature. . . . Orumamu could send his minions to punish children who had gotten in trouble or to supervise the water supply in times of shortage.

The Orumamu mask illustrated is not one of the more beautiful African masks by our standards—or even among others of its tribe—but questions of beauty were secondary to the guardian functions described above.

Some of the most striking African animal carvings used as headdresses in rites for ensuring fertility of the soil, ample rain, and good crops are those made in the western Sudan by Bambara people (Fig. 35). Prior to the rainy season, men belonging to agricultural societies prepare the carved antelope headpieces and then begin their rites in the dried fields. Their faces are covered with red masks, their bodies with fiber costumes. Upon their return to the villages, offerings and dances are conducted around the privileged performers, who imitate the movements of antelopes. The carvings represent both the male and the female antelope and are distinguished by curved horns for the former and straight horns for the latter. Intended to be seen from all sides and from some distance, the masks are given horns that extend extravagantly into space, and the mane is carved in an elaborate openwork pattern. Both the combative nature and the elegant grace of the animal are preserved. What seems an arbitrary schematization of the antelope into a succession of repeated rhythmic curves results from modeling sculpture more after other sculpture than after nature.

In many areas of Africa, there are secret societies that, within themselves, comprise miniature versions of tribal life itself. These societies perform various functions, which range from maintaining the social order to protecting the tribe against unfriendly demons. Both are roles of the Ekpo secret society of the Ibibio in southwestern Nigeria (Fig. 36). In one of the finest Ekpo masks the face is reconstructed in a menacing form, as a reminder to nonmembers of the hostile character of the spirits with which the society is concerned. If this head is looked at as sculpture, we can see how the artist conceived the various shapes not only as eyes, nose, and mouth but as variations and echoes of one another's form, or of a basic form. Their configuration—protrusion and recession—and vertical alignment guided their proportion and carving and produced an emphatic rhythmic sequence within the compactness of the head. The menacing quality of the mask comes in part from its battery of sharp teeth, which are visible because the jaw portion is hinged to permit movement during rituals.

The most spectacular examples of masks with moving parts were made by the Northwest Coast Indians of North America. The Kwakiutl and other tribes particularly delighted in fashioning masks within masks, which during ceremonial performances and dances were opened by strings pulled by their wearers, thus creating a type of dramatic revelation (Pl. 3, p. 26). In some masks three or four such revelations were possible, ranging from various animal or bird heads to human representations. These masks were beautifully carved and painted, and exceptional craft went into their hinging. The designs were part of a clan and tribal repertory, with motifs often derived from animals and birds. The colors are strong and the color areas cleanly shaped, changing with each successive revelation within a single movable mask. The Kwakiutl mask illustrated belonged to a *shaman*, the equivalent of a witch doctor, who was believed to possess supernatural powers to heal or to perform feats of magic. By means of the mask he impersonated a demon or spirit. The nonnaturalistic color and drastic reshaping of the facial features were calculated to evoke these supernatural forces. Art for these Northwest Coast tribes was a conscious form of competitive social ostentation, an attitude that accounts for their elaborate design and visual brilliance.

The mask worn by the Northwest Coast Indian differs from the African tribal mask in its relationship to the wearer. When the African actor ceases his role of impersonation, he relinquishes his relationship to the entity of the mask. In societies such as the Kwakiutl, the mask affirms the ancestry of the wearer; it proclaims his inherited rights and privileges and establishes his status in the tribe's social hierarchy. By contrast, African masks have no connection with the tribe's castes or classes. There are thus varying relationships between the social order of the living tribe and the supernatural world. In societies that have a tradition of the multiple mask, the wearer's status is directly tied to the myths, pedigree, and rituals he enacts. He acquires from the god, according to the French anthropologist Claude Lévi-Strauss, "by a continuous process of creation at each moment of social life, his titles, rank, his position in the status hierarchy."

## ART FOR THE DEAD

**Egyptian Tomb Paintings** Created thousands of years after the execution of the cave paintings at Lascaux, the tomb paintings of ancient Egypt present a very different kind of wall painting—one that, despite its situation, was nevertheless employed for purposes of sustaining life. The function of Egyptian tomb painting and wall reliefs was to serve the wants of the deceased in the hereafter, to prevent his second death from starvation or thirst and to ensure his comfort and link him with the living (Figs. 37–39). In a wall painting from Thebes (Fig. 39), we see a well-run estate being

*above:* 37. Wall painting, from Tomb 261, Thebes. c. 1500 B.C. $29\frac{1}{2} \times 41\frac{1}{4}$".

*right:* 38. *A Priest at Memphis Seated before a Table of Offerings*, from Tomb of Ra-hetep at Meydum. 4th Dynasty, c. 2600 B.C. Wall relief. British Museum, London.

*left:* 39. Tomb of Nakht (view of south walls), Thebes. c. 1422–1411 B.C. Wall paintings.

surveyed, or else the crops measured or harvested, and food production being recorded; at the far left are the standing figures of the deceased and his wife, for whose benefit these activities were undertaken. The deceased is always inactive, a passive observer of typical earthly pursuits. Depiction of unique events is rare in Egyptian art. In all the cultures mentioned in this chapter, death meant a change of status, not oblivion. About 5,000 years ago, the Egyptians began to bury painting and sculpture or models of objects, animate beings, and crops, instead of interring servants and animals with the deceased and taking badly needed food from the living for his wants. This was a tremendous step in civilization's advance. Through their murals, we gain an insight into the differences between the tribal food-hunting societies of the cave era and the hierarchical food-gathering cultures of the Nile Valley.

Setting aside its illuminating subject matter for the moment, we see that the formal organization of the Egyptian wall into clear, accurately divided zones, terminating at the sides, top, and bottom of the wall in strong borders, is in itself a sign of a highly organized society. Moreover, ground lines support the figures. The surface on which the painting has been done was artificially made and carefully prepared. The artists worked faithfully from preexisting art and codes to ensure the efficacy of their work. As in the cave paintings, the human figures, objects, and animals are disposed in such a way as to preserve their most recognizable and useful features. The human figures, in both paintings and reliefs, combine a frontal eye in a profile head, a frontal view of the shoulders, a three-quarter view of the midriff, and a profile view of the legs. Except for some occasional overlapping, Egyptian art furthers no illusion of depth. To render a larger scene that would normally be perceived as existing in depth, the Egyptians and most ancient artists used vertical zones, so that no action, figure, or object would be diminished through overlap or because of its greater distance from the viewer. Egyptian funerary art was not intended for the critical eye of the living, however, but solely for the welfare of the dead in the afterlife.

**Chinese Ritual Bronzes** In ancient China, if one is to judge by the art that has survived, greater attention may have been paid to the dead than to the living. As in Africa, Egypt, and Rome, veneration of departed ancestors was considered important for the successful conduct of life. Sacred rituals using special objects were performed to ensure rain and good harvests. Ornamented bronze ceremonial vessels (Pl. 4, p. 43) dating from the Shang period in the second millennium B.C. held offerings of food and drink for ancestral spirits and were used in sacrifices performed by the king and aristocracy. These vessels, as ritual accessories the equivalent of communion plates, rank with the most beautiful and finished bronze castings in the history of civilization. When used to propitiate an ancestor, the vessel might bear the inscribed name of the deceased or his clan, along with that of the donor. More than fifty types of bronze ritual objects were employed for such functions as the preparation and serving of food offerings. Besides their ceremonial function of linking the ruler and aristocracy, these objects found in tombs may be considered as ex-votos, or fulfillments of a vow in the form of gifts to the departed.

Although they lasted for a thousand years, practically nothing is known of the Shang rituals. Their intent seems to have included assuring the resurrection of the deceased and the vitality and fertility of the donor and his tribe. Bronze was looked upon as a semiprecious material, and the ritual vessels were aristocratic objects. After many centuries they have acquired a beautiful patina, a surface film resulting from exposure, in hues ranging from green, yellow, and blue to red. Both their shape and complex ornamentation were probably symbolic of concepts and powers that are now unknown. Their motifs frequently derive from mythical and real animals and birds—dragons, bulls, tigers, elephants, water buffaloes, snakes, deer, rams, owls, and cicadas, to name a few. Each motif had various associations or potencies that contributed to the total magical force of the vessel: the more ferocious or terrifying the design, the more effective the protective force. For instance, the owl seems to have been connected with the sun and heavenly fire, while the pheasant was related to mother earth. Used in combinations, symbols were employed to meet different needs. When we search the

*right:* 40. Haniwa horse. Japanese, A.D. 300–600. Terra cotta, height 38″. Indiana University Art Museum, Bloomington.

ritual vessels for these motifs, we often find only vestiges of the whole or individual distinguishing features incorporated into the elaborate designs. The bronzeworker broke up bodies into parts, or fused them, or had forms growing out of one another in a highly imaginative manner. As in African art, the original motifs were greatly transformed but did not necessarily lose their potency. The decorators seemed to have filled compulsively every inch of surface, often using for filler areas an abstract spiral form referred to as the *thunder pattern*. Parts of the vessel, such as the handle or lip, were at times converted into animal or masklike forms, heightening the mystical nature of the object. The shape of the Shang vessel illustrated here is derived from the appearance of two eagle owls set back to back. Frequently, as in this vessel, there appears to be a hierarchical disposition of forms in size and relief, which may have alluded to the structure of the myths or beliefs from which they came.

**Japanese Haniwa Funerary Sculpture** In the "Great Burial" (or Yamato) Period, from the 3rd to the 7th century of our era, protohistoric Japanese society placed small-scale clay funerary sculpture in the *tumuli*, or burial mounds, in which were buried clan lords and emperors. These mounds, few of which remain with their sculpture content intact, were surrounded by moats; from an aerial view, they are seen to have a keyhole shape. It seems possible that the humane, economically prudent use of ceramic "stand-ins" for human beings and animals to serve the needs of the deceased ruler may have come from China, where, as in Egypt, human immolation had at one time been practiced.

In the 3rd and 4th centuries, low-fired unglazed hollow clay cylinders—from which the term *haniwa*, "circle of clay," comes—were set into the ground around the tumulus and filled with offerings for the dead. By about the 6th century, human, animal, object, and architectural representations were set atop many of these cylinders and arranged in elaborate groupings on and near the mounds. These objects were the property of the dead, placed near their burials to serve them eternally. At the top of the mound, directly above the burial chamber and the sarcophagus, was placed a *haniwa* replica of the deceased's house, thus providing him with a permanent dwelling place. Gradually, around the house, there were added in successive periods and mounds, clay replicas of other houses, granaries, livestock, weapons, human attendants, and guardian figures, all recalling the ruler's earthly estates.

Far from being gloomy and funereal in mood, the Japanese *haniwa* sculpture shows a broad range of lively expressions and gestures despite its purpose. Lacking are the dense formal designs and involved cryptic symbols of the Chinese ritual objects. Little is known of the religious beliefs of the "Great Burial" Period, which ended with the 7th-century advent of Buddhism and cremation practices. The art styles that produced the *haniwa* objects and the Shang ritual vessel impress upon us, however, their makers' divergent tastes and attitudes toward life and death.

The horse (Fig. 40) was a favored subject as an aristocratic status symbol, and it was most frequently shown saddled and ready to be mounted. The horse's legs are frankly shaped as cylinders. Detail was kept to a minimum in these clay objects, and the design of the horse and other objects was intentionally simple, clear, and strong so as to be recognizable from an appreciable distance. In part because the sculptors worked quickly, this art has a fresh and varied quality. The eyes of the horse, like those of human beings in *haniwa* sculpture, were simply punched out of the clay. Legends grew up about the awesome and lifelike character of such horses. Such credulity may seem merely naïve to us, but for viewers of the 6th and 7th centuries, unacquainted with detailed naturalistic art, the *haniwa* sculptors provided the information essential to establishing the horse's identity. The living horse was then looked at in terms of art, rather than the reverse, as old Japanese legends testify.

**Zapotec Funerary Urns** Ceramics in the service of the dead from the same period as the *haniwa* can be found in the Zapotec culture of southern Mexico. The Zapotec peoples had important burial sites in the religious center and fortified city of Monte Albán, near present-day Oaxaca. From graves in this vicinity have come fired clay urns whose original contents are not known. Some of these urns are adorned with elabo-

*right:* 41. Zapotec funerary urn. c. A.D. 1000. Clay, height 25½″. Collection Sra. Machida Armila, Mexico City.

*far right:* 42. Bakota skull guardian, from French Equatorial Africa. 19th–20th centuries. Wood covered with copper and brass, height 30″. Ethnographic Collection, University of Zurich.

rately molded figures, probably gods, who wear magnificent feathered headdresses and complicated ornaments (Fig. 41). Unlike the relatively simple *haniwa* figures, the Zapotec urn stresses rank and ceremony, probably as a reflection of a powerful priesthood and monarchy. A large bird surmounts the headdress. With great skill and sensitivity to the pliability of clay and its capacity to withstand firing, the artist was able to suggest such accouterments as jade earrings, bells, beads, and thongs. The enthroned god holds an incense bag in his left hand. Building up these small forms into an aggregate that is widest at the top and yet without added support from the back was a notable feat. The rigidly frontal and symmetrical pose of the seated figure is a quite universal treatment for the deity, found in many religions having a highly dogmatic and authoritarian character.

**Bakota Skull Guardians** The use of sculptures as guardians of the dead was as widespread as the making of ritual funerary objects. Tomb guardians in the form of human or supernatural figures and animals have been found as far east as China. In Africa, the Bakota tribes have for centuries been remaking variations on a basic design of a figure that is literally tied to a container of human skulls (Fig. 42). Just as the configuration of this skull guardian has been altered within general limits by successive generations, so the oral tradition from which its meaning is known has undergone change. One interpretation is that this is a mother goddess who reigns over the dead; another, that the figure defends the living from an evil spirit. There is also a question of whether or not the lower part of the figure is a schematic representation of the arms or is a contraction for the torso and legs. (The part below the face is intended to be buried in the ground along with the container of skulls, but in ceremonial dances it is sometimes carried by the performers.) The guardian figure is made of brass attached to a wooden frame—an indication of its importance, since metal is not a common material in this area. The many surviving Bakota grave guardians show a decided variation in the treatment of the face, with the older examples being more naturalistic. Some Bakotas refer to the horizontal crescent surmounting the head as a "moon," while others call it a "headdress"; the panels flanking the central oval have been described as cheeks or as continuations of the face. Archaeologists have pointed out, however, that tribal hairdos and ornaments may have inspired these lateral shapes. While the original meaning of the guardian figure may be lost or obscure to the present-day tribe and its artists, what is significant is the value given to continuity with the past through repetition of what has proved to be an effective protection for the dead. Tolerance of deviation from a norm in this Bakota art allows a gifted artist to impart his own interpretation to the conventional theme as long as an accepted resemblance to its tribal model is preserved.

**New Ireland Funerary Art** The islands of New Ireland lie east of New Guinea, which in turn is just north of Australia. Every year from May to July, the rites for the recently deceased and for ancestors long dead are performed in New Ireland. These rituals and the accompanying dances and art forms are known, collectively, as *malanggan* (Pl. 5, p. 43;

Figs. 43, 44). Every year the art must be renewed, for when the *malanggan* rites are completed the masks, poles, reliefs, and statues of dead kings that were used are all destroyed or sold. The purpose of the rites is ostensibly to offer memorials to ancestors, but it does not appear that the sculpture employed is intended to influence or even please the dead. As a matter of pride and prestige, clans made up of men from different villages who have a common ancestry take it upon themselves to re-create these ritual objects, which are so elaborate as to require months of preparation. The *malanggan* rites furnish annual occasions for achieving unity among the clan members, both living and dead. To prevent a loss of face in the eyes of other clans, each tries to outdo the other in the skill and beauty of the objects, and there is no exact repetition of motifs from one year to the next. Each clan has its own symbols and designs, and the artists are urged to elaborate upon or re-create their works within these traditions. Although the repertory from which the artist works is general (sea life, snakes, birds, the human form, and decorative patterns) and there are no set meanings, many of the *malanggan* works do commemorate specific individuals, and generalized biographies of them are summarized on the poles and reliefs. (With their appearance during the ritual, the name of the deceased is called out, and he is mourned.) Clan members who are specialists at making these objects work under the scrutiny of elders in secret places or areas fenced off to keep out the women and children.

New Ireland artists employ a wider variety of materials than probably any other group of artists in Africa or Oceania. Characteristic of their style is a desire for splendor, which is achieved largely by brilliant polychrome applied in small, clearly delimited areas and in strong juxtaposition. Often the sculptures are carved from logs, but some are constructed of small pieces of wood, shells, bark, roots, fruit rind, feathers, or bits of cloth. Great care and precision goes into the joinery of the parts. Many of the sculptures have a solid core that appears to be suspended within a cage or open framework. The great ornamental poles were probably intended to be seen from all sides, since every square inch of surface is given over to patterning, much of which may have lost its original symbolic meaning. As public testimony to his skill, the *malanggan* ritual objects are as much a tribute to the living artist as to the honored deceased—a fact that has been confirmed by anthropologists. The appearance of *malanggan* in the rituals has strong psychological effects and stimulates emotional participation by the audience. But while serving religious ends, they also evoke strong aesthetic response.

**New Guinea Ancestor Skulls** In New Guinea, along the Sepik River, certain tribes employ actual skulls of the deceased for ancestor spirit abodes (Fig. 45). Over the skull,

*right:* 43. *Malanggan* pole (memorial festival figure, ancestor with shark), from New Ireland. 19th century(?). Wood, paint, sea-snail shell opercula; height 6′3/4″. Museum of Primitive Art, New York.

*below left:* 44. Cult house with *malanggan* style masks, from Medina, New Ireland. Collected 1931–32. Figures representing ancestors, totem birds, and fish, of wood painted with oil and earth color; house of wood, bamboo, palm, and croton leaves; 8 × 16′. Museum für Völkerkunde, Basel.

*below right:* 45. Ancestral skull, from Melanesia, Middle Sepik River, New Guinea. Face modeled in clay, eyes of cypraea shells. Übersee-Museum, Bremen.

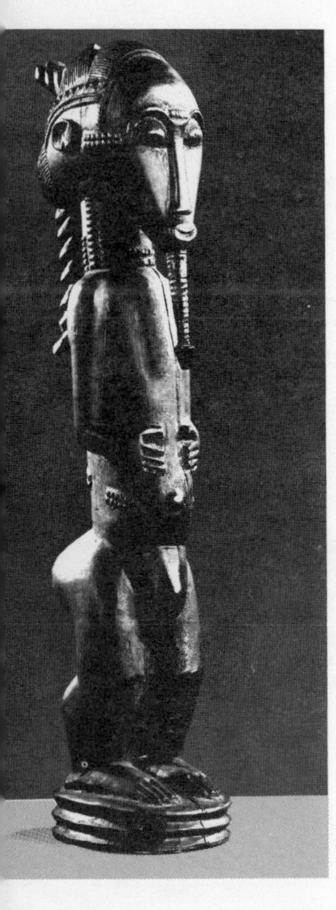

*above:* 46. *Ife King,* from Nigeria. c. 12th–14th centuries. Bronze, beads in crown painted carnelian; height 14½". British Museum, London.

*left:* 47. Baoule ancestor figure, from the Ivory Coast. Early 20th century. Wood, height 16½". University Museum, Philadelphia.

after it has been cleaned and dried, clay is applied and modeled to resemble the dead man as closely as possible. Ornamentation is added, in designs appropriate to his social rank and similar to what was worn by the deceased while alive. Shells are sometimes used to replace the eyes. These embellished skulls are often set atop mannequins and manipulated like puppets before the women of the tribe during fertility rituals. Both in Oceania and Africa, ancestor worship is linked with fertility rites, on the premise that the dead members are sympathetic to the tribe's increase. Since it is believed that the dead still need sustenance, offerings of food are also made to the ancestor skull.

**African Ancestor Sculpture** In Africa as in Oceania, there is the belief that the living are surrounded by the dead and that ancestors can play a significant role in the continuing life of the tribe. African ancestor figures are symbols and spirit abodes of the deceased. It is the hope of the carver and his patrons that the sculpture made for an ancestor will please him by its fine quality (*good* and *beautiful* are synonymous in many tribes) and that the markings, coiffure, and other tribal and individual attributes will be recognized by the ancestor as appropriate for his dwelling place. The ancestor can make his power accessible to the living—during ceremonies held to evoke this power, he passes it on to those who attend his effigy. Not only does ancestor sculpture express veneration or respect for the dead, but it also constitutes a surrogate for the living with the forces or powers controlling life. Sieber refers to these ancestral statues as "lobbyists," by means of which the living call upon their ancestors to intervene on their behalf with the appropriate spirits. Because the ancestor dwelling within is believed able to see, the eyes of these carved figures may have slits. Stress is often placed on the head, as the seat of power both in life and death, and the faces are characterized as benign rather than aggressive, because ancestors are considered friendly.

To Africans their art is intensely real, even when it seems to bear little resemblance to human or animal forms in nature. However, from the high culture of Ife, in Nigeria, which knew a monarchical system and pyramidal social structure, there have survived magnificent bronze heads and figures of royalty that have a naturalistic appearance and an ideal of classical composure (Fig. 46). Probably dating from between the 12th and 14th centuries—the equivalent of the medieval period in Europe preceding the Renaissance in Italy—heads such as that of an Oni, or supreme chief, were cast in bronze and presumably served as commemorations of the dead ruler. There is strong doubt, expressed by experts such as Bernard Fagg of the British Museum, that these were actual portrait likenesses of specific individuals. This degree of idealization within a context of naturalism would have its counterpart in the European ruler portraits discussed in Chapter 12. The Ife king is shown wearing the appropriate plumed and beaded crown, and the perforations around the mouth and chin may have been for insertion of beads or hair. Whether or not the vertical striations covering the face are related to actual scarification practice is not known. We can only speculate that these bronze effigies, too, served as spirit dwellings and were to be placed in shrines or honored locations.

The Ife heads readily draw our appreciation of their beauty because the physical subject naturalistically rendered is in itself handsome. Ancestor figures such as those of the Baoule tribe (Fig. 47), on the other hand, derive their beauty in the eyes of those sympathetic with African art from the visual rightness of the rhythms and proportions of the parts as seen in relation to the whole work. In the eyes of the Baoule themselves, however, the large head and elongated torso, the emphasis upon the navel, and the short squat legs all correspond to ideals of correctness and beauty prescribed for an ancestor figure. Again, the head is stressed as the seat of power both in life and in death; and emphasizing the navel and phallus confirms powers of fertility. Studies of ethnic physical types in Africa show not only that they are tremendously varied, but also that there is often some correspondence between sculptural and human proportion in various regions. The Baoule figure bears the stylized headdress and scarification marks appropriate to this tribe. The immobility of the figure is conditioned as much by the irrelevance of motion to the ancestor portrayal as by the fact that it was carved directly from a round log, with perhaps some thought to preserving its natural quality. In African sculpture, *connoisseurship*—or the discrimination of excellence—is similar to that for any other art. Only when hundreds of sculptures from a given region are patiently examined can an outsider begin to grasp why tribal members esteem certain carvings above others.

**The Lessons of Tribal Art** Much of the finest sculpture belongs to cultures not usually considered "civilized." The black in America who is seeking to discover his heritage will find that African sculpture has one of the longest continuous traditions of sculpture, but that this tradition has been jeopardized in recent years by the introduction of "civilization" to that continent. He will not, however, find an art dedicated to the celebration of "blackness," for in common with art throughout the world, the art of black Africa has been until recently without ethnic purpose. He will find that African art of both past and present is not nationalistic but tribal, not revolutionary but conservative—one arm of an establishment dedicated not to individuality but to the common good. Tribal art depends for its character upon its own language and hierarchies of social structure and upon religious and political beliefs. Each tribe has traditionally constituted an "in-group," in which everyone knew everyone else. Each person possessed considerable information about his own circumscribed society and natural environment, though adjacent tribes might be totally ignorant of each other's customs and art.

In terms of the complexities of mankind and its art, there is much that can be learned from the disinterested study of tribal peoples. The late psychiatrist Paul Schilder, in *Image and Appearance of the Human Body,* described the subtleties of vision and mental imagery in children and primitive peoples: "The process goes from the general to the individual and from complication to simplicity. The thinking of the child and the primitive person is fuller of meaning than the thinking of the adult. They see more relations; everything is connected with everything else. Their thinking is full of symbolizations and condensations. An object means much more than the adult mind sees in it; it is not only animated but connected with all activities in the universe." Thus it is a naïve assumption to think that so-called primitive societies were lacking in a coherent world view or life attitude because of the absence of a written language.

Claude Lévi-Strauss, in his essay "The Science of the Concrete," reminds us that one of the great purposes of art shared by all societies is that of *miniaturization.* He points out that most works of art are *miniatures,* being smaller in size or lacking in some of the properties of that which they represent. An African ancestor sculpture or Michelangelo's Sistine Ceiling (Fig. 198) have this in common. To his own question about the virtue of such reduction either of scale or in the number of properties, Lévi-Strauss responds:

> It seems to result from a sort of reversal in the process of understanding. To understand a real object in its totality we always tend to work from its parts. The resistance it offers us is overcome by dividing it. Reduction in scale reverses this situation. Being smaller, the object as a whole seems less formidable. By being quantitatively diminished it seems to us qualitatively simplified. More exactly, this quantitative transposition extends and diversifies our power over a homologue of the thing, and by means of it the latter can be grasped, assessed and apprehended at a glance. A child's doll is no longer an enemy, a rival or even an interlocutor. In it and through it a person is made into a subject.

Miniaturization is thus a graphic illustration of how art has helped man to come to terms with his environment. The work of art in all forms and at all times is in some way an object of knowledge, responding to a timeless impulse to know and to do.

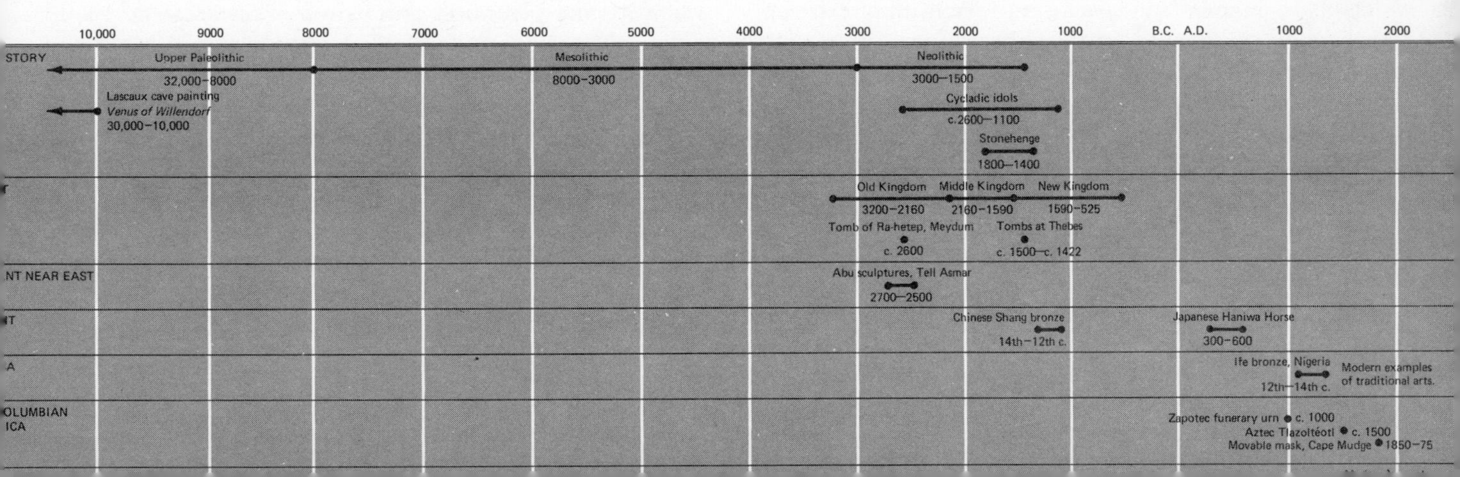

# 3

The history of religion tells us that gods have made men in their own likeness, but the history of art tells us that men have remade the gods into their own image. No more important purpose has been served by art than its giving a visible presence to gods. For millenniums, art provided visual reminders of celestial authority and, in the eyes and minds of men, made more intelligible the nature of their deities. The sculptured or painted presence of the god was the focus of worship and ritual, and it also gave to the faithful a feeling of reassurance and protection. Ancient Greek cities, for example, placed a statue of their tutelary god on the battlements to ensure their defense. Investing the god with material form also satisfied mortal curiosity and men's desire for familiarity with and recourse to their gods. The act of making a sculpture or painting of a god was both an honorific gesture and a means of coming to terms with the supernatural. The finished work of religious art also provided man with a visible ethic to guide the conduct of his life. Today we need not believe in the religions that inspired the images of Apollo, Buddha, and Christ to be impressed and moved by them. Their greatness as works of art transcends time and the boundaries of religious belief. Still, unless we can share to some extent the original concepts and emotions that produced this sacred imagery, we cannot fully appreciate the awe, wonder, and gratification with which they were received at the time of their creation. To content oneself with considering only the visual or aesthetic value of religious art is to miss the equally rewarding experience of learning about significant human attempts to discover and give form to the truth of existence. Furthermore, it becomes apparent how elastic is the potential of the human body, which has been represented in so many ways to accommodate such divergent concepts, and how flexible is the human mind that has accepted the religious art which follows as being real, or at least full of conviction and sincerity.

## APOLLO

On the temple of his sacred precinct at Delphi were inscribed the precepts of Apollo:

Curb thy spirit.
Observe the limit.
Hate hybris.
Keep a reverent tongue.
Fear authority.
Bow before the divine.
Glory not in strength.
Keep woman under rule.

In his study *The Greeks and Their Gods,* W. K. D. Guthrie has summarized Apollo's value to the Greeks by observing that Apollo is the very embodiment of the Hellenic spirit. Everything that distinguishes the Greek outlook from that of other peoples, and in particular from the barbarians who surrounded them—beauty of every sort, whether it lay in art, music, or poetry or in the qualities of youth, sanity, and moderation—is summed up in Apollo. Above all, he was the guardian against evil, the god of purification and of prophecy. Any good Greek could see in Apollo the preacher of "Nothing too much" and "Know thyself." Under his most important and influential aspect may be included everything that connects him with principles of law and order. Primarily, he represents the Greek preference for the intelligible, the determinate and measurable, as opposed to the fantastic, the vague, and the formless. Apollo was also looked to as a god of nature and was known as "keeper of the flocks." He was the god of the *palaestra,* or gymnasium, having been the first Olympic victor. He presided over the transition from boyhood to manhood, and he was variously shown as a warlike god who carried a silver bow or a patron of the arts who played upon a lyre. Concomitantly, he was thought of as the god of both physical and spiritual healing, capable of purifying the guilty and cleansing sin.

That any sculptor could somehow interpret all these attributes in a single human form seems impossible. In fact, the sculptor had to rely not only on his skill but on a sympathetic audience who would be inclined to read many of these traits into the sculpture. That such was the case, and that the artist's skill was of secondary importance, is borne out by stories from ancient Greece such as that of the father who enjoined his son to be like Apollo, but not like the

# IMAGES OF GODS

sculptor who made his statue. The image of Apollo in art originates in 7th- and 6th-century B.C. sculptures of standing youths, *Kouroi,* that spread throughout the ancient Greek world. These small and monumental statues of nude youths, frontally posed, arms at the sides and one foot often slightly in advance, have come to be called *Archaic Apollos,* but most were probably commemorative representations of deceased men or Olympic victors. Many of the smaller early Kouroi were votive sculptures, gifts by which the living venerated Apollo. One such, in the Museum of Fine Arts in Boston (Fig. 48) has inscribed on one of the thighs the words, "Mantiklos dedicated me to the god with the silver bow who strikes from afar." This votive sculpture, a gesture of homage to the god, may strike us as unreal in appearance; however, in the 7th century B.C., the Archaic period in Greek art, the spirit of Apollo was probably thought to be truly present in this sculpture. History teaches us that reality in art has always been determined by the art itself, not by measuring the art against actual life. Down to the last century, the credibility of a sculpture or painting was most often determined by comparison with other works of art. Thus, when the various sculptures of Apollo illustrated here are compared with one another, the reader makes certain judgments about which of them is most lifelike, without necessarily relating the works to his own body. There is no doubt that the Kouroi originally derived from Egyptian (Fig. 276) and Mesopotamian sculpture. The Greek contribution was athletic nudity and eventually a more lifelike appearance. A 6th-century B.C. hymn to Apollo helps us to understand the suitability of the Kouros type to the image of that god who was "like to a man, lusty and powerful, in his first bloom, his hair spread over his shoulders." After the 7th century, there is a gradual change not only in the image of Apollo in art but also in the human image in general. His slow but perceptible assuming of a more human aspect, his increasingly lifelike quality, depends first upon the sculptors' mastery of new skills with which to respond to and satisfy—and, in turn, to influence—changing tastes and conceptions of the god's nature.

In the *Tenea Apollo* (Fig. 49), done in the Transitional style of the mid-6th century B.C., the god is still represented

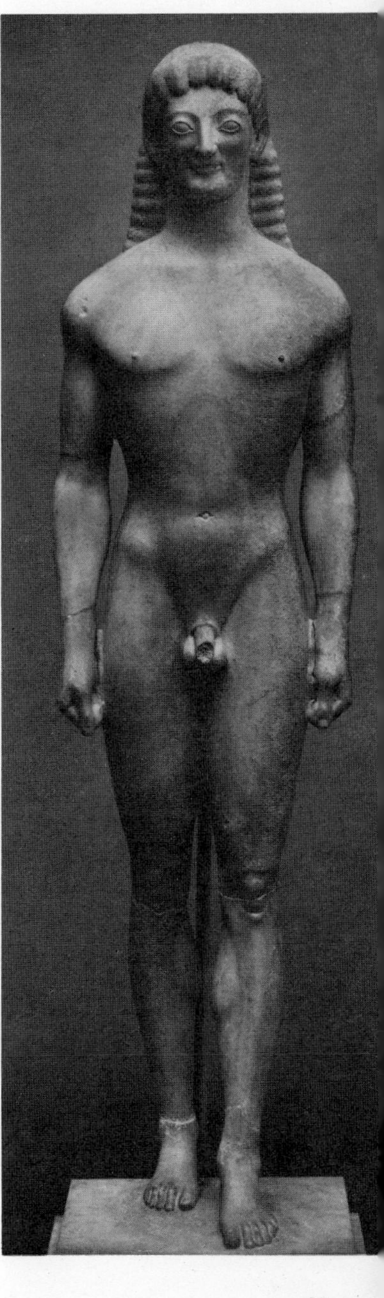

*above:* 48. *Apollo,* from Thebes (Boetia). c. 675 B.C. Bronze, height 8″. Museum of Fine Arts, Boston (Francis Bartlett Collection).

*right:* 49. *Tenea Apollo.* c. 550 B.C. Marble, height 5′. Glyptothek, Munich.

*above:* 50. Reconstruction of west pediment of the Temple of Zeus, Olympia. 468–460 B.C. Width c. 91′. Museum, Olympia.

standing erect, rigidly vertical and frontal. His body forms a perfectly symmetrical composition; the arms hang at his sides, and although one leg is extended forward, the body weight is equally distributed on both legs. The figure has taken on more convincing musculature and proportions. All these characteristics are Egyptian in origin but are appropriate to the interpretation of Apollo as an authoritarian deity, in line with the Greek view of him as the giver of laws. His complete nudity relates to his role as a supreme athlete. Unlike Egyptian figures, he is not flat-footed, and his feet have a more resilient contact with the ground. Nudity in early Greek art was generally reserved for commemorative sculptures honoring athletes victorious in the Olympic games. The 6th-century standing sculptures of Apollo were thus almost indistinguishable from the trophy sculptures erected for mortal, contemporary athletes. This ambiguity resulted because it was customary to idealize athletes rather than create portrait likenesses of them. It is often only through the dedicatory inscriptions on the base that the identity of the standing figure can be ascertained. From his first appearance in art, Apollo was interpreted *anthropomorphically,* that is, as having human characteristics, and was depicted in perfect physical form.

The pediment of the Temple of Zeus at Olympia (Fig. 50) shows Apollo at a legendary nuptial ceremony intervening in a disruption caused by the drunkenness of the centaurs. The idea seen developing in this Apollo (Fig. 51) paralleled other changes in Greek art. The rigid, frontal symmetry of the earlier statues (Figs. 48, 49) has been broken by the profile position of the head and by the gesture of the right arm, raised to restore order. Made in mid-5th century B.C., this Apollo departs from the Archaic figures in his softer, more sensuously modeled body, which results in a more subtle joining of the body parts and of the limbs to the torso. The treatment of the muscular fold of the pelvis, a Greek sculptural convention, affirms the perfect fit of the thighs in the socket of the torso, like the modulated juncture of a column capital with the lintel above. The new full-round conception of the body admits successive and varied silhouettes, not merely the front and side views of the other types. The body and the face, relaxed from the stylized expression of the *Tenea Apollo,* have become more beautiful in terms of actual human anatomy. Less mystically remote because of the increase in physical perfection, such statues prompted the 5th-century Athenian public to voice the opinion that their best sculptors could portray beautiful *men,* but not beautiful gods. Even the great sculptor Polyclitus was not immune to this criticism (Fig. 492). Scaled larger than the other figures in the composition and placed in the center—both of which are older devices for establishing hierarchy—the god has been assured his authority. The ideal proportions, physical development, and facial features immediately set the god apart from the mortals and centaurs who surround him. It was, however, the newer qualities of grace and physical self-confidence that endowed this Apollo with dignity and divine identity and with great self-control in a situation of emotional and mental stress. Thus, despite the emphasis on corporeality, the portrayal epitomizes conduct and restraint, as well as law and order, through presence and gesture.

Although close in date to the Olympia *Apollo,* the Classical *Apollo* (Fig. 52) of the sculptor Phidias carries even further the sensual possibilities of the body. The rigid axis, through the center of the body in earlier figures, has been eliminated, and the weight is placed on the right leg in a hipshot pose that creates a more active balance of the body—one of the great achievements of Classical Greek sculpture. In this system of *contrapposto* (or "counterpoise"), the movement of each portion of the body is an ideal compositional counterpart to the Apolline tradition of harmony between spirit and body. The strength of the still-idealized visage and the impressive physique, coupled with the resilient pose, assist in conveying a feeling of authority that has now become more humane than in the 6th-century model. The perfect proportioning of the torso is a striking lesson in moderation, in avoidance of physical or sensual excess.

At the end of the 4th century, the military conquests of Alexander the Great extended the rule of Greece throughout the Near East and into Egypt. This political domination spread Greek art and civilization to many different peoples and thus produced a heterogeneous culture termed *Hellenistic.* In general, the effect of this new internationalism on sculpture was an increasing development toward the more realistic depiction of nature and toward more complex and vigorous compositional mobility.

The Hellenistic *Apollo Belvedere* (Fig. 53) depicts the god in decided movement, with his draped left arm extended. It is believed that originally his left hand held the silver bow, his military attribute. The controlled movement permits illustration of Apollo's supreme physical grace and, by implication, of his intellectual discipline. While retaining obvious idealized traits in face and body, the *Apollo Belvedere* is the most lifelike, and hence the most nonsacred, of the Apolline sculpture we have discussed, and this change corresponds to political and sculptural developments in Greece as a whole. This last figure also suggests why the religion of Greece declined in power. The gods are almost totally conceived and presented in terms of man, an attitude that permits a fatal familiarity and identification between god and worshiper. This congruence of identity is apparent in spite of the fact that many of Apollo's attributes are beautifully incorporated within the sculpture. The handsome figure, with its athletic and dancer-like grace, retains a suggestion of the purity of mind and body and of the faculty of wisdom so cherished by the Greeks. In all these images of Apollo, the Greeks sought to present the beauty of his mind and of morality through the medium of a beautiful human body. And the mastery of sculptural mobility achieved by the artists, while powerfully evoking the personality or temper of the god, may ultimately have caused the weakening of his divine efficacy.

*left:* 51. *Apollo,* detail of west pediment of the Temple of Zeus (Fig. 50). c. 460 B.C. Marble, height 10′4″. Museum, Olympia.

*center:* 52. *Apollo.* Roman copy after Phidias' original of c. 460 B.C. Marble, height 6′5½″. Landesmuseum, Kassel.

*right:* 53. *Apollo Belvedere.* Roman copy, probably after Leochares' bronze original of c. 330 B.C. Marble, height 7′4″. Vatican Museums, Rome.

## BUDDHA

The Buddha is traditionally presumed to have lived between 563 and 483 B.C., in the region of Nepal on the border of India. Born a prince, he became a reformer of the Brahmanist religion and a great ethical teacher whose sermons in many ways paralleled those of Christ. Like Christ, Buddha emphasized meditation and good works and viewed this life as filled with pitfalls. And also like Christ, he did not work toward the establishment of a complex religious order in his own lifetime; the formal religion that evolved from his teaching came long after his death. Buddhism is composed of two main sects. The Mahayana (Great Vehicle) or "pious" sect looks upon the Buddha as a god possessing the power of miracles and protecting the faithful from harm. He is lord of the universe. This sect developed strongly in China and Japan from its origins in India. The Hinayana (Lesser Vehicle) or "rationalist" sect looks upon the Buddha as a great, but human, sage who provided a code of ethics that could deliver humanity from the sources of misery. His image in art was

*above:* 54. *Cushioned Throne with the Assault of Mara* (detail), from Ghantasala. Late 2nd century A.D. Grey marble, height 5′9¾″. Musée Guimet, Paris.

*right:* 55. *Bodhisattva of Friar Bala,* from Mathura. c. A.D. 131. Red sandstone, height 8′1½″. Museum of Archaeology, Sarnath.

*far right:* 56. *Parasurameshvara Lingham,* from Gudimallam. 1st century A.D. Polished sandstone, height 5′.

a reminder and not an actual presence, similar to images of Christ in Western art. The Hinayana sect was strongest in Southeast Asia, in Burma, Cambodia, Ceylon, and Thailand.

The history of the images of the Buddha goes back to the first centuries before our era, when he was not shown in human form but was represented by symbols—his footprints, the Wheel of Learning, the tree under which he achieved Enlightenment, an altar, or an honorific parasol recalling his princely origin. The faithful could achieve communion with Buddha by means of meditation on the symbols that induced his presence. One of the early sculptures that does not show the actual form of the Buddha (Fig. 54) is one in which an evil spirit menaces the divine throne. Although he is physically absent, attributes of the Buddha such as the throne and his footprints, as well as the reverent attitude of the court, are indicative of his sacred presence. This initial unwillingness to give tangible form to the Buddha has parallels in the history of Christian art, and there are no images of the Buddha or Christ dating from their own lifetimes. To have given tangible form to either of the gods may have seemed at first a contradiction of their divine being. An incentive for Buddhist artists to change was the growing competition with Hinduism and the exposure to Roman and Late Greek art.

Perhaps the earliest freestanding sculpture of Buddha was made in the Mathura region during the 2nd century A.D. and is termed a *Bodhisattva,* or potential Buddha. This powerful figure, the *Bodhisattva of Friar Bala* (Fig. 55), stands about 8 feet tall and was originally situated before a tall column. Atop the column was a stone parasol, 10 feet wide, which was carved with symbols of the heavenly mansions and represented the Buddha's royalty. The lion at his feet was also a regal attribute, symbolizing the Buddha as the lion among men. The rigid, frontal, and squarish formation of the body sets it apart from the Mediterranean art of the time and argues that the standing Buddha image was of Indian origin. The symbolism and body type, however, are markedly different from Hindu sculpture of the 1st century, such as the sandstone god Siva (Fig. 56). In this representation, the god is designated both by a human form and by his attribute—a giant phallus which was known as a *lingham.* Accessible only to Hindus, who could enter the sanctuary of the temple where it was housed and daily anointed with oil, the Hindu icon helps us to understand, nevertheless, why the Buddhists overcame objections to imaging the focal figure of their worship.

When the Buddha was finally given human form by the Gandhara artists, in the 1st or 2nd centuries of our era —roughly eight centuries after his death—his body was to be a materialization of concepts similar to those the symbols had conveyed. The tasks facing the early sculptors of the Buddha included the incorporation of thirty-two mystic signs of his superhuman perfection: among these were the cranial protuberance, symbolic of wisdom; elongated ear lobes, indicative of royal birth; a tuft of hair on his forehead, which like the sundial halo signified his emission of light; spoked wheels on the soles of his feet to symbolize the progress of his doctrine and the power of the sun; and a series of ritual hand gestures, or *mudras.* The Buddha's right hand pointed downward meant his calling of the earth to witness his triumph over evil and his Enlightenment or dispensation of favors; his right hand raised was to dispel fear and give blessings. By joining his thumb and forefinger, the Buddha set the wheel of his doctrine in motion.

Of greater challenge to the artist was the endowment of the Buddha's body with metaphorical significance; according to tradition, the face of the Buddha is likened to an egg, the eyes to lotus buds or petals, the lips to ripe mangoes, the brow to the god Krishna's bow, the shoulders to an elephant's head, the body taper to that of a lion, and the legs to the graceful limbs of a gazelle. The sculpture had to embody the sacred flame or fiery energy of the Buddha and his preterhuman anatomy. Finally, the sculptor had to impart to the statue that ultimate state of serenity, perfect release from pain, and deliverance from desire which the Buddha achieved in *nirvana.* According to his teachings, inward tranquillity was to be gained by first appeasing the senses, for only then could the mind become well balanced and capable of concentrated meditation. The sensuousness of Indian art is partly explained by this attitude that the senses should not be denied but should be used as the first stage in a spiritual ascent, whereby the faithful could ultimately be purged of attachment to the self and the world's ephemeral delights and could thus achieve a more perfect spiritual union with their gods and ideals. This confidence in the need for and mastery of the sensual suggests that Greek art such as the Apolline sculptures would have appealed to the early Buddhists.

Without question, the seated Buddha statue is indigenous to India and is a native solution to the artistic incarnation of the Great Teacher and god. The seated position was favored, for in the life of the Buddha it is recorded that after six years of penance he at last came to the Tree of Wisdom, where the ground was carpeted with green grass, and there vowed that he would attain his Enlightenment. Taking up the seated, cross-legged position with his limbs brought together, he said, "I will not rise from this position until I have achieved the completion of my task." The model or prototype for the seated Buddha seems likely to have been the earlier Hindu mystical system of *yoga,* which was constantly before the eyes of the early Indian artists and which was recorded as having been the means of the Buddha's achievement of nirvana. The objective of yoga is enlightenment and emancipation, to be attained by concentration of thought upon a single point, carried so far that the duality of subject and object is resolved into a perfect unity. The Hindu philosophical poem the *Bhagavad-Gita*, described the practice of yoga:

*above:* 57. *Buddha Preaching in the Deer Park.* A.D. 320–600. Sandstone, height 5′3″. Archaeological Museum, Sarnath.

*right:* 58. *Seated Buddha.* 6th–7th centuries A.D. Dolomite, height 6′7″. Anuradhapura, Ceylon.

> Abiding alone in a secret place, without craving and without possessions, he shall take his seat upon a firm seat, neither over-high nor over-low, and with the working of the mind and of the senses held in check, with body, head, and neck maintained in perfect equilibrium, looking not round about him, so let him meditate, and thereby reach the peace of the Abyss; and the likeness of one such, who knows the boundless joy that lies beyond the senses and is grasped by intuition, and who swerves not from the truth, is that of a lamp in a windless place that does not flicker.

Through yoga may be obtained the highest state of self-oblivion. It involves highly developed discipline in muscular and breath control and the ability to clear one's mind of all superficial sensory preoccupation in order to concentrate upon a single object or idea. The discipline of yoga seeks not only control of the physical body but a cleansing and rebuilding of the whole living being. The human body transformed by yoga is shown free not only from defects but also from its actual physical nature. The sensation of lightness, or release from the bondage of the body, induced by the practice of yoga produces the "subtle body."

It is often difficult to distinguish between the sculpture of the Mahayana and Hinayana sects. One of the most beautiful of the seated Mahayana Buddha sculptures, an example from Sarnath (Fig. 57), was made in the 4th or 5th century of our era. It shows the Buddha seated upon the lotus throne, making the mudra of the wheel-turning as he preaches his first sermon in the Deer Park, where he first achieved his Enlightenment and to which he has returned. Below his throne (in a segment not shown in the illustration) are a group of his followers and the symbolic wheel. The back of the throne is ornamented with the winged lions of royalty and the foliate ornamentation of the sun disk, or halo. This decoration derives from Iran and the cult of Mazda, the god of light, and its use represents an assimilation of earlier fertility and vegetative symbols. Air-borne minor deities flank the Buddha in reverent attitudes, not unlike the angels in medieval Christian imagery. The hierarchic formality of the whole composition indicates that the sculptor is no longer dealing with a specific event; the sermon has been solemnized into a more abstract sacred symbol. The earlier, more individualized and human interpretations of the Buddha have been replaced by the idealized figure that was to be the basis of later imagery.

In the Deer Park Buddha, there is no reference to skeletal or even muscular substructure; the body appears to be

Plate 4. Shang ceremonial vessel of the *yu* type. Chinese, 14th–12th centuries B.C. Bronze, height $9^1/_2$″. Smithsonian Institution (Freer Gallery of Art), Washington, D.C. (See p. 30.)

Plate 5. *Malanggan* spirit boat (figures representing deceased ancestors), from New Ireland. Painted wood, length 19′6″. Lindenmuseum, Stuttgart. (See pp. 32, 33.)

Plate 6. *Christ Enthroned, with Sts. Vitalis and Ecclesius.* c. 530. Mosaic. San Vitale, Ravenna. (See p. 48.)

*right:* 59. *Buddha,* from Gandhara. 3rd century A.D. Stone.

*far right:* 60. *Buddha,* from Mathura. 5th century A.D. Red sandstone, height 5′3″. National Museum, New Delhi.

inflated by breath alone. There is no trace of bodily strain caused by the posture. The seated attitude is firm and easy, indicating the Buddha's mastery of yoga. The proportions of the Buddha were almost canonical at this time, being based on a unit called the *thalam,* equivalent to the distance between the top of the forehead and the chin. The symmetrical arrangement of the body makes of it a triangle, with the head at the apex and the crossed legs as the base. The face, wearing the "subtle smile," is marked by the symbolic lotus-form eyes and ripe lips. The downcast eyes shut off his thoughts from the visible world. Such compositional devices were employed, for the most part, because the sculpture was meant to be contemplated and viewed metaphorically.

In contrast to the Sarnath Buddha, symbolic of the regal and mystical beliefs of Mahayana Buddhism, is a more austere and unadorned seated Buddha from Ceylon, exemplifying the Hinayana view of the Great Teacher (Fig. 58). Notwithstanding the severe weathering of its stone, the Ceylon Buddha has a less sensual, yet still firm aspect; the hermitlike figure has an appearance of complete absorption in meditation, indicative of the Buddha's renunciation of worldly concerns. It lacks the strongly stylized prettiness, or even effeminacy, of some later Buddha images in Southeast Asia.

Early standing sculptures of the Buddha (Fig. 59), created in the late 1st through the 3rd centuries at Gandhara, display an obvious relationship to early sculptures of Christ—and both types of imagery were indebted to Hellenistic and Roman freestanding figures. This influence resulted from the invasions of India by Mediterranean cultures and the subsequent occupation of some Indian territory by the Romans. Indian artists, working perhaps from Roman models, early produced a standing Buddha whose drapery and balance recall certain 1st-century B.C. Roman Imperial sculpture, such as processional reliefs of the Ara Pacis (Fig. 285). The Buddha is shown here in his capacity as the Great Teacher. The togalike monastic robe is cut in naturalistic channeled folds, so that we are aware of a counterpoised body structure beneath it. Further late-Greek influence can be seen in the face of the Buddha, which is a variant of the Apolline or Hellenistic ruler portrait type, with the addition of the mystic signs. The freestanding Buddha image also derives from Indian sculptures of royal personages.

In the art of succeeding centuries, notably in a 5th-century standing Buddha from Mathura (Fig. 60), Indian artists eventually departed more radically from Greek and Roman influence and developed a monumental standing Buddha

*top:* 61. Priscilla Catacomb (Greek Chapel), Rome. Late 2nd century. Gallery with three niches, ceiling open for light.

*above:* 62. *Raising of Lazarus.* Early 3rd century. Wall fresco. Sacrament Chapel, Catacomb of San Callistus, Rome.

more consistent with their own religious ideals. The Mathura standing Buddha is a sophisticated study in opposites. Against the vertical and immobile frontality of the body, the sculptor has designed an undulating sequence of drapery folds that prevent the eye from fastening on the boneless grace of the torso beneath. The transparency of the monastic robe suggests the shining forth of the Buddha's radiance. The hypnotic sequence of concentric disks leading into the ovoid head culminates in the downcast eyes that intimate the Buddha's withdrawal from earthly vision. The flat disk background, with its ornamental foliate motifs, is a foil for the sensual smooth volume of the head, while the rings of the halo and the outlines of the face and neck area play against the drapery rhythms. There is no abrupt transition or single detail to jar the eye or feelings; the totality of the design holds the eye soothingly within its borders and constantly returns it to the head of Buddha. The image is one of quiet authority that invokes love and respect without fear.

While repetition among the images of Apollo and Christ is frequent, Buddhist art exhibited far greater adherence to a prototype for almost 1500 years. Part of the explanation for successive replication in Buddhist imagery stems from a belief in the magical efficacy of certain prized statues; copies of these were thought to partake of the original's power. Furthermore, the Buddhist artist was not encouraged to work from a living model or rely on natural perception. With the help of fixed canons, it was his obligation to study the great older images, meditate on them, and then work from his inspired memory. Because the Buddha's beauty defied apprehension by the outward senses, the artist worked from a mental conception in a way that has interesting parallels, as we shall see, in the art of Michelangelo.

## CHRIST

**The Good Shepherd** Despite the many great paintings and sculptures devoted to Christ, in the last century he has been the subject of some of the worst art in history. Banal commercial religious wares have been responsible for the cheap Sunday-school image of Christ so often purveyed as art. Religious sentiment has, unfortunately, made most people and clergy uncritical of this debasement of Christ and art.

The first known paintings of Christ, dated no earlier than the 3rd century, are found in the Christian catacombs on the outskirts of ancient Rome (Fig. 61). Rather than secret refuges from persecution or underground churches where large congregations would assemble, as many people formerly believed them to be, these catacombs were burial chambers connected by long passages; they were known to and inspected periodically by the Roman government. Moreover, their lack of ventilation and restricted size precluded their use for large worship services. The Christ of catacomb painting, a humble,

rustic type lacking in distinct portraitlike features, is shown performing miracles (Fig. 62), in the guise of a teacher or a shepherd. The scenes from Christ's life, limited in number before the 4th century, were intended to encourage the hopes of the faithful with a promise of afterlife. Their optimistic message was that if one had faith, he too would achieve resurrection and salvation. The style of these small-scale images painted on plastered walls, many of which may have been done by non-Christian Roman house painters, is not new—any more than the beliefs of Christianity were completely new. The stress in the *Raising of Lazarus* is upon the Saviour's hand, not his body. The scene has a highly synoptic character, as if the artist were painting essentially a reminder of a story known by heart to those who saw it.

Among the first images of Christ, found in the catacombs and in funerary sculpture, are those showing him as the "Good Shepherd," which was a familiar image in Greek art (Fig. 63). There is ample evidence to confirm that the Christians recognized and valued the similarity between Christ as the shepherd and Orpheus, the son of Apollo who descended into Hades and sought through the charm of his singing and playing to save his wife Eurydice from the Underworld. The Greek mythological figure had much in common with both Apollo and Christ, since he was associated with salvation, sacrifice, love, and protection. The shepherd image was an ideal expression of the Early Christian community, which was characterized by a close relationship between priest and congregation: the priest was seen as the shepherd, the congregation as the flock. The artistic presentation of the shepherd amid nature was also fitting, for the Early Christian view of paradise was comparable to the Roman poet Vergil's descriptions of a new sylvan paradise, a beautiful nature in which the soul could repose, ruled over by a gentle shepherd. Christ as the shepherd, whose coming Christian theologians saw prophesied in Vergil's writings, thus ruled over a bucolic world as if in a Golden Age. Second-century Christian saints also describe the paradise in which the soul can find rest with the image of a magnificent garden.

In a 4th-century sarcophagus (Fig. 64), the shepherd is surrounded by winged angels harvesting grapes. Such small, childlike figures were customarily substituted for representations of adults in Roman Art of this type. Both the angels and the vineyard derive directly from pagan sources in which the grape harvest and wine alluded to premature death and regeneration. This explains the choice of theme for the sarcophagus of a deceased Christian who was well-to-do. Christian art that dates from before the 5th century mostly interprets the Jesus of the Gospels, or *the historical Jesus*—Jesus as the Messiah and not as a divinity. In the Lateran Sarcophagus, Jesus as the shepherd stands upon an altar, suggesting his death and sacrifice for mankind. His Resurrection provided hope and a spirit of optimism for the Early Christian community and its converts. There is no stress on Christ's militant or royal nature before the 4th century. The artistic prototype of the historical Jesus seems to have been late Greek and Roman statues of seated or standing philosophers (Fig. 114),

*above:* 63. *Calf-Bearer.* c. 570 B.C. Marble, height 5′5″. Acropolis Museum, Athens.

*below:* 64. *Christ as the Good Shepherd,* detail from the Lateran Sarcophagus. Late 4th century. Marble. Vatican Museums, Rome.

a type associated with the contemplative or passive life. Often late Roman artists would work at depicting pagan figures at the same time they were fulfilling Christian commissions. Sometimes carved sarcophagi were completed except for symbols or faces; thus they could be purchased by either pagan or Christian clients and finished to suit their purpose.

**Christ as King** Artists of the Early Christian era did not render portraits in the sense of direct likenesses of individuals. Portraits of Christ after the 4th century were based upon Roman Imperial portraits, which in turn depended upon formulas devised to show rank and dignity. This use of artistic formulas and *types* is termed *typological art*. The Church and public judged the success of Christ's portrait by whether or not he was given appropriately grave and noble features, had majestic bearing, made the correct gestures, or wore the right insignia and garments for the situation in which he was depicted.

In the 4th century Christianity received Imperial support and was no longer the private religion it had been in its earlier phases. The Church as a body was reorganized along the lines of the Roman Empire, and the priesthood became an autocracy. Theology and art were subjected to radical transformation and formalization. The external forms and the cult aspect of religion that had been criticized by the historical Jesus became prominent. In the 6th century, the Byzantine emperor Justinian ordered an ambitious mosaic series for the apse of the Church of San Vitale in the city of Ravenna, which he had just conquered from the Goths. The mosaic of the enthroned Christ flanked by angels and Sts. Vitalis and Ecclesius (Pl. 6, p. 44; Fig. 65), in the half-dome of the apse, reflects the transition from the historical Jesus to the *theological Jesus*. The incarnate Messiah has been replaced by the Son of God, the humanity and humility of the shepherd by the impersonality of a celestial ruler over the hierarchy of religious government. The doctrines that lay behind this mosaic were not those which had been taught by Jesus himself; in San Vitale the theology of the Incarnation and the Second Coming is the essential subject of the mosaic.

Like a Roman or Byzantine emperor (Figs. 286, 289), Christ holds an audience in which he grants and receives honors. Bishop Ecclesius donates the Church of San Vitale to Christ, and Christ gives the crown of mercy and martyrdom to St. Vitalis. This is preeminently sacred art; the more mundane attitudes of earlier Christian imagery have been replaced. The event transpires outside a specific time and place, an intention affirmed by the fact that these saints lived in different centuries. Also, St. Ecclesius presents a replica of the exterior of the church and, at the same time, the mosaic showing the donation is inside this very edifice. Christ sits upon the heavens, yet mystically he is also within the heavens, and beneath his feet flow the four rivers of Paradise. This mosaic demonstrates how theologians had reconciled the divinity and authority of Christ with that of the earthly emperors who acknowledged obedience to him. Christ rules the heavens, while the emperor Justinian, shown in an adjacent but lower mosaic, rules the earth. The relative informality of earlier Christian imagery has been replaced by a complex series of artistic devices to convey the concept of Christ as the Second Person of the Holy Trinity. (In Chapter 12, "Images of Authority," Roman Imperial sources of these devices are discussed.) Against the gold background of the heavens, symbolizing the ineffable light of God, the youthful, beardless Christ sits attired in the Imperial purple and gold. Contrasting with the attendant figures who must stand in his presence, Christ is frontal and larger; he appears oblivious to those around him. His ritual gestures of investiture and acceptance make a cross shape of his body, accentuating his centrality in the image and in Christian dogma. Although the mosaicists may have been inspired by St. John's descriptions of the radiance of Heaven, like the Evangelist they based the attributes and qualities of divinity on their experience of the highest form of earthly authority known to them, on the magnificent court ceremonies of the temporal monarchs.

Aesthetics changed in accordance with developments in theology. The San Vitale mosaic embodies changed aesthetic forms as well as dogma. Each figure, for example, is sharply outlined, with every detail clearly shown as if the viewer were standing close to each subject. The figures do not overlap,

*right:* 65. Interior, San Vitale, Ravenna; view across inner octagon into apse. A.D. 526–47.

and they are all seen as being near the surface of the mosaic, which accounts for their great size. There is only a limited depth to the scene and no attempt has been made to re-create atmospheric effects or the light and shadow of earthly perception. Positive identification of the role and status of each figure had to be achieved. The colors are rich and varied, but are governed in their use over large areas by symbolism. The composition is closed, or strongly self-contained, so that there is no suggestion that the frame cuts off any significant area or action. The figures display, at most, a limited mobility, for their static quality is meant to reflect a transcendent nature and to induce a meditative effect on the reverent viewer. Thus artist and theologian combined to give a physical presence to dogma by creating imagery of an invisible, divine world.

More than a century before the San Vitale mosaics were executed, there was painted on a wall of one of the Ajanta caves of northern India a scene of the Buddha in Majesty (Fig. 66) that bears a striking similarity in its use of formal devices—such as centrality, frontality, and pose and gesture—for showing authority. It is possible that both the Ravenna mosaic and the Ajanta fresco may have been influenced by Eastern sources such as Persian art, which, along with Roman art, provided models for the representation of rank in the late-antique world. The Buddha is enthroned between the sinuous figures of Bodhisattvas (exceptional beings who are capable of reaching nirvana but who renounce the possibility in order to teach others of its attainment) and two of his disciples. Courtiers are seen in the background. Buddha's gesture of teaching and his robe and posture are as ritualistic as those of the Christ image. Lions guard his throne, and he and the disciples have halos shown under ceremonial parasols, further symbols of royalty. The flower-strewn background and wall suggest the garden of a palace, a special place that only the faithful are privileged to see and comprehend.

The great Byzantine images of Christ and those in the Early Christian basilicas of Italy were found within the churches. By the beginning of the 12th century, however, French Romanesque sculptors had transferred sacred images to the exterior of the edifices, as seen, for instance, in the great relief carved over the doorway of the Church of St-Pierre, in Moissac (Fig. 67). But this did not as yet result in

*above:* 66. *Buddha in Majesty.* 5th century A.D. Fresco. Cave 9, Ajanta.

*left:* 67. *Christ Enthroned,* tympanum of the west portal, St-Pierre, Moissac. 12th century.

a conception of Christ as being of the world of the living. While adopting the ceremonial and sacred traits of the San Vitale image, the Moissac sculptor forcefully added new ideas to the conception of the lordly Christ. Wearing a crown, Christ is a feudal king of kings, surrounded by elders who are his vassals. His remoteness is reinforced by the great difference in scale between his figure and the representatives of humanity. All glances are directed toward Christ as to a magnetic pole. From his immobile frontal figure, the composition moves outward in waves. Angels and evangelical symbols, intermediate in scale between Christ and the elders but more closely proportioned to Christ, serve to impress upon the onlooker the hierarchical nature of the universe and to bridge the figures in motion with that of the motionless Christ. Here Christ is like the awesome Old Testament God, commanding and completely aloof. He is thus shown as the Redeemer and God of judgment at the Second Coming. His beauty does not derive from the comely proportions with which Apollo was endowed; rather it is of an entirely impersonal and unsensual nature, appealing to thought and faith.

**Christ as Judge** In neither the Apolline nor Buddhist religions is there an analogy to Christ's Second Coming and the Last Judgment, taken as themes for many of the most dramatic and interesting Christian works of art. The earliest Christian image of a Last Judgment is believed to be a scene from the 6th-century mosaic cycle in Sant' Apollinare Nuovo in Ravenna (Fig. 68). In this small work Christ is shown seated in the center and clad in a purple robe; he gestures to his right toward three sheep. Christ is flanked, on his right, by an angel in red and, on his left, by one in blue. The angel in blue stands directly behind three goats that, like the sheep, are facing toward the center. The episode is the fifth stage of the Apocalypse of St. John, in which Christ symbolically separates the sheep, or the elect, from the goats, the damned. The figure of Christ is almost completely frontal, and he expresses no emotion. It is an extremely simple but formal composition relying upon a knowledge of the scriptures, color, and gesticular symbolism, as well as the significance of left and right. The artist, in illustrating literally St. John's metaphor, sought to give the event an almost sacramental dignity and transcendence.

An early-12th-century French Last Judgment tympanum on the Church of Ste-Foy in Conques (Fig. 69) represents a tremendous change in interpretation of the judgment theme. This is one of many exciting apocalyptic sculptures done in southern France during the first half of the 12th century. In the Ste-Foy version, much more of the apocalyptic account has been encompassed by the artist, who relies far less upon metaphor and prefers to give a more tangible realization of the concrete details and mechanics of the Last Judgment. His art was a vivid memento, in its brilliantly modulated carved surfaces and abundance of human, divine, and demonic forms, of that fateful event, the day and hour of which "no man knoweth" (Matt. 24:36).

The large tympanum is set above the main doorway of the church, through which the worshipers must pass every day and, hence, serves as an ever-present reminder of their obligations. Moreover, to enrich his subject, the Ste-Foy sculptor and his theological adviser drew upon sources outside the Bible; the writings of such Fathers of the Church as St. Augustine were absorbed into the work. As an example, the weighing of souls (Fig. 70), which is not in the Biblical accounts of the Last Judgment, is perhaps borrowed from Augustine, who wrote, "Good and evil actions shall be as if hanging in the scales, and if the evil preponderate, the guilty shall be dragged away to Hell." The motif of the scales may also have come from Near Eastern art and indirectly from Egyptian sources in the Book of the Dead. The Egyptian funerary god Anubis, as watcher of the "weighing in," has been replaced by St. Michael. Contrary to the inviolable conduct of the Egyptian ritual, a devil here seeks to tip the scales in his favor as he sees that a soul on the side of Michael (on Christ's right, our left) has outweighed one on his side. This attempt at judicial corruption made by an agent of Satan was amusing in the 12th century, particularly in southern France, where law had become so important as a result of the feudal system and the rise of the Church.

The ordered and legal aspect of the final judgment is stressed by the artist at Conques in both his composition and his disposition of figures. Each zone and compartment of the scene is strongly separated by a thick stone border, on which

*left:* 68. *Last Judgment: Separating the Sheep from the Goats.* c. A.D. 493–526. Mosaic. Sant' Apollinare Nuovo, Ravenna.

*left:* 69. *Last Judgment,* tympanum of the west portal, Ste-Foy, Conques. 12th century.

*below:* 70. Detail of Figure 69.

are written the virtuous phrases, the teachings of the Church, and so on, appropriate to the location. This composition reflects a view of the universe as strongly ordered, so that everyone has a definite area to which he will eventually be consigned, just as the living at the time had little difficulty in defining their own status in the feudal system. Thus the image of the universe on the last day becomes a projection of the real world as it was involved in the social, economic, and political structures of the time. The authority and absolute dominance of Christ over the scene is achieved by his centrality and great scale. He sits immobile and frontal as a symbol of power, gesturing upward with his right hand toward Heaven on his right side; with his left hand he points downward to Hell.

The upper zone of the scene contains angels carrying the Cross, the symbol of the Passion and the Second Coming on the day of justice. The central position given to the Cross and the downward movement of the angels draw the eye centripetally to the Supreme Judge. On Christ's right, in the largest zone, is a procession of the saved, who proceed in homage toward the ruler of Heaven. They are led by Sts. Peter, Anthony, and Benedict, who symbolize the origins and rule of the Church. The saints lead a royal figure, believed to be Charlemagne, who had been a benefactor of the Abbey of Ste-Foy. The moral implied by this arrangement is that Charlemagne got into Heaven not by force of the crown which he carries but through the prayers and efforts of the holy men—an unsubtle admonition to the secular rulers of the time to support the Church. On Christ's left (our right), in another zone, are those consigned to Hell, nude and cramped in

awkward poses, experiencing all sorts of painful indignities inflicted with enthusiasm by demons.

The lowest zone is divided into two large porticoes known as *basilican castrum.* Between these, literally on the roofs at the point where the buildings come together, the weighing of souls takes place; it is thus also on the principal axis of the Cross and Christ. Next to the weighing-in on the left, armed angels are rousing the dead from their coffins, and on the right demons are pummeling the resurrected. In the center of the left portico (that on Christ's right) sits Abraham, who receives the souls of the deceased into his bosom. Entrance to Heaven is through a heavy open door, which reveals a fine

*below:* 71. *Christ,* detail of dome mosaic, Monastery Church, Daphnē, Greece. c. 1100.

*bottom:* 72. Comprehensive view of the dome at Daphnē. (See Fig. 71.)

medieval lock and set of strong metal hinges. The entrance to Hell is through the jaws of the Leviathan, whose head protrudes through the door to Hell (Fig. 70). The Book of Daniel (7:7) describes the terrifying Leviathan that God has created. Hell is ruled over by the seated Devil, surrounded by his squirming subjects. In the treatment of Hell and the Devil the medieval artist had his greatest freedom and could give vent to his fantasies, repressions, and humor. Here as elsewhere, by far the more interesting of the two sides is that dealing with the damned.

The 12th-century Byzantine mosaic of Christ the Pantocrator (Figs. 71, 72) in the dome of the monastery church of Daphnē, outside Athens, focuses attention on the face of Christ, his gesture of benediction, and the Bible held by him. It is an image calculated to evoke awe, reverence, and fear in the beholder. The severe expression is climaxed by the hypnotic glance, giving the effect of watchfulness. The celestial countenance is that of an immutable, stern judge who is both giver and enforcer of the law. An impressive face, it is not beautiful in the Classical sense, for it denies the importance of the flesh, of naturalistic rendering, and instead stresses the power of the divine will. There is an un-Classical imbalance in the Byzantine stress upon the eyes and in the intensity of expression. No Greek sculpture of Zeus hurling his thunderbolt conveys the wrath of which the Daphnē Christ seems capable.

**The Beau Dieu** The judicial and authoritarian aspects of the Byzantine Christ are continued but somewhat relaxed in the 13th-century French sculpture of the *Beau Dieu* (Fig. 73) from the Cathedral of Amiens. The figure of Christ stands between the main doors of the Cathedral and below the scene of the Last Judgment. Beneath Christ's feet are the lion and serpent symbolic of the evil he conquers. Both in his location and in his appearance, Christ has been made more accessible to the congregation. He stands before the doors to his house not as guard but as host, like a gallant feudal lord. This humanizing of Christ into an aristocratic ideal is reflected in his new familiar name, "the Handsome God," a title in many ways unthinkable at Moissac and Daphnē. This investing of Christ with a more physically attractive, a more tender aspect accompanies his reentrance into the world of the living and the reduction of the sacrosanct nature of the art itself. The transition has been from the Byzantine Pantocrator, Lord of All the Universe, to the more human dignity of the Gothic lord of men.

The *Beau Dieu* has an idealized countenance that bears instructive comparison with the head of the *Apollo* from Olympia (Fig. 74). The Gothic head is noticeable for its sharp features and subdued sensuality, indicating an essentially Christian attitude toward the body. This is particularly marked in the treatment of the mouth. The more pronounced

*left:* 75. *Head of Buddha,* from Gandhara. 5th century A.D. Victoria & Albert Museum, London.

*below:* 76. *Head of Christ,* detail from the *Coronation of the Virgin,* Reims Cathedral. 13th century.

*above left:* 73. *Beau Dieu,* detail of the west portal, Amiens Cathedral. 13th century.

*left:* 74. *Apollo,* detail of Figure 51.

ovoid outline of the Christ image, enhanced by the long tightly massed hair, and the axial alignment of the symmetrical beard, the nose, and the part of the hair give the deity an ascetic and spiritualized mien. Despite the generalized treatment of the forehead, cheeks, and hair, the Amiens Christ possesses a more individualistic character than does the Olympian god, who is totally unblemished by the vicissitudes of mortal existence. The eyes of the Gothic Christ are worked in greater detail in the area of the eyelid, and they have a more pointed upper arch than does the simplified perfect arc of the *Apollo's* upper lids. In both sculptures, details of the eyeballs were originally added in paint. The Gothic Christ lacks the masklike calm of the Classical Apollo.

Comparison of a Buddha sculpture with a 13th-century head of Christ from the French Gothic cathedral of Reims provides us with a summation of two radically divergent tendencies in the respective art forms of Buddhism and Christianity (Figs. 75, 76). The Buddhist head reveals the development toward anonymity in the celestial countenance, a refusal to glorify a specific individual. It seeks a pure incarnation of that spirit of Buddhism conceiving of the Buddha as representing the incorporeal essence of a religious attitude. The smile on the Buddha's lips recalls his wisdom and sublimity, which he attains in the *abyss*, or sphere beyond nirvana. The Reims Christ wears the marks of his passionate earthly sojourn in the worn and wrinkled surface of his face, and we sense that this deity has a unique and dramatic biography. There is no intimation of past experience, of trial and pathos, in the images of either Apollo or Buddha. The Christian face, however, speaks to us of a tragic personal drama; it displays or infers a far subtler range of feeling than the faces of the other two deities. The Gothic sculptor wished the viewer to read tenderness, compassion, pain, and wisdom in the lines of the divine face. The Reims sculptor may even have taken a French king—perhaps Louis IX (St. Louis)—for his model, so that Christ was now literally presented in terms of man, or *a* man. The Reims Christ represents the second half of the cycle begun in the catacombs when Christ emerged first as a humble man, then as an emperor and ruler of Heaven. Now the cycle moved in the other direction, to terminate in the images of Christ discussed in the section on Rembrandt (Chap. 11).

**The Deaths of Christ and Buddha** Western Christian art, like its theology, is dominated by the execution of its God. Buddha's death came tranquilly: for three days he lay on his right side, with his head resting on his hand, until he passed into the final nirvana (Fig. 77), in which he was freed from reincarnation. Buddhist art as a consequence does not know the pathos of such Christian images as the great 15th-century French panel painting known as the *Villeneuve* (or *Avignon*) *Pietà*, depicting the lamentation over the dead Christ (Fig.78). Used as a backdrop for the altar and thus seen in conjunction with the service, this large painting is a brilliant blending of the actual and the symbolic. The radiant gold background establishes the celestial nature of the theme, and the dark reddish brown of the earth reflects the somber mood. The arrangement, which has the Virgin both supporting and displaying the wounded and distended body of Christ, is not an attempt to show literally the events after the Crucifixion, but rather to represent the symbolical nature of the death of Christ and the Virgin's sacrifice of her son for mankind. The words stamped into the gold leaf at the top of the painting ("Oh, all ye who pass along the way, stop and see what is my grief") are from the Good Friday Mass. Within the formal deployment of the starkly outlined and self-contained figures, the unknown artist has created strong characterizations so that each, by a differing psychological response to the event, has a humanity which shines through his symbolic function. The donor at the left, whose powerfully modeled head is juxtaposed with the flat reddish profile of the Heavenly Jerusalem, is not an actual participant in or witness to the

*above:* 77. *Ananda Attending the Parinirvana of the Buddha,* Gal Vihara, near Polonnaruva. 12th century. Granulite, height 23′.

*right:* 78. AVIGNON MASTER. *Villeneuve Pietà.* c. 1470. Oil on panel, $5'3\frac{1}{2}'' \times 7'1\frac{3}{4}''$. Louvre, Paris.

*left:* 79. *The Crucifixion.* Early 5th century. Ivory panel, length 3³/₈″. British Museum, London.

*left:* 80. Reliquary in the form of a church with dome. Cologne School, c. 1180. Gilt copper, champlevé enamel, and ivory. Guelph Treasure, Staatliche Museen, West Berlin.

*right:* 81. *Crucifixion,* detail of Figure 80.

scene, but he meditates prayerfully upon its significance in a way that was intended to inspire the beholder. As Christ's body achieved an increasingly mortal form toward the end of the Middle Ages, so did those of his followers, and the artist's challenge became one of reminding us that the Redeemer who died was greater than a man.

Christ's physical and spiritual anguish on the Cross has no counterpart in Buddhist or Greek art. It was not until the 5th century, however, that the first Crucifixion scenes appeared, and these were in sculpture. Prior to that, there had been symbolic references in the form of an empty cross. One reason for the early absence of this subject, so central to Christianity and its art, is that crucifixion was an undignified punishment meted out by the Romans to criminals, their bodies often left to be devoured by wolves.

A small ivory relief carving from the beginning of the 5th century shows Christ on the Cross, with head erect and eyes open, fastened by four nails (Fig. 79). In this presentation, the sagging head and shoulders and the bent knees common in this type of death were avoided. There is no evidence of physical suffering, thus stressing Christ's divinity. At the right, below the crucified figure, is Longinus, the centurion who lanced his side; to the left, St. John and the Virgin, and at the far left, the hanged Judas. It was not until almost six centuries later that artists had the sanction of the Church to begin to show the pathetic tortured form of the crucified Christ and to close his eyes in death. On a *reliquary* (a container to hold relics, usually a bone from the body of a dead saint) made in the Rhineland in the 12th century (Figs. 80, 81), an ivory inset shows the body of the crucified Christ, with his head slumped to the right. This pose possibly originated in the sculptor's own conception of what this form of death involved, but more likely it derived from the tradition that in the last moment Christ's head bowed to his right. From medical evidence, it would seem that a dead man on a cross would have his head slumped straight downward, in a vertical line with the median of his torso. A more modest covering for the loins has replaced the simple 5th-century breechcloth. Even earlier than this example of 1180, the figures of Mary and St. John had taken up their familiar positions flanking the Cross, with Mary on Christ's right, and for centuries to come this became the fixed format. This panel is part of the gold and ivory decoration of a reliquary in the shape of a small enameled Byzantine cruciform church, made to receive the head of St. Gregory, brought to Braunschweig from Constantinople by Richard the Lionhearted in 1170. Reverence for the deceased saint and belief in the miraculous power of his remains account for the expenditure of substantial treasure on this small casket. The Crucifixion, also a theme of martyrdom, was an appropriate subject to honor the holy man on his reliquary.

One of the most impressive and personal interpretations of the theme of the Crucifixion is that by Matthias Grünewald (d. 1528), which occupies one of the main panels of the *Isenheim Altarpiece* (Pl. 7, p. 77). Painted probably between 1512 and 1515, the altarpiece was intended for the monastery church of the hospital order of St. Anthony in Isenheim, Alsace. The monastery's hospital treated patients with skin diseases such as leprosy and syphilitic lesions. The first step in a new patient's treatment was to be taken before the painting of the Crucifixion and to have prayers said at the altar for his healing. It was thought that skin disease was the outward manifestation of sin and a corrupted soul. The patient was confronted with the larger-than-life painting of the dead Christ, whose soulless body was host to such horrible afflictions of the flesh. Only the Son of God had the power to heal the sinner, for Christ had borne all the sorrows of the flesh that garbed the Word. The previous regal, authoritarian, and beautiful incarnations of Christ were replaced by the image of the compassionate martyr. The vivid depiction of the eruptions, lacerations, and gangrene of the body were intended to encourage the patient's identification with Christ, thereby giving solace and hope. From the late Middle Ages, partly because of the widespread pestilence, there are countless examples in the art and literature of northern Europe of the faithful being enjoined to identify emotionally with the Passion of Christ. Grünewald probably drew upon the vision of the 14th-century Swedish saint Birgitta, who wrote:

> The crown of thorns was impressed on His head; it covered one half of the forehead. The blood ran in many rills . . . then the color of death spread. . . .
>
> After He had expired the mouth gaped, so that the spectators could see the tongue, the teeth, and the blood in the mouth. The eyes were cast down. The knees were bent to one side, the feet were twisted around the nails as if they were on hinges . . . the cramped arms and fingers were stretched.

Grünewald's image of Christ goes beyond this description in exteriorizing the body's final inner states of feeling. The extreme distension of the limbs, the contorted extremities, and the convulsive contraction of the torso are grim and eloquent testimony of Grünewald's obsession with the union of suffering and violence in Christ. He focused on the final rigidifying death throes so convincingly that the feet, a single hand, or the overwhelming face alone suffices to convey the expiration of the entire body. The brutal stripping of the living wood of the Cross is symbolically in accord with the flagellation of Christ. Cedar, used for the vertical member of the Cross, was also employed in the cure for leprosy. The hopeful message of the painting can be seen in the contrast between the light illuminating the foreground and the murky, desolate landscape behind—a device signifying Christ's triumph over death. Miraculously present for this Crucifixion, John the Baptist intones, "I shall decrease as He shall increase." Men are enjoined to humble themselves in order to renew their lives in God. The static doctrinal and symbolic right half of the painting contrasts with the extreme human suffering and emotion to the left, seen in the grieving figures of St. John and the Virgin and Mary Magdalen. Grünewald's painting and views of religion seem to have stressed a communal response to tragic but elevating religious experience. Psychologically and aesthetically, each figure, like the composition as a whole, is asymmetrical and formed of an uneasy synthesis of polarities.

Through the images we have seen, it is possible to trace the changing conceptions of Christ, from his depiction as a humble messianic shepherd, through the kinglike God to be revered from afar, to the Godlike king who could be loved as a benevolent ruler, and finally to the Man of Sorrows, whose own compassion evoked the pity of suffering humanity. The transformation of sacred art proceeded differently for Apollo and the Buddha. Apollo's effigy began as sacred art and terminated in the profane imagery of a beautiful youth. The Buddha's early interpretation progressed from a humane individuality toward the sacrosanct impersonality of the 6th and 7th centuries. To comprehend the effectiveness of Greek, Indian, and Christian artists in uniting form and idea, one may exchange in the mind's eye the head of the Reims *Christ* for that of the *Apollo* at Olympia, the Lotus throne of Buddha for Christ's role in the Moissac relief, the nude figure of Apollo for the *Beau Dieu* of Amiens Cathedral, or finally, transfer the San Vitale Christ to the Grünewald altar painting.

**The Faceless Christ** In subsequent chapters there will be discussed many examples of the ways in which Christ was interpreted during the same century and in the centuries that followed Grünewald's altarpiece. In the 20th century the finest painting and sculpture are no longer primarily in the service of religion, and the most important art has been secular. Nevertheless, in 1948 two enlightened Catholic priests approached the painter Henri Matisse, a non-Catholic, to decorate a convent chapel at Vence, in southern France. Matisse's previous art had been entirely concerned with subjects that were sensual and that delighted the eye, such as

*right:* 82. HENRI MATISSE. *Ave (left)* and *le Chemin de la Croix (end wall)*. 1951. Murals. Rosary Chapel, Vence.

beautiful women and colorful interiors (Pl. 72, p. 361; Figs. 579, 580). A richly gifted decorator and draftsman, Matisse accepted this commission. Part of his chapel decoration (Fig. 82) consisted of two linear black-and-white ceramic murals that received soft changing color reflected from adjacent windows of yellow, green, and blue glass. One mural shows the Virgin and the Christ Child, and the other the Stations of the Cross. The first subject is drawn in a soft, lyrical curvilinear style that, with the full blossom designs surrounding it, evokes a joyful mood. What initially astounds visitors to the Rosary Chapel is the absence of facial features for the Virgin and Child. It is as if Matisse had decided that each viewer could project into the mural a face of his own creation, but the brilliantly economical outlines of the figures suffice to identify them. In the Stations of the Cross, Matisse consciously changed his style: he avoided the graceful silhouettes and allowed a more harsh, angular drawing—rather than gestures and facial expression—to express the tragic theme. The events are numbered and follow one another abruptly, consisting of the most rudimentary indication of the action and no concern with background. Realizing that the worshiper knows the episodes by heart, Matisse, like the catacomb artist, turned to a symbolical or synoptic rendering, but in a personal style possible only in his time. He exemplifies the sincere modern artist who cannot, as the medieval artist willingly did, repeat the conventions, types, and styles of his predecessors.

**Religious Art and Earthly Freedom** For the most part the ancient images in this chapter constituted *sacred art:* art which had a special prescribed style and function, set apart from the secular community: art which was dedicated, consecrated, and a living part of the religious ritual. The works were made holy by their association with a god and were treated with reverence and respect. Subsequently, their frequent destruction and defacement, as in the English Civil War and the French Revolution, gave testimony to their potency and to the strong feelings they could arouse. It is in religious art—as the historian of freedom, Herbert Muller, has pointed out, and as many modern artists agree—that the artist has contributed to the suppression of the growth of freedom. He has been the voice of a Church which historically has not championed political or civil rights, but has stressed the rites of the liturgy, of humility and intolerance. By persuading man through sacred art that the only true freedom was that of the spirit's release from earthly bonds, the artist and priest did not inspire their audience towards greater earthly freedom or always encourage a strong sense of personal worthiness. Worship of the god through his image was a duty and not a freedom. One can only speculate whether Buddha or Christ would have approved of art which inspired and restricted, educated and obscured, united and divided, encouraged and discouraged, freed and enslaved the spirit.

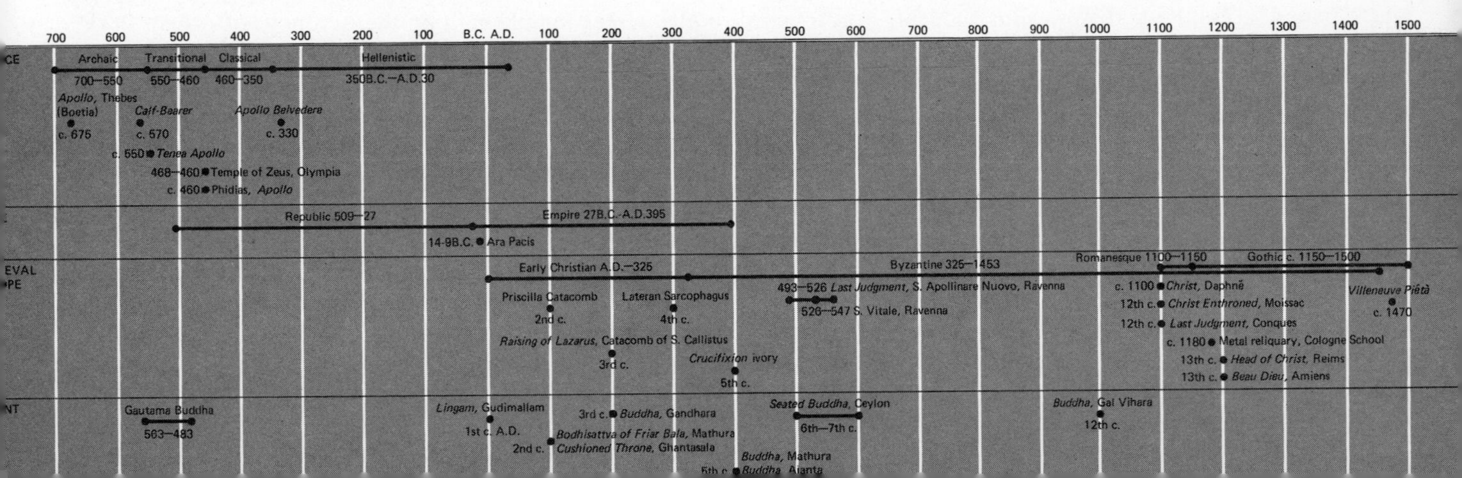

# 4

In his *Laws* of the 4th century B.C. Plato wrote, "Life must be lived as play, playing certain games, making sacrifices, singing and dancing, and then a man will be able to propitiate the gods, and defend himself against his enemies, and win in the contest." As the historian Johan Huizinga has pointed out (see p. 27), the highest and holiest function of the form and purpose of such play is to make man conscious that he is embedded in a sacred order of things. Play is thus involved in sacred performances or rites, during which something invisible takes a beautiful and holy form. This would include religion and sport as well, for during both the players are convinced that their rituals actualize and bring about an order of things higher than that in which they usually live. And the efficacy of their rites presupposes a hallowed spot, or as Huizinga has described it, "a sacred space, a temporarily real world of its own, expressly hedged off. But with the end of the play its effect is not lost; rather it continues to shed its radiance on the ordinary world outside, a wholesome influence working security, order, and prosperity of the whole community until the play season comes again." Thus the temple and the football stadium are in some ways alike.

What elevates a structure—whether it is a stadium, a palace, or a house of god—to a sacred order beyond the limits of its materials, what in other words distinguishes building from *architecture,* has been beautifully expressed by the modern Swiss-born architect Le Corbusier, in *Towards a New Architecture:* "You employ stone, wood and concrete, and with these materials you build houses and palaces; that is construction. Ingenuity is at work. But suddenly you touch my heart, by the use of inert materials and starting from conditions more or less utilitarian you have established certain relationships which have aroused my emotions. This is architecture."

The history of religious architecture is thus more than just a record of styles and engineering achievements. From the beginning of civilization, the construction of a temple or church has been an act of faith and gratitude performed by its builders—a joyful offering to a god from the living in return for his manifold gifts. Until the 19th century such architecture was in many ways a collective social endeavor by which architects expressed or symbolized the most sacred values of their cultures. In the last two centuries the architect has had increasingly greater opportunity for self-expression. In a variety of ways, public conceptions of the nature of the deity, Heaven, and the universe have been incorporated into the designs of religious structures. Religious architecture, like images of gods, is intended to make manifest to the intellect and to the emotions a feeling of what lies beyond the visible world and this life. Thus far in this century there are few sacred buildings of lasting distinction, and these have been created by gifted individuals who relied less on a consensus of congregational attitudes and conventional symbols than on their own artistic intuition and personal interpretation of the faith for which they were working. Today as in the past, the architect can be as much the teacher as the pupil, and while he has learned from the past, the views he expresses in architecture cannot help but influence the ensuing religious experience of those who worship in his church or temple. From antiquity to the present, there have been basic demands that the architect has had to meet in designing religious architecture: the structure's suitability as a house of God; its effectiveness for the performance of the liturgy; its conduciveness to prayer or communion with the god; its purpose as a meaningful expression of a congregation's beliefs.

## THE PARTHENON

The spiritual meaning of the Parthenon (Fig. 83), the celebrated Greek temple built on the Acropolis of Athens during the 5th century B.C. (448–438 B.C., the sculptural decoration finished by 432 B.C.), does not lie in its formation with cosmic symbols. Although the Parthenon's architecture does not literally represent the forms of myth and religion, it is nonetheless an inspired expression of the higher values of Classical Greece. Through analogies and through the circumstantial evidence of culture, the Parthenon reflects the world view of Periclean Athens and is a type of idealized spiritual self-portrait of that city. The reason for its building and for its location on the sacred hill of the Acropolis in the city's center (Figs. 84, 85) are important considerations.

# RELIGIOUS ARCHITECTURE

*left:* 83. Ictinus and Callicrates. The Parthenon, view from the northwest. The Acropolis, Athens. 448–438 B.C.

*below left:* 84. The Acropolis, view from northwest, Athens.

*below right:* 85. Model of the Acropolis, by G. P. Stevens. Royal Ontario Museum, Toronto.

Athena, goddess of the city-state of Athens, was known as the protector of heights and goddess of fortified places. During the Persian invasion of 480, work ceased on a partially constructed temple dedicated to her. When the Persians were defeated, construction of a new temple was begun on the same site and with the same plan by Callicrates as master builder, under the leadership of the statesman Kimon. When Pericles came to power at Kimon's death in 450 B.C., he had Ictinus build a larger and more impressive building with more columns and a slightly changed orientation. This structure made use of the available components of the temple begun earlier, including columns and the metope sculpture. The building of the Parthenon occurred in the flush of Greek confidence in the Athenian gods, Athenian moral values, Athenian mercantile success on the seas, and, above all, in Athenian culture. Ironically, construction of the great temple also coincided with the beginning of the fateful decline of Athens' political power and of what several historians have felt was her moral corruption. Many in Athens protested the great cost of the temple and were offended as well at Pericles' impatient offer to pay for it himself. To prevent the glory's accruing solely to Pericles, the Senate approved the project at public expense; these expenses were covered by funds taken from the Delian League, comprised of allies of the Athenian city-state, by loot from piracy and military campaigns, and by contributions from free citizens, who with their slaves donated work on a daily basis. The small size of the Parthenon, in comparison to the Egyptian temples (Fig. 303), reflects a marked difference in respective resources and, to some extent, the absence of a powerful priestly caste in Greece. Nevertheless, for a city of 100,000 people, the Parthenon was an ambitious undertaking. The Parthenon was a gift to the goddess of war and wisdom from free men who willingly submitted to her. Moreover, it was a votive offering in return for past naval and commercial success, for Athena was also the protectress of the navy. A recent study by Rhys Carpenter has provided historians with valuable new information on the Parthenon's construction.

*above:* 86. The Panathenaic frieze on the Parthenon, above the western entrance to the cella.

*right:* 87. The Parthenon, view from the west. Reconstruction by G. P. Stevens. American School of Classical Studies, Athens.

The extent of community participation in honoring Athena is commemorated in a long frieze (Fig. 86) running from west to east above the inner columns at the entrances to the sanctuary or *cella*, the interior room housing the statue of Athena Parthenos. This continuous relief is 525 feet long and its subject the Panathenaic ceremonies that took place every four years to celebrate Athena's birthday. A procession of representatives of all Athens escorted the wheeled model of a ship, from the mast of which hung a newly woven purple woolen sail, or *peplos;* on this peplos were embroidered in gold mementos of legendary battles in which Athena triumphed. When the procession reached the Parthenon, the sail was lowered, folded, and turned over to a priest, who draped it on the statue of the goddess in the sanctuary. In the relief, also, the gods are shown seated as guests at the ceremonial banquet in the sanctuary (Figs. 92, 93). It depicts the sequence and organization of the procession, which began in the city and which included the marshals, magistrates, sacrificial animals, libation-bearing maidens, elderly citizens, youthful musicians, charioteers, and armed cavalry. The location of the relief, about 40 feet above the base, and the consequent poor illumination and partial obstruction by the outer columns indicate that it was primarily intended for the eyes of Athena. To accommodate the mortal viewers on ground level, the sculpture at the top of the frieze is in higher relief.

The Panathenaic procession recalls the spirit in which the temple was built. Art was interwoven with the civic ceremonies accompanying dramatic performances, athletic games, and religious offerings and rites (Fig. 87). Public expenditure for art was conceded as necessary to enrich the lives of Athenian citizens. The ideal citizen of Athens was an active contributor to the affairs of the city. Within half a century this ideal was realized by, among others, Pericles,

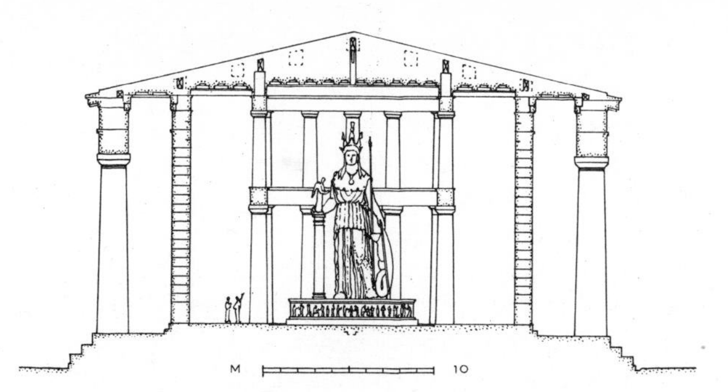


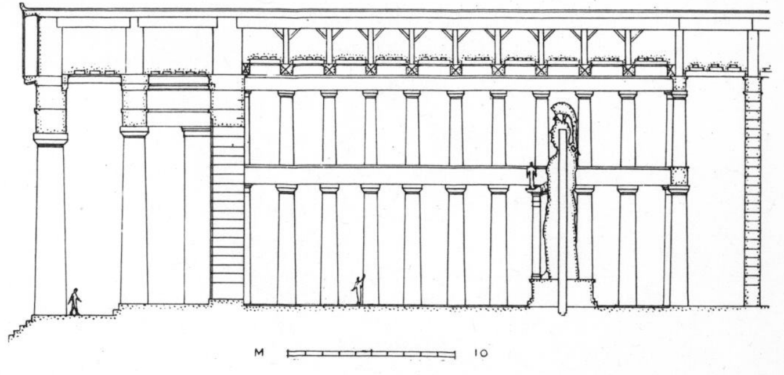


*above:* 88. The Parthenon. Cross section (*left*) and detail of longitudinal view of the sanctuary (*right*), omitting the storage chamber. Reconstruction by G. P. Stevens. American School of Classical Studies, Athens.

Sophocles, Aeschylus, Euripides, Anaxagoras, Socrates, Thucydides, and the sculptor Phidias, overseer of the sculptural decoration of the Parthenon. In conjunction with Pericles, it may have been Phidias who assigned the architectural design to Ictinus and an assistant named Callicrates. Many artists were recruited for the project, and according to Plutarch, who wrote centuries later, such was the spirited rivalry among the workers and artists to excel in quality and speed that, remarkably, the Parthenon was finished within the lifetime of those who inaugurated it.

The prime purpose of the Parthenon was to provide a worthy house of Athena. The temple form is the descendant of the *megarons*, or dwellings of Mycenaean kings, built on the Acropolis long before the time of the Parthenon. This temple was not designed as an interior space in which a congregation worshiped; for this purpose an altar was placed outside, in front of the eastern entrance. The cella of the temple housed the gigantic 40-foot effigy of Athena Parthenos, garbed in military costume. The statue's great size therefore required an unusually wide plan to satisfy the necessary height. Although the original is lost, we know that Phidias made this sculpture using gold for the dress and armor and ivory for the flesh. Appropriately, a ship's mast was used for the interior armature, indicating Athena's role as protectress of the navy. Entrance to the sanctuary was reserved for the priests and for privileged laymen on certain occasions. The laity were permitted to look into the sanctuary through the enormous eastern doors.

The orientation of the temple was worked out with painstaking care, as was true for all ancient sacred architecture. The temple has a roughly east-west orientation. The central axis is slightly south of due east, so that on Athena's birthday the rising sun shone directly through the doors onto her effigy. The location of the temple on the Acropolis was also calculated to permit the widest view from the city below, and from various points the Parthenon may be seen against the sky, the sea, or the mountains (Fig. 84).

**Architectural Design** The overall form of the Parthenon is basically that of the traditional Greek temple, with its walled interior divided into two parts. The windowless eastern chamber housing the cult statue was known as the *Hecatompedos* ("100 feet"), because of its 100-foot length. As seen in the plan and sectional reconstructions (Figs. 88, 89), there was an inner two-tier open colonnade that continued from the doorway to behind the statue, where it formed an aisle that permitted a view of the image from the rear. Natural illumination was provided by the huge doorway (32 feet high, 13 feet wide). Beneath the double-pitched marble tiled roof

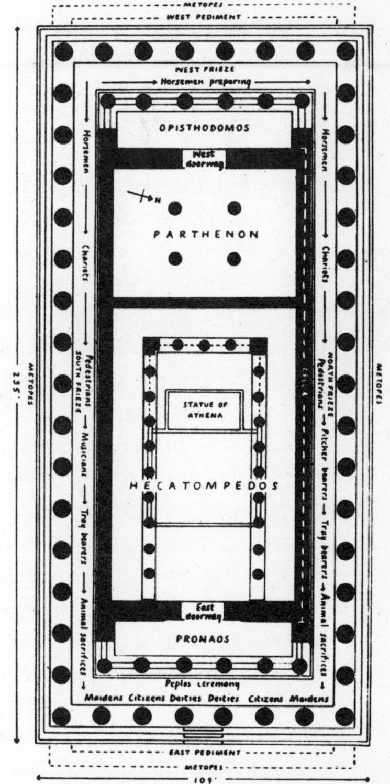


89. Plan, the Parthenon and Panathenaic procession, after N. Yalouris.

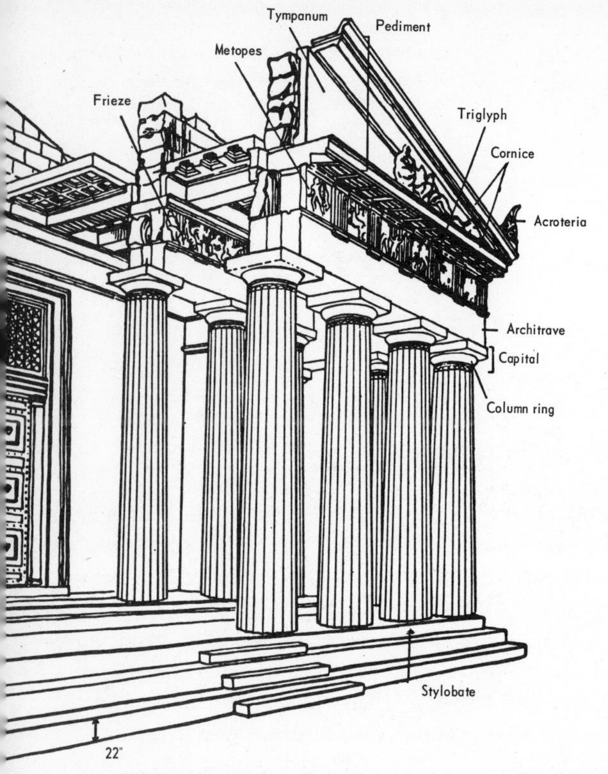


90. Sectional drawing, the Parthenon, after N. Yalouris.

was a flat ceiling of wooden beams. The sanctuaries of the Greek temples are of substantial historical interest because they are among the first large enclosed interiors, even though the space within was not so expressively shaped as in edifices of later periods—of Imperial Rome or Gothic France, for example (Figs. 106, 311, 312). The statue of Athena dominated, if not crowded, the sanctuary. The second, and smaller, western chamber was the storage space for ritual objects, important votive offerings, and the treasury of the Delian League and the state. This room was known as the *Parthenon* ("Chamber of the Virgin"), from which the whole temple took its name.

Since the Classical Greek architects believed that the splendor of a temple should not be confined to its interior, perhaps the most inspired part of the Parthenon's design is its exterior. This emphasis may be explained by the fact that the public ritual was conducted out of doors, and visually the temple was intended to appear accessible. Worship of the Greek gods did not entail the secretive ceremonial of ancient Egypt. The presence of important sculptural programs outside in the *pediments* (the gables, or triangular areas, formed by the sloping roof of a Classical temple) and *metopes* (panels which, with the triglyphs, cover the frieze zone above the architrave in Doric temples) also suggests that the temple was more "extroverted" than interiorized in its address to the general community (Fig. 90). The exterior Pentelic marble columns were a shimmering white, and the *triglyphs* were painted blue; the horizontal architrave blocks above the columns were hung with military trophies.

The temple was mounted on a three-stepped base that set it apart from the earth and the viewer, much as a pedestal does for sculpture. The height of the individual steps was intended to discourage their being climbed. The sanctuary's outer wall and entrances were surrounded by a handsome range of columns. These columns and the horizontal elements above them belong to the Classical order known as *Doric*. The masculine severity of this order was appropriate to a war goddess.

**Mind versus Chaos** The Parthenon tells more about the human than the metaphysical nature of the Greeks. Even in its ruined state it reminds us of the power of human intellect and of the Greeks' reverence for Athena as both the goddess of wisdom and an inclusive symbol of victory. The words of the 5th-century Athenian philosopher Anaxagoras could well have been inscribed on the Parthenon: "All things were in chaos when mind arose and made order." The temple, affirming its makers' belief in a rational unity of reality, is a visual analogy of the Greek idea of the world as ultimately knowable, static, and symmetrical. After its completion Athena's attributes were extended to include perfect equilibrium. A little over a century before, temple sculpture had been used to express the demonic and the common apprehension, if not fear, of the unknown. The Parthenon and its sculptural decoration, instead, express man's confidence in himself, in his place in the world, and in the dignity of his gods, who had human as well as divine qualities. To translate these religious and philosophical generalities into the specific components of the temple, it is important that we visualize the whole architectural ensemble, even though we can still perceive its radiant design from the ruins and appreciate how this accorded with Athenian speculation on the goddess' nature.

The Parthenon, like Classical sculpture, was designed according to the Greek ideal of *eurythmy*—the well-proportioned, harmonious, and pleasing appearance of the whole. It gave the immediate impression of compactness and completeness, and its beauty lay in the impossibility of adding, subtracting, or altering any part without disrupting the whole. Its ideal rhythm consisted of a lucid repetition of similar elements, such as the columns, which within themselves have a harmonious stability. Oswald Spengler has described the *Classical* as that which can be taken in at a single glance. While this seems an oversimplification, the Parthenon's major design does give itself thus readily to the eye. We are immediately aware of certain individual parts, then of their tidy and disciplined relation to other parts and to the whole—not unlike the relationships making up the *polis*, or Greek city-state, of which Athena was the embodiment. Each component has its own identity and designation within the nomenclature of the Doric order; if separated from the totality, the part and its location could be quickly identified. Parts with similar identity have a like measure and proportion to the whole, constituting the Greek ideal of symmetry. If we were presented with only one half of a Greek temple, it would be possible to predict or reconstruct the other half with maximum certainty.

Beauty and nature were interpretable to the Classical Greeks in terms of an ideal, or conceptually perfect, human body. Such a body, composed of harmoniously disposed and interrelated parts, was symmetrical and lucidly manifested its weight and support. The temple columns and their capitals are like legs easily supporting a torso. The taste for a round, tapered, and fluted column is indicative of a preference for the animate and sensitive proportion found in the best 5th-century figure sculpture. Each groove or *flute* can contain a man's back. As further evidence of the application of human scale, the intervals between the column axes can be expressed in terms of a column diameter and the width of a man's shoulders. The overall size of the Parthenon is itself more humanly oriented than is that of the mammoth Egyptian temple. Like the perfect idealized human form, the form of the Parthenon is based upon a mathematical module and a consistent set of ratios. There was an Athenian foot unit, and Professor William Dinsmoor's meticulous measuring of the Parthenon has revealed that Ictinus used mathematics rather than impulse to achieve the structure's perfect and unprecedented visual harmony. The ratio of the temple's height to its width on the east and west faces is 4 to 9; that of its width to its length is also 4 to 9; and that of the column diameter to the interval between columns *(intercolumniation)* is 9 to 4. The seventeen columns on the long sides are twice plus one the eight columns on the east and west, which again reduces to a 9 to 4 relation. With but a single module and ratio, the architect could calculate mentally all the proportions and dimensions of his building. It is likely that Pythagoras' work with numbers and his belief that everything could be expressed in terms of them influenced Ictinus. Numbers were believed eternal and incorruptible values because they existed outside the senses. Looking patiently at the Parthenon permits both the visualization and the intuition of its proportional system, which induces a strong sense of equanimity and of the structure's rightness.

91. View of the Parthenon stylobate, showing curvature.

**Optical Refinements** Further separating Ictinus' Parthenon from earlier Greek temples are the excellence and thoroughness of its optical refinements. There is not a perfectly straight line in the entire building. The purpose of every subtly curving edge may have been to correct the optical distortion of sagging that one experiences when looking at a long straight line or may have been to give a more sculptural appearance or a certain springiness to activate the temple's relation to the ground, and also that of its supporting columns to their load. Each step is convexly curved (Fig. 91), with this almost imperceptible curvature forming the perimeter of a tremendous circle having a diameter, according to Dinsmoor, of 3½ miles. The entire upper portion of the temple above the column level had a similar curve, and even the great door frames were curved. The columns near the corners have been placed closer together in order to provide a visual arrest for the eye as it moves along the peripheral colonnades. This placement also serves to align the triglyphs and metopes with the columns in such a fashion that two triglyphs are made to meet at the corner. The columns at each of the four corners have been slightly thickened so as not to appear spindly or thinner than the others since, because of their position, they are seen against the sky. The column shafts have been given a slight swelling, or *entasis*, as they rise from the base, to prevent the impression of sagging in the middle; they are also tilted back slightly to prevent the illusion that the building is falling forward. Use of such optical refinements, which required a consummate knowledge of mathematics and extremely difficult labor, augmented the beauty of the temple immeasurably. Though these devices are not all or immediately apparent to the eye, they impress themselves subtly on the mind and feelings. The brilliant execution of these refinements in the Parthenon surpasses any previous occasional but unsystematic use, thereby assisting Ictinus to bring the Greek temple form to perfection.

**Sculpture** The Parthenon was further enhanced by superb sculpture, in the form of the continuous frieze, metopes,

*top:* 92. ***Hermes and Dionysus*** (seated *left*) and ***Magistrate with Boy Folding Peplos*** (extreme *right*), from east frieze of the Parthenon. Marble, height 42″. British Museum, London.

*above:* 93. ***Hermes and Dionysus***, detail of Figure 92.

*left:* 94. Triglyphs and metope, the Parthenon. Metope 4′8″ × 4′2″.

two tympanum groups on the pediments, and decorative *acroteria*, or roof sculptures (Figs. 92–94). The roof ornament included lion heads and a sculpture group at the apex of the pediment, all of which have been lost. The metope sculptures, which dealt not with the historically recent Persian Wars but with legendary victories won by the ancestors of the Athenians over the Lapiths, the Centaurs, and the Trojans, lent animation to the horizontal and vertical lines of the temple. The metope figures are carved in strong relief and in a wide variety of movements at variance with the axes of their frames. The tympanums contained sculptural representations—on the east, of the birth of Athena from the brow of Zeus and, on the west, of the victory of Athena over Poseidon. These sculptures were supervised by Phidias. Many of them were painted and were carved in the round. Isolated, each figure has an autonomous beauty, and yet all fit harmoniously into a larger group. Despite the magnificence of these sculptures, as decoration they did not overbalance the temple as a whole but served as a crowning religious and aesthetic element.

Just as the Parthenon pays tribute to the high civilizing ideals and the ordering instinct of the Classical Greek mind, so does it also recall some of the limitations of that culture and its art. Ictinus was respectful of tradition, though not a slave to it. Within definite limits he refined and improved what had come before, but he did not revolutionize Greek temple architecture. The engineering of the Parthenon is extremely conservative; its post-and-lintel system was thousands of years old. The Greeks knew the principles of the arch and the dome but continued to associate certain traditional forms with their sacred buildings, and there was no structural adventurousness like that found later in Rome or in the medieval period of Western Europe. Typical of Classical art is a desire to codify what is perfect, and there is no aesthetic or engineering advance beyond the Parthenon in Greek architecture. The Greek ordering impulse found it hard to adapt to the tensions and changing times that followed. The cool aloofness and exquisite closed perfection of the Parthenon, like Classical sculpture, do not partake of the qualities of variety, the unexpected, emotional warmth, and psychological range encountered in ancient daily living. Herbert Muller has pointed out that the Classical Greeks had no respect for empirical knowledge and little sense of history; in the metopes, for example, the reliefs depict scenes from mythology rather than specific events. In Classical art time is suspended, and so there are many links missing between the Parthenon and life in 5th-century Athens.

Perhaps it is coincidental, but part of the downfall of Athens was her inability to sustain successful alliances with other countries. Political misfortune and disunity caused the initiators of the Parthenon—Pericles and Phidias—to fall from power, the latter ironically and falsely accused of stealing gold intended for Athena's statue. Longer than the city-state that produced it, the Parthenon and its noble but restricted ideals have endured as a beautiful abstraction. As Spengler has observed, the Greeks' mode of worship was a pious observation of form, not soaring aspiration.

## THE GOTHIC CATHEDRAL

The best approach to the Gothic cathedral in France is that taken by the medieval pilgrim, who, traveling on foot to a city such as Chartres, first saw the distant cathedral spires across the open fields. Physically, economically, aesthetically, and spiritually, the Cathedral still dominates the town of Chartres (Fig. 95). The cathedrals that rose above the medieval houses glorified not only Christ and the Virgin but also the cities that erected them; thus they symbolized man's awareness of the divine as well as his own self-consciousness. The Gothic was basically an urban style, for the very phenomenon of cathedral building presupposed the extensive development of cities in the 11th and 12th centuries. The growth of these cities in turn reflected important stages in European socioeconomic growth: the accumulation of wealth, organization of labor, an administrative efficiency, transportation and communication improvements, the establishment of relative political stability, and specific developments and techniques such as horseshoe nails and pulleys in mechanics. There also began to emerge significant intellectual resources and activity outside the monasteries.

During the 12th and 13th centuries, the hundred-mile area around Paris was covered with what one medieval writer called a "snowfall of cathedrals." Cathedral building was at that time an economic expenditure surpassed only by war. Today, it staggers the imagination that a city such as Chartres, having a probable population of only 10,000 in the 12th century, should undertake to erect, within a period of less than thirty years, a single structure that would now cost in excess of $75 million. Although built in some respects to satisfy civic pride, the Gothic cathedral was above all a gift to God. The rivalry between French cities to outdo one another in the size and magnificence of their cathedrals was undoubtedly motivated in part by secular concerns, such as economic benefits, but the deep and measureless religious faith and optimism of the builders were truly the prime movers. Like their cities, no two Gothic cathedrals are the same. In addition to great variations in size, the sheer variety and complexity of Gothic cathedral architecture prohibits us from writing about a fixed type as we could in discussing the Greek temple. This variety in itself furnishes evidence against the stereotype view of the essential unity, conservatism, and lethargy of medieval society. There was only

95. Chartres Cathedral, view from the city. c. 1194–1260.

one Church, however, and the cathedral does symbolize a basic spiritual unification. The so-called Gothic period was a time of continuing change; its architectural styles seemed constantly in process, their evolution reminding us of the vitality and discord of the Middle Ages.

The word *cathedral*, derived from the Latin *cathedra*, signifies that the bishop's seat is within. The bishops and their urban dioceses represented, in a sense, a rivalry with the Cistercian monasteries and their ascetic world-denying doctrines. The richly ornamented and elaborately designed exteriors of the cathedrals reflect a more affirmative attitude toward life on earth and a more explicit recognition of the civil community than do the austere, introverted monastic churches. From every prospect within the town, the forcefulness and rich variety of the cathedral's design make themselves felt. There was no prescribed approach, no one sacred way by which the worshiper was to proceed to the front of this house of God. In their original state, the cathedrals were not isolated by the open spaces or plazas that girdle many of them in their present condition (Fig. 96). A cathedral might have had squares of some sort on the west and north or south, but usually the city's secular buildings encroached directly upon the church walls, on its complex of chapterhouse, cemetery, school, prison, and bishop's residence. This tight proximity of the secular and the sacred parallels the role that the cathedral played in the community.

The Gothic cathedral was more than the religious focus of its society. Its bells regulated the day's secular activities, just as events in the life of Christ, the Virgin, and the saints provided the calendar for fairs, festivals, and the mystery plays. From the 11th century it became a seat of learning in both secular and sacred subjects. The cathedral satisfied the human need for spectacle, serving as backdrop and stage for its daily religious drama as well as for popular, often irreverent festivities. Churchmen regarded the public explosions on the Feast of Fools as safety valves against the rigorous proscriptions of Christian dogma. This explains the specific occasions that allowed such outrages as gambling and sausage-eating at the high altar, the worship of donkeys in the sanctuary (censed by burning shoe leather), or the election of a mock pope by the laity dressed as monks. At times the Heavenly Father's house served as playground for his children. Merchants used tax-free Church property during the great fairs that brought wealth to the city and funds for the cathedral's construction. At Chartres a fire destroyed most of the cathedral in 1194. It could be rebuilt because of wealth from the sale of indulgences, from gifts toward the enshrinement of the sacred relic of the Virgin's cloak, and from huge sums paid to church officials in rents and tithes. In addition, workmen gave time and labor, while wealthy confraternities of tradesmen donated substantial amounts of money for the cathedral's reconstruction. It was not unusual for business transactions to be conducted within the nave of the cathedral, and, on occasion, wine was sold in the crypt at Chartres.

The silence encountered today in the cathedrals is in great contrast to the clatter of voices about which the priests complained in medieval times. These disruptions lead to the building of screens *(rood screens)* in the 13th century, to separate the choir and altar from the congregation and to allow the priests to celebrate the Mass in privacy. The cathedral nave served variously as a lecture, hiring, and concert hall, as a repository for important civic documents and for commemorative monuments, as an arsenal, a municipal museum, and a trysting place. In many instances the bishop or deacons owned only the eastern portion of the church and not the nave, which belonged to the city.

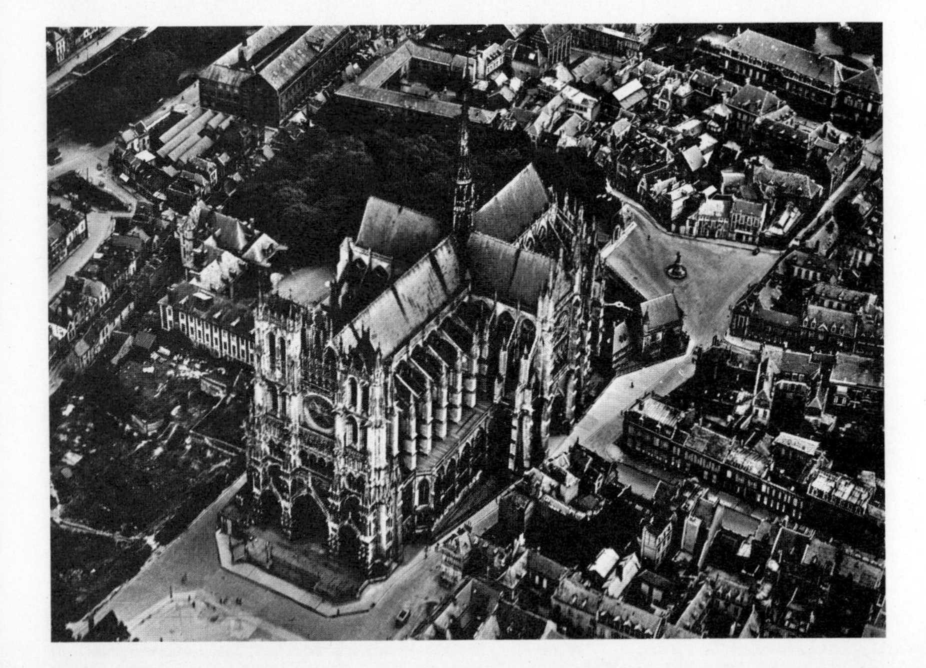

96. Amiens Cathedral, aerial view. c. 1220–88.

*left:* 97. Tombstone of Hugh Libergier, Reims Cathedral. 1263. Photo courtesy C. F. Barnes, Jr.

*right:* 98. Labyrinth, Reims Cathedral. Begun 1211. Drawing.

*below:* 99. VILLARD DE HONNECOURT. c. 1235. Vellum and ink, 9 × 6″. Bibliothèque Nationale, Paris.

**Architects** The fact that we do not know the names of many architects who worked on the Gothic cathedrals—such as the principal one for Chartres—does not substantiate the view that they were anonymous in their own time or were simply of the "folk" or of the priesthood. In reality, the names of many medieval architects have survived because of the medieval distaste for anonymity, the great esteem in which master builders were held, and the means by which they were honored. Jean d'Orbais and Hugh Libergier of Reims and Robert de Luzarches of Amiens are examples. Some builders were given such degrees as a doctorate in stonemasonry, and certain notable architects—Robert de Luzarches and Hugh Libergier, for instance—were entombed in churches they built (Fig. 97), and their effigies engraved on the burial slab. Moreover, the names of the architects or "masters of the work" were inscribed in a floor medallion at the end of a labyrinth incised on the nave pavement. The labyrinth (Fig. 98) was the architect's mark because it was associated with Daedalus, designer of the famous labyrinth commissioned by King Minos of ancient Crete for the palace at Cnossos as a place in which to secure the minotaur, a monster with the head of a bull and the body of a man. In medieval times, architects honored Daedulas as their creative ancestor. By crawling along the labyrinth on their knees, those who could not make the pilgrimage to Jerusalem were able to make the journey symbolically and, not coincidentally, pay their respects to the builder. The master builders of the cathedrals, the equivalents of present-day architects, frequently came from distinguished lay families, were trained by their fathers, and had roughly a middle-class and free professional status. They seemed to have been pious men of good moral character and education who were quite well off financially. They had opportunity for travel, since their services were often vied for on an international basis. Their education was in the craft of masonry or carpentry, Euclidean geometry, drafting, Latin and French, and various techniques and secrets of building that were passed on from one generation to the next. Much of their education was empirical, being based on what worked, and for centuries Gothic architecture developed by trial and error. The notebook (Fig. 99) of the 13th-century architect Villard de Honnecourt (fl. 1230–35) reveals a broad curiosity—about machines, sculpture, furniture, details of buildings, and animals. The master builder might well be versed in the making of objects and ornaments, furniture, and fortifications, as well as churches and castles. He looked to established successful prototypes rather than to originality as a basis for design.

The function of the master builder was to conceive the plan in consultation with a priest or the cathedral canons, or even the bishop, and to decide how to go about building the edifice. A financial adviser told him of his margin for the building's splendor, and thereafter he usually relied on a foreman to oversee the actual construction. Managing the business aspect per se was not the architect's job, and his tasks were more specific. Often responsible for selecting materials, he also procured the labor, estimated costs and quantities, settled labor disputes, and saw to the welfare of his artisans. A permanent workshop and planning office was established during a cathedral's building. By the 13th century the master builder gave orders only and had achieved a social status superior to that of earlier medieval architects.

Because of its prohibitive cost, plans were not drawn on parchment until the 14th century. Earlier, drafting of details or sections had usually been done on plaster slabs or wood panels, and these were not saved. Not until the 15th century, with the erection of Brunelleschi's Pazzi Chapel, was the whole building meticulously planned in advance. Many of the details of building and ornament were left to experienced and trusted masons, carpenters, and sculptors. When an architect on one of these great projects died, his successor respected what had already been constructed; still, while he might continue work on unfinished sections according to the original plans, he might also choose to introduce new ideas. The Cathedral of Chartres lacks a homogeneous style, for its sponsors did not insist upon any standard of architectural consistency other than excellence. It is a peculiarity, even a distinction, of the Gothic style that it is able to absorb such a heterogeneity of modes.

Although the Gothic cathedral impresses the modern viewer with its rich symbolism, the basic problems confronting the master builder were practical. His various considerations included adapting his plan to the demands of the liturgy and the performance of the canonical offices; providing for the proper disposition of relics and subsidiary altars; facilitating the movement of the congregation and of processions; and making provision for delivery of the sermon.

**Meaning and Organization** As discussed in Chapter 2 (p. 35), Lévi-Strauss has suggested that art throughout the world metaphorically miniaturizes that which it represents. As great as the Gothic cathedrals are in physical size, they too are imaginative models of the many things they stand for. Within the medieval metropolis, the cathedral meant *unity*—of religion, wealth, and politics. The Church sanctified a political monarchy, and the Gothic cathedral signified the solidarity of urban bishops, and often their cities, with the Capetian kings of France. This union served the contracting parties by weakening the respective powers of the monastic abbots and the nobility. As the spiritual defender of the realm, the cathedral was thus an official seal upon a mutual alliance between commerce, the Church, and the State. In the 12th and 13th centuries, the cathedral represented a growing French consciousness of cultural as well as religious and political unity. Money was one of the great forces that weakened the hold of feudal nobles, such as the Count of Chartres, upon the urban merchants, and by farsighted alliances, many city churchmen gained the financial support of the most dynamic class in French medieval society. Religious confraternities of burghers were formed, further tightening the bonds between the religious aspect of the cathedral and secular money, energy, and labor. Many stained-glass windows bear the names or effigies of secular urban donors or groups, and the figure of Peter of Dreux, Duke of Brittany (Fig. 100), kneeling below the figure of Christ between the south transept doors at Chartres, symbolizes the generous benefaction of the royal family.

Norris Smith has analyzed the implications of this social interaction on architecture as follows: "The medieval architect was less interested in manipulating the psychological responses of the worshiper than in erecting a suitable Palace of the Queen of Heaven. . . . the validity of the building lay in its relationship to the Virgin and to the unshakable reality of the institutions of church, monarchy and city, rather than in its power to arouse a response in a self-centered observer." Although this interpretation may be correct in part, no architect could fail to be aware of his clients—bishops and royalty as well as wealthy merchants—with regard to their aspirations for the cathedral. It may be closer to the truth if we suppose that the medieval architect combined and synthesized his objectives. In Paul Frankl's view men could pray anywhere in medieval times, "but a prayer chamber for the multitude, a church, must aim through its symbolism of form, to provide a suitable aesthetic framework for the prayers of the many."

The extent to which conscious symbolism entered directly into the developing form of the Gothic cathedral is difficult to assess. In the period of great cathedral building, there was a strong interest in symbolic interpretation, allegories, and metaphors. The cathedrals lent themselves to a wealth of allusions, to views that the material form of the church structure, for example, symbolizes the spiritual church. Since Early Christian times the church was seen as a metaphor of man's soul, and also as a representation of the Kingdom of Heaven and the mystical body of Christ. Both externally and internally, the cathedral served as a kind of

*left:* 100. Peter of Dreux, donor statue at the base of the south-portal trumeau, Chartres Cathedral. 13th century( ?).

sacred theater: its west façade provided a backdrop for mystery plays, and in its altar area the mysteries of the ritual were performed and the holy objects displayed. The architects were literate, educated, and in contact with the intellectual leaders, spiritual and lay, of the community. They consulted with canons, bishops, theologians, and priests on the theological program for the sculpture. Great theologians of the past had given much significance to the concepts of *measure* and *light,* but that these abstruse interpretations were consistently and systematically translated into medieval architectural design is conjectural. Of great influence were the already existing religious buildings, as well as the practical problems posed, after 1200, in erecting and supporting enormous vaults more than a hundred feet from the floor of the nave. The height of the nave at Chartres is 120 feet; at Reims, 125 feet; at Amiens, 138 feet.

Official handbooks of Church symbolism did not exist for the artist to consult. While there were important 12th- and 13th-century writings by such men as Durandus, these were not dogma, and the literary symbols contained within the treatises gave no assistance in matters of style or, in many cases, for evolving the shapes of parts. The cathedrals inspired reverent fantasies in many writers who worshiped within them, and their various interpretations of the same architectural features were formulated after the fact and were not consistent. What adds to the wonder of the cathedrals, and to their intellectual greatness in history, is that their architects did give—in one way or another—symbolic form to the highest ideals and much of the spirit of their age. Acquaintance with the Gothic cathedrals makes us aware of their profound and sometimes elusive connection with the societies which produced the Crusades, the feudal system, and universities and which enriched science and philosophy, contributed significantly to jurisprudence, and fashioned the poetry of the troubadours. To comprehend the meaning of the Gothic cathedral in its broadest and deepest sense, all these diversified activities must be explored, as modern scholarship has progressively undertaken to do.

By its great size and ornateness alone, the Gothic cathedral was truly acknowledged the house of God, but unlike a temple of Athena, the deity in tangible form did not dwell within. The cathedral was an ambivalent symbol of the new and greater Temple of Solomon, a symbol of Christ, the heavenly Jerusalem, and the universe. Its magnificence, in terms of the treasure expended on it, was deemed appropriate to its function as an offering from the faithful and as the spiritual residence of Christ or the Virgin. At Chartres the Virgin was more than a remote symbol; she was, as George Henderson has observed, a distinct personality, and like Athena she was involved in the affairs of the city. When the fire of 1194 ravaged the old Cathedral, it did not damage the cherished relic of the Virgin's cloak that was housed there. This was interpreted as a sign of the Virgin's will, a sign that she wanted an even greater residence. A further example of this direct relationship between the Virgin and the medieval Christian populace can be found in a book of her miracles and revelations to the people, which was composed at Chartres in 1210. It was through the cathedral that man was made aware of the invisible and infinite, that the divine became immanent. The master builder sought to devise a setting which would so stimulate the thoughts and feelings of the worshiper that he could realize the most important event of his life, the soul's communion with God.

*The West Façade.* All the major parts of the cathedral have a tradition extending back into the Middle Ages or, in some cases, even to antiquity. Their assimilation into the cathedral structure was a process involving not only formal adaptation and modification but also symbolic meaning. The sources of the *Gateway to Heaven,* as the west façade was called, can be traced to Syrian churches of the 6th and 7th centuries and to

*left:* 101. Façade, Abbey Church, Corvey, Germany. 873–85.

*right:* 102. West façade, Chartres Cathedral. Width 157′; south tower (*right*), height 344′; north tower (*left*), height 377′. Façade c. 1194–1260 (portals and lancet windows c. 1145); south tower c. 1180; north spire 1507–13.

certain Roman Imperial palaces fronted with twin-towered portals (Fig. 307). As Baldwin Smith has shown in a brilliant study, towered gateways were used as entrances to royal cities and abbeys in Carolingian times (Fig. 101) and were the scene of impressive ceremonial receptions upon a king's arrival. The transformation of the Early Christian basilica into a twin-towered edifice must be seen in the light of Charlemagne's revival of Roman political symbolism and his desire to show his ascendancy over the Church as well as the State. The emperor's symbolic participation in the religious service and his exalted authority were indicated in the towered façades of Carolingian and certain Romanesque churches by a *solarium,* or balcony, on which was located his throne and behind which was placed a large circular window. Sun symbolism was in that epoch equated with the authority of the king as well as of Christ. By the late 13th century, however, the symbolism of the west façade alluded entirely to Christ. Nevertheless, the façades of such Gothic cathedrals as Chartres (Fig. 102), with portals that had evolved in Carolingian times, "galleries of kings," circular windows, and double towers, still bear the impress of earthly royalty.

*The Circular Window.* The origin and significance of the great circular window of the west façade has been explored by Helen Dow, whose research indicates that circular windows go back to Babylonian times and had been known in Europe since Roman times. Unlike the well-known but misnamed Gothic "rose window," the circular window, with few exceptions, lacked stone tracery until the building of the Abbey Church of St-Denis, about 1140. The basic form of the rose window (Fig. 103), as found at Chartres, may have originated in old schemata of the symbolic wheel. Great Byzantine chandeliers, composed of pierced metal disks, were in use in France by the 12th century, either as hanging or as standing lamps. Lamps lent themselves to expression of the sun and light symbolism that had become associated with Christ in the Middle Ages. The circular form was rich in meaning, for it might signify virtue, eternity, God, or the Church. The great circular window also echoed the form and associations of the wheel of fortune, through which Christian virtue and its reward could be contrasted with the vicissitudes and transient nature of earthly existence. Ezekiel's vision of the wheel in the Old Testament made the window form an appropriate allusion to the Scriptures. The prominence of the window as well as its form symbolized the eternal and righteous eye of God. The word *nave* means "ship" in Latin, the window being, thus, the ship's guiding eye. Divine light and justice seem to have been two of the most important meanings of the window. As it had in its use by Charlemagne, the circular window in combination with the many sculptures of saints surrounding it conveyed the notion of a king surrounded by his armies. The full significance of this interpretation becomes apparent when the sculptural program of the west façade of Chartres is examined.

*The Sculptural Program of the Chartres West Façade.* The great main doors of the Gothic cathedral represented the Gates of Paradise. The purpose of the programs worked out with theologians for the sculpture occupying the honored positions around and immediately above the doors and for the imagery in the stained-glass windows was to manifest Church doctrine. It is questionable that these sculptures were directly intended to be didactic or self-evidently symbolic, for it would appear that the faithful relied upon the spoken word for their instruction in dogma and, hence, in the meaning of art. That elaborate theological programs were actually planned and carried out for cathedral imagery has long been known. In this connection, Adolph Katzenellenbogen contributed an outstanding study of the sculptural program of the west façade of Chartres (Fig. 104), which explained that the figures of the three *tympanums,* or semicircular relief panels over the doors, present Christ in his dual nature of God and Man, as well as the source of divine wisdom.

At the far right, the Christ child is shown seated on the lap of the enthroned Virgin, indicating her role in his Incarnation. In the pointed vaults bordering the tympanum are representations of the seven liberal arts (grammar, dialectic, rhetoric, arithmetic, music, geometry, and astronomy), the intellectual means by which to attain awareness of divine wisdom. The Virgin, esteemed for her wisdom, became the inspiration and guide of these arts—an indication of the growth of humanistic studies within the medieval Church. The left tympanum depicts the Ascension of Christ. Its peripheral vaults contain symbols of the zodiac and of diverse manual labor. The concepts illustrated here are Christ's

*above:* 103. Rose window, west façade, Chartres Cathedral.

*left:* 104. West portals, Chartres Cathedral. c. 1145–70.

transcendence of and rule over time, and the value of active physical labor, which, balanced with the contemplative life of learning, led the faithful toward knowledge of God. The central tympanum shows the Second Coming of Christ and the Last Judgment. Immediately below the central tympanum, on the rectangular lintel panel, are arrayed the twelve prophets who foretold Christ's Incarnation and who are to assist at the Last Judgment.

Flanking the doors of the Royal Portal are the *jamb figures,* whose purpose it is to proclaim the sympathetic concord existing between Church and State and between the Old and the New Testament and to publicize the illustrious lineage of the French monarchy. It was common practice in the Middle Ages to portray past or present kings and queens of France as important personages from the Old and New Testament; this custom emphasized that the royal line was a defender of the Church and enhanced it in the public esteem. The implication was that the virtuous qualities of the Old Testament kings were continued in the monarchs of France. This was all part of the medieval preoccupation with searching for parallels between the present and the past, the old and the new, the visible and the invisible. The elongated jamb figures, which date from about the mid-12th century, have a columnar aspect, and their form and purpose suggest that they comprise a second wall by which the Church is strengthened and defended. One must pass between the predecessors of Christ on the jambs before reaching him; this sequence signified the old leading to the new. To pass through the door was to move toward God through Christ, for Christ had said: "I am the door. Whoever enters me will be saved." The gallery above the circular window contains the effigies of French monarchs, hence the familiar name "gallery of kings" (Fig. 102). The gallery itself may have derived from the earlier medieval and ancient palace "window of appearances," from which the ruler presented himself to the public. While the effigies of the kings protected the western front of the church, the bishops' images were presented as defenders of its sides.

*The Bay System.* *Bays* are the rectangular cubelike compartments formed by each vault and its four piers. Professor Walter Horn has traced the origin of the bay system in medieval churches to early medieval secular wooden architecture as used in all-purpose structures, episcopal tithe barns, and houses (Figs. 105, 106). A few timber churches subdivided into bays have survived from the Middle Ages. In many sections of medieval Europe, residences, markets, and barns were structurally interchangeable. Tithe barns, which stored the one-tenth of a crop given to the Church by the faithful, were often of tremendous dimensions, since their construction from regular units permitted structures of great length. The Early Christian basilicas were not composed of bays, and the entrance of this technique into religious architecture, probably during the 9th century, is another important

*above:* 105. Market Hall at Mereville, France. 15th century.

*right:* 106. Nave, looking east toward the apse, Chartres Cathedral. c. 1194–1221.

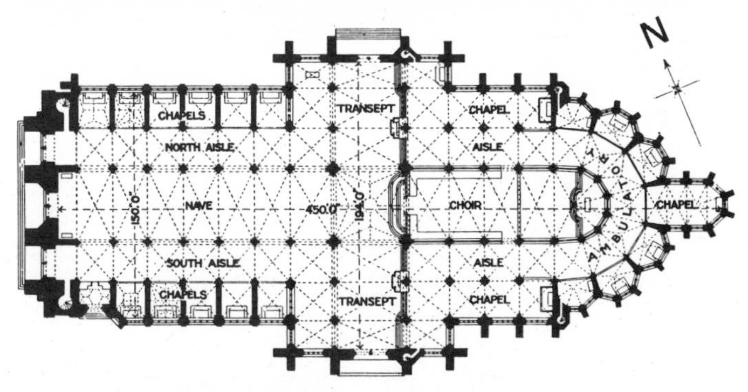


107. Plan, Amiens Cathedral.

example of drawing upon secular sources for religious architecture. The introduction of the bay into the basilican form skeletalized and partitioned the interior into similar units, thereby opening up great possibilities for expressive articulation of the space and for the use of geometrical or arithmetical premises in organizing the interior. The bay system was valued by the cathedral builders because of its familiarity and ease of handling. It met the Gothic need for a multiplicity of parts, and the implications it carried satisfied a feudal and hierarchical intent. The Scriptures may not have provided sources for specific architectural shapes, but Solomon (2:20) might be quoted as comfort to the successful architect: "Thou hast ordered all things in measure and number and weight."

*The Plan and Measure.* As had been formerly practiced in ancient and early medieval times, the orientation of the Gothic cathedral was meant to place the building in harmony with the universe (Fig. 107). The apse, containing the altar that symbolized Christ's tomb, was oriented consistently toward the east, the direction signifying rebirth. The western end was traditionally associated with death and evil; hence it was on this entrance that the Last Judgment was carved. The north was identified with cold and darkness, the world of the old order. The south signified the new dispensation. In addition to its symbolic value as a form, the demands of the liturgy caused the retention of the long-established cross plan; it facilitated procession through the nave, provided a large area for the choir east of the transept and ample space for the altar, and made feasible side aisles for accommodating the pilgrims who came to venerate the relics in the chapels. The basic plan of the Gothic cathedral had already emerged in Carolingian times, with the addition to the standard basilican elements (nave, aisles, apse, and an occasional transept) of a crypt, choir, and radiating chapels. In medieval times, cathedrals added many private side chapels to the apse, indicating the growth in strength of private families on whom the Church relied for funds and influence. The marked internal divisions of the church's plan signified the hierarchical order and authority of the clergy and its relation to the laity, who were prohibited access to the choir and altar areas. The plan thereby symbolized the stratification of the Kingdom of God according to rank and responsibility.

Scholars who have taken pains to draw accurate ground plans of medieval churches have found that in certain cases it is possible to discover a kind of scientific organization. One of the trade secrets of the master builder was a module on which he established both the scale and the proportions of his building. Recent surveys have shown that these proportions were often used in the plan and elevation of Gothic cathedrals, bridging what had been thought to be a gap in building practices between antiquity and the Renaissance.

Using any polygon, the master builder worked out the problem of building a tower and effecting the transition from a square base to a round spire. While all builders recognized the use of geometry as an aid to building, there were undoubtedly some who by temperament sought to use it extensively in a way that guaranteed them "true measure" and thereby heightened the cathedral's symbolic analogy to the measure that unified the universe. Otto von Simson argued strongly for the incidence of the latter attitude in his study of Chartres. His findings showed that a basic ratio of 5 to 8 was utilized in the plan and elevation of the Cathedral. Von Simson found further support for his argument in the fact that, in the Middle Ages, God was frequently referred to and even depicted as a geometer (Fig. 108). Church literature

*right:* 108. *Christ as Geometer*, from the *Bible Moralisée*. 13th century. Österreichische Nationalbibliothek, Vienna.

before and during the time of the cathedrals is rich in religious interpretation of numbers and geometry: to cite but two examples, the triangle symbolized the Trinity, and the square the relation of God the Father to the Son. In mystical numerology, almost any number could be interpreted as revealing some aspect of divinity or dogma. Numbers and geometry were thought to be important means through which the intellect and workings of God could be made intelligible to human understanding. The Gothic designer's taste for numerology is displayed in towers, fenestration patterns, piers, balustrades, arcades, statues, and doors. The parts of the cathedral do lend themselves to counting in numerical sequences, but not to a single grand program of interpretation as numerical symbolism. Selectively, rather than in a literal quantitative way, the master builder again realized a vital preoccupation of his time.

*The Interior and Light.* The dedicatory services performed in the sanctuary of the cathedral drew principally upon three Biblical sources to link the building to the past. The first was the account of the Temple of Solomon (II Chron. 2-6), the second was the Temple of Ezekiel, and the third was the description of the Heavenly Jerusalem by St. John. While the Bible does not describe in detail what Solomon's temple looked like, it does record a facing of gold and precious gems, and this description may have influenced St. John, who presents the most striking reference for the celestial city:

> And the building of the wall of it was of jasper; and the city was pure gold, like unto clear glass. And the foundation of the wall of the city was garnished with all manner of precious stones. . . . And the city had no need of the sun, neither of the moon, to shine in it; for the glory of God did lighten it.

Other Biblical sources speak of glass walls, and the increased use of stained glass in the 12th and 13th centuries may have been an attempt to strengthen the analogy between the church structure and the Heavenly Jerusalem. The design of the cathedral's exterior reflected much of the religious and secular history of man; the interior was considered the mystical heart of the cathedral, where God's epiphany takes place.

To enter into the initial darkness of the cathedral from the sunlit exterior is to experience once more the medieval worshiper's sense of proceeding from the material to the celestial world (Pl. 8, p. 78). Perhaps the most exalted efforts of imagination, the most inspired creations, of the Gothic builders are the internal colored light and the idealized space of the cathedral. Light and color are both form and symbol, the style and content of Gothic religious architecture. When the churches had their original complement of windows, the suffused polychrome glow never permitted total revelation of the space and detail or, significantly, of the measure of the interior. There was no comparable spatial or lighting effect in any other type of medieval building. The ranges of windows became luminous walls, and their deep and shifting reddish violet hues dematerialized the interior stonework, as if abstractly signifying spiritual triumph over material things. The space, lighting, and music of the cathedral interior transported the worshiper from an environment of familiar sounds, illumination, scale, textures, and dimensions into a world of intricate melodies of sound and color, changing vistas, elusive surfaces, and heights not determined by his own measure. The quick change from sunlight to darkness impelled the visitor to slow his pace in order to penetrate what initially seemed veiled from the eyes. The stained-glass windows were intended to keep out almost all external light and all reminders of the earthly world. Their task was to elevate and enlighten the mind and soul. Seen from the floor of the nave, 60 feet away, the narrative scenes on the windows did not lend themselves to easy reading, and details of the rose window were undecipherable. Within the relative obscurity of the interior, the sonorous reds and blues could be fully apprehended by the eye, and the gold of the altar achieved a finer luminosity.

The brilliance of the original cathedrals, however, was not confined to their stained-glass windows alone. In the 13th century, Durandus wrote:

> The ornaments of the nave consist of dorsals, tapestry, mattings, and cushions of silk, purple and the like. The ornaments of the choir consist of dorsals, tapestry, carpets and cushions. Dorsals are hangings of cloth at the back of the clergy. Mattings, for their feet. Tapestry is likewise strewed under the feet, particularly under the feet of Bishops, who ought to trample worldly things under their feet. Cushions are placed on the seats or benches of the choir.

But it was the light from the windows that inspired the greatest awe and inspired praise by Church theologians of the cathedral's "bright" and "lucid" structure. God was perfect light into which no mortal eye could look, and the light that man could see was but a pale reflection of God. Light was the source and requirement of beauty, the means by which God manifested his presence and his Creation to man. Light passing through the windows symbolized the Incarnation of Christ. Light symbolism, inherited from earlier Christian churches, was also known and used in ancient times. The power and uniqueness of its use in the Gothic cathedral inspired the great Abbot Suger, builder of St-Denis, to record his mystical ascension to God by means of meditation on the light of his cathedral:

> Thus when—out of my delight in the beauty of the house of God—the loveliness of the many-colored gems has called me away from external cares, and worthy meditation has induced

*left:* 109. Structural diagram of a Gothic cathedral.

*right:* 110. Buttresses, south side, Chartres Cathedral.

me to reflect, transferring that which is material to that which is immaterial, on the diversity of sacred virtues; then it seems to me that I see myself dwelling, as it were, in some strange region of the universe which neither exists entirely in the slime of the earth nor entirely in the purity of Heaven; and that, by the grace of God, I can be transported from this inferior to that higher world in an anagogical manner.

**Gothic Style** The Gothic style had its highest expression in cathedrals, and by 1400 it was to become an international style and be extended to secular buildings. In addition to the colored light, soaring spaces, and complex perspectives within the cathedral, other distinguishing features of the Gothic cathedral style include the pointed (occasionally rounded) arch, ribbed vault, and flying buttress, all of which had in some form been known or developed during previous architectural periods. These elements are usually combined in rhythmic numerical sequences. The subordination of components to larger parts and of larger parts to the whole has a strong feudal and hierarchical character. Unlike the organization of the Parthenon, however, there are no fixed numbers or proportions that govern the subordination of all of the parts. Like elements and sequences recur in different scales and combinations with other motifs. It is difficult to separate individual parts from their contexts because of their sequential arrangement and the density of the sequential groups; the viewer, nevertheless, is always conscious of looking at the parts of a greater but incomplete whole. Unlike the Parthenon again, no single prospect permits comprehension of the cathedral's total design. Like Gothic sacred music, the composition of a cathedral is polyphonic—it consists in the simultaneous combination of a number of parts, each constituting an individual theme that harmonizes with the others. There is evidence to suggest further analogy in the use of mathematics to regulate and proportion both musical and architectural structures. Surveys indicate, however, that many builders did not feel obliged to perpetuate older traditions and devised their own variant proportions to achieve more impressive visual harmonies.

To a greater extent than early medieval architecture, the Gothic cathedral reveals its skeletal framework, the multiple play of its vector forces, and the resolution of its thrusts and weight (Figs. 109, 110). The massive walls of the militant-looking Romanesque churches were largely dematerialized by an increased replacement of stone by glass between the main piers supporting the vaults. The cradling action of the flying buttresses involves the external structure in a new way, lending what might be characterized as a muscular appearance to the exterior.

The plan of a Gothic cathedral (Fig. 107) shows the enclosure of the nave and aisles to be a continuous series of points, a regular constellation of piers, which are connected by thin, parallel wall sections. While the medieval architect may not have used the word *space* or even thought of it in the terms of a modern architect, he had a great sensitivity for the effectiveness of certain distances between walls. Villard de Honnecourt's notebook shows a primary concern with

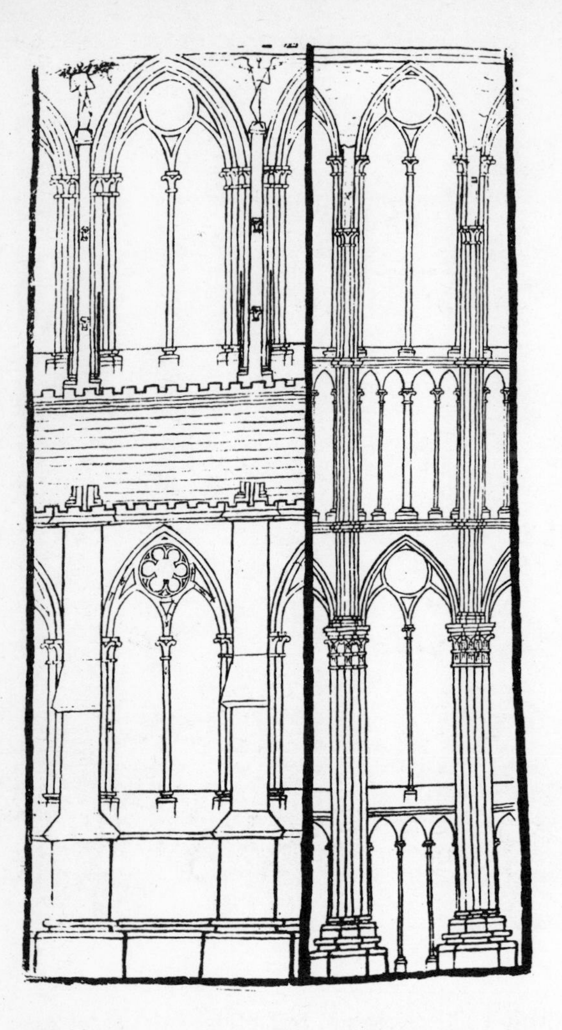

graphically designed screenlike walls (Fig. 111). Much of the physical character of the cathedral was undoubtedly determined by the engineering functions of load and support; the width of the building was probably fixed by what the builder felt he could safely vault and buttress. It is too limited a judgment, however, to look upon the architect's intent as being only to raise a structural tour de force. Many design decisions—such as the addition of pinnacles to buttresses, the clustering of slender shafts against the main piers, the use of pointed arches, and probably the ribbing of the vaults (Fig. 112)—were not purely structural and were intended to enhance the whole and increase its visual expressiveness. There is, for instance, a more pronounced articulation and sculptural treatment of the piers than is in fact necessary for their physical function as support. The proportions of the nave arcade, triforium, and clearstory (see Fig. 109) are the result of decisions deliberately arrived at for aesthetic, and perhaps symbolic reasons, decisions that were intended to bring the building closer to a visual and intellectual perfection. Only in part emotional and subjective, much of the experience we have in entering a Gothic cathedral derives from a rational and an intuitive awareness of the builder's logic, which he went to considerable trouble to make perceptible to the senses. The master builder's rich and complex inventiveness with three-dimensional form, as well as the various adjustments, alterations, additions, and refinements he made beyond a simple concern for the structural imperatives, have occasioned the opinion that in the Gothic cathedral it is function which follows form.

*left:* 111. Villard de Honnecourt. Drawing of exterior and interior elevations of the nave, Reims Cathedral. c. 1240.

*below:* 112. Vaults at the crossing of nave and transepts, Chartres Cathedral.

Plate 7. MATTHIAS GRÜNEWALD. *The Isenheim Altarpiece* (closed). c. 1512–15. Oil on panel; center 8′10″ × 10′1″, sides 7′7$^{3}/_{8}$″ × 2′6″. Musée d'Unterlinden, Colmar. (See pp. 56, 411, Fig. 561.)

*left:* Plate 8. Interior, Chartres Cathedral. 1194–1220. (See p. 74.)

*below:* Plate 9. Le Corbusier. Notre-Dame-du-Haut, view of interior south wall. Ronchamp, France. 1950–55. (See p. 83.)

113. LE CORBUSIER. Notre-Dame-du-Haut, view from southeast. Ronchamp, France. 1950–55.

## LE CORBUSIER'S CHAPEL AT RONCHAMP

The Parthenon and Gothic cathedrals such as Chartres came out of definite established traditions of religious architecture, and their architects sought neither novelty nor original self-expression. In 5th-century Greece and in medieval Europe, the most advanced architecture in terms of design and engineering was in the service of religion. The builders had, in architectural precedent and from scriptural sources, a preestablished public basis for symbolic meaning or religious associations with their architectural forms. In the 19th and 20th centuries, the finest and most advanced buildings in terms of design and structural techniques have been secular enterprises. The problem confronting 20th-century architects has been to evolve, from this generally nonreligious background, an architecture suited to religious purposes, one that would capture the feeling and tone of the sacred. The best modern architects have utilized a personal, empirical approach to each problem rather than depend upon conventional formulas. As a result they have avoided imitating church architecture—of any period. Those enlightened congregations and clergy who have allowed a gifted architect the freedom to create churches and synagogues appropriate to their time, place, and particular religious beliefs have thus inspired rather than inhibited good architecture. Modern architecture has often proved that a fine religious structure need not presuppose that the architect and his patron be of the same faith, as was also seen to be the case in the murals of Matisse at Vence (Fig. 82). Common to Phidias, Hugh Libergier, and the modern Swiss-born architect Le Corbusier (Charles-Edouard Jeanneret, 1886–1965) has been their inspiration by noble ideals as communicated in the idiom of their time.

Ironically, Le Corbusier's pilgrimage chapel of Notre-Dame-du-Haut (Fig. 113), located at Ronchamp in the Vosges Mountains of western France, near Switzerland, was inspired many years before when as a young architect he visited the Parthenon. In his notebook the youthful Le Corbusier set down his thoughts on what constitutes architecture and wherein for him lay the secret of the Parthenon's power. These ideas were later to have a strong influence on the Ronchamp chapel. Architecture, he felt, is an art of sensation, affecting our visual responses, inciting emotion through the senses, and bringing joy to the mind: "Architecture is the skillful, accurate and magnificent play of masses seen in light." The Chapel of Notre-Dame-du-Haut can be profitably analyzed on this basis.

Le Corbusier's assignment was to crown a hill with a new Catholic chapel intended to replace an undistinguished building destroyed in the war, on a site where for as long as men could remember pagan and Christian places of worship had been located. Surrounded by extensive hills and valleys, the elevated site had no accessible road. A specialist in residences and city planning, the architect had never before designed a place of worship, and he was not a Catholic. He was never-

*left:* 114. Notre-Dame-du-Haut, Ronchamp, distant view.

*below:* 115. Notre-Dame-du-Haut, Ronchamp, view of enameled doors, south wall.

*bottom:* 116. Notre-Dame-du-Haut, Ronchamp, view of interior south and east walls.

theless given a free hand in the project by the Archbishop of Besançon—on the premise, one can assume, that architectural genius is nonsectarian. In a letter to the Archbishop when the chapel was finished in 1955, after five years of planning and construction, Le Corbusier wrote:

> I wished to create a place of silence, of prayer, of peace, of spiritual joy. A sense of the sacred animated our effort. Our workmen . . . calculators . . . are those who brought this project into being, a difficult project, meticulous, primitive, made strong by the resources brought into play, but sensitive and informed by all-embracing mathematics, which is the creator of that space which cannot be described in words. A few scattered symbols, a few written words telling the praises of the Virgin. The cross—the true cross of suffering—is raised up in this space; the drama of Christianity has taken possession of the place from this time forwards. . . .

In 1910, Le Corbusier had written that "the Parthenon is drama," and this is the special quality which unites the three religious edifices in this chapter, which set them apart from secular structures in their vicinities. The way in which Le Corbusier achieved his dramatic effect is apparent from the moment the pilgrim or traveler first sights the Ronchamp chapel (Fig. 114.) Like the silhouettes of its Greek and Gothic predecessors, the silolike towers and sweeping roof line of the modern chapel reveal their general character from a considerable distance. But as one comes closer and mounts the hill, they become partially obscured and are then lost from sight—reminiscent of the ascent along the Sacred Way to the Acropolis or toward the Cathedral through the streets of Chartres or Amiens. As one approaches the crest of the hill, the chapel slowly reemerges, like a ship rising above the swelling ground formation the architect had landscaped; and as noted by Le Corbusier himself, its crescent roof also echoes a wave. The distant view of Ronchamp, like that of the Acropolis, prepares us for the structure's dramatic exterior, for its brilliant rough whitewashed walls with the dark raw-concrete roof fold hovering above. The use of whitewash for the exterior brings to mind the once-brilliant color of the Parthenon, which served to evoke the radiant wisdom and beauty of Athena. Further, it recalls the "snowfall of cathedrals," which were, as Le Corbusier himself noted, originally

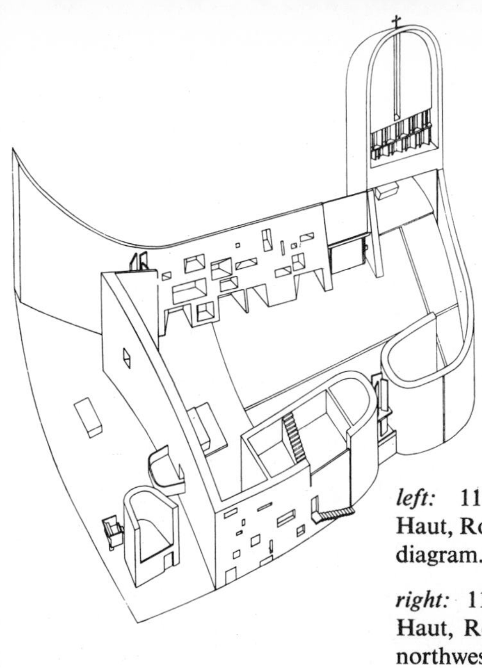

*left:* 117. Notre-Dame-du-Haut, Ronchamp, perspective diagram.

*right:* 118. Notre-Dame-du-Haut, Ronchamp, view from northwest.

white. When the summit has been reached, the first view of the chapel is that opposite the huge brilliantly, enameled processional door (Fig. 115) and the nonuniform and randomly placed splayed openings, suggesting the gun ports of a fortress, on the sloping south wall (Fig. 113).

When first seen from the hill's crown, the chapel's form creates a dramatic sensation that evades comparison. Le Corbusier wanted no possible association with any previous architectural style, and although interesting attempts have been made to liken the conjuncture of sloping roof with battered walls to forms found in crude Stone Age architecture, Ronchamp's architectural uniqueness prevails. Its qualities of a massive and militant aspect, the secretive darkened interior, and the prowlike encounter of the south and east walls evoke quick analogies with fortresses, sacred grottoes, and ships—none of which were consciously sought or intended by the architect as symbolic allusions or design sources. And the soaring, exuberant form seems to combine imaginatively the heavenward sweep of the spire, roof, and towers of the Gothic cathedral. Le Corbusier relied on the lucidity of mathematics not to illustrate theology but to give form to artistic intuition in creating an indefinable structure molding an indescribable space: "I defy a visitor to give offhand the dimensions of the different parts of the building."

This ingrained resistance to paraphrase and a succession of devices in the structure calculated to astonish the beholder are crucial to the architectural drama. As one instance of this, the massive walls do not bear the load of the roof, actually supported by triangularly shaped reinforced-concrete piers imbedded within the rubble-filled walls. Consequently, there is a 4-inch space between the roof and the walls, through which light penetrates the interior and imparts the sense of a floating roof (Fig. 116). Like the Gothic architect, Le Corbusier did not wish to emphasize the engineering aspect of the construction. The dramatic visual and emotional effects devised to induce a meditative and awed mood were most important. The great roof, which seems as if cradled by the towers, bows downward near its center like an enormous trough or sail catching the rain or wind; this covering is hollow and has external shell layers only about 2 inches thick but 7 feet apart. Its structure is like that of an airplane wing. The architect attributed the shape and construction to a crab shell picked up on a Long Island beach in 1946, which when inverted gave the idea for the roof.

When first asked to design the chapel, Le Corbusier refused. Only after several hours had been spent on the actual site and he had felt the impact of the sweeping natural panorama did the first ideas come and reverse his decision. He has written of his building "echoing" nature, as if it were some great sounding board for the natural forms around it. The metaphor and the relation to its site are poetical and imaginative, for the building does not literally illustrate by its formation the architect's comparison.

The spontaneous instinct of the pilgrim, once he has ascended the hill, is to walk around the structure in a clockwise direction. As is shown in the perspective diagram (Fig. 117), its various curving sides are more unpredictable in character than those of Gothic cathedrals. Because the great enameled door is used only for processions on special occasions, the north side contains the door for daily ingress, so that the newcomer usually walks one and a half times around before entering. On the west the wall (Fig. 118) is not pierced with

119. Notre-Dame-du-Haut, Ronchamp, view of east side.

apertures, and its curves reflect small interior chapels and the confessionals. From the roof parapet, there issues an omega-shaped waterspout or abstract gargoyle, from which the rainwater descends and splashes off geometrical shapes imbedded in a concrete pool below. The towers mark the interior chapels, and their vertical concrete louvers, giving texture and rhythmic variety, are permanently fixed. The north wall, though curved to a degree also, has a more markedly squarish character than the south, but its apertures are irregularly disposed in similar fashion, defying Greek and Gothic ideals of alignment and repetition.

The east wall (Fig. 119) is like a large open-air amphitheater or, with its upswept overhanging roof, like a great acoustical backdrop for the Word that is given from the external pulpit and for the sounds of the choir and of the Mass performed at the nearby altar. As many as 10,000 pilgrims have assembled for Mass here; in its use for services, this external church is analogous to the Parthenon's west façade and to the medieval cathedral façades used as backdrops for religious plays.

Unlike the sculptural riches of the Parthenon and the cathedrals, at Ronchamp there is but one piece of sculpture, a 19th-century statue of the Virgin of indifferent artistic quality, which survived the bombardment during World War II and which is housed in a glass case high up on the eastern wall. The image can pivot so that, whether the service is held at the inside altar or in the outdoor amphitheater, the statue overlooks the congregation. Despite the absence of specially executed sculpture, the Ronchamp chapel is in itself the most sculptural or molded in appearance of the religious buildings here considered, and its forms often refute or disguise their structural function. Le Corbusier consciously sought to avoid a building that seemed the product of a technological age, with the rigid rectilinear, repetitive, and invertible forms that have become so familiar in the steel-and-glass boxes of modern commercial architecture. He regarded this chapel as "a modern tool to open up fresh roads in a mechanistic society."

The actual building of Ronchamp was a curious blend of hand labor and modern practice, of traditional and new materials and tools, of intuition and sophisticated scientific calculation. Through the efforts of a small group of versatile laborers of different nationalities under an excellent foreman, the building took shape from materials at hand—such as the ruins of the previous stone church—and from wood, sand, and cement hauled to the hilltop. In the great variety of materials and techniques represented in its construction, there is a parallel to the building of the cathedrals. Both inside and out, Le Corbusier viewed this work as "sculpture in the round." Pulpits, altars, stairways, and wall recesses and projections were all shaped and proportioned to catch light or to cast striking shadows: "Observe the play of shadows . . . precise shadows, clear cut or dissolving. Projected shadows, precisely delineated, but what enchanting arabesques and frets. Counterpoint and fugue. Great music . . . ."

Many modern architects, observing what they feel to be "truth to the medium," refuse to disguise the materials or conceal the structural system employed, thus usually producing a starkly skeletal building. Le Corbusier, however, did not hesitate to cover the rubble and steel reinforcing frames inside the walls with concrete, which in turn was given a rough stucco finish and whitewashed. As he once wrote of the poet, the architect must give us more than "an exercise in grammar."

Within the church there is more to astonish. The chapel does not symbolize a rational, finite world, expressible in numbers or geometry in the way that Greek temples were microcosms of their universe; nor is it an evocation of the Heavenly Jerusalem of medieval society. Neither the north nor the south door is on the axis of the altar, and part of the dramatic effect of the interior scale results from entering on the building's narrow axis. Reversing the tendency on the exterior, inside one must turn on one's own axis. At first, standing in the darkened interior, one has the feeling of being within a fortress or cave, a citadel against death and a secret place for the enactment of religious mystery. Built to accommodate a maximum of 300 worshipers, the acoustically fine nave brings to mind Le Corbusier's words, "Inside alone with yourself, outside ten thousand pilgrims in front of the altar." Silence and wonder are evoked by the relative darkness, the slope of the concave ceiling and the floor, which diverge upward and downward toward the altar, the absence of familiar right-angle corners or easily recognizable wall designs, and the unfocused illumination that filters in under the roof and down through the deep reveals of the windows, some of which have colored glass.

Outside, the structure is so conceived as to appear to rival the power and grandeur of its natural setting; within, one is struck by its intimate, human scale, unlike the cathedral's vastness. Le Corbusier and his associates, years before, had devised a proportional system based on a standing figure with arm upraised, equaling a height of about 7½ feet. By using this measure and its subdivisions, called the *modulor*, in his designs the architect felt that he assured a human scale of reference. Thus he comes closer to Ictinus, whose intervals between the Parthenon's columns were a column diameter and the width of a man's shoulders, than he does to Hugh Libergier.

Despite its massiveness, the south wall of Ronchamp (Pl. 9, p. 78), one of the great wall surfaces in the history of architecture, does not overwhelm the worshiper in scale. Its beauty and expressiveness depend upon an inspired and subtle coordination of apertures that all differ in scale, proportion, and angle of their reveals, as well as on the paradox of such a massive wall serving as a kind of sculptural quarry. Within each niche the windows differ in size, color, or decoration. Often Le Corbusier painted a few words of praise of the Virgin on the glass: "Je vous salue Marie," "pleine de grâce." This wall, like the church as a whole, resists memorization or easy comprehension, which adds to its richness in design and appropriateness for its function: to provide an atmosphere for spiritual communion and to enhance the performance of the liturgy, with its attendant mysteries.

Le Corbusier cast off the obvious Euclidean geometric vocabulary and envelope of his earlier work and the symbolic axial symmetry customary in religious structures since the Parthenon and the cathedrals. Both in its parts and the whole, the chapel at Ronchamp demonstrates a decided asymmetry. Its most dramatic manifestation on the interior is the daring arrangement of the eastern end of the church (Figs. 116, 119). The Virgin's statue is set off to the upper right and balanced to the left by a concentration of perforations in the north wall that looks like a constellation of lights. At first a great wooden freestanding cross was stationed directly on axis with and behind the main altar. Subsequent transfer of the large cross off to the right of the altar was a type of stage direction not licensed by tradition or Scripture, but the change was sincerely motivated by a desire to animate more effectively and dramatize the otherwise quiescent religious symbols. Perhaps mindful of future criticism aimed at this rearrangement, Le Corbusier wrote: "This focusing is an act of architecture, an act having a real relation to architecture . . . architecture which puts all in order and regulates." The large cross is actually movable and during religious processions can be carried outside to be placed before the second altar. A second cross at Ronchamp is located atop the south tower: "Breaking the silence of the walls it proclaims the great tragedy that took place on a hilltop long ago in the East."

Unlike the reception accorded many other modern churches, the chapel at Ronchamp has been well received by pilgrims and by those living in the area. It continues to function successfully as a religious structure. Le Corbusier has produced one of the few modern religious structures that have the dignity, power, and beauty which bear comparison with the best of the past. He is a rare reminder that a modern architect, drawing from his own inspired imagination, can meaningfully symbolize the Virgin as well as the dynamo. In Le Corbusier's own words, "I have worked for what men today most need: silence and peace."

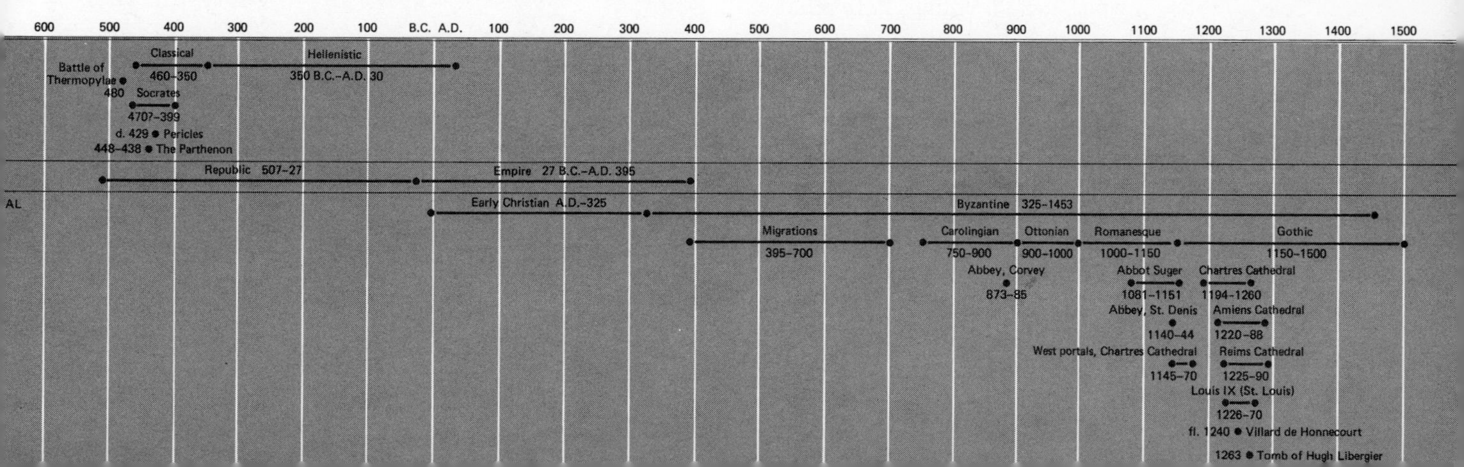

# 5

From the fall of Rome until the 14th and 15th centuries, the handmade, illuminated, and miniature-filled book was the carrier of much of the most important painting and literary content in Western Christian art. The historical worth and intrinsic beauty of the medieval manuscript are insufficiently recognized by the general public today. We have come to associate great painting with that done on walls and easels, both executed on a fairly large scale. But excellence in art does not depend upon either sheer physical size or the medium the painter chooses. Furthermore, the concept of a literally sacred art—in which the works of art, such as many of the medieval manuscripts, mystically partake of the liturgy—is also alien to present-day thinking and experience.

Illuminated medieval manuscripts, precious records of the cultural and civilizing interests of society during the so-called Dark Ages, reveal the varied development in art that prepared the way for Renaissance painting. They evidence the imagination and skill with which medieval men came to terms with their religious concerns. Far from being merely a public record of the medieval man, this form of painting also furnishes a valuable reflection of his private nature.

## SIGNIFICANCE

Christ is the only god who has the book as one of his principal artistic attributes, and in some respects Christianity is itself a book-oriented religion. Early Christian art includes images of a bejeweled throne on which sacred writings have replaced the figure of Christ. Many medieval Christian images show Christ holding a gem-encrusted Bible; a late-10th-century manuscript from Trier depicts Christ giving the benediction with his right hand and holding the sacred book with his left (Fig. 120). Christ is shown seated upon the heavens with the earth as his footstool. The extreme formality of the arc alignments and the axial symmetry of Christ comprise for the viewer a mystical and formal manifestation of Christ. Although of great importance, the book is secondary to the conspicuous vortex design in the navel area, possibly a symbolic reference to Christ's divine birth.

The sumptuous type of medieval illuminated manuscript, that used for liturgical purposes, often possessed magnificent book covers on which were set precious stones, pearls, carved

*right:* 120. *Christ Seated Upon the Heavens*, from *The Gospels of St. Maxim.* Trier, late 10th century.

# THE SACRED BOOK

ivory panels, enamels, and elaborate gold and silver work. These covers, treasures in themselves, were often donated by kings or queens. The precious materials were not intended primarily to delight the eyes but rather to create a binding appropriate for the sacred text and to symbolize mystical truths found in the Bible. The color, luminosity, and perfection of precious stones were interpreted as divine attributes or as symbolic of the blood of the martyrs, the Virgin's purity, the radiant presence of God, and so on. In some cases, medieval Christian patrons supplied pagan gems carved in antiquity. The gems were suitably blessed, the pagan spirits exorcised and made Christian.

Medieval artists and patrons did have an aesthetic, or concept of beauty, but it was predominantly religious: beauty was equated with God. We know from medieval churchmen as well as alchemists that gold was thought to possess magical powers; the color and luster of gold were the most appropriate light symbols of the period. Legends sometimes grew up about the miraculous powers of these richly adorned books, particularly those which had been used by saints.

A superb example of these magnificent book covers is that of the *Lindau Gospels* (Pl. 10, p. 95), which was made about 870, possibly in or near Reims. Within a carefully composed geometrical format, reliefs in bossed gold show Christ on the Cross, grieving angels, and, above Christ's head, the symbols of the sun and moon. Below Christ's arms are the figures of Mary and St. John. The thinness and malleability of gold permitted the working of intricate details on the agitated angels and a handsome relief modeling of the figure volumes. The quiescent image of Christ contrasts both with the movement of the attendant figures and with the densely set, variegated gems and their setting. The precious stones and pearls are mounted on decorative motifs of arcades and lions' feet, which allow light to pass behind them, and are set off by filigree borders.

The key to understanding the reverence accorded the medieval illuminated Bible lies in the meaning of the phrase "the Word." The Gospel of St. John begins thus: "In the beginning was the Word, and the Word was with God, and the Word was God." The words of the Bible were therefore sacred, and it was the task of the artist, when commissioned by royalty, to "clothe" the word in the richest and finest manner of which he was capable. Many manuscripts contained gold or silver writing on purple-dyed parchment. In a German book written at the end of the 10th century are the words, "May the Lord clothe your heart with this book." The precious nature of the materials and the care lavished on the book were in a real sense gifts to God from the faithful.

The profound significance of the word in Christianity helps to explain why illuminated manuscripts made of it a cultural and imaginative object to a much greater extent than had the ancient scrolls and pagan books. No earlier writings demonstrate an ornamentation of letters—specifically, of initials—comparable in calligraphic beauty. While many ancient books were written in handsome script, the manuscripts themselves were not made the object of imaginative or fantastic treatment. Ancient writing recognized no "privileged" words, except for the names of Roman emperors, and the task of writing was considered to be menial and fit only for slaves. With Christianity, the practice of writing passed from slaves to the priesthood, and down through the 12th century the development of the book is bound to the history of the monks. Certain words and letters did have special value or emphasis to the medieval monastic scribe, who gloried in the task of transcribing the Gospel that was from and for God. For the Christian, the act of writing was in itself sacred.

A medieval Bible was not produced for the private pleasure of a wealthy secular patron. The layman, in fact, did not own hand-illuminated books until the late Middle Ages. Even the royalty who commissioned the most elaborate manuscripts seldom kept possession of the book or appreciated all its intricate beauty. The book was meant not for the eyes of the public but for God and for his servants in the Church. There are many similar instances in art, such as the sculpture and painting in Egyptian temples or sculpture and stained glass in the Gothic cathedrals, of works that were inaccessible to the public but exposed to the sight of God.

The sacred book was a privileged object generally owned by a priest, abbot, or bishop, as the representative of the

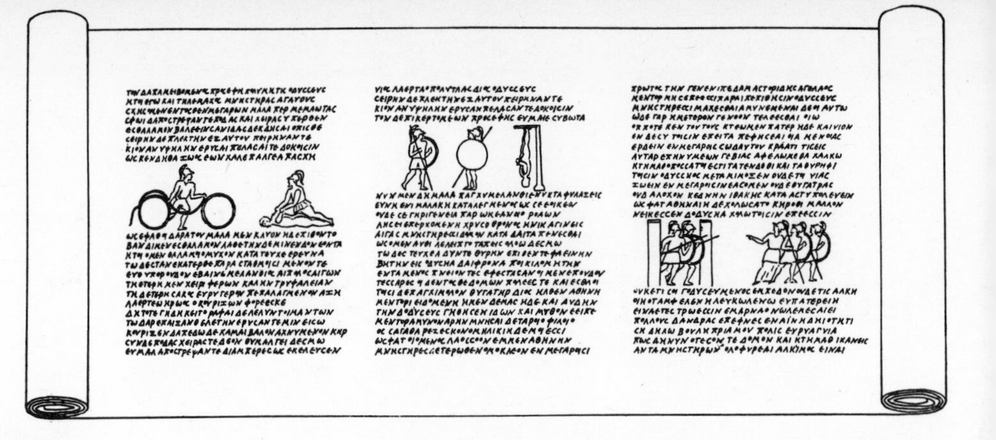

*below:* 121. *St. Erhard Celebrating the Mass* (detail), from *The Gospel Book of Abbess Uota* (Pl. 11, p. 95). Regensburg, 1002–25. Staatsbibliothek, Munich.

*right:* 122. Reconstruction of an *Odyssey* roll. 3rd century B.C.

Church of God. The congregation was separated from the book, just as it was remote from the sacred objects on the altar. They submitted to it for their religious instruction, and the gospels along with the sacraments assumed a central position in medieval Christian life. It is difficult for us to comprehend the dramatic experience of the congregation when the sacred book was revealed during the Mass, at coronations, or for special blessings. The Gothic cathedrals make manifest the complex religious ordering of life and the universe, and the sacred book presents the source and basis of that order. More than a collection of sacred stories, for its medieval public *the book was Christ*.

In some medieval churches the Bible was suspended from the ceiling above the altar by gold chains. It was carried in religious processions, and in Eastern churches it was placed upon a throne. Usually the Bible stood on the altar, flanked by candles and incense burners; the candles symbolized the light shed by the Gospels. A sumptuously decorated page of an early-11th-century manuscript made in Regensburg shows St. Erhard with an assistant celebrating the Mass (Pl. 11, p. 95; Fig. 121), under a canopy symbolic of Heaven. The saint is dressed in robes meant to be those of an Old Testament priest; to his right can be seen the sacred book, painted in gold, resting on the altar below a suspended gold crown and next to the Eucharistic objects. When the book was used during the Mass, it was kissed by the bishop; during the reading from it, knights drew their swords as a gesture of their defense of the Scriptures and the people put down their staffs. During investiture ceremonies, the sacred book was laid on the neck of the candidate, indicating that Christ was the head, the source of authority, of the bishop, who was about to assume leadership of the Church.

Clearly, the art within the decorated book is also sacred, the chief exceptions being certain nonreligious themes appearing in the margins of the texts. The miniatures and the figure rendering in medieval manuscripts give a first impression of unreality and naïveté. Nevertheless, it should be remembered that the artist was making images of sacred subjects, that is, of mystical themes, that were as vivid and real in his mind and the minds of the congregation as was actual life on earth.

## PRODUCTION OF MANUSCRIPTS

Sometime between the 2nd and 4th centuries the book form, or *codex,* evolved; it replaced the papyrus scroll, a single horizontal sheet written in columns and having its ends attached to rods. The ancients had occasionally included text illustrations or technical diagrams in their scrolls; those found in the Egyptian *Book of the Dead* and in Greek and Roman scrolls dealt variously with medicine, science, and mythology (Fig. 122). Roman illustrations were primarily wall or panel paintings reduced to miniature size. Between the 1st and 4th centuries *vellum,* or lambskin, gradually replaced the more expensive and less durable papyrus. With the development of the vellum book that, unlike a scroll, opened from the side, the artist was offered an entire page, more or less a framed picture; the composition could be as elaborate as he desired. Painting on papyrus had consisted of ink and watercolor, whereas the qualities of vellum encouraged the use of gouache and richer coloring. Vellum and the book form also permitted painting on both sides of the page without the dangers of flaking experienced with scrolls.

Acquaintance with ancient books was essentially a matter of hearing the text, whereas the Christian book was intended to be appreciated both aurally and visually. The sustained imaginative development of the illuminated book stemmed from decorated initials made by Irish monks in the 6th century and from illustrations made by Byzantine artists of Constantinople and Syria. The earliest West European development of book illumination took place in England during the 7th and 8th centuries, principally in Northumbria, the border region between England and Scotland. During the reign of Charlemagne, at the beginning of the 9th century, illuminated book production accelerated beyond the rate of the preceding two centuries in France and England. Christianity and the book were essential to each other's growth. The Carolingian Renaissance, the efforts of Charlemagne about 800 A.D. to revive aspects of Roman culture, gave the great impetus to illuminated book production in Western Europe. In the 8th, 9th, and even the 10th centuries, there were specific, clearly defined locales and geographical sources for book production—most frequently in monasteries. Thereafter, production became widespread throughout Europe, and during the 11th and 12th centuries an enormous quantity of manuscripts was produced. After the 13th century, urban centers such as Paris began to rival or surpass the monastic production of decorated books. The mobility of artists as well as of the books themselves during this later period makes tracing their origins more difficult.

A great variety of illuminated books was produced during the Middle Ages. Sacred books consisted not only of the Bible but also of limited excerpts from it—such as the Gospels or the Psalms—calendars of the religious feasts, prayers, blessings, commentaries, sermons, and lives of the saints. Generally these books had ornamented covers, frontispieces, canon tables, or tables of concordances for the Gospels; less frequently they contained a full page devoted to the Cross, portraits of the Evangelists or saints, illuminated initials, and miniatures illustrating the particular text. The examples we shall use to illustrate most of the foregoing types are drawn from various manuscripts produced at different times and places; yet these represent but a slight sampling of the inexhaustible wealth of imagery that emerged from medieval writing rooms or *scriptoria* (Fig. 123).

The notion of the medieval artist as a self-effacing craftsman resigned to oblivion is a glib one. At the end of many of the books, there exist hundreds of signatures of artists—many accompanied by short prayers, in which the artist asks for praise, avows his reverence, and curses his arduous labor and the obdurate nature of his tools: "I've come to the end, curse this pen and damn this ink."

## PARTS OF SACRED BOOKS

**Frontispiece** From a great Bible made during the first half of the 9th century at the Monastery of St-Martin in Tours, France, comes a painting of the Abbot Vivian presenting the

123. Geographical distribution of the scriptoria active in medieval Europe.

*far left:* 124. *Abbot Vivian Presenting the Bible to Charles the Bold*, from *Count Vivian's Bible*. Tours. 843–51. $19^3/_8 \times 14^5/_8$". Bibliothèque Nationale, Paris.

*left:* 125. *Scribe Presenting the Bible to St. Peter*, from *The Gero Codex*. Reichenau, c. 970. $9^3/_4 \times 7$". Landes- und Hochschulbibliothek, Darmstadt.

*opposite:* 126. *St. Matthew*, from *The Gospel Book of Charlemagne*. c. 800–10. Kunsthistorisches Museum, Vienna.

finished manuscript to the Carolingian King (Fig. 124). The depiction of an actual historical event is the exception rather than the rule in medieval manuscript painting. The monarch is shown enthroned in a space that suggests the apse of a church. Abbot Vivian and the other monks appear in a semicircle before the king, and the artist ingeniously managed to reveal the faces as well as the backs of some figures. The frontispiece commemorates the King's patronage and the purpose of the Bible as a gift, inferring the supremacy of the Emperor over the Church. The artists of the Tours school were deeply imbued with an awareness of the world of rank and protocol and evolved important devices to interpret these themes. Rather than put the spectator on the level with the monks, for instance, and thus obscure part of the Emperor's person, the artist chose an elevated viewpoint that freely discloses the entire scene. The disposition of the figures and their gestures, as well as the pose of the ruler and his central placement, are governed by the conduct of the ceremony.

Another donation scene is in a German manuscript of the late 10th century known as the *Gero Codex* (Fig. 125). The scribe is seen presenting the Bible he has copied and embellished to his patron saint, the apostle Peter. Peter is shown enthroned, larger in scale than the scribe, and placed exactly beneath an arch of a simple structure symbolizing a church. The saint's gesture is made without any accompanying sign of recognition of the monk's presence in his facial expression. The head of St. Peter may have been copied from a late Roman sculpture of a pagan subject. The separation of the monk's feet from any ground line does not signify that he is "jumping for joy"; in Europe painting had by this time ceased to attempt any suggestion of spatial depth. The visible world was reduced to symbols, and there was no need to preserve its three-dimensional qualities. Text and image shaped a common reality. With the absence of a convincing spatial setting, the figures acquired a relative flatness and weightlessness. Medieval painting was a symbolic and mystical art, whose power did not depend upon duplication of the world of appearances. The fact that the figures overlap the same architecture under which they at first seem to stand or sit is thus justified on the basis of a desirable clarity and an avoidance of cutting or segmenting the figure, gesture, or movement.

Some of the great German manuscripts made for eleventh-century Ottonian emperors possess magnificent coronation images for frontispieces, commemorating events in which the book itself played an important part. When Charlemagne's tomb was opened in the 10th century, the body was found seated on a throne, with the coronation Bible (Fig. 126) open on its lap. This Bible was used, in turn, by Ottonian kings at their coronation. A page showing the divine coronation of the German king Henry II, from an early-11th-century sacramentary painted in Regensburg (Fig. 127), depicts the arms of the king being supported by representatives of the Church. Seated above the ruler is the figure of Christ, who blesses the new king and places the crown upon his head. The use of gold and brilliantly colored patterns in the background and in the robes, as well as the geometric composition and

*below:* 127. *Christ Crowning King Henry II*, from *The Sacramentary of King Henry II*. Regensburg, 1002–14. $9^1/_2 \times 11^3/_4$″. Staatsbibliothek, Munich.

*bottom:* 128. *St. Valerian*, from *The Egbert Psalter*. Reichenau, c. 980. $11^1/_2 \times 7^1/_2$″. Museo Archeologico Nationale, Cividale del Friuli, Italy.

careful ordering of right and left, upper and lower zones, and center and subsidiary areas, makes this page exciting testimony to the power, wealth, and tastes of the Ottonian court. Charlemagne's empire had dissolved soon after his death; at the beginning of the 10th century, the Saxon kings of Germany gradually ascended in power. Called the *Ottonians* after the three emperors named Otto, they continued and advanced the cultural traditions of the Carolingians and allied themselves with the Church of Rome, an alliance that greatly influenced the course of medieval history.

**Cross Page** During the 7th and 8th centuries, some English and French manuscripts included elaborate pages devoted to the Cross. In the cruciform page of the *Lindisfarne Gospels* (Pl. 12, p. 96), the form of the Cross is seen against a dense field of interlaces. The conjunction of flowing lines and strict geometry may have been symbolic of the bringing of law to the lawless, for the interlacing has been subordinated to the limits and shapes of each area by strong linear boundaries; the right angles provided by the Cross and its frame are of Roman Christian heritage. This idea is only conjectural, however, for while the monks had converted the Saxons and Celts to the Cross, they themselves had been won to pagan art. Old barbaric notions of magic may have influenced manuscript painting, combined with the artist's desire to make the richest and most powerful presentation of the Cross.

The Cross page died out in the 8th century, but a painting of some 200 years later (Fig. 128) seems to continue pictorial ideas that were implicit in the earlier works. In a state of mystical trance, St. Valerian makes his gesture of blessing in such a way that his whole body becomes a cross fixed centrally within the frame. Behind the saint, symbolically rendered in dark colors against his light form, are menacing bestial forms. The all-consuming faith and trancelike withdrawal of the saint ensure his survival and final glory in a world of evil. This moving image illustrates the medieval conception of the holy man who must live in a dark and hostile world.

**Images of Evangelists** In many medieval Gospel books, the Evangelists were portrayed at the beginning of the scriptures for which they were responsible. Generally, the Evangelist was shown seated, usually in a side view; his symbol, adapted from the Biblical account of Ezekiel's vision, the lion for Mark, eagle for John, ox for Luke, and winged man for Matthew was often shown above him. In the *Echternach Gospels,* a late-7th-century Irish manuscript, the Evangelist Mark is not shown in person but is represented by his lion symbol (Pl. 13, p. 97). Remote from a literal image, this leonine figure presents a strongly imaginative equivalent. The sharpness of the lines that compose the body suggests that the painter may have been influenced by metal work. While the artist may have been unaware of true anatomy, he imparted a lively movement and ferocity to the beast. The design of the entire page is one of the most forceful in manuscript art. The geometric frame has an active life of its own, intruding into the central area and playing against the curves of the lion's body. Since the writing partaker of the color and calligraphy of the lion, the whole takes on a powerful consistency and discipline.

Of great importance to Western medieval art was the convergence in manuscript painting of the figure-oriented

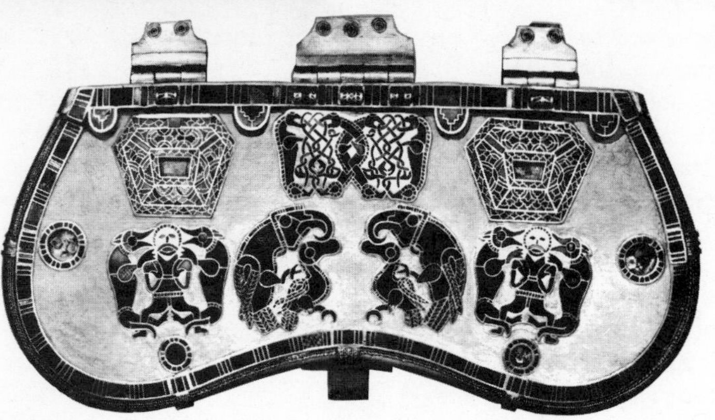

*left:* 129. *St. Sebastian*, mosaic from San Pietro in Vincoli, Rome. 7th century.

*below:* 130. Purse lid, from the Ship Burial at Sutton Hoo, England. Gold with garnets and glass. 7th century. British Museum, London.

*right:* 131. *St. John the Evangelist*, from *The Irish Evangeliarium No.51.* 8th century. $15^{3}/_{4} \times 8^{7}/_{8}$". Stiftsbibliothek, St. Gall, Switzerland.

*left:* 132. *Seated Philosopher*, sarcophagus from Sidamara. 3rd century. Marble, length 12′5″. Archaeological Museum, Istanbul.

*below:* 133. *St. John*, mosaic from San Vitale, Ravenna. c. 547.

Mediterranean tradition and the nonfigurative style of the North. A mosaic from Rome and a purse lid from a ship burial found in southeastern England, both of the 7th century, illustrate these divergent traditions (Figs. 129, 130). The mosaic figure of St. Sebastian, which comes from a Roman church, shows the robed saint holding a martyr's crown. His body is largely concealed, but the pattern of folds suggests the correct location and general proportion of the limbs beneath, and the position of the feet suggests that they still carry weight. The face, while lacking in individuality, is nevertheless convincingly human. The origin of the purse lid, with its garnet and gold plaques, is not known for sure, but it came from somewhere in northern Europe, possibly Scandinavia. Among the plaques are two showing a figure flanked by two rampant animals, which may or may not represent Daniel in the lion's den. Figures and animals are greatly schematized into flat, strongly outlined compartments, with no attempt to convince us of the corporeality of the subjects. The beautiful filigree and enamel work and the sureness of the outlining warn us that artistic skill need not presuppose naturalistic anatomical knowledge; these jeweled images were no doubt intensely real to their owner.

The human figure was exceptional in this Northern non-Christian art, and abstract or animal ornament was more common. It was in the manuscript art of Irish monks, who had access to illustrated books from Rome and to barbaric art both in England and on the Continent, that these powerful artistic tendencies were joined. The Evangelist portraits provided the initiative for this synthesis in the 7th and 8th centuries. A page of an Irish Gospel book of the 8th century, the *Irish Evangeliarium No. 51* (Fig. 131), gives evidence of the assimilation of the two traditions. In the frame are found the motifs from Northern pagan art—knotted forms, spirals, fantastic four-legged animals, geometric shapes, rows of dots. The figure of the saint, still of paramount importance on the page, has had imposed upon it the Northern taste for incisive curvilinear outlining, flatness, and arbitrary proportion. There is no impression of a body existing beneath the drapery. Despite the rigid frontality and symmetry of the figure, and also the lack of flesh color and portrait features, the synthesized saint evokes a powerful presence. Later, before the end of the 8th century, as a result of the Carolingian Renaissance, the Mediterranean and Classical figure style gained ascendancy.

The artistic origin of the prototypes for the Carolingian Evangelist portraits probably goes back to 3rd- and 4th-century Greek and Roman sculptures and paintings of seated philosophers (Fig. 132). The seated posture had, in antiquity, acquired connotations of the contemplative life, as opposed to the active life. Further sources may have been certain 6th-century Ravenna mosaics (Fig. 133) that depicted the four

*left:* 134. *St. Matthew the Evangelist*, from *The Gospel Book of Archbishop Ebbo*. Hautvilliers, near Reims, before 823. $10^1/_4 \times 7^7/_8''$. Bibliothèque de la Ville, Epernay.

*right:* 135. *St. Matthew the Evangelist*, from *The Gospels of Judith of Flanders*. England, early 11th century. $11^1/_2 \times 7^1/_2''$. Pierpont Morgan Library, New York.

Evangelists seated and accompanied by their symbols. Unlike the representations of ancient philosophers, who were shown dictating but never actually engaged in the inferior activity of writing, the images created by medieval artists included the inspired, pensive, puzzled, aloof writer, clearly identified with his profession. The artist could associate himself with the Evangelist, since both were involved in conveying the words of God.

One of the most exciting Evangelist portraits in medieval art is from the *Ebbo Gospels* (Fig. 134), produced near the city of Reims in the early 9th century. Nowhere in ancient art does one find so emotional an image. As much by style as by facial expression, St. Matthew is shown as a deeply inspired figure. His inner agitation, as well as the artist's own passionate enthusiasm, can be seen in the energetic drawing and nervous rhythms of the garment—qualities that overflow into the landscape background and the frame. The reserve or detachment of Classical philosopher portraits is unknown to this artist, who charges with excitement his color, composition, and the frame itself.

In contrast, an Evangelist figure (Fig. 135) from an English manuscript of the early 11th century, the *Gospels of Judith of Flanders*, presents a cool and elegant appearance. The elongated figure of St. Matthew and his gold-edged garment convey dignity and a restrained spirituality. The intricate, active qualities of the garment and frame are more expressive than the man's features or gestures in themselves. Expressiveness in medieval painting was not confined to gestures and facial expressions, for emotional tone was frequently conveyed in the drawing of the entire composition.

An early-11th-century artist working on the island of Reichenau, situated in Lake Constance, Switzerland, produced an image of St. Luke in which the Evangelist is shown in an ecstatic and hypnotic trance (Pl. 14, p. 97). In the Evangelist's lap are the five books of the Old Testament, and the prophets of these books are grouped about the Evangelist's symbol. The symbolic meaning of the image lies in the belief that the Old Testament prophesied the coming of Christ and that the Evangelists were the new heralds of his Incarnation. The trancelike state of the saint is appropriate to the time and place in which the image was painted. Monastic reform under the Ottonians called for an attitude of more intense piety and a renunciation of worldly pleasures. St. Luke is presented as a model of mysticism. Seen simultaneously are the saint and his vision, the image he appears to support, not unlike Hercules holding up the world. The miniature itself has a mesmerizing effect, with its rigid symmetry extending even to the enormous eyes and fixed gaze of the saint. The arch overhead is a symbol of Heaven, the drinking animals refer to those who are nourished by the Scriptures, and the brilliant gold background transports the scene outside time and place.

**Illuminated Initials** Writing was a privileged art in medieval Christianity. The written word came to have great personal value for the scribe, and between the two there evolved an intimate relationship unlike that between the ancient scribe and his text. St. Augustine, writing of the advantages of the priestly life, spoke of the opportunity to participate in the creation of the Book and the meditation upon the Word. The results of this relationship between scribe and letters can be seen in the great changes in the appearance of writing and the structure of the written page that took place from the 6th through 9th centuries. The increased beauty and intricacy of the writing indicates that the scribes did not always worry about a ready legibility of the text, which was usually known by heart. The variety of scripts, the scale differences of the lettering on the opening page of a Gospel, the variety of colors, and the addition of elaborate decoration to certain initials created a hierarchical structure based on increased valuation of words stressed in prayers, the liturgy, and chants or stressed because of their location. In contrast to the uniformity of Greek and Roman writing, no two pages of medieval text look the same, as can be seen in illustrations from the *Book of Kells* and the *Lindisfarne Gospels* (Figs. 136, 137). About the end of the 6th century, the initial was separated from the main body of the text; it was enlarged, set out into the margin, and formed with different kinds of lines and colors. The illuminated initial gradually took over the margin of the page and began to intrude upon the text itself, as in the page from the *Lindisfarne Gospels*, until about 800, when the initial began to occupy an entire page. The illuminated initial opened to the artist an entirely new world of meaning. The imagery enhancing the initial is not ordinarily illustrative of the text, but is the product of pure fantasy. Its justification probably lay in the belief that the magical power of the Word required commensurate visual garb.

During the Romanesque phase of manuscript art, the initial became the outlet for private sentiments of the monk

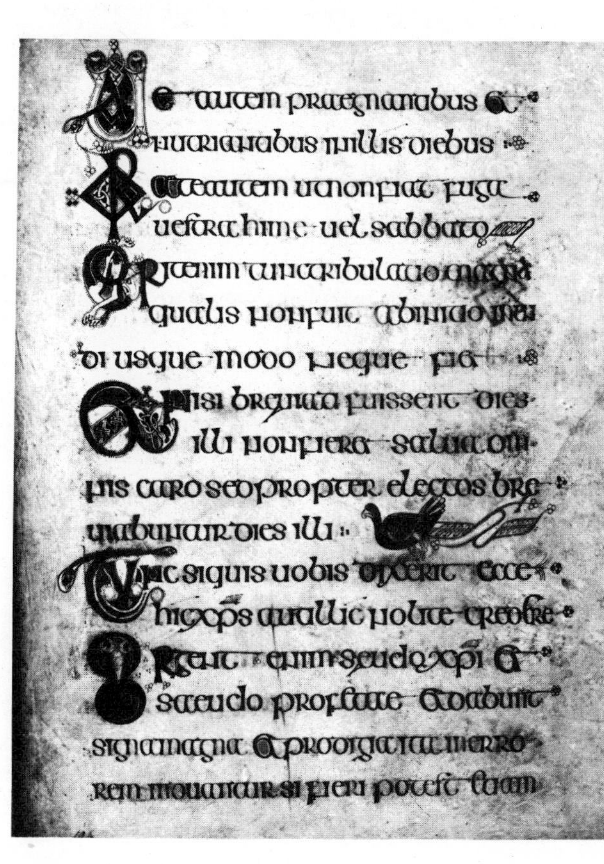

*left:* 136. Page for the Gospel of Matthew (24:19–24), from the *Book of Kells*. Northumbria, c. 800. 13 × 19½″. Trinity College Library, Dublin.

*above:* 137. Page from *The Lindisfarne Gospels*. Late 7th century. British Museum, London.

*left:* 138. Initials for Psalm 1, from *The Winchester Bible.* England, 12th century. Cathedral Library, Winchester.

*below:* 139. *Rufillus of Weissenau.* 12th century. Formerly in Hofbibliothek, Sigmaringen, West Germany.

illustrator and for themes that also reflected his immediate environment. Scenes of violence, brutality, and conduct not generally associated with Christianity overflow initials and margins. The great *Winchester Bible*, produced in England during the 12th century, contains a rich deposit of this type of imagery (Fig. 138). The two versions of the first Psalm are presented jointly; the initial B is filled on the left with episodes from the Old Testament that prefigure those of the New Testament on the right. At the upper left, David is about to slay a bear and rescue a lamb from its jaws. The antitype at the right shows Christ exorcising a demon through the mouth of an afflicted man. At the lower left, David is shown pulling open a lion's mouth to release a lamb, while at the lower right Christ, accompanied by the Archangel, harrows Hell by binding the hands of the devil and prying open the leviathan's jaws with the end of his cruciform staff. These acrobatic figures may have been inspired by actual performances of *jongleurs*, the itinerant mime-singing actors who performed lays, legends, epics, and sagas before audiences of feudal aristocrats gathered in manors and fortified castles. The initial itself has become the field for illustration, with the figures and action so composed as to move energetically within and over its curved frame. All the scenes stress the open jaws. The juncture of the two arcs of each B is an animal mask, from the jaws of which emerges intertwined ornament that in turn refers us to the very linear rendering of the entanglement of David and the beasts. Violent in theme, the jaws are identified with salvation and evil. This oral fascination has been traced to Anglo-Saxon literature such as *Beowulf*, with its detailed descriptions of monsters. The illustration from the *Winchester Bible* is but one of many instances in medieval religious painting and sculpture in which such mordant themes are encountered.

The initial had become a kind of safety valve for the artist of a religion that had a strongly prohibitive cast. It gave free play to demonic instincts, tastes for rapacious energy, and the convolutions of labyrinthine forms and processes. This type of art gives us an insight into the private torment and uncertainties of medieval religious life, as well as into the delight of the artist in the movement and freedom found in secular life. Comparable license was taken in the work of medieval sculptors who carved the capitals for monasteries and cathedrals, conjuring an otherwise proscribed world of monsters and phantoms of irreligious imagination (Fig. 557). It must be remembered that there was no artistic outlet for secular fantasy other than religious art. This intimate dialogue between the artist and his work, the personal conflicts and choices expressed in it—marginal to be sure in medieval art—was to become central in later periods (see Chap. 21). A marvelous self-portrait by the monk Rufillus of Weissenau (Fig. 139) is

*left:* Plate 10. *The Crucifixion*, upper cover of the binding of *The Lindau Gospels*. Reims or St-Denis, c. 870. Gold and jewels, $13^3/_4 \times 10^1/_2$″. Pierpont Morgan Library, New York. (See p. 85.)

*above:* Plate 11. *St. Erhard Celebrating the Mass*, from *The Gospel Book of Abbess Uota*. Regensburg, 1002–25. Manuscript illumination, $15^1/_4 \times 11$″. Staatsbibliothek, Munich. (See p. 86, Fig. 121.)

Plate 12. Cross page, from *The Lindisfarne Gospels*. Late 7th century. 13 × 9½″. British Museum, London. (See pp. 89, 93, Fig. 137.)

*above:* Plate 13. *Symbol of St. Mark*, from *The Echternach Gospels.* Anglo-Irish, c. 700. Manuscript illumination. Bibliothèque Nationale, Paris. (See p. 90.)

*right:* Plate 14. *St. Luke the Evangelist*, from *The Gospel Book of Otto III.* Reichenau, c. 1000. Manuscript illumination, $13^{3}/_{8} \times 9^{5}/_{8}''$. Staatsbibliothek, Munich. (See p. 92.)

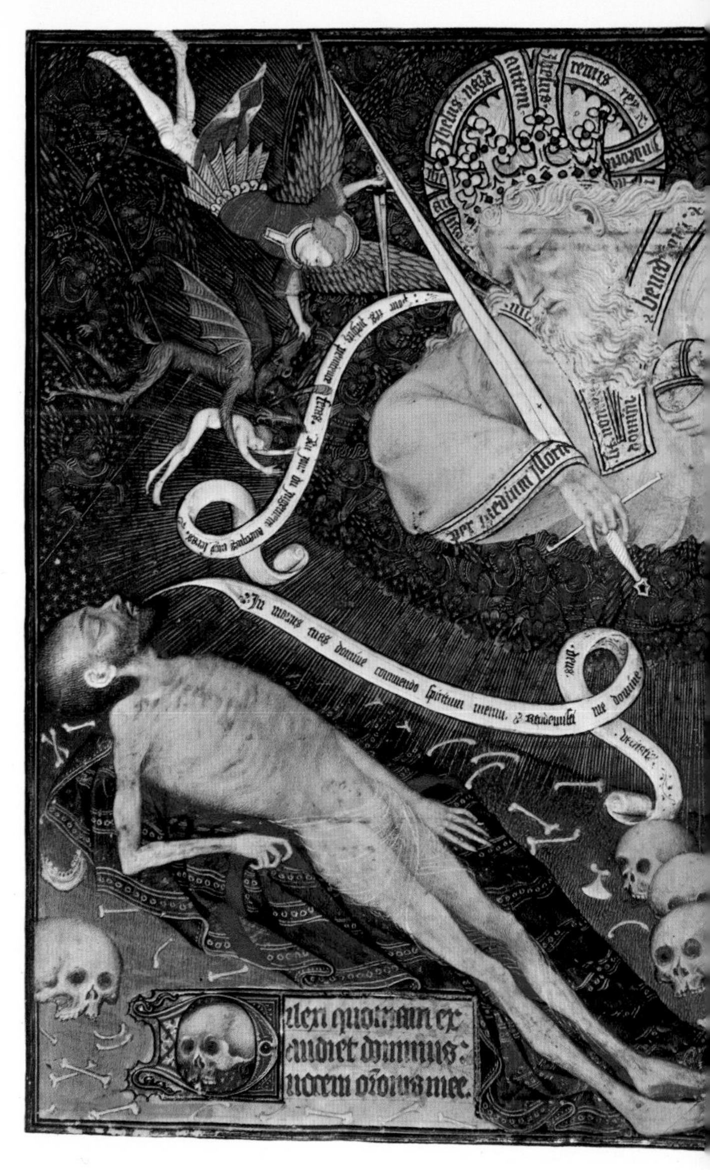

*below:* Plate 15. *Satan and His Locusts*, from *The Beatus of St-Sever*. c. 1050. Manuscript illumination, 14¼ × 11″. Bibliothèque Nationale, Paris. (See pp. 100, 101.)

*right:* Plate 16. THE ROHAN MASTER. *Dead Man Confronted by the Lord*, from *Les Grandes Heures de la Famille de Rohan*. Early 15th century. Bibliothèque Nationale, Paris. (See p. 101.)

the most overt expression of these concerns. Rufillus illustrates his tools, his face, his name, and the creatures—both sacred and profane—of his vivid imagination.

## STORYTELLING MINIATURES

Beginning with the 9th century, there was a revival of storytelling miniatures, a genre found in late Roman art. Frequently the artist had older manuscripts or copies of late Roman work from which he worked. Copying in manuscript art was not considered a dishonorable method but was, on the contrary, an important and accepted practice; originality was not the aim of the artists. Copying, however, did not preclude some display of individuality, and Carolingian copies of now lost Greek and Roman prototypes display important differences from what is known of the original styles.

Not all the decoration of medieval manuscripts was painted; many manuscripts contain outstanding drawings. Such manuscripts were not intended for royalty or for use in great public ceremonies but were what might be called nonofficial art, made for the private contemplation of the monks. The most notable medieval manuscript decorated with drawings is the *Utrecht Psalter*, produced in or near Reims about 833–35 (Fig. 140). It contains 166 illustrations of the Psalms and thousands of figures and objects, drawn in brown ink on the text pages without the separation of a picture frame. The source of the *Utrecht Psalter* was probably a lost Greek manuscript made centuries earlier. There was great freedom in the copying of the earlier manuscript, and the artists of the *Utrecht Psalter* felt free to infuse their drawing with an energy and impulsiveness not characteristic of the original. The drawings contrast strongly with the uniformity of the script, and the narrative compositions are more loosely structured than are the columns of text. The artists did not interpret the Psalms literally, but often added to them or contrived fanciful metaphors. These drawn figures are much more animated and freely rendered than those found in the painting of the time. The *Utrecht Psalter* comes close to being encyclopedic in its manipulation of figures and groups, and one can perceive the artists' enthusiasm for landscape forms, although a total integration of figure and background is absent. The psalter contains many images of the Mouth of Hell, as seen in the illustration for Psalm 102 (Fig. 140), which were to bear significant influence on later art. The manuscript as a whole was one of the most influential in medieval times because of the quality of execution and rich variety of subject matter.

Eleventh-century German artists, such as those who produced the *Golden Codex of Echternach* (Fig. 141), rank among the finest storytellers in the history of art. Unlike Roman

*left:* 140. Illustration for Psalm 102, from *The Utrecht Psalter*. Reims, c. 833–35. 13 × 9⁷/₈″ (entire page). University Library, Utrecht.

*above:* 141. *Adoration of the Magi; Divine Warning and Departure; Presentation in the Temple*, from *The Golden Codex of Echternach*. 962–1056. Germanisches Nationalmuseum, Nuremberg.

artists, the Ottonian painters conceived of the entire page as possessing an integral design. The placement of the figures or groups in each zone was carefully thought out in terms of the whole page. The climactic moments of the Adoration of the Magi and the Presentation in the Temple take place on the right side of the page, with the most important figures located beneath symbolic arches. The chronology of the events is rearranged in order to give the most important events privileged locations in the codex. Medieval art permits us to see simultaneously the inside and outside of a building; open doors signify that the action or location of the figures is indoors. The Ottonian artists created strong rhythmic designs and broad gestures played off against single-color backgrounds. While color is used symbolically in connection with the principal figures, it is also skillfully balanced against the background colors of the three zones. There is a distinctness and terseness in Ottonian miniatures that recalls the actual narrative style of the Bible.

Versatility and great imagination went into manuscript miniatures such as an 11th-century painting of Christ on the Sea of Galilee (Fig. 142). Through the precarious tilt of the dragonlike ship that seems about to swoop out of the frame, the undulating composition of sail and ship played against the agitated sea, and the anxious looks of the disciples, the painter has realized a spirited image of individuals in distress. The sleeping figure of Christ is the one stable element; even the frame has received impulsively flecked touches of gold.

*below left:* 142. *Christ on the Sea of Galilee*, from *The Gospels of the Abbess Hitda of Meschede.* Cologne. 978–1042. $6^5/_8 \times 5^5/_8$". Landes- und Hochschulbibliothek, Darmstadt.

*above:* 143. *Three Living Nobles and Their Dead Counterparts,* from the *Recueil de Poésies Françaises.* c. 1285. Bibliothèque de l'Arsenal, Paris.

To the modern viewer both of the preceding paintings perhaps seem lacking in truthfulness because they do not accord with our views of reality. Medieval painting had its own decided system and logic of conception, which contradicted perception; the visual world was only a reflection of a higher spiritual reality, and truthfulness in painting was based instead on *fidelity to the Scriptures.* For example, in such a painting as *Christ on the Sea of Galilee*, the scriptural passage against which it would have been measured reads: "And behold, there arose a great tempest in the sea, in so much that the ship was covered with the waves: but He was asleep." No mention is made of what the ship looked like, so that the artist had license to work from his own idea of an appropriate vessel. There is no horizon line to give depth, and the sea is rendered from above to ensure its identity, just as the boat is viewed from the more distinguishing side view. Clear identification, or readability, of forms precluded consistent or convincing perspective at this time. Textual brevity and abrupt changes of events have their visual counterpart in these terse images. The medieval idea of truthful representation of scriptural episodes was to scale the participants large relative to the picture area, give them simple declarative movements, and establish a minimal suggestion of surroundings when necessary. There is no shadow in these images because there is no reference to the sun or natural lighting conditions, and the brightly colored figures are flat because they move in a two-dimensional world.

One of the most dramatic, startling, and visually stunning medieval manuscripts is the *Beatus of St-Sever* (Pl. 15, p. 98), which was copied in Mozarabic Spain in the 11th century, from an older commentary on the *Apocalypse* by an 8th-century Spanish monk, Beatus of Liebana. Without knowledge of the text (Rev. 9:1–11), the viewer will find the imagery horrific but inexplicable. Familiarity with the text explains how the artist synthesized scriptural fact and his imagination. After the fifth angel has sounded his trumpet, the bottomless pit of hell is opened:

> And there came out of the smoke locusts upon the earth. . . . And it was commanded them that they should hurt only those men which have not the seal of God in their foreheads. They should be tormented five months. And the shapes of the locusts were like unto horses prepared unto battle; and on their heads were crowns like gold, and their faces were as the faces of men. And they had hair as the hair of women, and their teeth were as the teeth of lions and the sound of their wings was as the sound of chariots of many horses. And they had tails like unto scorpions, and there were stings in their tails. And they had a king over them, which is the angel of the bottomless pit.

To the medieval man of both the 8th and 11th centuries, the end of the world was imminent, and synoptic and powerful images such as these confirmed his fears and also satisfied his curiosity—one of the great historical purposes of art.

Like the sculpture of the Gothic cathedrals, medieval manuscripts were not entirely devoted to illustrating the Bible. Concern with death and moralizations about human vanity produced many images known as *memento mori* ("Remember that you must die") that were reminders of death. A late-13th-century collection of French poems contains a painting of three living nobles who confront with apprehension their skeletal counterparts (Fig. 143). Although there is some evidence of observation from life and of death, the figures still straddle the picture frame and exist in a world apart from the viewer. That medieval artists did develop certain devices and skills to make their images more natural can be seen in one of the most powerful and morbid images from the early 15th century in which a dead man is confronted by the Lord (Pl. 16, p. 98). *The Rohan Master*, as this painter is called today, convincingly depicts the emaciated, naked mortal stretched out on a bone-strewn ground behind the picture frame. From his mouth, in medieval fashion, there issue the words with which he pleads for mercy. The Lord answers that the sinful must be punished and that on the Day of Judgment he will be with the Lord. The dead man's soul is fought over by a devil and an angel against a tapestrylike background of blue and gold angels. The Lord's countenance and sword are not comforting, and the painting was intended to evoke awe and fear in the viewer. The simulation of withered flesh and bone through modeling and tinted colors and the receding tilted ground plane encourage an emotional identification with the subject; the spectator is projected into the painting in ways that were not possible in the 13th-century *memento mori*. New demands were being placed on the artist at the end of the medieval period, partially inspired by his acquisition of new artistic devices by which the visible world could be plausibly rendered, but the break from medieval symbolism and style was slow. The Rohan Master skillfully joins symbol and fact, the visible and the invisible, mortal and God.

The development of naturalism in medieval art was to bring about the destruction of that which gave conviction to its greatest manuscript art—the visual and textual consistency, the superb coordination of written word and image on a common two-dimensional surface. Changes in patronage and ownership of books were also influential. From the 13th century on, private persons commissioned and collected beautiful books; urban workshops directed by a master painter catered to luxurious secular tastes.

A 14th-century page (Fig. 144) painted or supervised by Jean Pucelle (fl. c. 1324), whose workshop was in Paris, attests the persistence of the medieval coordination of text

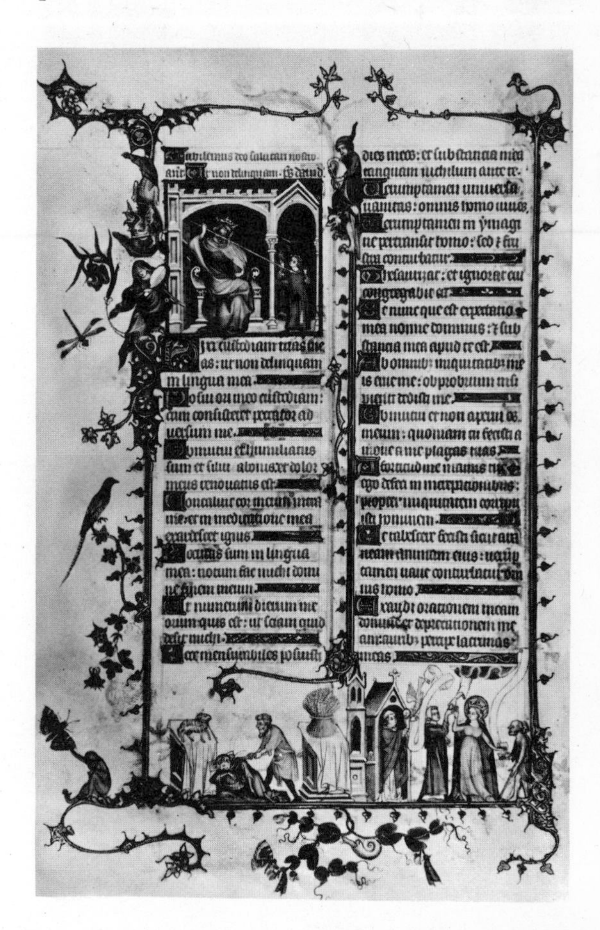

*right:* 144. Jean Pucelle. *David and Saul*, from the *Belleville Breviary*. c. 1323–26. Bibliothèque Nationale, Paris.

with decoration. However, in the new receding spatial box where Saul is threatening David with a spear, one sees the beginnings of the breakup of this unity of surface. The rudimentary spatial recession of the architectural setting punches a hole in the flatness of the page, and some of the strongly modeled playful figures in the margins seem to exist in front of the page surface. Pucelle also influenced the development of elegant and amusing margins, including at the left, for example, a dragonfly that was a pun on his name and served as his signature. The amusing marginal byplay between animals and insects is symptomatic of the increasing interest of artist and patron in introducing elements from nature—a development paralleled in the increasing natural reference of the cathedral sculpture of the time. The development of volume and articulation of figures in 14th-century painting derived from imitation of sculpture. The close textual ties of earlier illustrations were gradually being weakened, and a split was developing between the reality of the words and the images.

About a century later, a private prayerbook, the *Turin-Milan Hours* (Fig. 145), decorated probably by the Flemish Jan (d. 1441) and Hubert (d. 1426) van Eyck, reached a point similar to that from which early medieval painting had departed: namely, manuscript illustration based on the style or actual example of panel painting. One of the oldest manuscripts surviving from antiquity with a similar character is the *Vatican Vergil,* dated about A.D. 400 (Fig. 146); though of lesser quality, one of its illustrations gives us an idea of how far Roman artists had gone in achieving illusionism—but how short that route seems next to the mastery of Hubert and Jan van Eyck's paintings of a bedroom and landscape. The ancient Romans had never achieved a spatial organization such as that of the Van Eycks, in which the scene is rendered as if from the position of a theoretical observer standing at a fixed point.

In the Roman painting the parallel alignment of figures and setting makes the surface of the page perceptible and prevents the picture space from advancing any farther in our direction. A thousand years later the Van Eyck brothers were to transform the picture surface into a transparency, so that the bedroom of the miniature seems to be larger than the portion shown through the frame, and its space might conceivably extend into our own. Contrasting the Flemish and Roman landscapes, one sees that to achieve depth the earlier artist resorted to a raised viewpoint, whereas the Van

*above:* 145. JAN and HUBERT VAN EYCK. *Birth of St. John the Baptist*, from *Très Belles Heures de Notre Dame* (*Turin-Milan Hours*). 1416–20. Museo Civico, Turin.

*left:* 146. *Seated Philosopher with Figures Paying Homage*, from *The Vatican Vergil*. c. 400. Bibliotèca Vaticana, Rome.

Ordo grandimontensis Inicium habuit anno .1078. p Stephanum.

S. Stephanus

Petrus Damianus

Jo. Serapion

Isaac medicus

Zeno et Arnulphus

Isaac Benimiram medicus celeberrimus salomonis medici filius.

Zeno epus treuerensis a comite treuerorum theoderico captus.

Arnulphus ...

*left:* 147. MICHEL WOLGEMUT. *Nuremberg Chronicle.* 1493. Woodcut. Private collection.

Eycks constructed a space from the ground. Eye-level projection would gradually supplant elevation in spatial perspective of the 15th century.

In earlier medieval art, one might say that the subject of the painting, not the viewpoint of the onlooker, determined the scale and location of the figures, as was appropriate to the sacred eminence and superiority of the subject over the viewer. Part of the democratization of art at the end of the Middle Ages consisted not only of making it increasingly available to more people outside the privileged classes, but also in rendering the world of the painting through the eyes of the living artist and his viewer. Thus medieval painting, once a cross section of the heavenly order, became "a slice of life." The *Turin-Milan Hours* shows the awkward conjunction of the new illusionism and older manuscript decoration. The bedroom scene can be viewed by itself, out of the context of the decorated page, with no loss of interest or completeness. The stylized vines of the margin have a reality that is distinct from that of the flora in the Baptism landscape, just as the highly naturalistic and sculptural seated figure of the Lord differs in style and character from the flat linear outlining of the initial within which he appears. The text paragraph no longer lies on a flat page but seems to intrude into the unframed sky over the Baptism. The calligraphy of the letters is not of the same spirit in which the midwives and objects of the room are outlined.

These and other developments eventually made the book dispensable to serious painting in the 15th century. A changing conception of reality, new criteria for truth to the natural world, the loss of mystical associations between the Word and the written text, the great demand for more books and the ultimate response in the printing press and movable type all brought to an end more than a thousand years of great contributions to art by the hand-decorated book. Easel painting and murals were soon to preempt the attention of the best artists and patrons. Van Eyck's rendering of the baptismal scene—a sacrament which itself means rebirth—prophesies the new life, the new direction, for painting as it began to centralize what had been the marginal medieval concerns for celebrating the time, places, persons, and events of earthly life. But the development of the woodcut in the 15th century brought a new and viable synthesis of text and illustration to the printed book toward the end of that century (Fig. 147). The lines of wooden type and the carved wooden block illustration seen against the white page restored some of the beauty and unity of the earlier painted and calligraphic manuscripts—but not the sumptuous effects, grace, and power that had emanated from the hands which manipulated pen and brush.

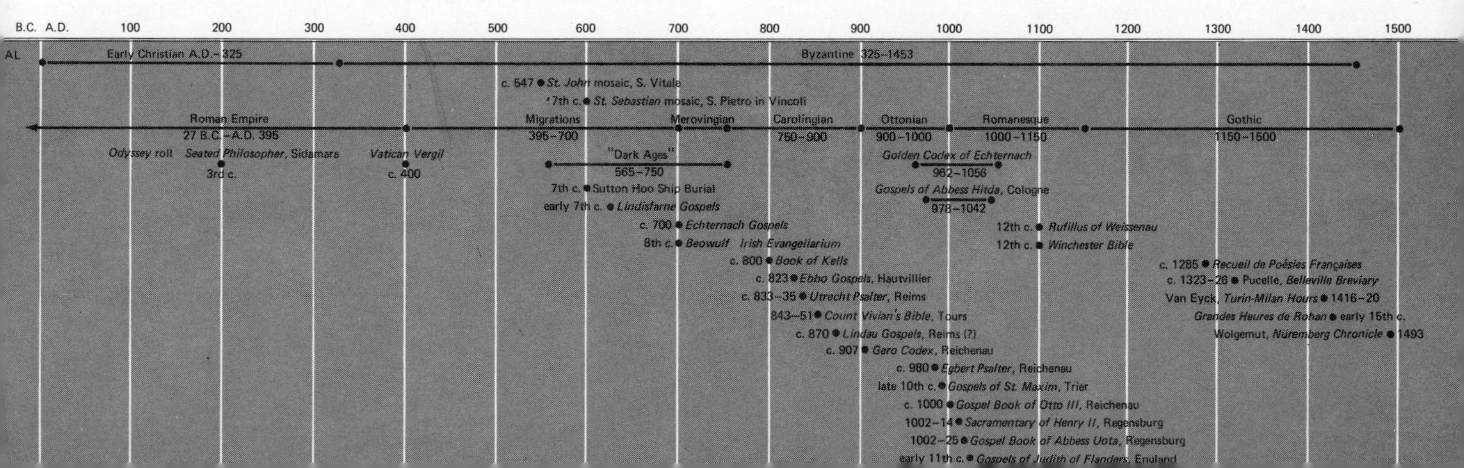

# 6

In the 13th and 14th centuries, medieval art began to evidence an absorption of secular values and an increasing awareness of human worth. At the end of the Middle Ages, in 15th-century northern France, Flanders (present-day Belgium), and Italy, there was a rapid development of illusionistic, or naturalistic, painting that displayed, to an unprecedented degree, a close correspondence between sensory experience and what was painted. The new premise separating 15th-century painting from previous art was expressed by the Italian artist Leonardo da Vinci, at the period's close: "That picture is the most praiseworthy which most resembles the thing to be represented." The new art, or *good modern manner* as it was known in Italy, appeared in both the North and the South at about the same time—roughly about 1420. In the North the great Burgundian court shifted its location from Dijon in France to Bruges and Lille in Flanders. With the change in location of this influential group, major Flemish artists such as Jan van Eyck, Robert Campin, and Rogier van der Weyden ceased to migrate.

## RELIGIOUS ART

In Flanders this development toward a naturalistic style began in book art, as discussed in the previous chapter, but received its greatest impetus in painting on wooden panels that were to be hung in churches, guild halls, and private homes. Flemish panel painting grew into a trend toward abandoning many medieval attitudes and artistic devices for the interpretation of religious subjects. No longer in consistent use were such symbolic attributes as halos and abbreviated settings. Also abandoned was the conventional surface adherence of figures caused by emphasis on strong linear contours and flat, bright colors, which resulted in an absence of depth and of bodies appearing to have neither weight nor volume. Use of generic facial types was replaced by strong characterization and individual portraiture. Fifteenth-century Northern art rejected depictions of a remote mystical world which the viewer could not penetrate and which barred any identification with himself and his values. The celestial sphere of earlier manuscript painting was replaced by what appeared to be a spotless mirror of 15th-century Flemish life. Nonetheless, this art did not abandon religious subject matter but continued to affirm the attachment of artist and patron to the Christian beliefs, for the essential objective of the Flemish artists was to garb mystical religious content with the appearance of the visible, material world.

The motives for this shift in Northern European art included the desire of the artist to present the real world as he saw, touched, and walked through it, as he experienced its beauty with all his senses. The affluent Flemish cities such as Bruges, Tournai, Ypres, and Ghent seemed appropriate incarnations of the Heavenly City, as well as means through which to express sentiments previously excluded from art. Rather than resist the new realism, the Church sought to utilize it for its own purposes. Because of the vivid and familiar aspect that naturalism could lend to invisible holy personages, the new art seemed a strong instrument for the exposition and support of religious dogma, which itself had become more tolerant of the facts of earthly existence. Unforeseen by the Church was the possibility that the artist could not negate his private and nonreligious feelings when he painted religious figures and the interiors and landscapes in which they moved. Thus the new art of the late Middle Ages was an uneasy synthesis of religious and secular values —with an undertone of conflict that was eventually settled in favor of the latter. This synthesis was the beginning of the disengagement of art and ideas of beauty from religion.

**The Use of Symbol** The key to the synthesis of this new art was the *symbol,* or the tangible sign of the invisible. Erwin Panofsky, one of the most brilliant scholars to study this period, has pointed out that the artists' and theologians' problem was to disguise religious symbolism under the cloak of real things, reconciling the idea of the symbol with empirical probability. Over a thousand years of Christian tradition had to be reconciled with the new naturalism and made into "corporeal metaphors of things spiritual." Use of the symbol was abetted by the fact that all reality came to be thought of as permeated with meaning. The process of looking discerningly at a Flemish painting becomes one of gradual penetra-

# 15th-CENTURY FLEMISH ART
# The Synthesis of Heaven and Earth

tion beyond the externals into submerged layers of meaning. The works of art discussed below have been chosen to illustrate the forms taken by the Flemish synthesis of Heaven and earth.

One of the earliest and most important 15th-century Flemish paintings to illustrate the symbolic synthesis of the mundane and theological is the *Merode Altarpiece* (Pl. 17, p. 115), assigned to the Master of Flémalle, who was probably the Tournai painter Robert Campin (c. 1378–1444). In the left panel the donor, a businessman named Ingelbrecht, and his betrothed kneel in a walled garden. Through the open gate can be glimpsed a street like those of Tournai, where the painting was done. The figure standing behind the open gate has been variously interpreted as the painter himself, a servant, or the marriage broker who arranged the betrothal of the patron and his wife. The garden and its flowers were, simultaneously, traditional symbols of the Virgin and familiar adjuncts to Flemish urban middle-class houses. The partially open door serves to link the left and center panels, but its rendering creates an ambiguous relationship between the donor and the scene to his right. As a result, one does not know if he is intended as an actual eyewitness to the event. The Annunciation scene of the central panel is depicted, for the first time in art, in a fully appointed middle-class parlor. Only the presence of the angel and the small child carrying a cross and hovering overhead on rays of light overtly announce a supernatural event. The child and cross, replacing the more customary dove in this Annunciation scene, signify Christ's Incarnation and Passion. In her physical appearance, posture, and surroundings, the Virgin is a middle-class type of the era. Her virtues are those esteemed in both the Virgin and the ideal Flemish housewife. Her sitting on the floor evokes her humility; the immaculate orderliness of the room and its contents alludes to her purity; the reading of the Bible and theological literature signifies her piety and awareness of her role. Meyer Schapiro has observed that what is seen in the room is a metaphor of what takes place within the Virgin's body. The handsome bronze utensil hanging in the niche above the angel's head refers to the Virgin's body as an immaculate vessel, and the lilies also are associated with her purity. The candle's wax and wick become the flesh and soul of Christ. The absence of flame from the candle and the fireplace is explicable on the basis of the divine light entering the room through the closed window; light had been the mystical metaphor of Virgin birth for centuries prior to this painting. In the words of St. Bernard, "Just as the brilliance of the sun fills and penetrates a glass window without damaging it, and pierces its solid form with imperceptible subtlety, neither hurting it when entering nor destroying it when emerging: thus the word of God, the splendor of the Father, entered the virgin chamber and then came forth from the closed womb." If extended, the rays of light would meet the side of the Virgin's head, consonant with the traditional view that she conceived through the ear.

The tiny infant carrying the cross symbolically links the middle panel to the third, in which Joseph is shown (Fig. 148)

148. Robert Campin, or The Master of Flémalle. *Joseph,* detail from right wing of *The Merode Altarpiece* (Pl. 17, p. 115). c. 1420–30.

steadfastly at work in his carpenter's shop. On the table in front of Joseph is a mousetrap, the presence of which is plausible as a household object of cleanliness. Its theological significance, as Schapiro has shown, pertains to Joseph's role as earthly husband of Mary and to Christ's Incarnation. Medieval theologians explained Christ's assumption of the flesh as a plan to redeem humanity from the devil: "The Deity was hidden under the veil of our nature, and so as is done by greedy fish, the hook of Deity might be gulped down along with the bait of the flesh" [Gregory of Nyassa]. Joseph was to conceal the birth of Christ from the devil, and the painter has shown him as neither too old to have fathered a son nor too young to disturb the attitudes of the faithful, but at the right age to deceive the devil. The mousetrap was a theological symbol explained by St. Augustine: "The devil exulted when Christ died, but by this very death of Christ the devil is vanquished, as if he had swallowed the bait in a mousetrap. He rejoiced in Christ's death like a bailiff of death. What he rejoiced in was his undoing. The Cross of the Lord was the devil's mousetrap; the bait by which he was caught was the Lord's death." The block into which Joseph is boring holes may correspond to a fishing-bait box lid and to spike boards attached to the ankles of Christ in 15th-century Netherlandish paintings of the Carrying of the Cross.

To look at the *Merode Altarpiece* only in terms of its complex symbolism is to neglect Robert Campin's ability as a painter. The panels are marvels of lucidity, in the way in which figures and objects impress themselves upon the eye. The composition, like the painting's meaning, is a synthesis of medieval and new devices. The elevated viewpoint and careful alignment of shapes tend to orient them toward the old surface pattern, even while creating the illusion of spaces and objects seen in depth. The objects strewn on Joseph's workbench and the table between the angel and the Virgin manifest this double character. The inconsistency of scale permits complete re-creation and visibility of objects shown in depth—for example, the window lattice and shutters and the second trap seen through the window over Joseph's right shoulder. The rightness of the artist's compositional sensibility is understood when we look at the panel as a whole and then mentally move any object slightly out of position. The creator of this work seems to have conceived of the painter's purpose as being both a reconstitution and a more perfect ordering of reality.

Both the Joseph panel of the *Merode Altarpiece* and Jan van Eyck's small painting of *St. Jerome in His Study* (Pl. 18, p. 115) might easily be taken for secular subjects. It is such painting that inaugurated the secular art of genre subjects. Van Eyck, asked by a Roman cardinal to paint St. Jerome, surrounded the translator of the Scriptures with all the accessories that would be found in a scholar's study. The result was a work in which the cardinal could identify himself with the saint as a leader of the Church, while Van Eyck, a man of substantial learning, could pay homage to Jerome's intellectual achievements. Among the objects associated with scholarship are books, writing materials, and the *astrolabe*, an instrument used in astronomy. Van Eyck was a mapmaker and—judging by the wealth of meaning in his painting—an avid reader. The painter's craft also necessitated translating the Scriptures into the vernacular of his society.

The miniature size of the painting ($8^1/_{16} \times 5^1/_4$ inches) attests that Flemish panel painting originated in manuscript art. Rarely did Flemish artists paint on the scale attempted by contemporary Italians in their mural art (see Chap. 7). Painting such as Van Eyck's gains much of its effect from its modest scale, which demands close viewing of its microscopic detail. The compositions do not consist of large, easily grasped relations between shapes. The sense of a precious object imparted by the St. Jerome panel resides in its small, concentrated areas of saturate luminous colors and in the hard brilliance of surface stressed in both technique and content.

When Van Eyck placed the human figure against a background of architecture and landscape (Fig. 149), he was able

*left:* 149. JAN VAN EYCK. *St. Barbara.* 1437. Brush drawing on panel, $12^3/_4 \times 7^1/_4$". Musée des Beaux-Arts, Antwerp.

150. JAN VAN EYCK. *Madonna with Chancellor Rolin.* 1436. Oil on panel, 26 × $24^1/_2$″. Louvre, Paris.

to adapt the medieval habit of showing the principal figure on a large scale, without forsaking his explorations of illusionism. St. Barbara is shown before the tower in which she was to be imprisoned by her pagan father for her Christian beliefs. The plausibility of her size was achieved by seating the saint on a rocky ledge in the foreground, where she reads from a book in her lap. The middle ground falls away sharply, and to her right and left can be seen workmen bringing materials or shaping them for the churchlike tower under construction. Both the subject matter of the panel and the panel itself demonstrate how artistic projects were carried out in the 15th century. The tower's construction is being supervised by a foreman who stands on a block at the right and is perhaps arguing with a workman atop the edifice standing with arms akimbo near a hoist. The shed near the foreman is where the stonecutters or sculptors worked, protected from sun and rain. The logistics of quarrying, transport, cutting, carving, stonemasonry, and mechanics of construction are presented in detail against a gently swelling landscape to the right and a distant city to the left. It was a visual reminder of the medieval view that every Christian was a builder.

In this brush drawing Van Eyck has also given us wonderful evidence of how he prepared his paintings even though the minute details of the St. Barbara panel would suggest that it was not meant to be carried further. Panel paintings were begun by carefully preparing and joining the wood segments together. Plaster or gesso was then applied to the surface and carefully smoothed. Upon this prepared surface the artist would then make his drawing, which served as the guide for the later building up of layers of color and glaze. In the St. Barbara panel, color was applied only to the sky area. Desire to recreate the brilliance as well as detail of the visible world was probably the strongest incentive for Van Eyck's improving on the old medieval technique of superposing layers of linseed oil over tempera painting; Van Eyck and Robert Campin combined their pigment with oil rather than egg as in tempera painting. The glazes intensified the color and, because the medium dried slowly, permitted reworking and admixture of colors. This technique was ideal for the simulation of light and its reflection. The oil-treated surface was semitransparent, and natural light that fell on it was partly repelled and partly absorbed, further adding to the jewellike quality of Flemish art. As is apparent in a painting such as Van Eyck's *Madonna with Chancellor Rolin* (Fig. 150), and also in the St. Barbara panel, all the shapes were first drawn on a plaster ground. Tints of hand-ground mineral or earth color were applied

*left:* 151. JAN VAN EYCK. Detail of *Madonna with Chancellor Rolin* (Fig. 150). c. 1436.

*right:* 152. ROGIER VAN DER WEYDEN. *Mary Magdalen*, detail of *The Descent from the Cross* (Pl. 19, p. 116). c. 1435.

directly to the gesso and then in layer after layer of glazes, so that the color acquired depth and volume as well as luminosity. Color became less separable as a property from the figures, and objects seen in depth tended to lie less consistently on the painting's surface than in earlier manuscript art. Van Eyck sought the illusion of three-dimensional sculptural roundness to increase his painting's verisimilitude to nature. He had also been a painter of stone and wood sculpture, which at the time was more naturalistic than painting.

Van Eyck's passion for exactitude and the virtuosity of his painted illusions could suggest an unimaginative art. Such criticism would fail to comprehend that more than manual dexterity is required to make on a two-dimensional surface a convincing representation of space, light, and three-dimensional objects. Let us consider, for instance, the subject and composition of the *Madonna with Chancellor Rolin*. Imposing figures inhabit a spacious and luxurious interior, beyond which extends a seemingly infinite panorama. Though empirically verifiable in every detail, the scene in its totality existed wholly in the artist's imagination. In esteem for his spiritual merit or possibly to fulfill a wish, the Burgundian chancellor commissioned for himself an audience with Christ and the Virgin in the Heavenly chateau. Though inspired by archaeological sources that Van Eyck incorrectly associated with Christ's lifetime, the final design of the interior has no definite earthly counterpart. The enclosed flowering garden seen through the colonnade is a metaphor for the Virgin and her purity. Two unknown and fascinating figures look out over a crystalline river that divides an earthly city on the left (identified as Maastricht) from the celestial metropolis on the right. Christ was the divine link between Heaven and earth; thus the benedictional gesture of his hand (Fig. 151) appears tangent to the symbolically seven-pillared bridge between the two cities.

Van Eyck's art was activity in sympathy with God's creation of the world, and the reality created in the painting is at once based on, yet remote from, his own. The painter has established himself as its sole arbiter—selecting, rejecting, refashioning what is to enter it. All material substance has been painstakingly and lovingly explored, given a heightened surface materiality, and fixed into a complex order. The painting contains a thousand glittering points to be discovered and enjoyed. To be shared with the painter is his wonder at the traits of optical perception, as seen, for instance, in the fact that small objects near the eye may block out distant objects of far greater magnitude behind them or in the fact that the eye cannot take in at once all that exists within the sweep of its gaze. Thus the wealth of a lifetime's accumulated visual and intellectual experience is given a new imaginative cohesion and existence on a rectangular surface measuring but 26 × 24½ inches.

To comprehend Van Eyck's re-created world, the viewer is always obliged to commence with the most minute detail. The face of the seventy-six-year-old chancellor, for example, betrays his hard and perhaps questionable career; and Van Eyck has reconstructed the man from his very pores. There is a hint of visual wit in the painter's having made the distant obdurate hill adjacent to the chancellor's brow, while above the head of Christ are placed the spires of the Heavenly Jerusalem, forming a kind of halo. Although Van Eyck was doubtlessly aware of the fallibility of his patron, his painting —like all of his art—is a radiant expression of optimism for the order of life, of faith that because of Christ's sacrifice the earth will again know Paradise. Van Eyck respects earthly rank as a counterpart of Celestial authority, and his imagery is aristocratic in form and content. Van Eyck and the Master of Flémalle reflect the divergent tastes and conflicting attitudes that existed among the aristocracy and the middle class of their time. The domestic Virgin in the *Merode Altarpiece,* for example, cannot be interchanged with the regal Madonna of Chancellor Rolin.

More man-centered in the expression of his religious sentiments than the Master of Flémalle or Van Eyck was the Flemish painter Rogier van der Weyden (1399/1400–64). He opposed their shared, more fairly equal focus on figures and objects, and in particular Van Eyck's pantheism. Van der Weyden's *Descent from the Cross* (Pl. 19, p. 116) is unusual in Flemish painting—it assigns the entire weight of expression and composition to the figures alone. To ensure its powerful and immediate impact upon the viewer, the painter compressed the action within a shallow boxlike space much like the sculptured altarpieces of the period. His intent was to provide an image for pious meditation through which the worshiper could empathize with the suffering of Christ and his anguished followers. The subject is the lowering of Christ's body from the Cross, and the theme is one of passion and compassion. The artist's purpose has been best summarized by Otto von Simson in a fine study of this painting: "The Christian artist must seek to approach God through the affect of compassionate love. He must seek to awaken these affects in others in order to help establish the bond of similitude between God and the contemplator of His image. This is the religious mission of the emotionalism of all Gothic art."

The Van der Weyden painting grows out of the compassionate emphasis and concern with the tragic in Christianity that had arisen at the end of the Middle Ages. The critical response of the worshiper's self-identification with the grief-stricken followers of Christ hinged upon lifelike rendering. It is not only their outward physical appearance that the painter conveyed with such power but also the refined range of emotional states that they manifest. This range includes varying degrees of active and contemplative participation in the moment—from the deathlike swoon of the Virgin, who mystically shares the death of Christ in her role as intercessor for mankind, through the levels of awakening comprehension of the event seen in the figures supporting Christ, to the full capitulation to grief of the Marys, and finally St. John's calm resignation as he seems to foresee the consequences of Christ's death. The bodies as well as the faces make transparent the protagonists' inner state. At the right, for instance, Mary Magdalen (Fig. 152) is caught in a suspended movement that is clearly the result of a total loss of self-consciousness. The emotional and psychological unity of the participants is marvelously embodied in the composition itself; the placement of and alliteration in the limbs join the whole in forceful rhythms. This complex unity was essential to the intent of Van der Weyden—to induce the whole congregation to share in the mournful experience.

As we have seen in the illustration from the *Gero Codex* (Fig. 125) and in Rogier van der Weyden's portrait of himself as St. Luke drawing the Virgin (Pl. 1, p. 25), artists in both early and late medieval times were not adverse to portraying themselves in religious compositions. The Van der Weyden self-portrait was an affirmation of the esteem in which contemporary Flemish ecclesiastical and secular patrons held the art of painting. While such inclusion could be interpreted as an exercise in pride, the painter actually represented himself in the role of worshipful servant to the Mother of God. Even when the artist did not specifically reproduce his own features, his painting might constitute a self-portrait of his nature. The *Adoration of the Shepherds* (Pl. 20, p. 117), executed by Hugo van der Goes (1440–82) and commonly known as the *Portinari Altarpiece,* is characterized by explosive tensions and alternate strains of serenity and turbulence that are revealing in the light of the artist's withdrawal to a monastery and his depressions and suicidal tendencies. The painting's large scale and ambitious panoramic composition rivaled the greatest works of such predecessors as Jan van Eyck and Rogier van der Weyden. Van Eyck's amplitude of setting and particularization of detail are present in the *Adoration,* as is Van der Weyden's insistence upon strong emotive qualities. Van der Goes' painting is, in fact, a magnificent summation of Flemish achievements, climaxed by the bold intrusion of the painter's personality.

Van der Goes mined the symbolism of his painting from the rich deposits of theological literature. Joseph is given prominence by being placed in the left foreground in front of a large pillar that is part of a ruined stone edifice. His representing stability both in the painting and in his place in Christ's earthly family make his connection with the sturdy pillar appropriate. He kneels and pays homage to the scrawny newborn babe who lies in the center of a circle formed by attendant angels, shepherds, and the Virgin. The pillar may relate to the apocryphal tradition that the Virgin leaned against it during the night when she gave birth to Christ, a description analogous to the birth of Buddha, whose mother stood beneath a tree and grasped it for support during childbirth. Van der Goes used the medieval device of scale discrepancies between the figures to set angels and mortals apart.

There is no shed for the Christ child, but the ruined stone setting relates to the decay of the Synagogue and the changing of the old order for the new that is signaled by the Nativity. Panofsky has shown that the vacant-looking building in the background bears the insignia of David, indicating that it is his house. The sheaf of wheat in the center foreground alludes to Bethlehem, "the house of bread," and to the words of Christ, "I am the bread which came down from Heaven." The flowers—lily, iris, and columbine—refer to the blood of the Passion, the pain that pierced the Virgin's heart, and her grief and sorrow.

The ox and ass, standing behind the manger in the stone building, had radically different connotations in medieval times, derived in part from a sentence in Isaiah: "The ox knoweth his owner, and the ass his master's crib." This was taken to mean that the ox recognized the Saviour, while the ass did not. The ass was often used as an anti-Semitic symbol referring to the Synagogue, which was also at times personified as a woman riding an ass. In older images the ass was shown eating, biting its tail, or tearing at the swaddling clothes, indicating its own stupidity and, by implication, that of the Jews for failing to recognize the Saviour. Van der Goes has shown the ass eating the straw of the manger. The ox is sometimes shown as engaged in a tug-of-war with the ass for the swaddling clothes, protecting the babe with its horns, or even reverently down on all fours before the child, identifying the event as a full epiphany.

Van der Goes has given the shepherds (Fig. 153) great importance in his painting, paralleling the magnified roles they began to play in the mystery plays, in which dialogue was fabricated for them because of their popularity with the audience. Van der Goes treats the annunciation of the Nativity to the shepherds and their appearance at the child's side in synoptic fashion, for the Annunciation is represented as

*above:* 153. HUGO VAN DER GOES. Detail of *Adoration of the Shepherds* (Pl. 20, p. 117). c. 1476.

*right:* 154. HUGO VAN DER GOES. *The Death of the Virgin.* c. 1478–80. Oil on panel, 4′10″ × 4′. Musée Communal, Bruges.

*right:* 155. *Phyllis Riding Aristotle.* South Netherlandish or French, c. 1400. Bronze aquamanile, height 13¹/₄″. Robert Lehman Collection, New York.

*far right:* 156. *Aristotle and Phyllis.* Netherlandish, c. 1480. Plate of copper, diameter 20″. Collection Irwin Untermyer. New York.

taking place simultaneously on a hill in the right-hand corner of the panel. The faces of the shepherds are a striking contrast in excitement and ascending levels of comprehension as they realize what they are witnessing. They are given an intensity of expression that borders on the fanatic. This study in psychological reactions to a situation, while occurring in a religious context and as a more or less marginal concern within the broad composition, anticipates later art, which extracted such moments from Biblical incidents and described them in purely secular situations (Pl. 31, p. 164). When the *Adoration* was sent to Italy after its completion, it elicited great interest and proved influential in subsequent Italian art.

In what may have been his last painting before his death in 1482, Van der Goes further developed his characterization of those participating in great moments of emotional stress. In the *Death of the Virgin* (Fig. 154), the assembled disciples are shown in the pathetic attitudes of a shared human grief, and yet distinguished in ways appropriate to the nature invested in each of them by the painter. Compressed within the confines of a small room are not only mourners and the deceased but also Christ as he descends with angels to receive the Virgin's soul. A brilliant glow emanates from him and penetrates the darkened interior, and an open space has been left for the viewer at the Virgin's bedside. Van der Goes was among the first to elevate the humble and ugly in art by showing them as possessing of true faith and enlightenment. Such dedication to the lowly perhaps accounts in part for his renunciation of early personal success and of the pleasures of secular life for a monastic brotherhood. Deep feelings of guilt concerning the adequacy of his devotion and a conflict between his worldly interests as a painter and those of a strongly ascetic man were thereafter to cause severe mental problems and illness. The intensity of feeling displayed by his subjects and the rigorous pictorial construction from which we, as onlookers, cannot detach ourselves convey Van der Goes' obsession for overwhelming the beholder's senses and reason with the emotional stress of witnessing the miraculous. Van der Goes' mental condition was a case in which the synthesis of Heavenly and earthly values could not be easily or finally achieved—an affliction by conscience that was known to many at the end of the Middle Ages.

## SECULAR ART

A considerable number of secular paintings, sculptures, and decorative objects were made by Flemish artists at the end of the Middle Ages; regrettably, almost all have been lost. We know that Van Eyck and Van der Weyden executed hunting and bathing scenes and that Van der Goes, before his retreat from public life, had been employed in such commissions as the decoration of the sails of a ship. Just as the great courts and the wealthy city burghers sponsored the development of religious panel painting, they also funded extravagant secular projects for which the finest artists were expected to contribute their services. Court artists or town-dwelling painters such as Van Eyck lent their skills to the painting of sculpture, furniture, and carriages, and to the designing of costumes, shields, banners, and the costly adornment of private fleets. In 15th-century Europe, art still served mundane purposes, and it was not considered demeaning for an artist to paint utilitarian objects.

In the view of Johan Huizinga, the mentality of the late Middle Ages craved to turn every artistic idea, sacred and secular alike, into a precise image; this "crystallizing tendency" of thought, "which encouraged and supported naturalism in arts," did not anticipate the Renaissance, but rather closed the medieval period. A brilliant demonstration of Huizinga's thesis is seen in two Flemish objects from this period: an aquamanile (Fig. 155), which dispensed either wine or water to wash the hands, and a copper plate (Fig. 156). One of the favored stories at the end of the Middle Ages concerned Phyllis, the mistress of Alexander the Great, who sub-

157. Parade shield. 15th century. Paint and gilt, height 32″. British Museum, London.

158. PETRUS CHRISTUS. *St. Eligius*. 1449. Oil on panel. 38½ × 33⅝″. Robert Lehman Collection, New York.

159. PIERRE THE FLEMING. *The Burghley Nef*. c. 1482–83. Nautilus shell mounted in silver, gilded; 13⅝ × 8″. Victoria & Albert Museum, London.

jugated her lover's teacher, Aristotle. In the objects shown here, the metalsmiths have given visual form to the idea that woman has the power to overcome the wisest of men. On the aquamanile Phyllis accomplishes this by physical force; on the copper plate by guile in the saddle. Both objects were for noblemen's tables and were ancestors to the modern "conversation piece." Such themes from antiquity also remind us that not only the Italians, but educated people of the North as well, were interested in the subjects of antiquity.

Another example of this secular art is a hand-painted shield used on parade occasions and done by an unknown artist (Fig. 157). On the shield of gilt and paint is depicted a knight kneeling before a beautiful lady. Behind the knight, in the position of a second or a benefactor of his profession, is the figure of Death. The heraldic emblems used in like contexts in the earlier Middle Ages had by then given way to chivalrous scene painting.

The Flemish veneration for the craftsman, joined with the purpose of homage to a saint, is seen in a depiction by Petrus Christus (d. 1472/73) of St. Eligius, patron saint of goldsmiths, in his shop as he waits upon a young couple about to be married (Fig. 158). The materials of his craft are displayed on shelves; and among the other objects, the mirror, which permits us to see the street and passers-by, may also have been a device to thwart the devil, who feared losing his image. In one of the earliest significant paintings devoted to the subject of business, Christus ingeniously created a type of marriage and professional portrait, and also treated a whole wall as a still life. Moreover, it is a forerunner of the numerous paintings concerned with events enacted at or near a table, to be discussed in Chapter 10.

Just how important jewelers and metal sculptors were to secular Flemish society is recorded by contemporary chronicles. The finest painters and craftsmen were employed by Charles the Bold for extravagant secular undertakings. One of the most famous spectacles was the wedding of Charles to Marguerite of York, the sister of the English king, in July of 1468, described by Baron van der Elst on the basis of chronicles of the event:

> A forty-foot tower was set up, painted with heraldic devices and adorned with mechanical boars, wolves, and donkeys, to be operated by puppeteers so that they danced and sang. . . . Inside the hall was lighted by bronze chandeliers shaped like

castles. They were surrounded by artificial forests, where wandered extravagant Gothic monsters. . . . A table was set for the bride and groom and for the most important guests under one canopy. Down the center stretched a huge lake framed in silver. In its waters floated thirty ships, each so marked as to represent a territory of the Duke's domain. Some of them were seven feet long and rigged like the galleons that dropped anchor . . . before the port of Bruges and Damme. This marvelous fleet of carriers brought food to the guests seated around the table.

Small but magnificent, a silver ship, by the Parisian goldsmith Peter the Fleming, survives to give witness to the dazzling display of late-15th-century banquets (Fig. 159). Known as *nefs*, such ships were set as status symbols next to the host at dinner. The hull of the *Burghley Nef* is a nautilus shell, mounted on a recumbent siren. A saltceller in the poop reveals the work's practical purpose. Though fantastic below the gunwales, the upper part of the ship corresponds to the latest design of the time. A crew of tiny figures mans the silver rigging, sails, and guns, while at the foot of the main mast Tristan and Isolde play chess.

The Flemish concern for law and punishment touched art in many ways. Convicted prisoners in some cities were forced to pay the expense of having bronze sculptures made of a hand or head by which to advertise to the public the nature of their guilt (Fig. 160). At the very end of the 15th century, the city of Bruges commissioned the painter Gerard David (c. 1460–1523) to paint two pictures on the theme of justice taken from the writings of Herodotus. In the *Punishment of Sisamnes* (Fig. 161), David shows the corrupt Persian royal judge being punished by flaying; the victim is stretched out on a table before witnesses who watch him being skinned alive. Afterward, Sisamnes' son was made a judge in his father's place and forced to sit on a chair covered with the skin of his father, as is shown in the scene in the right-hand corner. This painting was hung in the town hall of Bruges as an admonition to that city's justices. The moralizing purpose of medieval art thus continues, but it is treated in mundane terms and deals with civil behavior. While David's Italian counterparts of the Renaissance were most famous for reviving subjects from antiquity and for making studies of dissection (Figs. 181, 186), this painting reveals Flemish interest in both. Curious is the noticeable restraint in the expressions of the witnesses; only a small boy at the right shows any sign of repugnance. Gruesome pictures such as this remind us that the common view of art's purpose as being pleasing to the eye has many historical contradictions.

*above:* 160. Mask. c. 1499. Bronze, lips and throat pierced with holes for a ring now disappeared; 9⅞ × 5⅛″. Museum of the City Hall, Furnes, Belgium.

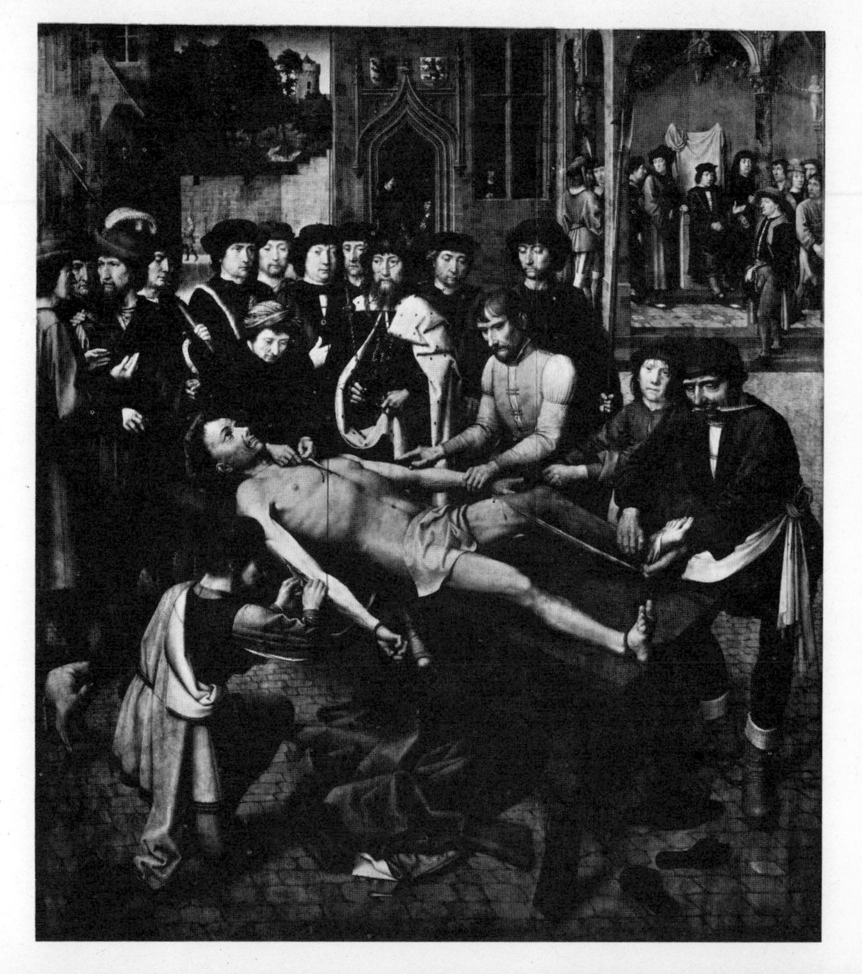

*right:* 161. GERARD DAVID. *The Punishment of Sisamnes*. 1498. Oil on panel, 5′11⅝″ × 5′2⅝″. Musée Communal, Bruges.

*far left:* 162. Rogier van der Weyden. *Last Judgment Altarpiece* (center panel). 1443. Oil on panel, height 7′. Hôtel-Dieu, Beaune.

*left:* 163. Rogier van der Weyden. Detail of a side panel from *Last Judgment Altarpiece*. (See Fig. 162.)

## THE LAST JUDGMENT

Having briefly noted various changes in painting occurring since the 12th century, we shall turn again to the theme of the Last Judgment, already discussed in terms of cathedral sculpture. The Flemish artist Hans Memling (c. 1440–94) created a version of this theme (Pl. 21, p. 118) which provides a valuable illustration of how the conception and execution differed from what was seen earlier—for instance, in the 12th-century tympanum of Ste-Foy (Figs. 69, 70). One of the most obvious developments was the increased naturalism that gave great emphasis to the geographical locale and to the details of the physical action of the resurrected. Through its stark naturalism, the judgment scene has become increasingly more familiar, thereby permitting the viewer to identify with the fate of those in the painting. The central figure of St. Michael weighing the souls has assumed an importance equal if not superior to Christ, who sits enthroned upon the rainbow described by St. John. The weigher of souls and the divine judge no longer seem uncompromising or inaccessible, as in earlier medieval versions of the scene. From the mouth of Christ there radiate the sword and the lily emblematic of his justice and mercy. At the sides of the rainbow kneel John the Baptist and the Virgin, whose prayers intercede on behalf of mankind. The spectator has the impression that in Memling's view man has greater hope for clemency than he did at Ste-Foy.

The left wing of the triptych shows St. Peter herding the naked elect up a golden staircase where they are robed prior to entering the Gothic portals of the Heavenly chateau. The right wing shows the infernal cascade of souls plummeting into the bowels of hell, where they are greeted by demons who exercise their punitive office with enthusiasm. The plausibility of the miraculous second advent of Christ and his judgment is achieved by couching the entire scene in as natural a setting and with accessories as realistic as was possible for the time. Christ and the citizens of Heaven seem suspended just above an earth that resembles a barren Flemish landscape, in a real sky that fades in color to almost white at the horizon.

Rogier van der Weyden's *Last Judgment* at Beaune (Fig. 162), done in 1443, provides an interesting variant on this theme. The scales held by the resplendent St. Michael, garbed in a costly Flemish robe of consummate workmanship, are tipped in inverse fashion from the position seen in Memling's and older judgment scenes: the saved soul is lighter than that of the damned. The painter was reverting to older traditions, going back to Greek times, in which the goodness of the hero's spirit was outweighed by the lesser virtues of his adversary or counterpart. This restores to the weighing ceremony the traditional connotations of up and down, right and left, which we see carried out in the organization of Heaven around Christ and in the elevated situation of Heaven as contrasted with Hell. Van der Weyden also deviated from his contemporaries by not having demons inflict corporeal punishment upon the damned (Fig. 163); their punishment is inward, the result of conscience. With masterful skill and insight, the

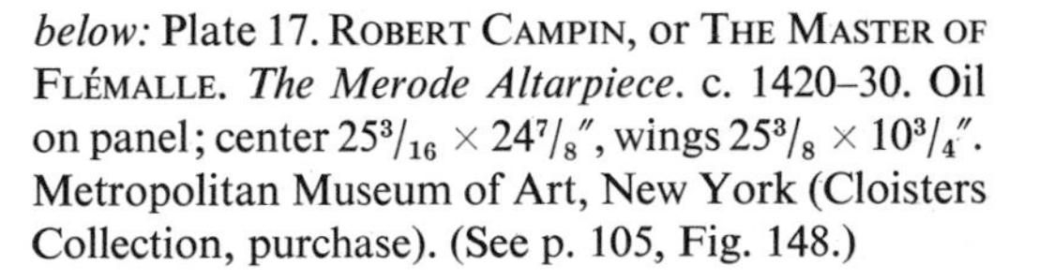

*below:* Plate 17. ROBERT CAMPIN, OR THE MASTER OF FLÉMALLE. *The Merode Altarpiece*. c. 1420–30. Oil on panel; center $25^{3}/_{16} \times 24^{7}/_{8}''$, wings $25^{3}/_{8} \times 10^{3}/_{4}''$. Metropolitan Museum of Art, New York (Cloisters Collection, purchase). (See p. 105, Fig. 148.)

*left:* Plate 18. JAN VAN EYCK. *St. Jerome in His Study*. c. 1432–41. Oil on panel, $8^{1}/_{16} \times 5^{1}/_{4}''$. Detroit Institute of Arts (purchase, City Appropriation). (See p. 106.)

Plate 19. Rogier van der Weyden. *The Descent from the Cross*. c. 1435. Oil on panel, 7′2½″ × 8′7″. Prado, Madrid. (See p. 109, Fig. 152.)

Plate 20. HUGO VAN DER GOES. *Adoration of the Shepherds*, center panel of *The Portinari Altarpiece*. c. 1476. Oil on panel, 8′3$^{1}/_{2}$″ × 10′. Uffizi, Florence. (See pp. 109, 110, Fig. 153.)

Plate 21. HANS MEMLING. *Last Judgment Triptych.* 1473. Oil on panel; center 7′4$^{3}/_{8}$″ × 5′4″, each wing 7′4″ × 2′4$^{5}/_{8}$″. Pomorskie Museum, Gdansk, Poland. (See p. 114.)

*right:* 164. Hieronymus Bosch. *Adoration of the Magi*, detail of center panel. c. 1499. Oil on panel, 4′6³/₈″ × 2′4³/₈″. Prado, Madrid.

artist transcribed the anguished expressions of figures in varying states of mental distress.

Van der Weyden's pessimism about mankind was surpassed in the thought and painting of Hieronymus Bosch (c. 1450–1516). His painting of the *Adoration of the Magi* (Fig. 164), executed at the very end of the 15th century, does not at first strike the modern viewer with its unpleasant associations. Nor is the painting technically an advance on the illusionism of Van Eyck and Van der Weyden from the first half of the century. Bosch's style is somewhat archaic, yet admirably suited to his moralizing imagination. This painting is a grim reflection of the Netherlandish artist's cynicism about man, the Church, and the materialistic interests of society, which had found a glorification in art itself.

In the central panel of the triptych, Bosch has placed a decaying hut in the foreground, with a broad landscape above and behind it. Before the hut are grouped the three Magi, who are clearly differentiated ethnic types from the far corners of the world. In the doorway of the hut stands a half-nude figure wearing golden chains, a crown of thorns over a metal hat, a crimson robe, a bell, and a frog. His leg displays leprous sores. This is the Antichrist, whom Bosch depicted from his acquaintance with Jewish tradition. An openly anti-Semitic inclusion, it presented a criticism of the Jews for not recognizing the true Messiah and for worshiping a false deity. The bell relates to the Antichrist as a bad shepherd, the crown of thorns and robe to his attempt at imitating Christ, and the chain and sores to Jewish traditions citing these as signs of the Messiah. The Antichrist holds an object known to Bosch's contemporaries as an *oven*, which was a symbol or prop for Hell, carried by the Antichrist in the mystery plays. To the right of the Antichrist can be seen the head of a donkey, referring to the Christian belief that the Jews worshiped the head of an ass. The decaying hut again refers to the fallen Synagogue. The shepherds who have climbed onto the shed and peer at the Virgin through a hole in the roof are the foolish shepherds or lost souls. The Magi who bring gifts represent humanity, which while longing for salvation is also foolish. This is borne out in the expression of the kneeling king, the heretical symbols on the cloaks of the Magi, and their warring armies in the distant fields. The placement of the Antichrist between the Magi, as well as the position of the Virgin and Child to the right, signifies the poles of choice open to mankind. Their ultimate seduction by the devil is represented by the wars which take place on the fields behind. The city in the distance perhaps refers to the New Jerusalem after the wars and the advent of a truly Messianic era. It is almost as if Bosch were prophesying the Europe-shaking Reformation that was soon to come with such dramatic force.

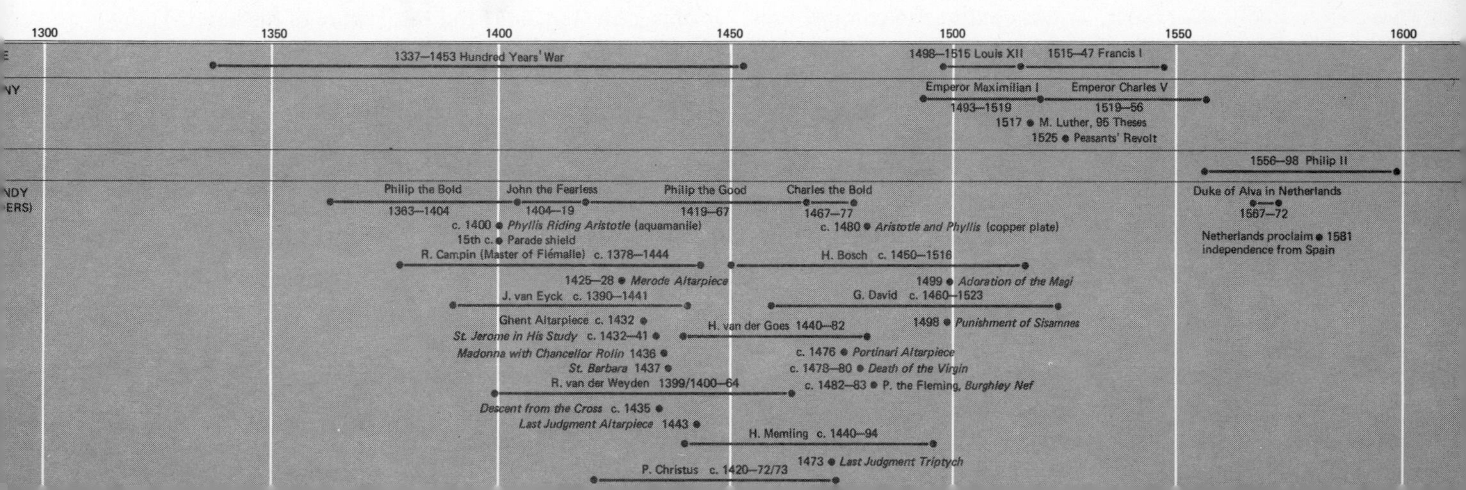

# 7

The predominantly secular character of Western civilization and of its art derives mainly, but not exclusively, from developments that took place in Italian culture of the 15th century. Although supported by the Church, artists of that time began to evidence new hopes for a happy earthly life. They drew heavily upon recent victories in the sphere of intellectual and imaginative freedom, and, together with philosophers, they asserted and accelerated their independence from religion. In medieval times it was thought that art was the projection of an invisible form into a visible world hierarchy; even then, however, the work of important artists had for contemporary connoisseurs a value independent of its content or sacred purpose. By the end of the 15th century, the new premise for painting was that a work of art should be a direct and faithful representation of a natural object. Symptomatic of this new, hard-won freedom was the appearance in the 15th century of theoretical writings on art, very different from the "recipes" left by medieval craftsmen. Elaborate theories of perspective and proportion were put into writing to guide the artist in his encounters with the visible world. As early as the first quarter of the 15th century, artists had formed a productive relationship with science, an alliance which lead to a rationalization of art and which endured through the next century until the Church's reaction to this secularization of culture.

Today, we consider history as continuous, but in the 15th and 16th centuries there was a strongly held view that a new culture, a new civilization, was born a thousand years after the fall of Rome and that it followed a millenium of cultural darkness. Even in our own times, writers continue to comment on the sudden outbursts of creative energy that occurred in the 15th century. This attitude, as well as the myth of the "Dark Ages," does disservice to the creativity and energy of the medieval period. The renaissance of city building, for example, was not a 15th-century phenomenon but actually took place during the 12th through 14th centuries. Ironically, Renaissance artists and writers traced the "rebirth" of art and the beginnings of a "modern style" back to Giotto, who lived in the late 13th and early 14th centuries. This should remind us, as it did not his countrymen, of the vitality and genius that nourished Western art before the events of the 15th century.

**Humanity in Giotto's Art** The Florentine artist Giotto (c. 1267–c. 1336) exerted great influence on the efforts of 15th-century Italian artists to unite in perfect harmony the divine and earthly aspects of existence. Giotto was able to project Biblical subjects into his paintings in ways that made the supernatural plausible and intelligible to all. He divested religious art of its aristocratic aloofness and theological abstraction, and he reduced its reliance upon symbolic accessories and gestures. What his contemporary Dante was to literature, Giotto was to painting—each translated the divine into a new vernacular that facilitated simple devotion. To his own age, Giotto's great achievement was the more lifelike appearance of his subjects, in contrast to the art of his contemporaries. The criterion was not the direct matching of Giotto's paintings with the real world, but a comparison with the art that had gone before. While it may be difficult today to appreciate this difference, Giotto remains a brilliant interpreter of the Bible, whose mastery of composition was indivisible from his abilities as a narrator. *Raising of Lazarus* (Fig. 165) is one of a great series of mural paintings adorning the Arena Chapel in Padua; it was painted about a thousand years after the catacomb painting of the same theme (Fig. 62). Dead for three days, the putrefying Lazarus was brought to life by Christ. To those who first looked upon this painting, it seemed that Giotto, in a similar way, had miraculously brought new life to art.

To read the story within the painting is to retrace the major compositional movements. At the left, as if having turned from the disciples, Christ effects the miracle through the magnetism of his gaze (Fig. 166) and the gesture of his hand. There is no distracting object behind him. The gold background traditionally used in most art of this time has been replaced by blue sky, which returns the action to earth. So powerful is the eye of Giotto's Christ that it impels the viewer across half the painting to the figure of Lazarus. A second bridge between the Resurrector and the resurrected man is formed by the gestures of two intervening figures. On the center axis the arm movements of the two figures who serve as intermediaries are not symbolic but instinctive, showing Giotto's relaxation of the figure's adherence to stereotype. Even when Giotto's people are motionless, they impress us as sentient beings. Gesture is

# 15th-CENTURY ITALIAN ART
# The Synthesis of Heaven and Earth

precious coin for the artist who expends it judiciously, and Giotto never squanders it. It must build the action and forcibly link or pace the composition, never distract by trivial movement or ostentatious detail. Not only the arm movements of the principals lead from Christ to Lazarus, but also the powerful but simple directional arrangements of the draperies, which retain a medieval quasi-independence of the body. Those of the figure behind Lazarus, whose face is veiled to ward off the smell of putrefaction, slow the eye's drive to the right and refocus its attention on Lazarus. The small bending figure of the man who has removed the lid of the tomb is so placed as to guide our attention to the figures of the kneeling women, who return the elliptical movement of the action to Christ. The figures are bonded together by ties that reflect both a deep inward awareness and a simple physical grace.

At all times the viewer's concentration is held within the frame. The painting is like a window through which we look into a clear shallow space, sufficient for the firm sculpturesque volumes that displace it. Giotto has developed a way of constructing a painting that is new. It is as if the viewer's eye were the apex of an imaginary pyramid or cone whose base is the rear plane, or blue sky, in the painting. The painting's surface is like a transparent plane intersecting the pyramid parallel to its apex and base. This form of visual cone allows Giotto to project his figures in depth with fair consistency, on the basis of their distance from the viewer—a way of seeing

*left:* 165. GIOTTO. *Raising of Lazarus.* 1305–06. Fresco. Arena Chapel, Padua.

*above:* 166. GIOTTO. *Head of Christ,* detail of Figure 165.

*right:* 167. Ambrogio Lorenzetti. *Effects of Good Government* (scenes in the city). 1337–39. Fresco. Sala dei Nove, Palazzo Pubblico, Siena.

*opposite:* 168. Ambrogio Lorenzetti. *Effects of Good Government* (scenes in the countryside). 1337–39. Fresco. Sala dei Nove, Palazzo Pubblico, Siena.

that was to be systematized mathematically in the next century. The frame works with the figures, serving as a measure and foil for their large scale, erectness, and resulting dignity.

As seen in this painting, Giotto's was a man-centered world in which Christ appeared as a man among men. His art fostered hope both in the humane vision of Christ and in the temperance, humility, and dignity assigned to man, who is shown as worthy of redemption. Giotto's rendering of the figure is integral with the spiritual values he assigned to his ideal of humanity. The painter made a historically influential equation between the weighty mass of his figures and their moral worth. The stability of their movements and disposition within the scene convey the impression that men have a meaningful part in a larger order.

**Landscapes of Ambrogio Lorenzetti** In Italy as in northern Europe, the artist's conquests of the visual world was a slow process attended by timid or hesitant efforts as well as by bold advances. After Giotto, the 14th-century artist who struck out in the most venturesome way to open up the space of his fresco and to create a more natural environment—thereby representing the abundance of earthly life—was the Sienese Ambrogio Lorenzetti (act. 1320–48). Commissioned by the city-state of Siena to decorate its town hall, Lorenzetti filled the walls of a room with allegories and commentary on the subject of good and bad government. Visually and historically, the fresco containing the effects of good government on the city and the country is the most exciting (Figs. 167, 168). Both views are original panoramic vistas, which depend not upon conventions or memory but on actual visual experience, based on the hill city of Siena and its natural surroundings. The spatial construction of the fresco is from the viewpoint of someone near the center foreground in the city, near the point at which the women dance as evidence of happiness under just rule. The architecture, figures, and landscape diminish in scale both in depth and laterally in relation to this vantage point within the city itself; the reference is not to the viewer or based on his distance from the painting. The entire city is rendered in focus, as if to accommodate the movement of the eyes as one searches through the fresco outward from the city's center. Lorenzetti was not working with scientific perspective or attempting photograph-like naturalism, since his was an empirical effort based on trial and error. The obliqueness of the streets, for example, is convincing but not scientific. There are minor inconsistencies, such as his failure to make figures in the landscape smaller in proportion to their setting, but the painter took the artist's license of bending a rule for purposes of clarity and vividness.

Not since antiquity and the Roman wall paintings (Pl. 50, p. 307) had a Western artist attempted an embrace of the visual world that was as sweeping as Lorenzetti's—or as topographically specific. The light of the entire scene is strongest in the area of the principal viewpoint, and it diminishes as it moves outward. Lorenzetti caught the continuity of light and natural space, and the kind of roving focus of the traveler (not dissimilar to what was happening in Chinese painting of the time, as will be seen in Chapter 16, "Art and Nature").

**Humanity in Masaccio's Art** More than a hundred years after the creation of Giotto's Arena Chapel frescoes, the Florentine artist Masaccio (1401–28) contributed to a fresco cycle of St. Peter in a chapel newly built by a silk merchant named Brancacci. No artist in the intervening period had fully grasped or extended the ideas of Giotto as did Masaccio in his fresco *The Tribute Money* (Fig. 169). The Brancacci Chapel became a fountainhead of ideas and inspiration for many artists

who followed, including Michelangelo (who supposedly had his nose broken there during a quarrel). In 1427 the city of Florence imposed an income tax which was advocated by Brancacci's party; the theme of the fresco is perhaps a subtle reference to this support. The events depicted by Masaccio are those attending the arrival of Christ and the disciples before the gates of Capernaum, where a toll was asked of them. In the 5th century St. Augustine interpreted this event as foretelling the toll that Christ was to pay upon the Cross for mankind. At this moment, for the first time, Christ singled out a disciple, Peter, to participate in a miracle—a prophecy perhaps of Peter's role in founding the Church and his aid in the redemption of mankind. Following Christ's instructions to him (the episode in the center), Peter takes the coin out of a fish's mouth (far left) and then pays the publican (extreme right). As in the work of Giotto, the main group is assembled in the center and close to the lower edge of the painting. Though the fresco was high up on the wall, the viewpoint of its construction is about level with

*below:* 169. MASACCIO. *The Tribute Money*. c. 1427. Fresco, 8′4″ × 19′8″. Brancacci Chapel, Sta. Maria del Carmine, Florence.

the heads of the group. The intense illusion of reality Masaccio achieved is contingent upon the fresco's construction from a fixed viewpoint. As defined by John White, "One of the most significant characteristics of artificial perspective is that it assumes an observer with his eye in one particular position at a fixed distance and direction from the scene before him." But this viewpoint may not always coincide with the spot in which the beholder finds it possible to stand, as is the case in the Brancacci Chapel.

The setting is new. The scene takes place on a broad plain before an extensive mountain range, seen in atmospheric depth; and though small in relation to the figure scale, the entrance to the city is drawn in correct linear perspective. The vanishing point of its diagonals is coincident with Christ's head, thus uniting the structural with the theological focus. Dramatic emphasis as well as structural clarity was furthered by the new perspective. While the human form still dominates in the painting—a requirement of Florentine art in this century—it has been set into a natural context. As if affirming this relationship, Masaccio's figures cast shadows upon the ground, conveying a marked sense of their relation to the surrounding world and their exposure to natural light. The artist's building blocks were the study of such qualities as the reflection of light and shadow by broadly treated volumes, the relation of solids to voids, and the rhythmic interplay of the human body with the forms of nature and architecture. The figures around Christ belong to an impersonal ordering and do not display spontaneous volitional movement.

Masaccio modernized but did not basically alter Giotto's ideal of a stable world governed by powerful laws. This modernization took the form of a greater awareness of and skill in rendering the anatomical makeup and coordination of the human figure. The corporeal body asserts itself even when sheathed in draped folds. Masaccio utilized newly discovered gestures and postures modestly but tellingly in enriching the human role in religious drama. This release of the human body from inertia was as important for the future secularization of art as was the Flemish celebration of the man-made object.

The strength of Masaccio's treatment of the faces of the disciples heightens the intrusion of the human into what had been exclusively the domain of the divine. Like many who followed, Masaccio drew strength from empirical as well as from theoretical inspiration, and while the faces of his human characters gained in intensity and plausibility, that of the adult Christ—because of his divine nature—became a troublesome problem. This dilemma is a sign of the transitional nature of the 15th century, which stood with one foot in the medieval period and one in the modern. Noteworthy are the great 15th-century portraits of secular subjects and a few faces of saints (perhaps because of their humanization), but renderings of Christ's face as eloquent as that at Daphnē (Fig. 71) are rare. There are, however, good grounds for believing that Masaccio did not paint the face of Christ and that this weaker conception was executed by his collaborator, Masolino.

Masaccio literally and figuratively brought a new shudder to painting. The theme of baptism in which a figure is immersed in water—or, as in Masaccio's *St. Peter Baptizing the Neophyte* (Fig. 170), has it poured over him from a bowl—was an old one. But for the first time the Florentine painter gives us the reaction of trembling flesh under the touch of cold water, and the instinctive but futile warming gesture of the man who has disrobed while awaiting his own baptism in the icy stream underlines this sensation. What may well have brought a shiver to Masaccio's contemporaries was his power to bring home to them in this performance of a sacrament their all too human and familiar frailty during such an ordeal. With Masaccio, the senses of his subject come alive, and flesh and temperature become tangible—the viewer and the viewed are brothers in the same skin.

**Secular Criteria for Art** What imparts excitement to the developments of the 15th century is the artists' pursuit of objective correspondences to nature, which released tremendous energies, gave rise to a pervasive spirit of free inquiry that in turn nourished venturesome ideas and produced bril-

*left:* 170. MASACCIO. *St. Peter Baptizing the Neophyte*. c. 1427. Fresco. Brancacci Chapel, Sta. Maria del Carmine, Florence.

*right:* 171. FILIPPO BRUNELLESCHI. *The Sacrifice of Isaac.* c. 1401. Bronze, 18 × 16″. Museo Nazionale, Florence.

*far right:* 172. LORENZO GHIBERTI. *The Sacrifice of Isaac.* c. 1401. Bronze, 18 × 16″. Museo Nazionale, Florence.

liant individual styles. A galaxy of talents crowned Italian art before the century was half spent. Masaccio and Veneziano, the sculptors Donatello and Ghiberti, and the architects Brunelleschi and Alberti—the latter being primarily a theorist—evolved, both theoretically and empirically, scientific bases for the means of representation. For most of the century these discoveries did not dogmatically circumscribe the artist. Furthermore, these abstract devices for rendering and ordering—perspective, proportion, anatomy, and the study of light—were not the sole prerogative of either sculpture or painting. Secular criteria were established for the making and judgment of all art. The rationalization of the means by which the artist could master the representation of the visible world coincided with the aggressive urban middle-class drive to systematize business conduct, explore the earth's surface in successful mercantile enterprises, and exalt man-made goods. Body and mind were to be in felicitous coordination, and this ideal enhanced the attraction of the ancient Roman sculpture known in that century. The supernatural was still respected; however, priority was given in art to the sensorily verifiable experiences, like the clear, measurable shaping of space and vital energetic bodies, as well as the convincing re-creation of familiar settings of home, city, and landscape. The artist continued to rely upon imagination for his basic conception, but he was now armed with new constructive and expressive means to suit his own taste and that of his time for emulation, but not literal imitation, of all that was material and measurable.

**The Baptistery Competition** The promise of the 15th century in Florence was evident during its first years, when, between 1401 and 1403, two artists in their twenties competed for that city's greatest artistic honor: designing and casting in bronze the east doors of the Baptistery, which faced the Cathedral. Finalists from among seven competitors, Filippo Brunelleschi, a goldsmith, and Lorenzo Ghiberti, a goldsmith and painter, still ranked as apprentices in the guild system. They presented their bronze relief panels depicting the Sacrifice of Isaac (Figs. 171, 172) as prescribed by the large jury of businessmen, artists, and theologians. The competition, the focus and pride of and the source of argument for the entire city, was carried out despite a recent devastating plague that had wiped out 30 000 inhabitants. And Florence had also successfully withstood the military threat of the Duke of Milan, who died suddenly in 1402 as he was besieging the city. The artistic enhancement of a holy building was a gesture of thanks for divine protection as well as one of civic pride. Both entries combined medieval and new ideas and forecast the vigor and creative imagination of Florentine sculpture.

Brunelleschi's was the more obviously dramatic of the two interpretations; his every figure (even the animals) was involved in strenuous movement. Cast in the round and then attached to the panel, Brunelleschi's energetic figures lean or twist into the viewer's space, overlapping the medieval frame. Their actions, however, lack the synchronized mutual integration of his competitor's design. Ghiberti divided the attendants from those engaged in the sacrifice by a diagonal landscape device rather than arrange the composition in horizontal layers. Despite its high relief, Brunelleschi's design still clings to an overall surface disposition of elements. The technical qualities of fine finish, down to the smallest detail of features, hair, and drapery, drew

*left:* 173. DONATELLO. *The Feast of Herod.* 1425–27. Gilt bronze, 23½″ square. San Giovanni, Siena.

greater admiration for Ghiberti, but he may also have impressed the jury by his ability to achieve a more natural and graceful suggestion of depth. Cast in one piece except for the figure of Isaac, Ghiberti's panel may thus have seemed to the artists better grounded in conservative standards of craftsmanship. Too, Brunelleschi's impetuous Abraham could well have appealed less to Christian theologians than did Ghiberti's interpretation of reticence and thoughtfulness. The businessmen, anticipating the costs of twenty-eight such panels on the future door, would have appreciated the lighter weight of Ghiberti's relief. Both artists included paraphrases from Hellenistic-Roman art: Brunelleschi in the attendant pulling a thorn from his foot, and Ghiberti in the torso of the young Isaac and the decoration of the altar. Even before the painters, it was the sculptors and, above all, the architects who saw in ancient Roman forms the basis for a new, beautiful, and expressive art.

Ghiberti won the competition and went on to design two great doors for the Baptistery. Brunelleschi became the greatest and most influential architect of the century, forsaking his great talents as a sculptor. The bitterness between the two that began with the competition never abated, for neither was a modest man. In his autobiography Ghiberti, the older of the two, wrote: "To me the palm of victory was conceded by all the experts and by all those who competed with me." There is some evidence of a split decision and no evidence that Brunelleschi admitted his rival's superiority.

**Psychology and Nudity** Almost contemporaneous with Masaccio's *Tribute Money* is a relief sculpture made by Donatello (c. 1386–1466) for the font in the Baptistery of San Giovanni, Siena. For *The Feast of Herod* (Fig. 173) Donatello drew upon Brunelleschi's newly discovered device of systematic linear perspective to create the appearance of the relief's orderly recession into depth. In the oldest extant example of a composition based on this system for transposing the three-dimensional world onto a flat surface with all distances measurable, the diagonals of the steeply sloping floor converge to a point marked by the elbow of the seated figure who gestures towards the severed head of John the Baptist. The diagonals of the upper part of the relief meet at a point slightly above, on the cornice of the wall behind the banquet table. This area of convergence corresponds roughly to a theoretical viewer's eye level. No artist of his century surpassed Donatello's ability to dramatize the workings of the human mind in situations of great excitement. He brought to art a great awareness of crowd psychology that vivified and united his figures with a range and depth of feeling unequaled at the time. These qualities were suited to the subject, which shows not the sacred moment of martyrdom but the animated group response to a sadistic murder. The reactions of the figures to the sudden appearance of John's head polarize around expressions of attraction and repulsion. Donatello bridged the gap between the two foreground groups partially by means of the triple arches and the table but also, and most importantly, by the fanatical stare of Salome suspended in her dance.

Though Donatello is referred to as a Renaissance sculptor, his life-size, painted wooden image of the Magdalen (Fig. 174) remains the expression of an essentially medieval Christian attitude toward the incompatibility of body and soul. Donatello often carved healthful and cosmetically attractive figures in an age that admired physical beauty, but he retained much of the penitential spirit of the late Middle Ages. Intended for the Baptistery of Florence, his sculpture is a merciless study of the body made less than human, first through self-indulgence and then through a self-denying asceticism. He renewed the late medieval dichotomy between inner truth and surface beauty. The Magdalen has become a living corpse, like a medieval reminder of death and the wages of sin. Only the zeal of the convert animates the leathery flesh of this skeletal figure, holding out the same hope as baptism. The spiritual intensity imparted to the sculpture by Donatello transcends its physical repellence and makes the work aesthetically compelling. The slight gap between the hands creates a life-giving tension that complements the psychological force emanating from the head, and essential to this focus is the self-imposed rigidity of the body. No sculpture in Western art is further from the Greek Classical ideal, and yet Donatello did make sculptures of the body which share certain Classical ideals.

It was Donatello who created, in his *David* (Fig. 175), the first life-size nude since the end of antiquity. The work was probably commissioned by a private patron for his home, for in 1430 the sculptor's society was not yet prepared to see a Biblical hero such as David commemorated in an unclothed representation. For unknown reasons, Donatello chose to show the vanquisher of Goliath wearing a hat and boots, accessories unthinkable for Classical statuary. Donatello's figure is a synthesis of postural derivation and personal observation of the body. Although the contraposto pose was borrowed from ancient statuary, the youthful model lacks the fluid contours and joints and the pronounced articulation of body structure, such as the joining of the legs and torso, found in ancient figures (Fig. 52). The *David* nonetheless furnishes an early-15th-century Florentine aristocratic ideal of youthful masculine beauty and intelligence, with the latter faculty triumphant over the brute strength of Goliath.

**The Sacred Conversation** The Venetian painter Domenico Veneziano (c. 1420–61), who came to Florence in 1439, drew insight and inspiration from Donatello and the insurgent art of his time to produce his masterwork, the *Madonna and Child with Saints* (Pl. 22, p. 135). Flanking the enthroned Madonna and Child at the left are Saints Francis and John the Baptist, while at the right are Saints Zenobius and Lucy. This is a devotional and honorific painting of a type frequently found in later Italian art, called the *Sacred Conversation*, implying the possibility of discourse between the figures. The formal symmetry by which divinity is honored is tempered by the forceful individualization of the saints. They belong at once to a timeless hierarchy, but have acquired personalities and states of feeling that prohibit their total submission to an impersonal order. We may speak of the saints' heads as portraits in an even more exact sense than in discussing the work of Masaccio or Giotto. Veneziano's most inspired characterization is that of John the Baptist. Ironically, the saint has been used as an interlocutor between the viewer and the Mother and Child. He himself is the most magnetic figure in the painting. Much may be read in his face—suffering, compassion, the gift of clairvoyance, and obliviousness to self. Taken as a whole, John has a late medieval head and the firm body of a Hellenistic athlete.

So strong is Veneziano's overall design that it does not disintegrate under the weight of the attention given to the heads. His color lacks the detailed, sumptuous radiance of the Flemings, but is more obviously constructive in its broader application, as in the greens and pinks of the loggia. The airiness and clarity of the scene depend upon many light, delicate tones with strong accents, such as yellow and red, discretely allied to the principal figures. The severe clarity and simplicity of the architecture never conflicts with the gestures of the saints but serves to underscore their slightest movement. Building on Masaccio's work, Veneziano introduced a convincing representation of brilliant sunlight, which shines from a single source on the rear wall just to the right of the Virgin and Christ. The light provides not only warm illumination of the background but a contrast with the cool foreground area.

**"Oh, What a Sweet Thing This Perspective Is"** Today it is possible for almost anyone to be taught in a single lesson simple perspective tricks and to suggest convincingly three-dimensional space on a flat surface. But in the 15th century the development of perspective devices was still a challenge and could produce great emotional excitement in the artist who discovered that, through these techniques, it was possible for him to explore a new artistic world. Consider for a moment that such artists as Masaccio, Donatello, and Veneziano, who were faced with the opportunity of depicting stories they had never actually witnessed, could now paint or model these

*right:* 174. DONATELLO. *Mary Magdalen.* c. 1454–55. Polychromed wood, height 6′2″. Baptistery, Florence.

*far right:* 175. DONATELLO. *David with the Head of Goliath.* c. 1430–32. Bronze, height 5′2¹/₄″. Museo Nazionale, Florence.

*left:* 176. Paolo Uccello. *The Flood.* 1446–48. Fresco. Chiostro Verde, Santa Maria Novella, Florence.

*below left:* 177. Rossi. Engraving after *The Flood* (Fig. 176) by Uccello. From Rosini, *Storia della Pittura Italiana* (Pisa, 1848).

incidents as if they were happening before one's very eyes. At their disposal were the new scientific as well as optical perspectives to achieve this illusion. Artists most concerned for the former had access to Florentine mathematicians interested in Euclidean geometry. One such artist was the energetic and inventive Paolo Uccello (1397–1475), who passionately loved the geometry possible in objects and the unifying space of scientific perspective but who would not submit totally or blindly to its use to dictate the form of an entire painting. As Uccello painted his fresco of *The Flood* (Figs. 176, 177) in the cloister of a Florentine church, he was weighing in his mind the effects of linear perspective against actual optical experience and making adjustments between the two. Thus within a single composition he includes two views of the Ark, its length at the left, and width at the right. Each has its own point toward which the diagonal lines of the ship converge, rather than a common vanishing point, which would be the case if the entire scene were constructed from a single, frozen viewpoint. As Giotto had done, Uccello was partly accommodating the shifting gaze of actual visual experience and the needs of pictorial organization, which could well differ from those of science and sight. Uccello recognized that linear perspective was not something toward which the beholder is neutral, and he exploited the sensational possibilities of this system through the deep dramatic funneling space created by the sides of the Arks. He then proceeded to populate this deep space, thereby varying the scale and postures of his figures. Shown in the same fresco are the beginning of the Flood (at the left) and Noah's awaiting of

the dove and the recession of the waters forty days later (at the right). The present battered condition of the fresco explains our use of an old engraving to assist the reader. The folly of men and women when faced with disaster is shown by the figures who continue personal quarrels and physical combat in the left foreground, and the futility of resisting the onslaught of the elements is seen in the man who tries to climb into a barrel and in those who try to cling to the sides of the sealed Ark. The arched, bloated body of a drowned child lies in the right foreground. The identity of the tall standing figure who looks to Heaven and whose ankles are clasped by a half-submerged figure is not known. That he is Noah is doubtful, though he is perhaps a priest who recognizes the truth of Noah's warning from God too late.

Here was a subject in which Uccello could indulge his curiosity and wonder about the appearance of the elements, the naked exposure of the body and human psychology, the shapes of objects such as the checkered collar around the neck of a struggling figure in the left foreground (which was a personal caprice or like a signature)—life and death in their most violent manifestations. His ego as an artist was gratified by proving he could convincingly render clouds, a wind-blown tree, drapery, animals, and the figure in unconventional ways.

Too often called a scientist rather than an artist, Uccello saw geometry and linear perspective as surveying tools for mapping what had in painting been unknown territory. Empirical study and intuition made him believe that there were certain geometric shapes common to men and animals which should serve truth and beauty as the artistic substructure of their re-creation.

Uccello's most brilliant demonstration of the power of rationalizing figures as well as space in art took the form of a 34-foot-long series of three battle paintings for a bedroom in the Medici Palace (Figs. 178–180). The left panel shows the Florentine chief, Niccolò da Tolentino, directing the battle against the Sienese, whose leader is shown just killed in the center panel; at the right, reinforcements attack the enemy's rear guard. Against the backdrop of the San Romano hills and fields, Uccello shows what began as a debacle turn into a victory. The bloodless combat and dazzling pageantry of the event recall the character of battles fought by mercenaries, who were greater threats to the civilians that employed them than to each other. Art, science, and reason were not alien activities for Uccello, who reportedly said, "Oh, what a sweet thing this perspective is." Today artists are using the computer to give them unimaginable perspective views of simple shapes, which can then be enlarged and transposed into illusionistic but abstract painting. Uccello used simple projective geometry to give him unfamiliar views and shapes of familiar objects, reveling in the ambivalence he could evoke between pure geometry and the idiosyncratic forms of armor, horses' flanks, and pennants. Uccello disciplined his soldiers so that they fought and fell within his ideal perspective and proportional framework. This artifice is continued in the gold and silver trappings and bright, unnatural colors of the horses which, unlike the receding lines and shapes, hold to the surface plane of the paintings. Uccello has thereby achieved cohesion of surface as well as depth, and he has temporarily synthesized the medieval and Renaissance ideals of picture-making in a magnificent decorative effort. It is probable that Lorenzo de' Medici enjoyed these panels from his bed—presumably while looking through his feet.

**Synthesis of Present with Biblical Past** During the 15th century the rulers of Florence satisfied their subjects and fellow citizens with frequent and lavish pageantry; for such tournaments and parades, in Florence as in Flanders, the best artists

*opposite below:* 178. Paolo Uccello. *The Rout of San Romano: Niccolò da Tolentino Directing the Battle of San Romano.* c. 1455. Tempera on wood, 6′ × 10′6″. National Gallery, London.

*below left:* 179. Paolo Uccello. *The Rout of San Romano: The Unhorsing of Bernardino della Carda.* c. 1455. Tempera on wood, 6′ × 10′7″. Uffizi Gallery, Florence.

*below:* 180. Paolo Uccello. *The Rout of San Romano: Micheletto da Cotignola Attacking the Sienese Rear.* c. 1455. Tempera on wood, 6′ × 10′5″. Louvre, Paris.

would be called upon to design ornament for their patron's armor. Fortunately preserved is a parade shield bearing the figure of David (Fig. 181) by Andrea del Castagno (c. 1421–57). Instead of decorating the shield with a coat of arms, Castagno has staged David's triumph against a natural backdrop. The vital figure of David is shown as if first confronting Goliath with loaded sling, and at his feet is the grisly evidence of the story's end. David was one of the great heroes of Florence, as well as a symbol of freedom, and on the shield Castagno shows him as vigorous and vigilant, ready to repel his enemy and, by implication, the enemies of Florence. In his figure of David, Castagno joined the posture of an ancient Greek statue with the results of his studies of human anatomy, for he was one of the first artists to study the body by dissection. This practical knowledge of musculature imparted energy, strength, and new expressiveness to his figures but, in the case of David, created an awkward synthesis with the archaic or conventionalized landscape. Castagno's art was more effective when figural studies were complemented by architectural perspective.

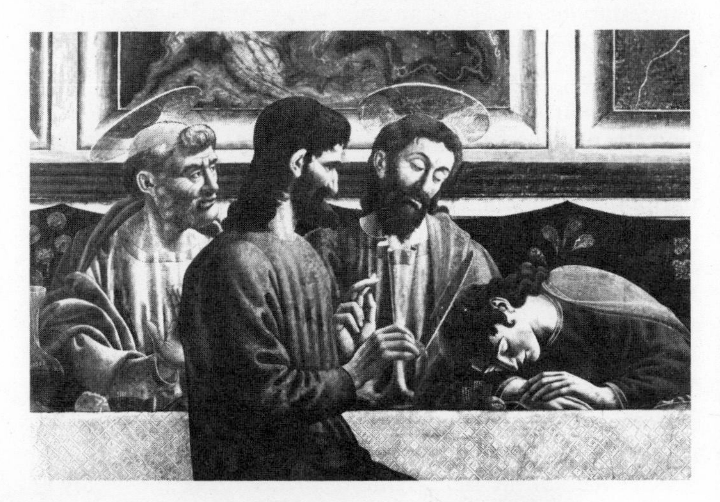

*above:* 181. ANDREA DEL CASTAGNO. *David.* c. 1450–57. Parade shield, tempera on leather; height 45½″. National Gallery of Art, Washington, D.C. (Widener Collection).

*below:* 182. ANDREA DEL CASTAGNO. *The Last Supper*. c. 1445–50. Fresco. Sant' Apollonia, Florence.

*right:* 183. ANDREA DEL CASTAGNO. Detail of Figure 182.

Shortly after Veneziano's *Madonna and Child with Saints* was completed, Castagno painted his fresco *The Last Supper* (Fig. 182), which was the prototype for several later 15th-century versions of the same theme. Although the subject is Biblical and the fresco's location was in the refectory of a Florentine church, Castagno's interpretation is in human and mundane terms. The disciples and Christ are shown seated at a long table in a severely beautiful pavilion, whose design is based on contemporary architectural tastes.

Marginal evidences of the increased interest in ancient art in the fresco are the bronze sphinxes at the ends of the bench and certain details of the architecture. As had their Flemish counterparts, painters such as Castagno often reconstructed or designed with the brush their own architecture and furnishings. Through linear perspective, Castagno created the forceful illusion of the pavilion's recession behind the end wall of the refectory. Within the resulting space of the room and seen against its coordinate system of verticals and horizontals are the impressive figures of Christ and the disciples. The initial appearance of the group resembles a social gathering, common to both Castagno's society and that of the ancient Hebrews, whose principal evening meal was an almost public occasion for assembling friends and a speaker. Castagno selected the moment when Christ prophesied his betrayal (Fig. 183). Judas is singled out by his placement across from Christ and by the absence of a halo. Because Castagno adhered to laws of perspective, Judas is actually larger in scale than Christ, who sits farther in depth—a relation of scale never seen in medieval art.

Christ has not, in fact, received the same emphasis given to the disciples who flank him and ponder the significance of his announcement. The group of Peter, Judas, and Christ is set off slightly by the accentuation of the marble pattern in the wall above their heads. The natural light entering the room through the windows at the right falls equally on all present. The individualization and humanization of the disciples is accomplished by their rugged countenances, the variety of their rhetorical postures, and the lack of restriction by the architectural framework. Despite the relative passivity of the figures, Castagno's ideals of latent muscular energy and cool hard-edge sculptural surfaces assert themselves. Such painting was thought to bring the dead and the past to life by giving them a vivid physical presence.

**Architecture and the Human Form** It was the locating of figures in architectural settings in the 14th and 15th centuries that accelerated developments in perspective. These settings acquired a beauty and interest of their own, competitive with the figures, as seen in the Castagno fresco and in the *Flagellation* (Fig. 184) by Piero della Francesca (c. 1420–92). One can conceive of the setting as existing prior to the presence of the figures, unlike medieval painting before the 14th century; indeed, there were drawings and paintings of architectural vistas without humans in 15th-century art. Piero was as devoted to geometry and perspective as Uccello had been, believing that its Euclidean shapes were the purest form of beauty. Pilate's palace invited an elegant conception; using a basic unit of measurement and geometry, the artist carefully constructed a handsome open edifice in which the flagellation takes place. Christ is located against the traditional pillar—here surmounted by a bronze statue symbolizing paganism—and he stands in the center of a strongly foreshortened circle inscribed on the pavement. Con-

184. PIERO DELLA FRANCESCA. *The Flagellation of Christ.* c. 1456–57. Tempera on panel, $23^1/_4 \times 32''$. Galleria Nazionale delle Marche, Urbino.

*left:* 185. PIERO DELLA FRANCESCA. *Head of Christ*, detail of *The Resurrection of Christ* (Pl. 23, p. 135). 1460.

ceivably, Piero was symbolically signifying Christ's divinity and central place in the universe. The entire pavement design and the careful measurement of the building's elevation coordinated with it may have had richer esoteric symbolism, known to very few other than the artist. Piero's *Flagellation* has been the subject of much serious inquiry by scholars, who have yet to reveal all its meaning or reach agreement on its content. Why is Christ upstaged by the three large foreground figures at the right? Who are these three men? How may we account for the recession of divinity from the central focus? Dr. Marilyn Lavin has given the most brilliant and persuasive argument, pointing out that the two older men were contemporaries of the artist and that they were fathers grieving over the disease that had felled their respective sons. The figure at the left, in exotic dress to suggest his interest in astrology and comparison with a wise man, is Ottaviano Ubaldini, who probably commissioned the work around 1466. His companion on the right, who shares the moment of enlightenment, is Ludovico Gonzaga. Ottaviano is shown explaining that, like Christ, their sons have gained eternal glory through their suffering. The handsome youth standing between these two men symbolizes their sons, the beauty of whose memory will remain always unimpaired. The overall message of the painting is thus that of the "triumph of Christian glory over the tribulations of this world." The asymmetric pictorial design was Piero's solution to the problem of synthesizing within a unified space the Biblical past with the present, the divine prototype with the contemporary event, Heavenly Jerusalem with 15th-century Italy. By placing the three well-dressed, contemporary Florentine types nearer to the spectator, the painter further humanized the action and the immediacy of viewpoint, encouraging the onlooker to identify with the mortals in the foreground. In the next century the ramifications of this recessive focus were to be more extensively explored.

Piero's style of drama avoids strong physical movement. Every figure has gravity of appearance and action, and the meditative or withdrawn moods precluded using the glance as a unifying device. In Pilate's aspect, moreover, Piero may have been interpreting the Biblical account of the misgivings felt by the Roman as a result of his wife's dream. By tracing the silhouettes of the figures, one can see that compositional cohesiveness derives somewhat from the figures' continuity of edge.

The solid, stable appearance of Piero's figures comes in part from a viewpoint slightly lower than the eye level of the subjects. This view, which was discussed by Piero in one of his two treatises on perspective, consequently stresses the length and firmness of the leg. Piero also situated his vanishing points in the area of Christ, noticeably off center, thereby creating an interesting visual pull between Christ and the foreground figures at the right. The 15th century knew no more thoughtful and gifted composer of pictures than Piero. None could so provocatively suggest to the viewer comparison of the beauty of architecture with that of the human form.

**Rationalizing the Miraculous** In view of their preoccupation with reason and physical laws, the most challenging religious subject for Italian artists was the miracle of the Resurrection. *The Resurrection of Christ* painted by Piero demonstrates how faith and reason joined to produce what may be the most profound painting of its age (Pl. 23, p. 135). Under a cool matinal light, Christ is risen, while at his feet lie the soldiers in deep slumber. The supernatural conversion is expressed in such subtle and diverse ways as to reflect the concentrated effort of a superior intelligence. Much of the shock immediately induced by the painting comes from the unexpected appearance of hieratic symmetry in a natural setting. Piero's passion for geometry as form and symbol explains the arrangement of the base of the tomb and the head of Christ into an isosceles triangle; and at its apex Piero painted the most powerful head of Christ of the entire 15th century (Fig. 185). In this head, and specifically in the hypnotic area of the eyes, is condensed the most crucial mystery of the Christian religion. Through the eyes, Piero conveys the concept of the risen Christ awakening into a world beyond mortal vision. The rigidity of Christ's face and pose and his obliviousness to the surroundings suggest spiritual or psychological rather than physical transformation. True to the account of the Resurrection, Piero shows Christ in human form. His body still has material weight, as seen by the discernible pressure of his leg on the tomb's edge. The dark

*right:* 186. ANTONIO POLLAIUOLO. *Hercules Crushing Antaeus.* c. 1475. Bronze, height 18″. Museo Nazionale, Florence.

hollows around the eyes speak of the Passion and the Entombment. Death is treated by Piero as a form of sleep, which gives additional meaning to the dormancy of the pagan guards, as yet unenlightened by the miracle.

Piero suffuses his message throughout the painting by means of contrasts, and all the contrasts involve the figure of Christ. He divides the painting into vertical and horizontal, right and left. But, as in medieval art, these directions must be viewed from Christ's standpoint. The landscape to Christ's right is one of winter and, like the wound in his right side, indicative of death. The tree trunk nearest the banner is an alliteration of his body, as the branches of both sets of trees are alliterations of Christ's head. To the Redeemer's left is the springtime of nature, alive and verdant again through his sacrifice. Thus the landscape symbolizes the world before and after his coming. The convergence of the trees on both sides toward the figure of Christ infers his relation to the state of the landscape, while the mound at the viewer's far left serves to balance the head of Christ and hold the focus within the frame. Piero's Christ is the God of all that lives. In Piero's paintings showing him before death, Christ is a gentle submissive figure. Resurrected, he becomes a masculine and militant being.

**The Athlete of Virtue** By now the reader must have noticed not only the athletic image of Christ in Piero's *Resurrection* and *Flagellation*, but also the gradual appearance of at least partial nudity and the heroic physiques given to so many Christian saints by artists working in the service of the Church. Did not Christian dogma condemn the body as sinful ? Colin Eisler has helped solve this seeming paradox by tracing the meaning and tradition of the "Athlete of Virtue," represented in Piero's paintings, for example, back to ancient Greece and to its glorification of the gymnastic heroes (see Chap. 3). This tradition continued through the Middle Ages in commentaries by theologians, who equated the body of Christ and the Church itself with that of the healthful, clean, or purified body of the athlete. In religious texts known to artists such as Piero, and later to Michelangelo, Christ was compared to Hercules and Olympic champions, and his Passion analogized to an athletic endurance contest. Christ's Resurrection proclaimed him the Eternal Victor. His virtue comprised physical manliness and mental fortitude, reminding us that medieval saints were equated with athletes of the spirit. The Italian Renaissance interest in antiquity allowed artists such as Piero and Michelangelo not only to examine the form of ancient Greek and Roman statues of heroic male figures, but also to consider these beautifully formed pagan bodies as metaphors for Christian spiritual values. Not surprisingly, the depiction of David and the martyred saints, such as St. Sebastian (Fig. 187), as the "forerunners" of Christ also fitted this image, one already suggested by Veneziano in his St. John the Baptist (Pl. 22, p. 135).

**Anatomy** Until recently it was customary to look upon art and science as incompatible and to differentiate between artists and scientists on the basis of temperament. Their broader cultural and disciplinary unity is often ignored. In 15th-century Italy, however, many artists contributed to the study of natural science. The development of mathematical perspective, for instance, was carried out by artists, while the study of human anatomy by artists was well in advance of that taught in the medical schools. Beginning probably with Castagno, and assuredly by the time of Antonio Pollaiuolo (c. 1431–98), artists undertook actual dissection of the human body in order to study the relation of its structure to its functioning. One of the appeals of ancient sculpture was that it provided what was thought to be accurate information concerning physiology and musculature and furnished artists with poses and gestures by which to increase the expressiveness and animation of their figures. Religious personages were given more lifelike traits as a result of this study, but artists such as Pollaiuolo celebrated the body as a model of energy, strength, and action.

Pollaiuolo was one of the first Italian artists to join ancient Classical form with Classical subject matter. However, the full enactment and revelation of the human body's considerable strength, rather than an inference of its potential force, is what separates Pollaiuolo's small bronze sculpture of *Hercules Crushing Antaeus* (Fig. 186) from the struggling figures in ancient Greek art. The Greeks would temporize the full manifestation of muscular tension in order to ensure conformity of the body's design with an ideal of fluid grace (Fig. 504). Pollaiuolo, who had the opportunity to dissect corpses, broke new ground for sculpture and discovered the means to convincingly embody the human energy demanded in gestures of violent pushing and pulling. The more angular and active silhouettes of his figures, in comparison with those of the Greeks, resulted from direct observation of how, for instance, the shoulder bones of the human form (such as that of Hercules) are pushed outward as the arm muscles are stretched and tightened. In Donatello's *David* (Fig. 175) body structures are only faintly articulated, but in Pollaiuolo's statue the skeletal-muscular systems operate clearly and their construction can be traced right down to the feet of Hercules.

In his *Martyrdom of St. Sebastian* (Fig. 187), it is clear that Pollaiuolo was fascinated with the expressiveness of the same body and pose seen from multiple perspectives. Forms are carefully arranged around St. Sebastian to overlap as little as possible. Here, the artist made the human figure break completely the old mold of symbolic and rhetorical gesture and achieved a convincing representation of physical strength in muscular action. But he was unable to give graceful resolution to the energies and movements of his figures, who seem overdeveloped and often static. More successful as a sculptor, Pollaiuolo failed in painting to integrate the new conceptions of the body with space. He used a plateau arrangement and an elevated viewpoint for the figures, which tends to flatten the foreground area. The deep landscape backdrop behind the plateau provides no aesthetic or dramatic ties with the foreground. The figure of St. Sebastian has a certain sentimental and soft quality, which does not permit it to dominate the scene by any means other than its elevation and centrality. In sum, Pollaiuolo's painting is more impressive in its parts than as a whole, and for its vigorous espousal of secular values rather than for religious ideals.

Although Florence dominated 15th-century Italian art, there were important painters working in other cities, such

*above:* 187. Antonio Pollaiuolo. *The Martyrdom of St. Sebastian.* 1475. Oil on panel, 9′6″ × 6′7½″. National Gallery, London (reproduced by courtesy of the Trustees).

*right:* 188. Andrea Mantegna. *St. James Led to His Execution.* c. 1455. Fresco (destroyed). Church of the Eremitani, Padua.

*left:* Plate 22. DOMENICO VENEZIANO. *Madonna and Child with Saints*, from *The St. Lucy Altarpiece*. c. 1445. Oil on panel, 6′7½″ × 6′11⅞″. Uffizi, Florence. (See p. 127.)

*below:* Plate 23. PIERO DELLA FRANCESCA. *The Resurrection of Christ*. 1460. Detached fresco. Pinacoteca, Borgo San Sepolcro. (See p. 132, Fig. 185.)

Plate 24. SANDRO BOTTICELLI. *The Birth of Venus*. c. 1485. Oil on canvas, 6′7″ × 9′2″. Uffizi, Florence. (See p. 138.)

Plate 25. MICHELANGELO. *The Creation of Adam*, detail from the ceiling of the Sistine Chapel. 1508–12. Vatican, Rome. (See pp. 147, 148, Fig. 198.)

189. GIOVANNI BELLINI. *St. Francis in Ecstasy.* c. 1485. Oil on panel, 4′1/2″ × 4′7″. The Frick Collection, New York (copyright).

as Piero della Francesca in Urbino and Andrea Mantegna (c. 1431–1506) in Padua. Mantegna had important contact with sculptures by Donatello in that city, and his work mingles this influence with an archaeologist's curiosity about the beauty of Roman art and its ruins and with personal researches into anatomy and psychological expression. In a fresco done at mid-century and lost during a bombing of Padua in World War II, Mantegna chose the viewpoint of an actual spectator in the chapel to depict *St. James Led to His Execution* (Fig. 188). The saint is seen pausing to bless a paralytic before Mantegna's personal and inaccurate reconstruction of a Roman triumphal arch. This low viewpoint coupled with the strong off-center locus of the vanishing point imparts dramatic tension. Contradicting theories of the time, Mantegna brings us very close to the action, which augments our emotional involvement in the scene. As did Masaccio, Uccello, Castagno, and Piero della Francesca, Mantegna first drew his figures as nudes, so that in the final fresco the firmness of their bodies is revealed even through their clothing. He shared Donatello's interest in eccentric perspective viewpoints and in making crowds active participants in the action. A strong undercurrent of restlessness, of potential as well as actual display of energy, runs all through his work. Mantegna's characters are believable as active empire and architectural builders, soldiers and executioners, rugged saints who tramped rough terrain—unlike the contemplative population of Piero's work.

**Man and the Earth** To appreciate the changed view of nature and art that had evolved from the Middle Ages into what is referred to as the Renaissance, one need only compare the 10th-century manuscript painting of St. Valerian (Fig. 128) with a portrayal of St. Francis (Fig. 189) done five centuries later by Giovanni Bellini (1429-1507). A holy man in approximately the same posture is common to both, but where St. Valerian turns his back, figuratively speaking, to a demonic world, St. Francis seems at first to be embracing the earth and the sky and its light. Both men were hermitic personalities, renouncing the material pleasures of the world, but the rural home of St. Francis is populated by harmless animals and a verdant private garden amid the rude rocky retreat. The gestures of both saints are symbolic, those of St. Francis indicating his miraculous reception of the *Stigmata,* the wounds of Christ, on his hands and feet. Unlike earlier paintings of the same subject, neither Christ nor a seraph is visible to us, and, as Millard Meiss has shown, the miracle is accomplished by means of the brilliant golden light of the sky into which the transfixed saint stares open-mouthed. This same scholar argues persuasively that the event took place at night and that what at first seems in the painting to be a figure in daylight is in fact the illumination from the radiant apparition. If we are to judge by the direction of the cast shadow of the saint and orientation of his body, the source of light is relatively low and on this side of the laurel tree, which reflects and moves in the

*right:* 190. *Venus de' Medici.* 3rd century B.C. Marble, height 5′. Uffizi, Florence.

supernatural glow emanating from a source out of sight beyond the left limit of the picture. Bellini continues the tradition of the theological significance of light, which goes back even earlier than the St. Valerian painter, but synthesizes it with the results of optical experience. There is a second, and this time natural, light source seen streaming through the clouds at the upper left, and it is explicable on the basis of the St. Francis literature which speaks of the nocturnal event causing an illumination comparable to the light of day.

From Flemish painting, this Venetian artist may have derived the use of some sort of oil medium that gave depth to his color and allowed overpainting. His shadows have a base layer of light blue-green which gives them volume. The meticulous reconstruction of the earth and distant cities is deceptive; while the rocky area resembles the geological formations near the site where St. Francis received the Stigmata, Bellini has synthesized many observations from nature and, like Van Eyck (Figs. 149–151), has used the actual to create an imaginary place that nonetheless belongs on earth. Thus Bellini affirms that by his day men and the earth belonged to each other no matter what their origin or destiny after life.

**Synthesis of Religious and Secular Philosophies** The interest of painters and sculptors in the art and literature of antiquity, which became most important in the last quarter of the 15th century, was to affect profoundly the pictorial synthesis of religious and secular values. As Erwin Panofsky expressed it, "In the Italian Renaissance the Classical past began to be looked upon from a fixed distance, quite comparable to the 'distance between the eye and the object' in . . . Renaissance focused perspective. This distance prohibited direct contact. . . but permitted a total and rationalized view." Classical culture was approached historically, as an integrated whole, and the ancient world became "the object of a passionate nostalgia." In the second half of the 15th century, this lead to the union of Classical form and Classical content, most strongly in architecture and mingled with naturalism in sculpture; it was least manifest in painting, which was dominated by fidelity to nature. But there were painters who expressed in individual works the longing of enlightened men of their age for a "rebirth" of ancient culture.

*The Birth of Venus* (Pl. 24, p. 136), a painting of 1485 by the Florentine artist Sandro Botticelli (1445–1510), celebrates the nude pagan goddess on a large scale for the first time since Roman antiquity. It was executed as a visual sermon in philosophy for a fourteen-year-old boy, Giovanni di Pierofrancesco, whose upbringing was in the hands of the most brilliant Humanist thinkers in Europe. The reconciliation of nudity and pre-Christian philosophy and art with Christianity was restricted to a small group of artists, scholars, writers, and aristocratic patrons such as the Medici family. According to Marsilio Ficino, the outstanding philosopher of the time, truth and beauty knew no distinction between pagan and Christian expression; both pagan literature and the Bible were revelations of the truth, of the same principles. The chaste beauty of Botticelli's Venus was inspired by the view that she symbolized not lust or sensual pleasure but pure intelligence or the highest attainments of the mind. Her role in the education of the young Giovanni was to inspire him to search for the true reality behind appearances and to discover the world's hidden harmony.

The figure of Venus was patterned after a specific sculpture—a Roman copy of an ancient Greek statue owned by the Medici (Fig. 190), the painting's format and the figure on the shore derived from previous Christian paintings of St. John baptizing Christ. The Humanists drew analogies between the miraculous birth of Venus and Christ, between her emergence from the sea and Christ's rebirth by rising from the water of Jordan. The painting's lesson included the birth of beauty in the human soul. The zephyrs who blow her to the shore are like angels, and the seashell was occasionally used by Renaissance painters and architects as a symbol of Heaven.

Botticelli's style was admirably adapted to rendering Venus in a way that would not arouse physical desire. The delicacy of his drawing and tinting of colors imparts sophisticated grace and strong pleasure to the eye and mind. Drawing was the basis of the work and deemed at the time the most appropriate for the education of the intelligence; strong color was avoided so as not to stir base emotions, which expressed a prejudice that would continue even into 19th-century art. Botticelli was an artist ideally suited to the aristocratic intellectual tastes of his courtly patrons, but he himself underwent a deep spiritual crisis and reversion to mystical Christianity toward the end of his life, upsetting the pagan-Christian synthesis announced in this famous painting and forecasting a similar and broader cultural change at the beginning of the next century.

**Art in the Service of the Mind** Though known as a man with universal interests, Leonardo da Vinci (1452–1519) did not share Botticelli's preoccupation with antiquity, philosophy, and literature—in short, the Humanism of his time. The direct experiences of eye and hand, which painting and drawing served best, and the active use of the mind in their support were what Leonardo believed in; and this explains his unprecedented empirical studies from nature accompanied by innumerable drawings and voluminous notebooks. Leonardo's modernity resides in his refusal to take untested assumptions as the basis for his art. Unlike many artists before him, his dedication to representing the visual world was not exclusively in the service of religion. Leonardo's few paintings deal mostly with religious subjects, but this is not the case with his drawings. On the basis of the paintings, one would surmise that Leonardo believed that through knowledge and imagination one should interpret noble themes, but with his drawings the compass of art takes in the entire earthly world for the enjoyment of the eyes. His unfinished painting of *The Adoration of the Magi* (Fig. 191) serves as an excellent example not only of his interests but also of his frequent inability to conclude his ambitious projects. The setting depends upon his observations of what might be called *natural science,* specifically studies of trees and geology. Fascination with geometry led him to introduce at the rear left a perspective rendering of a ruined structure that may relate to the fall of the old religious order. Lifelong interest in equestrian subjects and an inclination toward violent aggression account for the combat of mounted figures in the upper right. The foreground drama was the occasion for demonstrating his experience with psychology and the expressive capacities of the entire body. Against the reverent actions of the Magi, he contrasts the manifold and strong reactions of the onlookers, thereby giving full play to his researches into different age groups regarding facial types, gestures, and the drama of bodies in movement and

191. LEONARDO DA VINCI. *The Adoration of the Magi.* 1480–82. Oil on wood, 8′7/8″ × 7′11 5/8″. Uffizi, Florence.

192. Leonardo da Vinci. *Study for the Adoration of the Magi.* c. 1481. Pen drawing, bistre and wash; $8^1/_4 \times 5^7/_8$″. Uffizi, Florence.

inspiring future artists to broaden the psychological base of painting. The incomplete state of the painting shows its method of construction: First it was drawn and then the colors were applied, in tones from dark to light; the lighter tones have not been filled in. Dark backgrounds often create the lighter shapes, such as some of the heads in the center group, and this was one of the many devices by which Leonardo brought to painting new tonalities and more varied moods evoked by light. His light is never brilliant, but favors that of late afternoon, thereby muting differences among the forms it illuminates. In the *Adoration,* Leonardo makes tangible the elusive existence of light amid darkness.

Leonardo purposely did not employ a single perspective system for this painting, as he was later to do in his *Last Supper* (Fig. 219), but used different perspectives for different areas, giving the whole painting a synthetic quality. Rather than clearly establish at the outset a measurable space for the foreground figures, as Piero would have done, he sketched their movements and volumes. The figures themselves create their own spatial environment, which differs from the more measurable gridlike area at the upper left. The formal arrangement of the centralized Virgin and flanking Magi was like many of Leonardo's ideas subsequently frozen into artistic dogma.

Leonardo's finished paintings do not give as strong an indication of his imagination as his sketches often do. One of the studies for *The Adoration of the Magi* (Fig. 192) shows how he overlaid the perspective grid, used by artists since Brunelleschi, with rough notations of scrambling and tangled figure groups, horses bucking their naked riders, a recumbent camel, and phantomlike figures moving in the ruined palace or seated in the joists of the shedlike roof. No aspect of the story of the Magi or symbolism explains this fantasy. Man and beast move impetuously within the rational framework of space and architecture. So rich and abundant were Leonardo's ideas for the painting that seemingly he did not have the power or perhaps the time after seven months of effort to weld them together into a finished cohesive work. He had incurred difficult problems for himself by the large dark area about the Virgin (how might she have been painted finally to stand out from her surroundings?), created many detached gestures and heads, established frequent scale jumps, or discrepancies and background motifs disparate from the foreground. Yet for later artists such as Raphael, the unfinished work was rich in influential ideas. History has shown that many times finished paintings lose the freshness and intimacy of preliminary drawings, and Leonardo's unfinished work is all the more valuable in its frank disclosure of the powerful working of his mind and hand.

To the argument of whether men make the times or the times make men, one can point to Leonardo and the other leading artists of the 15th century as examples of the interaction of the two. Artists benefited from the civic pride, energy, and enthusiasm for art found in Florence; in turn, men and women gained from art greater understanding of their own humanity. The most lasting and creative contributions of the Italian Renaissance were not social, political, or religious, but artistic. The art that grew out of and away from the Middle Ages was influenced by the rise of science and the worldly interest of Italian tyrants and vigorous merchants who patronized art. Leonardo stands, on the one hand, for the artist who by means of art achieved greater self-realization and intellectual freedom than did his medieval and ancient predecessors, but who also served despots and enemies of Florence, for as he said, "I serve the one who pays me." Political and social freedom historically have not been the prerequisites of great art. The history of intellectual freedom embodied in Leonardo's thinking and inquiry is older than political and social liberty.

**Comparison with Flemish Art** In both Flanders and Italy of the 15th century, art was given an earthly stage, human scale, and natural location. Truthfulness to the visual world was the desire of Northern and Southern artists. Both achieved perspective whereby the three-dimensional world was convincingly transposed through a series of corresponding points onto a two-dimensional surface. Art was confirmed as an important means to enrich earthly life. The synthesis of the heavenly and earthly was changing and unstable, and the values of the latter were gathering into a strong ground swell at century's end. Art still guided men to the meaning of true spirituality, but also corroborated their celebration of the secular beauty and pleasures of the mortal environment. The self-confident societies of Bruges, Ghent, Antwerp, and Florence had produced artists obviously aware of their own talent, importance, and ambitions; and society's respect for artistic genius, familiar to us today, had its foundations established.

When we turn to the differences between Flemish and Italian art, it is apparent that science and ancient art had a stronger influence in the South. Painters in the North achieved verisimilitude to continuous three-dimensional space without recourse to the theories, systems, or geometry so prized by the Italians. Medieval art, which had a more lasting interest and influence in the North, came to be viewed as barbaric in the South—which gave the word *Gothic* unpleasant connotations. Geographically, historically, and ethnically, ancient Roman art seemed right for emulation to Italian artists.

Beginning with Giotto and continuing through Piero della Francesca, Italian style was characterized by a compact and immediately perceivable unity through the large, fluid continuity of the sculpturesque figures dominating their environment. The ideal composition resulted from the smooth interdependent functioning of figures and environment—the easy flow of statuesque figures in measurable space. Flemish style was characterized by a less mobile, if not static, complex additive ordering of the microscopic through the telescopic, in which the setting often rivaled the human being in importance. The Italians delighted in the relation of large, distinct, and more sensual figures set against one another and in credible space. Their color was important to shaping volume. It clung to the curving surfaces and was not intended to belie its distance from the viewer. The Northern artists favored dense groupings of contrasting rich tones of color and light, and intricate linkages of the edges of shapes lying at varying depths from each other. The brilliance of their color would at times make it hover in space and not hold to the actual depth of the plane it was painted on. The Flemings valued all that was given to the senses as a sign of divine meaning, and they searched for individuality in nature. Their criterion of realistic painting was largely a quantitative one of measuring and matching the subject against the painting. With the aid of geometry, Italian artists sought what they thought were the abstract principles behind the appearance of nature, the truly harmonious and beautiful form. Flemish art arrived at convincing spatial illusion through the trial and error of observation; their space, though additive, is still expressive. The Italians first developed it empirically and then through theory and preferred the overall lucid appearance of measured order. They favored the good and pleasing appearance of the human form, with supple coordination between mind and body. The Flemish accepted the unathletic yet natural movement that often accompanies profound inner feeling.

Later, in the 16th century, Michelangelo illuminated the differences between the art of the two areas and revealed his own prejudices:

> Flemish painting will, generally speaking, please the devout better than any painting in Italy, which will never cause him to shed a tear, whereas that of Flanders will cause him to shed many, and that not through the vigor and goodness of the painting but owing to the goodness of the devout person. . . . In Flanders they paint with a view to external exactness of such things as may cheer you and of which you cannot speak ill, as for example saints and prophets. They paint stuffs and masonry, the green grass of the fields, the shadows of the trees, and rivers and bridges which they call landscape, with many figures on this side and many on that. And all this . . . is done without reason or art, without symmetry or proportion, without skillful choice or boldness, and finally without substance and vigor.

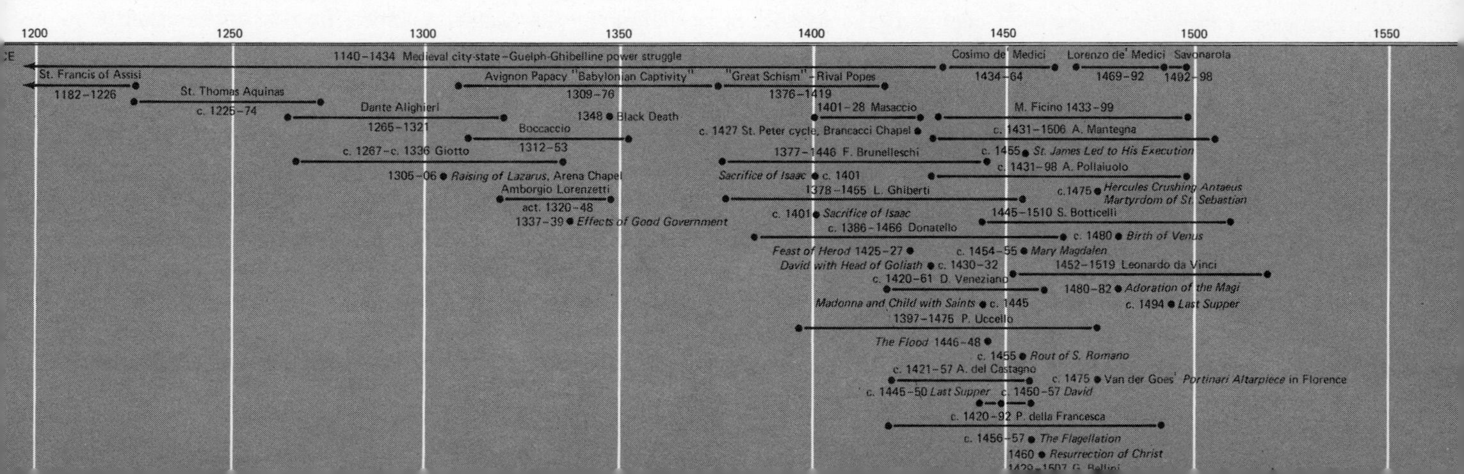

# 8

Imagine that you had the occasion to present the credentials of an experienced artist to a Congressional sub-committee whose task was to select someone to design and decorate a new Capitol building. Knowing our government's concern for examining character references and searching for possible undesirable associations, you must address yourself to the following: Your candidate traces his ancestry to an aristocratic family and does not believe in democracy or universal political freedom. He has celebrated in sculpture the assassin of a head of state. He places loyalty to his city of birth before that of his country. He has contributed designs for the expensive defense system of his city, but he deserted from that city during war. Tyrants have benefited from his service. While he is working your candidate can be surly, and on one occasion he is supposed to have threatened to kill his patron by throwing him off a high scaffolding. There is speculation that he is a homosexual. Many large projects that he has undertaken have remained incomplete for years. He does not believe that great art is or need be intelligible to the taxpayer. By a contract he once promised the most beautiful sculpture ever made. In all, the case would be a tough one to support and doomed no doubt to failure. Your consolation would be that you knew the import of official rejection of Michelangelo.

Some of Michelangelo's character "flaws" might receive a more sympathetic response from a younger generation today than they would have before about 1965. His desertion of Florence was not out of cowardice, for he returned during the fighting, and the incompletion of many of his projects was due to changes of mind made by such clients as the Medici of Florence and the Pope. While Michelangelo's "candidacy" and rejection are hypothetical, we have to acknowledge that in our time many fine artists have been blacklisted or denied access to government-sponsored exhibitions and commissions for comparable activities. Governments often have settled for what is less than the work of great artists, and the decision for art that is "safe" in every sense has become altogether apparent in Washington, where, ironically, some of Michelangelo's architectural ideas were used in debased form.

Michelangelo Buonarroti (1475–1564) was born in the Tuscan town of Caprese. At the age of thirteen, he was sent to Florence to study painting with the brothers Domenico and Davide Ghirlandaio. He remained there but a year when his work attracted the eye of Lorenzo de' Medici, who invited the young artist to join his household. There Michelangelo was introduced to the most brilliant group of intellectuals in Europe, and their acquaintance had a deep influence upon his attitude toward ancient sculpture and the intellectual purpose of art. He did not continue to see himself as a conventional craftsman. During these years in Florence, Michelangelo made drawings of the work of Giotto and Masaccio as well as of Roman and Greek sculpture; in 1492 he did dissections of corpses for anatomical study.

In 1494, just before the house of Medici fell from power, Michelangelo made the first of several flights in search of the security and tranquillity he needed for his work, but was never to find. After a short stay in Venice and more than a year in Bologna, he was able to return to Florence briefly before, in 1496, going on to Rome, where he carved his first *Pietà*, now in St. Peter's. He next returned to Florence for four years, beginning in 1501, to work on several civic commissions, including the *David*. In 1505 Michelangelo was called to Rome by Pope Julius II, one of the first great and troublesome sponsors of Michelangelo's art. It was the sculptor's fate to be frustrated and harassed by powerful patrons who encouraged grandiose schemes and then capriciously diverted the artist from completing them. Like many artists of his time and ours, he was constantly at the mercy of his sponsors' eccentricities. From 1508 to 1512, somewhat reluctantly, Michelangelo painted the ceiling of the Sistine Chapel, turning intermittently to his enormous, and preferred, project for the Pope's sepulcher; of this last only the *Moses* and the series of *Bound Slaves* ultimately saw realization (1513–16). From 1518 to 1534, Michelangelo divided his time between Rome and Florence, and also between sculpture and architecture. For Pope Leo X, he worked on the Medici Chapel in Florence. In 1529 he served as a military engineer on the Florentine fortifications.

From 1534 until his death, Michelangelo lived in Rome, painting *The Last Judgment* (1536–41) and the frescoes of the Pauline Chapel (1542–50). In 1546 he became chief architect for the rebuilding of St. Peter's, a project that was to excite his

# MICHELANGELO

remaining thought and energy. During the 1530s and 1540s he wrote many religious sonnets, dedicated to his friend Vittoria Colonna, who deeply influenced his spiritual direction. In his last two years, Michelangelo undertook a number of architectural projects, such as the redesigning of the Capitoline Hill in Rome, and executed only two uncompleted sculptures, both on the theme of Christ's death. He died in Rome in 1564, was laid in state and then interred in Florence.

The history of art includes many examples of artists who brought major talents to bear upon minor subjects. Vermeer (Pl. 34, p. 182) and Matisse (Pl. 72, p. 361) come quickly to mind as examples of men whose greatness lay in the *way* they interpreted the commonplace, giving to it the quality of the uncommon. Michelangelo brought great art to great ideas. He was the most technically gifted artist as well as one of the great intellects of his time and place. In itself, the fact that his surroundings were Florence and Rome and that his time was the Italian Renaissance should give some idea of Michelangelo's measure. The artist was obsessed with the infinite nature and mystery of God and his creation Man. Never did Michelangelo show an interest in rendering the details of objects or landscape; his was a Man- and God-centered art. Nor did he paint and carve in terms of specific living men: his aim was to depict the universal fate of humanity, and so far as is known, he made only one pencil sketch of a contemporary. Unwilling to be bound to an earthly material model, he felt impelled to work from divine inspiration in order to spiritualize his experience of reality and to achieve eternal and transcendent truth.

It would be futile, within a single chapter, to attempt a full history and discussion of Michelangelo. Instead, a few examples that represent seminal ideas and lend an awareness of the scope and depth of their maker's art will be discussed.

**Early Sculptures** Begun when Michelangelo was twenty-six, the *David* (Fig. 193) was carved between 1501 and 1504 in behalf of the Florentine republic, partly to commemorate the completion of a new civic constitution and partly to demon-

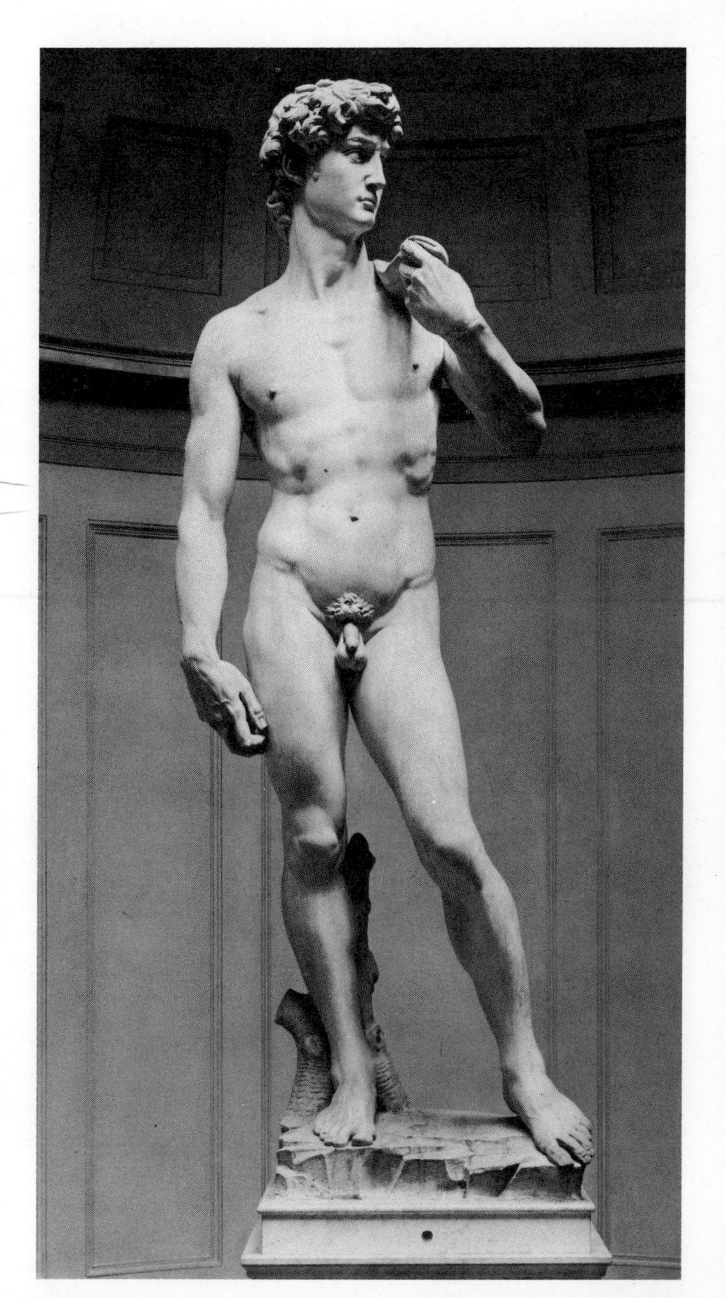

*right:* 193. MICHELANGELO. *David.* 1501–04. Marble, height 18′ (incl. base). Academia, Florence.

strate the city's artistic leadership and vigor. David was famous not only as the slayer of Goliath but also as a ruler, and his association with justice made him an appropriate figure to celebrate governmental reform. By a decision of a committee, the 18-foot statue was placed before the Palazzo Vecchio, the city hall, where it quickly became an emblem of civic freedom and the virtue of its defense. In the finely muscled, alert, and somber youth, the citizens could see an embodiment of what they felt were their own virtues. Michelangelo may have shared these ideals, but he also wanted the *David* to affirm his reputation as the greatest living sculptor. In his contract Michelangelo specified that his sculpture would be of unsurpassed beauty—and this despite the unusually thin block of marble he had been given, which would force him to exercise tremendous virtuosity. Not only did he demonstrate to the satisfaction of all his knowledge of ancient Greek art and the science of anatomy, but he also gave form to a deeply personal vision of a hero. In Michelangelo's view, only a handful of men in the history of the human race qualified as heroes. These were primarily Old Testament prophets or rulers who perfectly embodied a combination of the active and the contemplative life. In his youth, when the *David* was created, Michelangelo equated truth with beauty, and to *David* he gave the body of a Greek Apollo, but not that god's temperamental equanimity (compare with Figs. 51–53). By this time, the nude form in art had lost most of its medieval sinful associations, partly because ancient art and thought were now accepted as compatible with Christianity and with the tradition of the "athlete of virtue." Michelangelo believed that the nude male body was divine and that its ideal rendition in art would approximate the prototype conceived by God. He wrote: "And who is so barbarous as not to understand that the foot of a man is nobler than his shoe, and his skin nobler than that of the sheep with which it is clothed."

The quality of repose suggested by a front view of the youth's stance is not sustained, for there is a faint suggestion of tension in the torso muscles, which becomes more obvious in the neck and quite vehement in the angry visage. This climactic psychological element and the contrast in the states of mind and body are alien to Greek Classical ideals. There is a decided asymmetry in the disposition of the right and left sides of the body; the figure's right side is protected by the downward-hanging arm holding the stone, whereas the upraised left arm makes that side more open and vulnerable. Significantly, David looks to his left. From the Middle Ages there had been a tradition which associated divine protection with the right and the origin of evil with the left. It has been suggested that David is "frowning" at the sight of Goliath, assuredly the symbol of evil. Still, it would be a mistake to conceive of this work as illustrating a specific event or moment. David is, above all, a symbol of force and righteous anger, and the stone and sling signify the need for alert and courageous defense of principle. Like the pose of the *Colossus of Barletta* (Fig. 281), a late-antique Imperial statue, the militant and defiant attitude of David is a comfort to the good and a warning to their enemies. The angry concentration expressed in the features may also reflect displeasure with human weakness. Michelangelo was a Christian sculptor who could satisfy his religious belief with the idea of a Hebraic hero in the body of a Greek god.

194. MICHELANGELO. *St. Matthew*. 1504–06. Marble, height 8′11″. Academia, Florence.

Michelangelo considered David his alter ego, and he once wrote, "David with the sling, I with the bow, Michelangelo." The bow was a reference to his sculptor's drill, which like the sling was his attribute and means of serving God. After the *David,* Michelangelo was asked to do statues of the Twelve Apostles, but only the unfinished *St. Matthew* was actually undertaken (Fig. 194). Unconstrained as he had been for the *David* by the thin block he received, which dictated the relatively flat frontal pose, Michelangelo devised for the *St. Matthew* a posture that is a tense counteraction of twisting and frontal movements. In the grip of some powerful vision that forces his head to the side, the Apostle is unmindful of his body, which in an un-Classical way reacts by instinct. The strong compactness of limbs, with as little space as possible between the torso and arms, was a self-imposed restriction of the artist, who may have felt that it gave the most concentrated expression of the subject. His figure of Matthew violently twists about an imaginary vertical axis but is, in turn, inhibited by the limits of the block, which like mortal flesh is a form of confinement. The squarish shape and thick proportions of the figure, which to some degree also relate to the original block, show Michelangelo's resistance to accepted norms of the past.

The incomplete state of sculptures such as this has led to mystical, somewhat romanticized interpretations about the artist's intention to show the birth of the soul, his disinterest once the essential idea had taken form, or his desire to reveal the material source and end of all life. It is a fact that Michelangelo enjoyed work on difficult unfinished problems, but in the case of this Apostle figure, as was often to happen thereafter, demands for the sculptor's talents in Rome simply forced him to stop his work on it. The raw traces of tool marks and vestiges of the original block make the *St. Matthew* a fine illustration for some of the artist's views on sculpture, expressed years later. Michelangelo saw his destiny as being in the chisel and stone. Sometime between 1536 and 1547 he wrote, "The greatest artist has no conception that a single block of marble does not potentially contain within its mass, but only a hand obedient to the mind can penetrate to this image." Elsewhere, Michelangelo defined the art of sculpture as "the taking off that puts into the rough hard stone a living figure grown most great just as the stone had grown most small." This bringing forth of life from base matter was a spiritual act for Michelangelo, one in sympathy with God's creation of life. He once referred to God as the "Divine Hammer." Great art, he believed, depended upon the artist's possessing first within himself a perfect God-given conception (the *Platonic Idea*), whose "first-born" was a simple clay model. The second realization of the Idea was in the "rugged living stone" and possessed "such beauty that none may confine its spirit."

No artist before Michelangelo possessed such complete mastery of the human body and exceptional ability to render its richness as a material organism as well as its emotional, spiritual, and intellectual range. Possessing natural gifts as a craftsman and observer of his subject, Michelangelo was also a great student of the art of other artists and eras. The sculpture of ancient Greece and Rome and that of his own century all provided ideas and forms that were to be welded to his personal style. The greatest master for Michelangelo, his greatest influence as attested by the sculptor's own words, was God, the Creator. For the Greeks and certain Renaissance sculptors, beauty was achievable through fixed proportion of mathematical measure, but for Michelangelo proportion was a qualitative, not a quantitative, value. Proportion meant, for him, the extent to which his image corresponded to the Idea inherent in it. Furthermore, the physical beauty of his figures was not an end in itself; it was intended as a reflection of a spiritual beauty and was meant to elevate the thoughts of the beholder above material things. True beauty could not be obtained by merely copying the visible world. Michelangelo's art proceeds from the mind, through which he believed he could more truly comprehend the perfect form.

Michelangelo despised Raphael's optimistic judgment of the ability of his contemporaries, such as Castiglione, to achieve grace. The sculptor felt that Raphael had a naïve and mistaken faith in simple formulas of human conduct as a means of achieving true earthly happiness and excellence. The differences between their respective attitudes can be seen in Raphael's portrait of Baldassare Castiglione (Fig. 480) and Michelangelo's *Moses* (Fig. 195), intended for the uncompleted

195. MICHELANGELO. *Moses*. 1513–16. Marble, height 8′4″. San Pietro in Vincoli, Rome.

Michelangelo's contemporaries found in his style qualities that inspired religious awe and fear.

The spiritual antithesis of *Moses* is Michelangelo's *Bound Slave*, often misnamed the *Dying Slave* (Fig. 197). This, too, was designed for the Julius tomb. Though based upon a late Greek sculpture of one of Niobe's dead children, the figure is neither socially a "slave" nor a dying man. His prison is his body, which incarcerates the spirit. Were he dying, the figure might express a sense of joy, for death would return the spirit to God. Backing the figure is a half-finished ape, an animal that to an educated contemporary would have signified the dominance of lust, of the passions over reason. The human dilemma celebrated by Michelangelo is the torment of mortal life away from the Creator. Man's anguish is to have joined in himself a temporal body and an immortal soul, as expressed by the contemporary philosopher Marsilio Ficino in ideas parallel to Michelangelo's.

*left*: 196. MICHELANGELO. *Moses*, plaster cast, seen from below and 30 degrees to the right.

*right*: 197. MICHELANGELO. *Bound Slave*. 1514–16. Marble, height 7′6½″. Louvre, Paris.

tomb of Julius II. To Michelangelo, Moses was a moral and physical giant, a man whose imposing frame was the instrument of heroic physical and spiritual acts—of the leadership of his people in the Exodus. The enormous, vital head of Moses is the locus of divine visions, the fountainhead of law.

The interpretation of *Moses* depends, literally, upon one's point of view. Until recently, although the statue's intended position high on the papal tomb was known, all interpretations of pose and expression were based on an eye-level view (Fig. 195). Thus, scholars (including this author) tended to see the portrayal as Moses in righteous anger or seized by an ecstatic vision. The art historian Earl Rosenthal had the good sense to photograph a plaster version of *Moses* raised 9 feet above the ground, thereby altering our view both literally and figuratively. The sculptor carved the figure on its side so as to study it from the proper angle. The view from below modifies the scale of the disproportionately large head and beard, and it enhances the figure's composed strength. The gaze upward appears appropriate to the wise and contemplative leader of the Jews, and this sculpture gave particular pleasure to the Jews of Rome, even though their religion opposed the graven image. From below, the hornlike forms—the beams of light that apocryphal tradition had spring from Moses' forehead at the moment he saw the Lord—are barely visible. From an angle, nonetheless, the seated prophet is endowed with tremendous vitality and majesty. Here is why

*above:* 198. MICHELANGELO. Ceiling of the Sistine Chapel. 1508–12. Fresco, 45 × 128′. Vatican, Rome.

> Our mind, as long as our sublime soul is doomed to operate in a base body, is thrown up and down with permanent disquietude, and it often slumbers from exhaustion and is always insane; so that our movements, actions, and passions are nothing but the vertigos of ailing people, the dream of sleepers, and ravings of madmen.

This sculpture puts into tangible form ideas that Michelangelo was later to express in his poetry. Between 1547 and 1550, he wrote in a private lament to God: "For Thou not only gavest to time my divine soul, but didst imprison it in this frail body and weary flesh and must hand it over to its cruel destiny. How can I escape living thus. Without Thee."

To convey an interior state, a pathetic restlessness of soul, Michelangelo drew upon Greek principles of expressive body posturing. These avoided the coincidence in the same plane of parts of the body having a common point or axis. For instance, if the knee is forward, the left shoulder should be back and the right shoulder advanced. This balances forward and backward movements in criss-cross fashion. As the eye scans upward, each direction taken by the slave's body is countered by another immediately above, so that the composition is a self-adjusting mechanism in a soft, serpentine formation.

**The Meaning of Muscularity** Contemporary and subsequent artists selected figure types, postures, and muscular forms from Michelangelo's art without comprehending the essential life attitude in which these properties were rooted. Now it is even harder to understand the conceptualizing that Michelangelo gave to his re-creation of the body from art and life. In Renaissance theology God was praised as a sculptor, not as a painter. And Michelangelo regarded sculpture, with its sensual physicality, its mass and displacement of space, as the ideal means by which he, a creator second only to God, could surpass nature's own composition. A great dramatist of the human body, Michelangelo makes one sense the full movement and force of skeleton and muscle beneath a taut, leathery skin. He greatly enriched the figure's expressive repertory, yet contained its gestures within the cubic block from which they were cut.

Not since ancient Greece had figures been so splendidly endowed to perform superhuman feats. Still, this was not Michelangelo's drama. The true strength was either in latent tension or in tension turned against itself. With few exceptions, his figures do not use force against external obstacles, nor do they take energetic postures of work, love, war, or play. Heroic muscularity was for Michelangelo a prerequisite of God-like beauty, the mortal vestment of his Biblical heroes; in addition, it was a fit measure for their momentous personal struggles. In this sense, his message is that great physical strength is futile against God's will. From fragments of Greek torsos he learned to use muscular tension as a means of directing the viewer's thoughts to the figure's spiritual crisis, the conflict of soul and flesh, and toward spiritual exaltation. No living model could serve him, nor could the instinctive and practiced gestures that men make in their daily lives. It was Michelangelo's genius to make the unnatural seem natural. He even invented gestures for death, such as the contorted dangling arm of the dead Christ in the *Pietà* in the Cathedral of Florence (Fig. 207).

**The Sistine Ceiling** In his painting of the Sistine Chapel ceiling (Fig. 198), Michelangelo executed a humanistic-religious program of unparalleled magnitude. The commission from

Julius II was accepted reluctantly by Michelangelo, who longed to devote his energies to sculpture rather than painting, particularly to the grandiose tomb project. For four years, between 1508 and 1512, Michelangelo lay on his back and covered more than 700 square yards of ceiling with the great outpourings of a fired imagination. The strain of working while standing or lying prone on the scaffolding, under the dripping plaster, wrecked his health. At the end of his project, he wrote a poem describing his lamentable condition *(I' ho già fatto un gozzo. . . .)* *:

> I've grown a goiter by dwelling in this den—
> As cats from stagnant streams in Lombardy,
> Or in what other land they hap to be—
> Which drives the belly close beneath the chin;
> My beard turns up to heaven; my nape falls in,
> Fixed on my spine; my breastbone visibly
> Grows like a harp; a rich embroidery
> Bedews my face from brush-drops thick and thin,
> My loins into my paunch like levers grind;
> My buttock like a crupper bears my weight;
> My feet unguided wander to and fro;
> In front my skin grows loose and long; behind
> By bending it becomes more taut and strait;
> Crosswise I strain me like a Syrian bow. . . .

Despite his plaints and protestations, it seems likely that Michelangelo viewed this onerous task as penance, in which the ardor of his creative labors was expiation for sinful guilt.

The thematic program of the Sistine Chapel ceiling is an amazing fusion of Hebrew and Christian theology with contemporary Neoplatonic ideas. In all likelihood, Michelangelo had papal assistance in formulating the extensive program; and though the Pope gave him license thereafter to do as he pleased, the project undoubtedly satisfied the spiritual and political wishes of the patron. At the time that the ceiling was being painted, the papacy was waging war against foreign troops and heretics within the faith itself. The ceiling's decoration was touched by these contemporary events, and using complicated theological metaphors, the Pope had Michelangelo assert the Pontiff's confidence in his ultimate triumph over his enemies.

The subject of the ceiling is ostensibly that of the Old Testament God who created the world and punished man for denying his Lord. The nine principal scenes are depicted in rectangular frames, and their order does not follow strictly the chronology of Genesis. Above the head of the visitor upon entering the chapel are the Revilement of Noah, the Flood, the Sacrifice of Noah, and the Fall of Man. The common theme of all these episodes is God's punishment of man by means of the elements—earth, water, fire, and air. They illustrate how God chastises a world that has betrayed him and rejected Christ through false offerings and the partaking of the forbidden fruit.

The fulcrum panel of the ceiling, originally situated directly above the partition that divided the chapel in half, is the scene of God's creation of Eve from the side of Adam. Eve at this time symbolized the Church; thus in the ceiling's sequence the Church is mediator between man and God, furnishing the means of man's redemption. The second half of the ceiling is over the sacred area of the chapel, the altar. The overall theme of the remaining four subjects—the Creation of Adam (Pl. 25, p. 136), the Separation of the Waters from the Earth, the Creation of the Sun, Moon, and Planet, and the Separation of Light from Darkness—is the creative power of the Divinity.

In the triangular spandrels are depicted such precursors of Christ as David, who is shown killing Goliath, and Judith, who has beheaded Holofernes. Flanking the central rectangles are the Sibyls and Prophets. The agitated nude figures holding garlands and circular objects that are either large golden Eucharistic wafers or battle shields are altar attendants or human souls. The secondary motives of the ceiling were to assert the theological ancestry of the Pope and to imply that he was a new messiah acting as the earthly agent of God to punish the heretics. The Pope's family name means "oak tree," and there are also references in the ceiling to oaks. The spandrels depict the deliverance of the chosen people, perhaps as a prophecy of the actions of Julius II.

As in Michelangelo's earlier work, the figures are preterhuman in size and action. God is the Old Testament divinity who roars out of a whirlwind and speaks with a voice of thunder. His visage, as seen in *The Creation of Adam* (Pl. 25, p. 136), was strikingly similar to the bearded profile of Julius II. The purpose of the program was thus to strike fear and awe into the minds of the mortals who looked upon it—awe of the Creator and the Church, and of God's earthly representatives.

The Sistine Ceiling is a marvel of skill and endurance; yet the power of Michelangelo's art transcends mere virtuoso effects. There is a philosophical justification for all aspects of his style. He put his knowledge of the forms and the workings of the body into the service of spiritualizing human anguish and exaltation. The agitated, athletic figures of the Sibyls and Prophets mirror the profundity and excitement of visions inaccessible to ordinary mortals. In *The Creation of Adam* Pl. 25), Michelangelo infused Adam's form with the mingled response of a body awakening with reluctance at the separation of the spirit from its Creator. Adam is not joyful at his emergence into an earthly existence; the languid attitude of his arms and torso reveals his melancholy state, and the face has an expression of ineffable longing. With great significance, Michelangelo stressed the hands of Adam and God and the slight interval between them, which represented the measureless gulf that now separated man and his Creator. Attention is

---

* From *The Sonnets of Michael Angelo Buonarroti,* trans. John Addington Symonds (© 1948 by Crown Publishers, Inc.). Reprinted by permission of Crown Publishers, Inc.

drawn repeatedly to the contrasts and similarities between the bodies of Adam and God, fittingly reflecting a poem of the sculptor, possibly written during the years of work on the Sistine Ceiling: "He who made the whole made every part; then from the whole chose the most beautiful, to reveal on earth, as he has done here and now in His own sublime perfections. The human figure is the particular form in which beauty is most clearly manifested."

Little indication can be given in this brief space of the intellectual wealth Michelangelo brought to the program of his ceiling. Scholars such as Charles De Tolnay and Frederick Hartt have, in impressive and often conflicting studies, sought to unravel the many levels of meaning and alternative interpretations of its content. That such searching endeavors are appropriate to a full understanding and appreciation of Michelangelo's art is borne out in the sculptor's own views on painting:

> At its best nothing is more noble or devout, since with discreet persons nothing so calls forth and fosters devotion as the difficulty of a perfection which is based upon union with God. For good painting is nothing but a copy of the perfections of God and a recollection of His painting; it is a music and a melody which only intellect can understand, and that with great difficulty. And that is why painting of this kind is so rare that no man attains it.

**The Medici Chapel** Like the Sistine Ceiling, the Medici Chapel in San Lorenzo, Florence, on which Michelangelo worked at various times from 1520 to 1534, has been seen by some scholars not only as an artistic interpretation of a Humanistic program but also as a monumental attempt at propaganda (Fig. 199). The official purpose of the designs was commemorative, the creation of a sepulchral chapel to house the bodies of Lorenzo and Giuliano de' Medici, descendants of the 15th-century dukes of the same name. The date of the chapel's commencement is an important one, since it coincided with a decline in the power and aspirations of the house of Medici because of the death of two of its most important members. They, too, were to have been buried in the chapel (a plan subsequently discarded), which may have been intended as a grandiose allegory of princely and papal power, the Medici having produced several popes. The Chapel was to glorify the deceased occupants by using them as examples of ideal rulers and defenders of the Church.

Michelangelo did not himself assemble the sculptures as they are seen today. The four reclining figures, two on each of the sepulchers, were so placed by another sculptor. Below the figure of Duke Giuliano lie the figures of Night and Day; beneath the seated form of Lorenzo are the recumbent figures of Twilight and Dawn. That these sculptures signified time is conjectural, for Michelangelo wrote of them only as mourning figures turned to stone. As times of day, these images may signify the temporal life, which is one of ceaseless grief and restlessness. The suffering of the temporal life is given form in their ample, contorted torsos. On a sketch for the tomb over which are placed the Night and Day, Michelangelo wrote:

199. MICHELANGELO. Tomb of Giuliano de' Medici. c. 1524–34. Marble, height of center figure 5′8″. New Sacristy, San Lorenzo, Florence.

> We have with our swift course brought to death Duke Giuliano, and it is just that he take revenge upon us thus: that we have slain him, he thus dead has taken the light from us and with closed eyes has fastened ours so that they may shine forth no more upon this earth. What would he have done with us while he lived?

The moral of this lament may be that in death the Duke had vanquished the temporal life and time, being now outside time. Michelangelo had also planned to insert a mouse on the tomb to symbolize the gnawing, destructive action of time.

*far left:* 200. MICHELANGELO. *Lorenzo de' Medici.* c. 1524–34. Marble, height 5′10″. New Sacristy, San Lorenzo, Florence.

*left:* 201. MICHELANGELO. *The Medici Virgin.* c. 1524–34. Marble, height 7′5$^{3}/_{8}$″. New Sacristy, San Lorenzo, Florence.

*below:* 202. MICHELANGELO. *Brutus.* c. 1542. Marble, height 29$^{1}/_{2}$″ (without socle). Museo Nazionale, Florence.

The faces of the two dukes (Figs. 199, 200) show that Michelangelo did not create portrait likenesses of his subjects. He gave them instead a greatness and dignity that seemed to him a fitting commemoration for posterity. These seeming "portraits" are actually personifications of abstract ideals; Giuliano, moreover, did not live up to the principles glorified in his sculptural effigy. The figure of Giuliano may have embodied the Neoplatonic ideal of the active life, one of vigorous physical administration, shown by his open and commanding pose, the marshal's baton, and the coins in his hand, symbolizing a man who expends himself in outward actions. Lorenzo, his finger to his lips and his head partly in shadow, may have epitomized the contemplative life and saturnine disposition. In his meditative, introverted pose, he sits with his left elbow on a closed money box, which signified miserliness—in this case, perhaps, of the self. The Medici dukes are clad in Roman armor, recalling their election by the Pope as militant defenders to the Church. According to Hartt, these sculptured ducal effigies were in a sense a call to the leaders of Italy to rally in defense of the Church in her time of need.

Both lords look toward the Virgin and suckling Christ placed at the end of the chapel (Fig. 201). She is an incarnation of the Church, which took to its bosom the exiled house of Medici when formerly it had been expelled from Florence. She is the prophetic mother who gives her breast to the Child but at the same time draws back with the premonition of his sacrifice. According to a recent interpretation by Leo Steinberg, she is also the Bride of Christ: The symbolism of the Infant Bridegroom, "all his body, his straddling seat, reveals in the Child the divine lover electing his spouse."

Standing in the Medici Chapel, the visitor has the curious impression of being an intruder. Michelangelo's architecture is scaled to the heroic sculpture, not to the human being. The light entering from high up in the ceiling falls onto cold marble surfaces. The room itself is of exaggerated height and gives the impression of a deep, well-like space, unearthly and congenial only to the sculptured effigies. In 1534 Michelangelo voluntarily exiled himself from his beloved Florence for the rest of his life. Ostensibly he was working in Rome, and sentimental considerations were involved as well; but it is known that he hated the tyrannical Medici, who had gained an absolute rule and were responsible for the destruction of the Florentine republic. Michelangelo's bust of Brutus (Fig. 202) was commissioned by another political exile from Florence, and this celebration of the slayer of Caesar is explained by the esteem in which men like the sculptor and his patron held the murderers of tyrants. Presented somewhat in the style of Roman busts, Michelangelo's portrait of the noble Roman did not derive from a living model, and the artist alone conceived the features and expression appropriate to Brutus' character.

**The Last Judgment** Michelangelo's astonishing fresco of *The Last Judgment* (Fig. 203) should be viewed as part of the program of the Sistine Chapel, only two-thirds of which was actually carried out. It was proposed that Michelangelo execute a great fresco over the chapel doorway, having as its subject the fall of the rebel angels. *The Last Judgment* fresco over the altar of the chapel was to terminate this cycle. It is said, perhaps apocryphally, that when the Pope first saw the finished

*below:* 203. MICHELANGELO. *The Last Judgment*. 1536–41. Fresco, 48 × 44′. Sistine Chapel, Vatican, Rome.

fresco he fell on his knees in prayer. Michelangelo's painted vision is an awesome sight, calculated not to console the viewer with the promise of ultimate justice and mercy but to make him pause and reflect upon the adequacy and profundity of his personal faith. Michelangelo never intended his style to captivate the eye; he aspired instead to devotional images that would move those with little devotion to sincere meditation and tears, to reverence and fear. The subject presented in the dramatic fresco is the moments before the judgment. Some of the Biblical sources, according to De Tolnay, who has made one of the most thorough and satisfying analyses, were the books of Matthew (24:30–46), Revelations (1:7, 20:12), Daniel (7:13–14), John (3:19), Isaiah (13:6–9), and Ezekiel (37:1–9).

The seething masses of figures that comprise the great fresco do not fall into easily definable compartments or classifications; and in the absence of clothing or signs of rank, there is some doubt at first as to who are the angels or citizens of Heaven, the damned, and the saved. Beginning with the Resurrection scene in the lower segment, directly above the altar of the chapel, the agitated and turbulent tone of the final day is established. The dead are literally wrenched from the tombs. There is a persistent element of tension, or rebellious strength, in the bodies of those to be judged and a fierce determination by the damned to resist their fate. Michelangelo sees man as an independent spirit capable of defying God and universal laws even in the last hour. Christ the Judge responds to the feeling of the moment in a militant, almost wrathful gesture, as he vigorously enacts his role as supreme arbiter. The position of his right hand recalls that of ancient statues of Zeus and Roman emperors, or of generals riding triumphantly in the hunt or in battle as depicted on old sarcophagi (see Figs. 278, 280–282, 287, 288). With his left hand, he gently beckons the saved. There is no mitigating the sentence or the stern mood of Christ. The Virgin turns away, almost as if acknowledging her inability to sway her son. Around Christ are numerous figures of martyrs, brandishing the instruments of their martyrdom as if demanding justice. Soaring in the heavens are the wingless angels who transport the symbols of Christ's own martyrdom, as recorded in the Book of Revelations according to St. John.

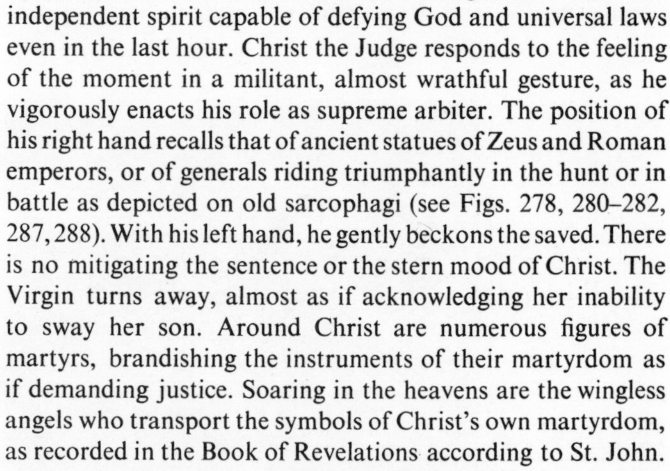

Late in the century, the Counter-Reformation was to look askance at Michelangelo's daring in depicting the angels with no visible means of support and to paint over much of the nudity of the figures. For Michelangelo, the angels and the saved rose in the heavens because of their faith, without the assistance of wings or a divine stairway. The ascent to Heaven is a difficult process for the elect, and a figure being hauled up by

*above:* 204. MICHELANGELO. *Minos*, detail of *The Last Judgment* (Fig. 203). 1536–41.

*right:* 205. MICHELANGELO. *Self-Portrait*, detail of *The Last Judgment* (Fig. 203). 1536–41.

*right:* 206. MICHELANGELO. *The Crucifixion, with the Virgin and St. John.* 1550–56. Black chalk drawing, $16^1/_4 \times 11''$. British Museum, London.

a rosary suggests that it is prayer and intense faith which achieve the final reward. In sympathy with the Church's own reformers who questioned the indiscriminate sale of indulgences, Michelangelo felt that ardent faith, more than good works or the intervention of celestial advocates, was responsible for man's salvation. The composition of the whole has a rotary movement of energetic figure clusters about the form of Christ. The overall circular layout may have conveyed for Michelangelo a symbolism related to that of the rose window of the Gothic cathedral (Fig. 103)—solar or cosmic symbolism, the Wheel of Fortune, eternity, and judgment.

The damned plummet or are dragged forcibly toward the depths and toward Charon's bark, the ferry of Greek mythology that carried souls to the underworld. In the lower right corner stands Minos, the underworld judge of Dante's *Inferno* (Fig. 204). Michelangelo does not, as Dante did, depict Minos as half man and half minotaur; he is given the head and body of a man and the tail of a serpent, which winds around his body, perhaps as a sign of the depths of Hell to which sinners are consigned. It is interesting to note that the face of Minos is a portrait of a Vatican official who criticized the fresco; when he complained to the Pope, the Pontiff replied that he was powerless to redeem the official from Hell. Michelangelo indicated the area of the damned not only by its location to the left of Christ but also by the powerful downward glance of God as he peers directly into its depths. Just below Christ, and to his left, kneels St. Bartholomew, holding in his left hand the skin of a man whose features are unmistakably those of Michelangelo (Fig. 205). The head of the saint has been thought to be that of Pietro Aretino, one of Michelangelo's most severe critics. *The Last Judgment* provided an opportunity for Michelangelo to profess his own strong sense of unworthiness and guilt.

**Christ's Death** During the last thirty years of his life, Michelangelo experienced a deep spiritual and artistic change. He grew dissatisfied with physical beauty, pagan subjects, philosophic truths, with art itself: "Thus I know how fraught with error was the fond imagination which made art my idol and my king." Art now appearing vain, a distraction from thoughts of God, Michelangelo made the dead Christ the theme of his last drawings and sculptures. He came to believe that salvation was dependent upon one's attitude toward Christ's sacrifice—that grace could come only through complete faith in the meaning of the Cross: "No brush, no chisel will quiet the soul once it is turned to the divine love of Him who upon the cross outstretches His arms to take us to Himself."

In perhaps his last drawing Michelangelo showed Christ on the Cross (Fig. 206), the figure's encompassing spread of arms emphasized by the mourning forms of Mary and St. John. The multiple outlines impart a tremulous appearance to the group. Long before, in search of the inner life of his subjects, the artist had abandoned the incisive sculptural edge in his drawing. Light and shadow replaced contorted musculature as the agents of pathos and of Michelangelo's spiritual sentiments. The more deeply he felt the content, the more frugal became his means.

Michelangelo's late life and work seemed, paradoxically, to reject what had taken a lifetime to gain. Having mastered his craft, the old artist submitted completely to private inspiration, with no self-consciousness about beauty or his art's appeal for others. Despising his flesh and obsessed with the spirit, whose immortality depended on Christ's broken body, Michelangelo sought a new art that, more directly than anatomical studies, brought spiritual meaning to the surface.

Two uncompleted *Pietàs* were the only sculptures executed by Michelangelo in the last years of his life. From 1548 to 1555 he worked on the *Pietà* in the Cathedral of Florence (Fig. 207), but after eight years of labor he removed the left leg of Christ.

*left:* 207. MICHELANGELO. *Deposition from the Cross.* 1548–55. Marble, height 7′5″. Cathedral, Florence.

*above:* 208. MICHELANGELO. *Joseph of Arimathea,* detail of *Deposition from the Cross* (Fig. 207).

*right:* 209. MICHELANGELO. *The Rondanini Pietà.* 1550–64. Marble, height 6′4$^{3}/_{4}$″. Castello Sforzesco, Milan.

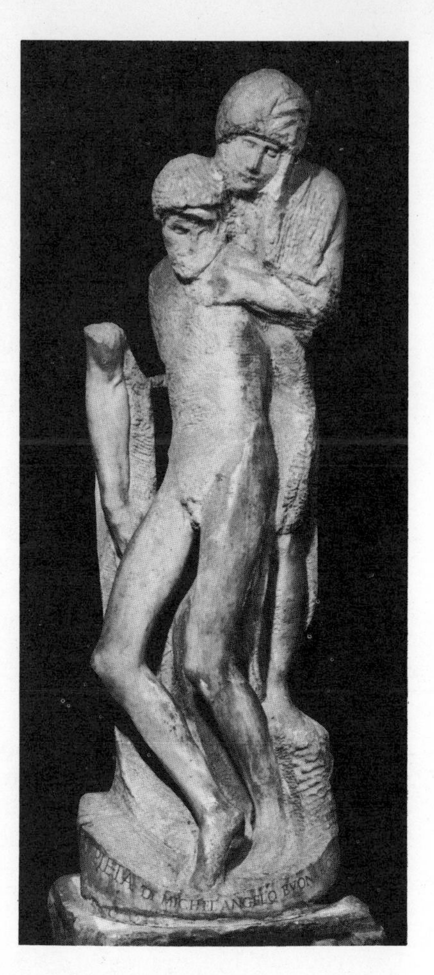

This has been interpreted by historians as a sign of angry dissatisfaction with the form of his work and as a sign of his desire to achieve greater compositional unity. No one considered other motives until Steinberg recently argued that in its original position the left leg of Christ was slung over the Virgin's thigh, forming a connection that was a symbol of sexual union. He has brilliantly traced the motif of the "slung leg" as a sign of sexual or marital union back to antiquity and pointed to its earlier occurrence in the pose of Christ in the Medici Madonna (Fig. 201). According to certain theologians and metaphors used by such priests as Savonarola, both Mary and Mary Magdalen were mystically espoused to Christ. Mary Magdalen appears in this work as "lover and penitent," a symbol of the Church Penitent, as the Virgin was of the Church Immaculate. Steinberg believes that the *Pietà* originally employed a direct sexual metaphor on a scale unprecedented in Christian devotional art; in view of the reformist atmosphere in Rome at the time, the aging Michelangelo may have felt that his intent would be misunderstood or that he had said too much in the "body language" of his art. How deeply he identified with this sculpture is shown by his self-portrait in the features of Joseph of Arimathea (Fig. 208), who tenderly assists in lowering Christ's body into the tomb that Joseph had prepared for himself. By contrast with Michelangelo's agonized expression in *The Last Judgment* (Fig. 205), the visage of Joseph reflects the artist's calm resignation toward death and toward his reunion with Christ.

Until the time of his death in 1564, Michelangelo worked intermittently on *The Rondanini Pietà* (Fig. 209), begun in 1550. Carved from what may have been an old Roman column, the vertical form of the Virgin supports the sagging body of the dead Christ, just removed from the Cross. Michelangelo apparently knocked off the original head and started another. Incomplete as the work is, the late style of the *Pietà* obviously scorned the supple, muscular, high-finish surface of the early sculpture. In its place were coarse textures and harsh junctures or angular interlocking of the limbs. Michelangelo sought to draw the beholder's attention away from surface qualities and toward a contemplation of the inner meaning of the subject. His vibrant late forms seem as if built from the inside out, affirming the importance of what the eye cannot see—the life of the soul and the Virgin's final spiritual communion with Christ.

The earlier authority of gestures gave way to successive changes during the carving, as if the artist sought symbolically to fuse the two figures. As part of his conversion to a medieval mysticism, Michelangelo turned away from Renaissance achievements of depicting a vigorous, healthy, and beautiful body in the Classical manner. It was not for lack of inspiration that Michelangelo struggled at the end. Though solemn in form and theme, Michelangelo's last work expresses the spiritual joy he felt in the meaning of his subject. Reputedly his final words to a friend were, "Remember the death of Christ."

*right:* 210. MICHELANGELO. Vestibule of the Laurentian Library. c. 1524–26 (stairway designed in 1558–59; completed by AMMANATI and VASARI, 1559). Florence.

*below:* 211. MICHELANGELO. Vestibule of the Laurentian Library, looking into the Reading Room. c. 1524–26. Florence.

**Architecture** Not a trained architect, Michelangelo approached the designing of walls as he did painting, like a figure sculptor whose ideas concerned relief compositions, skeletal armatures, systems of muscles and tendons, and tautly stretched skins. To design the Laurentian Library (Figs. 210, 211) for the Medici, he no more accepted Renaissance conventions of flat wall arrangements than he had the proportional systems of other painters and sculptors. The entrance hall of the library, like the Medici Chapel, is taller than it is wide, a deep well that offers the immediate experience of unfamiliar space and proportions. Into the relatively small space cascades a great stairway, subdivided more for grandeur than for traffic. The passive or reposeful effect of contemporary art and architecture was anathema to Michelangelo. His central stair is like a strong current irresistible to both ascent and descent. The grey stone and white stucco walls make one of the most dramatic contrasts in architecture. Doubling the columns in wall niches was not necessary for structural support but, like his constricted figures, imparted a feeling of contained energy. Using the design vocabulary of ancient and 15th-century architecture, Michelangelo devised

St. Peter's (Fig. 212), he used pilasters gigantic enough to rise through two stories and support a massive horizontal entablature. Not since Gothic cathedrals had the structural elements of a building been given such expressive stress. His vigorous articulation of walls is analogous to the muscular interaction in his sculptured bodies. Instead of neutral openings, windows became emphatic projections with sculptural frames that push aggressively forward and to the sides.

The colossal attracted the artist in architecture as it did in painting and sculpture. In his day the world was thought to center on the deteriorating Capitoline Hill (the Campidoglio), originally the cite of an ancient temple of Jupiter and then of the medieval city hall of Rome. The Pope approved Michelangelo's plans to redesign the crown of the hill as a great trapezoidal open square approached by a long inclined stairway (Fig. 213). At the end of the square stands the Palazzo dei Senatori; on either side the paired Palazzo dei Conservatori and Palazzo Nuovo. The plaza became an open-air theater for staging such public functions as the reception of chiefs of state. With its sculptural adornments preserved from antiquity, the plaza linked ancient and contemporary Catholic Rome. Pope Paul III had the statue of Marcus Aurelius brought to the square, because of the aura of Imperial symbolism investing this work. Michelangelo designed the pedestal for the image and placed it on a gentle mound, where converged a curvilinear grid dividing the area into twelve compartments. James Ackerman has shown that the mound and its zodiac design relate to Roman Imperial shields and that the curving lines emanating from the statue's base derive from a sun symbol in Imperial armored portraits.

his own grammar: the scroll brackets, for example, serve a purely expressive purpose. Michelangelo, like no previous architect, could bring a building to life and endow it with a kind of harnessed power.

Michelangelo's architectural commissions were for structures whose significance equaled the special quality of his elevated subjects in sculpture. For the west exterior wall of

To the façades of the two flanking palaces (Fig. 214) Michelangelo brought new architectural associations and symbols of authority. Here he joined one-story columns with colossal piers, and the vertical thrusts and continuity of these members balanced the horizontal elements of the low rectangular façade. More than at St. Peter's, Michelangelo has fused the organization of wall surfaces and the functions of load

*above:* 212. MICHELANGELO. St. Peter's, apse from the west. 1546–64 (dome completed by GIACOMO DELLA PORTA, 1590). Vatican, Rome.

*right:* 213. ETIENNE DUPÉRAC. Engraving after MICHELANGELO's plan for the Capitoline Hill, Rome. 1569. Metropolitan Museum of Art, New York (Harris Brisbane Dick Fund, 1936).

214. MICHELANGELO. Palazzo dei Conservatori. Designed c. 1546. Capitoline Hill, Rome.

and support so that, as in his figures, high drama comes from powerful counter-movements and a continuous adjustment of opposing forces. The pyramidal double stairway before the Palazzo dei Senatori, so influential in later palace design, served simultaneously to frame like a pediment the sculptures of river gods and the goddess Roma, to give access to the main floor (the ground floor was a prison and so marked by heavier masonry), and to provide a platform for the appearance of nobility. Stairways, plazas, and framed vistas excited Michelangelo because they demanded movement rather than the viewer's passive inspection permitted by earlier Renaissance architecture. The patterned oval pavement and the central statue force circulation about the plaza. The trapezoid encouraged movement toward the central palace, or it directed one's view across Rome to the new St. Peter's, where Michelangelo was planning the dome he did not live to see built. Thus Michelangelo gave significant shape to the two great monuments to Church and State in Rome and, in the process, applied the forms of antiquity to the advantage of a new and noble art.

The most gifted artist of his age, Michelangelo was also the most tormented. His writings reveal a man subject to depression, who thought himself mad and sinful. He could be timid, vengeful, and untrusting of those about him, often with good cause. Endlessly fascinated by the mysteries of creation, redemption, and salvation, he was strongly conscious of human frailty and fallibility. In short, Michelangelo was afflicted with magnificent visions that he felt achieved only a pale expression in his art: he sought to grasp the infinite, well knowing his own limitations. His visionary attempt resulted in the brilliant and daring paintings, sculpture, and architecture that inspire and awe the modern world. In tragic irony, Michelangelo felt himself a failure. By 1550 he had given up painting, and his last sculptures were left unfinished. He turned to architecture, the most abstract of the visual arts, to fulfill his lifetime need for a union with the Creator. Making his art the mirror of his personal growth and change, his ego and moods, Michelangelo seems in some respects a modern personality. In the art are magnificent bursts of inspiration, upheavals of superhuman energy, and the weight of disillusionment. No other artist had ever exhibited so intimate a bond between his personality and his art; none so fiercely insisted on maintaining his individuality.

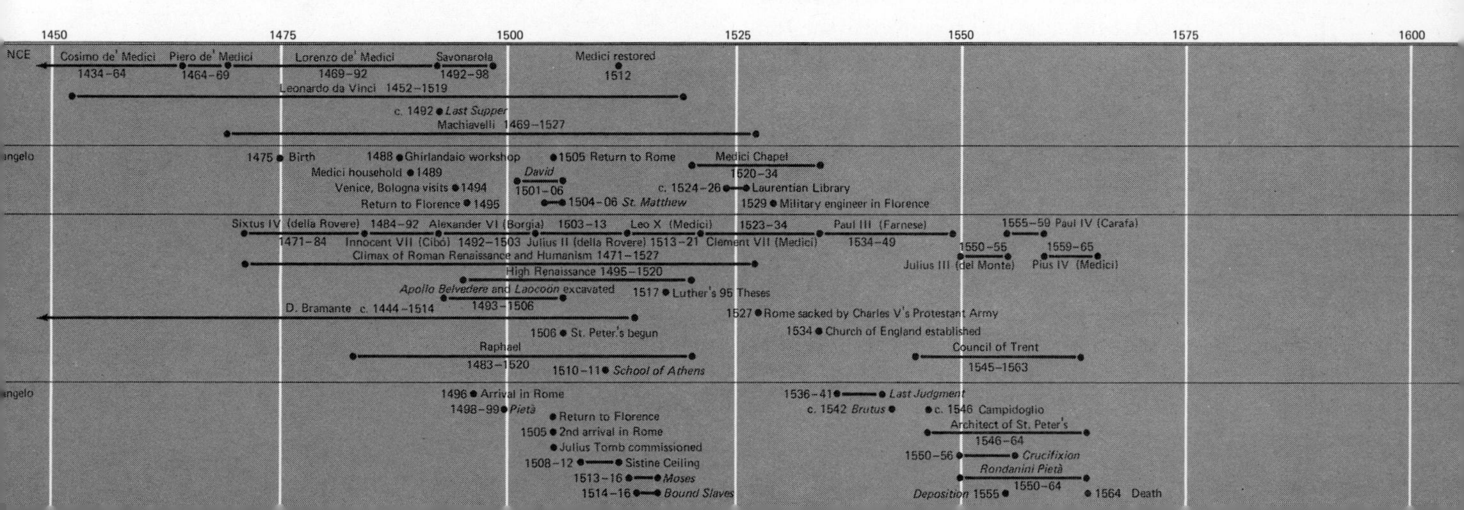

# 9

In our day it is the mass communications media that convey messages to the public. In the 16th and 17th centuries, painting, sculpture, and architecture were the great transmitters and their messages were primarily those of the Church. The purpose of religious art then was not only to illustrate or vivify the Bible and theology, as in the past, but also to engage in the war for mankind's spiritual allegiance being fought between religious factions throughout Europe. The word *propaganda* has acquired unpleasant connotations because of the recent history of its political use for distortion of truth, but in past eras a crucial purpose of art was the dissemination of information and opinion—or propaganda. The war of ideas that engaged many of Europe's finest artists penetrated to the art itself, for, like heretical literature, art that disseminated outdated, incorrect, or contradictory views had to be counteracted. For these reasons, changes in styles as well as in themes during the 16th and 17th centuries must be viewed within a militant context. The art of Leonardo, Michelangelo, and Raphael was highly acceptable to the Church of that period, but subsequent changes in Church policy and leadership, response to the Protestant Reformation, and demands for greater emphasis on piety and mystical faith caused extreme reactions and new alternatives to the work of these three great artists.

In this light, a painting from 16th-century Catholic Spain, *Christ Driving the Money Changers from the Temple* (Pl. 26, p. 161) by El Greco (Domenico Theotokopoulos, 1541–1614) can be meaningfully compared with *The School of Athens* (Pl. 27, p. 161) of Raphael (1483–1520), also painted in the 16th century. Raphael's fresco was located in the Vatican, in a room where the papal signature was affixed to important documents. Despite its position in a place of great importance to Christianity, the subject of the fresco is a portrayal of the great philosophers of antiquity, with the central focus upon Plato and Aristotle. Raphael was demonstrating the Humanist belief in the compatibility of pre-Christian thought with Church views in his own time. He has created a series of imagined but intensely lifelike portraits of many philosophers, situating them in an equally imaginary but dignified architectural structure inspired by the work of Bramante (1444–1514), a contemporary architect who strongly influenced Raphael.

The subject El Greco chose was the single occasion on which Christ used violence. This may have related to the strenuous measures taken by the Church to rid itself of heresy, which by then included acceptance of pagan philosophy and

# 16th- AND 17th-CENTURY ART
# The Synthesis of Heaven and Earth

art. Thus El Greco's Christ would drive not only the money changers but also the earlier Humanists from the Church. Through the archway above Christ's head appears a reference to Rome, specifying the target of the artist's commentary. The spaciousness of Raphael's setting, the balance, grace, and vital bearing of his philosophers, so beautifully realized in drawing, color, and composition—all are intentionally counteracted by El Greco. Against the older artist's lucid, metrical space, his fluid composure of groups and orderly alignment of all forms in recessive zones parallel to the picture plane, were now offered congestion, angular, disconnected passages, and dissonant color. El Greco painted not to soothe the eye but to irritate the complacent who took balm for reason.

To combat Protestantism the Church urged artists to affirm the sacraments, especially the Eucharist. In depicting St. Jerome, the Italian painter Domenichino (1581–1641), unlike Van Eyck (Pl. 18, p. 115), did not celebrate the saint's scholarship; he eulogized his great will in rising from the deathbed to receive for the last time the wine and wafer (Fig. 215). The struggle to share in the sacred Eucharistic mystery is represented with the full range of expertise developed by the 15th-century painters who brought art down to earth and glorified the marvelous organism of the human body. The task of Domenichino and his generation was to redirect men's thoughts toward Heaven, while working with the devices of earlier humanistic and secularized art.

**Individual License** Because 16th-century Protestants viewed as idolatrous the Catholic Church's use of art, no art appeared explicitly illustrating Lutheranism in the way that the *Spiritual Exercises* of St. Ignatius of Loyola was celebrated in painting. But the Flemish painter Pieter Bruegel (1525/30–69), of unknown religious affiliation, possessed a mind whose conception of the Bible and religious controversy departed from that of his Catholic contemporaries. His *Blind Leading the Blind* (Fig. 216), based on Matthew (15:12–19), could well have been a commentary on the religious leaders, equated with the Pharisees, then disputing theology throughout Europe. The church fully visible behind the blind men who stumble after each other seems a pointed reference. Painting for a select clientele, Bruegel could count on a sophisticated audience, which included devout churchmen, to recognize certain absurdities in the affairs of men. For him, art served the mind and was the means by which to illustrate knowledge and wisdom detached from the customary partisan causes undertaken by his fellow artists represented in this chapter.

*opposite:* 215. DOMENICHINO. *The Last Communion of St. Jerome*. 1614. Oil on canvas, 13′8″ × 8′4″. Vatican Museums, Rome.

*right:* 216. PIETER BRUEGEL THE ELDER. *The Blind Leading the Blind*. 1568. Oil on canvas, 2′10″ × 5′1/2″. Museo di Capodimonte, Naples.

*left:* 217. PONTORMO. *Self-Portrait*, detail of *The Deposition* (Pl. 28, p. 162). 1525–28.

Unlike Leonardo, Bruegel was interested in broad, even generic, human relationships, and our physical remoteness from his figures reflects the kind of intellectual detachment he assumed toward his subject.

To maintain that artists in the 16th century acted and thought only at the bidding of the Church is to overlook the individual initiative and personal feelings and fantasies of many of the greatest painters. Pontormo (Jacopo Carucci, 1494–1556/57), a contemporary of Michelangelo, was famous in his time for his art and for his eccentricity, which took the form of fanatical isolation and hypochondria; he exemplified the 16th-century concept of the lonely genius. His painting of *The Deposition* (Pl. 28, p. 162) is a deeply personal and disturbing meditation on the meaning of Christ's death, couched in a language that by comparison with the idiom of Raphael and Leonardo seems an alien tongue. The eye is at first jolted by apple greens, metallic greys, and shrill pinks and yellows—not the anodyne palette of Raphael, with its soft reds, blues, and flesh tones. The distortions of Pontormo's figures ultimately depend upon correct anatomical knowledge, but the demands for an expressive or emotional composition impelled the distention or abbreviation of limbs, dislocation of shoulders, and the elongated, boneless torsos. His figures are of a type, a strange family whose faces betray intense shock. The laws of spatial logic, and hence reason, are decisively put aside, as the entwined figures appear to be stacked vertically in some unreal place and moment. Unlike the rationale of a 15th-century painting, it is impossible to conceive of what these figures will do next or where they will go, any more than one can visualize the painting's space without them. It is the unnatural occasioned by mystical attitudes and themes that nurtured Pontormo's style. As was true of Michelangelo, an inner, personal vision, not nature, was his model. It is therefore difficult to determine how close his own portrait (Fig. 217), seen to the right of the Virgin, reveals his actual physical appearance.

**The Counter-Reformation Program** The Church did not always accept the license taken by an artist in the name of individuality; fearful of a corruption of its message, the Church evolved an official artistic program in the second half of the 16th century, and this reached fruition during the 17th. This program was intended to counteract the Protestant Reformation and its assaults not only upon the doctrine and practices of the Holy Roman Catholic Church but also on its art. The Council of Trent, which sat in the north Italian town of Trento from 1545 to 1563, was an arm of the Inquisition instrumental in crystallizing Church policy with regard to internal reform, as well as in plotting strategy against the northern Protestant heretics. In the last year of its meeting, the Council promulgated its views on art. In essence, this program reaffirmed the Church's belief in the importance of art, reiterated the opposition to idolatry, espoused the didactic purpose of art and its provision of an ethical model for the faithful, decried indecency in religious painting and sculpture, and insisted upon decorum, respect, and accuracy in interpreting theological or spiritual subject matter. The implications of the Council of Trent's view included an anti-Humanist attitude, a kind of Counter-Renaissance that favored an appeal to the emotions of the believer in the manner of Loyola's *Spiritual Exercises*. These exercises involved a self-induced ecstatic trance or meditation, comparable to yoga, in which the individual lost all self-consciousness and through visions identified himself with the feelings or state of his object of worship. Another implication of the Council's views was a stress on the supernatural, or a suspension of the rational, thus giving rise to numerous works of art dealing with miraculous themes. As a result of the Council's promulgations, theological truth and the strengthening of Church doctrines through visual representation became more important than artistic beauty.

**The Trial of Veronese** To ensure the carrying out of their decrees, the Council instituted a censorship of art by agents of the Inquisition. The most famous case brought before these agents, the Holy Tribunal sitting in Venice on July 18, 1573, was that of the Venetian painter Paolo Veronese (1528–88), who had painted a questionable version of the Last Supper (Fig. 218). The transcript of the trial illustrates, among other things, the uneasy synthesis of the spiritual and the secular in

*left:* Plate 26. El Greco. *Christ Driving the Money Changers from the Temple.* c. 1570–75. Oil on canvas, 3′10″ × 5′9″. Minneapolis Institute of Arts, Minnesota (Dunwoody Fund). (See p. 158.)

*below:* Plate 27. Raphael. *The School of Athens.* 1510–11. Fresco. Stanza della Segnatura, Vatican, Rome. (See p. 158.)

*opposite:* Plate 30. ANDREA POZZO. *The Triumph of St. Ignatius Loyola (Allegory of the Missionary Work of the Jesuits)*. 1691–94. Fresco on nave ceiling, Sant'Ignazio, Rome. (See p. 173.)

*above:* Plate 28. PONTORMO. *The Deposition*. 1525–28. Oil on panel, 10′3″ × 6′3½″. Santa Felicità, Florence. (See p. 160, Fig. 217.)

*right:* Plate 29. PETER PAUL RUBENS. *Descent from the Cross*. c. 1611–14. Oil on panel, 13′10″ × 10′1″. Cathedral, Antwerp. (See p. 171, Fig. 226.)

Plate 31. CARAVAGGIO. *Christ at Emmaus*. c. 1598. Oil on canvas, $4'7'' \times 6'5^{1}/_{2}''$. National Gallery, London (reproduced by courtesy of the Trustees). (See p. 175.)

the minds of the judges as well as the painter. When questioned about his profession, Veronese answered as follows *:

A. I paint and compose figures.
Q. Do you know the reason why you have been summoned?
A. No, Sir.
Q. Can you imagine it?
A. I can well imagine.
Q. Say what you think the reason is.
A. According to what the Reverend Father, the Prior of the Convent of SS. Giovanni e Paolo, whose name I do not know, told me, he had been here and Your Lordships had ordered him to have painted [in the picture] a Magdalen in place of a dog. I answered him by saying I would gladly do everything necessary for my honor and for that of my painting, but that I did not understand how a figure of Magdalen would be suitable there for many reasons which I will give at any time, provided I am given an opportunity.
Q. What picture is this of which you have spoken?
A. This is a picture of the Last Supper that Jesus Christ took with His Apostles in the house of Simon....
Q. At this Supper of Our Lord you painted other figures?
A. Yes, milords.
Q. Tell us how many people and describe the gestures of each.
A. There is the owner of the inn, Simon; besides this figure I have made a steward, who, I imagined, had come there for his own pleasure to see how the things were going at the table. There are many figures there which I cannot recall, as I painted the picture some time ago....
Q. In this Supper which you made for SS. Giovanni e Paolo what is the significance of the man whose nose is bleeding?
A. I intended to represent a servant whose nose was bleeding because of some accident.
Q. What is the significance of those armed men, dressed as Germans, each with a halberd in his hand?
A. This requires that I say twenty words!
Q. Say them.
A. We painters take the same license the poets and the jesters take and I have represented these two halberdiers, one drinking and the other eating nearby on the stairs. They are placed there so that they might be of service because it seemed to me fitting, according to what I have been told, that the master of the house, who was great and rich, should have such servants.
Q. And that man dressed as a buffoon with a parrot on his wrist, for what purpose did you paint him on that canvas?
A. For ornament, as is customary....
Q. Did anyone commission you to paint Germans, buffoons, and similar things in that picture?
A. No, milords, but I received the commission to decorate the picture as I saw fit. It is large and, it seemed to me, it could hold many figures.
Q. Are not the decorations which you painters are accustomed to add to paintings or pictures supposed to be suitable and proper to the subject and the principal figures or are they for pleasure—simply what comes to your imagination without any discretion or judiciousness?
A. I paint pictures as I see fit and as well as my talent permits.
Q. Does it seem fitting at the Last Supper of the Lord to paint buffoons, drunkards, Germans, dwarfs, and similar vulgarities?
A. No, milords.
Q. Do you not know that in Germany and in other places infected with heresy it is customary with various pictures full of scurrilousness and similar inventions to mock, vituperate, and scorn the things of the Holy Catholic Church in order to teach bad doctrines to foolish and ignorant people?...
A. Illustrious Lords, I do not want to defend it, but I thought I

* From *Literary Sources of Art History: An Anthology of Texts from Theophilus to Goethe,* ed. Elizabeth Gilmore Holt (© 1947 by Princeton University Press), pp. 245–248. Reprinted by permission of Princeton University Press.

218. PAOLO VERONESE. *Christ in the House of Levi.* 1573. Oil on canvas, 18′2″ × 42′. Academia, Venice.

*left:* 219. LEONARDO DA VINCI. *The Last Supper*. c. 1494. Fresco, 15′1$^{1}/_{8}$″ × 28′10$^{1}/_{2}$″. Refectory of Santa Maria delle Grazie, Milan.

*opposite:* 220. TINTORETTO. *The Last Supper*. 1594. Oil on canvas, 12′ × 18′8″. San Giorgio Maggiore, Venice.

> was doing right. I did not consider so many things and I did not intend to confuse anyone, the more so as those figures of buffoons are outside of the place in a picture where Our Lord is represented.
>
> After these things had been said, the judges announced that the above named Paolo would be obliged to improve and change his painting within a period of three months from the day of the admonition and that according to the opinion and decision of the Holy Tribunal all the corrections should be made at the expense of the painter, and that if he did not correct the picture he would be liable to the penalties imposed by the Holy Tribunal.

Despite the Tribunal's injunctions, however, there do not appear to have been any changes made by the artist.

Veronese's answers give a 16th-century definition of painting based on the composition of figures which were to be *read,* that is, which were to convey a message and be interpreted. Like a dramatist, the artist had to envision why each figure was present and what he would logically be doing. When it came to filling a large space with ornament and enrichment, Veronese claimed for the painter the same license given to poets—the freedom to include stories and information outside the Bible, bringing a past event to life in terms of one's own time. Veronese's criteria were his ability and personal judgment of fitness, fortified by what he had seen in great art of the past. The great scale of his painting and the sumptuous setting and elaborate social milieu were reflections of his personal delight in contemporary Venetian customs.

**Sacramental versus Psychological** Though not insensitive to secular life, Tintoretto (1518–94), another Venetian, painted religious images fully consonant with Counter-Reformation ideals. The Roman Church affirmed that, contrary to Protestant theology, to participate in the Eucharist was to partake mystically of the body and blood of Christ. This belief impelled Tintoretto to emphasize in his *Last Supper* the miraculous meaning and origin of the Eucharistic doctrine.

Tintoretto's art was typical of a Counter-Renaissance attitude which saw the style and content of such painters as Leonardo as too worldly. Comparison of Leonardo's *Last Supper* (Fig. 219) with Tintoretto's of a century later (Fig. 220) reveals the ideological gulf separating the two interpretations. Concerned for interior human motivation, Leonardo portrayed the moment when Christ foretold his betrayal. This permitted a virtuoso display of the artist's knowledge of facial and gestural expression and of the differences in individuals' reaction to shock. Set in an austere room, the scene has been treated illusionistically as a continuation of the refectory whose wall it adorns; thus, Leonardo could display his mastery of spatial organization and of the effects of certain lighting conditions. Tintoretto has suggested a rustic inn, and he made the meal a less formal occasion. Almost melodramatic, the lighting accords with the mystical sacramental moment chosen by Tintoretto. The artist's technique for attaining these effects was to set small sculptural figures in an open-ended box and then move different lights over the model.

Leonardo's composition is "closed," or completely contained within the limits of the picture area. The vanishing points and figural action lie either at the center or within the borders of the painting. Tintoretto's arrangement is "open"; space, light, shadow, and action seem to extend beyond the frame. Leonardo has organized his figures and table on an imaginary plane parallel to the picture surface, holding the viewer off from the action. Tintoretto's forms exist on a strong thrust diagonal to the picture surface, which makes them seem to recess in space. It is easier to isolate individual figures, objects, or units within the Leonardo scheme. Leonardo's work shows multiple rather than Classical unity.

*right:* 221. TITIAN. *Christ Crowned with Thorns.* c. 1570. Oil on canvas, 9′2″ × 6′. Alte Pinakothek, Munich.

The potential of the figures derives from the clear edge bounding each and the relative evenness of the light; they are clear in shape and illumination. Tintoretto's figures have a more inextricable relationship resulting from overlapped shadows and their construction through color as well as with light and shade. Obscurity and painterliness characterize Tintoretto's composition. Leonardo kept light and dark close to the middle register, avoiding strong contrasts over large areas. Extreme value contrasts in major areas create the dramatic and mystical effects of Tintoretto's composition. Leonardo, a Renaissance painter, eschewed clashing colors placed close together; Tintoretto made visual excitement out of strong disparities between colors. His light sources were multiple and irrational, Leonardo's fewer and more natural. Tintoretto's space pulls the viewer into the picture with a swift rush, but the eye is brought forward again by the large foreground groups and the angels hovering overhead. The edges and perspective focus of Leonardo's architecture lead the viewer into depth; the head of Christ in the foreground draws him back into an area near the picture plane. There is a meaningful focus on Christ in both paintings. Tintoretto set Christ's head in a mystical radiance, the most intense light of the painting; light, therefore, replaced perspective or geometry as the principal instrument of religious significance.

**Devotional Paintings** It was 16th-century Venetians such as Veronese, Tintoretto, and Titian (c. 1488–1576) who gave new implications to the verb *to paint*. In the 15th century artists colored areas already described by linear drawing, which gives their work a series of contours that are easy to grasp even when seen in black and white. The monochrome reproduction of the painting in Figure 221 gives the misleading impression of murky indistinctness. The relative coarseness and the fusion of silhouettes with the surrounding space derive from Titian's use of brush drawing in color to build his figures. Even his pen-and-ink or charcoal drawings synthesize distinct, continuous edges into a sketchy airiness. Color was Titian's prime means of expression and method of construction, color seen not in a vacuum but by natural or artificial light filtered through a palpable atmosphere.

Titian and Tintoretto responded to the physical sensations of brushing color onto a surface, savoring the pigment's weight, texture, and pliability, to make each stroke define a shape, degree of light, modeling, and exact color tone. Pressure could spread apart the pigment-filled brush, permitting the underpainting to radiate through and vibrate with the new color. To the elderly Titian came knowledge of the expressive power possible in the judicious selection of a few colored strokes, but his contemporaries, favoring the earlier virtuoso work, thought the style of *Christ Crowned with Thorns* the result of senility, trembling hand, and failing vision. Palma Giovane, a sometime collaborator, has described how the aged Titian worked:

Titian began his pictures with a mass of color which served as a bed or foundation for what he wished to express. I myself have seen such vigorously applied underpainting in pure red ochre, which was meant to give the half-tone, or in white lead. With the same brush, which he dipped in red, black or yellow, he created the modeling effect of the lighter portions. With four strokes he was capable of indicating a magnificent figure. . . . After he had thus applied this important foundation, he turned the pictures to the wall and left them . . . sometimes for months. When he afterwards returned to them, he scanned them with a concentration as severe as if they had been his mortal enemies, in order to find faults in them; and if he found something which was not in accord with his intentions, he went to work like a surgeon. . . . Thus by repeated revision, he brought the skeleton of his figures to the highest degree of perfection and, while one picture was drying, he turned to another. This quintessence of a composition he then covered over with many layers of living flesh, until the figure seemed to lack only breath. He never painted a figure *alla prima* [spontaneously], and was wont to say that he who improvises can never fashion a perfect line of poetry. He gave the last touch to his pictures by adjusting with his fingers a spot of black in one corner or heightening with a dab of red, like a drop of blood, the liveliness of the surface. . . . In the last stages of the work, he painted more with his fingers than with the brush . . .

Just as he reworked a single painting, so did Titian reinterpret certain themes and earlier compositions, not just for his many clients but, in later years, largely for himself. In his *Christ Crowned with Thorns,* he subdued the earlier strong facial reactions, obstructed focus upon hands, and generally suffused the entire scene with a drama of light and strongly textured color. To a certain extent, late works such as this were the painter's private devotional paintings, and in a secular sense they marked passionate devotion to painting itself.

**The Long View of Bruegel** In comparison with Titian's painting, Pieter Bruegel's *Carrying of the Cross* (Fig. 222), done a few years earlier, is a radical departure in Biblical illustration, yet conservative in terms of the relation of color to drawing. The pathos resulting from Titian's intimate focus upon Christ's ordeal is matched by an equally strong ethos arising from the viewer's remoteness from the figure of Christ, struggling under the weight of his Cross. The way to Calvary is plotted along a broad curving plane, and Christ is accompanied by a crowd that takes little notice of him but is diverted by all sorts of byplay. In the foreground are the weeping Marys and St. John, and nearby is seen an elevated wheel used for the torture execution of criminals in Bruegel's time. In a sense, Bruegel gives us a long view of Christ's ordeal: we see the Saviour in the broad context of a time and place, as a man among men, who like many before and after is unjustly put to death, providing the crowd with still another morbid spectacle. It is possible that the curving arc of the plain and the numerous references to circles would have suggested to Bruegel's limited but knowledgeable audience the continual recurrence of injustice. Some historians have seen in this painting the artist's bitter commentary on the brutality of Spanish rule over the Netherlands, or an oblique reference to the sadism of the Inquisition; but if this were true, it somehow escaped the notice of the Spanish Catholic royalty, who admired his painting. Bruegel's focus is the reverse of Titian's: it inhibits concentration on the personal and theological implications of Christ's Passion, and it increases the breadth of the artist's statement about history and human nature to a scale then unrivaled.

**The Mysticism of El Greco** The most mystical of the Counter-Reformation painters was El Greco, who believed in

*left:* 222. PIETER BRUEGEL THE ELDER. *The Carrying of the Cross.* 1564. Oil on panel, 4′7/8″ × 5′6 7/8″. Kunsthistorisches Museum, Vienna.

*opposite right:* 223. EL GRECO. *The Resurrection of Christ.* 1600–05. Oil on canvas, 9′1/4″ × 4′5″. Prado, Madrid.

*opposite far right:* 224. EL GRECO. *The Legend of St. Maurice.* 1581–84. Oil on canvas, 14′8 1/3″ × 9′10 1/2″. El Escorial, Spain.

the irrational basis of Christian dogma and the necessity of a uniquely personal style to embody his private visions. The events in his paintings are not depicted in 15th-century Europe, according to the rational perception of a detached observer, but are emanations of an ecstatic visionary who sought to show in one explosive moment things that defy intellectual comprehension. For this reason, his *Resurrection of Christ* (Fig. 223) seems antidotal to that by Piero della Francesca (Pl. 23, p. 135). El Greco presents the mystical levitation of Christ's body rising from the invisible tomb. The position of Christ's feet helps to engender this feeling of ascent and also recalls the posture of his Crucifixion.

El Greco was concerned more with metaphysics than with psychology. The cold, eerie light of the scene originates from Christ's transfigured person. His effortless upward movement contrasts with the forceful effects of the awesome mystical light, which has upset the sleeping tomb guards, dazzled those who have awakened, and exalted those present who comprehend the transformation. Through gestures at once rhetorical and symbolic, El Greco demonstrated the forceful process of spiritual enlightenment and the significance of the Resurrection. The gesture of Christ's right hand is a sign of the completion of what had been ordained, while its counterpart in the large figure at the lower right is one of simultaneous recognition and supplication. The extreme luminosity, the exaggerated elongation, and the inconstant silhouette of Christ's body reduce its corporeality and eliminate the suggestion of militancy seen in Piero's God. All that was tangible and substantial in the work of Piero has been made elusive and immaterial by El Greco. The stability of Piero's composition—its implied triangle of verticals resting on solid horizontals, all locked within a square format—has been replaced by an unstable irregular lozenge design in a vertical format. Just as the mystical nature of El Greco's Christ was freed from the logic of matter, so is the event abstracted from a specific earthly place and time.

The strength of El Greco's religious message did not weaken his inspired inventiveness as a painter. Great artists of the past and of his own time had early taught him lessons in drawing, color, and composition. As his art became more introspective, however, it posed unprecedented technical problems, so that the success of his solutions cannot be gauged against the work of others. To the viewer of today, El Greco's *Legend of St. Maurice* (Fig. 224) appears as a beautifully accomplished fact. He has solved the artistic problems so well that he has obscured

their original difficulty. One might usefully recall here that Counter-Reformation art often instructed the faithful in the merits of dying for their beliefs, in response to the Protestants who criticized the Church's veneration of its numerous martyrs. To affirm the sacred act of the martyr and to encourage worldwide missionary work, Roman Catholic artists were enjoined to recount the historical sacrifices of the martyrs. The story chosen by El Greco is that of the wholesale execution of a Roman legion which, with its commander St. Maurice, had been converted to Christianity. Refusing the emperor's ultimatum to renounce their faith, every man in the legion was beheaded at the site of what is today Saint Moritz, Switzerland. El Greco stressed the moment of decision when the legion officers surrounding St. Maurice considered the Imperial ultimatum. Accordingly, almost a third of the painting's surface is devoted to this small group in the foreground. The upper part discloses angels who descend from Heaven holding the crowns of martyrdom. To the smallest, most restricted area at the left is consigned the execution of the entire contingent.

El Greco boldly juxtaposed the largest and smallest figures in the entire painting. By means of the medium-size angels placed at the upper left and the large standard at the right, he set the eccentric composition solidly within the frame. The sculptural firmness of the foreground officers is replaced as the eye moves rapidly into depth by the diaphanous character of the tiny figures in the distance.

Essential to the style of these paintings by El Greco is the total absence of straight edge, evenly illuminated surfaces, continuous closed silhouettes, repose, and measurable space. Every shape seems in the process of change; rarely is the eye permitted to rest. Figures and clouds swell from tapered points, and rocks and pennants are edged in writhing contours. It is possible to follow the action of the painter's hand in the irregular cloud and flag forms. His thinking was focused on both particular objects and their adjacent areas, so that rarely is a figure or object seen in isolation. No dominant sustained vertical or horizontal axis structures the composition. Unity is finally the result of closely fitted oscillating or irregular parts, often at obtuse angles to each other or else in parallel series.

El Greco has been called insane, and, more recently, attempts have been made to suggest that he suffered from astigmatism. Neither was the case. His unique art was the product of a lifelong development, lucid calculation, and passionate religious conviction. He might have declared that his physical vision was normal but that his "inner eye" was abnormal.

**Sadistic License** Ironically the age of the Counter-Reformation, which saw restoration and increase of the Church's power, was also the lustiest and most perverse in its artistic celebration of sex. Art of the 16th and 17th centuries, ostensibly in the noble service of defending or expounding the true faith, was in fact the frequent outlet for erotic and sadistic interests of the artist, his ecclesiastical patrons, and his audience. Church scholars chronicled all forms of gruesome martyrdom, and in a Roman college for the training of missionaries, walls were lined with horrifying images of "successful alumni" who died as martyrs all over the world. Rather than discourage the young, such images fired their zeal. An engraving by Stradanus (Jan van der Straet, 1523–1605) of *The Martyrdom of Saint Agatha* exemplifies the public's fascination with sexual violence enacted upon feminine martyrs (Fig. 225). Ugliness and beauty are blatantly contrasted as symbols of sin and saintliness. Ironically, it was the Holy Inquisition, with its well-known methods of torture, that fed the public taste for sadism. The synthesis of Heavenly and earthly values at the time of the *Merode Altarpiece* (Pl. 17, p. 115) had already begun to attempt the absorption of sexual life, and in the period here considered there was an increasing frankness and exposure of this subject, which often tried the credibility of a synthesis.

**Synthesis of Flesh and Spirit** That there was no homogeneous Counter-Reformation style can be seen by the fact that, along with El Greco's paintings, those of Peter Paul Rubens (1577–1640) were highly acceptable to the Church. El Greco's opposite in temperament and style, the Flemish Rubens was able to reconcile a vital love of the flesh with a love of the spirit. His mythological pagan types, kings, peasants, and religious personages are interchangeable, sharing a common robust virility, effulgent health, and appetite for living. The deeply introverted El Greco distrusted the carnality

*left:* 225. STRADANUS. *The Martyrdom of St. Agatha.* 16th century. Engraving.

left: 226. PETER PAUL RUBENS. Detail of *Descent from the Cross* (Pl. 29, p. 162). c. 1611–14.

right: 227. PETER PAUL RUBENS. *St. Ignatius Exorcising Demons from the Church*. 1619. Oil on canvas, 17′6½″ × 12′11½″. Kunsthistorisches Museum, Vienna.

of the body with a medieval fervor, whereas Rubens seems to have been fulfilled through the sensuous painting of the flesh. The energy in El Greco's painting is mystical; that in Rubens' work is muscular.

When Rubens painted his *Descent from the Cross* (Pl. 29, p. 162), he involved his subjects in the arduous mechanics of lowering Christ's heavy body. The figure at the upper right having both hands engaged holds the death shroud in his teeth (Fig. 226). Despite the cumbersome process, the mourners are given grace of movement. The tenderness with which the body is received is intended to contrast with the brutality of the execution. Seen at close range, the painting of Christ's blood seems excessively lurid, but it must be remembered that this huge painting was for a large church and was to be seen from a distance by the whole congregation. Color helps us to realize how fully Rubens met the Counter-Reformation ideals of encouraging the faithful to identify with Christ's Passion. The flesh of the living has layers of color touched with the key red, which makes it glow with warmth and vitality. That of Christ has the grey of death and is contrasted with the ruddy-complexioned arms, the whiteness of the shroud, and the brilliant reds of his blood and the garment of St. John. The strongest and richest contrasts are thus grouped at the center around the broken figure, and the darker tones tend to merge with the deep blue-green of the sky. By focusing the light in the central area, away from the edges, the scene would thus appear to be more illusionistic in the darkened space of the church itself.

El Greco evokes unshed tears of anguish and disdains the materiality of this earth. Rubens induces the sweat of exertion and rejoices in sensuality. What El Greco shows lying beyond touch, Rubens addresses to our finger tips. While St. Maurice and his captains tread lightly on the earth, Rubens' race of giants grows from it. Rubens' Christ has known heroic physical exertion, that of El Greco only spiritual exercise.

Though comparison with El Greco may mislead the reader into doubting Rubens' religious sincerity, mystical asceticism has not been the only producer of great religious art. Rubens was passionately devoted to the Roman Catholic faith and spent a lifetime enriching the splendor of the altar with his paintings. Like the 15th-century Flemish artists before him, Rubens saw no contradictions in his attraction to the material world or the mythological past. He had optimistic confidence in himself and in the right and power of the Church. Like the Roman Catholic rulers and ecclesiastical patrons who paid for his secular art, he saw no sin in the healthy enjoyment of what lay outside dogma. When he painted religious subjects such as *St. Ignatius Exorcising Demons from the Church* (Fig. 227), he was attentive to the spirit of his theme. Just as St. Ignatius had recommended projecting oneself into the state of the subject of worship, Rubens' painting draws the viewer into the church to share the excitement of the miracle and the new hope of the sick who have been cleansed of the devil. Such projection is difficult if not impossible in the construction of El Greco's paintings. In Rubens' work, the foreground brilliance and posturing of the nearest figure draw us upward to the saint and back down into depth at the left where the devil quits the church.

228. PETER PAUL RUBENS. *The Last Judgment*. c. 1615. Oil on wood, 5′11⁵/₈″ × 3′11¹/₄″. Alte Pinakothek, Munich.

The diagonal in depth was a consistent stylistic device by which Rubens told a story, achieved dramatic and visual climax, and held his composition in forceful resolution.

The vigorous movement and sensual appearance of Rubens' figures are born in the rhythms of his brush and the creamy substance of his paint. To enjoy El Greco's color is to appreciate rare admixtures of tones, predominantly cool colors under a sometimes shrill light, restraint in the buildup of heavily pigmented areas, and, by comparison with Rubens, a less obtrusive trace of the brush. Showing warm light and lush sequences of opacity and transparency, Rubens' colors and glazes create the impression of pulse and blood lying just beneath the flesh. Rubens' brush swept with bravura across a form or delicately touched a tiny area demanding a highlight. The viewer looking at a Rubens' painting can sense the physical as well as aesthetic pleasure that the artist enjoyed as he worked. It is not difficult to comprehend Rubens' full involvement in the materiality of the medium that permitted him to re-create the sensuous world he loved.

When Rubens painted *The Last Judgment* (Fig. 228), he depicted the most sensual sinners in history. The damned flood downward from the seat of judgment and overwhelm the picture space, leaving the smaller and more remote upper regions for the elect. How paradoxical it seems that in this painting Rubens would acknowledge the sinfulness of voluptuous flesh, and then proceed for the rest of his lifetime to glorify the beautiful bodies of mythological heroes alongside similarly endowed saints and royalty. Just as so many artists before him, it is the spectacle of Hell rather than Heaven that calls forth his most inspired painting. Punishment rather than judgment, the provocative contortions and violent intertwining of condemned bodies rather than the composed bliss of the elect, predictably appealed to audiences drawn to depravity. Despite the diminished emphasis upon Heaven and imbalance between the saved and the damned, Rubens' pessimistic view of the fate of most of humanity is good Counter-Reformation propaganda.

Pieter Bruegel's *Triumph of Death* (Fig. 229), painted half a century before, seems to take a cynical attitude toward any efforts to buffer mankind from the facts of death. Unlike its medieval *memento mori* prototypes (Pl. 16, p. 98; Fig. 143), Bruegel's version of the encounter of the living and the dead is "catholic" only in its universality. Eyewitness to plagues and wars in the southern Netherlands, Bruegel could draw from personal experience concerning human vanity in the face of such disasters. Rubens championed the theological view of a Last Judgment and life in the hereafter. Bruegel, whose religious convictions are unknown, chose to show life stopping at the entrance to the coffin, with no assurance of an ultimate justice, of Heaven or Hell. There is no indication that the skeletal hordes dispatching the living or herding them into the open end of a gigantic coffin are the emissaries of Christ or the Devil. Instead of the Archangel with his valence, there is a skeleton beating a drum above the coffin, providing the insistent rhythm of death. Churches have been overrun by skeletons who perform irreverent services. The traditional figure of Death riding a pale horse is seen drawing a wagon load of skulls while nearby a king and a cardinal are in the grips of skeletons. In the lower right are the cavalier who dares death with his sword, the lovers oblivious to all, and the fool who crawls under the table. *The Triumph of Death* is so sweeping in its cataloguing of all forms of destruction on land and sea that it suggests the end of the world.

**The Religious Vision** Cataclysmic visions were fewer in the Counter-Reformation period than those of Heaven. So important was the Counter-Reformation concept of the religious vision that an increasing number of Roman churches in the

*left:* 229. Pieter Bruegel the Elder. *The Triumph of Death.* c. 1562. Oil on panel, 3′10″ × 5′3⁷/₈″. Prado, Madrid.

*below:* 230. Gianlorenzo Bernini. *The Ecstasy of St. Theresa.* 1646. Marble, life-size. Cornaro Chapel, Santa Maria della Vittoria, Rome.

17th century had their vaults illusionistically painted in grandiose compositions that permitted the faithful to look directly upward into Heaven. One of the largest and most powerful vault paintings was *The Triumph of St. Ignatius Loyola* (Pl. 30, p. 163) of Fra Andrea Pozzo (1642–1709). It celebrated the work and sacrifice of this order throughout the world and demonstrated the reception in Heaven of its leader and martyrs. Pozzo transformed the vault to give the impression that the church soars upward an additional two stories and is without any ceiling. Against the illusion of massive stable architectural elements, columns, and arches, Pozzo floated clusters of figures in a remarkable series of foreshortenings, so that from every point of view the scene is in perspective. The entire scene is suffused with radiance, accelerating the eye upward with no prolonged restraint. The message of the painting is that Heaven is directly accessible to the faithful.

The virtuoso 17th-century artists achieved illusions in a wide variety of media and a staggering range of subjects. The most gifted sculptor of the century and most ardent in his devotion to the aims of the Church was the Italian Gianlorenzo Bernini (1598–1680). Among his other talents were playwriting, stage design, painting, caricature, and architecture. His most spectacular production in sculpture is *The Ecstasy of St. Theresa* (Fig. 230). St. Theresa was a 16th-century saint best known for the visions she recorded. One of these, available to Bernini, describes the event portrayed in the sculpture:

> I saw an angel close to me, on my left side, in bodily form. This I am accustomed to see but very rarely. Though I have visions of angels frequently, yet I see them only by an intellectual vision, such as I have spoken of before. It is our Lord's will that in this vision I should see the angel in this wise. He was not large, but small of stature and most beautiful—his face burning as if he were one of the highest angels who seem to be all of fire. . . . I saw in his hand a long spear of gold and at the iron's point there seemed to be a little fire. He appeared to me to be thrusting it at times into my heart, and to pierce my very entrails: When he drew it out, he seemed to draw them all out also and to leave me all on fire with a great love of God. The pain was so great that I cried out, but at the same time the sweetness which that violent pain gave me was so excessive that I could not wish to be rid of it.

Bernini chose the moment between thrusts of the spear when the saint writhed in paroxysms of pleasure and pain. The erotic nature of both the vision and the sculpture is patent, but in keeping with the religious purpose of making the situation as vivid as possible. Bernini practiced the *Spiritual Exercises* of St. Ignatius of Loyola in order to absorb himself as deeply and accurately as possible into his subject. The nature of the vision excited his interest, particularly the coexistence of conflicting psychological states, imaged on the face of the saint with consummate virtuosity. Treating stone as if it were the wax of the models from which he worked, Bernini created the illusion of clouds, cloth, and flesh. The marble was warmed by light which entered from a concealed yellow glass window. There was no previous sculptural parallel to Bernini's deliberate and controlled use of light as both form and mystic symbol in his composition. The sculptural group is set behind a proscenium arch, and in the background golden shafts serve as radiant backdrops. Sacred sculpture and painted altarpieces, such as that by Rogier van der Weyden (Pl. 19, p. 116), had served as religious theater before. Bernini transformed the small chapel where the sculptural composition was housed into a sphere in which the differences between art and reality were suspended.

**Art for the Masses** The most influential painter of the 17th century was Michelangelo Merisi (1573–1609), known as Caravaggio after the town from which he came. His history of wild escapades and his attraction to violence contradicts the view that only pious men can paint great religious pictures. Dedicated to making art that would meet the needs of the masses, Caravaggio was a failure, for the people, conditioned by more aristocratic images of insincere piety, distrusted the stark reality of his types and the brutal realism with which he interpreted the Bible. It was among connoisseurs and artists that the recognition of his talent was achieved. When Caravaggio undertook the theme of religious revelation in his *Conversion of St. Paul* (Fig. 231), a painting intended for a darkened chapel, he startled parishioners by showing the rider flat on

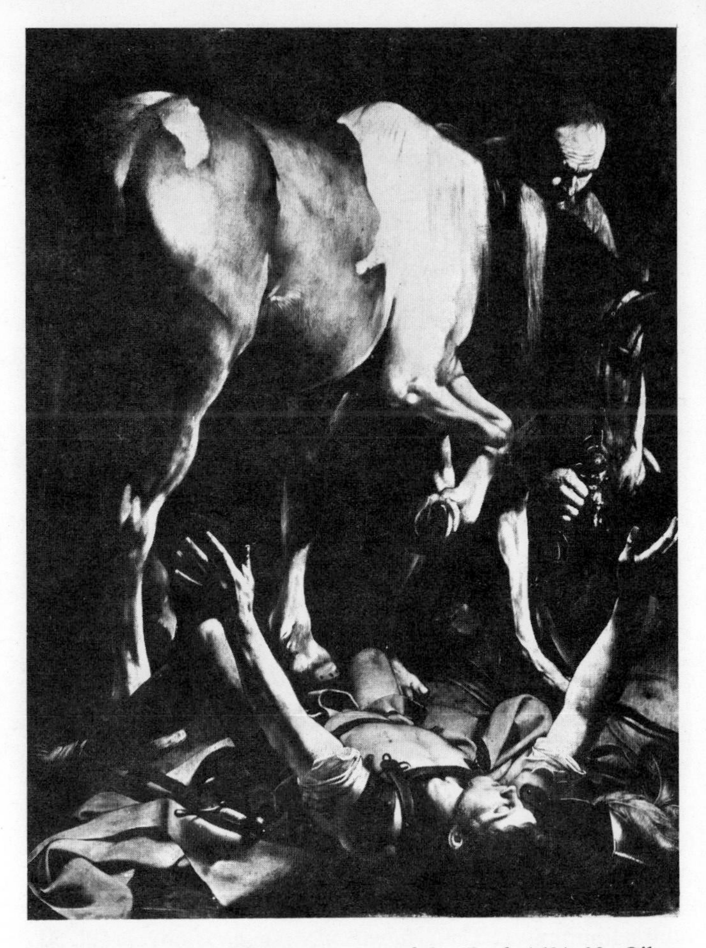

231. CARAVAGGIO. *The Conversion of St. Paul.* 1601–02. Oil on canvas, 7′6½″ × 5′9″. Cerasi Chapel, Santa Maria del Popolo, Rome.

his back, partially under his horse and with his head towards the viewer. Whether he wants to or not, the beholder is the vicarious witness to Saul's conversion to Paul, for he is made to feel as if the miracle takes place at arm's length. Cold, brilliant, penetrating light is the only evidence of God's presence, for Caravaggio could not bring himself to depict the supernatural as later Bernini and Pozzo were to do. Always he sought credibility in terms of the experience available to those of lowest estate or the uneducated. The action of the attendant who steadies the horse while contemplating the event is completely natural under the circumstances. The usefulness of the old man's gesture contrasts with that of the outflung arms of Paul by which the spiritual drama is revealed. Both gestures are instinctive and good theater. The indelibility of the conception resides in body surfaces made to seem firmer than those in life, or than Bernini's later carving in marble, and in the pure translucent light polarized against measureless shadows. Later artists such as Rembrandt (see Chap. 11) were to learn from

Caravaggio the dramatist that eyes or faces need not be highlighted or made focal points, but that light and shadow could compound, enrich, and dramatize the mystery of crucial events.

Still amazing is that Caravaggio worked directly on his paintings without recourse to preliminary drawings. Ironically Caravaggio's paintings of religious subjects had a strong influence on 17th-century secular painting. The painting of *Christ at Emmaus* (Pl. 31, p. 164) was intended for the guest room of a convent. It shows the two disciples Cleophas and Peter Simon seated with Christ, whom they had taken for a fellow pilgrim and invited to eat with them. The cockleshell on the disciple's tunic signifies that the men were pilgrims, like those who frequently used the convent's guest rooms. Caravaggio shows the moment when Christ reveals himself by blessing and breaking the bread. Coupled with the revealing gesture of Christ is the clarifying action of the strong light that poetically embodies the illumination of the minds of the disciples. Their reaction is violent, in contrast to the darkened face of the uncomprehending innkeeper. Caravaggio's message was simple, intended for the least sophisticated and humblest viewer: The common man may have direct knowledge of his God; the miraculous can occur without angels, halos, or opening of the skies; Christ's epiphany takes place in the heart of the faithful. The modest dress and table fare were obvious means to remind the faithful of Christ's humility. Not unlike the Flemish painters of the 15th century, Caravaggio detailed every surface provided by his subjects, from the contrasting complexions of the figures to the worm holes in the fruit. Caravaggio attached mystical feelings to the most tangible items. Unlike the Flemings, Caravaggio placed the action against a plain background and spotlighted only the figures and table. He involved the viewer more intimately in the scene through the violent foreshortening of the gestures and precarious balance of the fruit on the near edge of the table. The disciple at the left is so turned as to draw the eye immediately to the hand of Christ and thence to His face, the table, and the figure at the right. The strenuous, extended gesture of the latter, which seems to push into our space, is paralleled by the angle of the table before him, thus harnessing the number of strong movements that otherwise would mitigate each other. Caravaggio has demonstrated the expressiveness the profile is capable of. Often using models taken into his studio from the street, the painter was at his most forceful in painting rugged or picturesque types, and most disconcerting to the public when he attempted the holy subject of Christ's head.

Many Church officials, and it would seem the general public, found Caravaggio's painting vulgar or lacking in decorum and unnecessarily impoverishing of the holy personages. He was criticized for painting distracting objects, such as the still-life arrangement of the table, which undermined the drama of the moment. Because he avoided elaborate and traditional didacticism, Caravaggio's work was also condemned for not being self-explanatory. To those unacquainted with the Biblical story, the supper may have seemed like an ordinary secular event. And, in fact, the 17th century was to see a further obscuring of the lines that separated religious from secular painting.

Art of the 16th and 17th centuries was filled with vitality, and religious art nourished within itself even broader secular human interest than before. Simple lines of overall development do not exist, and in each period there are divergent and contradictory styles. Energy, affluence, recognition of individuality, great issues, and powerful patrons and institutions all combined for enormous productivity, which was as uneven in quality as it was in styles and viewpoints. Along with sincere and passionately inspired personal statements of faith, Counter-Reformation art also laid the foundations for banal, insincere, commercial religious art which afflicts too many churches today. Side by side with the continued emergence of many artists of genius, bad religious art came into being on an unprecedented scale. The means for making a convincing representation of a lovely pious Virigin and adorable Christ child were henceforth easily available to any painter who would trade on the sentiment of an undiscriminating congregation and clergy.

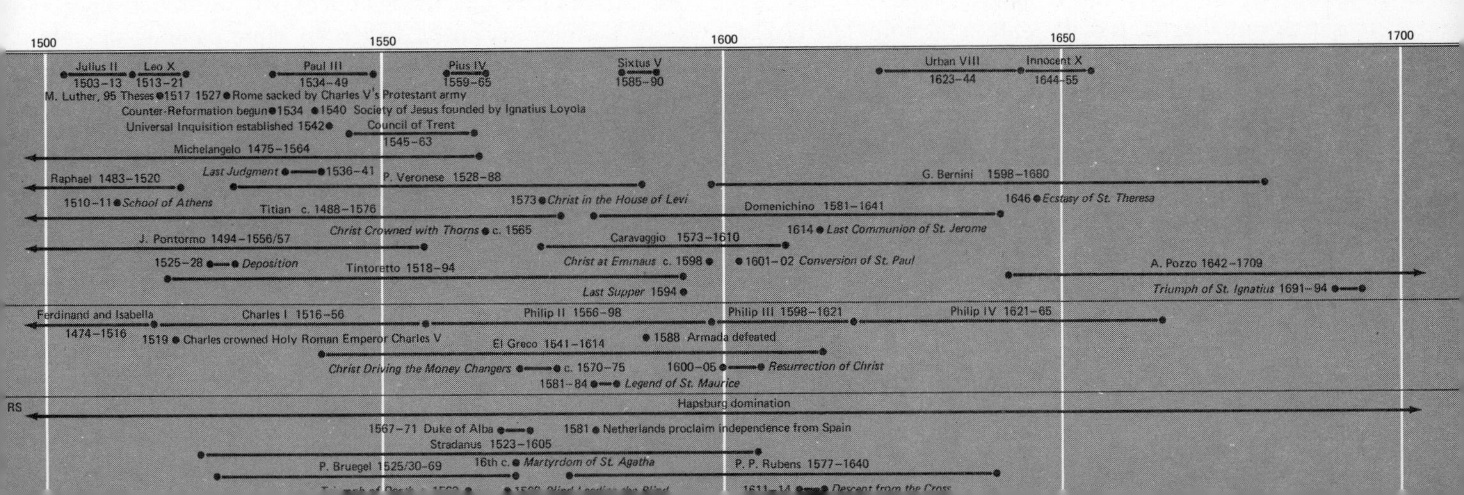

# 10

During the 17th century, European painting broadened its base to include varied and intimate secular objects, as well as great religious painting. Both Roman Catholic and Protestant Holland derived important secular art from the more customary intellectual sources, such as ancient literature, and from folk traditions and business, social, and domestic life—in subjects that examined the unethical, irreverent, sexual, vulgar, comic, and passive aspects of human conduct. These *genre* paintings explored the daily living of the peasant and middle classes and depicted persons of more human dimension than the imposing figures in 15th-century art. The Renaissance had rendered the outward appearance of men caught in heroic action or serious contemplation, but during the Baroque period the expression of vivid emotions and the workings of the mind became paramount. In 17th-century art the full range of human animation came much closer to realization.

Genre painting resists strict categorization, for it often overlaps into religious, allegorical, or historical art. Essentially, it consists in relinquishing climactic or historical moments in favor of activities that are a part of daily life. It usually deals with *types* of persons involved in *types* of common occurrences, although frequently a painter goes beyond typification and into portraiture to depict participants or chooses unique moments in the lives of his subjects. Early genre painting was based upon the growing tolerance of secular art, a basic optimism toward earthly existence, and curiosity about the way people pass their days. Although this art form avoids the ritual of religious and political imagery, it nevertheless concerns itself with the rituals of daily life in the home and tavern, the bank house and brothel. In this fidelity to everyday human life, genre art contributed to the evolution of a broadly imitative form of painting best defined as *naturalism*.

Social conscience was not the motivation for depicting peasant life, for the misery, oppressions, and tragedies of the lower middle classes did not find their way into 17th-century art. Favored themes were those of diversion, local or class customs, or quiet revery, themes which did not threaten established social order but which provided the upper classes with vicarious experiences. Thus genre art was not democratic, and it reaffirmed existing class distinctions. The security enjoyed in the 17th century by Church and monarchical state resulted in a relaxation of the demands made on painters, which enabled artists to execute both official work and genre painting.

In Holland, specialization arose during this century, so that artists painted only landscapes, portraits, still lifes, or genre art, depending upon their success with the market. Genre art, which was rarely commissioned, denoted the double edge of freedom and material insecurity that accrued to the artist during the Baroque period. In Holland, the market was overloaded by midcentury, and painters were forced to assume additional jobs or give up painting altogether.

While there is much aesthetic value in 17th-century genre painting, the public who bought or speculated in this art—churchmen, aristocracy, and middle class alike—was guided primarily by fidelity to appearance and could hardly be considered connoisseurs. Genre painting was intended for the modest scale of the home and for greater intimacy of viewing, so that its format was usually smaller than that of the grandiose paintings done for the Church or royal courts. Although not entirely uninfluenced by religious and official painting, the genre artist did have great license in making his paintings.

The table frequently appears in Baroque genre painting as a compositional and social catalyst. In religious art the table was occasionally used to hold books of Church scholars or devotional objects of a saint; it was most frequently identified with the sacred drama of the Last Supper (Figs. 219, 220) and Christ at Emmaus (Pl. 31, p. 164). Renaissance painters also utilized it to link the historical past with contemporary social customs, as noted earlier. In genre painting the table became the natural locus for social occasions or for portraying individual human activity.

The Flemish Pieter Bruegel presented such an occasion—the wedding feast (Pl. 32, p. 181)—in which the table serves as a meeting place for a segment of the community. Though not the first, Bruegel was the most gifted painter of his century in depicting the daily life of the Flemish peasants. The little we know of his biography indicates that he was not a peasant but a highly educated townsman, whose paintings were bought and admired by kings and intellectuals. Bruegel regarded his art as a means of recording his study of man, in the light of advanced

# THE TABLE IN BAROQUE SECULAR ART

contemporary secular theories and his own empirical experience. Bruegel's art reflects his astuteness as an observer and expresses neither criticism nor compassion. He saw the peasant as an unreasoning creature who passively submitted to forces greater than himself—to heredity, customs, and traditions. Bruegel's figures are thus motivated by simple, uncomplicated drives and enact their lives automatically, often with great vigor, if not with great cheer.

Not content with social reporting, Bruegel brought to art a gift of lucid analysis and a genius for storytelling that elevates his *Peasant Wedding* from a prosaic event to good theater. The setting is a grain-filled barn after the harvest, in which an overflow of guests celebrate the personal harvest of the farmer's daughter. She sits coyly and smugly beneath a symbolic crown hung on a green cloth. The full grain stacks and the ripe bride are meaningfully associated, as are the groom and the fertility symbol of the crossed sheaves hanging before his eyes. Art historians were unable to agree on identification of the groom, but the literary historian Gilbert Highet found him in the dark-clad, intoxicated figure in the center, just to the left of the rear figure holding a door used as a serving tray. The ill-mannered groom and his glaring parents seated opposite are wealthy townspeople, and, as Highet points out, Bruegel encourages our speculations on the wedding night and the married life of the bridal couple—though the painting's evidence makes the future quite clear.

232. CARAVAGGIO. *Bacchus*. c. 1590. Oil, $38^1/_2 \times 33^1/_2$″. Uffizi, Florence.

A few of the subthemes in the nuptial drama involve the friar's earnest pleas for subsidy from the obdurate landlord at the far right, who seems to enjoy the occasion less than does his dog; the bagpiper's longing gaze at the distant food; and the contrast between the little girl cleaning her plate and the bride's brother filling a jug at the left. The activity of the latter recalls Christ's changing of the water into wine at Cana, and the diagonal composition of the long table and triangular grouping in the left foreground can be found in 16th-century paintings such as those of Tintoretto (Fig. 220). The ample figures are hard-edged in their firm outlines, so that the pile of round jugs in the basket invites an ironic comparison with the peasants who emptied them and with the piled-up figures in the doorway who also wait to be filled.

The broad secularization of painting in the 17th century introduced themes involving satisfaction of the senses, in particular gratification of the palate. Baroque painters recorded all forms of table manners and dietary preference, with a gusto that is unmatched by the full-color photographic illustrations appearing in cookbooks today. For example, the young Caravaggio painted a well-fed, contemplative boy in the guise of Bacchus (Fig. 232), which is possibly a self-portrait. The wine god's attributes afforded the painter the objects of a still-life study, just as the model's features lent themselves to naturalism rather than Classical idealization. This inclusion of portraiture within a larger, defined context is termed a *portrait situation*.

*below:* 233. ANNIBALE CARRACCI. *The Bean Eater*. c. 1585. Oil on canvas, $22^3/_8 \times 26^3/_4$". Galleria Colonna, Rome.

*bottom:* 234. JACOB JORDAENS. *The Satyr and the Peasant Family*. c. 1612–18. Oil on canvas, $6'3^1/_2" \times 6'8"$. Musées Royaux des Beaux-Arts, Brussels.

As was evident in his *Christ at Emmaus* (Pl. 31, p. 164), Caravaggio was intrigued by the half-length figure, which forced the viewer's focus upon the subject. As well as a catalogue of the effects of light upon varied textures, the painting is a study in many types of balance, from the way the elegant glass is held, to the disposition of fruit and the wine carafe on the table, and even to the languorous position of the semi-reclining body. Curiously, the most immediate and seemingly stable shape is that of the glass supported by three fingers—which would suggest an unusually sober god of the grape. Later in the 17th century, artists were to show in extravagant ways the stronger effects and imbalance caused by alcohol, a tone that Caravaggio avoided in his restrained make-believe Bacchus.

A contemporary of Caravaggio, Annibale Carracci (1560–1609), for the first time in history centered a painting on a man eating (Fig. 233); a rugged anonymous peasant fills his mouth with beans while clutching a roll. The great polarity of Baroque painting is shown in the contrast between Domenichino's depiction of St. Jerome receiving the Eucharistic wafer (Fig. 215) and Carracci's *Bean Eater*. The former eats to partake of Christ's body and so ensure his future in Heaven, while the latter is concerned with satisfying his stomach and staying alive. The association of the human mouth with both sacred and secular rituals has an interesting mythological analogy in a painting by the Flemish artist Jacob Jordaens (1593–1678) that shows a satyr at a table with a peasant family (Fig. 234). Jordaens was illustrating a fable of Aesop in which peasants who had given shelter to a cold and hungry satyr invited him to their table. The satyr saw the man blowing on his hands and was told this was to warm them; then he watched the peasant blow on his soup and was told this was to cool it. The satyr thereupon left the table, for he wisely distrusted those who blow hot and cold with the same breath. Jordaens enjoyed painting the heavy peasant types right down to their bare feet. In this instance, the wisdom of the proverb had to compete with the artist's succulent rendering of flesh.

Jordaens' *The King Drinks* (Fig. 235) is a Flemish folklore celebration of Epiphany, an occasion for an entire clan to assemble and feast. At Epiphany "Kings's tickets" were sold in Antwerp. The old man has become reigning monarch by having drawn the lucky ticket among those at the table. His drinking signals an explosion of festivity. To each relative he has assigned a mock title for his "court"—the "Singer," the "Cock," the "Doctor," and the "Spinster." Here Baroque art has delighted in discovering the individual, consciously or not, lost in his abandonment to feeling. In such 17th-century paintings were introduced raucous, laughing figures, whereas formerly only angels or the Madonna smiled decorously as a sign of divine grace. The Renaissance and 16th-century theme of mythical satyrs and nymphs rioting at a picnic in an ancient wood has been restaged around the family table as an orgy of the senses.

*right:* 235. JACOB JORDAENS. *The King Drinks*. 1638. Oil on canvas, 8′7½″ × 9′4⅝″. Musées Royaux des Beaux-Arts, Brussels.

*below:* 236. ADRIAEN BROUWER. *The Smokers*. c. 1630. Oil on canvas, 18⅛ × 14⅜″. Metropolitan Museum of Art, New York (Michael Friedsam Collection, 1932).

Both in form and content, this is a painting concerned with the five senses. The figures make or respond to noise, catch the eye with exaggerated or grotesque expressions, fondle objects sensuously, inhale a variety of odors, and savor a staggering array of food and drink. In a way, this painting is also a study of cycles, distinguishing the flesh of young and old and presenting a broad range of expressions from anticipation to satiation. Jordaens displays great virtuosity in demonstrating the number of ways people may be portrayed with their mouths open. Faces border on caricature. The artist's insight into the ritual rather than spontaneous character of the event appears in the forced quality of some of the jeering expressions.

The painting itself assaults the senses of the viewer. Strongly flavored with reds, blues, and yellows, its silhouettes seem to weave back and forth and defy equilibrium. The dark jacket and relative stability of the musician standing to the "king's" left serve as foil and anchorage for the agitated goings-on. The costumes and flesh of the figures are painted so as to stress their appeal to the touch as well as to the eye. Depicting a scene at once hilarious and vulgar, the artist reserves good taste for the actual mechanics of painting, for color and design rather than subject matter. Above the "king" are the words, "It is sweet to be admitted to a friendly table."

Such a proverb written above *The Smokers* (Fig. 236) by the Flemish painter Adriaen Brouwer (1605/06–38) would con-

*left:* 237. JEAN LE CLERC. *Memento Mori.* 1615–20. Oil on canvas, 3′11½″ × 5′8½″. Isaac Delgado Museum of Art, New Orleans (gift of Mrs. William Helis, Sr.).

*below:* 238. QUENTIN MASSYS. *A Money Changer and His Wife.* 1514. Oil on panel, 28 × 27″. Louvre, Paris.

stitute a fine irony. Brouwer was preoccupied with the boisterous life around the tavern table; his small paintings catalogue drinking bouts, brawls, cooking, eating, gossiping, and gambling. His sitters appear to be fellow artists rather than peasants. Daringly, he devoted entire paintings to gross types with bulbous inflamed noses and gaping mouths, or to sleeping drunks with deluded notions of exalted status. His self-portraits show a discoloration and deterioration in his own face due to alcohol. Brouwer's *The Smokers*, probably done in the 1630s, is a personal avowal of manliness and the ethic of being oneself: The artist can drink and smoke with the best, take practical jokes, withstand pain, and not give a damn for whoever looks at his painting. Naturally disdainful of contemporary theories on composition and drawing, Brouwer sketched coarsely, but his characters and his painting convey the disorder of a tavern atmosphere, with its stale smells and murky lighting. The paint is applied ruggedly and with gusto, the technique also affirming his distaste for the delicate and precious. His strokes and tones convincingly render the garments and flesh of those poor in purse but rich in their enjoyment of earthly pleasures.

**Moralizing and Allegory** From Holland in the early 17th century came the morbid association of food with human vanity or life's brevity. In a large painting of an interrupted banquet (Fig. 237) attributed to the French artist Jean Le Clerc (1587–1633), a skeleton dramatically intrudes at the right. His presence warns *memento mori* ("Remember that you must die") and also evokes the fear on the part of Catholics that sudden death would not permit the last rites. The festive costumes and the highlighting of the man and woman to the right suggest that this may have been a marriage supper and that it is the bridegroom whom Death calls. The painter pulls out all dramatic stops in contrasting the vehement reactions of the revelers to Death's apparition. Rather than terror or awe, the sybaritic guests at the left seem to register dismay and displeasure at the meal's interruption. The broad stagey character of the gestures and the extremes of light and shadow unmistakably place the artist among Caravaggio's following.

**Business at the Table** Secular paintings of genre subjects involving the table go back to the early 16th century; one of the earliest of these introduces the theme of business. In *A Money Changer and His Wife* (Fig. 238), the Flemish painter

*above:* Plate 32. PIETER BRUEGEL THE ELDER. *Peasant Wedding*. c. 1565. Oil on panel, 3′8⅞″ × 5′4″. Kunsthistorisches Museum, Vienna. (See pp. 176, 177.)

*left:* Plate 33. DIEGO VELÁZQUEZ. *The Water Seller of Seville*. c. 1619. Oil on canvas, 41½ × 31½″. Wellington Museum, London (Crown copyright reserved). (See p. 183.)

Plate 34. JAN VERMEER. *The Artist in His Studio*. c. 1665–70. Oil on canvas, 4′4″ × 3′8″. Kunsthistorisches Museum, Vienna. (See pp. 188, 189, Fig. 250.)

Quentin Massys (1465/66–1530) showed the couple receiving a call from a client, who is visible in the small convex mirror on the table. The painting served as a double portrait honoring the husband's profession and his wife's piety. In the painting of St. Eligius by Petrus Christus (Fig. 158), secular objects help identify a holy man, but here a holy book has become the pious attribute of a businessman's spouse. The possible significance of her divided attention between the prayer book and the scales—a touch that might at first glance seem purely sardonic—was to certify the honesty of their business. In a figurative sense, the convex glass reflects the delight of the Flemish painters in mirroring the actual world. Its small curved surface allowed the tour de force of simulating greater space than that in which the couple actually sits. Paintings and prints such as this found their way to Rome and were known to Caravaggio, who probably was strongly influenced by their format and crisp, lifelike style.

The table also appears as an adjunct to business in *The Water Seller of Seville* (Pl. 33, p. 181) by the Spanish artist Diego Velázquez (1599–1660). A painter of Spanish royalty, Velázquez did not spare his brilliant talent in portraying a street vendor named El Corzo, his young clients, and the modest objects of his trade. The mundane act of selling water has been solemnized by the painter into an almost sacramental event, and it is not improbable that Velázquez had the sacrament of the Eucharist in mind. He may also have intended the scene to comment on the three ages of man, with the oldest passing on the gift of life. There is no intimation of the noise and jostling of the streets. The man drinking is in shadow, while in strong illumination the vendor and a young boy receiving a glass seem to share silently in a meditative union. Both in content and in form Velázquez has changed small coin into gold. The strongly individual qualities of El Corzo, of the youth holding a glass which contains a fig to keep the water fresh, and even of the jugs rise above typicality and are impressed on the memory. The tractable face of the youth contrasts with the lined face of the older man and with the jug upon which his hand rests. There is no overt attempt at pathos. The large objects and three-quarter figures, presented close to the viewer, have a restrained dignity and powerfully assert their worth. Immobility adds to their eloquence. The effect is obtained through a formal closure of shapes, a rough ovular form that holds the eye within the frame. The large jug leads the eye to the shadow of the smaller and to the hand of the man; the small jug is tangent to the boy's wrist which directs the viewer to the glass, to the boy's head, and to those of the other two figures; finally, the smock's curvature returns the eye to the large jug and anchors the oval to the frame at the right. A few tones—chiefly grey, terra cotta, white, and flesh color—are applied over large areas with deft and subtle nuance; reserved for the glass and droplets of moisture on the jug are the most brilliant highlights. The lucid lighting and the firm drawing of the forms are countered by the virtuoso painterly manner in which the rich pigment has been applied to the canvas.

Although possessing an ancient history as a profession, prostitution was not introduced as a theme for printmaking and painting until the 16th century. Mary Magdalen had been shown much earlier in religious paintings, but always as a penitent (Pl. 19, p. 116) or closed in a convent. A painting known as *The Procuress* (Fig. 239), and thought to be by Jan Vermeer (1632–75), is one of many done by Netherlandish artists on the theme of commercial love. Unlike predecessors who often dwelled on the ugliness of lechers, whores, and madams, Vermeer shows two well-dressed, handsome young men clearly able to afford their pleasure with an attractive professional. The drinker at the left smiles in our direction as an indication of his mood, but also as a way of welcoming the viewer as an accomplice. Unusual for Vermeer is the involved range of expressions and the interchange between his subjects. As was frequently done by other Dutch artists, his placement of the decoratively patterned rug over the table of the foreground afforded painterly enrichment. The paintings composed of men and women that Vermeer did later are quieter and more circumspect, describing encounters and courtships that are restrained and socially acceptable.

239. JAN VERMEER(?). *The Procuress*. 1656. Oil on canvas, 4′8¼″ × 4′3¼″. Gemäldegalerie, Dresden.

**Games and Music at Table** The pastime of gaming, with its elements of chance and cheating, delighted an age in which high morality was so vigorously championed by the powerful force of the churches. Though not the first card game painted in history—the theme had entered painting from the North earlier in the 16th century—Caravaggio's *Card Sharps* (Fig. 240) was the most influential. Lost during the last century, it survives only in photographs and numerous copies but, like so many of his other works, was definitely seen by foreign artists visiting Rome. Despite the acute characterization and delineation of the figures, this was not a painting simply extracted from some scene in a contemporary Roman tavern. The players, dressed in costumes of a fanciful character, are set against a background which is so bare that it eliminates conjecture as to locale and throws the actors into brilliant relief. Within the self-imposed restrictions of depicting a few figures at close range and within a tight space, Caravaggio has told a good story with great vigor. Artful arrangement of the poses allows one to see all phases of the deception and results in movement toward the center from both sides. He has shown the middle figure executing two gestures at once, and this skill at depicting one person doing two things simultaneously deeply impressed his contemporaries. In addition, he challenged future artists by his ability to render the human head three times in close proximity and from different viewpoints. Ironically, in view of the previous symbolism of light (Fig. 220), the profile of the card sharp at the right is given fullest illumination. Unquestionably, Caravaggio's interest in games was personal: on one occasion, as a result of a violent scoring dispute in a tennis match, he fatally stabbed his partner in the groin. Despite the artist's personal notoriety, *Card Sharps* was purchased by a cardinal—in itself a commentary on the inconsistent moral conservatism of the Counter-Reformation.

A Dutch painter who worked in Rome from 1604 to 1616 and who consciously took whole compositional and stylistic ideas from Caravaggio was Hendrick Terbrugghen (1587/88–1629). It is a euphemism of painters and art historians to say that one artist "borrows" from another, for there is no historical evidence that this was a two-way arrangement. The strongly centralized focus, the intense concentration of animated figures in a seemingly airless space, and the clear hard light that Caravaggio made possible for painters deeply appealed to the Dutchman. As lifelike as Terbrugghen's *Three Men Playing Dice* (Fig. 241) may seem, it is a reminder that, throughout the history of art, artists have painted pictures from other pictures—in other words, that art comes from life *and* art. Painters of the 17th century not only studied the faces and movements of their models but also looked to notable artists such as Caravaggio for means of achieving firm volumes, expressive gestures, effective lighting, and placement of half-length figures within a limited rectangular area. The merit of any pictorial synthesis lies in the extent to which an artist can unobtrusively integrate with his own what he has stolen, and thus impress his audience that he has gone beyond his predecessor, for instance, by making better use of modeling under clear light or in contrasting the expressive properties of hands and faces. Caravaggio's great reputation resides not only in the fertility of his ideas but also in the freshness and invention his conceptions continue to affirm when compared with most of those who had the opportunity to improve upon them. Though Terbrugghen's effort produced a good, vivid painting having perhaps more vibrant and sensuous color and fuller and firmer surfaces than its Italian source, it nonetheless stands in the same relation to the *Card Sharps* as a colonizer to a pioneer.

In *The Cheat* (Fig. 242), painted by the French artist Georges de la Tour (1593–1652), the table is again the setting

*opposite left:* 240. Caravaggio. *Card Sharps.* c. 1593. Oil on canvas, 3′3″ × 4′6″. Formerly Sciarra Collection, Rome.

*opposite below:* 241. Hendrick Terbrugghen. *Three Men Playing Dice.* 1623. Oil on canvas, 33 × 44⁷/₈″. Minneapolis Institute of Arts (The Dunwoody Fund).

*right:* 242. Georges de la Tour. *The Cheat.* c. 1630. Oil on canvas, 3′5³/₄″ × 4′11¹/₂″. Collection Pierre Landry, Paris.

*below:* 243. Valentin de Boullogne. *The Concert (Soldiers and Bohemians).* c. 1620–25. Oil on canvas, 3′11″ × 5′2¹/₂″. Indianapolis Museum of Art (William A. Zumpfe Memorial Fund).

for intrigue, deceit, and downfall. La Tour's use of this theme followed a stay in Rome, where he may have encountered the pictorial idea. The subject may be related to the Biblical parable of the Prodigal Son; this theme, the downfall and return of the errant son, was favored by Roman Catholic authorities in support of the sacrament of penance against the Protestants. Both the painting and the card game are highly contrived. The players are garbed in what for the time were outlandish costumes. The deck is stacked against the young man at the right in such a way that if the aces don't get his money, wine and the courtesan at the table will. The wily cheat has an affected air of nonchalance, as he reaches for an ace in his belt. The eyes and hands alone are sufficient to tell the story. All the hand movements have a suave boneless ease that serves to enact the deception and also to tie the figures together visually. The shadowing of the cheat's face recalls that of Judas in paintings of the Last Supper (Figs. 219, 220). This dark deed, however, is performed in daylight, which coolly illuminates the firm, smooth volumes of the bodies and the sparkle of the shiny accessories. The airless milieu makes possible a meticulous clarity of detail in presenting types who themselves seem all surface and no depth.

Caravaggio's influence was often passed on through Italian followers, who in turn taught painters such as the Frenchman Valentin de Boullogne (1594–1632). Such genre paintings as his *Soldiers and Bohemians* (Fig. 243) are important historically because they show the growing separation of painting not only from religious symbolism but also from secular allegory or moralizing. Earlier we have seen how ancient pagan monuments were used in conjunction with Christian subjects, as in Mantegna's *St. James Led to His Execution* (Fig. 188). Here Valentin uses a Roman architectural fragment for an inn table. In the 16th century, musical instruments often symbolized Christian virtues, godlike attributes, or intellectual and poetic gifts, but in this work they are instead the natural means of pleasure for low social types. The pocket-picking incident at the left was one of the ordinary hazards of frequenting public inns. Without the powerful concentration of Caravaggio's *Card Sharps,* Valentin has disposed his figures more casually in depth around the table, which is now set on a diagonal. The color is comparably softened, with a simple triad of reds, yellows, and blues played off harmoniously against one another and against the colder greys and the dark browns of the costumes and setting, in what is a more painterly style than that of Caravaggio. Instead of striving to create the illusion of actual textures, Valentin adapts the movement and weight of his brush and pigment to suggest a change of surfaces and stuffs—the hard sheen of metal, for

244. MAERTEN VAN HEEMSKERCK. *Family Portrait*. c. 1530. Oil on panel, 3′10½″ × 4′7″. Staatliche Kunstsammlungen, Kassel.

example. The relaxed mood of the entire painting arises from the effortless way that each figure twists in a different direction, turning in and out of the light, free to move in a more generous orbit than that provided by Caravaggio. The common device of an interlocutor between the viewer and the action, first used in the 15th century, is seen here in the soldier at the left who looks over his shoulder in our direction; it is, however, made less obvious by casting much of the face in shadow and giving greater prominence to the foreshortened blue sleeve. Less tightly composed than Caravaggio's scenes, Valentin's compositions introduced a relaxed air into French painting.

The table, a natural place for the family to assemble, was often used for a portrait situation. One of the earliest family portraits utilizing still life and the table (Fig. 244) was done by the Flemish artist Maerten van Heemskerck (1498–1574). The prosperous looking family is rather self-consciously arranged; the figures are posed in clear separation, not unlike the objects on the table, and their silhouettes are sharply delineated against the sky. Outdoor eating was not altogether unusual in the Netherlands, and yet Heemskerck's work has the contrived air of having been done in the studio, with a natural backdrop painted in later. The pose of the naked child and its mother may have been intended to recall paintings of the Madonna and Child—an association that would not be impious in the kind of well-to-do and proper family represented. Heemskerck, perhaps aware of the previous lack of easy interrelationships between figures in Flemish art, seems to have tried to infuse his work with the graceful movement of the Italian art he admired. The result is a rather stilted synthesis, but the painter's richness of observation keeps a certain compelling attraction.

The table as identified with the unity and humility of the family can be seen in *Peasants at Supper* (Fig. 245), painted by the French Louis Le Nain (1593–1648). The table is the means by which the family comes together each day and shares the quiet pleasures of home, hearth, and board. Absent from the painting, however, are the noise, movement, and disorder that one would expect to find during or even after the evening meal. There is no overt rapport between the figures: those in the foreground look toward the viewer, those in the shadows gaze into the fire. Le Nain, perhaps seeking to extol the probity of the peasant, cast him in an artificial mold, and each figure is very consciously posed. The child in the lower right corner, like the objects carefully distributed near him, serves as a visual stabilizer for the composition. Each person is carefully turned to counterbalance another figure, eliminating any impression of volition or spontaneity. The general air of decorum in the peasant hut resembles official painting of French royalty. Le Nain stressed the peasant's reflective capacity and graceful composure, rather than his life of arduous labor or moments of energetic diversion. The painting's strength lies largely in the realization of the materiality of figures, objects, and setting. The hard reality of the bodies and garments is heightened by soft gradients of shadow and the way the light rebounds from surfaces. Le Nain displays and elicits a certain detachment, a refusal to become deeply and emotionally involved with the subjects; yet he holds them aloof with obvious respect.

The Dutch painter Jan Steen (1629–79) has arranged *The Inn Garden* (Fig. 246) with more of the familiar casualness or disarray of a family outing. Seventeenth-century Dutch painting of the family stressed mutual good feeling and the enjoyment of food and congenial surroundings; any disquieting notes are absent. Sociologically, Steen's family is different from that of Heemskerck and not as self-consciously concerned with projecting a staid public image for posterity. Such pleasant views of the family had strong appeal in the Dutch art market, which was widely supported by people like those portrayed. Such painting flattered their pride and increased their enjoyment of national customs, games, social events, and peaceful diversion in convivial surroundings. Perhaps Steen, with his good eye for relaxed postures and situations, was—rahter than Rembrandt—a typical Dutch painter of the era.

For some Dutch artists, influenced greatly by Caravaggio, the table signified the opportunity for melodramatic enactment of debauchery or perverse conduct, but Pieter de Hooch (1629–*c*. 1684) satisfied his countrymen's middle-class taste by showing tables in settings of propriety and quiet sociability. His paintings frequently show tables in arbors, intimate courtyards, or neat interiors around which are gathered well-bred gentlemen who play an honest game of cards, imbibe with discretion, or converse wittily with pleasant hostesses. One of De Hooch's finest paintings is *The Mother at the Cradle* (Fig. 247). Here the table, though set off to the side, is identified with domesticity, with the care and vigilance of the wife for the children and the home. This ideal of insulated, constant security is measured out in the relation of the mother to the cradle and in the cool geometrical rightness and sun-warmed atmosphere of the rooms. Everything is in its correct place to compose an ideal home and a beautifully arranged painting. Even the dog has turned his head at a right angle to the floor tiles and is tangent to the door frame, taking the eye both into the vestibule and toward the mother. From the exterior comes not a suggestion of the sounds and sights of Holland's political anguish but only a dreamlike stillness, the reassuring heat of the sun, and the fragrance of well-tended gardens.

*left:* 245. LOUIS LE NAIN. *Peasants at Supper.* 1645–48. Oil on canvas, 3′8½″ × 5′2½″. Louvre, Paris.

*above:* 246. JAN STEEN. *The Inn Garden.* c. 1670. Oil on canvas, 26¾ × 22⅞″. Staatliche Museen, Berlin.

*below left:* 247. PIETER DE HOOCH. *The Mother at the Cradle.* 1659–60. Oil on canvas, 36⅜ × 39⅜″. Staatliche Museen, Berlin.

*below right:* 248. SCHOOL OF FONTAINEBLEAU. *Lady at Her Toilette.* c. 1550. Oil on canvas, 41⅜ × 27⅞″. Musée des Beaux-Arts, Dijon.

*left:* 249. JAN VERMEER. *A Woman Weighing Gold.* c. 1660. Oil on canvas, $16^{1}/_{2} \times 13^{3}/_{4}''$. National Gallery of Art, Washington, D.C. (Widener Collection).

**The Table and Self-preoccupation** In many ways 16th- and 17th-century art penetrated new areas of life. As taste for the intimate developed, painting invaded the bedroom, which in previous art had been allowed only as the setting for holy events (Fig. 145), such as the Virgin's death (Fig. 154). In the mid-16th century an unknown artist working at Fontainebleau Palace introduced into painting what might be called *self-preoccupation* (Fig. 248). Titian and the Venetians had depicted such subjects as Venus at her toilette, but the themes were from mythology. Here, the near-naked lady surely was readily identifiable at the French court. Similar paintings done of the mistresses of French kings became so popular they were copied. Shown before her dressing table, the young woman touches her necklace with one hand holds a ring with the other. This double gesture descended from Greek sculptures of Venus and can be seen in Renaissance paintings (Pl. 24, p. 136; Fig. 190). The ring has been interpreted as an erotic sign or as the indication of a desire for marriage. As in Venetian paintings of Venus in her bedroom, a maidservant is shown in the background, where a mirror again reflects the young woman's face. Conceivably, she was being presented as Venus. For contemporary sophisticated society the various objects and the mirror would have held meaning, but today we are not sure of their connotations. For instance, is the painting a veiled reference to vanity? Courtly taste, as much as artistic style, influenced the elegant sensousness of the torso. Such art was coolly detached toward nakedness, unlike the ripe flesh that later would melt under the brush of Rubens. In the focus upon jewels and fine materials, in the attitude toward sex, there is an unmistable preciosity.

After 1650, in Holland, Vermeer helped restore a quiet decorum to the theme of the table. Constants in his art are sunlit corners of elegant whitewashed rooms, furnished with carefully disposed tables, chairs, and paintings. The calm, handsome young women who inhabit Vermeer's interiors exemplify Dutch culture just before the disastrous wars of the 1670s. Standing near or seated at sturdy tables, they make lace, read, write, converse with military suitors, admire themselves, or sleep—and are conforting images of sedentary feminine diversion. In *A Woman Weighing Gold* (Fig. 249) are juxtaposed a painting of the Last Judgment and a girl holding a balance. A devout Catholic convert, Vermeer could have intended a symbolic significance—possibly for the religious conscience of the girl, who is faithfully fulfilling her responsibility. Her position is below the figure of Christ, which the Archangel Michael would assume to weigh the souls of the resurrected. The violence and terror of the Judgment Day scene make an ironic contrast with the stilled life of the room. Historically interesting is the religious painting seen, not hung over an altar, but now displayed in a private room.

Balance is not only the theme of the painting but the key to Vermeer's compositional ideas. Not unsympathetically, the woman is arranged in the setting, like the other objects, so that her hand and the scale must be grasped by the eye along with the picture frame behind, then seen in relation to the open box and her left hand. The casually arranged cloth on the table serves to draw us to both the source of light and the girl. The tangible, rigid armature formed by the right angle of the table against the wall and the alignment of the woman with the painting further the movement of the light and its refusal to be shaped into clearly defined patterns. In this small segment of the visible world Vermeer revealed the poetic potential of life.

**The Artist's Table** Vermeer's private life belied the tranquillity of his paintings. Before his death in 1675 he suffered financial setbacks, and his widow filed for bankruptcy. With great difficulty she succeeded in regaining possession of the painting known as *The Artist in His Studio* (Pl. 34, p. 182), which shows what appears to be an artist's workshop, a frequent genre subject of the time. A seated artist is painting a young model who holds a book and trumpet, symbols of fame. On a table to the left are a cast and sketchbook, objects that may symbolize the arts. Scholars have shown that the wall map is of the Netherlands in the 16th century, before Holland

*right:* 250. Jan Vermeer. Detail of *The Artist in His Studio* (Pl. 34, p. 182). c. 1665–70.

achieved its independence. The artist's elegant costume is also of that century, suggesting that this is not an actual self-portrait. The half-drawn drape, also, is an old device by which to suggest revelation of a past event. The painting is thus not directly about Vermeer's studio and his own lifetime, but it is a nostalgic evocation of the more affluent and ideal working conditions enjoyed by Dutch artists a century before. The painting of the studio model in the guise of Fame may have been an ironic personal statement by the artist, skeptical about the future reception of his own work and aware of the artificial nature of fame itself.

To realize this wishful image of an ideal, Vermeer gave the totality of his gifts as an artist. From this painting, one can begin to comprehend the imagination and inspired effort of the artist, which went much beyond his amazing technical achievement of simulating appearances. The fact that the viewpoint, angle of light, and placement of objects were all minutely calculated before brush met canvas does not detract from Vermeer's creative excellence, for these preliminary decisions were aesthetic judgments in the fullest sense of the word—the room arranged in terms of art. The eye moves into the painting slowly and logically from the large foreground shapes at the left to the artist at the right, and then to the model, with each area clearly apparent in its distance from other objects and the viewer. The careful, but not obvious, avoidance of simple alignment by means of parallel edges or right angles enriches the visual design and impels us to see each object in relation to another. Contrasts stress the idiosyncrasies of each shape, yet they do not destroy the feeling of inner rapport between everything within the painting. There are several strong rhythmic sequences, such as the ceiling beams, the brass chandelier curves culminating in the Hapsburg eagles, the horizontal vignettes of Dutch cities on the sides of the map, the black-and-white striping of the artist's blouse, and the alternating floor tiles. Against these sequences can be seen the random sparkle of upholstery nails on the chairs and the highlights in the fabric of the drapery. The drape holds all the painting's colors in less concentrated hues, with the exception of a small patch of blue that exactly matches the color of the model's dress; its dense, saturate pattern contrasts with the airy brightness and spaciousness of the room itself. Shadows never obliterate, but rather lead us to new revelations of tones and shapes. The composition is anchored at the left by the half-lighted drape seen against the most brilliant light on the wall behind it, and at the right by the judicious alignment of the edge of the map, the chair, the right easel leg, and the segmented black tiles that lead into the painting. Like the seated artist himself, the viewer is expected to weigh in his mind the rightness of each stroke in terms of the stuffs, luminosity, and hue of the object brought into being. The mahlstick held by the artist (Fig. 250) steadies his hand, like Vermeer's art a brilliant demonstration of wrist painting.

In the manner of Van Eyck, Vermeer reconstructed his world in terms of the smallest ray of light and the fragment upon which it fell. Unlike Van Eyck, however, he made his subjects and compositions free of the hierarchical demands of religious convention, so that he could bring to both arrangement and detail an unbounded revelation of his aspirations.

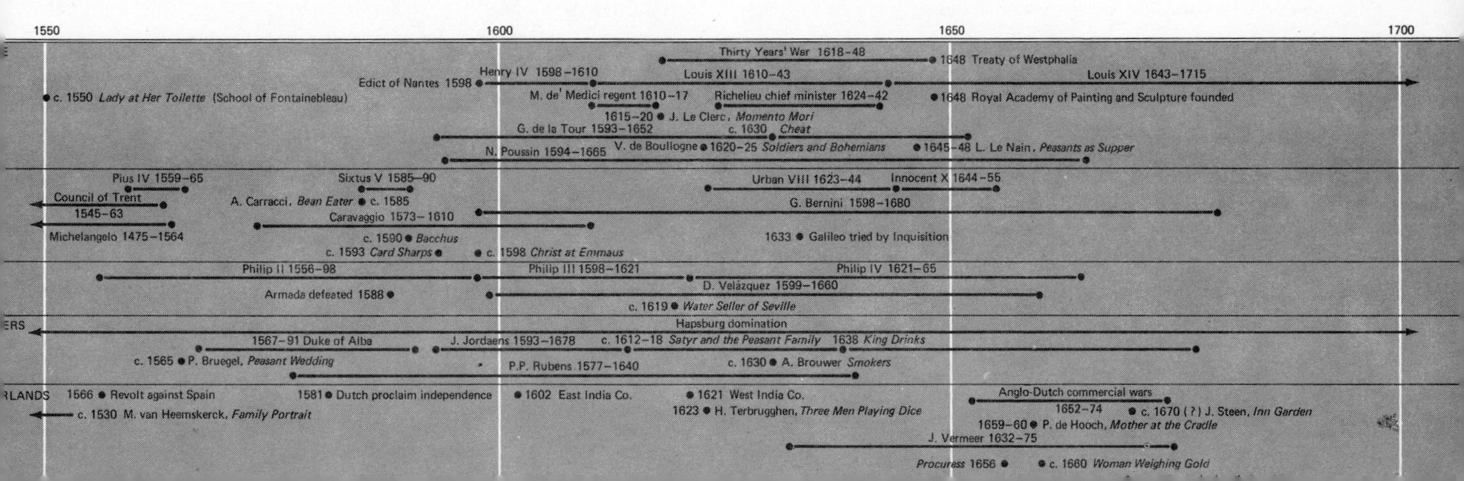

# 11

Rembrandt Harmensz van Rijn was born in Leiden in 1606 and died in Amsterdam in 1669. His father was a prosperous miller who wanted the young Rembrandt to be a scholar, and thus sent his son to a Humanist school from his seventh to his fourteenth year. For a short time, he was enrolled at the University of Leiden, and his early contact with great literature was to influence his later art. In 1620, he entered the studio of an unimportant Leiden artist and remained there for three years. At eighteen, he went to Amsterdam, where he studied for half a year with a well-known artist, Pieter Lastman. About 1632, he moved permanently to Amsterdam, where he began to have success as a portrait painter. In 1634 he married the wealthy Saskia van Uylenburgh. In quick succession they had four children, all of whom subsequently died; only his son Titus, born in 1641, reached maturity. Saskia died shortly after Titus' birth. By 1649, Hendrickje Stoffels was living with Rembrandt. Her willingness to become the painter's common-law wife brought her social hardship and actual persecution at the hands of a rigidly Calvinist society—a fact that makes Rembrandt's repeated interpretations of the theme of Christ and the woman taken in adultery all the more poignant. She stayed with Rembrandt through increasing financial difficulties, brought on by his omnivorous appetite for antiques and other *objets d'art,* many of which he used as props in his paintings. By 1657, Rembrandt was bankrupt and had lost his house and collection; two years later his graphic art was dispersed to satisfy his creditors. Contrary to the popular notion that Rembrandt was then reduced to a life of terrible poverty and neglect, he continued to receive good commissions and to devote himself to problems that interested him. He worked for the art firm set up by Hendrickje and Titus in 1658. In 1663 Hendrickje died, and in 1668 Rembrandt lost Titus, one year before his own death.

In his personal and artistic life, Rembrandt defied convention. For most of his life he recognized none of the accepted canons of social conduct, monetary management, adherence to the state Calvinist religion, and flattery of potentially wealthy and influential clients; most of all, he ignored proscriptions on what and how a Dutch painter should paint. He was an "un-Dutch" artist by his refusal to specialize or to show the merry-making, material comforts, or daily ritual of the middle class who controlled a buyer's art market. He puzzled this buying public by his avoidance of the art trends then fashionable, favoring more enduring notions of time and subject matter. From documentary evidence, it appears that Rembrandt considered himself a revolutionary in art because he did not acknowledge academic rules and followed only the nature and art of his own choosing. When Rembrandt was at work, as one historian has declared, he would not have stopped for a king.

His lifelong quest for personal freedom prevented Rembrandt from affiliating with any orthodox religion or political party. Unlike many painters of his time, he cannot be catalogued as a painter of portraits, genre, or religious subjects. No other artist of his generation was identified simultaneously with the different media of painting, etching, and drawing. He drew freely from older art, literature, history, and from the live subjects before his insatiable eye. Though he relied heavily upon the written word for inspiration, he distrusted writing about art, and the vast corpus of his work manifests a displeasure with artistic theory. From his varied sources he searched for the ties that bound humanity throughout history. Though compelled to individualize every subject in his art, Rembrandt never lost sight of mankind as a whole and saw life as a historical continuum from cradle to grave. With this view of the continuity of all life, travel was unnecessary, and Amsterdam became for him the microcosm of history. Rebel that he was in certain senses, Rembrandt accepted the role formulated by the artist during the Middle Ages—to move, delight, and instruct.

In his own lifetime, Rembrandt's biographers commented on the secret techniques by which he enriched etching and on the unusual thickness and odor of his oil portraits. He applied his paint in thick lumps—a technique called *impasto*—and built it up so heavily that one critic declared his portraits could be lifted by the sitter's nose. All that went into the making of art absorbed Rembrandt, and for the cookery of painting and printmaking he concocted his own recipes. The early biographers were impressed with his success as a teacher, for from the age of twenty-two he had many pupils; their tuition and the income from sales of their work allowed him to live well and to buy art. The students worked in upstairs rooms of his large Amsterdam house, drawing from casts, prints, and drawings and often from naked models. Among his many drawings are several on the subject of the studio (Fig. 251), illustrating his favorite lesson, which was to work not from knowledge of theories but from a visual experience of life. In one sketch, the young apprentices themselves have become the master's model. Such drawings, which the students may have been asked to copy, exemplified his teaching with regard to achieving strong relief by building from dark to light—contrasting shaded, recessive areas with the lightness of figures whose definition resulted from a rapid notation of directions made by their postures and clothing. To enhance the unity of the whole, which the subject alone could not give, Rembrandt would often impose shadows over his drawing. Their frequent arbitrariness shows that his imaginative intuition was extremely essential; apparently this irrational gift could not be taught, for none of the pupils rivaled the tutor. Although he learned much from his studies of other artists, Rembrandt's development of a highly personal style was founded in the main upon continous work, which in over forty years yielded roughly 650 paintings, 280 etchings, and 1400 drawings.

**Spiritual Art** *The Presentation in the Temple* (Fig. 252) is in many respects typical of Rembrandt's early paintings of religious subjects. This is not, it should be noted, *religious* painting, for it was not intended for use in a church. Rembrandt was a founder of what might be called private (i.e., nonecclesiastic)

*left:* 251. REMBRANDT. *Studio of the Artist*. c. 1635. Drawing, pen and wash; $6^7/_8 \times 9^1/_4$". Louvre, Paris.

*above:* 252. REMBRANDT. *The Presentation in the Temple*. 1631. Oil on panel, $24 \times 18^7/_8$". Mauritshuis, The Hague.

253. REMBRANDT. *John the Baptist Preaching*. 1636–50. Oil on panel, 24½ × 32″. Staatliche Museen, Berlin.

devotional painting: unlike the work of earlier artists, it did not illustrate dogma or propagandize organized religion. These paintings were small in format and intended for intimate contemplation in the home. Though Rembrandt was nominally Calvinist, a religion that looked with disfavor on paintings of religious subjects, his was in truth a private religion without theology, and his paintings, drawings, and prints constituted an individual and spiritual art. From his Roman Catholic mother, Rembrandt had derived his love and knowledge of the Bible, and his interpretations of Biblical stories have the freshness of personal discovery. The style that produced *The Presentation in the Temple* was doubtless influenced by the Scriptures, particularly by the frequent references to the symbolism of light. Against the looming backdrop of the impressive synagogue architecture, Simeon kneels with the Christ child and his parents before Anna, who stands with outstretched arms. The small group is illuminated by a strong shaft of natural light. The faces of the Child and the "just and devout" old Simeon are most strongly lit, recalling the passage from the Psalms, "God is the light of their countenance." Simeon, who knew that he could die in peace with the coming of the Messiah, appears to be looking beyond the head of Anna and saying, "O Lord . . . mine eyes have seen Thy salvation, which Thou hast prepared before the face of all peoples; a light of revelation to the gentiles, and a glory for Thy people Israel" (Luke 2:22–34).

Rembrandt knew the chief rabbis in the Jewish quarter of Amsterdam and had visited the synagogues. In his ardor to re-create the true image of the Scriptures, he ignored the archaeological backgrounds popular among the Italians and his Dutch contemporaries and drew inspiration from his immediate surroundings. The small painting is filled with observations of types, costumes, gestures, and poses, and contrasts the intense concentration of the central group with the rather indifferent presence of bystanders on the stairs to the right. The figures and architecture are so disposed in depth that the viewer also becomes a bystander off to one side in the shadows. The darkened areas were made luminous by Rembrandt's device of underpainting his canvas with warm bright colors and then scratching through the darker overpainting of the architecture to these high-keyed layers. The whole painting has a theatrical aspect, with the principals dramatically subordinated to the great space and strident contrast of light and dark. The faces as yet do not reveal Rembrandt's later deep understanding of human motivation. What we see is a drama of place rather than of persons.

Rembrandt's development as an individual and as a painter is reflected in a single painting that he began early in his career but felt compelled to rework as he grew older. His oil sketch *John the Baptist Preaching* (Fig. 253), begun about 1636 or 1637, was worked over intermittently until 1650. In this sketch, the ostensible subject is Biblical, but the theme is really that of an inspired individual addressing a group. At the time of this sketch's conception, Rembrandt was sympathetic to the Mennonites, a sect that decried a formal organized church and the ritual and sacraments of the Roman Catholics. Its ministers were laymen who preached not dogma but the virtues of mercy and charity, humility and obedience. Stress was laid upon the impulses of the heart, deeply felt silent prayer, and simple, warm spirituality. The Mennonites sought to return to the essential truths of the Bible instead of using it as the basis for an elaborate theology. They championed respect for the poor in spirit and love of one's brethren in Christ. Their sentiments may have influenced this conception of John the Baptist.

In loose array, all strata of society are gathered to hear John speak, with zeal and from the heart, of salvation. Rembrandt may have portrayed himself in one of the faces at John's feet. Rembrandt's later reworking of the sketch tended to concentrate the light upon John and those closest to him. As in the painting of Simeon, the illumination is appropriate not only for reasons of style, but also for the moment when the ascetic Baptist prophesied the Messiah as light coming into the world. John further spoke of the importance of fellowship, the need for brotherly love. Like the word of Christ, John's word is as a light to the path of the faithful. Rembrandt depicted a crowd divided in its attention, fragmented into those who hear, are moved, and understand, those who daydream or doze, and those who bicker or content themselves with trivial diversions. The various ethnic types and exotic costumes suggest the universal scope of John's message. At the center foreground, in line with the obelisk crowned by Caesar's effigy, stand three Pharisees in partial shadow, who have turned their backs on John and dispute among themselves. Rembrandt did not resort to the obvious device of illuminating only those who are the enlightened participants, for signs of vanity and folly can be found in both the light and the dark areas of the crowd. In the bright sections can be seen his earlier style of figure construction, with more opaque faces, a heavy reliance on drawing, and attention to picturesque detail. The later style treated figures and costumes in broader, less precise strokes and with fewer, more somber tones.

Rembrandt never traveled as did other famous Northern European artists of his century; yet his imagination and taste for remote lands and peoples filled his works with archaeological monuments, rugged panoramas unlike those around Amsterdam, and opulent and exotic accessories such as turbans, ornate bridles, monkeys, and camels. This small panel is charged with almost an overabundance of ideas and aesthetic means; the later alterations were in the direction of greater clarity and stability.

Rembrandt's continual restlessness and relentless self-criticism are also apparent in two states of his etching *The Three Crosses* (Figs. 254, 255). These etchings also show a great divergence from the early style of *John the Baptist Preaching*, a style that had brought him commercial and critical success. Each painting, drawing, and print seemed to open up new possibilities for the artist, who set personal goals of artistic perfection and inquiry above financial gain.

In itself, the third state of *The Three Crosses* seems to have a moving completeness. It is a readable drama whose religious

*above left:* 254. REMBRANDT. *The Three Crosses.* 1653. Etching, third state; $15^1/_4 \times 17^3/_4$". British Museum, London.

*left:* 255. REMBRANDT. *The Three Crosses.* 1653. Etching, fourth state; $15^1/_4 \times 17^3/_4$". British Museum, London.

subject is the Passion of Christ and whose universal theme is the loss of a man. In a centrifugal arrangement, Rembrandt detailed the several reactions to the execution, ranging from the indifference of the mounted troops and the satisfaction of the Pharisees at the lower left to the anguish of Christ's followers and the conversion of the centurion. The harsh barrenness of Golgotha intrudes on the scene in the rocks and scrub vegetation. The tortured bodies of the thieves flank Christ, and the descending light divides its focus among the three crosses. This division of interest and diffuse action impelled Rembrandt to make the fourth state. The successive states are like a chronology of the last hours of Christ on the Cross. The final etching shows the world in near-darkness, except for the torrential shaft of light above Christ's head. As in Genesis, the abrupt separation of light and dark suggests the creation of new life. The solemn centurion is the principal subordinate figure, stressing a comprehension of the meaning of Christ's death and the significance of conversion. The mood is altered not only by the inaction and rigidification of the few remaining accessory figures, but also by the rugged, stiff outlines of their bodies and their reduction to almost obscure presences floating in a sea of darkness. Black was felt and savored by Rembrandt as a tangible substance. Etching ink, crosshatching, and the close striations of the etcher's needle imparted the special qualities of a soft, absorbent black that he could not reproduce in his paintings. The appeal of etching may also have been that it permitted Rembrandt to emphasize the contrast between extremes of light and darkness, with their implications of life and death.

Rembrandt's conception of Christ is personal. Hanging from the Cross is the taut but meager body of an ordinary human being, with no attempt by the artist to achieve sublimity in an exceptional musculature. Christ's extraordinary strength and spirit issue from a strikingly erect posture, from the head and the radiance about it. More than Michelangelo, Rembrandt was drawn to the testimony of flesh to affirm Christ's suffering manhood.

Rembrandt had avoided the more obvious evidence of pathetic struggle in the figure of Christ. In *The Slaughtered Ox* (Pl. 35, p. 199), a small secular painting done two years after the Crucifixion series, however, Rembrandt evoked the violence of brutal execution. In the early Middle Ages the ox, symbolic of St. Luke, was thought to prefigure the sacrifice of Christ. It is not impossible that, with the Crucifixion theme so much in his mind during the time of this painting, the emotional associations of the two subjects may have overlapped. Further, Rembrandt's famous paintings of anatomy dissections, in which dead bodies are cut open and examined, may also have influenced his selection and treatment of the theme. The painting shows the spread-eagled carcass of the ox hanging from a rude wooden frame. The gutted animal seems self-illuminated with an almost phosphorescent glow. Massing his pigment in thick viscous patches, Rembrandt created a painterly equivalent of the moist, greasy, rich substance of the animal's muscle, fat, and bone. He showed with wonder the partially hollow interior of the flayed animal, formed of complex substance and color. Allowing it to dominate its gloomy setting and the timid woman peering around the corner, Rembrandt transfigured and heroicized the slaughtered ox and reiterated his fascination with the mystery of life and death.

To juxtapose an etching of the Crucifixion with a scene from an Amsterdam butcher shop is to bring together the poles of Rembrandt's broad interests. The past and present, the imaginary and the real, all of these alternate and interweave throughout his art. Rembrandt was a rebellious Dutchman who could not follow his fellow artists in meticulously documenting and praising their particular time and place. With grandiose projects half-formed in his head, he would still take the time to draw whatever immediately attracted his eye in the street or along the canals.

Michelangelo made his art in terms of Man (see Chap. 8), and Rembrandt in terms of men. No two artists in history had more antithetical views of art and humanity. For Michelangelo, Christ had to be shown as endowed with a sublime body to signify his divinity. But the Dutch artist could not think or paint in terms of philosophical abstractions; instead, it was the real and veritable that kindled his imagination. When Rembrandt painted his *Christ at the Column* (Fig. 256), he showed the Saviour as an imperfect physical specimen whose flesh hung on a bony frame. Unlike Michelangelo's ennobled conception of an impersonal and flawless skin, Rembrandt's small painting is dedicated to re-creating the particulars and material substance of the flesh belonging to a single man. The selection of a model (perhaps his son Titus) of such meager proportions, and his arrangement in a slack posture that bespeaks exhaustion of body and spirit, dismayed Rembrandt's critics and would undoubtedly have been scorned by Michelangelo.

Rembrandt must have posed problems like this to his students, for the painting suggests a studio study from a live model, and no column is actually visible. It is likely that drawing from life inspired Rembrandt to paint subjects from the Bible, which, when realized, often retained much of the character of their secular origin. Such a painting is a later version of *Bathsheba* (Fig. 257), although none of the preliminary drawings exist. Possibly Hendrickje, who was the model for many drawings, posed for Bathsheba. Her pose may have been inspired by Rembrandt's acquaintance, through 17th-century engravings, with Classical Roman sculptures that showed seated women, such as Venus, in profile. Recall Michelangelo's synthesis of *David* (Fig. 193); that of Rembrandt was to take a Protestant Dutch housewife and pose her in the manner of a Roman goddess to re-create the character of a tragic Hebrew woman.

In his later years, during the period when this painting was done, Rembrandt painted fewer crowd scenes and preferred to

*below:* 256. REMBRANDT. *Christ at the Column.* c. 1657. Oil on canvas, 13 × 10″. Wallraf-Richartz Museum, Cologne.

*right:* 257. REMBRANDT. *Bathsheba.* 1654. Oil on canvas, 4′10⁷/₈″ × 4′7⁷/₈″. Louvre, Paris (anc. coll. Vizzavona-Druet, Musées Nationaux).

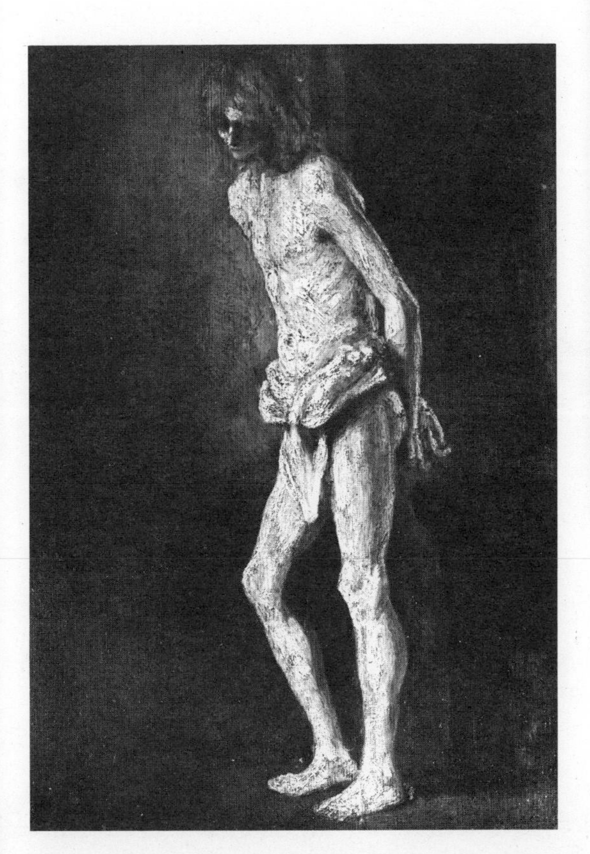

treat isolated individuals. He tended to immobilize his subjects, placing emphasis upon their inner rather than outer reactions to events. The great mysteries for Rembrandt were not those of theology but those of humanity. His painting of Bathsheba shows the wife of Uriah, chosen by David for himself, in a moment of troubled reflection. The theme is typical of Rembrandt, for it reveals the individual's passive submission to fate. He has depicted the moment of recognition, crucial to classical drama. Bathsheba is attended by a servant or David's messenger, who prepares her for the fateful meeting with the King. In Bathsheba's hand is the note that incites the tragedy. The expression on her face, the limpness of the arm holding the letter, the unthinking compliance with the actions of the maid—all compose the story of an individual caught in a web of circumstance over which she has no control, though she is aware of its eventual outcome. Moved by the vulnerability of people and their unwitting involvement in tragedy, Rembrandt reconstructed the Bible in human terms. While the painting gives an initial impression of factual account, Rembrandt added an aura of elusive, lyrical revery. Julius Held characterized this type of painting as Rembrandt's formula "of making his models appear both physically present and psychically remote."

Rembrandt's nudes were not in the Italian Renaissance tradition, for they lack its classical proportions, cosmetic perfection, and litheness. More in the Northern tradition (see Chap. 6), they are naked rather than nude, and the revelation of their bodies becomes almost an invasion of their privacy. With his intense empiricism, Rembrandt could not submit the naked body to norms imposed by other styles and cultures. His nudes are not generalized types; each body seems shaped by the character of its possessor. His naked bodies seem to retain the impress of clothes, and to show the effects of diet and an existence more sedentary than athletic. Gravity of mind and the pressure of conscience are sustained in these heavy bodies.

In an earlier painting, Rembrandt celebrated the beauty of a naked woman in amorous and more joyful circumstances

258. REMBRANDT. *Danaë*. 1636. Oil on canvas, 6′1/2″ × 6′8″. Hermitage, Leningrad.

(Fig. 258). On an elaborately ornamented bed, Danaë awaits the coming of the god Zeus, whose presence just beyond the curtain is announced by a golden light. The anguished, constrained cupid above Danaë symbolizes the chastity enforced upon her because her father the king had been warned of his own murder by a future grandson. In paintings of this subject by other artists, Zeus transforms himself into a rain of golden coins to gain access to Danaë's bed. Rembrandt uses the old symbol of divine luminosity and bathes the woman's pliant body in a warm glow. His Danaë is not the statuesque recumbent figure of the Italian Venus type, but in her gesture and radiant expression she exhibits a warmblooded anticipation.

Few of Rembrandt's paintings deal with miracles, for he saw the Bible in terms of men and women with distinct personalities, problems, and hopes not unlike those daily encountered in Amsterdam. When he painted *Christ at Emmaus* (Fig. 259), he set the scene in an austere, high-ceilinged stone room that dominates the figures by its scale. Only the radiance emanating from Christ immediately distinguishes the painting from genre art. To evoke the apparition of Christ, Rembrandt set him directly before a sizable hollow niche, which looms like a dark void recalling his miraculous emergence from the tomb. The niche also binds the figures and encloses the area of dramatic, but underplayed, action. By temperament unsympathetic toward Catholic theology and its association with the formal centrality of Renaissance compositions, Rembrandt shifted the focus of the painting to the left. Unlike Leonardo (Fig. 219), Rembrandt bathed the room in a deep but transparent shadow and in a powerful warm light which the figures seem to absorb with varying intensity. He gave to Christ an unaristocratic personality, stressing his gentleness, capacity for love, and ability to be at home with the humble. No painter before Rembrandt came as close to fathoming the Jesus of the Gospels or the historic Jesus (see Chap. 3). Rembrandt did portraitlike studies of Christ, probably based on a bearded youth from the Jewish quarter near his home. In the Emmaus scene, the bearded Christ retains the soft, gentle qualities with which Rembrandt endowed him in scenes showing his earthly ministry. Only the sad expression of the eyes suggests the suffering and fatigue of the Passion. Significantly, one of the disciples seems to study Christ's face for signs of the miracle, rather than follow his gesture of breaking the bread. Deliberately avoiding Caravaggio's rhetoric of gestures and accessory objetcts (Pl. 31, p. 164), Rembrandt himself said that he sought to convey the greatest inner emotion.

Another subject relating to an epiphany is the drawing of God announcing his covenant to Abraham (Fig. 260), done after *Christ at Emmaus*, in the mid-1650s. As recounted in Genesis (15, 17), God promised to give the ninety-nine-year-old Abraham a son and to make him the father of nations. Both themes had a deep attraction for Rembrandt, who was preoccupied with the family all his life and believed that the Jews

*below:* 259. REMBRANDT. *Christ at Emmaus.* 1648. Oil on panel, $26^3/_4 \times 25^5/_8$″. Louvre, Paris.

*right:* 260. REMBRANDT. *God Announces His Covenant to Abraham.* c. 1656. Drawing, pen and bistre; $7^3/_4 \times 10^1/_2$″. Kupferstichkabinett, Staatliche Kunstsammlungen, Dresden.

*below:* 261. REMBRANDT. *Tobias Healing Tobit's Blindness.* c. 1649–50. Drawing, pen and bistre, wash; $6^9/_{10} \times 5^1/_4$″. Kupferstichkabinett, Staatliche Museen, Berlin.

were the chosen people. Rembrandt saw in the community an extension of the family unit; and in rituals such as Christ's presentation in the temple, a linking of the two groups.

In the Bible it is written that at God's appearance Abraham fell flat on his face. This was a sign of fear and an indication of his unworthiness to look upon the face of the Lord. Rough as the sketch is, Rembrandt gave enough attention to the face of the Lord to evoke his kindly admonition, "Fear not, Abram, I am thy protector." Unlike Michelangelo, Rembrandt did not view Jehovah as the wrathful force but, instead, gave the Old Testament God the same benevolent aspect as his images of Christ. He flanked the Lord with two angels and above his head drew the dove of the Holy Ghost, thus introducing the trinitarian symbolism that recurs when the three men appear to Abraham and Sarah, and the Lord again promises them a son.

The rhythms of Rembrandt's hand as it moved over the grainy white paper, holding the reed pen, presented an intimate revelation. *God and Abraham* was not done from posed models, but the information and shorthand acquired from long study served him when he drew from imagination. The strokes that establish the broad gestures and the limits of movement for the figures of the angels do not form continuous constrictive outlines, but they overlap or leave gaps in the silhouette that suggest the fusion of the body with the surrounding atmosphere. In the prostrate figure of Abraham, several of the lines begin or end within the body's outline and have a hooked termination. With a single flourish of the pen, Rembrandt established where a limb was joined to the body and where and to what extent it projected from the body. The body and its clothing were conceived in terms of directional lines and weights. With the paper as a source of light, a few expert touches of dark establish the mood and detail of the Lord's face. To define such accessory elements as the clouds and the space, Rembrandt's hand swept over the surface in quick series of parallel lines.

The more that is learned about Rembrandt, the more it is realized how his preoccupation with certain themes satisfied many different personal interests and needs. His drawing of *Tobias Healing Tobit's Blindness* (Fig. 261) is but one of some fifty-five interpretations the artist made from the Book of Tobit. This Old Testament story of God's compassion toward men, with its emphasis on family unity and loyalty, appealed to Rembrandt, who not only had strong feelings of love and concern for his son Titus but also an abiding love for his own father, who had died blind. The drawing shows the subjects near an open window and Tobias examining the sightless eyes of his father before curing them with the gall of a fish held in a bowl by Tobit's wife. The archangel Raphael, who revealed the means of cure to Tobias, stands behind the father and son like a guardian angel or an attending physician. It has been shown that, here and in similar drawings, Rembrandt has accurately delineated the medical procedure for cataract operations as then performed in Amsterdam. Rembrandt depicted many themes in which sight or blindness is an important element—an understandable concern because of the relationship between vision and the artist's profession. The drawing possesses a weighted stillness and a concentrated attention on the part of the participants; Rembrandt also extended his characterization to the bodies of the parents, so that many of the strong accents of the drawing occur in their garments and give an expressive balance to the whole composition.

Rembrandt's etching of *The Sacrifice of Isaac* (Fig. 262) reverses the roles of Tobias and Tobit, for Abraham tenderly covers the eyes of his beloved son as he is about to deprive him of life. So intense is Abraham's grief in complying with God's command that even the intercession of the angel, who physically stays the sacrifice, does not immediately affect the father's anguished expression. In this last version, Rembrandt compressed the action in the close contact of the three figures, and the ass and servants were relegated to insignifiant roles. The black cavities framing the sacrifice suggest the tragic mood of the moments preceding it and the symbolic conversion of darkness to light by the angel's miraculous appearance.

One of Rembrandt's last paintings is the *Return of the Prodigal Son* (Fig. 263). Perhaps because of his close ties with Titus and with his own father, Rembrandt repeatedly interpreted the theme of father and son. In this picture, the wordless but profound reaction of all to the homecoming signifies the indivisible ties of the family. The sons who remained with the father display no jealousy or recrimination but are sympathetic witnesses to a sacred moment. Just as Rembrandt understated the drama, his frugal means added to the force of the painting. There is no emphatic action or elaborate interweaving of figures

*above:* 262. REMBRANDT. *The Sacrifice of Isaac.* 1655. Etching, $6^1/_4 \times 5^1/_8$". Albertina, Vienna.

*right:* 263. REMBRANDT. *Return of the Prodigal Son.* After 1660. Oil on canvas, $8'7^1/_8" \times 6'8^3/_4"$. Hermitage, Leningrad.

*left:* Plate 35. REMBRANDT. *The Slaughtered Ox*. 1655. Oil on panel, $37 \times 26^3/_8''$. Louvre, Paris. (See p. 194.)

*above:* Plate 36. REMBRANDT. *Portrait of Jan Six*. 1654. Oil on canvas, $44 \times 40''$. Six Collection, Amsterdam. (See p. 205.)

Plate 37. REMBRANDT. *The Jewish Bride*. 1668. Oil on canvas, 3′10$^{3}/_{8}$″ × 5′4$^{1}/_{2}$″. Rijksmuseum, Amsterdam. (See p. 205.)

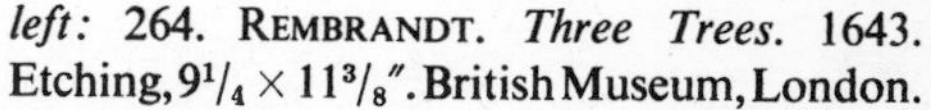

*left:* 264. REMBRANDT. *Three Trees.* 1643. Etching, $9^{1}/_{4} \times 11^{3}/_{8}$". British Museum, London.

*below:* 265. REMBRANDT. *The Omval at the River Amster.* 1645. Etching, $7^{1}/_{4} \times 8^{4}/_{5}$". British Museum, London.

and background. The individual forms are somewhat rectangular and blocklike. This suggestion of regularity and self-containment is offset by the dissolution of the edges of the forms and their fusion with the luminous ambience. There is a simple scale of emphasis, with the greatest wealth of color lavished on the rags of the son. With the reduction of the figures to a static condition, Rembrandt solemnized the human being and achieved a supreme drama of persons. This image of forgiveness and pity is a form of self-revelation that may reflect the artist's own resolution of conflicts with the world.

**Landscapes** From about 1640 to 1656, Rembrandt did a number of drawings, prints, and paintings of landscape, which earlier had appeared solely as a backdrop for figural subjects. Many of his landscapes are of the flat plains, picturesque thatched peasant cottages, and canals in and near Amsterdam. Dutch artists were known to make drawings from nature on the spot, but their paintings were completed in the studio and were often composites of different views. In his etching *Three Trees* (Fig. 264) Rembrandt shows the tiny figure of an artist sketching on a hilltop at the far right. In his more numerous figure compositions, humans dominate their setting or claim most of our attention, but in his landscapes Rembrandt was able to contrast their small scale and quiet routine activities with the grand sweep and endless variety of nature. By alternating zones of dark and light, Rembrandt suggested the depth and continuity of the earth's surface and dramatized the rugged trio of trees against the brightness of the clearing sky. A shaft of sunlight illuminates the fisherman and his wife at the left, while above them on the horizon is the silhouette of a city. From the rich sensuous blacks of the foreground shadows emerge the highlighted traces of bushes. Just as he could dignify the rags of a beggar, so he provokes our curiosity and pleasure in even the meanest vegetative scrub in his prints. The etching *The Omval at the River Amster* (Fig. 265)

*right:* 266. REMBRANDT. *The Anatomy Lesson of Dr. Deijman.* 1656. Fragment of oil painting, 3′4″ × 4′4″. Rijksmuseum, Amsterdam.

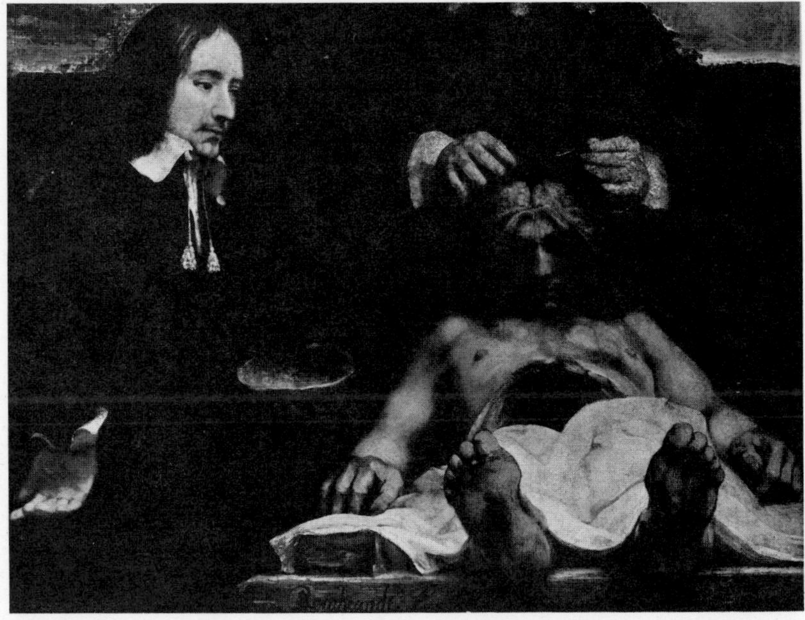

*above:* 267. REMBRANDT. *The Anatomy Lesson of Dr. Deijman.* c. 1656. Drawing, $4^3/_8 \times 5^1/_4$″. Rijksmuseum, Amsterdam.

*below:* 268. ANDREA MANTEGNA. *Dead Christ.* After 1466. Oil on canvas, $26^3/_4 \times 31^7/_8$″. Brera Gallery, Milan.

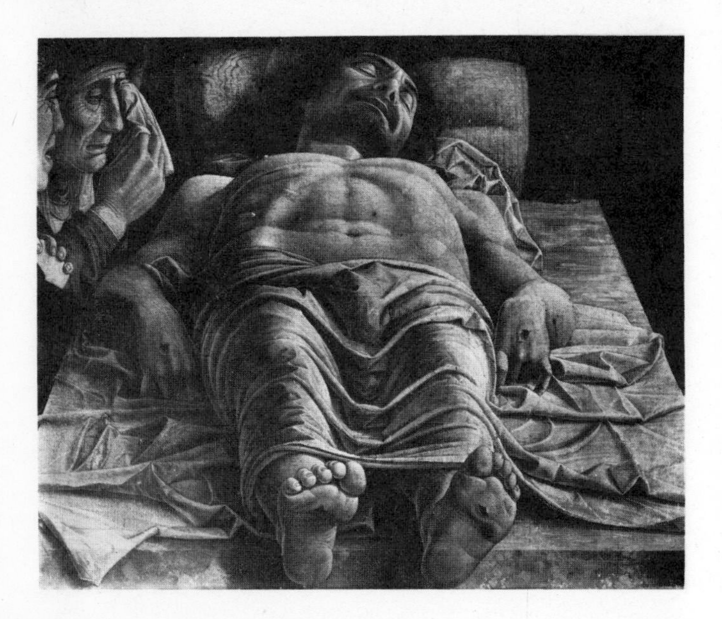

repeats Rembrandt's habit of combining large and small elements, of suggestively detailing the near and far. Secret places in nature such as caves or the shadowed copse seen at the left of the print enhance pictorial interest. To keep his compositions from disintegrating under accumulations of detail, Rembrandt graded the density and definition of areas and left as contrast large untouched spaces. The tangled wooded area at the left is built up from the inside out, whereas the houses and mill across the canal have more pronounced silhouettes and spare linear definition within. At no point does nature seem finite and arrested, but it is captured as if in a perpetual, transitory condition of illumination and growth, or of what it reveals and conceals. Rembrandt imposes an emotional character on the nonhuman, for as with his figures he virtually draws out the biographies of his buildings and trees.

**Anatomical Science** Rembrandt's insistence on personal discovery parallels developments in western European science and the empirical attitude reflected in the great anatomist Vesalius' opinion that the proper study of mankind is man. In describing the naked body, Rembrandt relied upon the practiced coordination of his eyes and hands; occasionally he even had recourse to the advice of famous Dutch doctors. The discoveries of advanced Dutch science coincide with those of Rembrandt most apparently in his painting *The Anatomy Lesson of Doctor Deijman* (Fig. 266). Only a sketch (Fig. 267) preserves for us the painting's original format; fire destroyed all but a fragment that shows the foreshortened view of the corpse, the chest and hands presumably of Dr. Deijman, and an assistant standing to the left and holding the removed top of the skull. Commissioned to make a group portrait of the doctor and his assistants or students, Rembrandt chose to depict a public dissection such as occurred in the Amsterdam medical amphitheater. In an excellent book, William Heckscher has shown that, while saluting the triumph of modern science over superstition and ignorance, the painting also combines the old moralizing ideas of *memento mori* and "the wages of sin are death" (Pl. 16, p. 98; Figs. 143, 229). The corpse was that of a hanged thief, and this was in a sense a punitive dissection comparable to that shown earlier by Gerard David (Fig. 161). Like Doctor Deijman, Rembrandt was heir to the Renaissance admiration of the body as both an object of beauty and the key to understanding life. The foreshortened cadaver has precedents in such works as Mantegna's *Dead Christ* (Fig. 268), and the dissection scene also has analogies with the segment of Michelangelo's *Last Judgment* in which men are divested of their skins (Fig. 203). A copy of Michelangelo's masterpiece was known to have hung in the Leiden medical amphitheater.

**Portraits** Rembrandt's early prominence, even before his arrival in Amsterdam in 1632, was based on his talents as a portrait painter. Like his fellow Dutch painters, he responded to the demand of the well-to-do middle class for portraits. Personal friends—writers and doctors—and interesting looking individuals he pulled in from the streets of Amsterdam also sat for their likenesses. In later years, Rembrandt experienced difficulties with clients who claimed that their portraits were not good likenesses, since they were accustomed to the slick, extroverted, and often smug images the fashionable painters achieved. After his bankruptcy, Rembrandt continued to receive important portrait commissions, one of which, from the governing board of the drapers' guild, resulted in the group painting known as *The Syndics* (Fig. 269).

An important contribution of Rembrandt to group portraiture was his successful solution of the problem of achieving an informal, unself-conscious, and convincing union of all the sitters. Since portraits were paid for on the basis of the amount of the figure shown, it was essential that all of the faces be clearly in evidence and that priority be given to the guild president. Rembrandt chose a moment during a meeting of the board with its stockholders, immediately after a query had been made from the floor. Within the painting, the figures are subtly united in their relationship to the president, who is rising to respond. The interlocked groupings and the positions of the bodies give a sense of this official relationship. The device of directing all attention outside the picture, toward the viewer, unites the figures at some external focus. The sobriety and similarity of apparel and the warm heavy atmosphere of the room—suffused with rich tones on the walls and in the near edge of the table covering—further the painting's harmony.

As in the best of Rembrandt's work, there is in *The Syndics* an underlying conflict between the apparent and the real. The

269. REMBRANDT. *The Syndics*. 1662. Oil on canvas, 6′7/8″ × 8′11 7/8″. Rijksmuseum, Amsterdam.

*right:* 270. REMBRANDT. *The Conspiracy of Claudius Civilis.* 1661–62. Oil on canvas, 6′5 1/8″ × 10′1 5/8″. Nationalmuseum, Stockholm.

*below:* 271. REMBRANDT. *The Polish Rider.* c. 1655. Oil on canvas, 3′10″ × 4′5 1/8″. Frick Collection, New York (copyright).

subjects were men of status and solid achievement who, on the occasion of the board meeting, presented an image of unshakable probity and solidarity. To the far right, however, is set into the wall panel a painting of a burning city, which in Rembrandt's time, as De Tolnay has shown, signified the ephemerality of worldly power. It was a commentary on vanity and a warning against pride to those of wealth. The faces of the men betray their inherent individuality and those human qualities which do not always accord with official roles. Rembrandt did not caricature these men, nor can their faces be read merely as units in a group program. In this discerning record the private history of each figure cannot be masked by the occasion, but to begin to dwell on the subtleties of each face is to remove oneself from the room and matters at hand. As prosaic an event as a business meeting, astutely viewed by Rembrandt, has been transformed into a work of art and a probing psychological study of the price and nature of power.

In 1662, the same year that he painted *The Syndics,* Rembrandt worked on a painting for the Amsterdam town hall (Fig. 270). Its subject was the ancient conspiracy of the Batavians, ancestors of the Dutch, who rebelled against Roman rule. Untypical for the Dutch artist of his time was the painting of a past event not actually witnessed by the painter. It is an ambitious example of Rembrandt's yielding to the urge to create a painting from his imagination. In its original state, *The Conspiracy of Claudius Civilis* was probably the largest painting Rembrandt ever undertook. When it was rejected, he removed it from the town hall and cut it down to the area he liked most, which made a work of marketable size. The nearly concurrent date of its painting makes the contrast between the group portrait of *The Syndics* and this historical work all the more interesting. Rembrandt's visionary inclination was inspired by the midnight meeting of the conspirators, when they swore allegiance until death upon the sword of Claudius Civilis. This highly charged incident is an ironic contrast to the mundane dispute in the stockholders' meeting. The confident reserve of the fiscally wise guild president makes an equally interesting comparison with the heroic presence of the one-eyed Claudius Civilis, who was to challenge the legions of the Roman Empire. The quiescent sunlight of the board room, with its connotations of security and permanence, gives way to the brilliant, inconsistent, and concealed radiance emanating from the conspirators' table, a strange light that transfigures their varied, rugged features and then fades into the surrounding gloom. The faces of the conspirators belong with their costumes and roles of the moment; the intriguing double life of the syndics is absent. Each figure has freedom of movement within a restricted space, preserving his individuality without weakening his relation to the group. Layers of glazes build up the surface into thick crusts; no color area is composed of pure single tones, and the colors seem suspended within a tangible atmosphere. Characteristic of Rembrandt's late style, as the paint became richer and more mobile, the outward action of the figures was reduced. Even in this histrionic episode, the participants have become more submerged within themselves.

Linked in spirit with the *Claudius Civilis*, and likewise an imaginative portrait, is Rembrandt's misnamed *Polish Rider* (Fig. 271). The proud and alert horseman is based upon eastern European light cavalrymen, whose heroic exploits in defending Christian Europe against the Turks were legendary even in Amsterdam. Their service as mercenaries in western Europe would have accounted for Rembrandt's acquaintance with his subject, since he shows the full military equipment of this type of soldier without specifying his Polish or Hungarian nationality or personal identity. The darkened background throws into relief the rider's manly beauty and the inspired painting of the horse and military costume, based on a triad of red, white, and gold. A clue to the portrait's meaning lies in the painting itself, in which the warrior rides his gaunt horse through an inhospitable landscape dominated by a massive fortress. The self-assured pose and unnatural radiance enveloping the horse and rider are perhaps suggestive of his symbolic role as a Christian knight errant in a world of peril. Descendant of Titian's equestrian portrait of Charles V (Fig. 296), Rembrandt's work makes horse and rider a more unified organism and gives the animal greater character. Rembrandt had, in fact, the opportunity to study the skeleton of a horse in one of the medical amphitheaters. Though without royal patronage for his theme, he combined the regal and triumphal associations of the equestrian motif with an idealized portrait, and at the same time reflected Europe's concern over the Moslem threat and his own private hopes that resided in youth.

The *Portrait of Jan Six* (Pl. 36, p. 199) epitomizes Rembrandt's ideals—dignified masculinity and a certain quality of cool correctness mingled with irrepressible human warmth. Rembrandt endowed the living subject of his art with traits of an active and a contemplative life, for in reality Jan Six was both a successful poet and a politician. Significantly, Rembrandt did not portray great contemporary Dutch political and military heroes. The most compatible subjects in his later life were men such as Jan Six who, like the painter himself, fully indulged both their worldly and intellectual appetites and ambitions. Personal rather than civic accomplishment seems most to have impressed Rembrandt. Such admiration for men who lived by strong individual codes was natural for an unconventional painter who resisted the formulas of his art. Jan Six stands to the right of center, takes no notice of the viewer, and does not assume a stable pose in the disposition of his limbs. With part of his face concealed in shadow, he is decidedly not represented as the extroverted affable or the prim type favored at the time.

The *Portrait of Jan Six*, like Rembrandt's most inspired work of any period, summarizes all that the artist had learned about his craft and the nature of men. By 1654, when the portrait was done, Rembrandt could produce painting that was both elegant and profound, in which he achieved great expressive power with economical means. The painting of Jan Six is in a sense a double portrait, a blend of studied contrasts that gives simultaneous insight into the public and the private identity of Jan Six. The automatic gesture of putting on a glove prefaces his going out into the streets; the tan gloves, scarlet cape, green-grey coat, and black hat are part of the gentleman's public identity. The actual public face has not as yet been "put on" or arranged, but the subject's features are relaxed in a momentary unawareness of others as his mind is absorbed in gentle reverie. The collar and row of buttons have a firm, tangible appearance that restores the viewer to the external man. Rembrandt did not try to dazzle with the virtuosity of his brush. He used a studied casualness in the single strokes of the gold braid and the vertical streaking of shadows in the cloak. Within the critical areas of focus, such as the hands and head, the strokes are accented and more strongly directed, grouped firmly together to suggest the rough and modulated substance of flesh against smooth cloth.

Rembrandt's ability to tell a story and to widen the narrative beyond its literal meaning was not restricted to group scenes, for it can also be seen in a painting with but two figures: *The Jewish Bride* (Pl. 37, p. 200), which was done in 1668. Though the work was possibly based on the Biblical story of Rebecca and Isaac, its essential theme was marital concord, and the models were probably Titus and his wife. Into this painting the artist projected his sentiments of family and erotic love. It proposes a frank, sensual attitude, one of sharing, unlike any found in Renaissance paintings of the family. The story unfolded in delicate, subtle gestures can be compared to marriage portraits by Van Eyck and Kokoschka (Pls. 73, 74, p. 362). The gestures of the man suggest love and possession, while the attitude of the bride conveys submission and encouragement. A gamut of affectionate feeling finds expres-

sion in this one painting. Its economy and restrained style make the slightest movement count. Colors emerge from shadow, with the strongest tones reserved for the area in most intense light. This highlight, significantly, does not fall on the faces but on the man's sleeve. The lightest parts are most thickly painted, so that in places the pigment actually forms a relief which catches shadow and light from the room where the painting hangs.

As we have seen, Michelangelo's humor in art could be bitingly vengeful, whereas Rembrandt's art has many amusing moments that are often at his own expense. Early self-portraits show the artist clowning or making preposterous faces at the viewer—not unlike some portraits by Adriaen Brouwer (Fig. 236), whose work Rembrandt admired. He liked to draw or etch himself as a young country ruffian or a dashing romantic

*above left:* 272. REMBRANDT. *Studies for a Self-Portrait and Beggars.* 1632. Etching, 4 × $5^{3}/_{8}$″. Rijksmuseum, Amsterdam.

*left:* 273. REMBRANDT. *Self-Portrait with Saskia.* c. 1635. Oil on canvas, 5′4″ × 4′4″. Gemäldegalerie, Dresden.

*above:* 274. REMBRANDT. *Self-Portrait.* c. 1660. Oil on panel, $13^{3}/_{4}$ × $9^{1}/_{2}$″. The Museum, Aix-en-Provence.

type. The mobility of his own face was endlessly fascinating. He could be unsparing toward his large, almost shapeless nose and scrutinize himself with the same unflattering candor he reserved for the ragged forms of street beggars (Fig. 272). Nonetheless, some of his human vanity showed through when he dressed in exotic costumes, included himself in a mythological or Biblical painting, or romantically shaded portions of the face without lessening the intensity of his gaze, as in the etching illustrated. No artist has left a more intimate history of changes in his face, fortune, and family, with the result that much of his work constitutes a private artistic chronicle.

A portrait of himself and his first wife Saskia (Fig. 273), done about 1635, shows what was then Rembrandt's ideal of a man and a successful artist: woman and wine in hand, fine clothes with a suggestion of the bold cavalier, and a fine table and surroundings. The format he used was one employed by other Dutch artists for brothel scenes. Rembrandt shows himself as a sociable extrovert, proud of his material possessions and willing to be liberal with them. The carefree attitude seen in this painting helps to explain his later bankruptcy, and it records his transformation from a miller's son to an elegant Amsterdam gentleman. It provides a personal inventory, giving a visual richness to the sword hilt and glass which rivals the rendering of his own face. The painting mirrors a materialistic preoccupation that precludes serious human revelation.

Rembrandt's self-portraits after 1650 reflect a succession of personal crises and show a more critical and perceptive self-appraisal. Where the early self-portraits were based in part upon his own availability as a model, his ostentation, and a wholesome self-esteem, the later portraits demonstrate an increasing desire to know himself. A self-portrait from the 1660s summarizes these late alter images (Fig. 274). There is no setting or elaborate costume, and for this painting Rembrandt chose to play no role. The portrait is thus totally self-conscious in the literal sense of the word. Although his life had been marred with suffering and bitterness, no mood of resentment or self-pity enters into this portrait. It is a calm and supremely comprehending study of the evidence with which age invests the flesh—the flesh has become a human poem. For Rembrandt, man is ultimately a solitary being. The world is found in his brain; the eyes now mirror introspection rather than outward alertness of the early portraits. Moreover, greatness of intellect is unrelated to exterior beauty. While no one knew better than Rembrandt the insecurity of existence, the artist's last portraits still show wonder and enthusiasm for life.

The principal means by which Rembrandt expressed his human consciousness was light. Early in his career, he used light as a device to organize his paintings, to achieve melodramatic effects, and to convey a transparent symbolism. As he grew older, he became aware of its more profound potential. The luminosity in his later paintings was no longer the convincing illumination of the room in which the viewer stands; nor was it subject to rational theories of the particular relation of solids to voids. The light in his mature works is a mysterious and enveloping radiance, tangible yet independent of local colors. Its qualities proceed from the nature of the subject. Rembrandt used light to play upon the polarity of inner and outer worlds, and he used a rich incrustation of paint with a materiality previously unknown. By doing so, he achieved an astonishing range of substances as well as infinite gradations of light and shadow. His art is a profound synthesis of a basic materiality and a spiritualization of forms.

Rembrandt has not always been acclaimed as a great artist. He was "rediscovered" in the 19th century, but not until our own century was the magnitude of his achievement realized. Today it is acknowledged that no other painter surpassed Rembrandt in his sensibility to paint and his ability to develop its expressive potential. His ideas and feelings about man rank him with the finest Humanists. His art is one of human beings, whose destiny he saw through the body. In Rembrandt's paintings and graphic works, man appears in both historic and private moments, as hero and victim. To the protagonists of the Bible, legend, myth, and history—remote from the artist's sight—he gave a personality and humanity unprecedented in the history of art. He showed rulers in their fallibility, Biblical heroes and businessmen in their frailty, and the King of Kings as a gentle human being. Moral expression, for Rembrandt, took precedence over physical beauty.

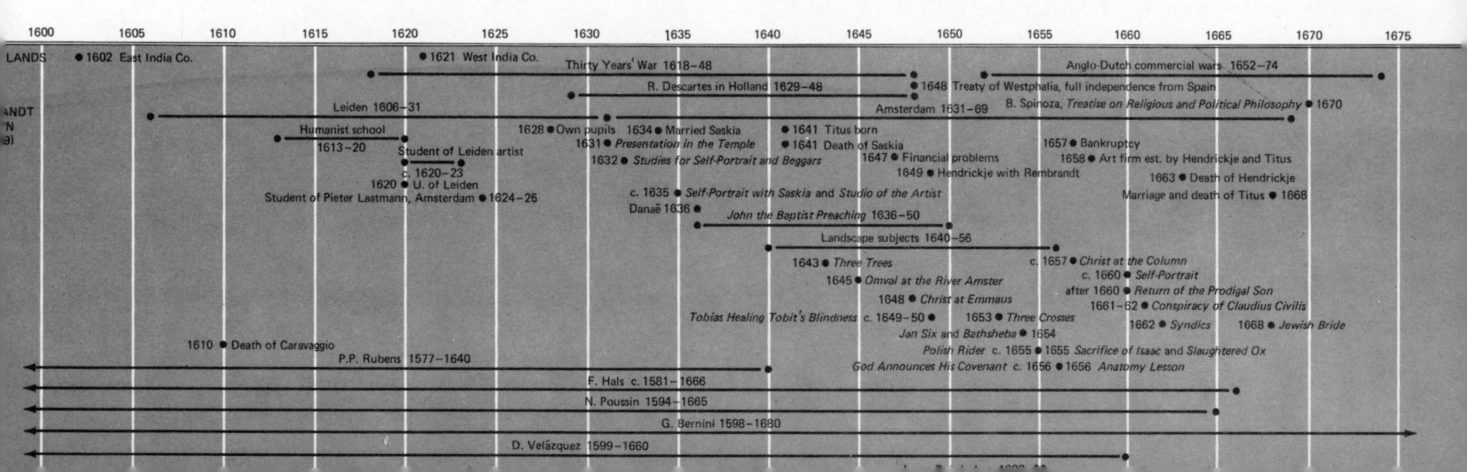

# 12

For the last hundred years or more—since the invention of photography and the growth of the mass media—the leaders of government have no longer called upon their finest artists for official portraiture. This separation of the best and most advanced art from the uses of political authority, and the consequent decline of the official state portrait are historically recent developments. The informality possible in the photograph corresponds to what modern leaders believe to be the tastes of the populace. Great portraits of past rulers, however, gave them more vivid life than did written chronicles; even today these sculptures and paintings satisfy human curiosity about the appearance of famous men. Here, we shall see how art has historically served the ruler in many vital areas, particularly as a means of projecting effective concepts of authority more than human personalities.

In antiquity art was an important means of making concrete the abstract concepts of kingship. The average man usually knew his ruler through art rather than through a physical presence. It was the artist who created an embodiment of the king's divinity and omnipotence, relying on his subject's likeness as well as on traditional prescriptions for making an interpretation of attributes that would be clearly understood by the people. Such public symbolism of authority extended also to the architecture associated with the residence, appearance or epiphany, and ceremonies honoring the ruler. The recurrence in the Mediterranean world, during the Middle Ages, of Egyptian and Classical hieratic symbolism was owing to more than its design appeal in painting, sculpture, and architecture. Succeeding cultures assimilated age-old devices to enrich art meant to glorify the reign of an earthly or Heavenly monarch.

## THE KING AS DEITY

The Egyptian pharaoh was regarded as divine, for he was the descendant and heir of the sun god, the ruler of the sky. An Old Kingdom statue of Khafre (Fig. 275) seated on a throne includes behind the head of the Pharaoh the carved symbol of the hawk-headed god Horus, lord of the rising sun. The hawk's wings encircle the ruler's headdress, symbolic of his origin and divine protection. The Pharaoh appears rigidly frontal, a timeless pose which was repeated without deviation during more than 3,000 years of Egyptian history and which was ancestor to the 12th-century enthroned Christ on the west façade of Chartres (Fig. 104). The transcendence of the Pharaoh over mortality is revealed through his aloof and immutable posture. There is no suggestion of bodily movement or facial expression. The stiffness and immobility of the human body and countenance were the means by which the sculptor, working with human anatomy, indicated the distinction of his king from mortals. In short, pharaonic imagery, dealing with a

*right:* 275. *The Pharaoh Khafre*. Giza, c. 1560 B.C. Diorite, height 5′6″. Egyptian Museum, Cairo.

# IMAGES OF AUTHORITY

cosmic kingship, sought deliberately to be as unnatural as possible. The only variation in the position of pharaoh statues is from the elbows down; the ruler is sometimes shown holding a staff of office or the crook and flail. The latter were the attributes of authority held by Osiris, the lord of the underworld and afterlife, who served as shepherd and judge of his people. The sacerdotal nature of pharaonic imagery parallels the ceremonious nature of Egyptian court life and the extreme formality of the kings' public appearances.

One of the oldest and most persistent devices for showing absolute authority and divinity of a ruler is that of *centralized composition*—setting the ruler between two flanking figures whose lesser stature is shown literally in their smaller scale or by subservient gestures. The pharaoh Mycerinus had himself portrayed erect and rigidly frontal between two goddesses, signifying not only his divine descent but also, for political reasons, demonstrating his acceptance by the local goddess of a province (*nome*) in his kingdom (Fig. 276).

Whether or not elements of naturalism, techniques such as bronze casting, and Egyptian symbols of kingship penetrated westward into Negro Africa or were themselves influenced by older Negro cultures is a problem that still occupies anthropologists and archaeologists. The West African civilization of Benin had a highly organized central government and a concept of sacred kingship analogous to that of European countries in the 16th and 17th centuries. A bronze relief plaque, dating perhaps from the 17th century, shows a seated Benin king (or *Oba*) flanked by two kneeling attendants (Fig. 277). His immobile posture and ritual gesture, larger scale, frontality, and possession of a hammer were all symbolic of authority.

*left:* 276. *The Pharaoh Mycerinus Between Two Goddesses.* c. 2500 B.C. Green slate, height 38½". Egyptian Museum, Cairo.

*above:* 277. *Benin King (Oba) and Attendants.* Nigeria, 17th century (?). Bronze, 16¾ × 15¼". British Museum, London.

Both in Egypt and in Benin, certain materials were royal prerogatives or monopolies for use in art. Both kings adorned their palaces with their own effigies. Both rulers were thought to be descended from dead kings and to be of divine nature. Elaborate ceremonies attended their public appearances. In certain African tribal societies, the ruler and important personages wore clothing (a warrior's surcoat, for instance), and nakedness was a mark of inferior social status. Egyptian pharaonic imagery allowed some facial likeness; that of Benin, however, insisted on a stereotype, so that the imperial image was representative of an abstract principle.

## WARRIOR KINGS

For a period of 3,000 years, pharaohs were shown in paintings and relief sculpture that proclaimed their godlike character and protection of the people. Shown in battle, at the hunt, in the company of other deities, and officiating at state ceremonies, the pharaoh's effigy was placed on the walls of tombs, palaces, and temples. One of the greatest of Egypt's rulers, Ramses III, who lived in the 12th century B.C., followed an established tradition by using the pylon of a great temple as a political billboard. In a relief decoration, he had himself shown hunting wild bulls (Fig. 278). This was not meant as a secular scene of frivolous sport, for all activities engaged in by a pharaoh were religious, symbolic of his fight against evil. Wild beasts as well as enemy tribes were viewed as the partisans of Set, an evil underworld deity. While the benevolent hawk god Horus flies above him, the Pharaoh coolly dispatches the fleeing animals with his spear. The reins tied to Ramses' waist seem unnecessary because of the perfect discipline and unison demonstrated by the chariot's horses. The symbolically small-scale troops also seem superfluous, for the divine ruler's victory was inevitable. The raised and extended front legs of the horses were a victory symbol throughout the ancient Near and Far East. The fallen, thrashing animal beneath the horses is interchangeable with bodies of dead warriors in battle reliefs. So effective was this combination of gallop and fallen prey that it persisted in imperial imagery into the 19th century and recurred with new connotations in Picasso's *Guernica* (Fig. 548). This relief of the hunt also demonstrates a fine synthesis of naturalistic observation (in fishes, reeds, and bulls) and the stylized or schematic formula with which Ramses and his retinue are depicted. The intrusion of pictographic writing extolling the Pharaoh demonstrates that the event and art transcended unities of time and space and possessed instead a higher reality.

A hunting relief from a 9th-century B.C. Assyrian palace shows King Ashurnasirpal II aiming at a lion poised on the rear of the royal chariot (Fig. 279). Assyrian palaces abounded in symbolically repetitious reliefs of imperial warfare, hunting, and religious ceremonies. The great size and number of reliefs were intended to impress visiting emissaries with the king's might. Assyrian kings were not deified; they were mortals who demonstrated their right to rule through physical prowess, actually jeopardizing their lives in stalking their prey or in hand-to-hand combat with their foes. The king's acclaim depended in part upon acknowledging the courage of his opponent, who was given an opportunity to attack. The Assyrian relief shown here indicates the type of hunt the king might conduct, utilizing captured lions that, if recalcitrant, could be goaded into fighting by the noise of cymbals and irritating wounds. Deliberate in his aim despite the beast's proximity, the King is about to release the fatal arrow. The muscular character of Assyrian kingship is reflected in the strong relief modeling, in contrast to the flatter Egyptian forms, which seem to lack bone and sinew. The overlapping of figures and objects in depth

*above:* 278. *Ramses III Hunting Wild Bulls* (detail of a pylon relief). Medinet Abu, c. 1180 B.C. Sandstone. Oriental Institute, University of Chicago.

*left:* 279. *Ashurnasirpal II Killing Lions.* Nimrud, c. 850 B.C. Limestone relief, 3′3″ × 8′4″. British Museum, London.

*left:* 280. *Prima Porta Augustus.* c. 19 B.C. Marble, height 6′8″. Vatican Museums, Rome.

*below:* 281. *Colossus of Barletta* (Emperor Marcian?). c. 465. Bronze, height 16′9″. Outside Church of Santo Sepolcro, Barletta.

and their abundant detail, schematized as it is, show a more earthbound orientation in Assyrian art than they do in Egyptian royal art. The profile view was favored in antiquity for its ready identification, clarity of exposition, and usefulness in rendering animals and figures in movement.

The richest legacy of imperial imagery derives from Roman art. The transformation of Republican Rome into an empire is reflected in two statues of rulers: that of Emperor Augustus (Fig. 280) was made in the late 1st century B.C.; the second work (Fig. 281), from the later Imperial era, probably represents Emperor Marcian who reigned from A.D. 450 to 470. The marble statue of Augustus is named for the cite of his wife's villa outside Rome, where it was found; the bronze cast of Marcian is usually referred to as the *Colossus of Barletta*, for its location in an Italian town on the Adriatic. Augustus' military uniform befitted the *Imperator*. In gesture he is the commander-in-chief exorting his troops. On his breastplate is the scene of a Parthian chieftain voluntarily returning eagle standards captured from Roman legions; a historic diplomatic feat of Augustus, the scene is approved by the figure of Jupiter and signifies a peaceful rule. Also symbolic are the figure of Alma Mater and the cornucopias, which attest to the prosperity under Augustus. The dolphin by his leg alludes to belief in the divine origins of the Emperor's family; the cupid astride it refers to Venus and fertility. Altogether on the breastplate are represented an actual event, divinities, and allegories demonstrating the universal Pax Romana for which Augustus was famed. Though deified by some of the conquered provinces, Augustus chose to remain *Princeps* in Rome, a "first citizen" nominally subject to the Senate in nonmilitary matters. Handsome and athletic, dignified but humane, the effigy of a ruler given to clemency as well as to war, the image recalls the grace and balance of the Greek *Spear Carrier* (Fig. 492).

Like a second bronze version of the *Augustus*, the Barletta statue also stood in a public place. It is a rare survival of the full-length Imperial statues of the time. Unlike that of Augustus, which was only slightly larger than human scale, Marcian's effigy towered impressively over the crowd, more than two and one-half times life size. No longer mortal and responsible to an earthly power, Marcian is deified in aspect and wears a crown. Both emperors were military figures, but Marcian's statue is the more aggressive. The quality of human mercy exemplified in Augustus is replaced by the severity of the later divine, uncompromising guardian of the Empire. In the original state, Marcian probably held a sword rather than a cross, his martial spirit giving comfort to his many non-Christian followers and evoking fear in his enemies. Symbols of power and accomplishment, the sword and the orb replaced the complex allegorical program of Augustus' armor. Relaxed fluidity of movements gave way to a firmer stance and rigidity in limbs and body. The sensuous softness of Augustus' form was succeeded by a tough, unyielding surface, as well as by a stiffer and more masculine treatment of the drapery.

Both works are ruler images. The head of Augustus echoes Classical Greek tastes (Figs. 51–53), displaying physical beauty, controlled and slightly softened treatment of hair and features, and an air of composure. The bronze head of Marcian has a geometric, blocklike form and an axial symmetry enhanced by the charismatic fixity of the enlarged irises. Augustus' more relaxed portrait does not belie an ability to speak eloquently and to extemporize. Marcian's tight-set mouth reminds us that on public occasions the post-Diocletian emperors spoke in formulas or communicated with prescribed signs, avoiding spontaneity and the trivial gestures that might have marred their godlike impersonality.

Between the Prima Porta and Barletta figures in date are two other works of Imperial art that reflect political and artistic changes. The equestrian statue of Marcus Aurelius (Fig. 282), made between A.D. 161 and 180, survived medieval destruction of Roman Imperial statuary because it was mistakenly believed to depict the first Christian emperor, Constantine. Originally, a fallen barbarian lay beneath the horse, and Aurelius' gesture is one of clemency to his foes. In his left hand he held the orb. Freestanding sculptures of mounted figures were in that era

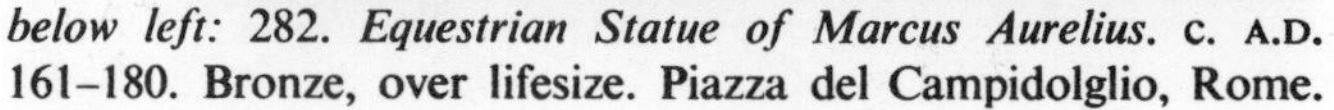

*below left:* 282. *Equestrian Statue of Marcus Aurelius.* c. A.D. 161–180. Bronze, over lifesize. Piazza del Campidolglio, Rome.

*above:* 283. *Commodus as Hercules.* c. A.D. 185. Marble, height 43½". Palazzo dei Conservatori, Rome.

*below right:* 284. HORATIO GREENOUGH. *George Washington.* 1832–40. Marble, height 11'4". National Collection of Fine Arts, Smithsonian Institution, Washington, D.C.

the prerogative of the emperor. So esteemed were Imperial effigies such as this that laws were written concerning human conduct prohibited in their vicinity; violation meant severe punishment. Public executions were performed before the monument, and a prisoner on trial could touch the statue, claiming sanctuary and the right of appeal to the emperor.

Aurelius' horse is rendered in meticulous detail, so that the bronze cast reveals strongly the modeled veins and creases in the flesh. The head of the Emperor is less detailed, however. To accommodate the beholder's gaze from below and at a distance, the hair portions are deeply drilled and the planes of the face are broadly modeled. There is an overall lessening of particularized features and portrait quality, making the figure and its gesture into more an ideal embodiment of the near-deific status of the living Emperor.

Toward the end of the 2nd century A.D. the gladiator-trained Emperor Commodus had himself depicted as Hercules (Fig. 283), thus proclaiming himself immortal. Nero had assumed the role of a living god in the 1st century, beginning a long tradition that centuries later in America produced Horatio Greenough's sculpture of George Washington in the manner of Zeus (Fig. 284) and situated Lincoln's enthronement in a Roman temple. The statue of Commodus reflects the vanity that caused this soldier-emperor to shoot five hippopotami with a bow and arrow from his box at the Colosseum before a cheering multitude. It also gives some indication of the caliber of ruler resulting from the choice of the army in its growing power over the Senate in electing and sustaining an emperor. Nonetheless, Commodus' bloody murder after a short and turbulent reign did not diminish the drive to deify the ruling authority of Rome.

## IMPERIAL PORTRAITS AND RELIEFS

Like their Assyrian predecessors, Roman emperors were shown in a wide variety of reliefs and paintings of battles, hunts, and ceremonial functions. One of the most beautiful and impressive reliefs of the Augustan age is the Ara Pacis ("Altar of Peace"), constructed and carved between 14 and 9 B.C. Built on the Field of Mars, a military parade ground then outside Rome, it was intended to publicize the Emperor's foreign and domestic policy. The Emperor and his family are shown on one of the exterior sides in a procession led by priests, which took place either at the founding or completion of the altar. Only a detail of the relief is shown here (Fig. 285), but it demonstrates the conscious informality of the groupings and the indistinguishability of Augustus (probably the figure at the left, the left half of whose body has been lost) from the others in the procession. Like other members of his family, the Emperor wears a laurel crown, but neither in posture, gesture, nor position is his preeminence stressed. The image Augustus sought to project was that of a ruler anxious to restore sincere religious observance and the unity of the family. Dilatory temple attendance and juvenile delinquency were not unknown in Augustus' time.

More then 300 years later, a great triumphal arch was erected close to the Colosseum and Forum to commemorate the victory of Constantine over Maxentius. It was adorned with new sculpture and with reliefs taken from older monuments. Two of the new reliefs showed Constantine receiving homage from the Senate (Fig. 286) and distributing gifts, according to tradition. In strong contrast to the more naturalistic figures of the Augustan relief, those of the Arch of Constantine jar the eye with their stunted bodies, large heads, repetitive gestures, geometric alignment, and total loss of individuality. The figures are flattened out and have lost all sensual appeal. The reliefs were relatively small and were not intended to fulfill the same function as, for example, the more than 60-foot, full-length statue of Constantine that was placed in his basilica. Although the best talent available at the time evidently did not work on

*right:* 285. *Procession of the Augusti*, portion of the frieze of the Ara Pacis. c. 14–9 B.C. Marble, height 5′3″. Rome.

*below:* 286. *Constantine Receiving Homage from the Senate*, frieze on the Arch of Constantine. Early 4th century A.D. Marble, height 41 3/8″. Rome.

*left:* 287. *Emperor on Horseback* (leaf of *The Barbarini Ivory*). c. 500. Ivory, 13³/₈ × 10″. Louvre, Paris.

the relief, it has a certain force and succeeds in conveying the court ideals of the period. In the Emperor's presence all activity was conducted according to a strict ritual. The importance of these reliefs lies in their culmination of the tendency toward a centripetal mode of composition, with total focus upon the strictly frontal and centralized figure of the Emperor. No previous ancient culture had realized so completely the artistic devices in the service of authority. Official taste of this epoch was indifferent to the organic qualities of flesh and blood. Expression of ideas superseded emphasis upon outward form, and the sensual life of the body glorified in Greece and early Rome passed into eclipse. A new and positive aesthetic evolved in accord with hieratic and spiritual ideals that would have been outraged by an interpretation like that of the Ara Pacis. A sophisticated, predominantly urban taste produced the Arch of Constantine statuary and the Barletta figure, and this provided the basis for such medieval Christian imagery as the Ravenna apse mosaic of Christ (Pl. 6, p. 44).

The eastern portion of the Roman Empire, known as *Byzantium*, was founded by Constantine in A.D. 330, with its capital city, Constantinople, named for the founder. Earlier Roman Imperial devices for imbuing art with the majesty and deeds of the ruler were continued and refined in the Eastern Empire in the centuries that followed. Art workshops were part of the Great Palace of the Emperors in Constantinople, erected during the reign of Theodosius in the second half of the 4th century. The ruler, who held a monopoly on many luxury materials such as purple dyes, sought to ensure that Imperial art would continue to remind his people of perpetual victory and divinely sanctioned rule. Coins, public statues, ivory reliefs on boxes, consular credentials, textiles, paintings, mosaics, army standards, and such precious objects as silver disks represented the Imperial effigy for a thousand years. The emperor was always shown as a majestic authority, whether in battle, hunting, officiating at public ceremonies, or attending the games in the hippodrome. The so-called *Barberini Ivory* (Fig. 287) is an outstanding example of the image of the early Byzantine ruler. A semiprecious medium imported from India and Africa, ivory had the advantage of softness for delicate and detailed carving, combined with durability and the capacity to take paint. Made about the turn of the 6th century, the Barberini panel was probably part of a series commemorating military and diplomatic triumphs of Emperor Anastasius I. The tripartite organization is a design scheme that can be traced back to Egyptian imperial imagery of the 1st Dynasty, notably in the votive palette of King Narmer (Fig. 288).

In both objects, the top zone is symmetrical, its uncompromising formality being reserved for images of a supreme deity. Flanking Egyptian gods represented in the form of bulls precede their later anthropomorphic treatment. On the ivory, a frontal bust of Christ appears in a medallion held by angels. The Christians had simply replaced earlier pagan Roman images of the emperor with those of their God and preserved the hieratic format. The second zone of the ivory shows the Byzantine Emperor on horseback, his standard largely obscuring the figure of an Asiatic chieftain. His stirrup is supported by an allegorical figure of Earth, and a flanking official presents him with a statue of Victory. On the palette, King Narmer is shown in a ritualistic gesture, with mace in hand, about to destroy his

*right:* 288. *Narmer Votive Palette*. Hieraconpolis, c. 3000 B.C. Schist, height 25″. Egyptian Museum, Cairo.

*right:* 289. *Disk of Theodosius.* c. A.D. 390. Silver, diameter 29 1/8". Academy of History, Madrid.

adversary with a single stroke. By the time of the *Barberini Ivory*, however, Byzantine emperors had reduced the frequency of such violent images, in a reflection of a Christianizing influence. While subordinate to their respective gods, both rulers assert their importance through their great scale within the zones they occupy. Anastasius is shown in not quite frontal pose so that he tactfully does not compete with Christ; he is relatively central within his field, but one flanking official is missing. In the lowest, most inferior register, both pieces have the greatest mobility and, symbolically significant, their least ordered portion. The enemies of Narmer flee or are dead, their disarray contrasting with the King's composed solemnity. Below Anastasius, on the left, are barbarians bringing tribute and, on the right, emissaries from India bearing gifts that include ivory. The relief carving in both works is of the highest quality—precise, clear, and adept in shaping compositional demands to political ones. The art of intervening centuries is testified to in the Byzantine relief, with its greater sensuousness, variety of movement, and body perspectives.

To someone unfamiliar with Byzantine art, it may appear stiff, repetitious, and unfeeling; there is no display of human warmth in the Imperial images, no dialogue between the figures. Unaccustomed to alternatives, Egyptian, Roman, and Byzantine artists accepted their assigned roles and succeeded in creating inspired art within officially imposed strict limitations. Much of the power of Byzantine art, like that of earlier Roman art, derives from its total realization of political and religious ideals. Like many other works, the *Barberini Ivory* and the silver *Disk of Theodosius* (Fig. 289), made at the end of the 4th century, show the possibilities of excellence in art that is not created in a republican society. Wearing the Imperial diadem, Theodosius is enthroned in the center of a gabled and arcaded structure that may have symbolized a façade of his palace. To the left and right of him are his sons, the princes Honorius and Arcadius, holding orbs symbolic of temporal rule. Flanking the whole are pairs of imperial guardsmen. An official kneels to receive a gift or investiture of power from the Emperor. According to court ritual, no one looks at the official. His hands are cloaked, showing his unworthiness to touch the divine person of the Emperor. In the area below is the earth goddess with the cornucopia symbolizing abundance under Byzantine rule; at this time, Christian emperors were not averse to using pagan symbolism. The Emperor's omnipotence is shown in hieratic fashion by his great scale, his centrality, and his location beneath an arch symbolic of Heaven. These attributes are more important than the individual personality or features of the ruler; hence the essential impersonality of the image. Again, the artist is depicting an abstract idea. An eye-witness description of an audience held with a Byzantine emperor by Liudprand of Cremona in the 10th century illuminates the environment that the artist was expressing, but not literally describing. Having been led into the audience chamber of the Emperor, Liudprand beheld the scene that he has described in the following way:

> Before the seat stood a tree made of bronze, gilded over, whose branches were filled with birds, also made of gilded bronze, which uttered different cries, each according to its various species. The throne itself was so marvelously fashioned that at one moment it seemed a low structure and at another it rose into the air. It was of immense size and was guarded by lions, made either of bronze or of wood covered over with gold, who beat the ground with their tails and gave a dreadful roar with open mouth and quivering tongue. Leaning on the shoulders of two eunuchs I was brought into the emperor's presence. At my approach the lions began to roar and the birds cry out. . . . I lifted my head and behold, the man whom I had just before seen sitting on a moderately elevated seat had now changed his position and was sitting on the level of the ceiling.

Unfortunately, no images of this marvelous throne and audience hall have survived the ages. The imaginative genius that contrived the tree and lions lives on only in the verbal record left by Liudprand.

The influence of Byzantine imperial imagery was felt all through the Middle Ages. One of its strongest manifestations is in 10th- and 11th-century Ottonian manuscript art depicting the Germanic emperors. An Ottonian emperor had married a Byzantine princess who brought to her husband's court works of art, and possibly artists, which helps to account for Eastern influence in Western Europe. Emperor Otto II had himself portrayed in a manner reminiscent of Theodosius (Fig. 290). Allegorical figures of four nations bring gifts to the impassive ruler who sits beneath an architectural canopy, itself a celestial symbol. The perspective of the canopy is rudimentary and inconsistent. To preserve the ruler's hieratic centrality within the arc of the canopy, the artist arbitrarily omitted the fourth column. To have rendered the depth of the painting consistently from the viewpoint of a spectator outside the picture would have meant subordinating the ruler to an external system governed by the viewer. Though suitable for thematic purposes, hieratic conventions could not be faithful to natural appearances.

The Ottonian portrait shares certain traits with a Japanese portrait of the great Shogun Minamoto Yoritomo (Fig. 291), by Fujiwara no Takanobu (c. 1142–c. 1205). Both were iconic representations of power. Takanobu, however, combined the impersonal symbols and stiff forms of the commander's ceremonial costume with a noticeable facial likeness of his subject. The Shogun is seated on a cushion throne, as he would be seen in the place of honor during a formal ceremony in the audience hall of his palace. This imposing portrait on silk was painted shortly after 1185, when Yoritomo overthrew the pleasure-loving Fujiwara regents, and the emperor retired from active rule. Yoritomo brought the *samurai*, the warrior caste, into power and created the military regime (Baku-Fu) that lasted in Japan until the 19th century.

Takanobu's painting inaugurated a portrait tradition in Japanese art. The style, a continuation from earlier periods, comprised large crisp silhouettes, clear ornamental surface patterns, a flat-toned, textureless flesh rendering, and an austere, seemingly airless surrounding. Mineral colors were mixed with glue to give opaque, unmodeled surfaces. By Western standards, the lines may at first seem uniformly drawn, but on closer inspection they reveal occasional deft changes in value while preserving a flowing, wirelike quality. The Shogun's individuality resides in the small, immobile shapes of the eyes, nose, and mouth. The position of the head and the hair style are traditional, as are the symbols of his office and power, the sword and scepter. Nevertheless, the injection of some of Yoritomo's distinctive features is evidence of an encroachment of the samurai taste for naturalism, in opposition to the abstract facial types characteristic of previous periods.

In Yoritomo's shogunate the code of Bushido came into ascendance. Yoritomo's portrait is therefore representative of a Japanese feudal ideal of the perfect knight, a code that Takanobu seems to have illustrated in many respects. The samurai was disciplined in the strict course of rational conduct: "Rectitude is the bone that gives firmness and stature . . . without rectitude neither talent nor learning can make of a human frame a samurai." He would at all times exhibit stoic composure and presence of mind: "A truly brave man is ever serene." The absence of animation in the portrait expresses the samurai view that it was unmanly to show emotion in the face and that

*left:* 290. *Emperor Otto II*, from the *Registrum Gregorii*. Trier, c. 985. Manuscript illumination. Musée Condé, Chantilly.

*right:* 291. FUJIWARA NO TAKANOBU. *Portrait of Minamoto Yoritomo*. c. 1185. Painting on silk. Jingo-ji, Japan.

*left:* Plate 38. JEAN CLOUET. *Francis I.* c. 1525–30. Oil on panel, $37^3/_4 \times 29''$. Louvre, Paris. (See p. 220.)

*below:* Plate 39. ANTHONY VAN DYCK. *Charles I.* c. 1635. Oil on canvas, $8'11'' \times 6'11^1/_2''$. Louvre, Paris. (See p. 221.)

Plate 40. ANTOINE-JEAN GROS. *Napoleon Visiting the Pest House at Jaffa*. 1804. Oil on canvas, 17′5″ × 23′7″. Louvre, Paris. (See p. 224.)

292. Andrea del Verrochio. *Lorenzo de' Medici*. c. 1478. Painted terra cotta, life-size. National Gallery of Art, Washington, D.C.

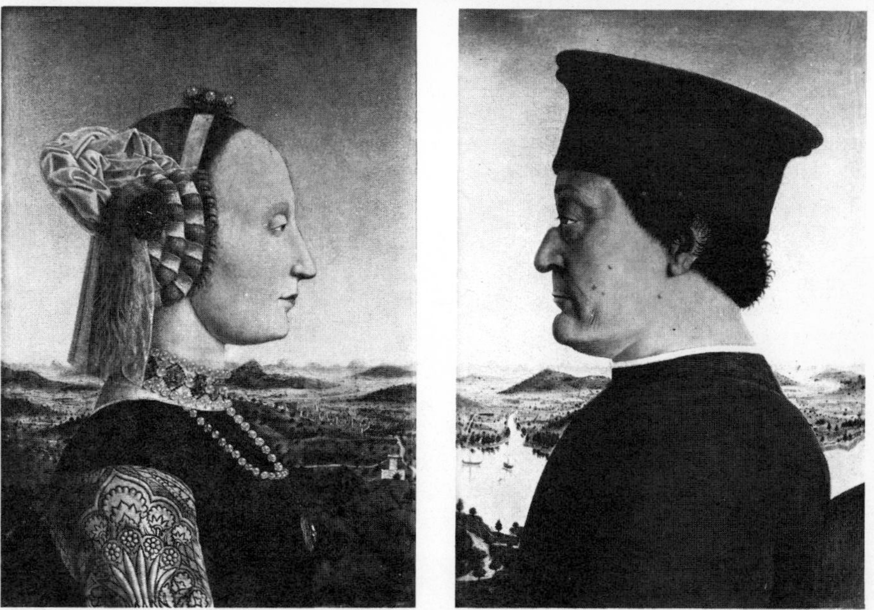

*above* and *right:* 293, 294. Piero della Francesca. *Battista Sforza, Duchess of Urbino* and *Federigo da Montefeltro, Duke of Urbino*. 1465–72. Oil on panel, each $18^1/_2 \times 13''$. Uffizi, Florence.

truly strong character was possessed by him "who shows no sign of joy or anger." An appreciation of culture was also part of his training. The samurai esteemed, and might even spare, an opponent who in the heat of battle maintained the presence of mind to compose or recall an appropriate couplet.

Yoritomo's portrait, which hung in a palace, may have been intended for worship. More likely it was a memorial to his military and administrative genius, to be venerated as an ideal by succeeding samurai. Thus the concept of a ruler's portrait serving as an ethical example was shared by East and West.

## STATE PORTRAITS

The finest sculptural portrait of a 15th-century Italian Renaissance ruler is that of Lorenzo de' Medici, done by Andrea del Verrocchio (1435–88) about 1478 (Fig. 292). This painted terra-cotta bust bears impressive witness to the Duke's power and excellence. The extent to which Florentine style was able to impart ideals of authority is further demonstrated when the bust is studied along with Machiavelli's statements in *The Prince*, written in 1513 and first published in 1532. Although Lorenzo the Magnificent died some twenty years before their writing, these precepts were influenced by Machiavelli's knowledge of his career and the tradition that produced him. Relevant to art is the importance placed upon appearances:

> We . . . encourage such Princes to fortify and guard their own capital city. . . . The Prince ought to go in person and perform the office of a commander . . . have no other aim, nor thought, nor take anything else for his proper art, but war. It is necessary for a Prince, desiring to preserve himself, to be able to make use of that honesty, and to lay it aside again as need shall require. Wherefore a Prince ought not to regard the infamy of cruelty, for to hold his subjects united and faithful . . . a Prince (ought) to serve himself of the conditions of the Fox and the Lion . . . and let him seem to him that sees and hears him, all pity, all faith, all integrity, all humanity, all religion . . . for all men in general judge thereof, rather by sight than touch, for every man may come to the sight of him, few come to the touch and feeling of him. A Prince ought to endeavor in all his actions to spread abroad a name of his magnificence and worthiness. He ought in the fit times of the year entertain people with Feasts and Masks.

Verrochio's Lorenzo is tough, sober, but contemplative. Subtle exaggerations make a somewhat leonine face. Like Lorenzo's palace (Fig. 324), the bust—with its firm roundness, simple dress, severe hairdo, and strong, thrusting nose—has a solid, even military appearance. The distinctly separate zones are composed on a frame of verticals and horizontals.

Skilled in war and politics, Lorenzo was also a cultivated man who formed at this court a brilliant artistic and intellectual circle, which included the young Michelangelo. On a scale less grand than Imperial Rome, the Medici also staged public pageants for the city of Florence.

Italian portraits of nobility in the 15th century, like the design of their palace façades, were strongly influenced by ideas from ancient Rome. In his double portrait of the Duke and Duchess of Urbino, Piero della Francesca (c. 1420–92) posed the subjects in profile (Figs. 293, 294), emulating coin and medallion effigies of Roman emperors. The profile view also served to conceal the Duke's damaged right eye, for while a fair degree of portrait likeness was considered desirable in this period, that which seemed ugly or deformed, along with conspicuous emotion, was to be concealed. The striking broken bridge of the ducal nose adds to the impressiveness of his birdlike profile. Un-Roman, on the contrary, was Piero's use of a landscape backdrop for the portrait. Artful placement of the heads above the horizon line perhaps implies that the Duke is, literally and figuratively, lord over the land he surveys. The couple's elevated viewpoint suggests that they are depicted on a balcony of their palace, and the Roman tradition of the ruler's association with a *loggia* or window of appearances has been seen in Figures 101 and 102 and will be discussed in Chapter 13.

State portraits of the past have little popularity or relevance today because of their extreme formality, their lack of warmth and individuality. These were portraits of concepts as well as of persons, and it is the alien character of absolutist political ideals that contributes to present-day public indifference or dislike. The formulas for the state portrait that originated in exceptional painting of the 16th and 17th centuries encouraged mechanical repetition in the hands of uninspired technicians; this continues even today in trustee portraits on our campuses or in corporation board rooms. With the rise of the state in the 16th and 17th centuries, it became the task of the portraitist to give material form to the immaterial entity of the state. The historian Garrett Mattingly, in *The Defeat of the Spanish Armada,* describes the climate in which state portraits emerged:

> The deepest longing of the troubled and divided sixteenth century was for unity and peace, and the only effective symbol men could find for the social order they craved was the person of the monarch. So the life of even the wickedest prince, most preachers taught, was sacred, and the duty of obedience was explicit no matter what the character of the ruler. Gradually that ultimate allegiance once given to the universal church was being transferred to secular sovereigns, in preparation for its further transference to an abstraction called the national state when men should think of it. The blasphemous doctrine of the divinity of kings was beginning to be in the air . . . everywhere in Europe. The sixteenth century belonged to the monarchs.

Early in the 16th century Jean Clouet (c. 1485–c. 1540) painted a half-length portrait of Francis I that is regal in subject and style (Pl. 38, p. 217). Required to portray grandeur, and therefore restricted in the gestures he could use, Clouet depicted the king with one hand symbolically on his sword and the other at rest on a cloth-covered table. Rational composure and power are thus conveyed in the hands alone. The outward swelling of the costume upward from the hands to the shoulders, culminating in the finely shaped neck, was consonant with what were thought to be ideal royal proportions; it was also in accord with the current fashion, which decreed exaggerating the breadth and masculinity of the king. Clouet gave only a subdued relief to the head, which is so disposed as to permit firm but delicate delineation of the long regal nose. The remote stare of the eyes is a fitting expression for a monarch, who was thought to exist and to govern in total isolation. Clouet's design stresses sharp contrasts of brilliant color, such as the red tapestry against the black and cream of the King's attire. Cool, nontactile surfaces add to the aloofness and unsensual character of the subject. State portraits were not supposed to be too literal or lifelike, and Clouet's almost abstract design of color, figure placement, and pose did much to create an aura that was symbolically unnatural. The style of a successful royal portraitist such as Clouet was of necessity identical to that of the ruler. As in antiquity, the state portraitist was enjoined to show the ruler as he should be, not as he was, and Mattingly points out that even from the pulpit men were told to revere and obey the most unscrupulous monarch.

The ruler who dominated the 16th century by his will, integrity, and sense of duty, along with his political and military success in putting together a global empire, was Charles V, the last German emperor crowned by the Pope. King during the Protestant Reformation, Charles warred with the heretics in Germany, yet sent a Lutheran army that sacked Rome in 1527; he was the power behind the Council of Trent and for most of his life overcame the intrigues of rival kings such as Francis I. The demand for imperial portraits such as those of Charles V was so great throughout Europe that not only copies of paintings but also engravings were used to disseminate the royal image. Eneas Vico (1523–67), an Italian printmaker, engraved a portrait of Charles V, based probably on a painting by Titian, in which the King's image was framed with allegorical figures of conquered territories, fame, and virtues (Fig. 295). All were set against a structure that resembled a Roman triumphal gateway or temple portico. Charles' roles as defender of the Faith, leader in war, and provider of prosperity are symbolized by the figures and garlands in the upper area of the print, while over the landscape at the left behind the structure his armies wage war. The ruins at the right refer to his conquests in Italy. The eagle above the portrait, on whose back stands the figure of Victory, is a motif from Roman triumphal arches, where it relates to the apotheosis of the emperor. Against the background activity of its frame, the Emperor's visage is serene but firm; utilizing Titian's characterization of Charles, Vico portrayed him as handsome and wise. When one reflects that it was during the reign of Charles V that great explorations were conducted in the New World and that territories as diverse as the Netherlands, Germany, Sicily, Spain, and Portugal were united, such extravagant homage from an Italian artist becomes understandable.

So successful was Titian (c. 1488–1576) in capturing the ideals of monarchy that Charles V ordered that no one else be allowed to paint his portrait. One of many influential state portraits that Titian did of Charles (Fig. 296) shows the Emperor riding on the field of Mühlberg, where he won a great

*above:* 295. Eneas Vico. *Charles V.* 1550. Engraving, $20^1/_4 \times 14^1/_4''$.

*right:* 296. Titian. *Charles V on Horseback.* 1548. Oil on canvas, $10'10^3/_4'' \times 9'1^7/_8''$. Prado, Madrid.

victory over two rival German rulers. In depicting Charles at the zenith of his power, Titian chose to adapt the old equestrian format from sculpture (Fig. 282) to easel painting. This increased the scale and monumentality of the ruler's image and, though in a seated pose, revealed him full length. His mastery of 16th-century ideas of horsemanship was validated in the noble bearing with which Titian endowed him. The gold and black armor, coupled with the aristocratic pose and the isolation of horse and rider, would seem to locate the action not in battle but as if on parade. The three-quarter pose of horse and rider permitted what Titian felt was the most striking view of Charles' face and displayed the beauty of the rounded, sash-covered breastplate. Many scholars have pointed out that Titian's clients favored his way of working, which was not bound to a strict likeness of the subject. After studying the sitter's features, Titian would then re-create him as he felt he ought to be. Although his painting is more sensuous than that of Clouet, Titian's state portrait has its own majestic quality.

During the 17th century artists of intelligence such as Anthony van Dyck (1599–1641) had discreet freedom to innovate, as long as they suited the taste and ideal of the patron. Rather than begin with an analysis of Van Dyck's finished painting of Charles I (Pl. 39, p. 217), let us consider the problem of representation as it might have been posed in the artist's mind. Charles I saw himself as a cavalier or perfect gentleman, a patron of the arts as well as the embodiment of the state's power and king by divine right. He prided himself more on his dress than on robust and bloody physical feats. Van Dyck had available to him precedents for depicting the ruler on horseback or in the midst of a strenuous hunt, but he set these aside. How then could he show the regal qualities and sportsmanship of a dismounted monarch in a landscape? Compounding the artist's problem was the King's short stature, just about 5 feet, 5 inches. To have placed him next to his horse, scaled accurately, could have presented an ungainly problem of their relative heights. Van Dyck found a solution to this last problem in a painting by Titian, in which a horse stood with neck bowed, a natural gesture that in the presence of the King would have appropriate connotations. Placing the royal pages behind the horse and farther from the viewer than the King reduced their height and obstrusiveness, yet furnished some evidence of the ruler's authority over men. Nature also is made to support and suitably frame the King. Van Dyck stations the monarch on a small rise and paints branches of a tree overhead to resemble a royal canopy. The low horizon line and our point of view, which allows the King to look down on us, subtly increase the King's stature. The restful stance yet inaccessibility of Charles depends largely upon his

*left:* 297. PETER PAUL RUBENS. *Henry IV Receiving the Portrait of Marie de' Medici.* 1622. Oil on canvas, 12'11$^{1}/_{8}$" × 9'8$^{1}/_{8}$". Louvre, Paris.

*above:* 298. GIANLORENZO BERNINI. *Louis XIV.* 1665. Marble, height 31$^{1}/_{4}$". Palace of Versailles.

pose, which is itself a work of art, derived from art, notably that of Rubens (Fig. 297). Its casualness is deceptive; while seemingly at rest in an informal moment, the King is every inch the perfect gentleman and chief of state. The cane was a royal prerogative in European courts of the time, and its presence along with the sword symbolized the gentleman-king.

Just as the subtle pose depicts majesty, Van Dyck's color, with its regal silver and gold, does much to impart grandeur to the painting and to achieve a sophisticated focus on the King. The red, silver, gold, and black of his costume are the most saturate and intense of the painting's colors and contrast with the darker or less intense coloring of adjacent areas. Largely from Rubens, Van Dyck had learned the painterly tricks by which materials and textures could be vividly simulated, so that the eye moves with pleasure from the silvery silken sheen of the coat to the golden leather sword harness and then on to the coarser surface of the horse, with a similar but darker combination of colors in its coat and mane. Van Dyck's portrait is evidence that, whatever one's sympathy for the message, the artist's virtuosity and aesthetic can still be enjoyed.

The royal esteem that painters enjoyed took the form of a monopoly granted to Titian by Charles V for his portraits. Peter Paul Rubens (1577–1640) even served as a royal ambassador; his life style was that of the aristocracy. Rubens was the greatest interpreter of Baroque rulers' expectations, for, with his broad education, he was able to synthesize pagan and Christian symbols for interpreting absolute monarchy and the divine right of kings. In 1635, for the triumphal entry of Archduke Ferdinand into Antwerp, Rubens received a corps of artists to decorate the entire city. Earlier, Marie de' Medici had commissioned Rubens to execute a great cycle of paintings dealing with her life as Queen of France and celebrating the reign of her late husband. In *Henry IV Receiving the Portrait of Marie de' Medici* (Fig. 297) Rubens mingled fact and fancy. Royal custom called for an important artist to portray the bride-to-be for the groom, who may never have seen her. Here, in double flattery, Rubens depicted the King as enraptured by the *painting* of his betrothed. The allegorical figure of France shares the King's admiring gaze. Two cupids, having seized the royal armor, signify that, for love, he had put aside thoughts of war, then being waged in Saxony—perhaps referred to in the burning city in the distance. Above sit Jupiter and Juno with their attributes, the eagle and the peacock, an ironic approval in pagan heaven of this Catholic union. In one of the most inspired postures in state portraiture, the King, attired in royal armor and bearing the courtly gentleman's cane, gracefully turns so that we see him in full length while the royal profile is directed toward the smiling visage of Marie. Even in the 17th century such conceptions demanded willing suspension of disbelief, but Rubens carried off the artifice with vigor and conviction, for the grand style and masterfull theatrics persuade us that the senses could verify an event of this character.

The deification of Louis XIV was a full-time project for the army of artists, musicians, writers, and poets gathered at the great court of Versailles in the 17th century. Among this brilliant coterie was the sculptor Gianlorenzo Bernini (1598–1680), who in 1665 carved the magnificent bust of King Louis XIV (Fig. 298) that remains in his bedroom at Versailles.

In his memoirs, Louis set down his views of the ideal Christian king:

> As he is of a rank superior to all other men, he sees things more perfectly than they do, and he ought to trust rather to the inner light than to information which reaches him from outside. . . . Occupying, so to speak, the place of God, we seem to be sharers of His knowledge as well as of His authority.

In carving his ideals of kingship, Bernini accorded perfectly with those of Louis. Verocchio had organized the bust of Lorenzo de' Medici (Fig. 292) geometrically and made it rest solidly on a broad base, with the subject's eyes turned down. Bernini's King seems airborne above a sweep of drapery swirling about a narrow base, the head turned unabashedly in a three-quarter view, its far-off expression a response to some "inner light." The wig billows about the serene countenance, while the gleaming marble recalls that Louis was the Sun King.

The most expensive portrait ever painted is reputedly that of Louis XIV (Fig. 299) by Hyacinthe Rigaud (1659–1743), who may have received over $70,000 for his work. Borrowing from Van Dyck, Rigaud attained the logical culmination of state-portrait development. The painting abounds in references to the kingly vocation. The column is a royal symbol derived from early Greece. The King stands in yards of purple lined with ermine and emblazoned with fleur-de-lis, the epitome of confidence and courtly grace. Carefully exposed, the shapely legs reveal their trained suitability for the dance. The high-heeled red shoes give the subject greater stature, for the King took pride in his manliness and in exemplifying the etiquette he demanded of his couriters. The elaborate full-length portrait encourages the viewer to inspect, not the face, but the splendid accessories of the King's office.

Napoleon was the last of the great rulers of Europe to employ the most important artists of his time. At Napoleon's request, the French artist Jacques-Louis David (1748–1825) showed the general leading his troops on a historic march across the Alps in 1800 (Fig. 300). Although Napoleon was

*left:* 299. HYACINTHE RIGAUD. *Louis XIV.* 1701. Oil on canvas, 9′1$\frac{7}{8}$″ × 5′10$\frac{7}{8}$″. Louvre, Paris.

*right:* 300. JACQUES-LOUIS DAVID. *Napoleon Crossing the Alps.* 1800. Oil on canvas, 8′10″ × 7′7″. Palace of Versailles.

*left:* 301. Ehrler. *Der Führer*. 1939. Oil on canvas. Whereabouts unknown.

still in the office of First Consul, this constitutes the last of the great imperial equestrian paintings. Following the orders of his subject, David showed Napoleon expertly mounted on a wildly rearing horse, pointing upward as if to the mountain peaks or to Heaven. In reality, however, it was not this romantic, commanding gesture that inspired 40,000 men to traverse the mountains; rather, the feat was accomplished by great staff work and five days of soldierly fortitude. Napoleon posed briefly for the rendering of his face, telling David that close resemblance was not important: "It is not the exact reflection of features, warts on the nose, that makes a likeness; it's the character and what animates the physiognomy, that needs to be painted. No one inquires if the portraits of great men are likenesses. It's enough that their genius lives in them." By showing the advancing army in the middle ground, seen from under the belly of the horse, David was following tradition and rational perspective, but Napoleon himself was displeased that his men were shown so small, as if they could be crushed by the horse's hoofs. The painting, with its obviously staged quality, is indeed contradictory to fact, for Napoleon crossed the Alps not on an unstable steed but on a sure-footed mule. As stand-in for the subject, one of David's students posed atop a ladder, pointing his arm till it dropped. Separate studies were made of Napoleon's white charger, which was shown rearing in the manner of 17th-century equestrian portraits. Despite such contrivances, David was sufficiently inspired to make the painting genuinely impressive. A dark foreground, spotlighting, and the pearly grey of the mountain setting and turbulent sky throw the striking figure of Napoleon into dramatic relief. Reviving an ancient symbol of victory, David has the wind at Napoleon's back, and the agitation it creates makes the face seem the serene center of a storm. The statement was that, like Hannibal and Charlemagne, with whose names *Bonaparte* is inscribed on the foreground rock, the soon-to-be Emperor would lead his country to new heights of glory.

Not a hereditary monarch like Charles V and Henry IV, Napoleon had to use art to help legitimatize his claims to power and, in one spectacular instance, to counteract a catastrophe that set his Egyptian army violently against him and threatened his support in France. After the fall of Jaffa, Napoleon's generals violated the surrender and slaughtered the entire garrison. Shortly afterward, bubonic plague nearly decimated Napoleon's army, a tragedy that to many seemed divine retribution. At great personal risk, Napoleon visited his suffering men at the hospital in Jaffa. Though not an eyewitness, Baron Antoine-Jean Gros (1771–1835), at Napoleon's order, utilized written accounts to produce a painting that is a fine example of counter-defamation propaganda (Pl. 40, p. 218). Shown in the midst of the plague-stricken, Napoleon calmly extends his ungloved hand to touch the bubonic boil in the armpit of a soldier. This gesture derives not from history but from art history, from scenes of Christ and the saints healing the sick and of the king, in a 17th-century imperial tradition, touching to effect cures. But no royal image ever made the public so aware of death, which is exhibited in gangrenous bodies at the base of the painting at the viewer's eye level. While confirming reports of the terrible casualties of the Egyptian campaign, Baron Gros also transformed Napoleon into a savior-king. In actuality, Napoleon, when forced to retreat from Acre and Jaffa, ordered poison placed by the wounded to enable them to take their own lives.

Knowing the historic effectiveness of art in political propaganda, Adolph Hitler banned art and used compliant, technically proficient mediocrities to revive state portraiture. A formal portrait of Hitler (Fig. 301) is as well crafted as Rigaud's *Louis XIV*. The placement of the Führer's figure above the viewer's eye level enhances a modest physical stature. Other heroicizing devices are the uniform and the gigantic sculpture of a powerful youth holding an eagle, the latter recalling the hawk god of pharaonic imagery (Fig. 275) and rulers portrayed with dieties (Fig. 280). The building instruments and blocks strewn over the foreground refer to the New Order's achievements in construction and to Hitler's obsessive self-image as an architect. The stadium, seen on the horizon, was the incubator of Nazi youth, whom Hitler served

*left:* 302. ROBERT RAUSCHENBERG. *Buffalo II.* 1964. Oil on canvas with silk-screen, 8 × 6′. Collection of Mr. and Mrs. Robert B. Mayer, Winnetka, Illinois.

as spiritual father. With his upward gaze and three-quarter view, Hitler posed as the visionary contemplating the future. Total frontality would have brought portraiture full circle to pharaonic forms. As in older state portraiture, the painter conveyed the abstract ideas of the regime rather than the personality or mood of his subject. It is skilled propaganda in support of the Hitlerian legend of invincible strength and immortality, admitting neither compromise, humility, nor compassion.

## PERSONALIZING THE PRESIDENCY

The final example is of the late President John F. Kennedy (Fig. 302), made by Robert Rauschenberg (b. 1925). The constant exposure of the president's image on television and in the press has destroyed the traditional, almost sacred character of the ruler's portrait. Rauschenberg accepted President Kennedy's popularized image and adapted newspaper photographs to his own complex, personal imagery. Rauschenberg's eccentric placement of the presidential photos within the composition disregards the world of rank, and their juxtaposition with other photographs neither conjures the attributes of the assassinated chief of state nor attempts to synopsize the Kennedy years. By the 1960s the image of authority had become susceptible to an artist's playful memory, nostalgia, taste for surprise, and wit; thus *Buffalo II* is an autobiographical assemblage of motifs culled from the artist's studio and from his urban environment. The Kennedy image, like that of other public and popular heroes, faded in and out of Rauschenberg's art. The artist's repertoire of press images permitted an idiosyncratic and unprogrammed way to conjoin past and present, common and rare, art and life. Titian's *Venus* is discernible, on its side and reflected in a mirror. Near the President's head appears a photograph of the American eagle, possibly a pun on the Egyptian hawk god Horus (Fig. 275), even though the dotted line leading from the eagle discourages the allusion. The enlarged hand, photographed during a presidential conference, draws attention to a small bird. The "key" to the work offered by Rauschenberg is the photo of an ignition key silk-screened onto the canvas. In *Buffalo II* the artist's private meditations fuse the ruler's image with art and non-art. The photograph, esteemed by the public as arbiter of what is true, real, and vivid, is paradoxically dimmed or made ambiguous by cropping, enlargement, and superimposition and then ironically contrasted with the tangible evidence of the artist's energetic presence left by his brush in the upper left. In Rauschenberg's view, it is the artist, not the ruler, who today fashions our vision of the world.

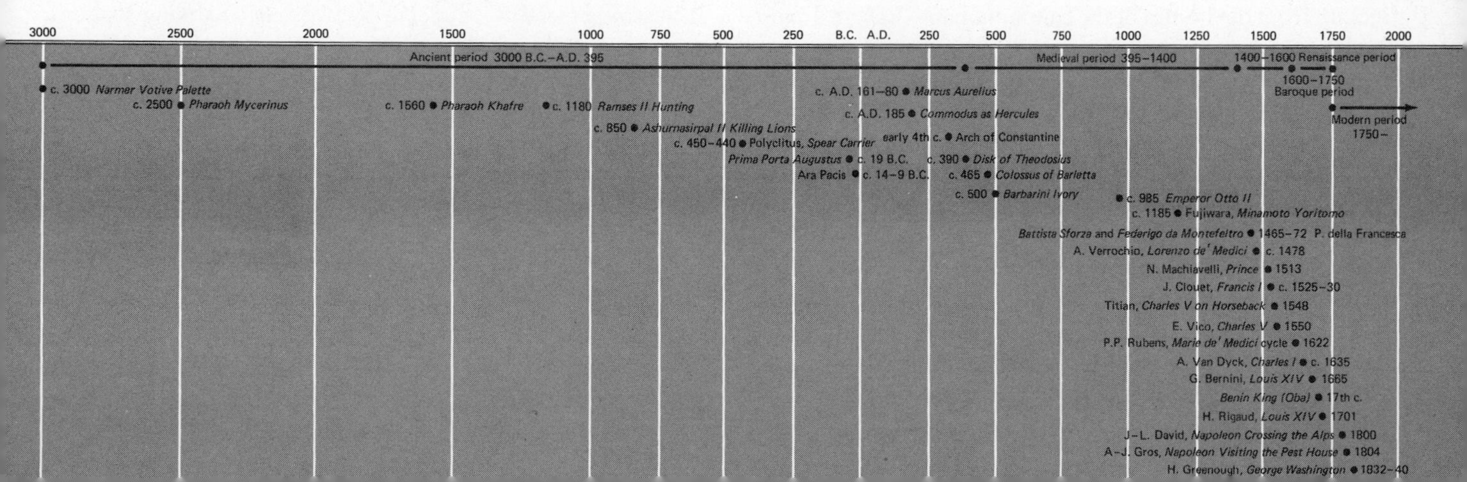

# 13

How misleading is the notion that architecture must always be an abstract art form was demonstrated earlier by the discoveries of scholars regarding the symbolism of religious buildings. Temples and churches, in turn, derived much of their symbolism or mystical associations from architecture that in ancient times had served kingship. Over a period of centuries certain architectural features such as gateways and palace façades acquired, not just from written sources but in the minds of both the masses and rulers themselves, connotations of authority. When kings acted like gods, and gods were interpreted as kings, it is not surprising that the ancient architecture of palace and temple should have acquired royal and divine associations. The influence of ancient royal architecture descended through the Middle Ages and into the Renaissance and Baroque periods. In modern times, its propagandistic and symbolic values were revived by Mussolini and Adolph Hitler. It is clear, then, that the history of architecture often mingles with the history of ideas and that architecture has been used as a powerful instrument by rulers to strengthen their image in the minds of their subjects. The destruction wreaked on so many palaces is a substantial tribute to the effectiveness with which monarchy has been identified with its masonry.

In their formal relations with the public, ancient rulers used specially designed architecture as a backdrop for ceremony. But even without such public rituals, the architecture —by its symbolic associations, grandeur, durability, and distinction from the homes of the common man—was, in a sense, a substitute for the ruler, a constant reminder of his power whether he was at home or abroad. Ancient coins usually bore the king's image, and often there was also a simple rendering of the entrance to his palace—which for most people was all they would know in their lifetime of the royal residence. The dome over the United States Capitol, for example, is today sufficient to identify this country and evoke its form of government. Ironically, however, the dome has anything but a republican source and history, rooted as it is in ancient symbolism of Heaven (Fig. 212) and serving to proclaim the divinity of Near Eastern and Roman monarchs.

Unlike our own and other present-day governments, those of the past regularly called upon their best architectural talents to construct public buildings. Like religious architecture since the 19th century, the best modern architecture has on the whole developed independently of the state, under the patronage of private persons and business. For this and other reasons, it has become difficult for us to appreciate that what seem to be dead and impersonal ancient ruins once embodied so many of civilization's most important political values.

## ANCIENT GATEWAYS

Ancient Egypt and Mesopotamia cradled much of human civilization and evolved important architectural symbols, notably the imposing gateway to a city or to a palace-temple complex. The great *pylons,* or gateways, to Egyptian temples such as that of Ramses III at Medinet Abu also served to front the palace when it adjoined the sacred precinct (Fig. 303). Upon the huge walls of the pylons, the pharaohs had carved and painted records of their victories and descent from the gods, with whom they were often shown in company. Roman emperors were later to do the same on their triumphal arches. Set into rectangular recesses on the face of the pylons were flagstaffs from which flew pennants signifying the god or pharaoh in residence (Fig. 304). The pylon form consists of a central zone for the great doorway, possibly surmounted by a solar disk; both disk and doors were originally covered in lustrous metal. Completed by two taller flanking sections, the pylon ideologically represented the gateway to Heaven, with its hieroglyph denoting the sun setting between two mountains. In all probability, this tripartite division derived its form from that of Mesopotamian fortified gateways (Pl. 41, p. 235). The great scale of the pylons was intended to overwhelm those who approached them frontally, along a prescribed path that was often flanked by guardian sphinxes. The massiveness of these gateways is explained in the declaration of a pharaoh who announced to his god that he had built him an august house which would endure for a million years. The act of passing through the gate was a symbolic one, for within

# THE ARCHITECTURE OF AUTHORITY

lay the Egyptian equivalent of Paradise. Although they have been destroyed, it is known that when palaces adjoined the temples (at right angles to the forecourt and central axis) provision was made for the pharaoh to appear on a balcony or at a window (the *window of appearances*), from which he could look down on his subjects and on the ceremonies in the first open court behind the pylon.

In Mesopotamia, most of the prevalent mud-brick architecture has survived to a lesser extent than have the stone structures of Egypt, but the shape and meaning of its great symbolic gateways are known, and through an archaeological reconstruction one can see the famous Ishtar Gate of Babylon (Pl. 41, p. 235). The simple tripartite design consists of two flanking square towers with an arched portal between. Crenellated battlements for defensive purposes crowned the gateway. The arch was a symbol of Heaven, simulating its apparent curvature, and the decoration in blue enhanced the comparison. The king would often appear enthroned under the arch

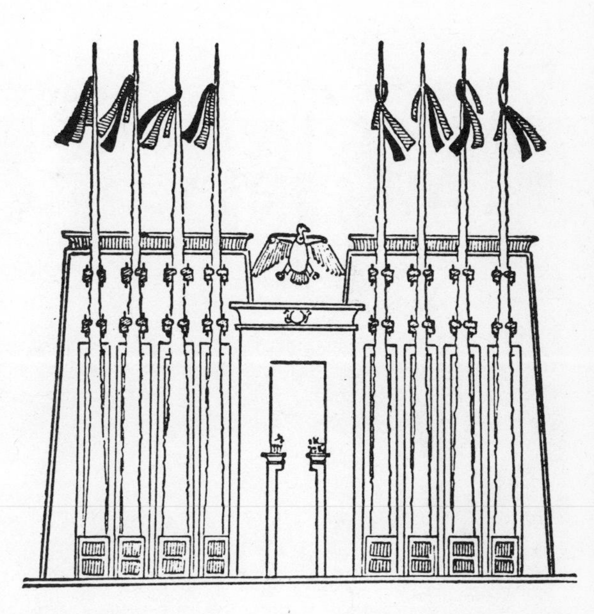

*left:* 303. Funerary temple of King Ramses III, Medinet Abu (Thebes). 20th Dynasty, 1198–1167 B.C.

*above:* 304. Drawing of a pylon from the Temple of Khons, Karnak.

of the gateway to his palace or the city and there hold public audience or administer justice. The animals modeled in ceramic tile distributed over the wall surfaces of the Ishtar Gate are spirit guardians, and the king's epiphany to his people was thus staged with tangible evidence of his support by the gods. The persistence of this type of tripartite, arcuate portal can be seen in various examples in this chapter, for not only the Egyptians but the Romans and medieval lords as well found it ideal both for practical defense and for its long-standing associations of kingship (see also Figs. 101, 102).

When Agamemnon marched off to rescue Helen, thus beginning the Trojan war, he passed through the Lion Gate of his citadel Mycenae (Fig. 305), which dates probably from the mid-13th century B.C. The gate is so named because of the heraldic lions carved in relief above the actual opening. The utilization of sculpture and symbolic figures to heighten the appearance and significance of an important entrance had analogies in the Assyrian human-headed winged bulls who guarded royal palace entries. The device of the lions flanking a single column is interpreted as an emblem of the royal house of Mycenae, for the ruler lived in the only structure fronted by columns. The column of the relief rests upon an altar, intended to signify the closeness of the royal house with the city's goddess and the descent of the royal family from Zeus. The association of the house of the ruler with columns has persisted down to the 20th century, and rulers have often had a column included in their portraits (Fig. 299). While the column itself may not have had specific symbolism, early in its history it came to indicate a special place—the royal house—of king or god, and this continuing association was more important than aesthetic considerations of design.

As Rome acquired dominion over the ancient world and gradually absorbed the varied cultures of the conquered peoples, her emperors adapted to their own use the imperial architectural devices of their enemies. As reminders of Roman rule, triumphal arches were built in conquered cities, and special ceremonies celebrating the emperor's visit were performed before this background. A reconstruction of the Roman city gate from Miletus (Fig. 306) has a place for the emperor's effigy in the niche above the central portal; this niche is crowned by a triangular roof line, the use of which was an Imperial prerogative, and was probably flanked by statues of Roman gods. The columns, niches, and porchlike design possibly derived from architectural features of the Imperial palace in Rome, an edifice that no longer exists. Of interest in studying Baroque development of palace design some 1500 years later is the articulation of the Miletus gate,

*above:* 305. The Lion Gate, entrance to the citadel, Mycenae. c. 1250 B.C.

*right:* 306. The City Gate from Miletus (restoration). c. A.D. 160. Staatliche Museen, East Berlin.

*right:* 307. The Palace of Diocletian at Spalato (Split, Yugoslavia). A.D. 4th century. Reconstruction model after E. Hebard.

*bottom left:* 308. The Colosseum, Rome. A.D. 70–80.

*bottom right:* 309. The Colosseum, aerial view.

with its projecting flanks and focus on the center by means of the interrupted pediment above the Imperial effigy. Here are early symbols of centralized authority achieved by a subordination of the flanking parts and by a manipulation of projection and recession that climaxes in the middle niche.

One of the best-preserved Roman palaces is that built by Emperor Diocletian at Spalato, on what is today the coast of Yugoslavia, from which at the beginning of the 4th century he ruled his half of the Empire. The west gate had the Mesopotamian design, but was augmented with niches for sculpture flanking the door and an open arcade above, denoting an imperial residence and calling to mind the window of appearances. A reconstruction of the palace (Fig. 307) shows the mile-long arcaded loggia that afforded the Emperor and his court a pleasant stroll and view of the Adriatic. The broad cruciform avenues of the palace, which bisect the overall square into four different areas, served not only ordinary traffic but also the many liturgical processions required. Immediately behind the colonnaded sea wall are the audience and ceremonial chambers, the state banquet hall, and the Imperial apartments. The octagonal structure jutting out above the others is Diocletian's tomb. Opposite is a temple precinct. The two square, atriumlike structures were residences for members of the court and the palace guard. The palace was in effect a walled city, with its own martial order of landscaping. The layout provided for many long colonnaded vistas whose dramatic focus was on Imperial symbols such as ceremonial courts or on some other space intended for an appearance of the ruler himself. Axial symmetry, found initially in the layout of Roman military camps, became an Imperial symbol in implementing the strict organization of buildings and space on a vast scale. Nowhere is this seen more impressively than in the city of Rome itself.

## ROMAN CIVIC STRUCTURES

**The Arena** The single monument that best commemorates the Imperial, and uncivil, playground is the Colosseum (Figs. 308, 309), built between A.D. 70 and 80 by Vespasian and his son Titus, on the site of an artifical lake on Nero's palatial estate. The Colosseum was inaugurated in A.D. 80 with the killing of 5,000 animals in the arena. Within the

*right:* 310. Plan of the Baths of Caracalla, Rome. A.D. 211.
*bottom right:* 311. Baths of Caracalla (reconstruction).

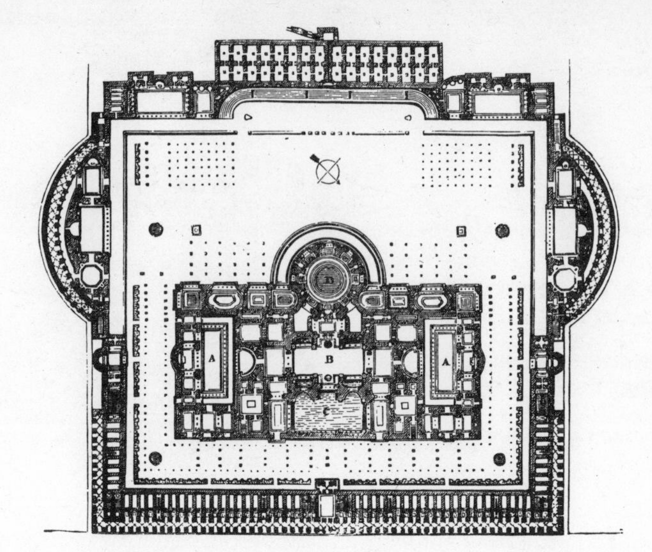


three succeeding centuries, this imposing figure paled beside the expenditure of 5,000 pairs of gladiators and 11,000 animals in one day or in comparison with the bill of $2,500,000 for gladiators paid by Marcus Aurelius for a single series of games. The martyrdom of Christians was, numerically, but a minor item on the arena's bill of fare.

While many of the architectural forms and principles used by the Romans had been known earlier, no previous culture had brought so many ideas and techniques together on such a grandiose scale. Whereas the finest styles and most perfect buildings had previously been reserved for the gods and kings, the Romans also made fine architecture available for public use. The development of the arch, buttress, barrel and groin vaults, and the masonry and concrete dome were Roman contributions utilized for the needs of the living populace, but they also constituted symbols of Imperial benefaction.

The Colosseum rises in several tiers above the ground, covering 6 acres and forming an open-air oval amphitheater with diameters of 615 and 510 feet; the arena itself is 281 × 177 feet. It probably accommodated 50,000 spectators. The partially ruined exterior shows its three tiers of arcades, the upper two of which were filled with sculpture. Above the arcades was a wall punctuated by windows, shields, and supports for the ship's masts to which the ropes for the canvas awning shading the spectators were fastened. Sailors manned catwalks to manipulate the awning, which was at times painted like a billboard of political propaganda. On the exterior, the 160-foot wall gained a muscular and rhythmic emphasis from the columns engaged to the piers of the arcades. Travertine marble attached with metal clamps covered the outer wall. At ground level, eighty archways gave access to the arena. The exterior had a handsome masculine simplicity in the clarity, vigor, and starkly expressive design of its serial openings and horizontal courses.

The open arena was supported on a great brick, stone, and concrete skeleton of piers, arches, vaults, and corridors. This network permitted quick entrance and exit of the masses, whose tickets—like those of a modern stadium—showed them their entrance arch and seat designation. The concentric, continuous vaulted galleries on the second and third levels permitted shaded strolling during intermissions. Beneath the arena, with its floor of sand (often covered by wooden boards), was a network of rooms, cages, ramps, and elevators run by counterweights and pulleys that brought the beasts directly onto the field. Elaborate sewers served not only for the disposal of blood and waste but also for draining water when the arena had been flooded for mock naval battles. The natural springs that had fed Nero's lake serviced the Colosseum. On a given day, the arena might in the morning contain a miniature fleet in combat, and in the afternoon hold artificial mountains and forests through which animals and hunters would stalk each other. The ingenuity, energy, and ambition of the Colosseum stage managers became taxed increasingly and drawn to perversion as the centuries went by and the public demanded new and bigger thrills from their rulers.

**Imperial Baths** The Colosseum and its slaughterhouse function for purposes of public diversion are not the sole

*right:* 312. Basilica of Constantine, Rome. A.D. 310–320. Reconstruction after G. Gatteschi.

keys to understanding Imperial architecture and Roman society. No other government provided its people with architectural facilities for enjoying life that were as extensive, practical, and handsome. The Roman Imperial bathing establishments, or *thermae,* provided recreation in a healthier sense. While Rome had hundreds of small public baths, there were eventually nine major thermae, which could serve several thousand people at a time. Roman concern with personal hygiene goes back to the city's earliest history. By the time Emperor Caracalla built his enormous bath, there was a long tradition whereby all Romans set aside at least the late afternoon to go to the thermae, there to tend both body and mind. The Imperial baths were, in truth, miniature cities. All are presently in ruins, but those of Caracalla, built in A.D. 211 and appreciably restored in modern times, are typical.

The Baths of Caracalla (Figs. 310, 311) were built upon a great walled platform, which was 1,080 feet on each side and covered 270,000 square feet; outside the thermal complex were shops. Underground were furnaces for heating water and steam to warm the gigantic rooms, great *hypocausts* or ducts, and service corridors large enough for horse-drawn vehicles to pass through. Within the walled area were colonnades, gardens, fountains, sculpture, lecture halls, and libraries (in the east and west semicircular segments of the plan), as well as athletic fields and the great central complex of bathing halls, dressing rooms, and grand concourse. For the first time in antiquity, sports and bathing practices were brought together, permitting both athletic exercise and cleansing of the body. The cultural facilities permitted audition of new plays and of speeches, examination of art objects, and reading. Juvenal's prayer for "a healthy mind in a healthy body" could thus be realized. Further, the baths were ideal for socializing and the exchange of news and of political views. Personal reputations and politics were, needless to say, both in jeopardy at times of mixed bathing in the nude.

A bathing ritual began with skin-scraping and a "dry bath" of steam; then followed immersion in a domed hot pool *(caldarium)* to the south, passage to the central concourse *(tepidarium),* for cooling off and conversation, and finally a dip into the cold pool, in a chamber *(frigidarium)* open to the air on the north side of the complex. The warm central hall contained an estimated 1,600 people at one time. No previous society had provided such extensive *indoor* facilities for civic enjoyment.

This conquest, or creation, of vast internal space was made possible by engineering. Enormous brick and concrete vaults were raised upon huge buttressed piers. The *groin vault,* the intersection at right angles of two barrel vaults of equal diameter, permitted support of the structural load on four piers. This in turn freed great wall areas for fenestration. The Romans were masters not only of spatial organization but also of the use of lighting. This light fell, moreover, not upon rude concrete but on marble and mosaic floors and pools, polychromed marble walls, and gilded stucco and coffered ceilings. Exteriors were often stuccoed and painted to simulate marble, for the Romans lavished their art and costlier materials on the interior. Within the baths the average Roman found delight and grandeur for the eye, endless gossip for the ear, culture for the mind, and the means of making fit or pampering the body. At the Baths of Caracalla they could, in addition, satisfy the needs of the soul, for included in the basement was a shrine to the god Mithras.

The emperors built and supported admission to the baths to keep the political allegiance of the public, but it is the formal design and organization of the environment created by these buildings that put the Imperial stamp on the baths as well as on all great Roman public monuments. The shaping and control of a vast impersonal interior space and its vistas, the precise ordering of the sequence of rooms according to function and scale, with the whole garbed in the costliest materials, comprise as much an image of Imperial authority as was the emperor's own effigy.

**The Basilica** The most influential Roman Imperial structure for the history of architecture was the *basilica,* or public assembly hall. Its layout, with a long central hall terminating in an apse and often with flanking aisles, was a decisive influence on the form of the Early Christian basilica and, ultimately, on the Gothic cathedral (Figs. 106, 107). While Roman basilicas varied, they were generally rectangular and had either double-pitched wooden roofs or masonry barrel and groin vaults, as is seen in the great Basilica of Constantine (Fig. 312). Basilicas served the military as drill halls, were

*left:* 313. Inca fortress at Sacsayhuaman, near Cuzco, Peru. c. A.D. 1400.

*below:* 314. Nijo Castle wall. Kyoto, Japan. 1602.

found as separate chambers in the Imperial baths, saw use as stock exchanges, and were host to the administration of justice. What imparted an aura of royalty and divinity to the basilica was the law by which the effigy of a god or, more usually, of the emperor had to be enshrined in the basilica's apse. The Christians, when they found the basic plan of the basilica adaptable to their liturgy, substituted the image of Christ for that of the emperor in the apse. Though most edifices of this kind have been destroyed, it is known that they were often sumptuously decorated in their interiors and also that some basilicas may have had small flanking towers or cupolas above the corners. The entrance façade, which along with the occasional addition of an arcade on the parapet level would have related to palatial symbolism, indicated that the basilica was the seat of royal power. The Early Christian bishops took over the contrasting plain brick exteriors and luminous colorful interiors as fitting symbols of the house of the Lord. Ancient visions of the Heavenly Jerusalem were conditioned by the most sumptuous of earthly structures, one of which was the basilica.

## MEDIEVAL FORTIFICATIONS

**The Wall** The advances of technology and the enforcement of law and order have decreased in our time the importance of the wall as a structure for protection and defense. Fortifications on the limits of cities are almost nonexistent today, and confidence in police security has been such that private houses and the business districts of many cities have been constructed with great quantities of fragile, destructible glass. But recent civil disturbances here and in other countries have perhaps revived the importance of the wall, the construction of which was for many peoples throughout history a matter of life and death. The businessmen who have bricked up the fronts of their establishments, and the administrators who have omitted windows from the designs for new schools, evidence the return of this consciousness, although their concern is primarily defensive and rarely extends to include aesthetics.

In the history of architecture, some structures—such as the Great Wall of China—transcended the purpose for which they were intended; they involved considerable engineering feats, and by their imagination and sensibility to formal beauty they were distinguished as aesthetic achievements. The Incas of Peru were among the greatest wall builders and designers of all time. Their ruined fortresses, such as Sacsayhuaman (Fig. 313) near Cuzco, Peru, consist of irregular polygonal stones often of great weight. The stones were beveled and notched to fit so snugly together as to resist penetration by

*right:* 315. Castle of Angers, France. Present form, 1228–38.

a knife blade, much less afford a toehold. To eyes conditioned by abstract art, each stone is in itself an impressive sculptural form, particularly since most surviving Inca sculpture is in other materials. As an aggregate the walls are marvels of random pattern, rather than linear logic, and stunning in their reception of light and projection of shadows, which accentuate the molded surfaces. The logistical problems of quarrying, transportation, and construction, coupled with the artistry of these walls, suggest that the Incas did not build in haste or fear, but with confidence and pride in a culture that could devote so much time and skill to placing stones atop one another.

Gunpowder and the concept of the castle were introduced to Japan in the 15th century by Europeans, but the design of stone walls, such as those of Nijo Castle (Fig. 314), evolved from the vernacular tradition and are hardly derivative. Ranging in height from 20 to 130 feet, they consist usually of rough, wedge-shaped stones whose smaller faces turn outward. No mortar was needed; the stones by their tapered shape, weight, and gravity were secured in place and have withstood earthquakes. Those at the wall's edges or corners were regular, smooth faced, and built up in elegant curving profiles. They derived from formulas to which, it seems, only their builders were privy, and in some recorded instances the builders hid their work with screens until it was completed. Natural and geometric forces conjoin in a Japanese fortress wall as they do in a teahouse or palace interior. Though serving the same function, the walls of the Japanese castle could not be confounded with those of the French castle of Angers (Fig. 315), built in the 13th century. Not only the native materials of slate and granite, but also the even layering, the regularity of striping, and the submission to repetition mark the walls at Angers as European. Their sloping base, rising from rock scarped to meet it, had a military purpose but contributes to the handsome appearance. This rationalized design permitted countless masons to work quickly in unison without the choices and problems faced by their Japanese counterparts—with impressive aesthetic as well as practical results. One can almost date Western medieval walls by the degree of straightness of each stone course and by the precise uniformity of each block, ancestral to but not causal for our present-day unimaginative use of bricks. To consider the history of walls in the abstract, as pure design, is to ignore their purposes and the complex relationship of practicality and taste.

**Connotations of the Castle** With the breakup of centralized government after the fall of the Carolingian Empire in the 9th century, the castle came into existence to provide local defense against invading Norsemen. Between 1100 and 1300 castles flourished, and in terms of political and economic importance they became the secular and architectural rivals of the cathedrals. As the cathedral was the earthly home of the Lord of Heaven, the castle was the home of the lord of the land. The visible and invisible nature of the compartmentalization of medieval society was symbolized in its walls, which reminded that either one belonged or did not belong, believed or did not believe, served or opposed. The character of the walls had to enforce these reactions, and there is no other architecture as closely determined in its form by the demands of survival in a hostile environment. But while these structures conjure up brutal and aggressive associations, one of their great original purposes was the preservation of civilization from the destruction of invaders from northern and eastern Europe. To those defending them the great stone walls often meant the difference between fear or hope, life or death, law or disorder, freedom or imprisonment, culture or barbarism.

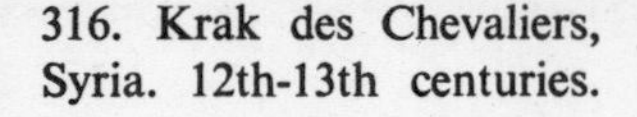

316. Krak des Chevaliers, Syria. 12th-13th centuries.

*opposite:* Plate 41. The Ishtar Gate of Nebuchadnezzar II, from the Processional Way, Babylon (modern Iraq). c. 575 B.C. Reconstructed by Koldewey. Staatliche Museen, East Berlin.

Medieval castles differed from earlier fortresses, such as the ancient walled cities of Babylon, Rome, and Constantinople, by their private rather than communal nature. They were the strongholds and residences of kings and nobility. The feudal system was dominated by a military society, whose rule by force of arms was architecturally signified through stone walls and towers of castles. Their wide dispersal in Europe and the British Isles bespeaks the decentralization of government or rule by personal lordship and explains why castles were crucial to local histories. Regionally, castles alone could determine who controlled the immediate area; they were therefore of primary political concern to kings and nobles, and documents such as the Magna Carta reserved to the nobility the right to own them. Wars were often settled in the Middle Ages by the outcome of a single castle siege.

Warfare was not the only purpose of the ruler's fortified residence; during peacetime it could serve him as hotel and hunting lodge, treasury and archive, armory and warehouse, and as a prison for political enemies. To the peasants and nearby villagers it was often a seat of local administration and justice, a place to pay taxes, and a reminder of service to be rendered in return for military protection or refuge. Local knights had to serve their lords forty days a year behind his walls. The castle exemplifies the contractual as well as hierarchical nature of medieval feudalism. Its influence on all ranks of society was considerable, for its cost of construction and upkeep was enormous.

No architecture received more careful consideration from its owner than the castle, for his life and power depended upon it. The construction of these fortified residences depended upon the growing specialization and availability of labor and upon the most sophisticated technology of the Middle Ages. By the end of the 12th century, quarrymen and rough masons cut and prepared the stones for shipment by carters, who turned them over to freemasons for final dressing and laying. Woodmen cut the timber and carpenters built the scaffolds, joists, floors, and roofs. Miners cut foundations and cellars from rock in many cases and dug moats or built skirtlike mounds beneath the walls. Limeworkers, hodmen, smiths who forged metals, watchmen, and clerks completed the work force, which was under supervision of a master mason, an architect, or the lord himself. Master masons drew praise and high pay for speed and strength of construction, ingenuity of design, and the visual impression of the castle. Walls were often whitewashed, which accounts for the name of the "White Tower" of the Tower of London (Fig. 318), and when decorated with pennants proved a dramatic spectacle.

Until the 14th century, the castle dominated warfare and the land. Its topographical location was crucial—ideally it would present as many natural obstacles to attackers as possible, while permitting in peacetime the garrison's access to and control of important travel routes. In many areas, the castle was the key to the kingdom. The Order of the Hospitaller Knights, which guarded the Levant for Christian pilgrims after the conquest of Jerusalem, built Krak des Chevaliers (Fig. 316) on a strategically located hill in such a way as to narrow the approach of an attacking force toward the most strongly fortified section. The line of the walls echoes that of its site. On level ground, moats held the enemy away and discouraged undermining the towers. The sloping base of many fortified walls, as at Angers, was intended to make undermining difficult, and the transition from rectangular to cylindrical towers was similarly motivated.

The pure geometry and strong forms of castle architecture, which have appeal today because of the recent concern of sculptors and architects with simple and brutal form, was not dictated by taste but by the harsh realities of killing and staying alive. Architects had to be military engineers and strategists. Circular mural towers, extending out from the walls, allowed defenders in them to protect the battlements and give covering fire to those on the ground beneath. Stepped battlements gave a colorful silhouette, but, more importantly,

Plate 42. GIOVANNI PAOLO PANNINI. *The Piazza Navona Decorated in Honor of the Birth of the Dauphin*. 1729. Oil on canvas, 3′7″ × 8′1½″. Louvre, Paris. (See p. 267.)

*above:* 317. Harlech Castle, Merionetshire, Wales. 1283–90.

*above right:* 318. Tower of London. 1078–90.

protected archers. *Machicolations,* battlements that projected outward from and helped articulate the wall, allowed the dropping of missiles, oil, and fire on those below. The twin-towered gateways, often citadels in themselves, as in English castles such as Harlech (Fig. 317), became increasingly aggressive in design, to allow the defenders to better attack the foe by charging forth and withdrawing, which the *portcullis* (iron gate) and drawbridge permitted. In fact, the development of castle design was extroverted toward aggressive defense.

By the 13th century castles were ideally concentric and consisted of a double ring of walls linked by towers, which gave the garrison bowmen better angles and greater openings to counter assaults. Flat, lead-roofed towers held machines to hurl missiles like those of the besiegers. Once an attacking force penetrated an outer wall or front gate, there were, as at Krak, other walls to negotiate and devastating hairpin turns between gates where fire could be poured through "murder" holes in the roof of the entrance causeway. Defenders could leap out through concealed sally ports to attack their enemies in the rear. Finally there was often the great multistoried inner tower or *keep,* or the citadellike entrance itself, a stronghold of last resort. Originally cubical, as in the Tower of London (Fig. 318), the ideal 13th-century keep was shell or circular in form, as at Windsor (Fig. 319), to deflect missiles. The

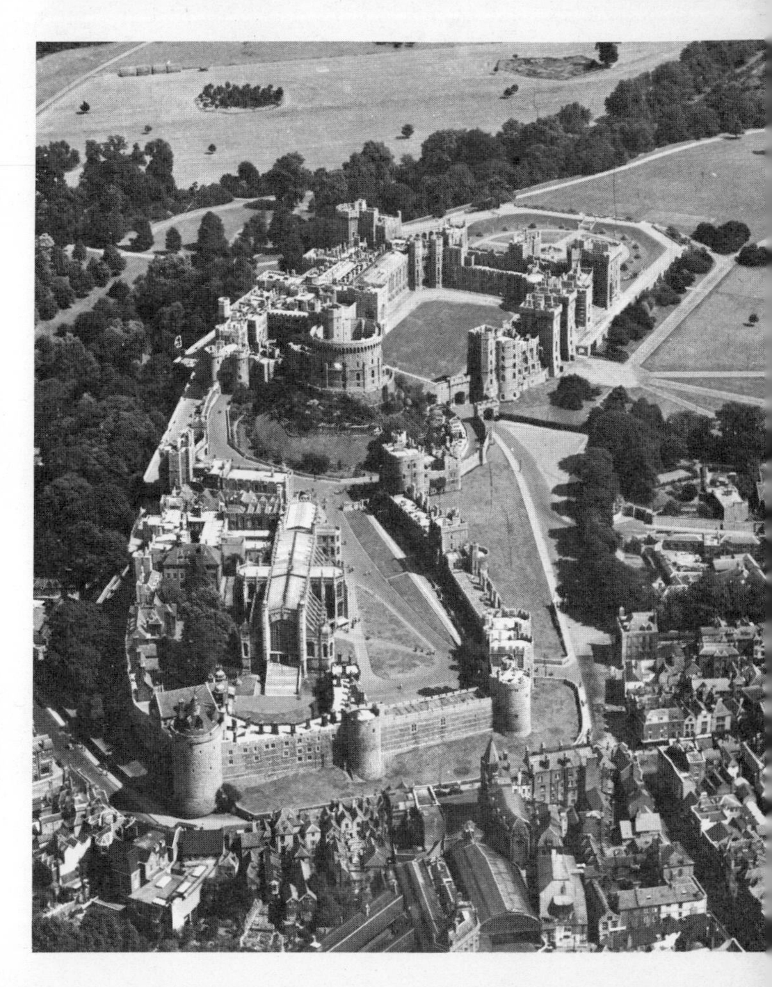

*right:* 319. Windsor Castle, aerial view from the west, Berkshire, England. Keep begun 1170.

the tradition of symbolism seen in the Imperial Roman gateway (Fig. 306). Peacetime garrisons of 300 in a castle could swell to 2,000 during war, yet a handful of well-provisioned defenders in a keep could hold off an army for months. Bad morale and starvation, rather than architecture, caused many castles to fall.

By the end of the Middle Ages castle design was so perfected that fortresses such as Angers became impregnable and were bypassed. Wars shifted to the battlefields and to fortified cities, so that castles were built to serve only as palatial residences; that at Windsor (Fig. 319), for example, has no history of war and continues to be occupied today. Many similar castles, destroyed neither by war nor by kings jealous of the power of the nobility, continued as elegant residences for royalty and aristocracy. Spartan outer walls often belied the luxury within, shielding fine, ornamental gardens and spacious, beautifully decorated domestic apartments. Beginning in the 12th century, castle owners whitewashed the outer walls to enhance the stark beauty of their fortresses, but the more splendid work of painters, tapestry weavers, sculptors, and furniture makers was reserved for their own quarters.

severely beautiful Castel del Monte (Fig. 320), built in Apulia by Emperor Frederick II, was a fusion of keep and walls in an octagon. The shape resulted in an interior plan of eight rooms of equal size on each level. The gateway is framed by a medieval version of a Roman temple façade. The window above the portal served a practical function and also continued

**City Halls** During the Middle Ages not only towns but also the homes of the wealthy and seats of municipal government came to be fortified. More important than castles to the history of later palace design was the architectural development of the town hall in European cities that won political independence. In Bruges, the present-day town hall (Fig. 321) was originally a cloth makers' guildhall as well as a seat of

*top:* 320. Castel del Monte, near Andria, Apulia, Italy. c. 1240.

*right:* 321. Town hall and square, Bruges. Late 13th century. Belfry height 279′.

*right:* 322. Palazzo Comunale, Siena. 1288–1309.

government. The 279-foot tower, which contains a belfry and clock, rivaled that of the local cathedral in height, articulation, and expense. Such communal halls served as watchtowers and signs to tell visitors on the roads that they were coming to a free city. In the absence of a tradition of symbolic architectural designs for city halls, that of Bruges is an interesting mixture of castle and cathedral design elements, which articulate its great expanse without causing it to lose scale. Its symmetry and austere elegance make it still an ideal ceremonial backdrop. The expensive stone rebuilding of an originally wooden structure and the employment of skilled architects who could interpret the pride and militancy of Bruges are among the most dramatic evidences of civic consciousness in urban history.

In Italy, communes that successfully achieved independence centralized government in a chief magistrate, or *podestà,* whose authority was signified by the town hall. Architects had to develop a form of building that was nonroyal and that fortified the town hall against rebellions of dissident political factions within the city itself. The wealth of many Italian cities encouraged considerable private building, and, from the Middle Ages, ordinances governed the character of houses near the town halls. The halls themselves show the effects of this conscious, rationalized planning. The Palazzo Communale of Siena (Fig. 322), with its soaring tower and impressive red-brick façade, dominates a huge fan-shaped square (where the famous horse races, or *Palio,* are still run). The embattled histories of cities such as Siena explain the fortified aspect of the building, with its stepped battlements. The blind arcade that runs below the third story of the two wings flanking the center may be a vestige of the Roman Imperial use of arcades to designate the seat of authority. Characteristically medieval are the pointed arches and predominance of tripartite windows in the upper stories. The entrance to the tower, which served practical as well as symbolic purposes, was enhanced with a portico containing sculpture. The numerous doors remind one of the frequent and ubiquitous use made of these town halls in the daily life of the medieval citizenry.

## RENAISSANCE PALACES

**The Meaning and Role of Taste** The history of palaces after the Middle Ages is a demonstration of the evolution of taste. Taste presupposes discrimination and judgment as to what is or is not acceptable; in art, it presumes a highly developed society which encourages competition between individuals and groups and a diversity of art forms. Much in the manner of portraiture, palaces are the result of taste exercised by ruling classes for the purpose of affirming their individual merit and their rank as a group. Under the leadership of kings and influential families, absolute standards of taste have been established in various periods, so that in one country or city, such as Rome, palaces of different eras are markedly different in appearance. Structured by a class-conscious society, tastes are not of equal value, and, historically, the socially dominant, leisure classes have become the founders, arbiters, and guardians of taste. The rationale behind this phenomenon, as Meyer Schapiro has pointed out, is that, unlike the lower classes whose conduct is influenced by exterior compulsions, an upper class can act freely, from considerations of aesthetic pleasure alone. This then leads to good taste and to palaces that are incarnations of an upper-class taste extended to social as well as political conduct. To those who exercised it, taste was thought to have an evolving history, to progress and improve along with society. Ideas of tact, for example, could determine whether a 15th-century palace was to appear as a fortress or an elegant home, just as the role a monarch or aristocrat wished to play before society could determine the pose and setting he adopted for his portrait (see Chap. 12).

**Palace Façades** Many of the most beautiful walls in the history of architecture were those designed as palace façades. Particularly from the 15th century on, architects had the opportunity to give greater articulation to palace façades; and as palaces and castles gradually lost their function as fortresses in both the city and the countryside, even greater flexibility of design was possible. Rather than pose significant engineering challenges, palaces offered the architect the best opportunity to display his talents as a designer and decorator. Throughout the history of palace design, there recurs the imperative of announcing the dignity, power, and taste of its owner. For practical as well as symbolic reasons, the formal façades of palaces furnish little notion of what their interiors are like. In comparison with an often cold, austere exterior, palace interiors might be lavish and brilliant in décor. The public face of the aristocrat, according to the Renaissance code of courtiers, should not betray his inner feelings; and a cardinal rule of urban palace façades was to not betray the privacy of the inhabitants or their true natures. The architect had the problem of conforming to current social laws of the aristocracy, which meant achieving the right tone in terms of the amount of formality or sumptuousness; these considerations influenced the degree of freedom permitted to the designer. In practical terms, this conditioned the choice and finish of stone and other materials, the proportional relation of width to height and base to upper stories, the disposition of windows and doorways, the number of openings, the amount and kind of ornamentation, and the scale and character of horizontal dividing elements and the roof line.

How all these parts were interrelated and design focus achieved was a reflection both of taste and of changing symbols of status. To understand certain constant features of palace façade design, it is important to know that the ground floor was not used for entertaining or for living quarters by the owners but was reserved for servants, storage, and stables. Stairways came to be increasingly important after the 15th century, gradually becoming more than an inconspicuous means of moving between levels. The true first floor—what in the United States would be the second story—was the *piano nobile,* where receptions and entertaining were conducted. Its ceilings, which were often the highest in the palace, looked down on large salons and banqueting halls. Sleeping quarters were usually on the third floor. During the Renaissance many rulers had self-enclosed small private apartments within their large palaces. Physical comfort was placed second to marks of prestige inherent in large-scale elegant structures, for the most part unheated and lacking such conveniences as plumbing. The conventional proportion of the palace was a greater width than height. Urban palaces like those of Florence and Rome frequently had inner courtyards surrounded by colonnaded loggias, and in some instances there was also a walled garden at the rear. Later drastic changes in interior décor, owing to the fact that many old palaces have continued to be used, explain why this discussion is concentrated on their exteriors.

Chronologically, the Ca'd'Oro and Palazzo Medici-Riccardi (Figs. 323, 324) were built at about the same time, but their designs mirror the radically different environments of Venice and Florence. The Venetian palace, called the *House of Gold* because of the gilded ornament lavished upon its interior by a French artist, has one of the most delicately beautiful screen arcades in all architecture. The canal-level arcade is broader and simpler than those above, signifying its more prosaic function as a gondola landing from which visitors quickly mounted stairways. The entire left half of the façade is dematerialized into a rich pattern of light and dark. Emphasis of the piano nobile is subtly achieved in the open clover-leaf arcade terminating the lower rhythmic sequences established in the railings and colonnades. The Near Eastern and medieval flavor of the Ca' d'Oro design reflects Venice's maritime contacts with Oriental lands and also its remoteness from the significant changes in architecture then evolving in Florence.

The Palazzo Medici-Riccardi, designed by Michelozzo (1396–1427), looks militant and solemn because of the heavy rusticated, or rough-hewn, stonework of the lower story and the barred windows. The turbulent history of the Medici in 15th-century Florence makes such precautions understandable. In keeping with the primarily social function of the piano nobile, the stonework changes at that level to a more finished variety. Double arcaded windows framed by a strong round arch punctuate the wall at regular intervals, maintaining the independence of the story by not aligning with the large windows of the street level. Round-arched windows were medieval carry-overs, and the palace still has a fortress look. Each horizontal level is distinctly marked by a *stringcourse,* or horizontal band between stories, whose slenderness and fine-scaled rhythm contrasts with the powerful overhanging cornice of the roof. The ponderous base, the clear delineation of the upper zones, which seem to grow progressively lighter, and the dramatic termination of the cornice and roof partake of the same style as Verrocchio's bust of Lorenzo de' Medici (Fig. 292). Both bust and palace have an aspect of solid impenetrability. The façade is quite flat, without embellishment of the doorway, accentuation of a main window, or vertical division into central body and side wings. The preponderant proportion of wall surface to openings assures a massive and compact effect.

If there was an analogy in architecture to the 15th-century secularization of painting, it was in the growing rivalry of churches by ambitious palace design. The architect most responsible for giving secular architecture an importance comparable to Renaissance church design was Leon Battista Alberti (c. 1404–72). His façade for the Palazzo Rucellai

*right:* 323. Ca' d'Oro, Venice. 1422–40.

*below:* 324. MICHELOZZO. Palazzo Medici-Riccardi, Florence. Begun 1444.

*below:* 325. LEON BATTISTA ALBERTI. Palazzo Rucellai, Florence. 1446–51.

(Fig. 325) has a less martial and more Imperial Roman tone than Michelozzo's Palazzo Medici-Riccardi. It was the first Renaissance palace with repeated superimposed orders, like those of the Colosseum (Fig. 308). Alberti sought consciously to re-create the appearance of ancient Roman palaces, and this aim accounts for the finely cut and more or less uniform masonry, the flat vertically aligned pilasters dividing the whole façade into rhythmic rectangular bays, and the substantial cornice, which along with the horizontal stringcourses serves to balance the verticality of the aligned windows and pilasters. The arched windows, however, are still medieval in character. Alberti's ideal of harmony, and hence of beauty, rested on the proper mathematical proportioning of all parts of the structure in relation to other parts and to the whole. For Alberti, Classical beauty meant that nothing could be added or taken away from a perfect, ideally based design. The pronounced flatness

*left:* 326. ANTONIO DA SANGALLO and MICHELANGELO. Palazzo Farnese, Rome. 1530–89.

*below left:* 327. CARLO MADERNO and GIANLORENZO BERNINI. Palazzo Barberini, Rome. Begun 1628.

and grid arrangement of the entire façade is derived from Alberti's interest in transposing an architectural idea into linear organization on a two-dimensional surface whose own logic could be independent of the building's actual structure. One of many architects without formal architectural training who practiced after the Middle Ages, Alberti was largely responsible for making the architect a wall decorator or arranger, rather than a builder involved with engineering problems and the discovery of new ways to enclose space. With rare exceptions, the great architectural engineers of the Middle Ages do not again have counterparts until the advent of the notable 19th- and 20th-century engineers. Though the right side of the façade remained unfinished, Alberti's design for the Palazzo Rucellai influenced later architects in terms of its fine balance of vertical and horizontal elements and its tendency toward a general harmony and uniformity, with some subtle distinctions in the two upper stories.

The overall use of heavy stone became outmoded in Roman palace design of the 16th and 17th centuries and was reserved thereafter for country villas. The Palazzo Farnese (Fig. 326), designed largely by Antonio da Sangallo (1483–1546), with the top story facing the interior courtyard and various other details done by Michelangelo, reserves the use of stone for the corners, providing a new framing device for the façade and the main portal. The windows of the two upper stories are surrounded with elaborate tabernaclelike combinations of columns and pediments resting on brackets. Alternation of curved and triangular pediments helps to distinguish the piano nobile, and the tabernacle forms give greater sculptural projection and emphasis against the flat stucco walls. The main portal begins to protrude somewhat, and is enhanced by the ornamented and balconied window directly above. At this window the Farnese Pope would make his public appearances, not unlike the practice of the pharaohs in antiquity or even of rulers in our own day; Mussolini, for example, continued this practice in his appearances from a balcony of the Palazzo Venezia in the center of Rome. Michelangelo's addition to the Sangallo façade incorporated into one expressive unit the earlier symbolic devices of the gateway, window of appearances, and coat of arms for the first time in palace architecture. The site was also modified to create a slight rise for the central doorway.

Although Sangallo and Michelangelo succeeded in making the façade of the Palazzo Farnese more expressive in terms of its strongly framed windows and powerful jutting cornice, the exterior wall was still basically a flat surface and the palace a block in general outlines. In the 17th century, more three-dimensional articulation of the exterior wall occurred with the development of recessive or projecting wings for urban palaces and villas. The Palazzo Barberini in Rome (Fig. 327), begun in 1628 by Carlo Maderno (1556–1629) and completed by Bernini, has a façade that is more openly symbolic of centralized power. This was appropriate to a family that gave so many important popes to the Church. Bernini's completed façade has qualities of dignified grandeur, lightness, and openness not seen before in palace design. His extensive use of glass partially accounts for this effect and also reflects the wealth and security enjoyed by its inhabitants. Each story has

a distinctiveness, yet the overall design is unified through harmonious scale and proportion, as well as by a rigorous vertical alignment of the bays. The top-floor windows are recessed within their architectural frames, thus animating somewhat the inherent flatness of the façade and also further emphasizing the piano nobile below. The piano nobile is made dominant by the greater size of its windows and its projecting balcony, also through the range of engaged columns flanking its arched windows.

The autocratic rule epitomized by the Barberini has an echo in the way in which windows and columns have lost their independence and are all subordinated to the total effect. The use of projecting wings and the narrow recessed portions flanking the middle section helps to focus attention on the central balcony. Bernini's most spectacular architectural symbol of centralized authority, which entailed thrusting extensions of the façade deep into the viewer's space, was his inspired colonnade for the huge square before St. Peter's (Fig. 388). In his design of the Palazzo Chigi-Odescalchi (Fig. 328), Bernini's use of giant orders for the pilasters and an unbroken vertical continuation of two stories was very influential in the planning of subsequent palaces. Though poorly altered by later architects, and given more bays and entrances than Bernini himself had stipulated, this façade was perhaps as fruitful a source of ideas for Baroque symbols of nobility as Roman Imperial architecture had been.

**Palaces of Kings** It was in the French Palace of Versailles that many of the traditional architectural symbols of authority were joined, refined, or elaborated upon. Versailles symbolized the complete centralization of power in one man, Louis XIV (Figs. 298, 299). The palace, which was built on a malaria-infested swamp and cost the lives of thousands of men, became not only the residence of the royal court but also the seat for the entire administration of government. The main building of the palace, over 600 yards wide, was in itself a completely self-contained city. It provided living quarters, business offices, kitchens, banqueting halls, ballrooms, chambers of state, and even its own theater. In size and splendor, there was no other palace in France or elsewhere in Europe to rival it. For members of the French court or high government officials, not to be able to live at Versailles was tantamount to exile.

Aerial views of Versailles (Fig. 329) illustrate the symbolical relationship of the palace and its environment. On one side lay the city of Versailles, which had been built up as the

*top:* 328. GIANLORENZO BERNINI. Palazzo Chigi-Odescalchi, Rome. Begun 1664.

*right:* 329. LOUIS LE VAU and JULES HARDOUIN-MANSART. Palace of Versailles. 1669–85.

palace grew. From that direction, great avenues slashed through the city and converged on the main parade ground before the palace. Just as in ancient times, all roads now converged upon the capital of the world. The central road came from Paris and, like the palace, shared an axis with the Champs-Elysées and the Louvre, over 9 miles away (Figs. 391–394). The geometry of long straight avenues connecting broad squares and royal buildings was a Baroque authoritarian symbol.

The public side of the palace faced the town and the people, the source of the King's finances and manpower. The funnel shape of the city plan reflects this relationship. The rear façade of the palace was addressed to many square miles of private gardens, an area of private pleasure reserved for the King and his court. Here, Louis' rule over nature was made patent by the rigid but beautiful geometry of the gardens, planted according to the plans of André Le Nôtre (1613–1700). The palace, which significantly stood on the highest ground, was thus the fulcrum between two worlds, public and private, the focus of man and nature.

The approach to the palace was through the traditional Court of Honor (Fig. 330). This gigantic court was recessed toward the center of the palace in a series of stages. Moving toward the main entrance, a visiting ambassador would not enter a fortified, blocklike castle, but gradually would be embraced by long elegant palace wings that reached out like hospitable arms to draw him in. In the innermost courtyard, marble busts of Roman emperors were mounted on the walls. Exactly in the center of the palace and above the main doorway, framed by double columns, was the King's bedroom, which opened onto a balcony from which Louis could make public appearances and observe military reviews. The Egyptian window of appearances was here given its most resplendent setting (see pp. 226, 227, Figs. 303, 304).

Within the palace, Louis had an army of artists and artisans lavishly decorate the ceilings and walls with murals depicting events in the lives of the gods, with whom he felt a kinship. The famous Gobelin tapestry and ceramic industries were founded as royal monopolies to supply Versailles with miles of tapestries, carpeting, and moldings. Over 140 types of colored marbles were assembled from all over Europe for the wall and stairway decorations. Hundreds of stucco and marble sculptures of gods, nymphs, nudes, and, naturally, of French royalty were carved and set in the rooms and gardens. No expense was spared in making this the artistic center of the Western world; indeed, it became the model for all European royalty. The Palazzo Medici-Riccardi (Fig. 324) would have been as inappropriate to Louis XIV as Versailles would have been to Lorenzo de' Medici. Louis had no need for a fortified residence, since his armies ruled all of France and much of Europe. He did not need rusticated masonry walls to suggest his strength. The huge floor-to-ceiling windows and the great Venetian mirrors in the famous Hall of Mirrors were as expressive of the Sun King as the thick walls and barred windows of the Florentine palace were of the Renaissance rulers. Since Louis was the "Lord of Light," his earthly palace became a materialization of this concept.

The gardens were designed to be used by the six or seven thousand people who lived at the court. On the upper levels of the gardens, Louis held fabulous banquets, which were often accompanied by brilliant displays of fireworks. Over 1,300 waterspouts were built for the many fountains, each designed around a marine motif. In shaping the water so variously, Louis showed his rule over nature, as was implied in the virtuoso clipping of hedges and trees. Long garden prospects shaped even the natural space. Great open-air stairways, whose design went back to those built by Bramante for the Vatican and by Michelangelo on the Capitoline Hill (Fig. 213), not only carried the promenader from one level of the garden to another but also gave a sensation of leading directly to the clouds. The gardens and palace of Versailles constituted a private city that required the most advanced mathematics and skilled engineering of the time to build.

Contemporaneous with Versailles is the great Japanese pincely palace of Katsura (Figs. 331–336), built near Kyoto

330. The Court of Honor, Versailles (Fig. 329).

*left:* 331. Katsura Palace, Kyoto. 17th century.

*below:* 332. Katsura Palace, view from the Palace toward the Middle Shoin.

under the direction of Prince Toshihito and his son Prince Toshitada. The palace occupies 16 acres, bounded by bamboo thickets and screens and adjoining the Katsura River, the waters of which were diverted into the gardens. As much as by totally different architectural traditions, Versailles and Katsura were formed by different concepts of authority and of man's relation to nature. At the time of its construction, in the 17th century, the imperial family was feeling the oppression of the shoguns, and Prince Toshihito had no effective political power. His palace was thus symptomatic of his retreat from the outside world, whereas the French King used his palace to symbolize the world centered in his person. Except in the temples, the Japanese builders avoided symmetry, and the approach to Katsura was carefully designed to be informal and natural and to provide by its turnings unexpected vistas of the beautiful gardens and ultimately of the palace itself. The accent on artifice or on the mastery of the elements demonstrated at Louis XIV's Versailles was altogether alien to the attitudes of the Japanese aristocracy toward nature, which was more passive and romantic.

The main building at Katsura immediately reveals the absence of a strong central focus: There is no formal stairway or forceful accent on a main door, nor is there the familiar European blockish quality and self-sufficiency with regard to setting. Under the direction of the Prince, Katsura, like its predecessors, was made to appear perfectly adapted to the seemingly unplanned variety of its natural surroundings. The main building is an *echelon* or zigzag arrangement of three large *shoin*, or halls, consisting of some forty modest-sized rooms, few of which have designated functions. The large, slightly convex roof is the dominant design motif, and its weight is crucial for structural stability. The architecture is basically a skeletal post-and-beam construction, with paper walls that are not load-bearing as in European palaces. Many of the external and internal walls at Katsura are made to slide open, thereby allowing multiple changes in room layout and vistas into the gardens. The aristocracy stoically accepted any discomfort of climatic conditions, feeling that architecture should serve essentially the spirit rather than the body. Unlike European architects, Japanese designers based their work more on aesthetic preference than on ideal geometry when it came to formulating a proportional system.

The building is raised off the ground by posts (Fig. 332), both because of the sloping site and as protection against

*left:* 333. Katsura Palace, Middle Shoin seen from the first room of the Old Shoin.

*below left:* 334. Katsura Palace, the New Palace and lawn seen from the Middle Shoin.

floods; the basement is walled to keep animals out. The uniform floor level at Katsura was also a break with the traditional aristocratic symbolism of different levels that was found in earlier imperial palaces. The modern Japanese architect Kenzo Tange, who has written a fine study of Katsura, points out that these deviations from the historical aristocratic norm reflect a new influence of the ideas and energy of the lower classes, who were responsible for the Noh plays, puppet theater, and the tea ceremony so vital to Japanese culture and enjoyed by the aristocracy. Prince Toshihito employed as his director of construction a garden and tea expert named Nakanuma Sakyo, who came from the newly prosperous merchant class, while the chief gardener is known to have been of low birth. Though advice was forthcoming from fellow noblemen and Zen priests, the Prince seems to have been susceptible to new ideas from outside of the court as well.

Katsura does continue most of the characteristics of Japanese imperial architecture. Its beauty depends largely upon the utmost restraint in decoration, as seen in the spareness of its rooms and the clean contrasts between vertical and horizontal elements (Figs. 333, 334). Japanese designers thought of space in two-dimensional terms, and the interior of the palace might be described as an additive sequence of flat patterns. Similarly, the symbolic gardens were to be viewed sequentially and with much attention given to contemplating what was underfoot. Neither within nor without the palace does one have the sense of a total integrated form, in contrast to the European palaces with their more static blocklike arrangement, planned and fixed vistas in and from the interior, and predictable overall symmetry. The openness of Katsura becomes in itself an aristocratic symbol, for the houses of the farmers were closed against the elements. Unlike the highly finished decoration of Versailles, that of Katsura is, intentionally, often left rough or incomplete in order to harmonize or suggest analogies with nature. The Japanese brought to a high art the enclosure of space for human enjoyment.

The lesson offered by the garden was that of the underlying harmony of all life in the universe—not, as at Versailles, for example, one of man's self-glorification at the expense of nature. The Katsura garden is the loving creation of gardeners who were fine artists. Mingling ponds, mounds, beaches, and groves, the Katsura gardens are totally unpredictable on the basis of any one part. The ritual tour enjoyed by 17th-century royalty followed prescribed water routes or the discrete paths and stepping stones contrived to appear as integral parts of nature. Constantly changing views were unfolded to the eye, just as textures subtly changed underfoot. Except for the buildings, the gardens possess no reference to human scale or activity, so that at one moment they are recognized in their normal aspect, and in the next they may appear as endless depths, expanses of sea and mountains. Worn stones and moss and aged trees preserved the viewer's impression of being surrounded by timeless serenity. Impeccably cared for, the garden's correct informality is preserved by the elimination of mud and unsightly collections of leaves. In such an environment, men could cleanse their minds of mundane concerns.

*left:* 335. Katsura Gardens and *Shokintei* (teahouse).

*below:* 336. Interior of the Katsura *Shokintei*, with hearth and tree trunk used to support a partition.

The building most appropriate to such a setting is the teahouse (Fig. 335), where the *chanoyu*, or traditional tea ceremony, is performed. Usually a one-room structure surrounded by a small-scale garden, at Katsura the 17th-century tea pavilion, the *Shokintei* (Fig. 336), contains additional rooms. A religious ritual practice by Zen monks before the image of Buddha, *chanoyu* later became secularized into a form of social meditation but preserved the rules and solemnity of its origin. A few invited guests assembled at the garden gate and, in prearranged order, passed leisurely through the garden, cleansing their hands in a rude stone basin and usually entering the teahouse through a low door, as a symbol of humility and the democratic nature of the ceremony. In an alcove of the austere tearoom would be placed a painting, a simple flower display, or a single beautiful object that, after thoughtful inspection by the entering guests, served as a source of discussion. Following strict ritual, the host prepared the tea with intentionally crude but handsome utensils. Simplicity and naturalness were the notes struck by the environment, the tea objects, the gestures, and the subsequent conversation, which ideally never touched on business or politics.

From the Buddhist temple the tea ceremony passed to a deceptively simple, light, wooden-framed structure topped and stabilized by a heavy thatched roof. Between the exterior wooden supports were rough, mud-covered lath walls and translucent rice-paper screens. Openings in the wall were intentionally disposed in an irregular way, both for visual effect and to guide the light properly for the tea ceremony. Painstakingly and at great cost, the owners of the teahouse constructed a building that gave the impression of austere rusticity and natural imperfection. Devoid of interior furniture, with the guests sitting on rice mats arranged over the floor, the tearoom has an air of emptiness and contemplative space.

Arthur Drexler has explained the significance of this quality of "emptiness" according to Zen and Taoist ideas as the means of expressing the sole reality:

> The purest style of tea house architecture . . . claimed to be concerned not with the material of the building itself, but with the emptiness within. . . . It was important to produce a space that would reflect the transiency of things in this world . . . and to this end asymmetrical compositions were preferred: Only what is incomplete is still within the process of life and is therefore imperfect.

This worshipful attitude toward imperfection extended to introducing an untreated tree trunk as a partition support in the room, thus linking those within to the natural world without.

## MODERN CIVIC ARCHITECTURE

Rare are the modern public buildings, housing civil authority, that can be enjoyed both for their beauty and for the way in which the particular character of governmental institutions has been embodied in the overall design. More familiar to us in our republic are city halls and county, state, and federal buildings that mingle (or mangle) architectural motifs borrowed from the temples, churches, and palaces of ancient Rome and the Renaissance and Baroque periods. The governments that inspired the dome and giant orders were not elective; yet American federal architecture is basically in-

*left:* 337. KALLMAN, MCKINNELL & KNOWLES. Boston City Hall, west façade and south side. 1968.

*below:* 338. Boston City Hall, skylight shaft.

distinguishable from the products of autocracy as well as from that of the Soviet Union, Nazi Germany, and Fascist Italy. Massive bleak walls of heavy masonry, squared and monotonously aligned windows, endless flights of steps, and grandiose cornices are traits that describe equally well all the foregoing styles of 20th-century architecture. Throughout American history, Democratic and Republican administrations have shared in the bad taste and contradictory tendency toward architectural timidity and fiscal extravagance that produce the earth crushers typical of the United States capital.

**Boston City Hall** The Boston City Hall (Fig. 337), completed in 1969 by the firm of Kallman, McKinnell & Knowles, resulted from the rare and spectacular example of a municipal government, not previously known for creativity, giving up the stifling claims of "consistency" and tradition, to which civic-planning groups have neurotically clung. By holding its big scale, and not attempting to appear larger or smaller than it is, the structure is monumental. By reflecting in its design the interior governmental activities and by mirroring the governing process, it is meaningful. The designers have imaginatively tackled one of the most persistent problems of architecture—how to make the walls of a large building interesting and not monotonous. Every side of the building is a surprise, because each façade has incorporated the spatial division behind it, without compromising power of shape and without creating illogical sequences or rhythmic discord. The three upper stories, which form a stepped, cornicelike crown, house the offices (the "rabbit warren"), while the meeting rooms of the city's administration are each signaled below. The fortresslike appearance is mitigated by the large entrances inviting visitors into the nine-story lobby, which is in itself like a shopping center of civic services. The building is thus a rectangle around a hollow core, permitting varied and dramatic lighting throughout (Fig. 338) and avoiding the gloom and tedium so often associated with government office buildings. The structure was erected on a sloping site, which the architects accommodated by a daring mixture of materials. The brick plaza and foundation walls, apparent from the southeast, help to link the new complex with the historic red-brick structures nearby; the plaza presents a magnetic attraction for the crowds, who are drawn to and not away from the entrances. There are no concessions to conventional symbols of authority, such as columns and domes, and a ramp inside

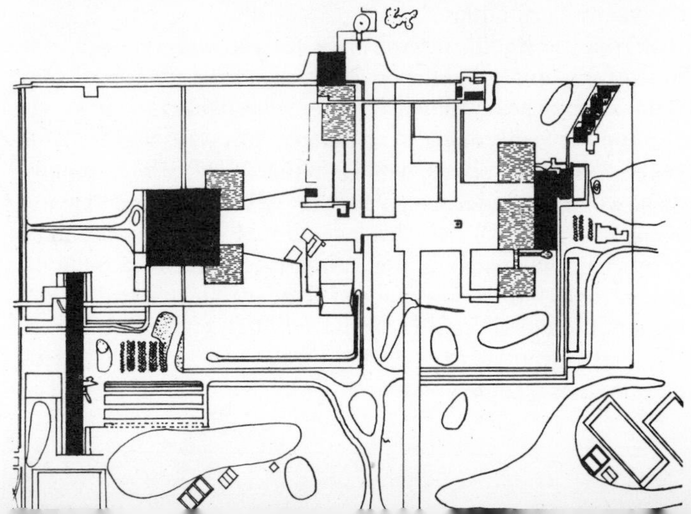

replaces the usually endless flights of stairs. And yet the building's materials and design give an impression of durable dignity and an appealing ruggedness and openness.

**Chandigarh** There is no question that the architects of the Boston City Hall drew heavily on the ideas of Le Corbusier (see also pp. 79–83), or that they were particularly influenced by his designs for the capitol buildings at Chandigarh in Punjab, India (Figs. 339–346). They were inspired by the raw concrete sculptural forms, the structure wider at the top than at the bottom, and by the ramps, lightwells, and recessed sunbreaker forms. They also appreciated the efforts of Le Corbusier to combine monumentality with workable architecture that could serve important and complex functions. In this last they were more successful than the master, though the problems of Le Corbusier were more difficult, his scale of achievement more heroic, and his failures more disturbing.

When Nehru proclaimed India free from fettering traditions, he selected Le Corbusier to create a city that would instruct young Indian architects, denied experience under the British, in how to build anew an old civilization that had not yet achieved stability. Chandigarh was thus to symbolize the creative strength of the new republic, so that tribal allegiances would be transferred to the state and country. For Le Corbusier, the toughest technical problems involved the site and the climate: The complex was to be built on a vast plain rising slowly to the Himalayas, against which the buildings would always be seen. The tropical setting meant extremes of terrific heat and monsoon rains. The labor force was plentiful but unskilled, the finances modest, and the technology crude. In addition, the culture was alien to a European who had planned, but never built, cities for other continents. Leaving the city proper to be designed and supervised by his associates, Le Corbusier made the basic decisions about the placement and design for the capitol complex. He made these decisions by intuition, studying moveable flag poles to determine the locus and height of his buildings against the awesome mountainous backdrop. For the architect, there could be no haphazard or timid solution.

The capitol compound (Fig. 339) thus occupies a large pedestrian plaza, a series of tangent squares with tree-lined avenues, reflecting pools, and mounds and terraces that are still in the process of being landscaped. The east-west axis is marked by the Law Court and Secretariat; adjacent to the latter is the General Assembly. The culmination of the north axis, which was to have been a governor's palace, is now a Museum of Knowledge. The considerable distances between the buildings resulted from Le Corbusier's aesthetic decisions about the relation of architectural forms, to each other and to the mountain range, and about the space of the plaza. Although they underscore the separate government functions housed within each structure, the distances make pedestrian or bicycle movement (still the principal means of getting about) between the Secretariat and the Law Court an ordeal during monsoons or 115° heat. Traffic of different types is accommodated by separate routes which—if Chandigarh grows beyond the planned population of 150,000 to about the size of Los Angeles—should prove adequate and effective. At present, however, the excessive costs of landscaping such a vast space and the small amount of motor traffic make the plaza a barren waste in many areas, a problem also throughout much of the rest of the city.

*opposite:* 339. Le Corbusier. Final plan of the capitol complex, Chandigarh, India. 1951.

340. Le Corbusier. The Secretariat, Chandigarh, India. 1959.

Le Corbusier rejected the symmetry of such urban centers as that around the Place de la Concorde in Paris (Figs. 391–395), but not the scale or open space of that ensemble: his 400- and 800-meter squares do in fact relate to distances along the axis from the Louvre to the Arc de Triomphe. Each building is stamped with his style and symbolic gesture—each appears as an architectural fist against the onslaught of nature. His concessions to the sociology of his client can be found in the variegated design of the wall-like Secretariat (Fig. 340), which signifies the different levels of administrators, who live in sectors of the city and in homes similarly classified into fourteen levels. The great length of the building anchors the space of the capitol square at one corner, but raises endless problems for the efficiency of the inside. The compact rectangularity of the building serves design but not the need for office expansion.

The General Assembly building (Fig. 341) has a magnificently designed, pseudoportico front (Fig. 342) for its square plan. The detached, raw concrete façade answers the powerful challenge flung by the Law Court (Fig. 345) half a mile away. Ceremony, symbol, and visual effects take precedence in the Assembly building over practicality, for the legislators are segregated by design (Fig. 343), and the great cooling tower ceiling of the main chamber is sufficiently compelling to distract those who would engage in parliamentary debate. Inspiration for the tower came from an industrial cooling tower in another Indian city, and its exposure above the roof line answered the challenge of the dramatic mountain peaks in the distance. The 40-foot-high forum that circles the main assembly hall (Fig. 344) has a column-supported black ceiling; it is a dramatic assembling area for the legislators. One is constantly moving from narrow to wide, short to tall, dark to light spaces in this building, a situation in which the stage-setting upstages the actors but delights the audience. The Assembly governs by consent of the governed, but the former must try to operate in a structure which came into being from a single arrogant will. All great architects must be arrogant, appropriating to their conceptions land, sky, materials from the earth, wealth, and labor. But architects, like government advisors, must temper brilliance by common sense or produce hardship, if not disaster, for the people compelled to live with grand design.

The great form of the Law Court (Fig. 345) provided no protection for citizens waiting in front of the building in rain or heat so as to enter the court rooms; consequently, a covered area has been added. Monsoon downpours funnel into the entrance court, whipping even those ascending the ramps within (Fig. 346). The "air-conditioning" purpose of the double roof and sunbreakers did not work, fixed glass windows generated heat, and protection from glare scarcely prevented judges from changing the designs of their courts. In her intelligent commentary on Chandigarh, Norma Evanson has suggested that many discomforts could have been prevented without serious design alteration. But despite the failures of utility, Le Corbusier kept alive the tradition of monumental architecture, when it seemed alien to the course of history and was identified with political dictatorships. Dictatorship by the architect has its flaws, but also its compensation. The capitol buildings at Chandigarh are strong and

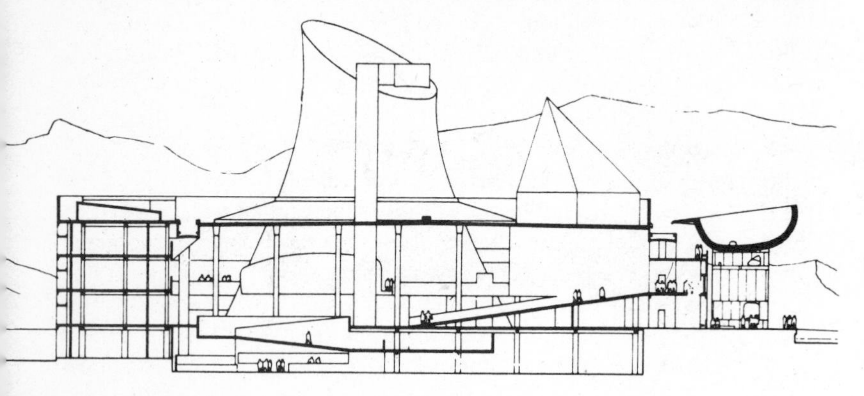

*above left:* 341. LE CORBUSIER. The General Assembly, Chandigarh, India. 1959–62.

*above right:* 342. Portico of the General Assembly, Chandigarh.

*left:* 343. Section of the General Assembly, Chandigarh.

*above left:* 344. Forum of the General Assembly, Chandigarh.

*above right:* 345. LE CORBUSIER. The Palace of Justice (Law Court), Chandigarh. 1952–56.

*right:* 346. Entrance to Palace of Justice, with ramp at the rear, Chandigarh.

have an energy that diminishes complaints about them. No modern architect designs with Le Corbusier's authority and sculptural sensivity; as a model for future Indian cities, however, Chandigarh promises disaster. The vernacular Indian tradition of dense groupings of buildings and covered passageways meets the challenge of heat, wind, and rain far better than do his solutions. But used by imaginative architects, Le Corbusier's ideas now bear fruit elsewhere, as the Boston City Hall clearly demonstrates. Great as his gifts were, Le Corbusier failed at Chandigarh to prove that a whole city could be shaped externally, rather than internally by the people themselves.

2000 1750 1500 1250 1000 750 500 250 B.C. A.D. 250 500 750 1000 1250 1500 1750 2000

Ancient period 3000 B.C.–A.D. 395
Medieval period 395–1400
Renaissance period 1400–1600
Baroque period 1600–1750
Modern period 1750–

RRANEAN
ND

c. 1250 ● Lion Gate, Mycenae
Temple of Khons, Karnak ●—● c. 1200–935
1198–1167 ● Temple of Ramses III, Thebes
A.D. 70–80 ● Colosseum, Rome
c. 160 ● City Gate, Miletus
211 ● Baths of Caracalla, Rome
310–20 ● Basilica of Constantine, Rome
4th c. ● Palace of Diocletian, Spalato
Tower of London ● 1078–90
Windsor Castle keep ● begun 1170
13th c. ● Krak des Chevaliers, Syria
1228–38 ● Castle of Angers
c. 1240 ● Castel del Monte, Andria, Italy
1283–90 ● Harlech Castle, Wales
1288–1309 ● Palazzo Comunale, Siena
late 14th c. ● Bruges Town Hall
c. 1400 ● Inca fortress, Sacsayhuaman, Peru
Ca' d' Oro, Venice ● 1422–40
Michelozzo, Palazzo Medici-Riccardi, Florence ● begun 1444
L. B. Alberti, Palazzo Rucellai, Florence ● 1446–51
A. Sangallo and Michelangelo, Palazzo Farnese, Rome ● 1530–89
C. Maderno and G. Bernini, Palazzo Barberini, Rome ● begun 1628
G. Bernini, Palazzo Chigi-Odescalchi, Rome ● begun 1664
L. Le Vau and J. Hardouin-Mansart, Versailles ● 1669–85

RLD

Inca fortress, Sacsayhuaman, Peru ● c. 1400
Kallman, McKinnell & Knowles, Boston City Hall ● 1969

Nijo Castle wall, Kyoto, Japan ● 1602
Katsura Palace, Japan ● 17th c.
Le Corbusier, Chandigarh, India begun 1951 ●

# 14

A city cannot be a work of art. . . . To approach a city, or even a city neighborhood, as if it were a larger architectural problem, capable of being given order by converting it to a disciplined work of art, is to make the mistake of attempting to substitute art for life." In these words Jane Jacobs, one of the most incisive urban critics in the United States, condemns architects and planning commissions who design whole cities on the drawing board. Because of repeated oversimplification of the complex life processes, the results of modern city planning and urban renewal have invariably been rather monotonous: aesthetic demands have conflicted with or superseded human need. Too often architects have been insensitive to the daily customs and problems of living and indifferent to those things that make city living enjoyable. Older cities are most livable, lovable, and beautiful when art has responded to life. Until this century the urban feature that met complex social and aesthetic needs was the city square. Before the age of the automobile it was public places, not great religious structures and palaces, that had the strongest daily artistic impact on urban societies. At a time of crisis for city dwellers, it is worth remembering that—far from being meaningless empty areas—squares, piazzas, and forums have historically been the points of reference for men's orientation of themselves in relation to their gods, their rulers, and their fellowmen.

There are a few encouraging signs that Americans are becoming conscious of the need to return more of the city to the pedestrian and to create urban areas for the enjoyment of people of all ages and incomes. Those who have visited Europe will recall the pleasure felt on walking unexpectedly into large and small squares with fountains, sculptures, and shaded arcades, whose builders and dates often were not listed in the guidebooks. Only in recent years have we become more aware of the square as an urban art form, intended for the daily use of the general public. Since ancient Greece, when the city included both public buildings and *spaces,* the square has been an urban air-conditioner and public parlor, the place of communal refreshment, and a source of civic pride. Because of these lovingly preserved spaces, many inhabitants of European cities have a strong sense of identity with their historic past.

## THE AGORA

The buildings that dominate the early history of architecture are temples, castles, and palaces, erected to serve gods and kings, priesthood and aristocracy. When were ordinary citizens first served by builders worthy of the name *architect*, men of imagination and taste as well as skill, capable of translating into stone and wood collective secular ideals? In other words, when did architecture begin to consider the common man? The earliest type of civic complex that rendered such a service was the *agora* (Fig. 347), developed in Greece during the 5th century B.C. in such cities as Athens and in Greek colonies on

# THE LIFE AND DEATH OF THE CITY SQUARE

## Pleasure to the People

the west coast of Asia Minor. In Greek antiquity the word *agora* denoted a central urban zone that was the spiritual, legal, political, and commercial heart of the community, so that the idea of the city gradually became synonymous with agora. Long before Classical Greece, in the earlier civilizations of Egypt, Mesopotamia, Crete, and Mycenae, there were marketplaces, often at the junctures of main city arteries and frequently adjacent to the temple or palace of the ruler. Their excavated ruins, however, do not reveal that they served all the varied and important functions essential to the Greek city republics.

The evolution of the Greek agora began in the 7th century B.C. in Athens. Most American cities were established only a few years or decades ago, and even the oldest date back a little more than 200 years, which makes it hard for us to comprehend how certain architectural concepts can mature and ripen over a period of 500 years. The Athenian agora began on a city site, near the Acropolis or fortified hill (Figs. 83–85), probably at an important crossroad or a natural source for water. At first markets were set up in temporary wooden stalls. Until the 5th century B.C. the Greek acropolis, with its temples and sometimes palaces (as at Athens), was the dominant civic complex. From the 5th century on, the agora of men increasingly replaced the acropolis or agora of the gods in importance for the daily life of the city. This change coincided with the great mercantile growth and success of such urban centers as Athens itself. In the case of Athens, the agora was never submitted to an overall arbitrary geometric plan. It assumed a roughly rectangular form (Fig. 348), enclosing a large open space, for the most part kept free of permanent monuments to permit plural uses. The agora served a dense conglomeration of functions: it was the focus of political elections and meetings, veneration of the gods, proposals and enactments of law, the exchange of goods, the storage and use of civic archives, painted and sculptured tributes to heroes of the republic, and strolling and daily communication. Plane trees and colonnaded walks added to the pleasurable ambiance, attracting peripatetic philosophers as well as gossips and idlers.

*opposite:* 347. The Athenian agora, viewed from the north toward the west side. 5th century B.C. Reconstruction model after J. Travlos, American School of Classical Studies, Athens.

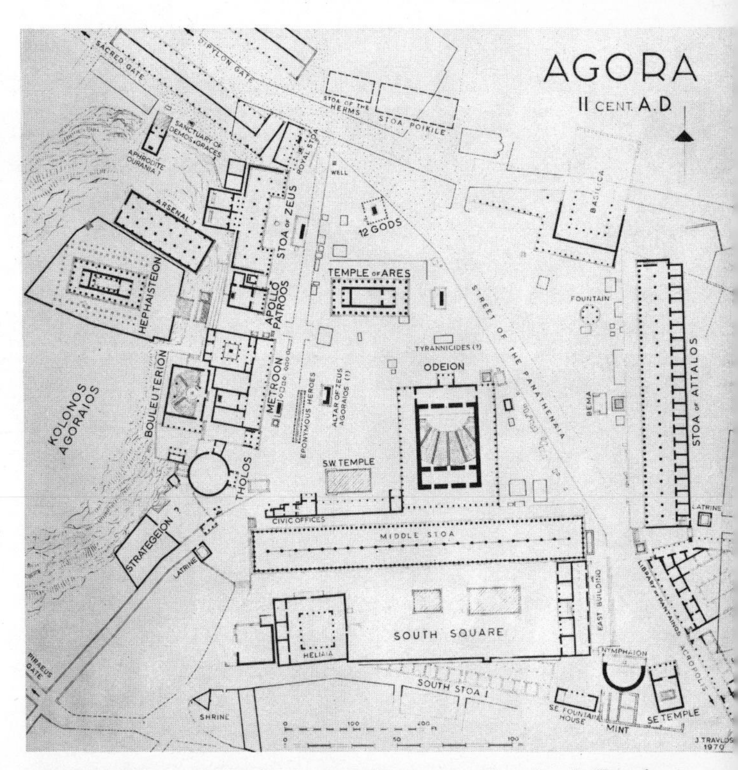


348. Plan of the Athenian agora. Reconstruction by J. Travlos, American School of Classical Studies, Athens.

The successive stages of the Athenian agora attest to its response to the somewhat anarchic character of the city's form, as well as to its adaptation to the irregularities of the site and to older shrines and buildings. The west side (Fig. 347) was reserved primarily for legal and religious activities (the Council House, shrines, and temple), while the eastern and southern areas were generally used for commercial transactions. The quarters of the pottery makers and bronze casters abutted the agora, as did the temple of their patron deity Hephaestus. The agora was never completely shut off physi-

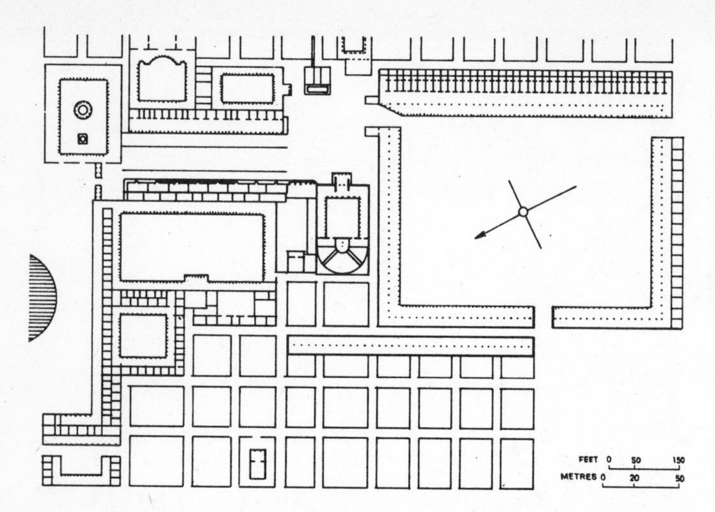

*left:* 349. Plan of the agora at Miletus. c. 160 B.C.

*above:* 350. Harbor and north agora at Miletus. Reconstruction model after H. Schlief, Staatliche Museen, Berlin. (See Fig. 306.)

cally from the city, a practical and symbolic characteristic. The nongeometric alignment of the buildings reflected a *functional,* not an architectural, aesthetic unity.

In the Greek colonial cities of Miletus and Priene in Asia Minor, the agora, in the 4th century B.C., acquired a more regularized outline. Here it was adapted to the planned checkerboard street pattern and was allotted two or more blocks. The agoras in these two port cities were also more specialized than that of Athens, in keeping with their commercial importance. At Miletus (Figs. 349, 350) the horseshoe plan emerged. The agora was formed by two L-shape porticoes with a main street running along the open end. Beyond the street was a continuous portico. Thus two of the entrances were at the corners of the agora, prophesying the access routes in medieval squares, which similarly avoided having entrances in the middle of the sides. Such unexpected views afforded greater variety, interest, and drama.

The element that gave the Greek agora its distinguishing architectural physiognomy was the *stoa* (Figs. 351, 352), the colonnaded, roofed portico (like a covered walkway) of one or two stories. While sometimes freestanding, the stoa usually had a wall at the back and stairways at the ends. Occasionally there were rows of shops, offices, and storerooms against the rear wall. The distance between the columns on the interior —that is, the row between the front colonnade and the wall— usually was twice as great as that between the exterior columns. The preferred order for the external columns was the Doric, admired for the sobriety and dignity it lent to the edifice and to the agora as a whole. At Athens, the south portico was known as the Painted Stoa, for its rear walls once bore paintings (now lost) such as the *Victory of the Greeks at Marathon.* Too, military trophies could be displayed there. Stoas thus served as picture galleries, just as agoras, with their statues and portraits, were the equivalent of outdoor museums. In its concentration of art works intended to inspire patriotism and civic virtue, the Athenian agora rivaled the best-endowed religious precincts, such as that at Olympia.

The stoa was the architectural descendant of colonnaded porticoes used by the Egyptians in the outer courts of their temples and of the columned façades of Cretan and Mycenaean

*left:* 351. Stoa of Attalus II, in the Athenian agora, viewed from the front toward the Acropolis. c. 150 B.C. Full-scale reconstruction by the American School of Classical Studies, Athens.

*opposite:* 352. Stoa of Attalus II (Fig. 351), in the Athenian agora, viewed from within the colonnades.

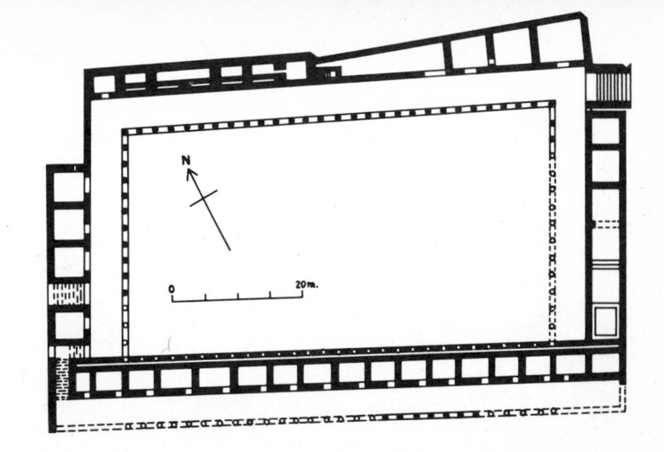


*left:* 353. The Palace at Knossos. c. 1600–1500 B.C. Reconstruction.

*above:* 354. Plan of the lower agora at Pergamon. 2nd century B.C.

palaces (Fig. 353). Thus the urban stoa secularized and democratized an architectural form originally employed in sacred and royal structures. The Greeks admired the external rhythmic elegance and internal flexibility of the stoa, its possibilities for partitioning, as well as the shelter it provided from wind, sun, and rain. The Stoic philosophy takes its name from the discourses originally held in the Athenian stoas. The stoa was not restricted to the civic center, for it was also used in theaters, religious precincts along important avenues, and gymnasia, but its greatest influence on subsequent cities of other cultures was in conjunction with city squares and major streets.

The agora was formalized into a regular, self-enclosed plan by the 2nd century B.C. in cities of Asia Minor, such as Pergamon (Fig. 354). And, in fact, the modern restoration of the Stoa of Attalus II in Athens (Figs. 351, 352) is based not on the older, more amorphous principles of agora construction but on the original gift of that Pergamene king. Hellenistic tyrants predictably sought to eliminate the anarchic features of the agora and to make of them monuments to their personal power. Ironically, just at the time when a pervasive architectural harmony was achieved in the agora, the republican polis, which had given it birth, was dying. This was not the last time that an architectural form evolved under republican ideals would be preempted by despotic rulers; and, as is evident from such monuments as the Capitol building in Washington, D.C., the reverse process has also occurred in the history of man's cultural experience.

## THE ROMAN FORUM

For those who seek through history a precedent for a humane environment, the cities of the Romans induce two deeply conflicting reactions. Ancient Rome may symbolize all that is squalid, oppressive, inhuman, and depraved, or it may appear as a model for the mastery of civilized assembly and for the movement of masses of people. There are historians who stress Roman ingenuity at stealing ideas from subjugated cultures; there are others who divine a Roman genius for deploying building materials and structural forms to shape public spaces with unprecedented effectiveness and magnificence. Historically, both views are correct, and the two can be conjoined when we focus on one of the great urban achievements of the Romans—the *forum*.

The Roman forum combined the acropolis and the agora into one great precinct, either over a long period of time, as in the original Roman Forum, or in a single concentrated building campaign. The latter was the case in the Forum of Trajan (Figs. 355, 356), begun in A.D. 107, the last and most influential great Imperial forum. The word *forum* means a place of assembly or communal meeting. Not only were temples and shrines located in the forums, but the great basilicas included in the forum complex synthesized the sacred and profane into one structure. The basilica was a development of the stoa, a multi-aisled, wall-enclosed structure with entrances at the center of the long sides and lateral apses for Imperial statues (Fig 312). Serving commercial and legal purposes, as well as that of

*above:* 355. Forum of Trajan, Rome. c. A.D. 2nd century. Reconstruction model after Bender. Museo della Civiltà Romana, Rome.

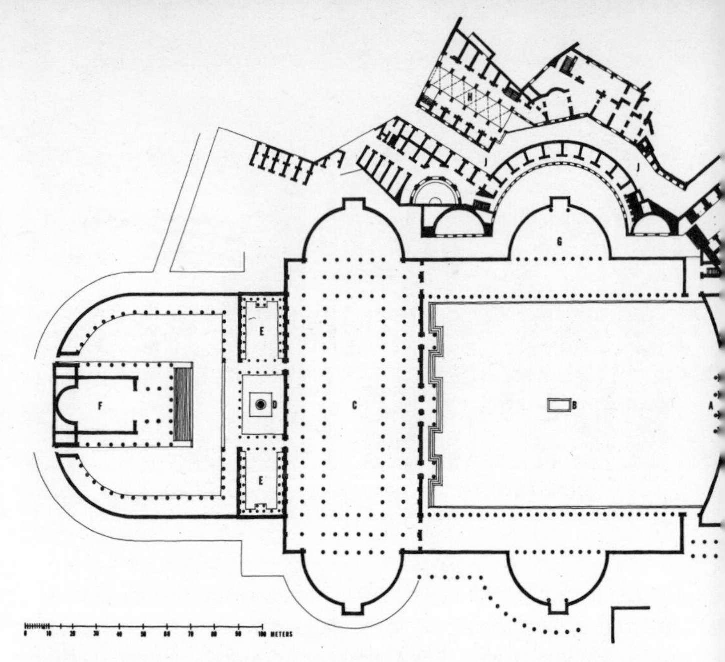

*right:* 356. Plan of Trajan's Forum. A) Arch of Trajan; B) Forum; C) Basilica Ulpia; D) Column; E) Libraries; F) Temple of Trajan; G) Trajan's Market; H) Aula Traiana; J) Via Biberatica.

emperor veneration, the basilica was like an indoor forum, the counterpart to the great open-air colonnaded forecourts outside, and it served as such on rainy days. As we can see in the plan of Trajan's Forum (Fig. 356), laid down by his Syrian architect Apollodorus, the basilica transversely intersects at one end the long axis of the main courtyard. Behind the basilica were two brick libraries for Greek and Roman literature flanking Trajan's triumphal column, and beyond that was a temple. Consonant with the astrological ideal of cities and precincts in harmony with the heavens, all the components of Trajan's Forum were rigorously aligned along a series of axes. The longitudinal axis was dominated by a statue of the Emperor which one saw immediately upon entering through the triumphal arch. The Romans were the first to develop a square oriented around a centrally placed monument. By contrast with the Greek agora, its most probable source, the Roman urban precinct symbolized in its symmetry, frontality, and centralized focus the Imperial presence, benefaction, and rule.

One approached Trajan's Forum through narrow, crowded, dark, unpaved, and ravinelike streets, typical of most of Rome's thoroughfares. Although there were miles of colonnaded walks, the planned and architecturally designed streets between the big Imperial civic complexes were few. To leave behind the jungle of tenements and maze of streets for the majestic clarity, space, and radiance of the forum must have been a moving experience. Passing through the triumphal arch that led to the

*below:* 357. Trajan's Market, viewed from Trajan's Forum.

*right:* 358. Isometric reconstruction of Trajan's Market.

forum was comparable to entering into a city of gods and emperors, where the sun fell on marble pavements, colonnades, and gilt-bronze roof tiles. There are no records of citizen protest committees fighting the destruction of housing and shops on the proposed site of Trajan's Forum, but large-scale urban renewal came in with the Romans, and, as today, tenants suffered dispossession without the benefit of new quarters.

The forum was every Roman's daytime home and place of business or amusement. He could have his lawsuit tried, be harangued by politicans, hear a funeral oration, pay homage to one of his gods, do his marketing, dictate his correspondence to public secretaries, obtain the news, or review a conquering general's trophies and pictorial accounts of his triumphs carried on wooden placards. At four in the afternoon he left the forum for the Imperial baths (Figs. 310, 311), another city within the city. No doubt people idled in the forum; however, by means of strong axial arrangements and the setting up of compelling vistas or goals, architects such as Apollodorus did everything possible to encourage purposeful activity. These same arrangements also provided a splendid arena for state rituals. No previous builders had employed with such boldness, skill, taste, and scale materials that, like the great open space of the forum itself, could only be described as luxurious. The Empire was drawn upon (or exploited, depending upon one's taste or distaste for the Romans) for the finest materials and workmen to serve the emperors. These, in turn, justified their power when, by creating public spaces, they made the otherwise unbearably crowded, foul, dangerous city of Rome an exciting place to live in. To the Romans there was only one city of consequence, Rome itself. In a society that permitted competition and rewarded the ambitious, the forum made endurable the predicament of living in a six- or seven-story wood, rubble, and brick tenement that could burn in minutes or collapse from its own weight or the contractor's corruption. That there was no total city planning to benefit the poor can be explained by private enterprise, an approved system of individual land exploitation that reaped the profits necessary for a few thousand to live in a grand style. Such a situation finds some parallel in large cities today, for high performance in the competitive activities of the forum was a passport out of the ghettos.

**The Market of Trajan** Antiquity's most dramatically designed and innovatory public social space was the great market (Fig. 357) that Emperor Trajan had built next to his forum. It rose to a height of some six or seven stories against the hill behind. Because of Imperial sponsorship, the market offered Imperial cashiers and foodstuffs for the public dole. Private merchants could also rent shops. Analogies for this great market can be found in a modern multilevel shopping center and, on a smaller scale, in the irregular plan, diagonal vistas through archways, and handsome brickwork of San Francisco's Ghirardelli Square (Fig. 401). In the early 2nd century A.D. a now nameless designer of genius utilized the most sophisticated formal and technological ideas for planning the market and its construction in concrete and brick. He created a complex that rose on three hemicycular levels to a series of asymmetrical cubic structures, containing streets, ramps, passageways, and more than 200 rooms of varying sizes (Fig. 358). The semicircular lower structure echoed the graceful shape of the Forum across the street; otherwise, the market was not subjected to implacable symmetry, to the tyranny of columns and continuous horizontal entablatures, or to the marble facing and costly ornament of the forum. Instead, concrete rooms, made spacious by new types of vaulting, were faced in brick, arched passageways rose directly from great piers, and walls opened amply to admit light and air. This highly original complex, ideal for its climate and its business, has been described by William MacDonald:

> At the Markets the center line of the hemicycle was not used to control the overall plan and no balanced rectilinear silhouette was attempted. There were no peristyles or courts because the Markets existed for the life of the shops and streets. The result both functionally and visually was an urban unit, a city quarter with an irregular skyline, curving and turning streets, changing vistas, and an elaborate internal communications system. The place is so large and its plan so complex that it could not have been comprehended at once; it invited exploration and disclosed itself only part by part.

The large-scale groin and barrel vaults of this market (Fig. 359) were soon emulated all over the Empire, dramatically increasing the possibilities of enclosed space for civic use.

*right:* 359. Trajan's Market, interior of the actual remains.

*left:* 360. Market and city hall at Tübingen. Medieval.

*right:* 361. Market square, town hall, and cathedral at Bremen. Medieval.

## MEDIEVAL SQUARES

The history of Western civilization is often maddeningly contrary. If one had only urban public spaces as a record, it would be logical to expect that one would witness from antiquity to the Renaissance a steady development of the planned, spacious, symmetrical forum, since the Romans had founded so many cities throughout the Mediterranean and western Europe. However, with the fall of the western half of the Roman Empire in the 4th century A.D., there began a period of about 700 years during which Roman cities declined and little urbanization occurred. The 12th to 15th centuries saw the urban renaissance: more than a thousand new medieval cities emerged all over Europe. The changing character of open urban space responded to different forms of societies than had existed under the Roman Empire. The planned, regular, and grandiose monument-oriented character of the Imperial forum was supplanted by its opposite. Many medieval cities that developed in the 12th and 13th centuries did *not* have public squares to begin with, since tradesmen and merchants used

*left:* 362. Piazza della Cisterna, San Gimignano, Italy. Medieval.

*below:* 363. Plan of the Piazza del Duomo and the Piazza della Cisterna, San Gimignano. Medieval.

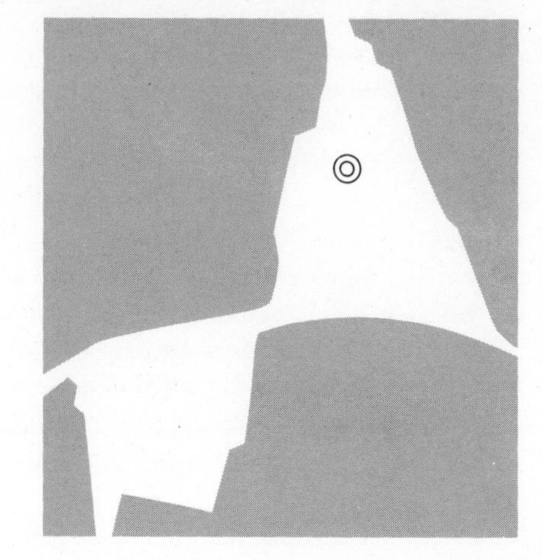

areas either just outside or just inside the city gates for their transactions. Even in medieval cities that grew up around a monastery or castle, public spaces were not submitted to the dictatorial planning of an equivalent of the Roman caesar (Fig. 360). Their appearance, size, shape, and subsequent evolution responded to a many-sided tug of war among several groups: the city's communal administration, usually a council composed of representatives of various urban middle-class factions such as the companies and guilds; the urban nobility; and the clergy. The emergence of important public squares in castle towns reiterates the ancient competition of agora and acropolis, in which the urban burghers won their civic freedom from feudal lords.

In defiance of the geometer's circle and rectangle, medieval civic spaces were irregular, often in the shape of wedges and triangles. The latter may have reflected the original funnel shape created when lines of temporary stalls were set up near gates or in open spaces to derive the greatest benefit from the flow of pedestrian traffic. The steady, widespread economic growth of Europe from the 12th century on swelled city populations with artisan producers of goods, merchants, and bankers, who, along with peasants or tradesmen lacking urban property, clamored for space in the cities to barter or sell their merchandise. Streets were widened in certain places; buildings were demolished to carve out a market space at right angles to the street; cemeteries adjoining churches were paved over and converted to the interests of the living community; land was reclaimed by covering streams; and suburbs that had grown up at the gates were encircled with new perimeter walls. By the 15th century public squares punctuated all European cities. Building sites framing or near these open spaces were precious, and houses located on the squares were often the most distinguished in the town. Houses served as places of business as well as residences until the era of the Medici, who separated the two in the 15th century. The respect for individual dwellings accounted for the narrow streets and eccentric shaping of the squares. Urban greenery was restricted to private walled gardens attached to the houses and was not to be found in the marketplaces.

Medieval European squares were closed on all sides by public and private buildings and, usually, could be entered only by narrow streets at the corners or by a rare broad street debouching into the center. The access routes generally were inflected to curve or angle around existing houses and to provide defense against weather and military assault. Blocks of adjacent dwellings determined the intimate size of the squares, and only in the 15th century did there develop a desire for uniformity of façades, scale, and proportion in the city block. In the medieval city major public buildings were quite commonly embedded into surrounding structures and street patterns. A cathedral could be left exposed only at its west and transept portals, and a city hall, such as that in Bremen (Fig. 361), might be open to view only at its front. The adjacent squares often took their proportions from the principal edifice flanking one side. If the building was tall, like the towered city hall at Bruges (Fig. 321), the square could be narrow and deep. A broad guild or town hall only three or four stories high would impose upon its square the dominance of width over depth. The *parvis,* an irregular space open before the west portals of cathedrals, was holy ground. Here one could assemble, hear a sermon, or even tether horses. Those using this ground enjoyed immunity from civil laws. Along its transept side, however, a cathedral or church could have a public market, or where squares developed in groups, as at San Gimignano (Figs. 362, 363), an arcade or narrow opening might link open spaces of varying uses and legal histories.

Individuality of plan, caused by gradual evolution, reflected the diversity of the structures that rose to define and close the square, and the steep roof silhouettes of the surrounding buildings precluded a uniform skyline. The streets that entered the squares from the corners afforded the visitor little foretaste of what the square would look like, and from within the square its actual size was masked by its many angles and the magnetic attraction of each building. Unlike the Forum of Trajan, which had an Imperial statue located in the center, medieval urban spaces held their permanent furniture, such as fountains and sculpture, well away from the main lines of traffic, thus ensuring flexibility in the use of the open space.

By the end of the Middle Ages great urban squares such as those at Siena (Fig. 364), Florence, and Bruges were used not only for commerce and religious pageantry, but for legal proceedings—including executions (Fig. 365)—and sports.

*right:* 364. Piazza del Campo, Siena. Late medieval.

*left:* 365. *Execution of Savonarola in the Piazza della Signoria, Florence.* c. 1500. Panel. Museo San Marco, Florence.

*above:* 366. Piazza della Signoria, Florence. *left:* ARNOLFO DI CAMBIO. Palazzo della Signoria. 1298–1314. *right:* Loggia dei Lanzi. 1376–82.

Jousting tournaments of knights or squires could be watched from temporary bleachers or from the windows of the houses. The horse race or *Palio* at Siena (see p. 239) and the soccer game in the Piazza della Signoria (Fig. 366) in Florence are modern counterparts of medieval urban sports. Most of the squares were paved by the end of the Middle Ages, not just for sanitary purposes but also for beauty and to satisfy civic pride.

Medieval town councils were responsible for maintaining the walls of the city, seeing that the land within the walls was properly distributed, passing ordinances, settling disputes, and listening to petitions. There was, however, no systematic planning or large-scale urban renewal. The councilors could well have had the responsibilities of a city engineer or designer. Surviving documents reveal that 13th century Siennese householders were urged to make their windows onto the main square consonant in shape with those of the new city hall. In the 15th century residents of a certain quarter of Avignon objected to enlarging a small parvis on the grounds that it would encourage the influx of small boys, noise, violence, uncertain defense, and poor hygiene (bad winds); moreover it would lower the aesthetic tone or beauty of the place.

Rare is the city square that has survived from the 12th, 13th, and 14th centuries unaltered in plan and elevation. Most

*below:* 367. Façade of city hall at Lübeck, Germany. c. 1250.

*right:* 368. FRIEDRICH HERLIN. *Market Square at Rothenburg,* detail of an altar painting. 1466. St. Jacob's, Rothenburg, Germany.

*right:* 369. Cathedral of San Lorenzo (1345–1490), Perugia, with a Renaissance portal, and the Fontana Maggiore (1278).

of the beautiful European squares of medieval origin have undergone changes in outline, and new buildings or redesigned structures now front them. Nevertheless, their plan often persists. Some medieval squares were partially faced with arcades that belonged to a private house or a city hall, as in Lübeck (Fig. 367), but it remained for the Renaissance to regularize this feature. Medieval university towns, such as Bologna, provided extensive arcading of streets to facilitate the passage of faculty and students.

Medieval builders and those who may have been responsible for the design of urban spaces knew how to manage with sensitivity the distances between sides of a square. The cathedrals manifest the ability of the architect to absorb an infinite variety of decorative and structural features while achieving a sense of order and perfection appropriate to the City of God; similarly, medieval squares bounded by secular buildings exemplify diversified order and orderly diversity (Fig. 368). Medieval urban aesthetics presupposed a harmony that could be served in the whole while not predictable on the basis of its parts. Consistency of quality, rather than repetition of form, was a conscious objective in the architecture that framed late medieval squares.

The strongest testimony to medieval urban designers' practicality and aesthetic sensibility to space is the linkage they made of disparate squares to achieve economy and beauty of open space in or near the town center. At Perugia (Fig. 369) the cathedral and town hall are at right angles to each other and separated by a space whose focus is a magnificent medieval fountain. The two buildings share an ample but, from the ground level, complex space, difficult to diagram in the mind in terms of its borders. Use of the fountain and activities appropriate to both institutions took place in front of these respective structures, while the daily communal promenade through the entire complex could and still does occur at noon and before dinner. The eccentric location of the entering streets still gives this exciting urban center a sense of closure and tangible space. Wherever one stands there are new, unpredictable prospects to discover. The sloping site has been accommodated by the terrace adjoining the cathedral, thus adding richness to the area's elevation.

## THE RENAISSANCE: OLD CITIES AND NEW SQUARES

With the exception of a few small cities or towns, there were no real Renaissance cities, for only in theoretical treatises of the 15th and 16th centuries were cities completely designed. In Renaissance painting one can see the 15th-century artist's conception of an ideal city square (Fig. 370)—a re-creation of

*below:* 370. Piero della Francesca and Luciano Laurana. *View of an Ideal City*. c. 1460. Panel, 1′11⅝″ × 6′6¾″. Galleria Nazionale delle Marche, Palazzo Ducale, Urbino.

an ancient Roman forum, replete with circular temple, colosseum, triumphal arches and columns, and geometrically designed pavements. Decorative "furniture" is symmetrically disposed about the square. Arcades are present but not continuous, reflecting diversity rather than uniformity of the buildings. The square is still scaled to the human figure and is comparable in size to larger medieval squares. The Renaissance artist sought to correct what he felt was a lack of clarity and to establish a beauty related to geometric principles. The isolation of a major building in the center of a square resembles the location of the Florentine Baptistery, but the latter was atypical of medieval urban architecture.

The enactment of Renaissance ideas largely took the form of their imposition on such medieval squares as the Piazza della Signoria in Florence (Fig. 366). Michelangelo advanced the idea of continuing the beautiful arcade of the Loggia dei Lanzi, which dates from the 14th century, completely around the piazza. Such an arcade would have imparted a unifying regularity and emphatic rhythm to the frame of the square, a rhythm that we can visualize by looking at his design for the Capitoline Hill (Fig. 213), probably the finest Renaissance square. The Loggia dei Lanzi was a revival of the ancient portico or stoa (Figs. 351, 354), and, like its ancestors, it served as a public art gallery. It contributed to the popularity of the arcarde or arched colonnade in conjunction with a square.

In the 16th century the artist and art historian Giorgio Vasari (1511–74) designed the famous Uffizi Galleries (Fig. 371), the name of which denotes its original use as an office building. The Uffizi gave form to that century's taste for uniformity and symmetry, at the same time treating the street or square between the galleries as a controlled perspective, a self-conscious work of art. The bridge between the galleries nearest the Arno River provided both closure and a perspective focus toward the river. When viewed from the river, it framed Arnolfo di Cambio's ruggedly handsome 14th-century Palazzo della Signoria, jutting angularly into the main piazza. The addition of a row of sculptures, originally including Michelangelo's *David* (Fig. 193), from the front of the Palazzo into the square, created a new axis without disrupting the flexibility of the open area. The city planners of the Renaissance placed stronger emphasis upon statues in public places than had their medieval predecessors.

*opposite left:* 373. FILIPPO BRUNELLESCHI. Hospital of the Innocents. Begun 1419. Piazza Santissima Annunziata, Florence.

*opposite right:* 374. AMBROGIO DI CURTIS. Piazza Ducale, Vigevano. 1492–98.

Placing the work of a great artist in public occasioned important changes in urban space. In Padua, for example, to accommodate Donatello's equestrian statue of the mercenary general Gattamelata, a church courtyard was leveled (Fig. 372). Thus the sculpture, which stands out from the corner of the Church of St. Anthony at a 45-degree angle, became the pivotal point for two squares that buttressed the church, to make them spacially continuous. The man on horseback, as Lewis Mumford has pointed out, symbolized the great political changes that took place in Europe at the end of the Middle Ages, when municipal power was replaced by that of the despot. Emperors and dukes arrogated to themselves the design of public squares or even whole cities. Paradoxically, the ideas formulated during the 15th-century Florentine communes provided inspiration to tyrants from the 16th century on.

*left:* 371. GIORGIO VASARI. Uffizi Galleries, Florence. 1560–80. View toward the Palazzo della Signoria (Fig. 366).

*below:* 372. Piazza del Santo and Basilica of Sant'Antonio, Padua.
*lower left:* DONATELLO. *Equestrian Statue of Gattamelata.* 1445–50.

One influential Renaissance square was that of Santissima Annunziata in Florence (Fig. 373). In 1419, Filippo Brunelleschi designed an arcaded front for the orphanage forming one side of the square. Arcaded public buildings were already common in the Middle Ages, but Brunelleschi's innovation was to make the arcade's proportions systemic to the rationale of the plan, elevation, and interior of the whole structure. In the 16th century Antonio da Sangallo (1455–1534) added to the church itself an arcade that, harmonizing with Brunelleschi's work, framed the square's space more consistently and allowed it to interpenetrate with structures constituting its borders. The first fully planned Renaissance square may have been the Piazza Ducale (Fig. 374) in Vigevano near Milan, built between 1492 and 1498 under Ambrogio di Curtis, engineer to Ludovico the Moor. A ruthless razing of older buildings made possible the square's perfectly rectangular form, but the arcades masked the entering streets and preserved the closure of the original piazza. The result resembles the completely enclosed agora, though a better analogy might be drawn with the interior courtyards of Renaissance palaces. This public development of an architectural form formerly reserved for the private use of royalty recalls the evolution in antiquity of columns and colonnades from royal house to civic square. The square at Vigevano served ducal and civic pride in contrast with, but not in negation of, the older city.

The most spectacular example of an urban square as a synthesis of medieval and post-medieval ideas is to be found in Venice's Piazza San Marco (Figs. 375, 376). The history of the Piazza can be traced to the 9th century, when the cathedral was founded, and this most magnificent pedestrian square in the world is a tribute to architects whose contributions were made over a period of a thousand years. By the year 1000

*left:* 375. Piazza San Marco, Venice. *lower left:* Doge's Palace. 1309–1424. *lower center:* Basilica of St. Mark. 1063–94. *center left:* Jacopo Sansovino. Library of St. Mark. Begun 1536.

*below:* 376. Plan of the Piazza San Marco, Venice.

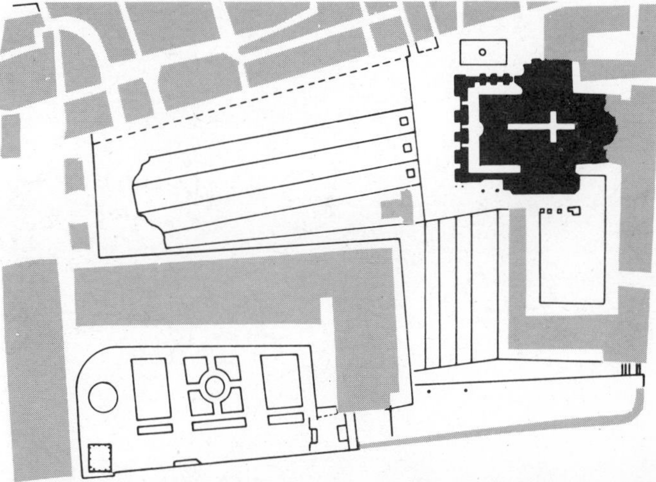

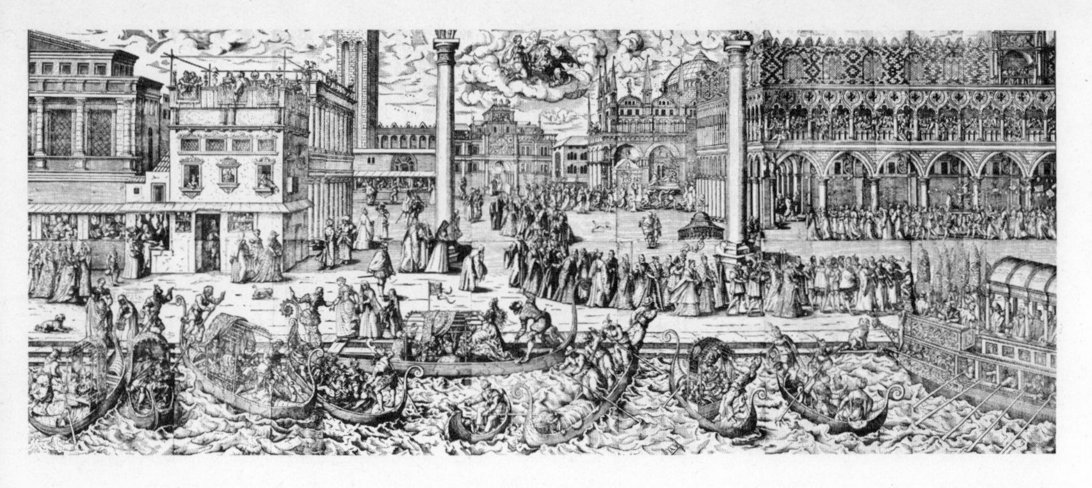

377. JOST AMMAN. *Procession of the Doge in the Piazza San Marco, Venice.* Woodcut by G. A. VAVASSARE, after TITIAN. 1697. Metropolitan Museum of Art, New York (Whittelsey Fund, 1949).

there was a parvis and a marketplace, presumably constituting the basis of the two squares (the piazza and piazzetta) that join at right angles. In 1329 the original bell tower, or *campanile,* was built like a hinge at this juncture. The columns of the Lion and St. Theodore, which frame the entrance to the piazzetta overlooking the lagoon, were erected in the 12th and 14th centuries, respectively. These freestanding columns, with their triumphal connotations, give a discrete limit to the south side of the piazzetta, while imparting a majestic impression to those disembarking from the canal. It was between these columns that criminals were executed. In medieval fashion the piazza is tangent to, and not intersected by, the main urban artery, in this case the Grand Canal (Fig. 377). (This arrangement allowed better flow of commercial traffic.) In the 15th century the arcaded north side of the square, which housed city offices, was begun by Pietro Lombardo (c. 1435–1515) and Bartolomeo Buon. Adjacent to these offices is the beautiful clock tower, erected in 1499 by Caducci. This tower symbolically signaled the tyranny of time, a new form of the regimentation of life for a great mercantile power. In 1505 Alessandro Leopardi erected the great flagpoles in front of the cathedral (Fig. 378). Nowhere else in the world do flagpoles contribute so much to their setting, by their scale and by the movement of their banners. Between 1536 and 1537 Jacopo Sansovino (1486–1570) designed the library opposite the magnificent 14th-century Doge's Palace, thereby completing the flanks of the piazzetta (Fig. 375). Almost 150 years later Scamozzi added the new administrative offices which formed an L with the library and completed the symmetry of the long sides of the piazza. Like the archives within, the colonnades of these buildings were eloquent reminders of bureaucratic control over the lives of the Venetians. Not until the early 19th century was the narrow end of the piazza closed off by the Napoleonic portico, which also bridged the divergent heights of the two administrative wings. Entering the piazza through the Napoleonic portico gives a spectacular funnellike view of the cathedral. The doges called upon the best architectural talent to create and preserve in the Piazza San Marco reminders of the power, history, and magnificence of Venice. Today Venetians know who they are because their past is symbolized before their eyes.

When one stands in the Piazza San Marco he has the rare feeling that there is no more important or interesting place

*left:* 378. GENTILE BELLINI. *Procession in the Piazza San Marco.* 1496. Oil on canvas, 12 × 24′. Academy, Venice.

*opposite left:* 379. ALBRECHT DÜRER. Project for a fortress city. 1527.

*opposite center:* 380. Plan of Palma Nuova. 1593.

*opposite right:* 381. PIETRO CATANEO. Plan for an ideal city. c. 1554.

to be in the world at that moment. From sunrise, when the pigeons assemble in legions to be fed, until the sidewalk cafés put away their tables after midnight, the drama and the delight of the piazza are people and architecture. This was the point at which all of Venetian high society assembled in the days of Titian and Tintoretto, the ballroom of Europe in the 18th century, the stage for religious pageants that go back before Bellini's great painting (Fig. 378). The Piazza San Marco is that special place where one knows important things have happened and will continue to happen. No other spot in the city gives that feeling. To leave its luxuriously textured façades and pass into the narrow dingy streets is to be reminded of Marco Polo's description of his fellow Venetian noblemen, who, to preserve their rank despite poverty, wore the costliest silks over rotting underwear. The public façade was and is everything in Venice.

The Piazza San Marco is not a perfect work of art. There are other smaller squares that come closer to perfection in the sense of fulfilling their designers' plans and that are marked by consistency of style and uniform excellence of execution. But we do not value Vigevano's piazza (Fig. 374), for example, above that of San Marco. Greatness tolerates some imperfection, incoherence, and lack of formal unity. The inconsistencies of the piazza are tributes to the living process of its formation over a millenium. The great Basilica of San Marco, for example, represented the lootings of Constantinople by the Crusaders, and the building is one massive trophy. Isolated and separated from one another, the buildings of San Marco would still be impressive, some beautiful and some rather monotonous. Taken together, as a context, they contrast yet complement one another to make the whole greater than the sum of its parts. The Piazza San Marco is an incomparable whole, like the Athenian Acropolis, the Bible, and the Venetian Republic itself. One perceives this, not through hypothesis, plans and photographs, or the evocation of laws or rules, but through intuition gained from being there dawn to dusk.

Venice should teach modern city planners how old cities can adapt new ideas while increasing their beauty and desirability as places to live. In the main, the dreams of 15th- and 16th-century urban planners were at the service of royalty, not of municipalities. The development of geometry as an artistic device, and more specifically the study of perspective, helped to transform the artisan into a learned painter and the master builder into an architect, whose plans could be executed by others. The development of urban planning was a solution to military and political problems rather than sociological ones. How could a duke or prince effectively protect his domain with its new satellite towns or outposts, taking into account changing methods of warfare and the invention of gunpowder? Theoreticians like Alberti, Filarete, Scamozzi, Leonardo, and Michelangelo worked on the problem by first determining the ideal defensive walled perimeter of the city. Polygonal geometrical forms were the solutions, because they permitted crossfire by the defenders.

The device of a polygonal piazza at the exact city center was used in many schemes, such as those created by Albrecht Dürer (Fig. 379), designed for a king and presumably to house Protestant refugees, and by the designer of Palma Nuova (Fig. 380), a Venetian outpost town. These open urban spaces were nuclear for the plan of the whole city: the main streets either radiated outward from their sides or extended from their corners to the city's perimeter. Thus the shape of the central square echoed that of the city. From the ruler's standpoint, this was an egocentric plan, making little or no architectural concessions to the diversified sociological functions of the city. Broad streets like spokes in a wheel facilitated access to the walls in all parts of the city, and the main square could serve to mobilize the troops. The plan of Pietro Cataneo (d. 1569) for an ideal city (Fig. 381) rejoins acropolis or citadel and agora within the tight frame of the ruler's power. The principal squares are aligned with the ruler's residential axes. The ideas conceived by artists as exciting explorations in the rationaliza-

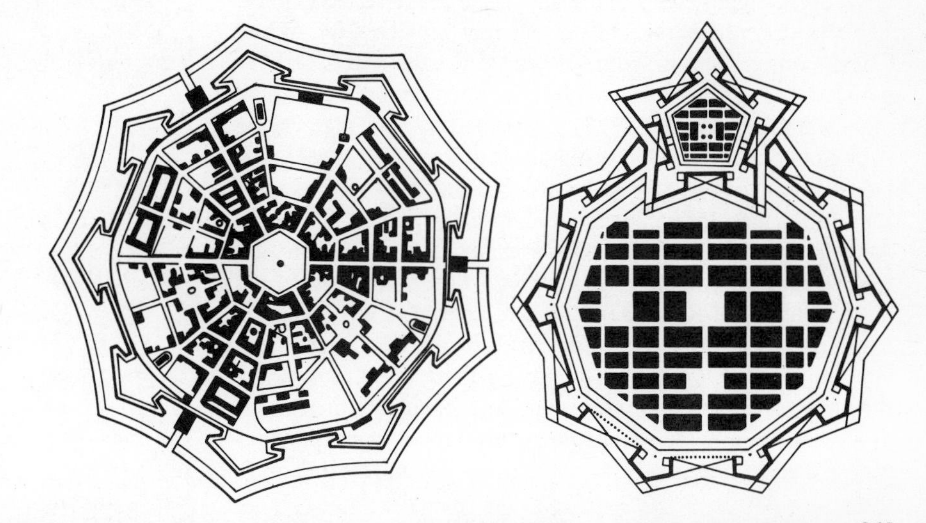

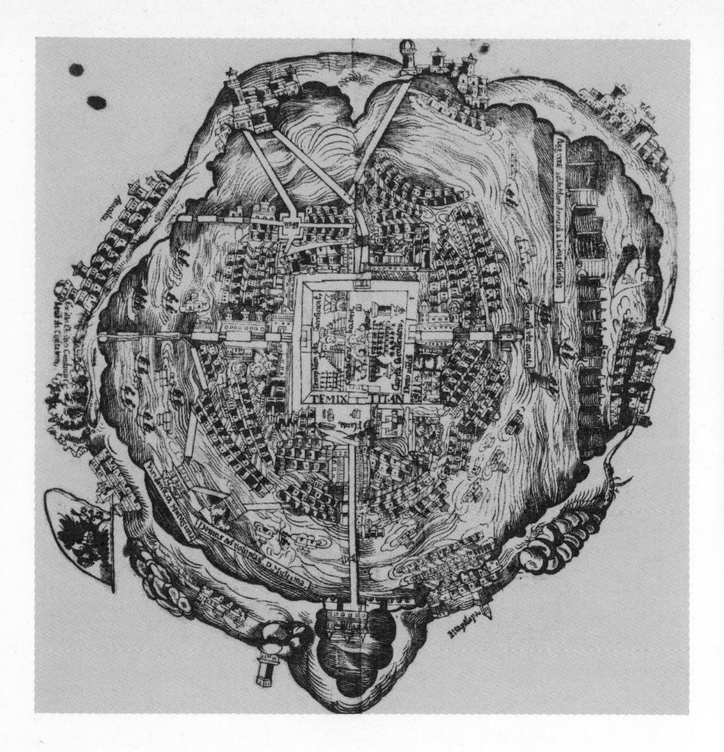

*left:* 382. Cortés(?). Plan of Mexico City. Instituto Nacional de Antropología e Historia, Mexico City.

*above:* 383. Great Temple of Tenochtitlán. 16th century. Reconstruction drawing after Ignacio Marquina. Instituto Nacional de Antropología e Historia, Mexico City.

tion of sight and space were adopted by those who would suppress the free element and subject urban life to authoritarian regimentation.

## TENOCHTITLÁN: THE AZTEC AGORA

The regularized city square has been associated with absolute political power throughout the world. It is possible that Albrecht Dürer's plan for a royal city, in its emphasis on perfect proportions and accurate measurement of the areas for different urban components, took its inspiration from Italian Renaissance theorists and ancient Roman writers. However, the centralized square flanked by the palace of the ruler may have been suggested by the plan of the great Aztec capital, Tenochtitlán on the site of present-day Mexico City. When Cortés conquered the city in 1519, he sent back letters accompanied by rough maps of this gleaming metropolis in the midst of a gigantic lake (Fig. 382). These letters and plans were printed in Dürer's home city of Nuremberg in 1524, three years before the artist published his treatise on fortifications containing the plan for his ideal city. Dürer showed an interest in Aztec gold sculpture and would certainly have been impressed with the power of royalty encountered by the Spaniards. Much in the manner of Renaissance urban renewal, the Aztec ruler Montezuma, in the 15th century, transformed a cluster of old villages into a capital city, imposing three great causeways through its heart to the civic center. Appropriate to the capital of a priest-dominated society, the central rectangular precinct was a dense concentration of religious structures and open spaces, entered through gateways embedded in the walls. Tenochtitlán was ruined by the Spaniards and is today buried under Mexico City; thus we must rely upon reconstructions (Fig. 383) to experience a public space that at once signaled the established earthly power of Montezuma and his uneasy alliance with the gods. The great plaza was an agora of the gods, who were specifically honored in the temples atop the great pyramidal structures. The plaza also embraced a school for novices, handball courts, sacrificial altars, and a theaterlike arrangement of more than 140,000 human skulls obtained

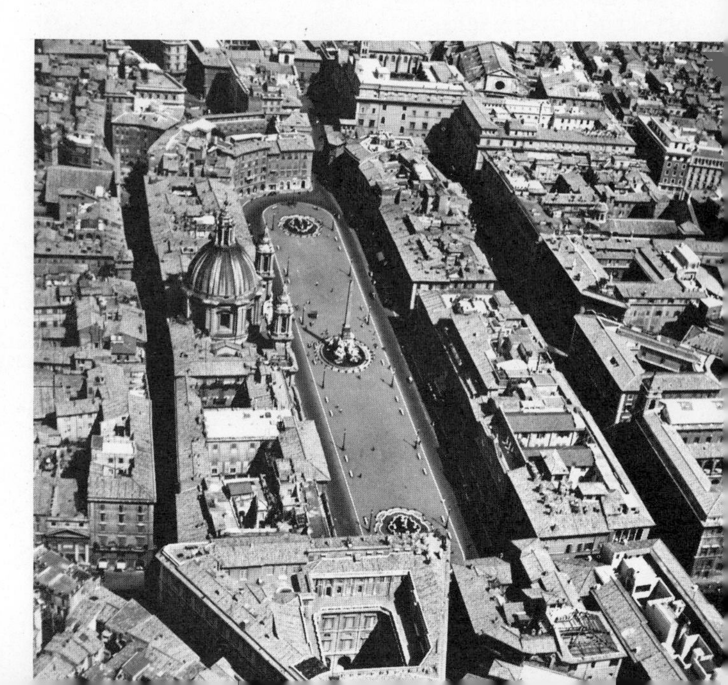

from sacrificial victims. The great plaza quadrated the city plan into four precincts, in themselves miniature cities with arcaded marketplaces. Montezuma's palace and those of the chiefs of other Aztec clans bordered the main plaza, attesting to the family alliances that supported the priest-king. Built around patios, these palaces were like miniatures of the city plan, recalling the Renaissance palace court and piazza. The monumentality of the great pyramid that supported twin temples dedicated to the two gods would have appealed to European readers of Cortés' descriptions, since it coincided with the taste for major buildings concentrated around a square. Long before Tenochtitlán, earlier pre-Columbian cultures had mastered the organization of great lateral spaces for temple precincts and cities, but always such organization served gods, kings, and the dead. The living were consigned to less orderly quarters just as in medieval and Renaissance Europe.

## PIAZZAS FOR PLEASURE

It is in Italy that one most frequently experiences the contributions of the square to the urban good life. On a hot summer day there is no more festive public square to receive the tired native or tourist than the Piazza Navona in Rome (Fig. 384). Its great fountains are heard before they are seen. The instinct to wade in Bernini's Fountain of the Four Rivers (Fig. 385) is so strong that one can understand why in the 18th century, during the great August Roman carnivals, the whole square was flooded by plugging the drains. People would walk or ride through the lagoonlike square or witness gondola jousts. The piazza stands on the site of an ancient Roman circus, an arena for Greek foot races, boxing, and chariot competitions, and this accounts for one of the Piazza Navona's most striking features, its oval format.

In the 17th century the square was enriched by Borromini's great Church of Sant' Agnese, its wide and curving façade calculated to honor the piazza's broad axis and to activate the space. One is conscious of Borromini's will exerted upon the piazza. The more restrained palaces flanking the church housed members of the Pamphili family. Pope Innocent X, born a Pamphili, sponsored the piazza's new design, which included the commission of a monumental fountain to be crowned by a mighty Roman obelisk. For a time it seemed that the commission would surely go to Borromini, but through a ruse Bernini's design was brought to the attention of the Pope. Innocent was so delighted with the plan that he immediately placed the project in the hands of Bernini. Resisting the temptation to upstage his rival's architectural design, Bernini located his Fountain of the Four Rivers so that it did not split the central axis of Sant'Agnese, but he in turn imposed his intent on the space of the piazza. The church, the fountains, and the square are theater, a dramatic competition of artistic drives in the service of papal ego. As can be seen in Pannini's painting (Pl. 42, p. 236), papier-mâché and temporary wooden structures, which harmonized with the marble and travertine fountains, were built for celebrations sponsored by the French cardinal in honor of the birth of the dauphin in 1729. No previous public square was so dominated by its embellishments, nor has any square ever engendered a spirit so perennially ebullient with the bustling business of pleasurable living.

Bernini's burgeoning ideas were influenced by his experience with set designs and rustic grottoes sponsored by Roman nobility. He demonstrated a genius for achieving spectacular effects with water as well as with sculpture. Literally and figuratively, the fountain was a tour de force: a dove—symbol of divinity, peace, and the Pamphili—crowns the obelisk, which signifies eternity, wisdom, and solar symbolism. Below,

*opposite:* 384. Piazza Navona, Rome. 17th century form taken from an ancient Roman circus.

*right:* 385. Piazza Navona, Rome. *left:* CARLO RAINALDI and FRANCESCO BORROMINI. Palazzo Pamphili. 1645–50. *center:* BORROMINI. Church of Sant'Agnese. Begun 1652. *right:* GIANLORENZO BERNINI. Fountain of the Four Rivers. 1648–51. (See also Pl. 42, p. 236.)

*left:* 386. NICOLA SALVI. Trevi Fountain, Rome. 1732–62.

the surprisingly hollowed rock is flanked by personifications of great rivers from four continents. The latter suggested the world-wide success of Roman missionaries. The great fountain was intended to regale and remind Rome of the resurgence of the city's power as well as that of the Church. Today, circling the square in a carriage or on foot, one is still entertained by dazzling sights, sounds, and fresh smells of cascading water, a rejuvenating experience that in Bernini's day carried his and the Pope's dreams for greater renewal of the city. The Piazza Navona continues to serve with remarkable efficiency as the airconditioner for an entire sector of Rome.

From Bernini's ideas about sculpture and fountains came Nicola Salvi's design from the 18th-century Trevi Fountain (Fig. 386). Here, the fountain is served by the square, a restricted space that receives a chaotic spill from a palace wall 50 feet wide. To view the fountain visitors stand with their backs to a church placed obliquely opposite. One steps down from the street level to that of the basin, and all levels and angles yield surprises in the forms taken by water issuing from artificial grottoes and clefts. Only a society addicted to sensual display could have produced such visual pyrotechnics.

For 18th-century Rome, Francesco de Sanctis designed the most imaginative combination of public stairway, street, piazza, and stage in the world. The Spanish Steps (Fig. 387) join the hilltop church of Santa Trinità al Monte with an old flower market below in the Piazza di Spagna. Nearby are the traditional quarters for artists, and their models used the stairway as a hangout. Pietro Bernini, the father of Gianlorenzo, designed the fountain for the piazza in the form of a ship, which appears to be sinking when the drains are plugged to flood the piazza. To begin the descent of the stairs is like stepping on stage, with all of Rome as the audience. The design flatters the extrovert or natural performer. This great stairway, which pulses in and out, has a double nature: a formal appearance that lends itself to informal activities. The axial structure of the bifurcated stairs that frame the obelisk at the top and the sweeping delineation of space are elegant reminders of papal benefaction. There is ample room for spontaneous congregation and dispersal; the broad landings and stairs invite sitting, strolling, and sightseeing. Unlike Michelangelo's no-nonsense flights of steps leading to the Capitoline Hill (Fig.213), the Spanish steps make ascent and descent a leisurely aesthetic experience, for the stairway is a place as well as a passage, an end as well as a means. Aesthetically and psychologically, de Sanctis succeeded in bringing together the city's human, architectural, and topographical elements.

*left:* 387. FRANCESCO DE SANCTIS. The Spanish Steps, Piazza di Spagna, Rome. 1721–25.

## PIAZZAS FOR POWER

**St. Peter's Square** If a great architect is successful, he makes his audience forget the problems with which he struggled. To ignore them, however, is to forget that art history is made up of personal dramas, suspense, and anxiety. Imagine the problems confronting Bernini when, at the behest of Pope Alexander VII, he began in 1656 to build the great square before St. Peter's (Figs. 388–390). Logistically, his challenge was to create, in a crowded city, an open space that could contain thousands of people who, in receiving the papal

blessing at Easter, stood for the world. Symbolically, the form of the enclosure had to convey the all-encompassing authority of the Church. His piazza was to be a prelude to the most important edifice in Christendom, the objective of year-round universal pilgrimage. The basilica itself presented problems, because the façade, built by Carlo Maderno, was too wide and too high in relation to the dome. The façade was also a reminder of a humiliating disaster for Bernini. In 1637 the great sculptor had designed a pair of bell towers to flank the façade. Shortly after construction began, cracks developed, and work had to be abandoned. Because of his artistic monopoly of papal projects, Bernini could count upon the loud and bitter criticisms of his architectural and sculptural rivals.

*left:* 388. Basilica of St. Peter and the Vatican, Rome. Apse and dome (1547–64) by MICHELANGELO; dome completed (1588–92) by GIACOMO DELLA PORTA; nave and façade (1606–26) by CARLO MADERNO; colonnades (1656–67) by GIANLORENZO BERNINI.

*above:* 389. GIANLORENZO BERNINI. St. Peter's Square, Rome. 1656–67.

Bernini's solution strongly suggests that he studied the Forum of Trajan (Figs. 355–359). It entailed a pair of freestanding colonnaded "pincers" extending from St. Peter's like missionary's arms, which, in the artist's own words, "embrace Catholics to reinforce their beliefs, heretics to reunite them with the Church, and agnostics to enlighten them with the true faith." The wedge shape of the parvis served to shrink the width of Maderno's façade when seen from a distance in the piazza, thereby placing stronger emphasis on the dome. By adding a second fountain to match the first by Maderno, Bernini completed the lateral axis of the oval section of the square, which included a great obelisk. The oval provided ample dramatic space for a multitude, making the Pope visible either on the Benedictional Loggia above the entrance to St. Peter's or at his apartment window in the Papal Palace. The simple travertine colonnade revived the ancient stoa. It contained two aisles for pedestrians and a central street for carriages; thus, one could use the square in all weather. The visitor enters the piazza either on the long axis or from the sides through the colonnades, thereby assuring a breathtaking experience of the molded sweep of space. The handsome colonnades (Fig. 390) reflect a sculptor's sensitivity to the interaction of solids with space and to the expressiveness of alternating light and shadow on a vast but not monotonous scale.

*left:* 390. GIANLORENZO BERNINI. Colonnades, St. Peter's Square, Rome. 1656–67.

**Place de la Concorde** What the piazza at St. Peter's is to the architectural symbolism of religious authority, the Place de la Concorde (Figs. 391–394) in Paris is to the urban expression of monarchy. For physical size and centrality of role in an extensive urban complex, the Place de la Concorde is without rival. Its original name has been changed, and its core is now a gas-lighted traffic island for pedestrians. Nevertheless, one can still stand at the base of its obelisk and look in four directions to observe the impressive monuments terminating radial lines from that spot. To the north is the Church of the Madeleine at the end of the Rue Royale; to the south is the Chamber of Deputies, the former Palais Bourbon, across the Pont de la Concorde. Eastward lies the Tuileries, originally the royal gardens that fronted the dome-centered wing of the Tuileries Palace, which until 1871 was part of the Louvre. Westward extends what was intended as a triumphal axis for the new Paris, the boulevard of the Champs-Elysées, which mounts a sloping hill for a mile to the Arc de Triomphe in the Place de l'Etoile. The designers coordinated a palace, religious, legislative, and residential buildings, a bridge, circular piazzas, streets, a boulevard, and triumphal arches, and in so doing abandoned the traditional closed square. The Place de la Concorde is bounded on two sides by the Seine and by the trees of the Champs-Elysées. Only the two remaining sides have structures: the raised terraces of the Tuileries and the twin buildings of the Maritime Ministry and the Hôtel Crillon, which flank the Rue Royale and frame the Madeleine. Planned vistas are achieved at the expense of intimacy and human scale, a worthwhile price to authoritarian minds and taste. The Place de la Concorde is the baldest display of the artist's arrogance in the service of political power to be found in a European city. It is the heart of a gigantic urban playground for the pomps and parades enacted by political and social authority. Here, art supported by military might has conquered urban space. The resulting architectural arrangement has satisfied absolute and constitutional rulers from Louis XV and Napoleon to the successors of De Gaulle.

In the mid-18th century the Place de la Concorde was a raw site, undeveloped, the approximate western terminus of Paris.

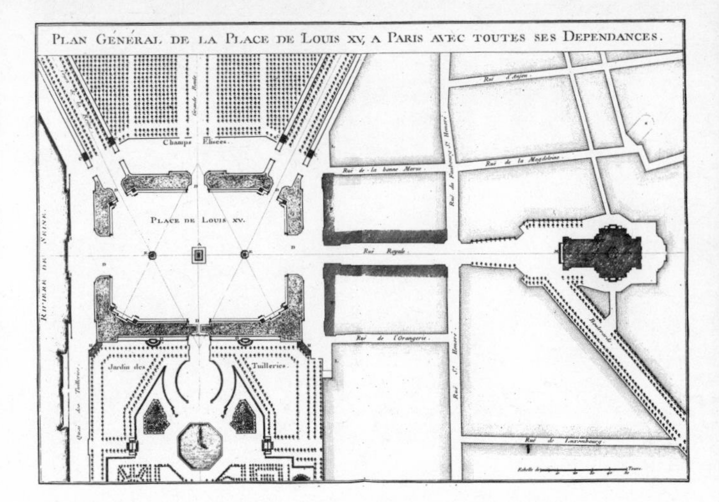


Its growth was linked to the western expansion of the city. In 1763 Louis XV directed Jacques-Ange Gabriel to build a square, in the center of which would stand a gigantic equestrian statue of the King to commemorate his victory in Austria in 1748. The square was thus named Place Louis XV. Gabriel drew up a plan in which a 15-foot-deep grass-lined ditch, bridged at six points, girdled a flat, lawn-covered esplanade, whose geometrically placed and symmetrical paths converged on the monument. This level site for promenades recalled earlier gardenlike squares between castles or palaces and towns. A low balustrade around the square, along with the ditch, were

*above:* 391. Plan of the Place de la Concorde, Paris, from PIERRE PATTE, *Monuments érigés en France*. Designed and built 1753–70 as the Place Louis XV.

*left:* 392. JACQUES-ANGE GABRIEL. Place de la Concorde, Paris. 1753–70. *upper right:* Church of the Madeleine facing the Rue Royale. *center to left:* Avenue des Champs-Elysées. *right:* Tuileries Gardens. *foreground:* Pont de la Concorde, leading to the Left Bank.

*below:* 393. The Louvre (1546–1878) and Tuileries Gardens (1564–1680), flanked by the Seine (*lower left*) and the Rue de Rivoli, Paris.

*left:* 394. Avenue des Champs-Elysées, viewed from the Place de la Concorde toward the Arc de Triomphe, Paris. Begun 1828.

*above:* 395. JEAN-FRANCIS CHALGRIN. Arc de Triomphe at the Place de l'Etoile, Paris. 1806–35.

the modest means by which the square received spatial articulation. The raised terraces of the Tuileries and the twin buildings to the north, which emulated the architecture of the Louvre, provided a degree of vertical closure on two sides. Unconcerned about the dissipation of space, Gabriel represented the 18th-century distaste for the architecturally enclosed square and the preference for essentially two-dimensional geometric planning to coordinate monument, architecture, and nature over vast distances. This is one reason why the Place de la Concorde is difficult to understand at ground level and is best seen in aerial views, like the diagrams Gabriel drew up for the king. The more open city mirrored the ruler's confidence in his military capabilities. Encouraged by the grandiose precedent set by Louis XIV (Fig. 329), Louis XV sought to remake Paris along the lines of Versailles.

The King saw the possibilities of coordinating the old Palais Bourbon on the left bank with the square and the Madeleine Church. This necessitated bridging the Seine, and Louis ordered work begun on the Pont de la Concorde. (Ironically, the bridge was finished in the 1790s with masonry from the Bastille.) He thereby made the river and the bridge part of the new city center. Louis turned over to the public not only the land for his square, but also the park area of the Champs-Elysées and the property around the Madeleine Church. It remained for the Revolution to "liberate" the Tuileries. The King's statue stood on axis with the central avenue of the Tuileries, laid out a century before for Louis XIV by André Le Nôtre. This axis was, in effect, an extension of the heart of the Louvre, but in fact it began with the dome of the Tuileries Palace and was to be continued up the Champs-Elysées (Fig. 394). Thus the original purposes of the Place de la Concorde were to beautify Paris, to give it a new center, and to provide the stage for public pageantry, such as the fireworks display honoring the marriage in 1770 of the King's heir with Marie-Antoinette of Austria. (Many people died by falling into the ditches around the square during the nocturnal excitement.) During the French Revolution, the guillotine replaced the equestrian statue, and 2,600 people, including Louis XVI and Marie-Antoinette, were executed in this square, newly christened Place de la Révolution. Under the Directory the guillotine was replaced by a plaster statue of Liberty, and in 1795 the square received its present name for the first, but not the last, time.

When Napoleon came to power he made important additions to the complex. As had his Valois and Bourbon predecessors, Napoleon lived in the Tuileries Palace, which closed the great court of the Louvre on its side facing the gardens. The Emperor built a triumphal arch at the gardens' entrance, so that his troops could parade in front of the palace, then through the arch, the gardens, the square, and up the Champs-Elysées. Looking up the long axis from the palace toward the hill at the end of the Champs-Elysées, Napoleon decided this perspective, too, needed a climactic monument and gave orders for the erection of an Arc de Triomphe in the center of the Place de l'Etoile (Fig. 395). His aim was to glorify the victorious armies of France. Thus the beginning and the end of this long vista were framed by monuments of Roman descent. Further, Napoleon was responsible for the Italianate arcaded Rue de Rivoli, which borders the north side of the Tuileries, making of the area a semiclosed and even more formal square. In the 19th century the gardens and the apartments overlooking them were the social and residential hub of Parisian society. Ancient Roman, Renaissance, and Baroque Italian ideas about architecture and imperial planning were combined with the French taste for clarity and linearity of organization.

*above:* 396. GIUSEPPE MENGONI. Galleria Vittorio Emanuele, Milan. Dedicated 1867. Iron and glass construction.

*right:* 397. Times Square, New York.

In 1835 Louis-Philippe ordered the erection of the Egyptian obelisk in the center of the Place de la Concorde. To restore focus on the square, the German architect Johann Wilhelm Hittorf built, in 1854, two flanking fountains in imitation of Bernini's design at St. Peter's (Fig. 389), which similarly had created a strong lateral axis to counterbalance the major thrust of the space. The ditches were filled in, which destroyed the articulated nature of the square. However, the greater level space accommodated public safety and increasing traffic, both foot and mounted. The history of the Place de la Concorde and its adjacent streets and squares indicates the strong influence of a new urban mobility, which in the 18th and early 19th century carried with it the implications of a militaristic regime and rigid social stratification. Until the horse-drawn bus in the 1820s, only those who could afford carriages and horses enjoyed the squares and boulevards. Demarcated and beautified by trees, the Champ-Elysées was designed for different types of traffic. The Place de l'Etoile is a circle upon which twelve major streets converge. To cross to it is, for the pedestrian, an adventure at best. Integrated with the street system, the open pedestrian square loses its importance as traffic increases and is replaced by the boulevard lined with trees, broad walks, and cafés.

The Champs-Elysées reminds us that distinctions between streets and squares may be too finely drawn. Medieval towns widened their streets for market squares, and the Piazza Navona was ideal for the oval circulation of both wheeled vehicles and pedestrians. The Champs-Elysées is broader than most

earlier squares, reflecting the Baroque taste for streets that were wider than the adjacent buildings were high. The broad avenue also facilitated grand military parades, such as those which take place on Bastille Day. The extremely generous sidewalks accommodated not only pedestrians but, beginning in the 19th century, outdoor cafés of considerable variety. Gradually, the great Parisian boulevards built under Baron Haussmann came to supplant the royal *places* as the forums of public life, except in winter.

**Milan's Galleria** Milan was the first city to have an all-weather, all-season civic heart for pedestrians. The most spectacular example of the confluence of pedestrian street and square, all within a glass-covered structure, is the Galleria (Fig. 396), designed by an amateur architect, Giuseppe Mengoni, and dedicated in 1867. Two colorful, geometrically designed, tiled streets—643 feet and 344 feet long—converge to make a Latin cross. The longer axis leads to the square fronting the Milan Cathedral. One would oversimplify to call the Galleria an early shopping center. Restaurants set their candlelit tables outside (yet still inside) on the tiled pavement, and diners could dance to one of several orchestras that played simultaneously in the evenings. The eclectic architecture set the right tone of elegance, of the old and the new. The Milanese knew they were living in the year 1867, for the Galleria's 88-foot-high glass roof told them so; but, like their operas at nearby La Scala, the architecture connected them with the past. The repetition of forms, instead of being monotonous, serves as a foil for the variety of signs and displays, giving a discrete order to diversity.

## THE MODERN SQUARE

The modern city squares seen in the daily newspapers are more often than not actually urban parade grounds. To those who use them they symbolize national rather than civic solidarity. Few American readers can recall the personal pleasures or even patriotic moments that took place in a city square. How many of us can say that city squares are important focal points in the culture or day-to-day living of our communities? Our largest open civic spaces are usually parking lots! We worry over vehicular, not pedestrian circulation. The gridiron cities of the United States were laid out for profit, not pleasure. Our national ethic of keeping busy scorns public places for promenades. Even public parks are of concern to police and city officials as potential battlegrounds. Ironically, the smog that is slowly killing us may yet force the pedestrian square back in to American life. New York's Fifth Avenue may someday become a foot mall and Park Avenue live up to its name.

The most famous square in the United States is not a square at all. New York's Time Square (Fig. 397), at the juncture of Broadway and Seventh Avenue, is closed to buses and cars only on election night, New Year's Eve, and at the end of wars. Otherwise it is a traffic officer's nightmare, the pedestrian's peril, and neon-sign maker's paradise. In recent years Pop, Op, and Light Art have made us more aware, and perhaps more appreciative, of the imagery and technology of its enormous advertising displays. The stores and movies located in the area cater less to New Yorkers than to tourists. Despite its drawbacks, however, Times Square is the place, day and night, that never sleeps. Contrasted with the new Lincoln Center of the Performing Arts (Fig. 398), about a mile north of it, Times Square may seem indescribably tawdry and chaotic, but it is a wildly interesting environment—a 24-hour-a-day Happening.

A case could be argued that Lincoln Center, rather than being stately and elegant, is pompous in mood and authoritarian in style, even reminiscent of Italian Fascist architecture of the 1930s, that it caters to the tastes of a social and financial elite rather than to the common man who stands in long lines for his opera tickets. The vast scale of the complex contributes to its impersonal character. The stoa and arcade, which in Europe were scaled to the human form and were dictated by practicality as well as by aesthetics, have been translated into a gargantuan stage setting to mask the generally undistinguished architecture. The huge arcades provide some protection from the aggressive New York elements, but the formality of building placements, a complex of interconnected

*below left:* 398. Lincoln Center for the Performing Arts, New York. 1962–66. Component units: Guggenheim Band Shell; Metropolitan Opera House; Vivian Beaumont Theater; Juilliard School, including Alice Tully Hall; Philharmonic Hall; and New York State Theater.

*below:* 399. HENRY HOFMEISTER, H. W. CORBETT, RAYMOND HOOD, and others. The public plaza and ice-skating rink at Rockefeller Center, New York, photographed in the winter. 1931–39. *right:* The RCA building, containing Radio City Music Hall.

*left:* 400. Lawrence Halprin & Associates. Fountain and plaza, forecourt of the Civic Auditorium, Portland. 1970.

squares, suggests a drill field. The center's main fountain is an unimaginative concession to European prototypes. Only Henry Moore's large sculpture mounted in a basin filled partly with water (and often with trash) provides visual relief from the architectural regularity. For years architects have taught that consistency of style is crucial to city planning, but the dreary results of most urban developments make one realize that the chaos of Times Square at least has vitality. The last thing Times Square could be called is visually dull!

Rockefeller Center (Fig. 399), built in New York city between 1931 and 1939, contains a square that does serve people. However, only when it could be conceived as economically feasible did those financing the project approve its construction. Intelligent placement of the limestone slab skyscrapers rewards looking upward. During the winter the sunken portion of the square is a public ice-skating rink that can be observed by hundreds from the street level above. Lacking competition, a mediocre fountain sculpture seems better than it actually is. Stone planters fill the area with shrubbery and flowers in the spring and summer. Their sides serve unintentionally as welcome benches for tired visitors, though formerly it was against the law to sit on them. There are interesting shops in the area, both above and below ground level. This square has been a rare urban success as a place for people. As a pilot project for the city, however, Rockefeller Center has been a failure. In the last few years many new skyscrapers have been set back from the street to provide larger open spaces in front of them. More like the cathedral parvis than the urban square, they serve to widen the sidewalks and stretch out the distance to the main entrance of the building, instead of providing areas of communal enjoyment. The windy New York streets restrict to some extent the ambitious use of water in fountains, but the limited imaginations of clients and architects have been a greater inhibition to the introduction of this art form to the city. Recently, when confronted with a challenging project for a fountain square, a New York business balked, and instead the city of Portland, Oregon, can now lay claim to having realized an exciting venture.

The 200-foot-square forecourt of the Portland Civic Auditorium (Fig. 400) has been described by Lawrence Halprin, who designed it, as a "people's park." At its dedication the architect took off his shoes and socks and jumped into the water, followed by hundreds of delighted Portland citizens. Every minute 13,000 gallons of water cascade down concrete waterfalls 18 feet high and 80 feet wide, culminating in a pool 10 feet below street level. One can even pass behind the falls into a grotto. In the pool there are concrete platforms that seem to float and that rise to a series of amphitheaterlike steps leading back to the street. It is a square in which to sit, walk, crawl, watch, or wade. Traffic is screened off by a landscaped earthen mound or berm. As at the Trevi Fountain in Rome (Fig. 386), the indifferent architecture of the main building facing the square now serves as a backdrop.

Every civilization lives and dies by its myths. The United States must now learn to get along without the fantasy of the metropolis as an ethnic melting pot. We are beginning to realize that different ethnic groups prefer their own neighborhoods and will accept some cultural segregation if they have their own places to create and perform. Rather than ignore the natural instinct to resist loss of identity, those who design and manage our cities should make provision for serious adult play. This need is satisfied by open urban spaces where rallies, festivals, pageants, concerts, and art exhibitions can be played out, as in the homelands of many immigrants to our cities, and as on college campuses all over the nation. Street corners are not substitutes for squares. Vest-pocket parks and pedestrian malls in shopping centers help, to be sure, but the plaza is still a viable means to bring together small communities in different parts of large cities for cultural and political purposes. When in 1970 New Yorkers of Italian descent protested FBI "oppression," they did not assemble at Lincoln Center, but rather at Columbus Circle, which today hardly lives up to the second half of its name or to its original function of giving space to soapbox orators. Traffic had to be channeled elsewhere for a day. Chicago's Civic Center, dominated by Picasso's sculpture (Fig. 554), has been a rallying ground for unions and adherents to divergent causes. Berkeley students fought a small but bitter war over a "People's Park," and hundreds of students and nonstudents confronted Palo Alto police and city officials over the use of a tiny, ambitiously named plaza. The argument

401. Ghirardelli Square, San Francisco. 19th-century industrial complex redeveloped from 1964.

that well-designed public squares constitute a loss of profits and tax income can be refuted as fiscally of socially myopic.

There is a brilliant and happily imitable example in the United States of a group of architects and a businessman who learned from the past to combine the old and the new in architecture and thus provide a rich variety of activities for a large, heterogeneous pedestrian group without destroying the city. This is Ghirardelli Square in San Francisco (Fig. 401), born out of the shell of an old chocolate factory and other commercial buildings that comprised a block near the waterfront. In the early 1960s this capacious 19th-century manufacturing building, not unlike many around the country, was ripe for demolition as an eyesore on prize real estate. The factory was purchased by an enlightened civic-conscious businessman and redesigned by a team of architects who accentuated its multilevel elevation and magnificent vistas. Garage space is below the large block, while on the upper levels are restaurants, trees, shops, an art gallery, and the International Children's Art Center. The result is both a public square and a shopping center, and it draws more San Franciscans of all ages than tourists. The architects maintained the style of 19th-century commercial architecture and added new buildings in the same type of brick, plus many beautiful details ranging from lighting to signs, kiosks, and door handles. In this case business had the good sense to make its architecture interesting and enjoyable. The gigantic old Ghirardelli sign was kept, and it proves that commercial signs can be handsome additions to a city's profile. Its 19th-century lettering, visible for miles across the bay, responds to San Franciscans' taste for traditional style and elegance.

Let those who seek a vision of better urban living begin by discovering the best of the past. If cities have hearts that can be manifested by space and architecture, then they are visible in the design of public squares. Too much of the urban renewal in the United States, as well as the design of older American cities, is not without taste only—it is heartless.

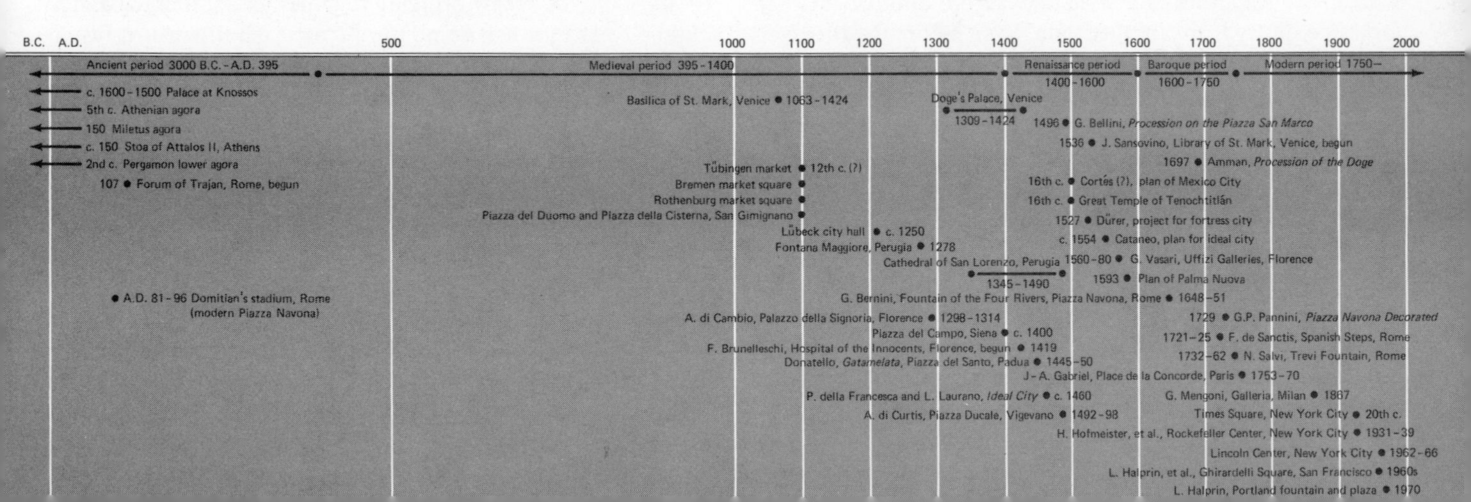

# 15

Like a river changing in depth and width, receiving new springs of ideas, or altering its course and leaving isolated bodies of water to dry up, art's history has continual movement that is not checked or governed by the calendar. At the beginning of the 19th century, the former synthesis of "heavenly" and "worldly" values was found to be ineffectual and irrelevant; this development was not entirely new, but rather resulted from a process of gradual enervation during the two preceding centuries. Like many other fields, art has a dialectical history in which there have often been conflicts of opposites to motivate the artist. The newer synthesis that perplexed and inspired many 19th-century painters centered on the ways in which, and extent to which, their art should be influenced by both past and present. Should one's style and subject imitate the past in interpreting the present? Should the artist's themes be of the moment, yet in a style that did justice to the Baroque or Renaissance masterworks in the Louvre? Or should *both* form and theme be grounded in the artist's own time?

In themselves, such questions were not raised for the first time after 1800, for they had already been posed and solved at various points in history. Since the 17th century, for example, Dutch as well as French artists had been interested in showing their own time and place without resorting to a paraphrase of the styles of other periods and countries. Portraits, still lifes, and landscapes were modes that permitted an artist to interpret aspects of his time, while he also did mythological or historical painting in a style taken from another artist in another country from another time. Even before the 19th century there had been excellent alternatives to the view that the purpose of art should be to educate and ennoble its public. Genre and the foregoing types of painting of people, objects, and nature sidestepped these noble aims, and the high value given them by private collectors had established a base for a nonintellectual painting, esteemed for how it was made rather than for its subject matter.

In the 19th century, principally in France, a number of conditions conspired to change the answers to these questions and to produce viable new syntheses in terms of what was to happen at the beginning of the present century. Many of the leading independent artists were separated from the patronage and ideals both of church and state, as well as from formal art-school training. Progressive artists after 1850 could hope for support from an increasingly large, middle-class, art-buying public and from the emergence of increased numbers of art dealers. For many important artists, personal study in the Louvre or other art museums came to replace academic art schools. Artists relied upon other artists and sympathetic art critics and dealers for criticism and encouragement. Independence involved substantial risks, but the ideal of contributing to culture and gaining personal fulfillment from artistic activity was a strong incentive. The heroic focus in advanced painting shifted away from saints, statesmen, and warriors to the masses, to the private citizen and to the artist himself.

Some of the dramatic changes that occurred in art in the course of the 19th century are apparent when a large canvas of Jacques-Louis David (1748–1825), *The Battle of the Romans and Sabines* (Fig. 402), is juxtaposed with *Moulin Rouge* (Fig. 403), a lithographic poster by Henri de Toulouse-Lautrec (1864–1901). Purposes, sources, and styles are separated by much more than merely ninety years of time. David's painting was intended to hang in the great palace of the Louvre, which in 1800, though still serving in part as a residence, had been converted into a museum for the nation. Toulouse-Lautrec's posters were pasted on walls and kiosks around Paris as advertisements for a Montmartre dance hall. David attempted to unify his society by bringing together an aristocracy and a middle class that had come to distrust each other as a result of the French Revolution. Toulouse-Lautrec's message was spelled out literally; his job was to bring together the general public with the virtuoso performers in a night club for purposes of business and pleasure. True to tradition at the beginning of the century, David drew upon a historical episode—that is, borrowed from the past—to make his moral point for the present. His source for the painting was literary, Petrarch's *History of Romulus*. The incident chosen was the moment when the wife of the Roman leader interceded to stop his personal combat with Tatius, chief of the Sabines and her kinsman. David assumed an educated audience that would com-

# TO BE OF ONE'S TIME
# The Synthesis of Past and Present in 19th-Century Art

*left*: 402. Jacques-Louis David. *The Battle of the Romans and Sabines*. 1799. Oil on canvas, 12′8″ × 17′¾″. Louvre, Paris.

*right*: 403. Henri de Toulouse-Lautrec. *Moulin Rouge, La Goulue*. 1891. Color lithograph poster, 5′5″ × 3′10″. Philadelphia Museum of Art (gift of Mr. and Mrs. R. Sturgis Ingersoll).

prehend the idea of how women could mediate in class conflict through intermarriage. Toulouse-Lautrec derived the subject of his poster from frequent visits to the Montmartre cabaret Moulin Rouge and direct observation of such stars as La Goulue ("The Glutton") and Valentin le Désossé ("The Boneless One").

David based his style on ancient Greek and Roman art. The past thus provided him with models of pose and composition, as well as confirmation of the archaeological accuracy of details. To assure anatomical exactitude, he first drew from skeletons posed in the manner of the final painting, and then from live models similarly posed in imitation of ancient works of art. It was not David's opinion that the artist should be original, that he should innovate, but rather that he should take from the past and perfect his choices. Toulouse-Lautrec's style, though to some extent indebted to contemporaries such as Edgar Degas (Figs. 416–18), was largely formed by personal taste, visual perceptiveness, and the idiosyncrasies of his hand. Just as the dancers in his poster prided themselves on their ability to improvise and to create highly stylized, even grotesque and surprising movements, so did the artist value his talent for direct observation and spontaneous translation of their movements in a style that was equally exaggerated and individualistic. Both David and Toulouse-Lautrec were affirming the superiority of art over nature—the former by homage to the exalted impersonal styles of the past, the latter through expressing his own temperament.

For David, as for many artists since the 15th century, his model for the rhetoric and arrangement of pictorial presentation was the theater and its performers on a stage. Toulouse-Lautrec's figures were inimitable in a double sense: not only were their postures uniquely unstable, but the artist's conception negated measurable three-dimensional stage space and the illusionistic devices that permitted the audience physically to identify with his personages. His poster has a decided surface emphasis, whereby all the shapes and colors are flattened out, and it is the silhouettes rather than facial expression and modeling, as in David's work, that impart character and expressiveness. The segmented treatment of Valentin and the ambiguity of the yellow globular shapes at the left (probably a lamp) presuppose changes in the value of the human figure, compositional balance, and clarity from those which had obtained in David's day. Toulouse-Lautrec's art is symptomatic of the turn-of-the-century interest on the part of independent artists in capturing and developing those properties and experiences which are to be found only in the graphic medium of painting and prints, that is, which do not readily lend themselves to paraphrase in other media. David's work is *discursive* painting, about whose subject one could read and talk without reference to how it was made. In relation to painting, the poster reflects 19th-century changing attitudes toward history and constitutes a form of popular social history of the moment. This democratization of history was accompanied by broad changing attitudes toward the artistic suitability of subjects drawn from daily life.

**Death and New Heroes** At the beginning of the last century historians and painters began to show that history involved

*right:* 404. FRANCISCO GOYA. *Execution of the Madrileños on May 3, 1808.* 1814. Oil on canvas, 8′8¾″ × 11′3¾″. Prado, Madrid.

*left:* 405. THÉODORE GÉRICAULT. *The Raft of the Medusa.* 1818–19. Oil on canvas, 16′1⅜″ × 23′9″. Louvre, Paris.

masses of people, and accordingly the reactions of the common man to his fate gradually replaced those of the epic leader. In Chapter 12, "Images of Authority," we saw how David (Fig. 300) and Baron Gros (Pl. 40, p. 218) interpreted history through the feats of a great military hero. Since the Romans, war had been shown in terms of kings and generals, the victors and their generosity toward the vanquished. During and after Napoleon's reign, war and the concept of the hero underwent a change in European painting. When Francisco Goya (1746–1828) painted *The Execution of the Madrileños on May 3, 1808* (Fig. 404), he did not choose to record a battlefield scene. The French occupation general Murat, who ordered the killing of hostages in reprisal for the civilian uprising in Madrid, was not even shown. Goya had originally been sympathetic to the Napoleonic invasion of Spain, in the hope that it would bring modern ideas to his country. His painting is a manifestation of partisanship, not as an oppressed Spaniard but as a human being protesting brutality and injustice. He does not glorify war as artists had done before him, but instead shows the slaughter of defenseless civilians by a firing squad. The anonymous, doomed yet defiant Madrileños are the real protagonists and heroes, though pathetic ones; the conquerors are machine-like in the cold precision with which they carry out the execution at brutally close range. To impress his audience with the true horror of the moment, Goya brilliantly illuminates those about to die before the volley of the shadowy troops and sprawls lifeless figures in the foreground in the unnatural contortions of violent death. Rather than histrionic pose, the hostages manifest instinctive reactions of grief, resignation, and outright defiance at the last moment, and Goya contrasts their disarray and shapeless grouping with the close formation of the soldiers, the unfeeling single-mindedness of those disciplined to carry out any order. Goya may or may not have actually witnessed the firing squads in action on the night of May 3, 1808, but it is certain that he did not require the intermediary of a writer to furnish his strongly felt subject matter.

One of the great 19th-century paintings (Fig. 405), which deals with a mass catastrophe having political implications, was based not on a history book but on contemporaneous newspaper reports and interviews by the artist with the survivors. The French painter Théodore Géricault (1791–1824) had ambitions of doing a monumental painting on a noble theme that would rival great works of the past such as Rubens' *Last Judgment* (Fig. 228) and Michelangelo's awesome fresco of the same theme (Fig. 203). However, he wanted the subject to be contemporary, in order to prove that he could paint modern history on an equally heroic scale. In 1816, the wreck of the government ship *Medusa* off North Africa and the ensuing tragedy of more than a hundred persons cast adrift on a raft for several days provided Géricault with a sensational and topical subject. Shipwrecks had often been depicted in the past, but this overworked theme had never been treated with the stark immediacy and intense focus upon human suffering that Géricault brought to his huge canvas, with its emotional sincerity and imaginative staging. He had the ship's carpenter reconstruct a model of the actual raft, which he then set afloat; he studied not only the faces and bodies of those hospitalized by their ordeal but also the heads of dead criminals and putrefying limbs from the Paris morgue. He made numerous drawings and painted sketches of various incidents of the shipwreck, but finally he passed over such dramatic moments as the mutiny in favor of showing the handful of survivors rising like a human pyramid to signal a ship in the distance.

The eye level of the viewer is at the lower part of the painting, so that one is confronted with a jumble of corpses and the old man's grief over his dead son. This device of engaging the viewer in a direct confrontation with death was learned from Baron Gros. Though Géricault worked from over a hundred preliminary drawings and studies, the final composition evolved slowly by trial and continual change. Its roughly triangular design had precedents in Renaissance painting, with hieratic implications of social and political authority; but here the compositional pyramid formed of suffering bodies rests on an unstable base, and the climactic figure is a Negro slave who has his back to us. Professor Lorenz Eitner has demonstrated, in many studies on this work and its period, that the figures adrift on the wind- and sea-tossed raft were a contemporary metaphor for the tragic condition of modern man and his soul.

The scandal of the *Medusa* episode arose over what was interpreted as the negligence or calculated cruelty of the ship's captain and officers toward the crew and passengers in cutting the lines connecting the overloaded raft with the lifeboats. This act provided ammunition for political foes of the Bourbon monarchy. Stories of mutiny and cannibalism persisted long after the event, which saw the death of most of the unfortunates on the raft. While Géricault's motives for the painting may have been in part political and humanitarian, they still afforded the opportunity to prove his great gifts as an artist.

In the first half of the 19th century the most significant change in art was in subject matter, and artists such as Géricault drew liberally upon the ideas and styles of older artists such as Michelangelo and Rubens. With the decline and fall of Napoleon, artists of independent convictions were confronted with the absence of an inspiring leader to celebrate in painting, and their shift of focus to humanity and its suffering and joys produced a new, humane art.

For the majority of artists working in France who sought the support of the government, there was little problem about fitting their subject matter to maintain the political, social, and cultural status quo. When in 1827 the painter Jean-Auguste-Dominique Ingres (1780–1867) was commissioned to decorate a ceiling for the gallery of Charles X in the Louvre, he created a theatrical pantomime of the deification of the Greek

*left :* 406. JEAN-AUGUSTE-DOMINIQUE INGRES. *The Apotheosis of Homer.* 1827. Oil on canvas, 12′8″ × 16′11″. Louvre, Paris.

*right :* 407. EUGÈNE DELACROIX. *The Death of Sardanapalus.* 1827. Oil on canvas, 12′11$^{1}/_{2}$″ × 16′3″. Louvre, Paris.

poet Homer (Fig. 406). Before the backdrop of a Classical temple is seen the enthroned poet, who is being crowned by Fame. Before him sit personifications of his *Iliad* and *Odyssey*. The attendant figures to the left and right are famous poets, musicians, and artists who pay homage to the great epic writer. The painter Poussin, seen at the lower left, points toward the ceremony. Such paintings informed the public and the art world of the artists of the past who currently enjoyed official favor.

With what markedly different artistic effects and social connotations the pyramidal composition could be employed is attested to in the diverse conceptions of Géricault and Ingres. The formal organization of the *Apotheosis* was a quotation from Raphael's work (Pl. 27, p. 161), used in the service of authoritarian ideas about painting, culture, and society. It was Ingres who complained that Géricault's *Raft of the Medusa* was unhealthy in terms of its focus upon death and the disagreeable, which he felt would not ennoble the minds of the public. His own poised and robust figures are models of personal hygiene and control over mind and body. Color as an emotive device is severely checked, as are other expressive instruments such as dramatic light and shadow, painterly texture, and strong brushstroke. Ingres represents the 19th-century conservative artist who could not come to terms directly with his time, perhaps feeling that contemporary costume, customs, and events lacked the dignity and beauty of the past and that, although living individuals were suitable for portraiture (Fig. 481), they were inappropriate for historical painting. To those few artists who sought to build upon the past yet come to grips with the present and openly express strong convictions, Ingres' view of history seemed false, and his style in large figural compositions frigidly antiquarian.

Eugène Delacroix (1798–1863), a contemporary and rival of Ingres, is an example of the independent artist who was at the same time a literary painter, drawing upon the past for stylistic and thematic ideas. His *Death of Sardanapalus* (Fig. 407), also painted in 1827, was based on Lord Byron's poetic account of the last Assyrian king, who destroyed his harem and himself before capture by the Persians. Delacroix transferred the orgy of death from the battlefield to the boudoir, and his self-image and sadistic attitude toward women found release in this painting. In the 19th century, it was Delacroix who did great paintings of passion, who more than any other painter of his time built upon the effects of strong colors such as red, green, and black. From Rubens he learned much about rendering the figure in strenuous action and about building his forms through color. The scene of carnage in the Assyrian king's harem afforded Delacroix the opportunity to dazzle the eye with the brilliance of exotic trappings and the rich contrasts of the flesh of the horses, slaves, and dying women.

**Synthesis of Symbol and Event** Such vicarious reliving of romanticized past history did not always content Delacroix, who like certain others had strong egalitarian political views which did not accord with those of the rulers of France, and on occasion he used painting as the means of their expression. As a young artist, Delacroix had posed for one of the dead figures on Géricault's celebrated raft. From the slightly older man, Delacroix received the impetus to make a monumental history painting that would rival great Baroque compositions and yet do justice to the concerns of his day. His opportunity came during the revolution of 1830, which led to the overthrow of Charles X and his replacement by Louis-Philippe. Originally titled by the artist *The Events of July,* the painting commonly known as *Liberty on the Barricades* (Pl. 43, p. 285) was meant to express Delacroix's hopes for a more enlightened government as well as to gain the ruler's favor. Though in Paris at the time of the uprising, Delacroix like Géricault had to rely upon newspaper accounts, journalistic prints, and other visual sources, as well as on memory, for his painting of a skirmish that took place at a bridge connecting the Ile de la Cité with the Right Bank of Paris, with the insurgents successfully fighting off the government troops. Included was the Parisian boy of the streets who, while under gunfire, bravely retrieved needed ammunition from the dead troops and planted their flag.

408. Honoré Daumier. *Rue Transnonain, April 15, 1834.* 1834. Lithograph, $11^7/_8 \times 17^1/_2$″. Metropolitan Museum of Art, New York.

Delacroix's stirring painting, with its swirling smoke, vigorous movement, and strident red, white, and blue tones, synthesized the old and new while capturing the momentary nature of the event. From past traditions came the allegorical half-nude feminine figure symbolizing France and liberty; from the specific moment came the excitement of the place and participants, among whom Delacroix may have placed himself as a figure in a top hat. From Géricault came the pathetic motif of the naked corpses and the dense pictorial triangle, here climaxed by the heroic Amazon. The motif of the dying revolutionary looking up to the symbolic flag-bearing woman is a translation from a Napoleonic battlefield scene by Gros, where a wounded enemy soldier gazes upward at Napoleon as if to a savior; similar expressions of this motif can be seen in Gros' *Napoleon Visiting the Pest House at Jaffa* (Pl. 40, p. 218). Thus Delacroix was showing a transfer of allegiance from an individual leader to a principle or an abstract concept. This is very likely the last great painting in which an important artist frankly confessed his political activism and optimism in support of a government. Subsequent disillusionment with Louis-Philippe also made this Delacroix's last partisan painting.

**The Artist as Political Critic** At the cost of personal imprisonment and the official prohibition of his political caricatures, Honoré Daumier (1808–79) was the most outspoken critic of the French state. With his thousands of drawings and prints taken from daily life, Daumier is the first modern artist for whom the attitude "one must be of one's time" became a lifelong ideal. His lithograph *Rue Transnonain, April 15, 1834* (Fig. 408) is a stark disclosure of the murder of a worker and his family by government troops in retaliation for labor's defiance of the state. The print's title is taken from a tenement in Paris in which all the working-class occupants had been systematically slaughtered. Daumier grimly but subtly depicted the death of three generations.

409. GUSTAVE COURBET. *Burial at Ornans*. 1849. Oil on canvas, 10′3⅞″ × 21′8¾″. Louvre, Paris.

As in the work of Géricault and Delacroix, Daumier's superb draftsmanship and style were predicated upon older art. The foreshortened corpse of the father is a reworking of past images of the dead Christ (Fig. 268), and the artist must have known that this antecedent would not be lost upon a public that still read art in terms of art. In the 19th century there was an increase in the practice of artists' adapting pictorial designs previously reserved for religious themes to the service of more mundane values. This is another manifestation of the secularization of religion, which had begun at the end of the Middle Ages; yet it also produced a new and viable spiritual art. Whereas significant modern art has not celebrated directly the Bible and the Church, it does deal sincerely with the life of the human spirit. Historically, the religion of humanity comes closest to explicit realization in the art of the last century.

**Courbet and the Burial of Historical Painting** It is ironic that the birth of modern art should be found in connection with themes of death. One of the most crucial paintings for the emergence of modern art, *Burial at Ornans* (Fig. 409) by Gustave Courbet (1819–77), deals ostensibly with a funeral ceremony near a French provincial town. Gathered at the grave side are relatives and friends of the deceased, the priest and his assistants, and just entering the scene at the left the pallbearers with the draped coffin. In the foreground the grave digger kneels by the open grave. A leaden grey sky looms over the event. Such a routine daily ceremony would hardly seem to provide the basis for a painting that shocked its first Parisian audiences. In retrospect, one might say that more than just a coffin went into the open grave at Ornans. Earlier funeral paintings of religious (Fig. 154), historical, or literary figures had answered the implicit question of who died, as well as why and how. Painting some fifty life-size portraits of his neighbors, Courbet composed a huge canvas whose subject is the burial of an unidentified person dead of an unknown cause. Courbet provided most of the answer to the significant question of *what,* not who, died and was buried at Ornans:

> . . . the art of painting can consist only in the representation of objects visible and tangible to the painter. An epoch can be reproduced only by its own artists. I mean by the artists who have lived in it. I hold that artists of one century are fundamentally incompetent to represent the things of a past or future century. . . . It is in this sense that I deny the existence of an historical art applied to the past. Historical art is by its very nature contemporary. . . [1861].

Figuratively speaking, one might say that Courbet cast into the grave the previous history of art, in so far as it was to be imitated in his time. To be of one's time meant for Courbet that anything he had not seen for himself was ethically impossible as a subject. It was therefore the death of everyman that he painted. There is no suggestion of a life beyond the grave, no promise of a soul or its ultimate ascent to Heaven. A man now survives in the memory of those he leaves behind. The hero or protagonist becomes the enduring community. Ordinary men and women are the actors and actresses of history, and their costumes signify its change. Judged by the prevalent critical standards of art, which glowingly praised Ingres, Courbet's painting was a failure because nothing of consequence was being recorded, and there seemed to be no subject in the traditional sense and no moral. The figures seemed wooden and not gracefully modeled, there was no carefully organized composition, and the thickly painted surfaces offended the eye of the contemporary public.

Courbet's style did reject any overt use of older pictorial compositional devices such as the pyramid, harmonious reciprocal physical movement, neatly drawn contours, and smoothly finished surfaces. The basic color range stresses the blacks and greys of the clothing and sky, against which are set the ruddy coloring of the begrieved faces and various accessories of the clergy. The absence of conventional methods of ordering the figures resulted from Courbet's conscious desire to preserve the look of the unarranged. His subjects were not athletes, and he caught them in their unimpressive natural postures or movements. Color and an allover dispersal of strong accents were relied upon to hold the painting together. It is

*left :* 412. EDOUARD MANET. *Luncheon on the Grass.* 1862–63. Oil on canvas, 7′3/4″ × 8′10 3/8″. Louvre, Paris.

*below :* 413. MARCANTONIO RAIMONDI. *Judgment of Paris.* c. 1520. Engraving, 11 5/8 × 17 1/4″. Metropolitan Museum of Art, New York (Rogers Fund, 1919).

that was veiled in terms of antiquity. As long as Couture or any other artist couched sex in a dead language, he was safe from critical and public censure. By contrast, Manet's *Luncheon on the Grass* (Fig. 412) created scandal largely because it represented a contemporary scene, and in it, relative to the animated goings-on of Couture's painting, nothing was happening between the sexes. Merely to have shown a naked woman in the woods might have been acceptable, but Manet had the effrontery to add the company of two gentlemen dressed in contemporary fashion and to show his nude unreservedly eyeing the viewer. In one of his many witty inversions of the prevailing public taste, Manet clothed the woman bathing in the background and stripped the woman seated with her male companions, depositing her clothing in the foreground. In this vein, the painting was originally entitled *The Bather.*

Manet's painting forms an important bridge between the past and present. It is essentially a studio problem in which the artist synthesized landscape, still life, genre, portraiture, and the nude—at the same time making the painting appear a spontaneous encounter. He borrowed the basic compositional structure from a 16th-century engraving by Marcantonio Raimondi (Fig. 413), after a lost cartoon by Raphael, adapting from it poses and the triangular arrangement of figures. Notwithstanding this impressive legacy of different types of painting, Manet brought his eyes and aesthetic judgment to bear on his visual allusions in welding the whole together. The richest painting is in the still life, not in the faces. His desire for a more immediate visual impact and convincing optical effect lead him to reduce modeling, sharpen silhouettes, and force us to discern his fine nuances of closely matched tones.

The absence of any dialogue or interaction among the figures removed a basic compositional prop, but it also enhanced

the sophisticated character of the subject. With Manet, we begin to see the breakdown of psychological reciprocation, the mutual awareness or exchange between figures in close proximity that, from the time of Giotto (Fig. 165), artists had developed into a high form of pictorial rhetoric. The detached air of his figures may have seemed socially appropriate to Manet, but it was also a reflection of his own attitude toward life. It was Emile Zola who said, in writing about Manet, that when looking at his work in order to appreciate what he was doing "one had to forget a thousand things about art." Since Manet, this has been the case with most of the leading painters and new art movements, for again and again the public has had to set aside or widen its notions of what art should be in order to understand what the artist has done.

Shortly before his death, the ailing Manet brought together in one great painting a number of refractory motifs that

incorrect to say that Courbet cut himself off completely from the previous history of art (Fig. 22), for it is precisely the way he used the past that helps us to understand the attitude of so many modern artists on this subject:

> I have studied the art of the masters and the art of the moderns, avoiding any preconceived system and without prejudice. I have no more wanted to imitate the former than to copy the latter; nor have I thought of achieving the idle aim of art for art's sake. No! I have simply wanted to draw from a thorough knowledge of tradition the reasoned and free sense of my own individuality. To know in order to do: such has been my thought. To be able to translate the customs, ideas and appearances of my time as I see them—in a word, to create a living art—this has been my aim [1855].

**The Modernity of Manet** Edouard Manet (1832—83) manifested his respect for museum art as a means of discovering his individuality by drawing and painting copies of such artists as Titian (Fig. 221), Hals (Pl. 70, p. 359), and Velázquez (Fig. 17); yet in the 1860s and 1870s he became the foremost painter of modern urban life. Like Courbet's, his style was distinctly personal; but inconceivable without the previous history of art. From the old masters he learned how colors worked together and the culture of the brush by which they were to be applied. His painting *Funeral in Montmartre* (Fig. 410) rejects the opportunity for sentiment in favor of a remote viewpoint, treating the scene of a burial on a cloudy day as a pure painterly problem of matching tones of greys, blacks, and creams under given lighting conditions. As a result of this approach, it is impossible to focus for any length of time on the actual funeral procession, since our attention is pulled toward the deceptively shapeless areas of color, their stroking and nuances. In no previous painting that we have considered has the actual painting process rather than the theme dominated our awareness to a comparable degree.

Manet's generation—which included Degas (Figs. 416–418), Monet (Pl. 45, p. 295), Pissarro (Fig. 419), and Renoir (Pl. 47, p. 296; Fig. 420)—was disenchanted with artistic manifestations of political partisanship, piety, and strong emotional involvement. Their ideal in painting was a detached confrontation of the world, with alert observation and wit. The act of painting was alone approached with passion by Manet. In comparison with the historical or literary compositions of Ingres or Delacroix, which were intended to be read as much as viewed, those of Manet were largely independent of literature and were grounded in his immediate environment. His painting had its validity in artistic rightness, in the handling of color and shape, and in their similitude to the world of aesthetic sensations.

The present-day fame of an artist such as Manet may mislead one into believing that he enjoyed similar repute in his own time or that he was representative of the art then being produced. Both in numbers and according to the gauge of public approval, it was artists such as Thomas Couture (1815–79), Manet's teacher, whose work best represented the preferences of the public of their time. In the 19th century, academic and conservative rather than forward-looking art was the true mirror of social tastes. Couture's *Romans of the Decadence* (Fig. 411) served as commentary on the moral decline of modern Paris

*above right:* 410. EDOUARD MANET. *Funeral in Montmartre.* 1870. Oil on canvas, $28^5/_8 \times 35^5/_8$″. Metropolitan Museum of Art, New York (Wolfe Fund, 1910).

*right:* 411. THOMAS COUTURE. *Romans of the Decadence.* 1847. Oil on canvas, 15′1″ × 25′4″. Louvre, Paris.

Plate 43. EUGÈNE DELACROIX. *Liberty on the Barricades*. 1830. Oil on canvas, $8'6\frac{1}{2}'' \times 10'8''$. Louvre, Paris. (See p. 281.)

Plate 44. EDOUARD MANET. *A Bar at the Folies-Bergère*. 1881–82. Oil on canvas, 3′1½″ ×
Courtauld Institute Galleries, London. (See pp. 284, 287.)

summed up what had been the source of his pleasures as a painter. *A Bar at the Folies-Bergère* (Pl. 44, p. 286) brings together a beautiful young girl, still-life objects on the bar, and the mirrored reflection of a world of sociability and diversion. For the first time in art a mirror occupies the entire background of a painting. When the crowd is encountered in Manet, it is for purposes of social pleasure rather than for the enactment of fateful events. Manet's world is one in which no claims are made on the delighted viewer; it is there to delight the eye, like the barmaid and her wares. The poetic depths of his painting lie not in psychological insights but in a subtle visual counterplay, in the contrast between the world seen directly and its mirrored reflection. The head of the daydreaming barmaid is the intermediary between the tangible objects of the foreground and the elusive optical effects of the mirror behind. What is behind the viewer, that is, what reappears in the reflecting surface, tends to mingle with what is before his eyes, confounding the separation of the two spheres. Enigmatically, the reflection of a top-hatted man is caught in the mirror at the right—like a phantom image, for it is not meant to be the artist nor anyone visible on our side of the counter, and the barmaid takes no notice of him. Her reflection is of another pose.

Further, the scene reflected in the mirror requires a viewer on our side of the counter, but there is no indication of any such person. Undoubtedly aware of these visual paradoxes, Manet quite likely preserved them intentionally to spice his painting.

The unheroic, undramatic nature of his paintings has led to the mistaken view that Manet had no real interest in subject matter. For the discriminating and aristocratic sensibilities of Manet, Paris was essential to his art—a city whose provision of worldly pleasure caused Balzac to describe it as a "great consuming eye." Manet's brush needed such an inspiring motif. Without disguising its traces, his brush re-created the handsome wine bottles, the ripe orange color of the fruit, and the elegant cut and softness of the woman's costume. These subtle effects of color and light and texture could not be captured in a drawing, for, like Courbet, Manet sought what was only possible in painting. The problem of distinguishing so many reflecting surfaces was one for a master painter. Concern for actual perception induced Manet to cut off the trapeze artist and leave only her legs at the upper left. Here is the mirror image of the visible world, perceived by the human eye to be blurred and obscure. It was in the 19th century that painting as a whole most faithfully approximated the true experience of vision.

**New Candor toward the Body** For conservative artists such as Ingres, the worth of any painting other than a portrait depended in large part on its choice of subject and its affinity with approved styles of the past; but for Manet, as for his Dutch predecessors in the 17th century, it resided in *how* any subject was painted. Ingres could not content himself with frankly painting an anonymous naked model in the studio, for by training he was compelled to add accessories and a title from literature or mythology to appeal to the beholder's intellect and good taste. For many, Manet's painting of a barmaid seen with wine bottles lacked the intellectual value and dignity of an Ingres nude, such as that posed holding an antique vase and titled by her creator *La Source* or *The Spring* (Fig. 414). Ingres' passion was to purify the silhouette of the feminine body, which accounted for his adaptation of an antique pose identified with beauty. Omitting the prop of the Classical urn would have lowered or even vulgarized the final painting in his eyes. To be of one's time meant, for Ingres, to accept the timeless beauty of ancient and Renaissance art, as acknowledged by the public and most of his fellow painters. Thus one might say that his ideal was, in essence, to be of another time.

When Ingres wanted to show the naked bodies of women bathing, he garbed them with remote identities; he depicted them in the manner of *La Source*, or as nymphs or harem girls

*right:* 414. JEAN-AUGUSTE-DOMINIQUE INGRES. *La Source*. 1856. Oil on canvas, 5′4½″ × 2′8¼″. Louvre, Paris.

*left :* 415. Honoré Daumier. *The Hot Bath.* 1839. Lithograph, $8^1/_2 \times 10^7/_8$". Minneapolis Institute of Arts (gift of Mrs. C.C. Bovey, 1924).

*below left :* 416. Edgar Degas. *The Tub.* 1886. Pastel on cardboard, $23^7/_8 \times 32^7/_8$". Louvre, Paris.

*below :* 417. Edgar Degas. *The Cotton Broker's Office in New Orleans.* 1873. Oil on canvas, $28^3/_8 \times 35^3/_8$". Musée des Beaux-Arts, Pau, France.

in the exotic Near East or North Africa. With Daumier, instead, the act of bathing was divested of its exotic and erotic associations to become a mundane act of hygiene and even of comedy. Daumier's *The Hot Bath* (Fig. 415) was inspired by the Parisian ritual of hauling boiling water up flights of stairs to one's flat, pouring it into a tub, and then immediately immersing oneself in the scalding depths to obtain the maximum thermal benefit. He shows the prudent but agonizing bourgeois stoically lowering himself into the boiling water and instinctively elevating his nose in an expression of his divided instincts and notions of Heaven and Hell. The dramatic agony of the Christian martyr was thus humorously supplanted by the discomfort of the anonymous modern Parisian apartment dweller.

When Edgar Degas (1834–1917) shows us a woman bathing, it is like a glimpse through a keyhole, for unlike the perspective of Ingres and Daumier, which is that of the Renaissance, his viewpoint is close to and above the bather (Fig. 416). This Degas pastel drawing is but one example of his disenchanted view of women. Our closeness to the figure, which Renaissance theorists such as Alberti warned against, tends to produce curious foreshortenings, emphasizes the body's awkwardness and angularity, and in general defeats the feminine beauty that Ingres strove to draw and paint. Degas saw washing as a hygienic act that an animal could perform; thus he dwelt on the woman's struggle to contort herself into the meager basin.

Degas gave up formal art-school training after two years and, like many other independent painters, continued his education on a personal basis, by making copies in the Louvre. His desire was to honor the lessons learned from Giotto and other great artists of the past while painting the contemporary Parisian scene. Art was for him a personal fusion or resolution of contradictions, the intellectual and the sensual, and a love for drawing and color. It was in his pastels that these last two found perfect union. While he admired fixity of pose in certain aspects of traditional art, he could not bring himself to render static postures. If Manet has preserved for us the tones of his time, Degas has captured its movement. Rejecting the academic repertory of approved body movements, he drew from both the practiced and the unthinking, routine gestures of his subjects as performed in their day-to-day existence. These gestures tended, as in his bather, to stress the purely physical activity rather than the intellectual and emotional life of his subjects, who were very often chosen from the lower classes.

**Degas and a Modern Viewpoint** *The Cotton Broker's Office in New Orleans* (Fig. 417), with its institutional green walls and customary business gestures of men in their black suits or shirt sleeves, exemplifies what being of one's time meant for Degas. Many of the figures are members of the New Orleans branch of the Degas family, whom he visited in 1872, so that the painting is a modern group portrait or genre scene whose daring informality is a 19th-century counterpart of Rembrandt's innovations in *The Syndics* (Fig. 269). The spatial construction is from the viewpoint of someone actually in the brokerage office and standing in a corner, so that the room moves diagonally away from us into depth. Degas would not compromise the conditions of actual vision for the artificial frontal perspective of the Renaissance, with its location of the viewer at a greater distance from the foreground figures. Faithfulness to the idiosyncrasies of vision led to Degas' overlapping of his figures, and his disdain of the formal caused him to pose his relatives and their business associates in suitable and unselfconscious poses. With its fidelity to an American business office, Degas had hopes (unfulfilled) that the painting would be purchased by some English or American industrialist.

In the prodigious output of Degas there is an unmatched visual record of contemporary theater and ballet, rehearsal halls, café life, horse racing, modish shops, brothels, and laundries—in sum, the world of diversion and artifice, its places of performance and of preparation, and those whose professional talents made the Parisian spectacle possible. Paradoxically, professionals of the lower classes fascinated Degas, who memorized their specialized gestures, and yet he showed no sympathy or feeling toward them. Some expression of warmth occurs only in a Degas print of prostitutes celebrating the birthday of the madam. The psychological isolation of people in public has been captured in Degas' *Absinthe Drinkers* (Fig. 418), which was mistakenly interpreted in Victorian England as an indictment against the debilitating effects of alcohol. Degas was not a social critic but, rather, a sharp sociological observer of his time. For *Absinthe Drinkers* he posed an artist friend, Marcel Desboutin, and his wife. Their divergent and distracted expressions convey the boredom that afflicts café-goers who consistently rely for enjoyment upon chance public encounters. This fidelity to visual experience meant that new compositional forms had to be evolved, and in 19th-century art such as that of Degas the viewpoint from which the picture was made became the most specific in the history of art. The spectator functions as a definite part of the scene, and the remoteness of the stage construction seen in David and Ingres has disappeared. The second phase of the modern revolution, occurring roughly between 1850 and 1885, was the radical change in form which accompanied that of subject matter. Degas did not place the figures at the painting's center, or even to left or right of center, as a Renaissance or Baroque portrait painter would have, but he located them eccentrically to the upper right as if toward the periphery of our field of vision. Degas thus contributed to the devaluation of the painting's center as the prime location for a subject and, consequently, to the upgrading in visual importance of the peripheral field.

**The Spectacle of Paris** For Degas and Manet, painting continued to be figure-dominated. Degas did few landscapes and no still lifes or panoramic city views, but preferred instead indoor subjects under artificial light. It was Monet, Pissarro, and Renoir, the open-air painters, who interpreted the great outdoor spectacle of Paris itself. Under Louis Napoleon, numerous boulevards were built in Paris after 1850 to let in "light, air, and infantry." When Claude Monet (1840–1926) painted *Rue Montorgueil, June 30, 1878* (Pl. 45, p. 295), he did so out of a love for flags and not to evoke the historical source of the holiday. Rather than depict the barricades of the past, he reveled in a contemporary flag-bedecked Paris boulevard seen from a window. Unlike Delacroix (Pl. 43, p. 285), Monet did not deal with historical painting in terms of violent heroic military action but, rather, as the thrilling aesthetic experience of sunlight playing over a city street transformed by red-white-and-blue decoration. To the public of his day, it appeared that Monet suffered from an eye disorder, for they were not accus-

*right :* 418. Edgar Degas. *Absinthe Drinkers.* 1876. Oil on canvas, $36^1/_4 \times 27''$. Louvre, Paris.

*left*: 419. CAMILLE PISSARRO. *Place du Théâtre Français*. 1898. Oil on canvas, $27\frac{3}{4} \times 36\frac{1}{4}$". Los Angeles County Museum of Art (Mr. and Mrs. George De Sylva Collection).

*below left*: 420. PIERRE-AUGUSTE RENOIR. *Place Pigalle*. c. 1880. Oil on canvas, $25\frac{1}{2} \times 21\frac{1}{3}$". Collection the Right Honorable R. A. Butler, Cambridge, England.

*below*: 421. HONORÉ DAUMIER. *The Uprising*. c. 1860. Oil on canvas, $39\frac{3}{4} \times 42\frac{7}{8}$". Phillips Collection, Washington, D.C.

tomed to seeing in painting what they saw ordinarily from their own windows. From Monet's elevated and remote viewpoint, the street and flags dissolved into countless individual sensations of light and color. Each touch of his brush gave their equivalent, and the purpose of his discontinuous touches was to reproduce the scene's brilliant shimmer. Figures observed in the street were reduced to disconnected spots of dark color, which were captured on the canvas by masterly single strokes. The depersonalization of the urban crowd is explicable on the basis of the remote physical perspective of the artist. By disengaging his strokes from a uniform fused mass, Monet was being visually honest—that is, seeking to convey true empirical perception—but also calling attention to the independent existence of the touch of color applied *on* the canvas. Paradoxically, there was created both an overall illusionistic image and its opposite effect, which was a random disposition of colors over a flat surface. It is this allover pattern and roughly equal density of the strokes which weaves the compositional fabric. The new intensity of Monet's color, born of a desire for consistency with visual appearance, was to impress later artists such as Seurat (Pl. 48, p. 297) and Gauguin (Pl. 49, p. 298) with its emotional, symbolic, and decorative possibilities.

The later boulevard views of Camille Pissarro (1830–1903) capture the free and unpredictable ebb and flow of city traffic (Fig. 419). Mobility was for the Impressionists a satisfying sign of modernity, and the physical transformations that did much to beautify and mobilize Paris after 1850 were joyfully celebrated rather than criticized in their paintings. The Impressionists, unlike Degas and Manet, painted directly from their subject on the spot and relied upon their thorough artistic training to compose with great rapidity a perfect painting. Pissarro makes no attempt to contain precisely or to centralize the subject, and like our field of vision the painting's borders trim the scene on all sides, so that we are made strongly aware of seeing only a segment of a larger fluctuating world. Because there is no horizon line, the street appears to parallel the painted surface, thus accentuating the ambivalence between spatial depth and the picture plane.

Pierre-Auguste Renoir (1841–1919), who was more committed to the figure because of his academic training, tended to personalize his street scenes more than Monet and Pissarro did, so that some figures retain their identity. His paintings are sometimes treated as if focused on one spot, such as a woman standing next to him, and the rest of the image slips into a blur that is analogous to peripheral vision. This change in social and optical focus can be appreciated by comparing Renoir's *Place Pigalle* (Fig. 420) with Daumier's *The Uprising* (Fig. 421), which is dated about twenty years earlier and shows rioting figures on a Paris street. The Impressionists had political convictions but kept them out of their paintings. Daumier continued the militant partisanship that characterized advanced painting of the first half of the century, and he translated the crowd at least in part into individuals—in fact a family. Though the work is unfinished, the drawing of the heads shows that Daumier intended all to be in focus. For the Impressionists, the new boulevards constructed between 1850 and 1870 were not to be shown as battlegrounds or parade sites, but as the loci of the truly Impressionist experience; they were to be places where one walked casually and without destination, responding to aesthetic perceptions such as the sight of beautiful women, sunlit trees, and elegant shops. From Impressionist painting such as that of Renoir, one could never glean Honoré de Balzac's famous lines about Paris: "Paradise for women, Purgatory for men, Hell for horses." Moreover, Impressionist painting, unlike the large-scale historical paintings, was intended primarily for middle-class homes.

At the end of the century, Pierre Bonnard (1867–1947) painted a beautiful screen, patterned as an object and partly in style after Japanese art, with the subject of a Paris square (Fig. 422). Influenced by the late-19th-century Paris Shadow Theater performances, in which silhouettes were illuminated on a screen, as much as by Japanese prints, Bonnard presents the flattened cut-out shapes of a row of horse-drawn cabs and three cloaked women at the top of the screen and below the figures of a woman and child seen against a great empty space. The shimmering Impressionist colored mosaic had given way to large monochromatic shapes and the consequent emphasis on flat surface pattern. The third phase of the modern revolution continued with subjects already established, but these were now given new meaning through new formal ideas. Art began shifting away from imitation of nature and stressing the unnatural. By inventiveness of personal style, the artist made the familiar seem unfamiliar. The rightness or veracity of the work of art was not determined by matching it against a

422. Pierre Bonnard. *Paris Square*. 1897. Four colored lithograph screen panels, 4′5⁷/₈″ × 1′6⁵/₈″ each. Museum of Modern Art, New York (Abby Aldrich Rockefeller Fund).

423. AUGUSTE RODIN. *Gates of Hell.* 1880–1917. Bronze, 18 × 12′. Rodin Museum, Philadelphia (given by Jules Mastbaum).

specific place and moment, but by its internal coherence of color and shape and their emotive appeal. The imperative of independent artists after 1885 was to explore deliberately the expressive possibilities of the materials of art themselves, such as line, shape, color, and surface organization. The Impressionist fleck of color had been expanded to a larger, firmly bounded flat color area; illusionism was abandoned, but representation remained. Modeling of forms, rational perspective, nuances of light and dark or value construction, natural illumination and shadows, as they were traditionally known and used to achieve illusion, all began to be ejected from progressive art. The stress was now upon artifice, on the treated surface itself. Both at the beginning and at the end of the 19th century, artists believed style was everything, that is, the essence of art; but for David and Ingres this implied an imitation of Classical and Renaissance styles, whereas for Bonnard and Toulouse-Lautrec it was the expression of a highly personal style.

**The Gates of Hell** The single most important work of sculpture in the 19th century was the *Gates of Hell* (Fig. 423) by Auguste Rodin (1840–1917). Rodin is repeatedly referred to as an Impressionist sculptor, though such statements are highly inaccurate. In this gigantic portal he has shown a view of society and a manner of realizing form that directly oppose the goals of the Impressionists. Mounted on an architectural frame inspired by great Gothic portals (Fig. 104) and Renaissance doorways are almost 200 naked figures who enact the artist's tragic vision of humanity disillusioned and frustrated while relentlessly driven by passion. Rodin sought to rival medieval sculptors (Fig. 70) and also Michelangelo (Fig. 197) by presenting an epic image of the modern soul. The three naked figures atop the *Gates* were deprived of hands to suggest the futility of resistance to death. The tombs at the base of the doors announce that the drama above them takes place in the afterlife. Presiding over the dismal scenes of fruitless striving sits, not Christ, but *The Thinker*—Rodin's symbol of the artist as both judge and prisoner of his own time, as a man gifted with intelligence but cursed with passion. Thus man has replaced his god on the cross of suffering, and death brings neither celestial solace nor the fires of Hades—only eternal movement. Bereft of ideals, the aimless mobs and the individuals of the portal know unity only through despair and loneliness. Man carries within him the eternal divergent goals of longing and dissatisfaction, so that Hell for Rodin is not a drama of place, but one of people. The lack of apparent order or composition contrasts with medieval Last Judgments (Fig. 69), and it reflects Rodin's disbelief in the theological view of the world, as supported in thought and composition by such predecessors as Michelangelo. Rodin made the naked human form respond to a host of feelings, through gesture and movements that had no precedent in the history of sculpture. These derived from observations of the living model, and as a psychologist of the body, an observer of instinctive gesture, and an interpreter of flesh, Rodin had no peer.

In Chapter 14, the Piazza of San Marco (Figs. 375, 376) was discussed as an example of the imperfections possible in a great work of art. Rodin's *Gates of Hell* also achieves greatness despite incompleteness, inconsistency of style in architecture, and weakness in compostion. Rodin himself, conscious of these imperfections, likened the state of the sculpture to the incompleteness of cathedrals. He worked on the project from 1880 until his death in 1917, which implies further that its imperfections related to the protracted, living process of its origin. This epic could no more assume the appearance of fixed order than Rodin's sculptures of individual human forms (Figs. 3, 491, 493, 497) could betray conscious stylization. His aim was to achieve the natural in form and meaning; the closer he came

*left:* 424. James Ensor. Detail of *Entry of Christ into Brussels* (Pl. 46, p. 295). 1888.

*below:* 425. Edvard Munch. *Evening on Karl Johan Street.* c. 1892. Oil on canvas, 33¹/₄ × 47⁵/₈". Casino Communal, Knokke-le-Zoute, Belgium.

to this goal, the less obtrusive could be his system of work. It might be argued that his *Gates* are not art, but life itself—a vast collection of beautiful parts which nevertheless are valued as a single incomparable whole.

**Painters of Personal and Social Crises** From what we have seen in the second half of the 19th century, one might derive the notion that advanced painting was entirely devoted to depicting a second Eden on earth. While this was true of Impressionism in France, there were prophetic developments of a different, grimmer nature in other countries. The ugly and hostile aspect of city life, never assessed by painters such as Monet, was measured out by the Belgian James Ensor (1860–1949) and the Norwegian Edvard Munch (1863–1944). Ensor's *Entry of Christ into Brussels in 1889* (Pl. 46, p. 295) is a bitter commentary on society's perversion of a religious event into a vulgar carnival; the painting reflects the artist's personal disillusion and feeling of alienation from society. Ensor identified with Christ and felt that he himself had been unjustly evaluated and persecuted by the public and critics after his youthful acclaim as the savior of modern Belgian painting. The actual events that Ensor witnessed in the streets of Ostend and Brussels, in which political factions assailed each other verbally and physically, became the basis of this personal metaphor. The inconspicuous figure of Christ at the painting's center is drowned in waves of grimacing masks (Fig. 424) and commercial slogans. Ensor was probably influenced by the vernacular art of the contemporary Belgian marionette theater—by its sets, masks, and aggressive action which included caricatures of religious themes. Ensor had also seen Seurat's painting of the *Grande Jatte* (Pl. 48, p. 297), and he may have been inspired to redo French paintings of such communal sociability. The airy openness of Monet's boulevard has been replaced by a claustrophobic crowding of the street. The subtly inflected touch of Monet's brush contrasts with Ensor's assaults on the painting surface, his violent twisting and streaking of thick pigments. Ensor brought to his paintings sharp insights into the psychology of crowd behavior under conditions of extreme stimulation and with the resulting loss of inhibition. The masks become intimate revelations of the depravity inherent in their wearers. Ensor compulsively jammed every inch of the painting with distasteful, hostile figures, thereby weakening the total composition. The painting is important mostly for the arresting qualities and expressive power of its details, as the means by which Ensor brought to art a frank self-realization in his harsh themes and brushwork.

In Munch's painting *Evening on Karl Johan Street* (Fig. 425), the crowd is divested of its individual identity and given no attributes of human warmth. Through magnification of psychological overtones the faces have become dehumanized, presenting less expression than the blank windows, which are given an exaggerated treatment that makes them seem to pulsate. While the street pulls the eye strongly into depth, physical passage is actually blocked by the phalanx of the crowd. This is a painting whose true subject is anxiety over one's place in a world that is inhospitable and menacing. Munch imparted to his paintings psychotic distortions of the color and shape of familiar objects—faces, trees, the rooftops, the sharp recession of the street. In previous art, the distressed individual was seen within the painting as if perceived by a rational onlooker; with Munch, however, the total environment of the painting was colored and shaped by the subjective state of the artist. Though influenced by Scandinavian writers of the time such as Strindberg, Munch's insights, like those of Ensor, derived in large part from personal crises. In no previous period had the artist's personal uneasiness in his society been so frankly painted.

**The End of Conversation Painting** The themes of sociability so prevalent in 19th-century painting were not new to the history of art, as was evidenced in the discussion of the table in art of the 16th and 17th centuries (Chap. 10). Common and crucial to Baroque table paintings was the demonstration by the subjects of their awareness of others, and pictorial composition was supported by connecting figures through their gestures and facial expressions. Renoir's *Luncheon of the Boating Party* (Pl. 47, p. 296) continues, and brings to a glorious culmination, this theme and its sophisticated rhetorical devices. The last of the great conversation paintings, its subject and form strongly depend upon people clearly manifesting their mutual awareness. Thereafter, when shown together by other artists, the figures revealed a diminishing (or nonexistent) sense of mutuality or personal interaction. Renoir, who was cognizant of older art, once again brought the table to life and depicted his friends enjoying the delights of good food and drink, the countryside, and one another's company. The painter's bride-to-be is seen at the lower left, playfully occupied with her dog. Across the table is the artist Gustave Caillebotte, whose posture of sitting on a chair that is turned backward and whose sportsman's shirt did not accord with conservative notions of decorum either in public or in art. As in 17th-century Dutch and French paintings, Renoir gives us a history of the commonplace. The moral of his painting, which was that of Impressionism on the whole, was to be yourself. The painting's colors are mostly red, white, and blue for festive rather than for patriotic reasons. It is worth the viewer's attention to examine how each color is varied throughout the composition, thereby tying objects, figures, and setting into a radiant, harmonious whole. Just as the subjects manifest complete relaxation, so is the beholder enjoined to savor at leisure such beautiful passages of the painting as the still life on the table or, as Renoir had learned from Rubens (Pl. 71, p. 360) the delights of contrasting colors and textures in a beautiful woman's dress, hat, and flesh. Renoir would soon abandon such themes of informal diversion and the Impressionist style in favor of conventional subjects involving nudes. He treated these with a tighter surface finish and firmer modeling, so as to align his work with the more disciplined masterpieces of the past.

**The Family in Life and Death** When Vincent van Gogh (1853–90) painted his *Potato Eaters* (Fig. 426), he was living in one of the poorest areas in Europe, where he found his subjects in Dutch peasants. His dark tones matched the character and mood of his grim environment. In this painting he showed his reverence for those who lived by what they could retrieve from the reluctant soil of Brabant. The solemnity of the figures around the simple table and its humble fare evokes memories of religious paintings of Christ and the disciples (Pl. 31, p. 164; Fig. 259) or the partaking of Communion, and this analogy may well have been in Van Gogh's mind. The cheap religious print hanging on the wall is like an attribute of their piety. Living more poorly than his parish during this missionary period in his life, Van Gogh had failed to win their

426. VINCENT VAN GOGH. *The Potato Eaters*. 1885. Oil on canvas, $32^1/_4 \times 44^7/_8$″. Stedelijk Museum, Amsterdam.

*left:* Plate 45. CLAUDE MONET. *Rue Montorgueil, Fête Nationale du 30 Juin, 1878*. 1878. Oil on canvas, $24\frac{1}{2} \times 13''$. Musée des Beaux-Arts, Rouen. (See p. 289.)

*below:* Plate 46. JAMES ENSOR. *Entry of Christ into Brussels in 1889*. 1888. Oil on canvas, $8'5\frac{1}{2}'' \times 14'1\frac{1}{2}''$. Collection Louis Franck, London. (See p. 293).

respect as a preacher, and it was only with difficulty that his subjects were persuaded to pose individually for him. Self-trained as an artist, he had not learned how to interweave gracefully the glances and movements of his figures in the manner of even the most mediocre academic student, let alone with the skill of Renoir. Van Gogh fiercely asserted the individual identity of each peasant in his portraiture and captured that sense of angular movement conditioned by hard physical labor, but he also achieved a feeling of their sharing in the fruits of common toil. The glow of the oil lamp served to illuminate their faces, but also to endow them with a sympathetic radiance. Van Gogh had become disillusioned with the orthodox church, and he came to believe that those deserving of reverence were not the saints of the past but the humble plowmen, "all those who wear the stigmata of a whole life of struggle, borne without ever flinching." Distrustful of his memory and of painting pictures of unseen subjects, he believed that the Bible could best be illustrated in the guise of the men and women of his own time and place. Once again the secular subject of figures at a table acquired religious overtones.

Munch was in some ways a Norwegian Van Gogh, and he created a *Frieze of Life* that dealt, in paintings and prints, with ordinary men and women and the crises with which they were continually confronted in life. It was patterned after the great painting cycles of the past that recorded the life of Christ, the Virgin, or saints. Like Van Gogh, Munch endured great personal suffering and sought to transform himself through art. The anguish of others became a metaphor of his own. In his *Death Chamber* (Fig. 427), the theme of tragedy and death that was so prevalent at the century's beginning returns, but now it strikes nameless victims and is presented in a homely setting. Based on his own sister's death, the print is like a modern version of the medieval *memento mori* (Fig. 143), except that Munch's focus is now upon the great grief that each of the living must bear within himself. The stark use of black and white and the strong outlining of silhouettes sharpens the sense of sorrow's containment and the unbridgeable isolation of every man in such moments of crisis. For Munch, Impressionism was too superficial an art, an attitude that failed to deal meaningfully with feeling and the suffering in life. Like Van Gogh, it was his desire to give to men and women that quality of holiness formerly imparted by the halo and to induce the viewer to remove his hat before such paintings as if he were in church. Both artists continued, and carried even further, a tradition of more than 400 years standing of humanizing the sacred and saintly. Unlike more financially successful conservative artists who repetitiously exploited the formats and devices of older religious art, Munch and Van Gogh created inspired paintings and prints out of their strong, genuine feelings for their fellow men, hoping thereby to unify mankind as was once done by the organized Church.

**The Good Life of the Past and Present** The abstract, idealized art of the 19th century was not provided by its progressive painters but by artists such as Pierre-Puvis de Chavannes (1824–98) who championed conservative values of history and culture. Admired as the most important painter of his time by artists of widely different convictions and tastes, Puvis continued the tradition of making paintings intended as symbols of an entire cultural epoch and civilization. He did not consider 19th-century society as worthy of or appropriate for such treatment in painting. When he was commissioned to decorate the museum in Lyon, Puvis chose to interpret abstract concepts of what Lyon meant in antiquity, for him the golden age in that

427. EDVARD MUNCH. *The Death Chamber*. 1896. Lithograph, 15½ × 21½". Munch Museum, Oslo.

*left:* 428. PUVIS DE CHAVANNES. *Vision Antique.* 1885. Oil on canvas, wall size. Musée de Lyon.

city's history. His *Vision Antique* (Fig. 428) was to decorate a museum room filled with ancient Greek and Roman works of art. The painting was not based on actual history, and unlike David (Fig. 402), Puvis was unconcerned with action. Instead, it is his imaginative evocation of the beauty and serenity of the region's countryside and population. In effect, he was painting life as it ought to have been and should be. The viewer was expected to ponder the intellectual premises of the painting. Each figure is distinctly isolated and is shown in a reflective mood, in a landscape setting that itself encourages meditation. A dominant tone of cool grey establishes the remoteness of the scene and reflects the painter's disdain for the strong color and taste for outdoor immediacy found in Impressionism. Puvis' painting illustrates art governed by rational notions of what art ought to be, and such was the artist's divided personality that he produced the most gruesome and sadistic private drawings in French 19th-century caricatural art.

When Georges Seurat (1859–91) undertook a large painting in the same years that Puvis was working on his mural, he too dealt with an eternal, idyllic life, but it was that of the weekly holiday outing enjoyed by the working classes, not as portrayed in an imagined Greek setting but on an island in the Seine in northern Paris. In his *Sunday Afternoon on the Grande Jatte* (Pl. 48, p. 297), Seurat's personal vision transformed a prosaic event into a poetic occasion. What seems at first to be a gathering of familiar persons in a mundane setting becomes the source of a haunting paradox. While outwardly appearing to share in the enjoyment of the place and moment, the figures do not communicate. The gaiety of the moment derives essentially from the warmth and brightness of the colors, not from expressive traits of the figures themselves. Ignoring the potential for movement, Seurat chose to present what might be termed still*ed* life. Seurat believed that monumental painting such as that of Piero della Francesca (Pl. 23, p. 135; Fig. 184) required keeping gesture and movement to a minimum and, moreover, that composition could be achieved without conventional psychological and emotional rhetoric.

The landscape is painted from a single viewpoint, but each figure within it is rendered from an individual perspective, as if the artist were directly opposite each of his subjects. Seurat restored to advanced painting the monumental size and impressive volume of the figure that Impressionist painting gradually destroyed. The shadows cast by the sun do not accord with a single light source. Convincing as the intensity of sunlight is, the painting was done in the studio by artificial light, for unlike the Impressionists Seurat had explicitly avowed a theoretical basis of working. He distrusted the intuitive and spontaneous. Despite the apparently informal dispersal of the figures, none can be shifted from its position. A taut compositional scheme is contrived by the relation of silhouettes and aligned shapes that link foreground, middle distance, and background. The whole painting has the fresh appearance of instantaneous execution, but each silhouette was meditated upon in extensive preliminary studies and purged of the superfluous. For his purposes, Seurat's edges are more expressive than his faces. The large, solemnly static figures are, ironically, constituted of minute, volatile touches of color. A strict systemization of Impressionist color style, Seurat's aesthetic of meticulously divided strokes of color ensured each color's brilliance by adjoining it with its optical complement—yellow with violet, red with green, and so on. His stroke varied in size and direction, depending on the shape he was painting and the scale of his canvas. By contrast with the work of Munch, Seurat's distortions were objective and were grounded in consciously formulated aesthetic theory. Seurat achieved an air of the casual through minute calculation. From the recurrent, uneventful moments in the life of mundane city dwellers, he created an impression of the eternalized and heroic.

**Primitivism and the Good Life** The most famous independent artist of his day, who found that he could better be of his time in Polynesia rather than Paris, was Paul Gauguin (1848–1903). In previous centuries, artists frequently left their own countries and traveled for purposes of study (often to Rome, as has been pointed out), but in most cases they eventually returned to their home country. Gauguin left Paris for the South Pacific for the first time in 1890 for varied reasons, one of which was economic. Also, Paris seemed to him to suffer from an excess of civilization—and from an inadequate appreciation of his gifts. Among the Polynesian natives he sought the simple evidence of the true meaning of life and religion, but nonetheless he looked at his subjects through the eyes of a sophisticated and Christian European artist who sought to sell his works in France. Much of what he painted was dependent upon visual encounters, on remembrances of Parisian painting such as that of Seurat or Puvis, and on his own amateur studies in religion and in ancient and primitive art. He was critical of Impressionism as being too imitative and as lacking in imagination, qualities of the mysterious and spiritual, and the capacity to arouse strong feeling. Yet, his painting *Day of the God* (Pl. 49, p. 298) is unthinkable without the work of the Impressionists that Gauguin had emulated in the early 1880s and without the innovations of Seurat's *Grande Jatte*. In place of Parisians enjoying the pleasures of the open air and the beach, Gauguin painted South Sea natives in their vaguely distinguished secular and sacred rituals, ranged about his own version of a Polynesian deity. Their postures are in part paraphrases of Egyptian art, in part natural movements. The positioning of the foreground figures is of his own invention, perhaps to symbolize the powers of creation possessed by the idol behind them.

Gauguin's form of Symbolism was unsystematic and largely intuitive. His imagination led him to gestures, shapes, and colors that he believed would have an instinctive universal meaning. Gauguin is the prototype of the modern artist who, while discrediting the form, premises, and values of conservative or academic art, strives to continue its unifying social function and utopian imagery on his own terms. By personalizing past influences and means of conveying meaning, unlike conservative artists who drew from an official public iconography, Gauguin helped to open the gulf between artist and public, with respect to understanding art, which has not since been closed. Even more influential for later art than his symbolic programs and treatment of the figure, however, are the brightly colored amorphous shapes in the water in the foreground, which resist definition but create a strong visual and emotional experience.

Unlike Monet, Gauguin did not paint directly the source of his feeling in nature; rather, he sought equivalents in shape and color for conveying the feeling itself—to define an object precisely to eliminate its mystery. Thus he alone could judge the rightness of what he painted—a premise that introduces the dilemma and risks of the modern critic and audience. Whereas the Impressionist might argue in defense of his painting, "This is how I see it," Gauguin would very likely argue that he was painting the look of emotion, or that "This is how I feel it." Gauguin summarizes the problems and possibilities of the modern artist at the end of the 19th century. As was already noted, he yearned for the universal role that art had played in the days of the great allegorical and religious paintings, when artists could subscribe to public values or symbols and interpret a theology in which they believed and by which they could be genuinely inspired. But Gauguin was also heir to new ideas of personal expression that mitigated against public painting such as illustrative or dogmatic art. Like his progressive contemporaries, he had a horror of literature as providing the basis of art. The expressive power of his means, drawing and color, which he had learned in France from fellow artists, musicians, and poets, defied verbal translation. The artist was thus obliged to communicate feeling in terms which were possible only in painting.

**The Ethic of Modern Art** Much of advanced 19th-century art was based on ordinary worldly encounters, which did not need interpretation in the sense of the involved subject matter of previous centuries; instead it surrendered its meaning to direct experience of the painting. The public has been slow to comprehend this attitude or approve. Gauguin vacillated in his conviction of purpose and sometimes wrote out programs for his work, or he compromised his flat abstract surface patterns with modeled figures. It remained for artists in the 20th century to develop Gauguin's legacy further and more consistently. The 19th century witnessed the logical culmination of tendencies in art since the end of the Middle Ages, which was devoted to simulating the world of appearances. At the century's end came the beginnings of a deliberate fidelity to the world of feeling, and of positing art itself as the subject of art and the basis for valid abstraction. One of the great ethical bases of modern art had been established—that of working directly from private empirical experience in an individual style, personally acquired, as a more direct means of realizing true self-expression.

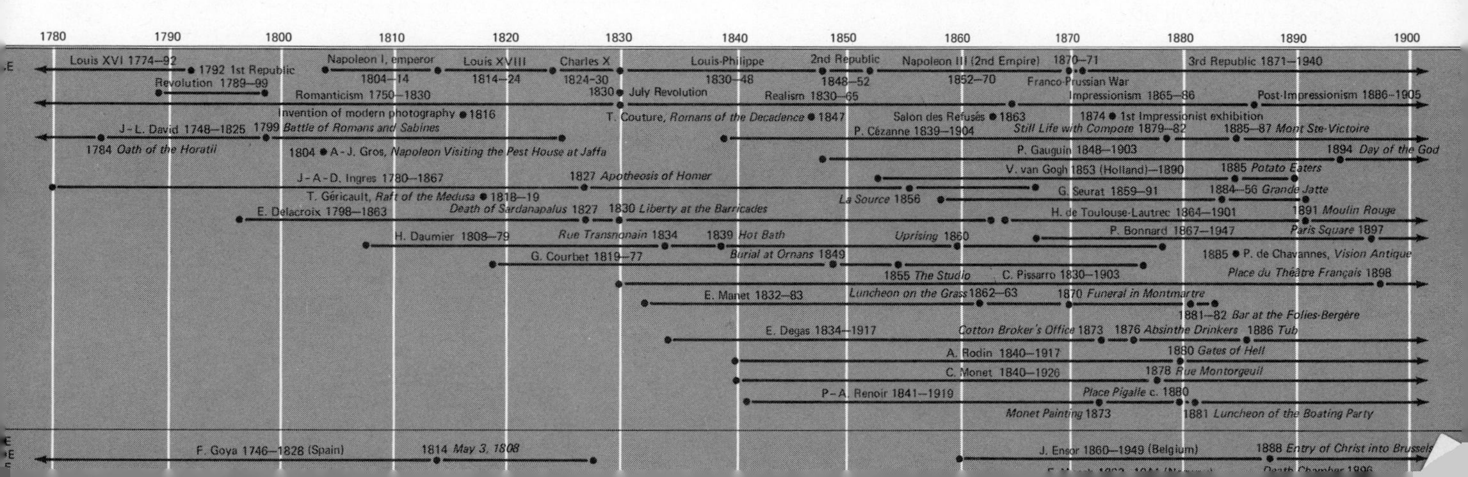

# 16

Whether a painter or sculptor chooses to make his art *about* nature, he is always creating his art out of the things of nature. Whether he works with ink on silk or rice paper, with animal-hair brushes on wood or canvas, in mineral pigments, clay, marble, or in bronze, the earth is the prime source of his art supplies. Science and technology may permit him to refine his tools and natural materials, but he is still working with matter in order to interpret matter. In some respects this relationship explains the deep attachment many artists have to their materials and the special kinship between the stuffs and the subject matter of art that treats the land. The earth is the source, sustenance, and future of their lives, and as with their gods, countless artists have sought to make nature into their own image. Nature has given man his form, but through art man has given new forms to nature; art is, in other words, nature having passed through man. The Swiss artist Paul Klee has captured the essence of this process:

> He is like the trunk of the tree. Afflicted and moved by the forces of the stream he conveys what he has perceived into his work. The treetop expands in all directions and becomes visible in time and space and all the same things happen with his work. . . . It would never occur to anyone to demand of the tree that its top be shaped just like the roots. Everyone knows that what is above ground cannot be just a reflection of what is below. . . . The artist, like the trunk of the tree, is really doing nothing else than accumulating what comes from the depth and passes it on. He neither serves nor commands; he is an intermediary. . . . Beauty has merely passed through him.

There is no continuous history of landscape painting ranging from ancient times down to the present. The first true landscapes did not appear until Roman art of the 1st century B.C., and subsequently in Western art there was a thousand-year interruption of this theme from the end of antiquity to the 14th century. Landscapes reappeared first in the margins and backgrounds of medieval art, and not until the 17th century did they become a central concern in the European artist's focus. The absence of landscape painting in past periods of history does not imply that men were totally unaware of or uninterested in nature. It is better accounted for in the lack of incentives and the artistic means by which to render nature in art.

The painting of nature has seldom been done by those who lived closest to the land. It was not peasants, but educated and inquisitive townsmen, who evolved the sophisticated coding systems by which mountains, trees, earth, and water found their equivalent on the painted surface. Topographical recording and the literal imitation of specific natural locations have a shorter art history than do many other purposes of landscape

429. Hsu Tao-ning. *Fishing in a Mountain Stream.* c. 1000. Scroll painting on silk, 1′7″ × 6′10½″. Nelson Gallery–Atkins Museum, Kansas City, Missouri (Nelson Fund).

# ART AND NATURE

art. Indeed, at various times in the past accurate surface imitation would have been inimical to prevailing artistic ideals.

**The Beginning of Landscape Painting** In the 1st century B.C. the Romans developed the first true landscapes in painting. These are to be found on the walls of private houses, notably at Pompeii, which was preserved in the volcanic ashes erupted by Mount Vesuvius in A.D. 79. There, artists had been commissioned to disguise the walls of urban villas with frescoes painted illusionistically to simulate deep space, architecture, and the countryside. These landscapes did not recreate specific locales but were imaginative, mysterious places that could have had sacred and idyllic connotations. The shrine next to the tree in Plate 50 (p. 307) suggests such ties with religion. The Romans looked upon the Egyptian goddess Isis as a nature deity, and the shrine may relate to her worship. The dominant bluish tone adds to the fresco's unreal or enchanted mood. Such a painting gave its owner the prestige of being both educated and a Roman of good taste. Much Roman painting derived from Greek art, and the elaborate architectural elements painted on some Roman walls may have originated in lost Greek painting done as scenery for stage plays. It was the Romans, however, who developed the illusion of natural prospects extending laterally and to a horizon line deep beyond the borders of the painting. Without the unified geometric perspective system of the Renaissance, which no ancient peoples attained, the Romans managed to create an art convincingly close to empirical visual experience. Though the Roman artist did not make all receding lines converge on a single vanishing point (which would have suggested a fixed point for observing the scene), he was alert to the appearance of objects, trees, hills, and the land and realized depth through atmospheric coloring, overlapped shapes, and the diminution of figures and objects relative to their distance from the viewer. The prime Roman device for representing depth in nature was the elevated viewpoint, a technique used in Early Renaissance painting before systematic perspective was known (Pl. 17, p. 115).

For the Roman urban dweller, these landscapes afforded spiritual comfort and escape from the annoyances of his everyday environment. He was brought into contact with the beauties of the countryside by painting, just as the reading of Vergil removed his thoughts to the idyllic pastoral life. Today the travel poster is perhaps the most familiar means by which we indulge in such imaginative displacement.

The emergence of landscape art in China a few centuries after its appearance in Rome is similarly based on religious purposes, literary analogies, and the escapist desires of its collectors. A landscape painting (Fig. 429) by Hsu Tao-ning (late 10th–early 11th cent.) indicates that by the year A.D. 1000

Chinese art possessed a consistent, integrated world view with a focus on nature, not man. Landscape painting had developed from beginnings in about the 4th century A.D. in magical funerary functions and animistic beliefs and afterward passed into the service of Confucianism and then Taoism. Chinese pictorial writing was the source of painting, and all artists were first trained in calligraphic brushwork. Artists were frequently scholars, poets, and philosophers, and their painting was intended for an audience of these groups, constituting therefore an elite or aristocratic rather than a public art. Though its aesthetic values were appreciated, landscape painting remained closely tied with mysticism and a function of facilitating the beholder's communion with the reality of the universe. It demonstrated the belief that all things in nature, no matter what their size, were of worth.

Though Hsu Tao-ning's painting is not the literal recording of a specific mountain site, it shares many qualities with the mist-shrouded, jagged, soaring peaks of northern China. Its subject, fishing in a mountain stream, is an activity as timeless as it is universal in that country. Never in Chinese and Japanese painting was the artist enjoined to imitate surface appearance; literal imitation was thought to be vulgar, an impediment to true insight and the genuine spiritual and aesthetic experience of nature through art. The sign of a great painter was his ability first to fathom the meaning of what he was painting and then to impart this wisdom to his art. For this reason, Chinese and Japanese painting was in great part based on copying the works of venerable masters. Nature was shaped according to conventional types, signs, and symbols in order to convey thought and feeling. The painter learned by heart the various ways to render mountains, water, and trees, the principal ingredients of landscape art. Despite typification that extended to every stroke the artist might make, the sublime artist—as he was regarded by those who followed—was able to transmit his unique personal reactions to a given subject. The ideal mode of painting was one that gave the appearance of being effortless (made possible in part by mastery of types and strokes), as if, figuratively, the artist allowed his landscape to paint itself. To do this, he had to be able to identify with the subject he was painting and be a part of the vital movement, the resilience or resistance of the water, trees, and mountains. Painting became a form of deep and serious communion with nature, permitting the artist and the compatible beholder to realize a sense of oneness with the perfect unity, creative energy, and essence of the natural world—from its infinite space, to the mountain range, and down to the smallest pebble. The great purpose of painting was to bring joy to the soul. A city dweller who possessed a landscape painting was supplied with a source of religious experience and a release from urban cares. These paintings were to be approached with reverence, humility, and intense concentration.

The scroll painting, developed by such 10th- and 11th-century masters as Hsu Tao-ning and probably executed at tables, is one of the great vehicles of Oriental painting and the finest format for Oriental landscape. These paintings were not meant to be viewed in their entirety, and rarely were they intended to be savored by more than one or two people at a time. The scroll was to be unrolled gradually, from right to left, in reflection of the temporal progress of a traveler through a landscape. Thus a succession of motifs customarily is revealed in an area about 2 feet wide. The classic format of scroll painting initiates the scroll with a depiction of the ground near the bottom of the silk, or paper, as if inviting the viewer to enter. In the next passage, the viewer is led into the middle distance by a path or stream, and subsequently to the distant peaks, and finally back again. This sequence is repeated, with variations, throughout the whole. At any point, the viewer can look to his right, from whence he has come, or to the left, the area still before him. Some scrolls trace the course of a river from its source to its termination in the sea, a subject ideally suited to this format. There are no dramatic episodes, no climactic events. Man is not the measure of the universe in this art; he plays an important but small role in the unfolding of time.

The construction of a Chinese or Japanese landscape painting does not assume a fixed position of a spectator outside the painting. Oriental painting never used the Western window-frame device, which tends to separate the viewer from the scene and suggest a single viewing point. The Eastern paintings were constructed from many viewpoints. Usually the artist began at the top with the most distant forms, such as the faint outlines of mountain peaks, and then, in the manner of Chinese writing, worked downward and forward to the bottom. The total spatial construction depends upon the moving focus of the traveler within the scene. The painter wanted the effect of an infinite and unmeasurable space extending beyond the limits of the frame and the eye, a space in which all things in nature lived. This space could be suggested by pale washes of ink or by entirely blank (that is, unpainted) silk or paper. The space was illuminated by no strong single source of light but rather by an overall diffused light, concentrated more in certain areas than in others. Shadows were rarely shown.

Color was seldom used in Oriental landscape painting; ink and wash were preferred. Free of descriptive purpose and seeking to infuse their paintings with qualities not given directly to the senses, artists found an ideal instrument in the gradients achievable with ink.

In China and Japan, Zen Buddhist painters developed a technique of splashed-ink painting. During long meditation, the artist conjured up the vision of his painting in his mind and waited for the moment of perfect unity with it—in Zen terms, the *moment of enlightenment*. When he achieved this instantaneous revelation, his task was to set it down as rapidly as possible in order to sustain the ecstatic vision. The ink was then literally splashed onto the surface, in conjunction with controlled brush strokes also. A Japanese master at this type of painting was the 15th-century artist Sesshū (1420–1506). In his painting *Fisherman and Woodcutter* (Fig. 430), a dozen quick strokes establish or, rather, insinuate the environment. There are varying degrees of form definition. The relative concentration of the ink establishes what is near and far, and the traceable movements of the brush create forceful directions for the eye as well as suggest the substance of the landscape. This type of painting was not for amateurs, for it demanded firm, disciplined control of the brush, a sure sense of tonal values, and great sensitivity to solid-void relationships, with particular care to the use of empty space. Only what was caught in the web of the artist's consciousness emerges, and once the idea was fixed on paper, the brush was spared. The artist signed his name with a woodblock, and often he, a priest, or a poet might inscribe a message or line of poetry directly on the painting. Moreover, the paintings were frequently inspired by poetic passages. The placement and weight of the dark ink was with an emphasis on total composition. The writing and the position of the figures testify to the sureness required of the artist in locating his forms within the space of the painting, for he had no systematic network of edges or ground lines to guide him.

There are important similarities as well as differences between the painting of nature in East and West. The Flemish painter Pieter Bruegel (1525/30–1569), like his Oriental counterparts, was a man of culture in close association with geographers, philosophers, and writers who shared many of his views and appreciated his paintings (Pl. 32, p. 181; Figs. 14, 216, 222, 229). The development of landscape art in the 16th century was related to other forms of exploration. There is a thesis that Chinese landscape painting also had its roots in geography. Like many of the Chinese painters, Bruegel traveled widely, storing in his memory and sketches a vast repertory of motifs. His finished paintings were not of specific locales but were attempts to present a cosmic view of the infinite extension, depth, height, timelessness, change, and order of nature. The purpose of Bruegel's art was to demonstrate his comprehension of nature and man's relation to it. Like Hsu Tao-ning, Bruegel found the world governed by laws over which man had no control and to which he passively submitted. In *The Return of the Herds* (Fig. 431), men and animals bow before the impending storm. Man loses his

*above left:* 430. Sesshū *Fisherman and Woodcutter*. Late 15th century. Brush painting.

*left:* 431. Pieter Bruegel the Elder. *The Return of the Herds*. c. 1560. Oil on panel, 3′10¼″ 5′2⅝″. Kunsthistorisches Museum, Vienna.

432. SESSON SHOKEI. *Wind and Waves*. Ashikaga Period, 16th century. Hanging scroll, ink and slight color on paper; height $8^3/_4''$. Formerly Nomura Collection, Kyoto.

individuality against the overwhelming backdrop of the world in which he lives; it is the face of nature, not man, that acquires expressive power and individuality. Bruegel, again in the manner of Oriental painters, had an animistic view of the earth, which he conceived of as a great organic body, as described in the words of the 15th-century philosopher Nicholas of Cusa: "The earth is a great animal, the rocks are his bones, the rivers his veins, the trees his hair."

The towering mountain to the right in *The Return of the Herds* has a gaping cavern in its side, like a great wound. Bruegel often sketched cracks and fissures in rocks and the evidences of erosion and decay in nature. He was also attracted to signs of regeneration, however, and this painting was one of a cycle devoted to the seasons, which pictures the death and rebirth of the land. Before Bruegel, Oriental artists had done cyclical paintings of the same subject, but in Bruegel's painting important formal differences appeared. He painted a continuous earth surface and sky, and gave a greater sense of tangibility to space. His viewpoint was more consistently that of an external observer in a fixed position. He sustained a complex integration of the many parts of the scene and covered the entire picture surface with paint, drawn forms, and particularized textures. Like Hsu Tao-ning and Sesshū, Bruegel wished the viewer to lose himself within the painting as he searched out its smallest parts—the village at the mountain's base, the harvested fields, the gallows—and to realize it was not the human beings that imparted drama to the scene, to recognize that man's efforts to change the face of nature have produced little more than flyspecks.

**Storm and Cataclysm** Weather and water were interpreted with great effect in such Japanese painting as *Wind and Waves* (Fig. 432) by Sesson Shokei (c. 1504–89). The absence of any horizontal line and the cumulative curved forms aligned in one direction instill a feeling of the wind's presence. The precarious tilt of the boat and the backward curving thrust of the foreground tree imply the unseen force. A few stylized strokes coalesce into wave forms, but it is the broad undefined area of the painting even more that suggests the magnitude of nature's power. Sesson did not attempt to emphasize the human drama by placing the boat and its tiny figures in the foreground. Chinese and Japanese artists saw in the bamboo and pine that bowed before the wind a model of ideal human conduct. They emphasized less the danger of the moment than the habitual means by which men and trees accommodate to the adversity of wind and waves and submit to cosmic forces.

Nothing in Chinese or Japanese painting is comparable, in form or subject, with a series of drawings made by Leonardo da Vinci (1452–1519) in depiction of cataclysms. Where Sesson showed a convincing natural tempest, Leonardo created a vision of the world's destruction in a roaring convulsion (Fig. 433). Leonardo's religious paintings reflect his admiration of order and the harmonious existence of man with nature; but his notebooks and drawings reveal a preoccupation with disorder and a belief that the world was a precarious balance of powerful forces. Were these forces unleashed, he believed, the obliteration of all life would be accomplished with greater violence than had occurred in the Deluge.

Leonardo made scientific studies of a wide variety of phenomena, such as the flow of water and rock formation, in order to comprehend all of nature. He used theory and empirical observation to interpret his experience. The scope of Leonardo's

433. LEONARDO DA VINCI. *Cataclysm*. c. 1516. Chalk and ink on paper, $6^3/_8 \times 8''$. Royal Collection, Windsor Castle (copyright reserved).

P.Cezanne

*left:* Plate 55. PAUL KLEE. *Botanical Theater*. 1934. Oil and watercolor, $19^5/_8 \times 26^3/_8$″. Collection Mrs. K. Bürgi, Belp, Switzerland. (See pp. 316, 317.)

*below:* Plate 56. WASSILY KANDINSKY. *Picture with White Edge, No. 173*. 1913. Oil on canvas, $4'7^3/_4'' \times 6'7''$. Solomon R. Guggenheim Museum, New York. (See p. 319.)

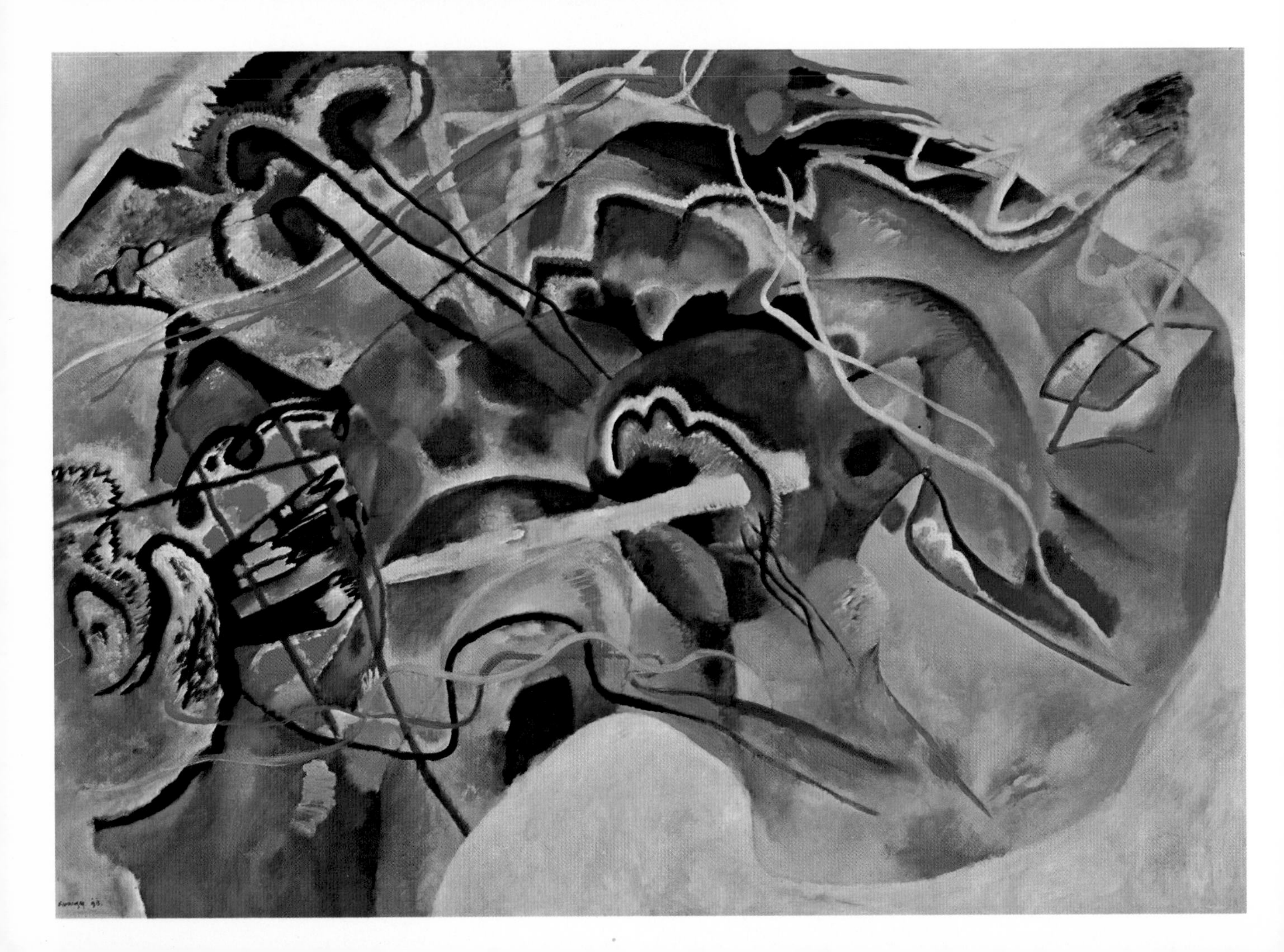

434. Hasegawa Tōhaku. *Pine Wood.* Early 17th century. Folding screen, ink on paper; height 5′1″. National Museum, Tokyo.

interest was so broad that there existed no complete models of drawing for him to imitate even if he had so desired. The cataclysm drawing reproduced here (Fig. 433) shows Leonardo's own devices for tracing the movements of water, wind, and dust clouds. A mountain undermined by the action of water is disintegrating, and its surface, scoured by powerful winds, reveals the ancient marks of earthquakes on its sides. As the mountain peels away and collapses, clouds of dust-filled air and waves move outward in a centrifugal pattern. Accompanying the sketch are long, vivid, and precisely written statements detailing the sequence of destruction, the violent psychological and physical reactions of men and animals to disaster, and the "pitiless slaughter made of the human race by the wrath of God." These statements and drawings show that Leonardo was haunted by visions which may have been induced by widespread prophecies that the world would be destroyed at the end of the century. Into these visions there entered the artist's misanthropy, pessimism about a natural harmonious order, and deep personal disquiet.

A modern painter who responded to inner sensations and created private images to some extent related to nature is the Chilean-born artist Matta Echaurren (b. 1912). His large work *The Earth Is a Man* (Pl. 51, p. 307) is an *inscape*, or a landscape of the mind, a psychedelic transformation of his experience of the volcanic landscape of Mexico. Matta's tropical palette of yellows, reds, and blues and his vague retention of a horizon line, with its contingent major divisions of sky and earth, preserve some of the qualities of the Mexican landscape and suggest a vivid experience from certain hallucinogenic drugs native to that country. The painter's transformations are elaborated into a visionary fusion of genesis and apocalypse, of coalescence and dissolution. Unlike Leonardo's visionary cataclysms, those of Matta are not susceptible to literary programming, nor are they based on scientific geological and climatic studies. Matta's turbulent imagery may reflect the anxiety of the times around World War II, as Leonardo's drawings reflected the disturbing apprehensions of his countrymen about the end of the world.

In his painting Matta created an untraversable and uninhabitable world in constant flux, with fantasized flora, primeval birds, molten eruptive geology, and a solar eclipse. In the upper area is the eclipse, which surprisingly intensifies the light permeating the entire painting. Every shape and area is in the process of changing, and outlines are smooth, undulant, and unstable. Matta gave his shapes an insubstantial and elusive quality by wiping the paint on with a cloth at certain points, thereby dissolving one color area into another and obliterating sustained reference to the pigment and its materiality. The poetic ambiguity of his space comes from soft transparencies of shapes, avoidance of logical recession, and unpredictable areas of phosphorescent brilliance or absorbent darkness. There is an ambivalence of direction in the composition, so that lateral and vertical movements are reversible, thus enhancing the cyclical nature of the theme. Putting Matta's work into historical perspective, William Rubin wrote that, "Whereas the rationalist Greeks had used the external image of man (microcosm) to represent the order, logic, and finite mechanical perfection of the universe (macrocosm), Matta invokes a vision of galaxies to suggest the infinity and mystery within man."

**The Fugitive in Nature** A distinguishing talent of Oriental painters was the ability to evoke the elusive qualities of a landscape seen in a mist. One of the most beautiful examples of this type of painting is a depiction of a pine wood (Fig. 434) on a folding screen by Hasegawa Tōhaku (1539–1610). His inspiration came from the early morning view of pines around Kyoto. With but three or four ink tones, and leaving broad areas of the paper untouched, he suggested the appearance of a pine forest

*left :* 435. CASPAR DAVID FRIEDRICH. *Capuchin Friar by the Sea.* 1808–09. Oil on canvas, $3'6^{7}/_{8}''$ × $5'6^{5}/_{8}''$. Staatliche Museen, West Berlin.

*right :* 436. GUSTAVE COURBET. *Seaside at Palavas.* 1854. Oil on canvas, $15^{1}/_{4}$ × 18″. Musée Fabre, Montpellier, France.

suspended in a soft vaporous atmosphere. The one tree represented in distinct focus serves as a stable base for contemplation as well as for compositional purposes. The strokes are not intended to imitate the surface aspect of the tree but to convey a more subjective impression of the sharp, compact, vertical clusters of needles and the asymmetrical, individual character of every tree. Each screen panel is complete in itself and yet adds to the scope and depth of the whole composition. Fugitive as thought, the painting offers something tangible and solid at one point, then lets shapes melt into the measureless void. Mingled here are delight in an everyday scene, perhaps an esteem for the pines as analogues of human dignity and endurance, and an awareness of spiritual immanence in nature.

The technique which underlies Tōhaku's painting is but one of many basic differences between his work and that of the French Impressionist Monet. Too often Oriental painting such as Tōhaku's is incorrectly termed "impressionistic," implying both similarities to and influences on French Impressionism. In *Bordighera Trees* (Pl. 52, p. 308), for example, Monet did not select from nature properties that could be transcribed into lines or set down with clear, firm boundaries. When Monet confronted the trees, he was not concerned with hidden essence, philosophical symbols, or memory images; rather, he was concerned with sensations of sunlight and color directly experienced at the moment and place he painted. Chinese and Japanese landscapes are without—and did not seek to achieve—the brilliance of Monet's sunlight.

Tactile sense, volume, solidity, continuity, and sometimes even identity of objects are generally absent from Monet's art. The painting's fabric is composed of an overall accumulation of short divided strokes of bright color. The work reveals a discontinuous edge, but a continuous touch (Pl. 45, p. 295; Pl. 86, p. 433). The spectrum of color and the mixture of tones in a square inch of *Bordighera Trees* (Pl. 52) have no counterpart in Eastern painting. A square inch taken from the bushes at the lower right contains in dispersal many touches of green; a few flecks of red, the complementary color induced in the eye by exposure to green; yellows and whites from the sun and reflected light; violet induced by the yellow; and some oranges and blues from areas either seen through the bushes or adjacent to them. The strokes do not follow lines established in nature itself, and each seems different from the others. This technique was not acquired from a tradition, but developed from Monet's earlier painting and from his immediate encounter with the landscape as he worked quickly to fix with the brush what was fleeting before his eyes. The inventiveness and energy of his painting is clear at every point on the canvas. The tree trunks, from root to branch, show no formularized pattern but express continuous discovery of the action of light upon color and form. No part of the surface is unpainted. The ground is covered with the thick tangled web of Monet's strokes, heavy-laden with oil pigment. Monet did not compose his painting by arranging his landscape like furniture; he made the whole work together through the equivalence of visual weights or densities of color in each area. In his personal study of the effects of mixed color on the eye of the beholder, Monet learned which tones expand and which contract, which advance and which recede, and how a few highkeyed areas serve to counterbalance deeper tones. It was not color in the abstract, but nature's color, that excited Monet. The landscape was not an excuse but, in fact, the reason for him to paint.

In contrast to Sesshū's landscape (Fig. 430), *Bordighera Trees* shows finite space that does not swallow up those who live within it. It is a personal space that is directly relatable to the location viewpoint and feelings of the man who painted near the Bordighera trees. His excitement, betrayed in his brushwork, comes from direct confrontation of the scene in nature. In the 15th century, Jan van Eyck often included within his paintings minute, paradisaical landscapes, seeming wonders of light and color (Fig. 151). And one might say that not until 400 years later, in the secular Eden of Monet's luminescent, sun-soaked landscapes, was a comparable optimism expressed.

**Piety and Pride before Nature** In Oriental landscape painting, artists took an appreciative and humble stance before the vastness of their physical surroundings. Frequently a scholar or monk was shown seated beneath a tree or standing on a hill, contemplating nature and meditating upon the source of his art and faith. In Western painting we can see an echo of this interest in solitary communion with nature in *Capuchin Friar by the Sea* (Fig. 435), by the early 19th-century German artist Caspar David Friedrich (1774–1840). Against the bleak, stratified expanses of land, sea, and sky, the single vertical form of the monk, his back toward us, confronts infinity. To his contemporaries Friedrich painted "the tragedy of landscape"—nature steeped in sadness and the yearning by man to embrace the universe. The drama for contemporary German audiences was that of the individual soul, symbolized by the reverent friar, striving to achieve harmony with the soul of the world. Unlike the medieval image of St. Valerian (Fig. 128), Friedrich represented the view that the holy man must not turn his back upon the world, but must assume the enormous task of penetrating its mysteries by his thought. Perhaps symbolically, the painting lightens in its upper reaches, suggesting the elusive object of man's thoughts and desires, a theme on which Paul Klee was also to comment in his *Limits of Reason* (Fig. 575).

Almost half a century after Friedrich's painting, Gustave Courbet commemorated his first encounter with the sea in his *Seaside of Palavas* (Fig. 436). One can imagine no Chinese or Japanese painter who would similarly depict himself saluting nature as an equal. In a letter to a friend, Courbet commented on his discovery of the sea and added this thought, which reads like a caption to the painting: "O sea! Your voice is tremendous, but it will never succeed in drowning out the voice of Fame as it shouts my name to the whole world." Courbet was not the first immodest artist in history, but none had so brazenly portrayed his self-confidence before his "competition," before the challenge of making infinity tangible (Figs. 22, 409).

Courbet was one of the painters who influenced Monet to focus directly upon nature itself, rather than merely utilize landscape as a backdrop for human action or for purposes of moralizing. Courbet's life view was that of a materialist in the most positive and dignified sense of the word. No artist in history loved more deeply the physical substance of nature, its closed, secret places and its vast openness. These last two polarities in his art are beautifully demonstrated in his *Source of the Loue* (Fig. 437). From his oil pigments, using a brush and palette knife, Courbet wrested those properties which permitted re-creation of the material substances of water and rock. Beyond such technical accomplishment, moreover, Courbet's response to nature was meditative and not confined

437. GUSTAVE COURBET. *The Source of the Loue*. c. 1864. Oil on canvas, 3′3½″ × 4′4″. Albright-Knox Art Gallery, Buffalo.

to its surfaces, for in the grotto painting the deep cavities from which the river issues lead our thoughts toward contemplation of nature's invisible depths. The grandeur of the cave painting depends upon the absence of humans, which concentrates the drama on the weathered rock and the relentless action of the river. Courbet painted out of doors, directly from nature, and often in the space of a few hours. In subjects such as this grotto, he would first prepare his canvas with a dark color. To friends watching him paint such a subject, he once said: "It surprises you that my canvas is so dark. Nature without the sun is dark and obscure. I do as the sun does. I clarify the salient points and the picture is made."

**Nature and Artistic Order** The 17th-century French landscape artist Nicolas Poussin (1594–1665) regarded nature as a noble and orderly setting for the enactment of grandiose classical tragedies. Moreover, its mood is directly determined by the human drama enacted within it. The subject of *The Funeral of Phocion* (Pl. 53, p. 309) is drawn from Plutarch and concerns the Athenian general Phocion, unjustly executed by the state he had loyally served. At his request, Phocion's body was carried from Athens to his native city to be cremated, and his ashes were scattered on the earth. The solemnity of the return of Phocion's body is to be read in the mien of the litter bearers and in the gravity of the landscape itself. Basing his ideas on principles of Greek and Roman rhetoric and of music, Poussin conceived of painting in terms of "modes" by which one could interpret happy, calm, or sad events. To control the effect of his art, he did not allow his own emotions to influence the act of painting, which was to be governed only by a rational adherence to these modes. Nature and art were thus constrained by Poussin's intellect. He felt it to be the painter's task to impose his will on nature and art, to study carefully everything within the painting, to avoid the spontaneous and the trivial, and to make each stroke a controlled expression of his will. He believed, as did the philosopher René Descartes, that the faculty of reason could determine the true nature of physical order. Nature appears in Poussin's painting as an unopposed harmony, not unlike an aspect of a mechanistic universe. Nature's order was the model upon which Poussin based his painting, showing ancient Classical architecture juxtaposed with precisely formed trees and mountains. The calm stability of the landscape is further stressed and perfected in the walls, columns, and pediments of the city.

Much of the scene's tranquil atmosphere comes from the soft late-afternoon light falling over the landscape from the left. This lighting, which was partially a device to suggest that the event took place in the remote past, illuminates the critical passages of the story and creates successive light zones that gently alternate with soft shadows and lead the eye into depth. Poussin insisted that extreme values of light and dark be smoothly modulated by intermediate ones; thus he provided a measurable and logical transition from the darkened foreground to the most brilliantly illuminated area on the distant horizon. The dark foreground areas hold the viewer apart from the scene, in order to elicit a detached, sustained awareness of the action and the painting's well-thought-out structure. Furthermore, the painter avoided rough edges, jarring angles, or disturbing color combinations to effect an easy, graceful flow from one area to another. His colors were mostly dark browns, greens, and greys, with the strongest colors, the reds and whites, reserved for small areas in which they were essential to identifying the figures. The large trees at the right and left and the clouds were used as subtle coordinates of and containment for the action, providing within the picture frame a second, natural framework for the scene. In the right foreground are stone ruins which provide visual anchorage for that portion of the canvas; but these also serve to remind us that Poussin meticulously constructed his entire painting as if using building blocks, with each shape and shadow and tone having an unalterable position in the whole.

Poussin's definition of art was "an imitation made on a surface with lines and colors of everything that one sees under the sun. Its end is to please." His work did not truly embody this definition, however, for his painting is based on literature and is a *conceit,* or a conception of the mind, not a scene as directly encountered. He did not reveal colors as they actually appear under sunlight, and he favored drawing over color in the construction of form. His vision was highly selective, and his painting was strongly addressed to the intellect.

Poussin's definition of art was more closely realized in the 19th century by Paul Cézanne (1839–1906), who admired the older painter. This admiration was directed principally toward Poussin's logical method, his systematic means of setting down his thoughts. But unlike Poussin, Cézanne was firmly committed to reproducing strong sensations of color, light, and air, the lessons he had learned from the Impressionists. He felt that the old masters had "replaced reality by imagination and the other abstractions that accompany it. . . . They created pictures, we are attempting a piece of nature." In *Mont Sainte-Victoire* (Pl. 54, p. 309), Cézanne painted what he saw; he emphasized consistently the lines and colors of surfaces; and he directed the whole toward delighting the senses. He made no demands upon literary erudition. By the 1880s, he had given up somber, figural dramas in landscape settings, and the mountain became a personal obsession and the climactic focus of his paintings from nature. Meyer Schapiro defines this attraction on the basis that the mountain externalized Cézanne's "striving and exaltation and desire for repose." No single form, but an idealized nature as a whole, may have held somewhat the same appeal for Poussin. The mountain in the *Funeral of Phocion* was for Poussin, as for the Chinese, the dwelling place of public gods.

Cézanne's painting exacted a greater struggle than that of Poussin in putting nature in order, for Cézanne's harmony involves a difficult and arduous balancing of unlike forces—stability and instability, energy and repose (Pl. 63, p. 347; Fig. 486). Poussin made careful plans for a painting and could foretell precisely how it would look upon completion. Each shape such as a tree or a building was probably carried to its completed state before the overall composition was finished. Cézanne's method was more empirical and relied upon momentary intuitions and judgments. He repeatedly worked over the whole painting and would alter what he had already painted or what he saw if it did not fit into the total aesthetic organization. Unlike a composition of Poussin, Cézanne's landscape cannot be separated into definable parts or tidy zones. Cézanne's building blocks are simultaneously color and drawing, and these means constantly fuse, overlap, or grow out of each other. In the fields, for example, he used a line segment to give firmness to a section that would otherwise have been spatially ambiguous or without some sense of direction. He was at once intentionally concerned with presenting a stabilized view of nature in depth and with achieving a coherent surface pattern. The left-hand area between the pine trunk and the frame shows this concern. In isolation, lacking any specific object reference, the section appears to be a succession of colored patches that alternately move forward and backward, but with consistent reference to the surface. Put back into its original context, it falls in place and contributes to the valley's recession. Cézanne coordinated the foreground shape of the tree trunk in its edge, color, and axis with the adjacent areas. Just above the horizon line, he painted sections of pine branches whose agitation heightens the mountain's massive immobility. Appropriately, the mountain is the only object seen in its entirety. The branches also bring the viewer's eye back to the foreground plane.

Unlike Poussin, Cézanne tolerated sharp juxtapositions of warm and cool colors, saturate and dilute tones, such as those found in the area of the sky. The directions of Cézanne's brushstrokes are in actuality as essential to the painting's structure as they are to the imitation of textures in the landscape. They indicate the direction in which a solid moves into depth (as in the foothills of the mountain which vitalize the large area of the sky) and accelerate or decelerate the eye's movement through the painting (as in the zone of the field). Cézanne sought an equilibrium between emotional and intellectual response to nature and painting, but never did the modern master domesticate the natural world to the extent that Poussin did. Cézanne preserved the irregularity, energy and contradictions he saw, wishing to claim by his brush nature in all its fullness. As he expressed it, "The landscape thinks itself in me and I am its conscience."

**The Dutch Landscape** During the 17th century, the great period of Dutch landscape, artists of that region delighted in expressing hearty enjoyment in the external appearance of earthly matter, instead of evoking nostalgia for the ideal past depicted by their French and Italian contemporaries. While figures were usually present, to establish the scale of the scene and to suggest the harmonious relationship of man and nature, there was no storytelling. Nature did not serve merely as a backdrop for significant human events, nor was topographical exactness usually a requirement. Dutch artists were now free from older formulas for composition and color. They would make drawings directly from a motif and complete their paintings in the studio; they reserved the right to synthesize and rearrange their notes and experiences in a selective naturalism.

438. JACOB VAN RUISDAEL. *Wheatfields*. c. 1650. Oil on canvas, 3′4½″ × 4′3½″. Metropolitan Museum of Art, New York (bequest of Benjamin Altman, 1914).

Another innovation of these Dutch artists was the discovery of and fondness for uncultivated nature, often juxtaposed with evidences of man's work with the earth. This synthesizing and selectivity, coupled with the modest formats of their commercially viable easel paintings, continued the process of miniaturization, by which the artist and his audience could cope with a natural world greater than themselves. In the landscapes of the 17th-century painter Jacob van Ruisdael (1628–82) and those of the 19th-century painter Vincent van Gogh, we can readily perceive the dramatic and poignant enactment of the miniaturizing purpose of art.

In Ruisdael's *Wheatfields* (Fig. 438), the only importance assigned to literary subject matter and the human figure is the contrast between their insignificance and the immensity of nature. The landscape is not conceived as the projection of the moods of men within the painting; indeed, nature's indifference to man seems somehow a comfort to the Dutch painter. He shows wheatfields, human attempts to cultivate nature, but he accentuates the wild scrub along the road, the eccentric positions of the trees, and the shifting shapes of enormous cloud formations that defy human alteration. The rough silhouette and tangled mass of vegetation are characteristic of Ruisdael's style.

In *Wheatfields* the road is brought almost to the viewer's feet to lead him more directly and quickly into the landscape. Poussin avoided the emotional involvement that Ruisdael felt was so essential. By alternating zones of shadow and golden light, Ruisdael controlled the pace at which the eye moves through the landscape. The forward roll of the clouds seems to counter the inward thrust of the earth, so that the composition assumes a foreshortened wedge shape in depth as opposed to Poussin's arrangement of successive zones largely parallel to the picture surface.

Ruisdael gave to his painting a vivid sense of nature in movement—its processes of growth and decay, the shifting light as the sky changes, and the violent force of winds that propel the clouds and contort the trees. He was stirred by the wars within nature herself, between the natural forces of life and death and man's ultimately feeble attempts to conquer land and sea. A solitary individual himself, Ruisdael sought in his painting to come to terms with a great impersonal, indomitable force outside himself.

The painting of nature was an even more deeply personal instrument for Vincent van Gogh—so much so that his *Landscape with Sun Rising* (Fig. 439) may belie the painter's stated intent. Writing from St-Remy to the painter Emile Bernard in December, 1889, Van Gogh described a painting that is probably the one reproduced here:

> The sun rising over a field of young wheat, lines fleeting away, furrows running up high into the picture toward a wall and a row of lilac hills. The field is violet and yellow green. The white sun is surrounded by a great yellow halo. Here . . . I have tried to express calmness, a great peace.

What a shock the last sentence is! The viewer is pulled immediately and violently by the arrowlike flight of the fields into the painting's depth, but not to another and prime focus of the scene—the sun. Compounding the painting's tension between perspective and spiritual focus is the leftward tilt of the land, which also competes with the pull of the sun. The sun is the only stable form in the entire work, but it is placed at the right and the very top of the painting, the most difficult point of access. No previous landscape painter had looked at and painted the actual sun so directly. This act of Van Gogh was as startling as that of the medieval artist at Daphnē (Fig. 71) who painted the powerful face of his god. For Van Gogh it was from the sun's force and brilliance that nature, art, and he himself gathered vigor and life. In his last years, the basis of this being lay in attaching himself, through the hard work of his art, to man, the soil, and the heavens. He wrote of "plowing on my canvases as they do in their fields." The striving for impossible goals of perfection and possession and the accompanying purge of great feeling perhaps explain why Van Gogh could write of the finished work as being calm.

Van Gogh wrote to his brother and friends that his paintings should be framed in white and hung in white kitchens or against plain backgrounds. This was both a sign of his humility and a realization of how his paintings could be shown to best advantage. They can be seen in the strongest sunlight, unlike those of Ruisdael or Poussin, and still surpass the intensity of the actual scene. Van Gogh wanted not simply an equivalent of nature but a more intense re-creation of it. He wanted his drawing and color to smell of the earth. The fields that Van Gogh painted are in a sense disappointing. He made them exciting by coding their forms in his strong pure tones, boldly set against one another in a torrent of staccato touches. We are always conscious of the life of the painter's hand, its obvious power, trained responsiveness, yet inexplicable individuality (Pl. 58, p. 328; Fig. 426). Van Gogh wrote, "What a queer thing *touch* is, the stroke of the brush." Perhaps his wonder and uncertainty stemmed from his use of the brush as a direct and spontaneous extension of his internal state of being. He used the touch to decipher the inner character of what he felt was the true soil of Provence. Wherever he went, Van Gogh absorbed through painting the sights and effects that alone could give him peace.

**Nature Seen Close Up** A common theme from nature is the close-up of a small cluster of plant life in which the artist searches for the individuality of the part. With botanical accuracy, the German artist Albrecht Dürer (1471–1528) in his *Study of Plants* (Fig. 440) depicted the flora in a tiny area of marsh. This was more than a purely secular scientific investigation, for in his natural subject Dürer sought the minute and multiform evidence of God's creativity. Dürer's quantitative surface reproduction would have been anathema to Chinese and Japanese artists, who felt that optical fidelity concealed rather than disclosed the essential quality of nature. Dürer, however, found challenge and meaning in the multitude of shapes, colors, textures, and in the precise proportions and inclinations which described each plant form. The clustered natural forms demanded different and less strict compositional solutions than his large religious and figural paintings had involved. He did not impose an obvious stilted ordering on the plants but carefully preserved the appearance of a casual, overlapping disarray, while unobtrusively contrasting and harmonizing the stalks and leaves with one another. In his own words, "Art, however, is in nature, and whoever can draw it out, he possesses it."

To enact his fantasies of nature in such paintings as *Botanical Theater* (Pl. 55, p. 310), the modern Swiss painter Paul Klee (1879–1940) staked out a small uncontested territory of

*left :* 439. VINCENT VAN GOGH. *Landscape with Sun Rising.* 1889. Oil on canvas, 28 × 35⅝″. Collection Mrs. Robert Oppenheimer, Princeton, N.J.

*below :* 440. ALBRECHT DÜRER. *Study of Plants.* 1503. Drawing, 16⅛ × 12⅜″. Albertina, Vienna.

his own, one inaccessible to such optical aids as Dürer's perspective or the modern microscope. Klee searched for a totally new and poetical approach to lend familiarity to obscure and minute aspects of nature, such as the intimacy of the night world of plants. His viewpoint is not that of a detached scientific investigator, but a conception that evolves in the mind when the eyes are closed. Through his meditations, Klee's art became a fusion of the interior and exterior world in a way never previously seen in Oriental or Western art. His oil and watercolor *Botanical Theater* seems disarmingly familiar at first. There is no horizon line or sky, no definable light source or measurable distance between the viewer and the plants. No means exist to compare the space and the scale of the painting with oneself or a real landscape. There is no botanical guide to catalogue the plant life. Klee's world seemingly has its own laws of size, light, growth, and species. He believed in the interrelation of all phenomena, and his objects have a dual character, being part vegetal and part animal. The pungent color that floats over and permeates the shapes, and the prickly textures in and around the plants recall experiences of sight, smell, taste, hearing, and touch. It is as if Klee were able to project himself into the subhuman night world and perceive the scene through the senses of its occupants.

Klee's drawing method was to some degree automatic; he let his pen and brush explore the surface as if guided by impulse and the feel of the materials. The creative act sprang from inner watchfulness and listening and from an uninhibited response to the free associations induced by imagination as he worked. When a spiral was begun, for instance, it might emerge as a snail, or two leaves might change into a pair of eyes:

> Art is a simile of the Creation. . . . Today we reveal the reality that is behind visible things, thus expressing the belief that the visible world is merely an isolated case in relation to the universe and that there are many more other, latent realities.

Klee felt that his art would comfort his viewers by reminding them that the mind itself is not confined to earthly potentialities.

Klee strove for union with the "heart of creation . . . in the womb of nature . . . where the secret key to the universe is safely kept." His paintings are small—done, one might say, within the radius of the artist's elbow and the action of his wrist. This modest size encourages intimate and prolonged discourse between viewer and subject. The miniature scale was essential to Klee's style, for, in his words, "style is the ego."

The art of Paul Klee may be termed *imagistic,* for it took form from his imagination, and the root of the word *imagination* is "image." Imagistic painting gives form to that which is unattainable for the outward senses. Klee felt that the artist's moral imperative was to search his inner being for inspiration and "to render visible those impressions and conceptions not in themselves visible."

## NATURE AND ABSTRACT PAINTING

At the beginning of this century the artist's decision to move away from illusionistic painting of nature frequently entailed important concerns and commitments that extended beyond the world of the studio. The implications of the way a man paints reach into his psychological and emotional makeup, and style is part of the artist's world view ("style is the ego"). Furthermore, the artist will often preserve in his nonillusionistic work a certain residue of his earlier imagery based upon his perception of nature. This can be seen by juxtaposing works from both styles accomplished by a single painter.

As a young painter in Holland at the turn of the century, Piet Mondrian (1872–1944) was inclined toward passive depictions of the Dutch countryside without action or figures. As in his painting of a windmill (Fig. 441), Mondrian searched for solitary prospects, small segments within the vast panorama of nature that reflected an inherently stable and tranquil world. Mondrian selected a viewpoint that allowed him to align principal axes within the scene, those of the bridge and windmill, with those of the picture frame, thus permitting stable pictorial construction. The reflections in the placid water echo and reinforce the directions of the mill and bridge, and a grid pattern is recurrent. Many brush strokes, such as those at the left and in the pond, are unrelated to literal observation of nature but serve to strengthen the design armature of the whole composition. The artist's viewpoint, with the large foreground area given over to the reflecting surface of the water, has contributed to a perceptible flattening of the space, which, coupled with the pronounced use of repeated motifs, gives a strong surface rhythm and pattern to the painting. During Mondrian's subsequent growth as an artist, as well as in his writings, his obsession with the possibilities of rhythm became patent. Rhythm was a critical link by which Mondrian hoped to unite "the individual with the universal."

Hundreds of paintings intervened in Mondrian's career from *Mill by the Water* to *Composition in White, Black, and Red* (Fig. 442) of 1936, but in mood and design the latter work is a condensation of the former. Though it gave up representation of the specific in nature, his later art preserved the ideal of manifesting the underlying harmonious order of nature in its broadest sense. The structural components of the later work, straight lines meeting in a rectilinear grid, were present in the mill painting. Junctures now become crisp right angles, and all the rectangular shapes and pure colors lie completely at the surface. Irregularities traceable to the hand of the artist are absent. Crucial to the continuity of form and meaning between the two paintings is the relation of the asymmetrical composi-

*above:* 441. Piet Mondrian. *Mill by the Water.* c. 1905. Oil on canvas, mounted on cardboard; $11^7/_8 \times 15''$. Museum of Modern Art, New York (purchase).

*right:* 442. Piet Mondrian. *Composition in White, Black, and Red.* 1936. Oil on canvas, $40^1/_4 \times 41''$. Museum of Modern Art, New York (gift of the Advisory Committee).

*left:* 443. WASSILY KANDINSKY. *Landscape with Factory Chimney.* 1910. Oil on canvas, 26 × 31½″. Solomon R. Guggenheim Museum, New York.

tion to the frame, treated as if what is within its borders were an incomplete, fragmented view of a greater order. The irregular quadrature of the later painting is controlled not by directly perceived shapes in nature but by the artist's intuition of balance between black lines and small red and large white rectangles. Mondrian's compositional reflexes had been conditioned by his paintings of land, sky, water, and trees. The painting's title accurately describes what is *on,* not *in,* the picture plane. Mondrian believed this type of painting was important for humanity because it presented in purified artistic form a model of equilibrium, a condition imperfectly experienced in nature but eternally sought in all forms of life. Seeing as the painter's task the expression of a vision of reality, Mondrian desired the purest expression of life through the freeing of color, rhythm, and form from their particularized appearance in nature. In the varying dimensions of the rectangular areas, with their impeccable arrangement and perfect balance of tension, he felt such artistic liberation could be accomplished: "Space becomes white, black or gray; form becomes red, blue or yellow."

Another pioneer of abstraction after 1900 was the Russian painter Wassily Kandinsky (1866–1944). His early art shows a strong attraction to the countryside. By 1910, when he painted his *Landscape with Factory Chimney* (Fig. 443), Kandinsky had proceeded to a point where it was increasingly difficult to match his painting with an actual landscape. He had reduced distinctions between land and sky, trees, hills, and buildings, between space near and far; his paintings coalesced into strong arbitrary color harmonies that were less and less governed by perceived sequences of hues. Kandinsky did not seek a stable viewpoint or a geometrically based order, but instead he presented a turbulent, heaving earth. Against the broad, sweeping curves of the hills are ragged and diffuse color patches, which produce intense color sensations and contribute greatly to the excited mood of the whole. Unlike the Impressionist painters, Kandinsky did not paint the mood induced in him by contact with nature, but rather superimposed upon the landscape an already existing emotional state. Kandinsky's predilection was for wild, hilly terrain laced with precipitous diagonals—the kind of landscape that might provide an adequate carrier of his feelings. These qualities flood over into a later painting, *Picture with White Edge, No. 173* (Pl. 56, p. 310). Though not intended as a landscape, it shows that his mind and the movements of his hand could not expunge earlier experience, for within this seeming abstraction there remains a pictorial sign language of wavelike hills and jagged peaks and trees.

Taken as a whole, *White Edge* has an apocalyptic mood. Dating from the eve of World War I, it may have been indirectly inspired by Kandinsky's response to the tense atmosphere in Germany, where he was working. Its brilliant color evokes a sensation of clashing sounds. Kandinsky believed that sensory experiences overlapped and that each color had its equivalence in sound, so that painting became an orchestration of elements having inherent expressive associations with which the painter could strike chords in the soul of the viewer. Framing the dense and saturate color mass in the painting is an irregular white edge, a color that Kandinsky wrote of as a "pregnant stillness." Like Frenhofer, Balzac's fictional painter (see p. 394), Kandinsky sought a perfect fusion of drawing and color and achieved an exquisite but nonetheless controlled chaos.

Kandinsky's departure from illusionism was gradual, hesitant, backsliding, and rarely complete in the years between 1910 and 1914. His writings show a deep awareness of and misgivings about a possible important loss to art in abandoning nature and the familiar as a frame of reference. What impelled him in the direction of *White Edge* was a growing distrust of modern materialism, science, organized religion, and illusionistic art—all of which he came to regard as impediments to free expression of the human spirit. Inner freedom was for Kandinsky the sole criterion for both ethics and aesthetics. The creative process ideally meant a suspension of consciousness and a purely spontaneous and intuitive activity, though Kandinsky did in fact impose some critical judgment:

> I have painted rather subconsciously in a state of strong inner tension. So intensely do I feel the necessity of some of the forms that I remember having given loud-voiced directions to myself, for instance, "But the corners must be heavy." The observer must learn to look at the picture as a graphic representation of a mood and not as a representation of objects.

444. Jackson Pollock. *Seascape*. 1934. Oil on canvas, 12 × 16″. Collection Lee Krasner Pollock, New York.

*Seascape* (Fig. 444), an early painting by the American Jackson Pollock (1912–56), projects the moody image of a storm-tossed boat seen against a disquieting sky. The canvas is filled with dense pigmentation, rough shapes, and strong movement. The subject was appropriate to the strong and aggressive temperament of the young artist. From his first works, Pollock asserted his rebellious nature and the need to impose his will and muscular energies on both nature and art. The small format and the limits of the canvas are strained to contain the violence of his painting.

Created sixteen years and hundreds of paintings and drawings later, Pollock's *Autumn Rhythm* (Pl. 57, p. 327) continues, refines, adds to, and subtracts from the seminal qualities of *Seascape*. From the scale of the conventional easel painting Pollock had gravitated toward what might be called a "portable canvas mural," a huge work roughly 8½ × 17 feet. In 1947 the painter wrote:

> I prefer to tack the unstretched canvas to the hard wall or floor. I need the resistance of a hard surface. On the floor I am more at ease. I feel nearer, more a part of the painting, since this way I can walk around it, work from the four sides and literally be *in* the painting.

Vermeer's painting of the artist in his studio (Pl. 34, p. 182) demonstrated a system ideal for wrist painting; the artist's subject was reduced to the scale of a traditional easel format. In Pollock's work of the late 1940s, scale was not strongly predetermined but resulted from the interaction of the artist and his evolving image, which established the size of the painting (Fig. 4). Further, Pollock was impelled to arm as well as wrist painting; the rhythm and energy of his whole body found outlet in the creative act. For both technical and aesthetic reasons, he gave up oil for enamel paints. In this way, he was freed of oil paint's historical associations, and the more viscous enamel medium also permitted a continuous spinning out of the linear fabric—the heart of Pollock's mature style. The dripping and spattering of paint as Pollock walked around and over the horizontal canvas was a technique thoughtfully and deliberately arrived at as the inevitable means by which to impose his visions and feelings on the painting's surface and the viewer's eye.

Accidents and chance were encouraged, but controlled and corrected. "I *can* control the flow of paint: there is no accident, just as there is no beginning and no end." The automatism of Kandinsky continued in Pollock's colored drawing, but with less disposition to repeat obvious landscape and object forms. Pollock literally wished to be *in* his painting, more deeply involved in its creation than had ever been physically or psychologically possible.

> When I am *in* my painting, I'm not aware of what I'm doing. It is only after a sort of "get acquainted" period that I see what I have been about. I have no fears about making changes, destroying the image, etc., because the painting has a life of its own. . . . It is only when I lose contact with the painting that the result is a mess. Otherwise it is pure harmony, an easy give and take, and the painting comes out well. . . . I want to express my feelings rather than illustrate them.

The expression rather than illustration of feeling is therefore the content-form of *Autumn Rhythm* (Pl. 57).

Just as Pollock felt that he must not lose contact with the painting, so must the beholder give it full and sustained attention, and not look for an image of leaves and clouds. Seen in its own terms, *Autumn Rhythm* constitutes a new, physically impenetrable, and unstable environment. Its tangled web or netlike configuration possesses inconstant densities, suspended in ambiguous relation to the surface. The eye is permitted to look through the web as if into a tinted void that is given atmospheric properties by the spattered color. This web is woven by the intimate calligraphy of the artist into a composition punctuated by nodes of coagulated color, congested tangles, and open and airy passages. Like a graph, the surface is a record of the artist's hand responding to his internal state as he works over the entire surface, its fluid lines serving as traces of impulse and decision. There is neither beginning nor end, but at the four sides the configuration tends to turn back in upon itself as if signifying the limits of the nucleus. The parts and their relation are unpredictable, and no segment is duplicated. The key to the color harmony of the painting is the predominance of black, against which are browns and whites in lesser quantity, and the pervasive color of the canvas itself, which has become a positive element in the artist's conception. The title was supplied after the painting was done, perhaps when Pollock found some correspondence of qualities or mood between the two. He placed his finished works outside his barn in a field, not to appraise their similarity to nature but to decide whether they held their own as autonomous objects.

## SCULPTURE AND NATURE

Until the 20th century, sculptural themes from nature were usually decorative foliate motifs for architecture, synoptic landscape backgrounds for figures in reliefs, or personifications of the seasons, fertility, and the like. In this century, a number of circumstances have contrived to focus the minds and talents of many important sculptors upon nature as a source for metaphorical sculpture, upon images that allude to animal life or processes in nature. The dominance of the illusionistic interpretation of the human figure in sculpture, which had obtained for milleniums, was weakened early in this century. Constantin Brancusi (Figs. 445, 488, 501), and Jean Arp (Fig. 446), followed in time by David Smith (Fig. 447) and Alexander Calder (Fig. 448), to name but a few, moved their imagery into new areas that drastically altered the form and very substance of sculpture. Since the 1960s, a number of artists have involved themselves with nature in such a literal way as to have transcended sculpture or traditional art forms; they have nonetheless continued that essential purpose of art which enables man to come to terms with his environment.

*Bird in Space* (Fig. 445) by Constantin Brancusi (1876–1957) resulted from a gradual evolution in his thinking and art which had begun with an heraldic image of a standing and speaking mythological bird. In a series of images, of which perhaps the most crucial is illustrated here, Brancusi purified his form to include only what he considered the essential or absolute expression—and hence reality—of flight. By eradicating specific reference to any particular species and by transforming the standing image to one of soaring elevation, Brancusi evolved a private metaphor that fulfilled what Sidney Geist has termed "an image of spiritual flight, at once the nocturnal and euphoric flight of erotic dream and the flight of the soul in its urge to transcendence."

Brancusi provided the sculptors of this century with a model for an art of simple and pure forms, a work that was indivisible, consisting of really only one shape having a unified surface. Traditional criteria of beauty which depended upon the harmonious relationship of parts to each other and to the whole were no longer applicable. The hard purity of the surface reflects its surroundings and the light with the result that, when strongly illuminated by the sun, the form seems to dematerialize through its radiance. Paradoxically, the form of the sculpture depended upon the artist's polishing it by hand, but the finished work denies all evidence of sculptural process, thereby permitting the viewer total focus on the image of mystical ascension. This new self-sufficiency of form is enhanced by the absence of an illusionistic base or adherence to a wall for structural support. Brancusi designed his own supports for his sculptures, looking upon them as integral to the works.

Although the beginnings of his art and his feelings about the self-sufficiency of sculptural form coincide with those of Brancusi, the sculpture of Jean Arp (1887–1966) has a quality of elasticity, a pulse and softness that give it an identity and appropriateness for interpreting themes from nature. Arp's *Growth* (Fig. 446) is but a single example of a lifetime of work dealing with the unseen forces and processes shaping life. In this small bronze sculpture, Arp has evoked the internal fluid pressure of life's force in the soft serpentine ascension of the form and its multiple protuberances. Although the theme is generic, the form suggests associations with various plant and human shapes. Movement is achieved through the flowing surface continuity, the absence of clearly delimited parts, and the smooth finish that permits unobstructed play of light and shadow. The sculpture seems to of pulsate, enlarge, and strive

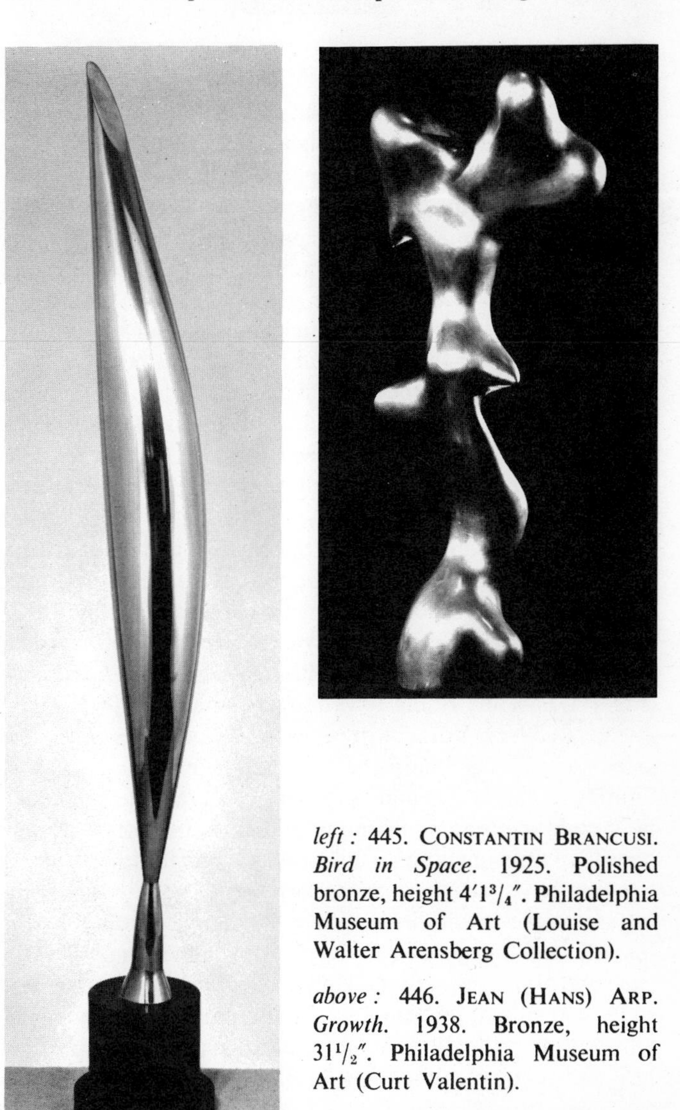

*left :* 445. CONSTANTIN BRANCUSI. *Bird in Space*. 1925. Polished bronze, height 4′1¾″. Philadelphia Museum of Art (Louise and Walter Arensberg Collection).

*above :* 446. JEAN (HANS) ARP. *Growth*. 1938. Bronze, height 31½″. Philadelphia Museum of Art (Curt Valentin).

*left* : 447. DAVID SMITH. *Hudson River Landscape*. 1951. Steel, length 6′3″. Whitney Museum of American Art, New York.

*below* : 448. ALEXANDER CALDER. *Lobster Trap and Fish Tail*. 1939. Mobile, steel wire and sheet aluminium; height 8′6″, diameter 9′6″. Museum of Modern Art, New York (gift of the Advisory Committee).

upward. Arp has treated the lower area in a way that suggests it continues below the level of sight into a root.

To his abstract sculpture Arp gave a sensuality and grace equal to that bestowed upon the antique figures of Apollo (Figs. 49–53). Like Klee's, Arp's purpose was to show the importance and relatedness of common, recurrent phenomena in nature and to recompense for a human vanity that viewed the world as man-centered. A witness to wars and revolutions, Arp wanted an art that countered both human bestiality and society's adulation of the rational and technological. In affirming the peaceful, the handmade, and the irrationally conceived, he longed for man's return to a more simple existence and "an elemental, natural healthy art" that would release men from material cares and self-consciousness. "Works of art should remain as anonymous in the great workshop of nature as the clouds, the mountains, the seas, the animals and man himself. Yes! Man should once again become part of nature."

The American sculptor David Smith (1906–65) forged, twisted, and welded steel into his *Hudson River Landscape* (Fig. 447). While riding on a train back and forth between Albany and New York, he drew several ink sketches of impressions the moving landscape made upon him. In actuality, Smith's sculpture has more projection and recession than can be seen in a photograph; nonetheless, it possesses a unique quality of drawing in space, and its steel configuration appears to have been lifted from a flat surface. Smith was not representing a specific locale or particular landscape feature, for he himself said this could be any landscape; but he found the flow, contrast, and rhythm of the Hudson River Valley appropriate to his way of making sculpture. The sculptor liked to view his work outdoors, with the countryside seen through it, particularly in winter, with the snow forming additional and complementary shapes on the twisted steel form. The use of steel was not anachronistic, for its tensile properties made possible the personal style that conveys Smith's private vision of nature.

The *mobiles,* or moving constructions, of Alexander Calder (b.1898) involve the artist and sculpture with nature in a revolutionary new way. Calder was the first sculptor to build an art upon the premise that a construction could move. In the early thirties he experimented with a variety of mechanical power sources, but abandoned them as being too restricted in rhythms and too difficult to integrate with the entire sculpture. He had found a simpler, more appropriate power source: nature with its wind and gravity. Calder's mobiles such as *Lobster Trap and Fish Tail* (Fig. 448) are based mechanically upon a counterbalance of linear elements, which may be suspended from a ceiling or poised upon a fixed point. His colored, flat metal shapes suspended from catenary wire arms have an ancestor in the pure bright colors and biomorphic contours seen in the painting of Mondrian (Fig. 442) and Miró (Pl. 82, p. 414). Calder was largely responsible for bringing color back to sculpture. Like Arp, he enjoys the ambivalent references of his shapes and configurations, which can be viewed as abstractions or as processes in nature such as the movement of leaves, snow, or clouds. Calder's genius lay in making sculpture which, either in movement or at rest, resulted in a harmony of satisfying configurations and their shadowed reflections. The use of flat forms and movement contributed to the larger process of sculpture's gradual dematerialization in this century. In his *stabiles,* motionless sheet metal constructions, such as *Teodelapio* (Fig. 449), Calder developed a form of sculpture without conventional mass or volume. From small models, he supervises metal workers in iron foundries, who enlarge his works to considerable size, employing welding and riveting to stabilize and join the big metal plates. The self-supporting stabiles, like *Teodelapio,* set up in a street in Spoleto, Italy, show Calder's great judgment in finding motifs that hold their scale (that are not too big or too small for the sculptural idea) and in selecting colors that are right for the forms.

**Snelson's "Atom"** During the last ten years or so, there have been many artists whose work has refuted the idea that art and science are mutually exclusive. One of the most gifted is Kenneth Snelson (b. 1927), an artist whose scientific background has long interested him in the relationship between tension and compression in discontinuous structures. Unlike Arp, David Smith, or Calder, Snelson does not make metaphorical sculpture, the understanding of which depends upon recognition of clues such as fragments of familiar shapes in nature. His sculpture *Atom* (Fig. 450) resulted from the desire to create in art an analogy with other kinds of structures, notably those that "stay together because there are forces involved in them." Sculpture for Snelson means creating things in space, and these "things" may derive from what is invisible to the naked eye. After reviewing the theories of scientists on atomic structure, Snelson came to the conclusion that their picture of the atom was "garbled" and "inconsistent" from one field of science to the next. He saw these differences as stemming from *aesthetic* judgments as well as from "convenience" on the part of scientists. Snelson feels that his sculpture gives a fairly consistent picture or reasonable model of an atom. It is based on the structure of the element and on the way he imagines electrons in motion, their orbits occupying a spherical field around the atomic nucleus. "What I am describing is the spatial and structural meaning of what are called electron shells. . . . My belief is that the electron in motion is the basic element of space occupancy. . . . This model shows how electrons can occupy a shell simultaneously without interfering with each other." Snelson has relied upon technology to give him the material—steel—and the means to depict a "frozen statement of an orbit." Unlike a scientific model, Snelson's does not give a scientist more satisfactory statistical data than he had; rather the artist has drawn upon the invisible in nature to obtain ideas for sculptural forms which satisfy his artist-scientist desire for knowledge and beauty.

*below :* 449. ALEXANDER CALDER. *Teodelapio.* 1962. Height, 60′. Spoleto, Italy.

*right :* 450. KENNETH SNELSON. *Atom.* 1964. Stainless steel, 27 × 12 × 12″. Courtesy Dwan Gallery , New York.

**Earth Works** A number of contemporary artists during the last few years have become physically rather than figuratively involved with nature. While their incentives vary with their personalities, they have in common a desire to escape the "art system" and to avoid what they feel is the commercial debasement of art; they prefer instead a direct intervention in nature with results that provide artistic rather than monetary satisfaction. For these artists "art system" has meant the creation in a studio of durable aesthetic objects to be exhibited for sale in galleries, to be reviewed by critics, and ultimately to be hung in museums or private collections. To many artists this is another form of business speculation, like stocks and bonds or grain futures. Artists such as Robert Smithson, Michael Heizer, Dennis Oppenheim, and Hans Haacke are interested in expanding or changing the existing physical limits of art—canvas, picture stretchers, and studio and gallery walls—and involving themselves in less permanent, intangible, and commercially nonnegotiable enterprises. Their works, unclassifiable as objects in the sense of paintings or sculptures, most closely approach landscape architecture and often demand considerable physical as well as mental effort. Their conscious aim has been to deflate the "myth" of mystery, beauty, quality, genius, and virtuoso handling, which they feel have been propagated by art dealers and critics to shore up the market price of paintings and sculptures.

They have exchanged the studio for a place or site in nature—a wheat field or meadow, quarry or land-fill area, desert or ocean floor. They have replaced the conventional artist's tools—brush, chisel, and welding torch—with the pick and shovel, lawn mower and harvesting machines, rental equipment such as bulldozers, and aqua lungs, all of which belong to systems of construction, farming, and exploration. Finally, they have ignored the traditional artist's materials—oil pigment, stone, and bronze—which, though they derive from nature, are processed or refined by the time the modern artist uses them. Instead these workers of the earth are putting themselves directly in contact with the raw materials of nature itself, utilizing ecological systems as others have modeled clay. They are not landscape architects, who satisfy the pretentious

*above:* 451. ROBERT SMITHSON. *A Non-Site* (Franklin, N.J.). 1968. Aerial map. Courtesy Dwan Gallery, New York.

*right:* 452. ROBERT SMITHSON. *A Non-Site* (Franklin, N.J.). 1968. Beige-painted wood bins filled with rocks; length 9′2″. Courtesy Dwan Gallery, New York.

tastes of wealthy clients, nor do they resemble ancient artists who built earth mounds for religious and communal purposes. And they have no intentions of symbolizing, therein linking their thought with the widespread literalism of American art of the 1960s. They seek instead to intervene in nature only temporarily and for no further purpose than the enactment of their own ideas of art. It would appear that this attitude interrupts, if it does not conclude, the age-old purpose of miniaturization in art.

Such art has been variously called *earth work, ecological art,* and *abstract geology*. It has found advocates in those who feel that art should belong to everyman, rather than just to the rich, and who wish to be more a part of their natural environment by conceiving and executing projects that work within the systems of nature. Implicit in these projects is their ultimate disintegration or reintegration with the earth. Like man himself, all that will remain are photographic records, which may or may not be exhibited and sold. The aim of earth workers has not generally been to focus upon the neglected beauty of nature, nor to make us examine a dry riverbed or slag heap with appreciative eyes. Sites may be chosen to stress wild disorder, brutal ruptures, or placidity and are often selected at random or with aesthetic indifference.

The art of Robert Smithson (b. 1928), who pioneered this type of work in 1966–67, is a "system" devised to cope with "a bleached and fractured world [that] surrounds the artist. To organize this mess of corrosion into patterns, grids and subdivisions is an aesthetic process . . . that has been scarcely touched." The earth is a "jumbled museum" which Smithson explores and reorganizes through the strategy of what he terms his *non-sites*: maps, aerial photographs, and boxed earth samples of an area, such as that near Franklin, New Jersey (Figs. 451, 452). All three components are similarly shaped and serialized according to a private "system" and give us three different perspectives of the original site. The artist has described being "engulfed by nature," and he has tried "to give evidence of this experience through a limited revision of the original unbounded state." This has meant gathering into his metal bins samples of rocks or fragments of raw matter, which for him represent the unbounded "physical abyss" one can experience in nature.

Whereas Smithson was able to exhibit his non-sites in a gallery, Michael Heizer (b. 1944) could show only photographs of the 30-ton granite mass in a cement depression that he made in Silver Springs, Nevada, in August of 1969 (Fig. 453). About his work Heizer wrote:

> The position of art as a malleable barter-exchange item falters as the cumulative economic structure gluts. The museums and collections are stuffed, the floors are sagging, but the real space still exists. This dry lake was leased indefinitely, with the option to buy. What is sold here is land, not art. Potentially, the most malleable aspect of this work is the deed to the property.

Heizer has photographed his work at successive periods, as the sides of the depression have crumbled, as it has filled with water and silt, and as it has moved toward indistinguishability from the area around it. Heizer does not see his work as being competitive with nature, for "man will never create anything really large in relation to the world."

Another young earth worker, Dennis Oppenheim (b. 1938), takes a different view: "Artists have always been frightened by things like the Grand Canyon. These forms may be impossible to duplicate or rival, but they are important. Now we have to take them on in their own ballpark." Oppenheim's projects involve intervention in the topographical configuration of sites that he selects; he alters, by using metal chips or a harvesting machine, the actual contours of a swamp or wheat field. He

453. MICHAEL HEIZER. *One-third of Displaced-Replaced Mass* (Silver Springs, Nev.). 1969. Thirty tons of granite mass in cement depression with rainwater fill; mass 15 × 5½ × 4½′, depression 23 × 6 × 5′. Sponsored by Mr. and Mrs. Robert C. Scull, New York.

454. DENNIS OPPENHEIM. *Directed Seeding* (Part I). April, 1969. Fensterwolde, Holland. Courtesy the artist.

has, for example, contracted with farmers in Pennsylvania and Holland to harvest their fields in patterns contrary to normal agricultural procedure. In Holland (Fig. 454) this produced series of undulating contours that created, when seen from the air, the illusion of a terraced rather than flat site. Oppenheim has been interested in the system which seeds, harvests, bales, and sells the wheat and considers these separate stages as art. He sells bags of the Dutch wheat harvested under his supervision. This view presumes that art does not reside in an object, but can be found in all the components of a system which the artist becomes aware of and only slightly alters to suit his purpose.

**The Articulation of Nature** Today's artists are not totally remote from the past. Consider a painting of the earth by Hieronymus Bosch (Fig. 455) in comparison with *Condensation Cube* (Fig. 456), by the German-born Hans Haacke (b. 1937). Bosch had the vision, uncanny for his time, that the earth existed within a closed system, symbolized by a transparent sphere. Haacke accepts the same premise and thanks to technology can build his model but without Bosch's global symbolism.

To understand the thinking of a gifted and articulate younger artist who is no longer interested in making sculptural objects—fixed, isolated works to be interpreted by a viewer—consider the problems Haacke posed in making his highly individual "weather box." He assigned to himself the task of creating something "which experiences, reacts to its environment, changes, is non-stable . . . that cannot 'perform' without the assistance of its environment . . . [that is] sensitive to light and temperature changes . . . that lives in time and makes the 'spectator' experience time . . . [that] articulates something natural." Using Plexiglas, a product of technology, he fashioned a series of carefully proportioned boxes into which distilled water could be introduced and then sealed. Potentially these could be mass produced and cheaply sold. When exposed to sunlight and temperature change, hydrodynamic changes resulted. Thus the product and precision of technology has been put in the service of creating a work characterized by random behavior, by organic movement feeding on natural forces. He feels that human beings are more at home with natural rather than mechanical motion, natural rather than clockwork time. Aesthetically and intellectually Haacke favors the mutual enhancement of the geometrically shaped container and the organic happening on the inside. He uses the laws of nature and science as tools, not as ends, and thus he is not a science illustrator. The viewer can enjoy the prismatic light reflections as the light and bubble patterns change over a long period of time. Haacke would have deplored artificially colored glass or liquid; what he has done is to isolate and articulate a natural phenomenon, whose appreciation he feels requires exceptional sensibility. His work is tied to *systems* thought and art in that it involves transfers of energy, matter, or information without the viewer's participation or empathy. The viewer is a witness, not an interpreter, as in the past history of painting and sculpture.

Art, like science, is a record of man's interaction with nature. Landscape art is not of importance because it gives geographical information about China, Holland, or southern France; it has value because of the way these places were seen,

Plate 57. JACKSON POLLOCK. *Autumn Rhythm.* 1950. Oil on canvas, 8′9″ × 17′3″. Metropolitan Museum of Art (George A. Hearn Fund, 1957). (See p. 320.)

Plate 58. VINCENT VAN GOGH. *The Artist's Chair*. 1888. Oil on canvas, $35^1/_2 \times 28''$. Tate Gallery, London (courtesy of the Trustees). (See pp. 332, 333.)

felt, thought of, and then given aesthetic form by their makers. For artists such as Bruegel, Dürer, and Leonardo, art did have some cartographic function, but this was not its sole or primary purpose. Inherent in all the art discussed in this chapter has been the artist's desire to know about creation, his gods, and the nature of reality—where he and other men stood in relation to the universe. The act of painting and making sculpture from nature has in itself been as important perhaps as the knowledge imparted by the finished works of art, for it is during the art process that the artist feels most strongly his communion with nature. For some, painting from nature helped the artist to fathom its essential order and to re-experience its genesis, but for others it was the occasion for putting nature into a more perfect and personal order while nonetheless preserving its violent aspects.

Artists have derived from nature the means or motifs to externalize their feelings or images of themselves; an awareness of life not given to the eye, the reconstruction of an ideal past, understanding of the present, and even a prediction of the future; escape from the difficulties of daily existence, or terms on which to meet reality; satisfaction of a need for objective knowledge, or the stimulation of fantasy. In an ecology-conscious society, we are aware of man's potential to pollute and destroy the earth. If the earth is to be further obliterated, it will not be because of the artist. Art continues to give a model of what it means to live in a civilized way with nature.

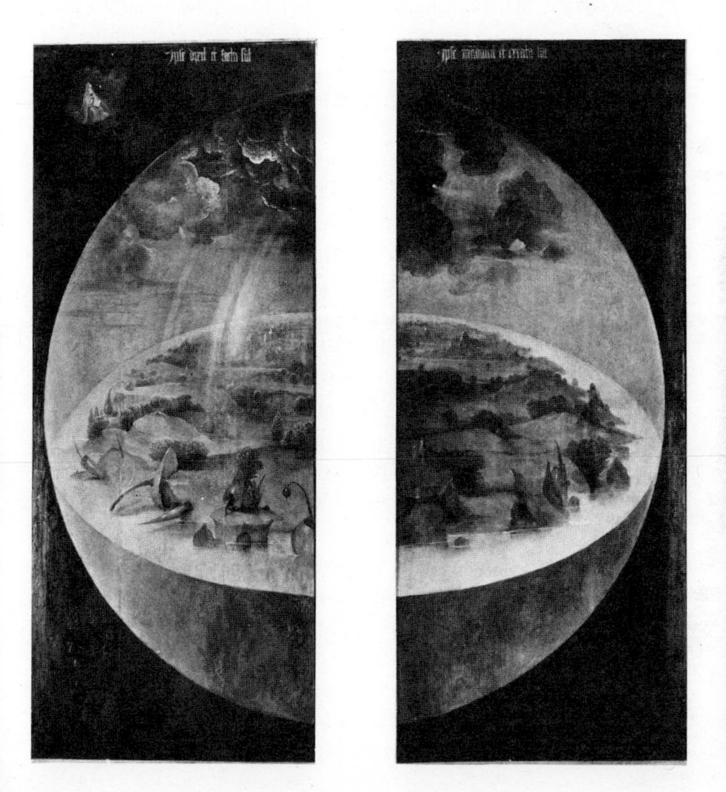

*left:* 455. HIERONYMUS BOSCH. *Creation of the World,* closed wings on the triptych *Garden of Earthly Delights.* c. 1505–10. Oil on panel, 7′2″ × 3′2¼″ (each wing). Prado, Madrid.

*below:* 456. HANS HAACKE. *Condensation Cube.* 1963–65. Clear acrylic plastic, water, and climatic conditions; 11½″ cube.

900 1000 1100 1200 1300 1400 1500 1600 1700 1800 1900 2000

Ancient period 3000 B.C.–A.D. 395
Medieval period 395–1400
Renaissance period 1400–1600
Baroque period 1600–1750
Modern period 1750–

before A.D. 79 *Sacred Landscape* (Pompeii)
A. Dürer, *Study of Plants* ● 1503
H. Bosch, *Garden of Earthly Delights* ● c. 1505–10
Leonardo da Vinci, *Cataclysm* ● c. 1516
P. Bruegel, *Return of the Herds* ● c. 1560
1648 ● N. Poussin, *Funeral of Phocion*
c. 1650 ● J. van Ruisdael, *Wheatfields*
C. D. Friedrich, *Capuchin Friar by the Sea* 1808–09 ●
D. Smith, *Hudson River Landscape* ● 1951
J. Pollock, *Seascape* ● 1934
*Autumn Rhythm* ● 1950
Matta, *Earth Is a Man* ● 1940–42
K. Snelson, *Atom* ● 1964
R. Smithson, *Non-Site* ● 1968
H. Haacke, *Condensation Cube* ● 1963–65
D. Oppenheim, *Directed Seeding* ● 1969
M. Heizer, *One-third of Displaced-Replaced Mass* ● 1969
G. Courbet, *Seaside at Palavas* ● 1854
*Source of the Loue* ● c. 1864
C. Monet, *Bordighera Trees* ● 1884
P. Cézanne, *Mont Ste-Victoire* ● 1885–87
V. van Gogh, *Landscape with Sun Rising* ● 1889
P. Mondrian, *Mill by the Water* ● c. 1905
*Composition in White, Black, and Red* ● 1936
W. Kandinsky, *Landscape with Factory Chimney* ● 1910
*Picture with White Edge, No. 173* ● 1913
C. Brancusi, *Bird in Space* ● 1925
P. Klee, *Botanical Theater* ● 1934
J. Arp, *Growth* ● 1938
A. Calder, *Lobster Trap and Fish Tail* ● 1939
*Teodelapio* ● 1962

c. 1000 ● Hsu Tao-ning, *Fishing in a Mountain Stream* (China)
late 15th ● Sesshū, *Fisherman and Woodcutter* (Japan)
16th c. ● Sesson Shokei, *Wind and Waves* (Japan)

# 17

To understand the fascination that objects have had for the painter, it helps to examine a few of our own fundamental attitudes. No one is neutral toward objects. Aside from the specific function for which an object has been made, its continued use and the mind's tendency to make analogies have often invested it with multiple associations or symbolic purposes. In the Middle Ages, for example, the relics of saints and kings or objects used by them had great value, as if some of the holiness or power of these revered figures had rubbed off on what they had handled. Even today the personal effects of a dead man or of a celebrated figure can have special meaning. To witness the public's fascination with the late President Kennedy's rocking chair, or the spirited bidding for hotel bed sheets used by the Beatles, is a reminder that people still invest inanimate objects with irrational meaning and value.

We also tend to forget that paintings themselves are objects. They begin as wood panels or canvases that are stretched over rectangular wooden frames and on which pigment has been applied. Throughout most of art's history, this fundamentally static character has been disguised by illusions of naturalism and movement. As will be shown in this chapter, artists have long had the ability to look searchingly at objects and to invent many possible relations with the framed surface. The artist can create an unfamiliar context by using his frame like a camera lens, forcing the spectator to focus upon objects within a severely limited environment. The small size of most objects chosen for painting allows an artist to preserve their exact scale, a condition that can vivify a painting. Since the objects are painted imitations, they cannot be touched or used; we are obliged to appreciate them solely with our eyes, thus experiencing them in a new way. Probably for the first time, we become aware of an object's color, shape, volume, texture, and surface reflection of light—the aesthetic properties that commonly unite the interest of artist and viewer.

Like the physical circumstance of the painting itself, objects lack movement, and many artists have been fascinated with their fixity, their quality of *just being there*. The combination of picture and objects has often been used to produce a restful visual experience satisfying the need of artist and viewer to see things put in order. Placing two or more objects next to one another can establish a *dialogue* for the painter, stressing various forms of interchange or reciprocation between objects, creating types of order or harmony that have metaphorically been models for human existence. Changes in composition as well as in the choice of objects often parallel important shifts not just in styles but in broad developments outside the sphere of art. This type of painting is important in the sociology and psychology of art. It is the one form of painting in which the artist has generally been superior to his subject and could dispose of it when he was finished. Beginning in the 17th century, it was the one form of painting in which the subject was not considered superior to the painting itself. Many beautiful paintings have been created from the most modest or unlikely subject objects. Before the 17th century, it was perhaps still-life painting that most readily allowed the discriminating viewer to contemplate and appraise the judgment and coordination of the artist's eye and hand. Even the most illusionistic rendering of objects does not require total self-effacement on the part of the artist, for we can come to recognize many still-life painters by their choice of objects, by their arrangement and lighting. There are endless ways in which a round wine bottle can be convincingly transposed to the flat surface of a painting. Throughout the history of art, men have delighted in the challenge of reworking the same subject and even repainting the same picture. Meyer Schapiro has given an illuminating summary of the unique importance of the still life:

> Without a fixed place in nature and submitted to arbitrary and often accidental manipulation, the still life on the table is an objective example of the formed but constantly re-arranged, the freely disposable in reality, and therefore connate with an idea of artistic liberty. The still-life picture, to a greater degree than the landscape or historical painting, owes its composition to the painter, yet more than these seems to represent a piece of everyday reality.

**Objects in Antiquity** The largest surviving pre-Roman body of painting concerning itself with objects is that found in Egyptian tombs (Figs. 37, 39). The pictures of foodstuffs and vessels in Egyptian reliefs and wall paintings do not constitute pure still-life painting, or rendering of inanimate objects for

# ART, OBJECTS, AND THE OBJECT OF ART

their aesthetic value alone. They are accompanied by representations of the deceased whom these objects were to serve in the afterlife, of workers who were to make and gather the objects in the service of the dead man, or of the gods who were to receive the objects as offerings. Their purpose in Egyptian art was thus utilitarian. As long as ancient art was god-centered and deeply rooted in magic and religion, no legitimate tradition of still-life painting could develop. But ancient literary sources recount that, by the 4th century B.C., urban Greek artists had achieved highly illusionistic techniques of representing objects in stage sets and on portable panel paintings and frescoes for homes and shops. Though none of this Hellenistic art has survived, its emergence in the 5th and 4th centuries B.C. accompanied an increasing secularization of artistic subject matter in both painting and sculpture. It was part of a public taste for enjoying and capturing the immediate material existence, as well as of a growing religious and political relativism. Much of the still-life art produced by Greek artists dealt with food and the vessels and plates with which meals were served, reflecting the tastes and social customs of the artist's patron and his guests and the delight of city dwellers in the products of the country. The Greek imitation of the fruits of nature, with its connotations of sociability and connoisseurship, had later parallels and influence in Roman painting and mosaic, many examples of which have survived.

One such mosaic, representing the floor of a Roman dining room, is known as *The Unswept Room* (Fig. 457). Dating from the 2nd century, it is probably a copy by Heraclitus of a lost work from the Greek city of Pergamon. It was not uncommon for guests at a fashionable banquet to litter the floor with bits of food. The scattered objects in *The Unswept Room* mosaic are table discards, the refuse of a discriminating, ritually ordered banquet such as would be held in the *triclinium,* or dining room. The mosaic consists of small, roughly squared cubes of white and colored stone set into a cement base. The color range and intensity of the stones, or *tesserae,* used by Roman mosaicists surpassed the palettes of fresco and panel painters in antiquity. The minute size in which the stones could be cut permitted subtle tonal gradations and intricate curves, so that the artist's medium did not inhibit his choice of objects or illusionistic intent. Not only the shape and color of the objects but also the relief effect from cast shadows, and the naturalistic mouse in the lower left corner, would cause an unsuspecting guest to tread carefully in the rooms and would doubtless provide conversational diversion between the courses. Study of this seemingly random composition reveals the brilliant calculation and sensitivity to complex balance exercised by the artist. Objects do not overlap or touch; nor are shadows tangent at any point. There is no single organizing axis or consistent light source. The mosaic is rendered in perspective, so to speak, from any point in the dining room. The careful spacing between shapes and shadows and the overall density established in each large quarter of the floor results in a harmonious ordering of a highly sophisticated type. Comparison of this mosaic with Egyptian paintings of objects illuminates the changes that had

457. HERACLITUS. *The Unswept Room,* copy of a Hellenistic mosaic by Sosos. Rome, 2nd century A.D. Vatican Museums, Rome.

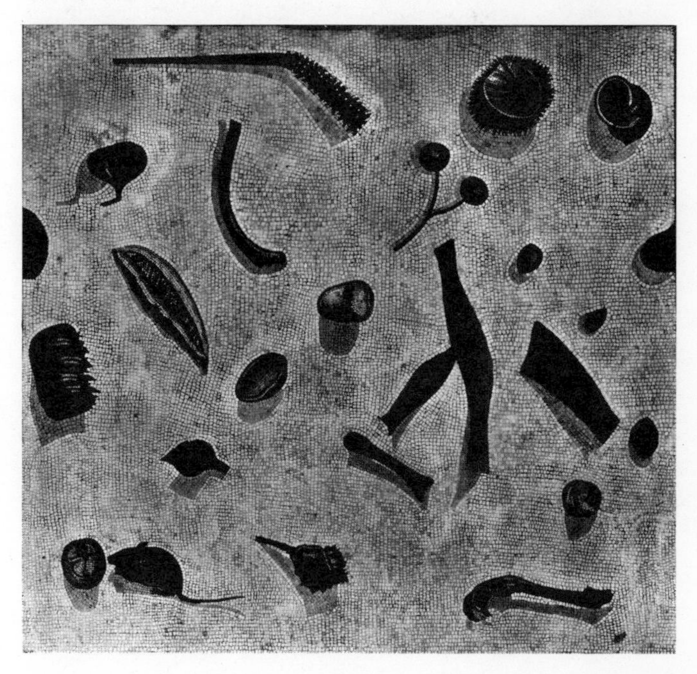

*left :* 458. *Throne with Scroll and Symbol of the Evangelists Luke and John.* Early 5th century. Mosaic. Santa Prisca, Santa Maria Capua Vetere, Italy.

*below :* 459. DOMINGO CRESPI ( ?). *Instruments of the Passion,* from *The Breviary of King Martin of Aragon.* 1395–1410. Bibliothèque Nationale, Paris.

taken place in the relationship between man and his environment—from a sense of fear and a deep need for security in the next world to an attitude of relaxed pleasure and confidence.

**Objects That Symbolize Persons** From the 4th through the 14th and 15th centuries in Western art, the achievements of the Romans in the naturalistic rendering of secular objects and their making of them the complete subjects of works of art were apparently forgotten or ignored. The life of the objects in art underwent significant transformation. For about a thousand years in painting, mosaic, and sculpture, objects served in the main as attributes, symbols, or accessories for Christian heroes. The throne, for instance, occupies an important place in Early Christian imagery. The presence of the throne as a venerated object and symbol had various origins; it derived from religious sources such as the Biblical description of the throne of Solomon, from pagan traditions, and from the artists' familiarity with the thrones of Roman emperors (Fig. 289). During the important Council of Ephesus in the 4th century, a throne, empty except for the Gospels placed upon it, had the place of honor as a sign that Christ chaired the conclave.

A 5th-century mosaic (Fig. 458) from a church in Rome illustrates how an object could thus replace the image of Christ himself. We saw a similar symbolic use of the throne in our discussion of early portrayals of the Budda (Fig. 54). The regal, authoritarian tone of the mosaic is attributable not only to the sumptuousness of the throne, with its inlaid precious stones, elegant drapery, and brilliantly colored cushion beneath the scroll of sacred Scripture, but also to the formality of the object's placement. Not unlike the arrangement in mosaic images showing Christ in Glory (Pl. 6, p. 44), the throne is frontal, placed centrally between symbols of the evangelists John and Luke, and dominates the whole ensemble in its size. The central axis of the throne is shared by the Scriptures and the dove of the Holy Ghost, which reveals to the eyes of the enlightened beholder the source and omnipotence of Christian

law. In contrast to the whites, greys, subdued and pastel tones of *The Unswept Room* mosaic, Christian mosaics had by the 5th century acquired a more consistently rich, dark, and luminous color and surface quality. The decorative border of the mosaic also displays less caprice or spontaneity in design than did the decorative motifs in earlier Roman art, symptomatic of the formality and stylization that developed in Christian art along with the codification of Church dogma and power.

Whereas the Christian mosaic of the throne was valued in its time for the exalted nature of its subject and the preciousness of the medium, Van Gogh's late-19th-century painting of his own chair (Pl. 58, p. 328) has come to be valued for its artistic merit and powerful revelation of the artist's feeling about himself and his relation to others. It is questionable whether Van

Gogh was conscious of the earlier tradition of the subject as a symbol of a human presence or of a god. Largely through instinct and an urgent need to attach himself to others, he came to endow objects—his shoes, pipe and tobacco, books, gloves, and flowers—with human associations. The objects that moved him were modest, and their appearance was shaped by use.

Although the subject is inanimate, Van Gogh's painting of his empty chair can nonetheless induce disquiet in the viewer. The heavy dark outline of the chair aggressively asserts its object character, as does the substance of the thick, strong yellow pigment re-creating the wood and straw. Unlike the impressive frontal throne of Christ, seen from slightly below and eternally stabilized against the backdrop of Heaven, Van Gogh's chair is painted from above and turned at a severe angle to the floor tiles and the corner of the room. No attempt was made to align the objects into a simple deliberate pattern.

Each part of the whole vigorously appeals to the eye, prohibiting tranquil inspection, and in this way the chair's magnetism as an object and as a visual form is brought home to us—for it is to it that we must constantly return our gaze. Whereas the throne in Christian art helped to relate man to his god, to orient him to the universe, Van Gogh's chair was the artist's link with sanity and human love.

**Objects and Narrative** The storytelling capacity of objects was recognized more than five and a half centuries ago by a Spanish artist, possibly Domingo Crespi (fl. c. 1409), who decorated a private book of religious lessons and prayers for King Martin of Aragon. The section dealing with the events leading up to Easter includes a large painting filled with an assortment of objects whose conjunction would be incomprehensible to anyone unfamiliar with the details of Christ's Passion (Fig. 459). As recounted in the Bible and the apocryphal gospels, the devout reader of the royal breviary can single out an object and put it into the context of the events leading to Christ's death. But this ability to reconstruct the religious drama owes much to previous painting. Even in the Middle Ages, with its emphasis on textual interpretation, artists took the license of filling in details omitted by Scripture (for instance, the insertion of medieval tongs or pliers, by which the nails were removed from Christ's hands and feet). Purposes of clarity and ready identification influenced the even dispersal of the objects, each carrying with it poignant associations. The mystical nature of the painting allows the painter to suspend objects and fragmentary heads and hands in space.

**Objects as Attributes** It was from the medieval tradition of objects as attributes of Christ, the Virgin, and the saints that their independent secular painting emerged in the 15th century. A German painting, *Cupboard with Bottles and Books* (Fig. 460), was executed by an unknown artist during the years 1470–80; it has been interpreted as a pharmacy sign, perhaps from a hospital, because the tag on the flask reads, "For toothaches." The lower half of the composition is a neatly distributed but static display of objects hanging on a wall or standing upon a shelf. Within this recessed niche, the objects are susceptible to varying intensity of light and shadow. The cupboard above is shown with one of its doors partly open, as if it had pivoted into the viewer's space. Paintings that astonish the eye by illusionistically moving away from or toward us had a tradition as far back as ancient times (Pl. 50, p. 307), and their reappearance in the 15th century, both in northern Europe and in Italy, is thought to be a conscious revival of this ancient practice.

There is a strong possibility that this German advertisement may have been inspired by compositions of polychrome inlaid wood, called *intarsia,* which were developed in Italy before the middle of the 15th century and for which such major artists as Piero della Francesca and Uccello willingly supplied drawings. Because of its associations with Roman nobility, Italian rulers such as the Duke of Urbino commissioned *intar siatori* or inlay artists to decorate entire rooms of their palaces with this type of illusionistic art. Fra Vincenzo da Verona was active about 1480 in designing optically deceptive inlaid decoration for a church in Modena. Showing his mastery of complex

460. *Cupboard with Bottles and Books.* German, 1470–80. Oil on wood, $41^3/_4 \times 31^7/_8$". Geib Collection, Rochester, New York.

*left:* 461. Fra Vincenzo da Verona. *Cupboard and Niche with Objects.* c. 1480. Wood inlay. Louvre, Paris.

*above:* 462. Juan Sanchez Cotán. *Quince, Cabbage, Melon, and Cucumber.* c. 1603. Oil on canvas, 25¾ × 32″. Fine Arts Society of San Diego, Calif.

perspective problems, in the panel illustrated (Fig. 461), Fra Vincenzo simulated a partially opened cupboard, whose latticed shutters angle toward the viewer with such convincing effect as to arouse the impulse to open them further or close them. Piled on the lower shelf are liturgical objects such as a cross and a censer, while the hourglass and skull above symbolize, as they had since antiquity, the theme of mortality and human vanity. Instead of depicting living and dead figures, the artist employed objects for his *memento mori.* The French art historian Charles Sterling, in his excellent history of still life, points out that inlay artists utilized the most advanced techniques of perspective developed by 15th-century painters and geometers and that, ironically, their inlaid work in turn began to influence 16th-century painters to attempt illusionistic compositions which seem to advance toward the viewer.

**Wordly and Pious Objects** Heir to the illusionistic tradition and subject matter that went back to ancient Roman mosaics, Caravaggio (1573–1609) painted a solitary basket of fruit (Pl. 59, p. 337) that, like the vivid relief of his figure paintings (Pl. 31, p. 164) was to have a substantial impact on 17th-century art. This lowliest of subject matter, by artistic standards of the time, was boldly centered in the painting, preempting the customary place of a noble figure. Within this strong formal emphasis, the artist preserved the informal disarray of the fruit spilling over the basket and out of the picture. Rather than perfectly formed and fresh clean fruit, he showed fruit that was dust-covered and deteriorating from worms and the long interval required by the painting. Caravaggio was not appealing to the sensation of taste, nor was he moralizing by using the fruit to signify the transiency of life. Rather, he was giving a lesson in seeing, compelling his audience to look long and hard at what they ordinarily took for granted. That he finds the basket of fruit worthy of comparison with figure subjects may be supported not only by the time which must have been required for patient detailing of its properties but also by the fact of its illumination with the same kind of hard lucid light.

Caravaggio and the Spanish Carthusian friar Juan Sanchez Cotán (1561–1637) furnish persuasive evidence that the serious painting of fruits and vegetables can satisfy both worldly and pious temperaments. Shortly before taking monastic vows, when he was about forty years of age, Cotán did a series of still-life paintings, and their sober profundity far exceeds in quality his sentimental religious figure paintings (Fig. 462). Like a second frame, he employs a stone window casement in which a quince and cabbage are hung near a melon and cucumber resting on the ledge. The carefully staggered disposition of the objects suggests musical notation, but whether or not this was his inspiration, Cotán hit upon an ingeniously simple device to separate and dramatize the individual objects and their relationship. It is known that Cotán was interested in geometry, and this painting may have resulted from personal meditations on contrasts between shapes conceived in nature

*right :* 463. Francisco de Zurbarán. *Still Life with Vessels.* 1633–40. Oil on canvas, $18^{1}/_{8} \times 33''$. Prado, Madrid.

*below :* 464. Mu-Ch'i. *Six Persimmons.* Southern Sung Dynasty, late 13th century. Ink on paper, width $14^{1}/_{2}''$. Daitoku-ji, Kyoto.

and in the human mind. By cutting open the melon and using a niche which interrupts the strong cold light, he expands the variety of ways in which we can know his subject. The gradual advance of the objects from left to right culminates in the cucumber precariously balanced on the edge of the sill, so that the artist counteracts the impression of a monotonous horizontal alignment and seems to make a partial loan of one of the objects to the viewer's space. Caravaggio's testimony to the worth of such a theme and the intriguing potential of emphatic side lighting must have encouraged Cotán to digress from his customary pious subject matter.

The 17th-century Spanish artist Francisco de Zurbarán (1598–1664), a contemporary of Cotán, exhibited a duality of interests that produced official religious and royal imagery as well as meditative still lifes. His art on the whole reflects the painter's existence at court and in the cloister, and it captures the domestic environment of objects. That Zurbarán carried over attitudes from one mode of life to another can be seen in his *Still Life with Four Vessels* (Fig. 463). Four beautifully made, variously shaped, but relatively modest objects are disposed along a stone ledge, like a litany, in a line parallel to the picture plane. This arrangement suggests offerings placed before the altar in a Spanish cathedral of the time. The mood of the whole echoes, in inanimate fashion, that of Zurbarán's images of humble monks. Unlike Dutch paintings involving objects, this picture gives no suggestion of casual use or sociable situations. The objects are presented for serious contemplation, not unlike the monks' practice of meditating at length upon a passage of Scripture. Their symmetrical placement is deceptive, for Zurbarán was deeply aware of the individuality and worth of each vessel and elicited a range of contrasts far beyond the objects' number and superficial appearance.

**Objects of Meditation** Oriental painting does not include the Western category of still life. Despite the fact that Chinese artists produced magnificent objects with a history of important religious and aesthetic use in temple, tomb, and home, they never created entire paintings devoted to inanimate objects. Closest to Western still lifes of fruit detached from the tree is *Six Persimmons* (Fig. 464), by the Chinese artist Mu-Ch'i (fl. c. 1269). Mu-Ch'i's six pieces of fruit, painted in ink on paper, are divorced from any setting or support; they hover in an undefined space as if suspended in the viewer's consciousness. It is only their proximity to the lower edge of the hanging that suggests a normal relation to a table or the ground, or at least an acknowledgment of the pull of gravity. Because the painting has been cut, however, it is impossible to comment on the relation of the objects to the total field.

The spiritual speculations of the artist are suggested by the fact that the persimmons are rendered in various stages of their life cycle. For this reason alone, the French term for still life, *nature morte,* or "dead nature," would seem inappropriate. The Chinese painter dealt only with living things, and he found

465. BAUGUIN. *The Five Senses*. c. 1630. Oil on panel, $21^5/_8 \times 28^3/_4$". Louvre, Paris.

the life cycle of the persimmon as important as that of man. Each fruit has a singular shape, tone, weight, density, and relation to the adjacent fruit. Unlike Zurbarán's regular spacing, the deployment of Mu-Ch'i's persimmons seems naturally informal. They are related by overlap, tangency, and discrete intervals, yet these objects do not share even an invisible ground line. No two stems are the same, nor are their proportions and direction predictable. To alter any of the foregoing subtle relationships would be to disrupt their internal harmony in the eyes of a sensitive viewer. The many aesthetic judgments made by Mu-Ch'i resulted from sustained concentration and final revelation. Zurbarán's vessels and Mu-Ch'i's persimmons remind us that an artist's attitudes toward life may be manifested through the smallest, most modest subjects.

**Objects and the Senses** In the 17th century, painters of objects began to depart from the rigorous "inventory" style of alignment and to dispose them in more informal ways and with a greater sense of depth. A French painter named Bauguin (fl. 1620–40), who derived much from Caravaggio, constructed a painting of objects that to his contemporary audience evoked the pleasures of the table as well as the gratifications of all the senses (Fig. 465). Their seemingly casual disarray implied recent use, and in a continuance of the illusionistic tradition of visual tricks, the mandolin seems to jut out toward the viewer's reach. In painting such as this, it is not the meaning or purpose of the objects that dictates their locations. Not trusting to gambler's luck, Bauguin invites us to discover his reasoned decisions for pairing and juxtaposing different objects, such as the repetition of fluted edges in the mandolin and purse, the geometric order of the gaming board and the disorder of the adjoining table area, the shape of a flower against the octagon of the mirror, the pure geometry of the glass versus the natural irregularity of the melon. Sophisticated audiences in the 17th century shared the artist's enthusiasm for visual perception and the exercise of intellect. They appreciated the correct shadings of the mandolin calculated on the basis of the light source and varying surface angles and admired the mental scheming that produced musical and pictorial harmonies.

**Objects to Satisfy Sociability and Vanity** The object became central to painting in the late 15th and 16th centuries. In 17th-century Holland, still lifes were an art form of aesthetic as well as symbolic significance. In contrast to the situation in Roman Catholic countries, the Dutch Protestant Church was not an important sponsor of art, and still-life paintings were developed to satisfy the needs and taste of a secular, largely middle-class clientele. These paintings were modest objects, intended for hanging in the home among other prized domestic possessions. Still lifes were also purchased as financial speculations, so that the Dutch artist, anticipating his modern counterpart, did not always know his future buyer. The aesthetic subject matter and passive quality of the Dutch still lifes, in accord with the insulated atmosphere of the middle-class Dutch home (Fig. 247), recall the tranquilizing effect of the pleasant scenes painted inside urban dwellings of ancient Rome (Pl. 50, p. 307). It was from Dutch paintings after 1620 which described partially eaten meals, with their consequent suggestion of physical deterioration, that still another evocation of the themes of *vanitas* and death emerged. The Dutch love of finely painted objects testifies to a distaste for the passions of epic and dramatic images, which did not suitably reflect the secure and complacent character of Dutch culture and prosperity in the 17th century. The still-life paintings record Holland's acquisition of material wealth and an extensive overseas trade that returned to the home country exotic objects, foods, and wines. The fact that most Dutch still life refers to meals also makes of these paintings emblems of the Dutch pride in hospitality. They are fit companions to portraits of affable Dutchmen who invite us to share their wine and company (Fig. 244). There was a wide range of still-life painting, involving different types of meals and degrees of opulence or modesty, depending upon such factors as the different cities where they originated and their date. Toward the end of the 17th century, the still lifes were composed of more precious, exotic objects and began to display more complex arrangements and a more feminine air.

The Dutch enjoyed seeing inanimate objects organized in stable compositions. Objects were placed close to the viewer, as if soliciting him to share intimately the knowledge and experience of the artist. Both the painstaking creation and the appreciative seeing of the art were best accomplished while seated. Absorbing the satisfactions of a Dutch still-life painting demands the same kind of savoring as is required in doing

right: Plate 59. CARAVAGGIO. *Basket of Fruit*. c. 1596. Oil on canvas, $18^{1}/_{8} \times 25^{3}/_{8}$″. Pinacoteca Ambrosiana, Milan. (See p. 334.)

below: Plate 60. PIETER CLAESZ. *Still Life*. 1643. Oil on panel, $29^{1}/_{2} \times 35$″. Minneapolis Institute of Arts. (See pp. 336, 339.)

*left:* Plate 61. JEAN-BAPTISTE-SIMÉON CHARDIN. *Still Life*. c. 1732. Oil on canvas, $15^7/_8 \times 12^3/_8$". Norton Simon Foundation, Los Angeles. (See p. 339.)

*below:* Plate 62. EDOUARD MANET. *Still Life with Carp*. 1864. Oil on canvas, $28^7/_8 \times 36^1/_4$". Art Institute of Chicago. (See p. 340.)

justice to a delicious meal. As illustrated in a work (Pl. 60, p. 337) by Pieter Claesz (1596–1661), the Dutch artist and his patrons delighted in a calculated chaos that was very much unlike the pristine neatness of Cotán and Zubarán. The objects are represented in disarray, as they might be seen after a meal by someone who had just pushed back from the table. A suggestion of the meal's original order and the timepiece at the left impart a slightly morbid touch of temporality. Before undertaking the painting, the artist spent a great deal of time thoughtfully arranging the objects in search of shapes that "rhymed," means of linking disparate forms and easing the eye's course through the painting, and an angle of illumination that offered a maximal range of values to set off both the materials and the shapes of the objects. Just as the highlight of the meal might often derive from a single tang, such as that obtained from a lemon peel, so was the painter's cuisine dependent upon a touch of color against a prevalent monochrome or within a narrow range of subdued tints. The transition from vertical to horizontal forms, from near to distant items, was accomplished through careful adjustment of objects and lighting. The drama ultimately became one of light, illuminating and annealing the multiple shapes and textures.

**Elegant and Inelegant Objects** Using elegant objects, the 18th-century French painter Pierre Subleyras fashioned an alter image of Francis I, Duke of Este and one-time commander of the French army in Italy (Fig. 466). The objects are indicative both of the attributes of the Duke and of the early-18th-century ideal of a ruler. Francis I is visibly represented by a handsome marble bust carved by Bernini in 1651–52. Ironically, the bust itself was made from its subject's portrayal in two paintings, so that we see the Duke ultimately through the eyes of four artists. The white gloves and red carnations resting on a finely embosed silver platter announce his courtly mien. The body of the exotic plumed bird refers both to his participation in the aristocratic pursuit of the hunt and to his taste for gourmet food. The armor and the astrolabe suggest his interest and prowess in military and astronomical science. The bronze sculpture of Hercules supporting the world reminds the viewer of Francis' ethical guide. The frightened woman and children in the painted background may signify the terrors of war and the threat to life against which the Duke stood as protector. Both the painting and the bust epitomize the 18th-century aristocratic ideal of intermingled formality and informality—seeming one thing, but in fact being another.

The beauty of Subleyras' painting was in certain respects assured before the work was undertaken by the intrinsic quality of the objects chosen. This was art about art. In another 18th-century still life, however, a superior work of art was made of inferior objects. The French painter Jean-Baptist-Siméon Chardin (1699–1779) found in simple household utensils a source of wonder and matter for life-long exploration (Pl. 61, p. 338). Even more than could specifically religious or political accessories, the objects chosen by Chardin reveal the strong morality of the painter. The sturdy basin or pitcher, worn and recolored from daily use, was for Chardin silent evidence of frugality, temperance, and constancy. It served his passionate interest in the mysterious effects of light upon material substance—in other words, reality as given to the eyes.

Like Zurbarán, Chardin aligned his objects on a shelf beyond reach and set out for visual research. Unlike the cool, dry, and hard surfaces of Zurbarán, Caravaggio, and Cotán, Chardin's warm and elusive equivalences of his subjects took shape not from firm outlines but from manipulation of light values and the viscous properties of paint. The durable was created by the inconstant. With the exception of the works of Rembrandt (see Chap. 11), nowhere in the Dutch still-life painting that Chardin admired are we as conscious of the physical nature of the oil medium, the touches of the brush, and the sheer material substance of the painting's surface. From a few pigments, Chardin coaxed a rich gamut of tones such as those in the copper basin. When closely studied, these variegated tones contradict the initial impression of the basin's solidity and simplicity, for Chardin established each tone in response to minute sensations of light and dark given directly to the eye.

*right :* 466. Pierre Subleyras. *Still Life with Bust of Francis I, Duke of Este*. 1730–45. Oil on canvas, 4′5¼″ × 3′4″. Minneapolis Institute of Arts.

**Picture-Makers and Painters** Subleyras and Chardin exemplify the distinction between *picture-makers* and *painters*. Picture-makers, such as Subleyras, wish us to experience the object in a literal manner, to observe their success in closely matching the distinctive properties of objects in a seemingly airless space. It is as if one might reach out and pluck a flower from within the picture frame and thereby perfume the air. Neither the oil medium nor the hand of the artist intrudes upon the viewer's awareness of the illusion before his eyes. Rembrandt and Chardin (Fig. 611), while they create plausible illusions of objects, also impart to them visible evidence of artifice, the traces of oil and brush, and make it impossible to separate the object from its unique painterly environment.

Edouard Manet was such a painter. (Pl. 44, p. 286; Figs. 410, 412). To enjoy his painting is to savor nuances of color and the subtle matching of tones, the tasteful dispersal of color accents over the field of the canvas, the bold application of shapes to the painting's surface. His paintings of objects were not intended as inventories or as incentives to philosophizing. Manet's constructions of broad, strongly edged, and relatively flat areas of closely linked tones appeal more quickly to the eye than do any of the previously considered paintings. The painted fabric of Manet's objects and background is more apparent and more loosely woven than that of Chardin and the Dutch still-life masters. There is a more consistent awareness of the flat picture surface; breadth, direction, and twists of his brushwork call attention to the surface as well as to the object. Manet reserved the most brilliant tone for the small patch of the lemon off to one side. Less brilliant hues such as coppery brown and pinks occur more frequently than the yellow, but less frequently than the greys. Manet gave to the greys and whites, which fill the largest part of his painting, the greatest range of nuance. *Still Life with Carp* (Pl. 62, p. 338) was painted for the cultured vision of a sophisticated, but at the time limited, audience. The objects included were important not only because they set up challenging tonal problems, but also because in themselves their qualities created a discriminating and pleasurable aesthetic experience.

Whereas Manet could accept the generally perceived shape, if not the tone, of objects, Cézanne insisted upon reexamining all properties of his subject as if he were seeing it for the first time (Pl. 54, p. 309; Fig. 486). Cézanne could not unquestioningly repeat anything that was given to the senses, but instead he was impelled to re-form, recolor, and reorganize whatever entered within the boundaries of his canvas. Zurbarán and the Dutch could admire the craftsman's art in making handsome objects, but Cézanne felt no allegiance to the glassmaker, the ceramicist, or even to the farmer whose apples he painted (Pl. 63, p. 347). His reconstruction of objects was motivated by a desire to search out their essence, to increase their visual interest, and to meet the particular compositional and expressive demands of the painting. Neither perversity nor ignorance of perspective techniques led him to reshape the compote in Plate 63 into an asymmetrical, flattened oval; rather, his main consideration was the pictorial need of added coordination with the frame to increase the stability and visual weight of the composition. High-keyed tones at the upper left balanced the cloth at the lower right, and the dislocation of the base of the compote was necessary to harmonize with the assembled apples and glass. This meant stretching the basin of the compote.

Each successive decision made in the painting solved some aesthetic or compositional problem raised in a preceding stage of the canvas, instead of satisfying a concern with fidelity to the appearance of the object. Previous painters had allowed the objects to compose their paintings; Cézanne relied upon the painting to compose the objects chosen. The apples illustrate this point, for Cézanne *realized* them in paint both from the outside edge inward and from the inside out. The direction of their stroke-faceted surfaces was coordinated with, and must be seen against, the directions of the knife, the cloth, and the pile of fruit itself, and ultimately the directions of all other movements in the painting. Each daub of the brush on an apple was calculated to fix the light value, hue, curve or flatness, warmth or coolness of a particular area of *sensation*. Any part of Cézanne's painting yields to the pull of adjacent areas because of the thoroughness with which all have been fitted together. Cézanne devised such blunted shapes as those in the mouth of the glass and the compote and used the ingenious connection of objects and touches of bright color to achieve an ambivalent relationship between the picture's surface and the objects in depth. Cézanne repeated the objects, but never his mode of painting them. The importance of Cézanne's contribution and the value of his art has been succinctly expressed by Meyer Schapiro:

> At the threshold of our century stands the art of Cézanne, which imposes on us the conviction that in rendering the simplest objects, bare of ideal meanings, a series of colored patches can be a summit of perfection showing the concentrated qualities and powers of a great mind.

**Independence from Imitation** Fortified by Cézanne's assertion of the artist's obligation to restructure the visual world, the Cubist break with the imitation of the object as seen in nature was a relatively quiet revolution. Picasso (see Chap. 20), Braque (Fig. 468), Léger (Pl. 87, p. 433), and Gris (Pl. 64, p. 347) did not select radically new subject matter or issue violent manifestoes attacking those who represented the literal form of the object as perceived in three-dimensional space. At no time during Cubism's most important years (1909–14) did these artists completely renounce the object. Their objects, however, were derived from a restricted and immediate area of their environment. More specifically, the objects were associated with a favored café, the studio, and the artist's home, the latter two frequently being one and the same. An old photograph of Braque in his studio (Fig. 467), made between 1910 and 1916, shows walls, tables, and floor covered with randomly juxtaposed objects; further the object character of Braque's paintings themselves is stressed by the inclusion of several of them leaning against a table in the middle-ground. The objects found in Cubist paintings are not costly or rare possessions, but were prized for aesthetic or personal reasons and were utilized in daily activities, often conveying an intimate sense of conviviality. Death, moralizing, personal crisis, world events, and so on were all excluded in favor of themes of simple, mostly domestic pleasure. Although the objects conveyed human sentiments, they were rendered in a way that showed the artists' unsentimental attitude toward the older tradition of still lifes. Nor did the Cubists ever arrange objects in the prosaic sequence of their original setting.

If we compare Bauguin's still life, *The Five Senses* (Fig. 465), with *Guitar and Flowers* (Pl. 64, p. 347) by Juan Gris (1887–1927), the significance of the Cubist revolution in form may become clearer. Bauguin follows the shapes, textures, and colors of the objects quite literally, whereas Gris asserts his right to rework all the objects in his painting. Gris has destroyed the closure and autonomy of objects, so that they fuse with other shapes or are joined in complex patterns on the painting's surface that have no natural counterpart. Color is not confined within distinctly bounded areas but is disposed in broader zones. The artist's brushstrokes are similarly independent of the objects and are used to create decided directions, textures, and visual patterns that are essential to the painting's structure. There is no manipulation of light and dark according to a fixed light source, as found in Bauguin's work, but an effect of flickering light and shadow is maintained within new rules laid down by the artist. It is difficult to look beyond (that is, to ignore) the surface of Gris' painting, into a spatial volume as is possible with the 17th-century work. With the modern painting, one is very conscious of the artist's inventiveness in imposing a new structure upon objects (such as the guitar) that otherwise had remained unchanged for hundreds of years. Gris wants the viewer to be very aware of the constructed aspect of his work, in which no area is neutral or merely "fill." Space and object both become part of an intricate pictorial scaffolding that holds the composition tautly suspended within the frame. Bauguin could conceivably have finished the painting of each object separately, always keeping in mind its final appearance and arrangement. With Juan Gris and other Cubists, the artist began without such assurance, without a fixed conception of the finished work, and while improvising moved back and forth over the whole picture surface at all stages of the painting's development. He continuously adjusted every element to its adjacent areas and the overall design. It is an approach which requires that the spectator judge for *aesthetic rightness* rather than for fidelity to the appearance of objects arrayed under light on a studio table.

By drawing our attention to the physical aspect of artistic creation, to the painting's pigment and strokes, Gris is also affirming the object character of the painting. Although he simulates some movement into depth and forward, we are conscious primarily of the painting's surface. The tangency of compositional elements with the edges of the canvas at various points and the many vertical and horizontal accents reiterate the physical dimensions of the painting. Gris does not depend upon the intrinsic or preexisting beauty of objects, but wrests aesthetic value from each touch and from the firm and lucid total design he has invented. To appreciate his achievement demands not that the viewer try to reconstruct each object from seemingly scattered components in the painting, as if it were a jigsaw puzzle, but that he should savor the pleasures of the work in its painted parts and in the harmony of the whole. Gris' discipline and method may be compared to those of the musician, whose improvisations are governed by a profound knowledge of musical structure.

Georges Braque (1882–1963) assembled pieces of a newspaper *(Le Courrier)*, a cigarette package with its government seal, and simulated wood-textured paper and pasted them to each other and the paper surface over which he drew with charcoal (Fig. 468). Thus he chose not to simulate in paint materials that were flat in nature and susceptible of incorporation in his compositions. This *collage* technique (from *papiers collés,* meaning "pasted papers") frequently appears in Cubist art, often with wit and playfulness; here, for instance, Braque

*left:* 467. GEORGES BRAQUE in his studio. c. 1910–16. Maeght Gallery (LIFE Magazine, © 1949 Time, Inc. All rights reserved).

cut out a heart from a newspaper article about Italy and alliances. Use of daily newspapers helps to date these compositions and makes them quite literally of their time. The assembled objects were common and readily identifiable, linking the composite artistic image to the world of familiar activities. Unlike older illusionistic painters, Braque actually built his composition outward from the surface toward the spectator. With charcoal drawing he integrated the pasted paper segments with each other and with the white background, introducing shading for purposes of compositional accent without reference to a consistent light source as was seen in the Bauguin. Thus even light and shade were now made subject to the artist's will. It was the Cubists such as Braque, Picasso, and Gris who gave to modern art a declaration of independence—a freedom to choose the materials of art and to decide how they may be used, without adherence to conventions about what was noble or faithful to the world of appearances.

**New Ideas on Expression** It is unnecessary to refer to the original objects in order to evaluate and enjoy *Gourds* (Fig. 469), a painting by Henri Matisse (1869–1954). Line, color, and composition, though influenced to a degree by his contact with the visual world, became primarily personal inventions. The standards of control and quality in his art were supplied by Matisse's exceptionally good taste and dependence upon artistic intuition. *Gourds* gives itself immediately and fully to the eye as a fresh sensory experience, the viewer being affected before any reasoning process occurs. The choice, limited number, and forceful rendering of objects eliminates questions of their meaning. Their clarity of contour and careful dispersal without overlap emphasizes their familiarity and durability. The objects' internal coherence within the frame and the broad, flat areas of pure bright color quickly establish for the eye the rightness and importance of the total harmony.

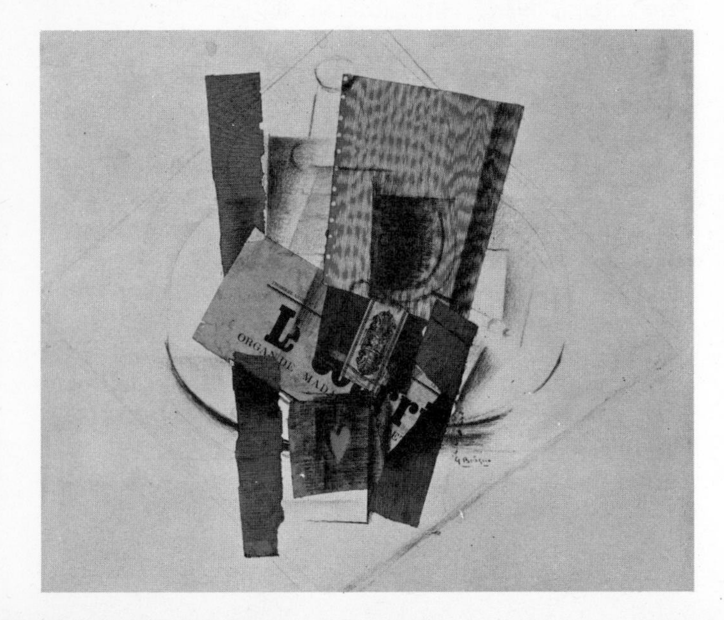

Matisse "dreamed" of an art having "balance, purity and serenity." His imagery endures because of the range and provocativeness of his contrasts. His shapes and colors possess a tenuous tie with the visual world. Painting from memory rather than from direct perception, Matisse liberated drawing and color from the specific properties of objects so that they in turn could release his feelings of joy and serve his views of expression in art (Pl. 72, p. 361; Pl. 89, p. 434; Figs. 82, 580, 581).

> What I am after, above all, is expressiveness. Expression to my way of thinking does not consist of the passion mirrored upon a human face or betrayed by violent gesture. The whole arrangement of my pictures is expressive. The place occupied by figures or objects, the empty spaces around them, the proportions, everything plays a part [1908].

As with the term *expressivo* in music, we do not ask "expressive of what?" Matisse's drawing is expressive because it clearly derives not only from skill and taste but also from strong will.

The irregularity of objects in *Gourds*, though also occasioned by the subtle demands of the painting's surface structure, does not extend to the extremes of the Cubists' manipulations. Matisse delighted in the formal completeness of objects as well as in the entire painting. Instead of the linear framework of the Cubists, he set up a seemingly loose dispersal of shapes on a strong asymmetrically divided blue-black background, achieving a daring balance of his few objects against their ground. He made effective use of intervals as well as of linear correspondences and played upon the visual weight of a color when seen in areas of varying size and in different contexts. In *Gourds* were sounded new color chords, such as blue-black-reddish brown, which did not originate in established sequences before Matisse's eyes but came to him instinctively as he responded with pleasure to a particular tone he had set down. "I cannot copy nature in a servile way; I must interpret nature and submit it to the spirit of the picture. When I have found the relationship of all the tones, the result must be a living harmony of tones."

**Objects as Private Symbols** The Italian painter Giorgio de Chirico (b. 1888) could not, in another sense, accept the visual world as a basis for expressing his views of reality. In De Chirico's *Grand Metaphysical Interior* (Pl. 65, p. 348), the painting of objects involved fanciful images that were not imitated from what is given directly to the senses. The stimulus of external sensations was replaced by the artist's inner attentiveness to "strange sensations." The objects of De Chirico's

*left:* 468. GEORGES BRAQUE. *Le Courrier*. 1913. Collage, 20 × 22 1/2". Philadelphia Museum of Art (A. E. Gallatin Collection).

*opposite:* 469. HENRI MATISSE. *Gourds*. 1916. Oil on canvas, 25 5/8 × 31 7/8". Museum of Modern Art, New York (Mrs. Simon Guggenheim Fund).

painting can for the most part be inventoried and identified, but their context and connection elude definition. Indeed, what is crucial for the painter is that they *are* enigmatic. The objects are set in an interior which is not a room in the sense that it knows human presence. It is an interior because behind a window shade suspended at the right is not a blue sky, but a green exterior. Within this interior is a naturalistic painting of an Italian villa; the familiar exterior world is thus displaced, consigned to a picture frame to become one more inexplicable object. Painted with equal illusionistic precision in an adjacent framed panel are various normally unrelated objects. The framed panels are supported by a network of drafting instruments, ordinarily to be associated with rational design. De Chirico endowed these tools with obscure meanings that we can perhaps sense but cannot fix in precise terms. They have been used as part of a calculated irrationality. The light and shadow in the room and its spatial construction are also independent of traditional usage or the position of the viewer. The shadows, shapes, space, and the pervasive stillness are an uncanny ambient made compelling by the exactness of its rendering.

The word *metaphysical* in the title refers to De Chirico's belief that the artist should paint a higher reality than that of the senses. He therefore sought to restore mystery to art and to paint the obsessive hallucinatory images which he felt mirrored the state of his soul. He became alienated from the empiricism and pictorial rationale of previous artists. De Chirico's world is that seen when the eyes are closed—a cool, dry, inert, and uninhabitable environment meant to be traversed only by the eye. The intimate personal nature of his choice of objects is in contrast to the social and hedonistic connotations of those used in Cubism or in Matisse's work: "I fill up the empty spaces in my canvas as the structure of the picture requires with a body or an object according to my humor." Objects in older still lifes exhibited some unity of origin and use, involved some shared frame of reference. Perhaps influenced by Cubism and its collage technique, De Chirico's irrational dislocation and juxtaposition of objects from the everyday world he distrusted were important in loosing the inhibitions and fantasy of later artists who felt that "to be true to oneself" in art demanded response to the fringes of consciousness and the deepest recesses of the self.

For Marcel Duchamp (1887–1968) the meaning and value of a work of art depended on its interpretation in the viewer's mind. "The spectator brings the works in contact with the external world by deciphering and interpreting its inner qualifications and thus adds his contributions to the creative act." The painter of *The Bride Stripped Bare by Her Bachelors, Even* (Pl. 66, p. 348) was against traditional notions of meaning, whereby the painting illustrates the title and is fully understandable on the basis of a preexisting common knowledge. *The Bride,* instead, was intended as a cynical commentary on art, the machine, reason, sentimentality, and sex. Duchamp's intentionally dry, academically precise painting of objects was meant to discourage praise of the virtuosity of his hand. He baffled attempts to trace the origin and meaning of his objects and deflated technology by creating irrational machines that cannot produce anything. For those who may be seeking the sentiment suggested by its nominal subject, there is little likelihood of empathy with Duchamp's *Bride* or her "bachelors." Done during a period of personal crisis, *The Bride* is a complex metaphor or private myth, modern in its obscure personal origin, incompleteness, and ambiguity. Duchamp used his metaphor with wit in order to mechanize love and humanize the machine, to depersonalize art but personalize the act of *viewing* art. He was giving form to a "world of unknown quantity," of which the visible world is only a shadow. Art should be made, he felt, only by intuition and revelation. "The artist acts like a mediumistic being who, from the labyrinth beyond time and space, seeks his way out to a clearing."

*The Bride* consists of two glass panels mounted in an aluminum frame measuring roughly 6 × 9 feet. The shapes were applied to the glass with paint, varnish, and lead wire; the craks in the glass resulted from an accident in shipping, a random addition of which the artist approved. Technically, the work is marvelously made. Objects are not represented on the glass surface; they exist on the glass, as if knowing no other habitat. From Duchamp's notes, it appears that the top panel is the "bride," and the lower one the "bachelors." The "bride" herself, at the upper left corner, consists of intricate and suggestive plumbing forms. To the right is a perforated cloud shape. At the lower left are nine objects recalling those used in dry-cleaning plants; Duchamp called these his "malic molds," or "bachelor machine." Below them is "the slide," or waterwheel, realized as if in an idealized extension of space. Duchamp painted his objects on the window so that, in looking through the glass, we see our own world, not one imagined by the artist. Within an object-filled room, the forms of *The Bride* seem to hover and move, existing in ever-changing contexts when viewed from different angles.

**The New Literalism** The art of De Chirico transposed familiar objects into unfamiliar situations. Duchamp invented objects that insolently parodied objects, human situations, and the body itself. *Target* (Pl. 67, p. 349), a work by the American artist Jasper Johns (b. 1930), is *itself* the painted object. There is no illusionism, and the painting has no reference to anything outside itself. The subject is a two-dimensional target coincident with the painted papered surface on which it exists. When the artist wished to introduce three-dimensional objects, he made plaster casts and closeted them in a row of boxes with movable lids set above the principal motif. He presents us with no riddle and asks only that his work be taken at its face value. Johns removed two-dimensional objects—in this case a target, elsewhere the American flag or stenciled numbers—from their accustomed surroundings and connotations. He did not, however, put them into De Chirico's uncanny and enigmatic settings. Johns exaggerated the vividness of the object through increased or intensified size, color, and texture. In short, he wished the viewer to have "a direct painting experience." Johns' position reflects the current view of art as an empirical experience for the viewer, with the work of art regarded as an independent object of entirely surface importance and brought into being by any means the artist may choose.

This permissive notion of means is illustrated in *Broadcast* (Pl. 68, p. 350), a work from 1959 by Robert Rauschenberg (b. 1925). The artist's premise was that any material, if employed literally, could be used in art, and from his New York environment he culled a host of objects that he brought together into *combines.* The objects have a general character of personal souvenirs, like entries in a diary of the artist and the city. There is no illusionism of objects involved. As such, they have been used before in their everyday existence and are used directly again in the combines. According to Rauschenberg, "A pair of socks is no less suitable to make a painting with than wood, nails, turpentine, oil and fabric." He has combined a stuffed angora goat with an auto tire, a stepladder with a thermometer, scraps from billboards with photographs of celebrities, mirrors, baseball bats, Coca Cola bottles, and, in one instance, live grass. His selection of objects was not indiscriminate but involved careful judgments of the eye. In *Broadcast* he mounted two working radios and adjusted them so that each can be tuned to only one station. One transmits news and sports, the other music. Near the radios are appropriate photographs of racing, police beating a rioter, and the word *Help.* The improvisation of parts and the overall structural effect of the paint produce a jazz quality in harmony with the sounds transmitted by the second radio. *Broadcast* is thus environment painting in a broader sense than we have heretofore encountered. Rauschenberg's combines are like fanciful time capsules, bearing witness for the future to his life and times. Rauschenberg has included smells and sounds along with sights, and the pathetic, comic, vulgar, and exuberant means by which modern society has expressed itself as brashly as the artist.

Art, such as we saw at the opening of this chapter (Fig. 457), can be made from discards—from the table, from the life of a city, and from a supermarket. Both Heraclitus and Rauschenberg have given society's leavings a second, more durable life through art. When the American painter Andy Warhol (b. 1925) exhibited *Campbell Soup Can* (Fig. 470), it infuriated not only the public but many critics and artists as well. Traditionally, artists have been their own worst critics. One is reminded of what Emile Zola said about Manet—that to appreciate what he was doing "one had to forget a thousand things about art"—and if one is to enjoy Warhol's work, to be sure, it is necessary to forget a thousand things about painting. At the same time, however, there are some things from the past worth remembering on his behalf. The strongest criticism leveled against the work is that, aside from its magnified scale, the painting presents no imaginative transformation of the subject, no apparent exercise of artistic judgment. Such fidelity to the object has already been seen in 17th-century still life, however. And, while perhaps not of a high order, imagination was involved in both cases.

Warhol flattens out the can (which appears bent as is often the case when it has been opened), but in this respect his flatness of style belongs to this century and is characteristic of commercial as well as noncommercial art. (One might indeed argue

that *any* painting put up for sale is an object of commerce.) The beautiful handmade objects of German and Dutch painting were of their time, and by selecting a mass-produced product and its container, Warhol continues such expression of his own era. If the artist continues to be free to choose any subject today, Warhol certainly has the right to draw inspiration from advertising or the supermarket. To the charge that painting such as this is all subject matter and shows no stylistic individuality on the artist's part, the answer is that in past centuries subject matter was often the most important element to both the public and the artists themselves. Only after the initial shock—or repulsion—toward a new subject matter has worn off can one judge the painting on its aesthetic merits or demerits alone. Furthermore, Warhol does not believe in individuality of style, and his calculated self-effacement before his subject is as old as the most naturalistic still-life picture-making. The great irony is that for much of this century the public has cried out for art that it can understand and that clearly relates to its experience; yet when artists such as Warhol deliver what the public seems to have been clamoring for, this same public is outraged. Fortunately for Warhol, he has had more success than the Ford Motor Company had with its Edsel model, which was designed exclusively from exhaustive market research of the public's wants.

Since 1961 Roy Lichtenstein (b. 1923) has been making paintings which relate to those of Johns and Warhol by their vernacular motifs and by their calculated avoidance of a number of characteristics that the public of the sixties has come to expect of American artists. Lichtenstein's choice of imagery —including comic strips, household objects, stamps, currency, paintings by artists such as Picasso, Monet, and Mondrian, Greek temples, hot dogs, guns and gun-slingers—at first outraged his audiences because it seemed unworthy of art, mechanical or too imitative in execution, and tasteless. His series of *Brushworks,* of which one is reproduced here (Fig. 471), continues the tradition of making art from art. In addition, it represents Lichtenstein's positive objective to seek alternatives to the legacy of past art—alternatives to the Renaissance integration of objects and the ground they are seen against and to the Cubist reformation of the motif and integration of it into the weblike structure of the field. Lichtenstein draws an image thrown onto the canvas by an opaque projector and then uses the commercial printer's device of Ben Day dots, achieved with a uniformly perforated screen. The brushstroke, before Lichtenstein, had been identified with manual virtuosity, the expression of feeling, and with a guarantee of aesthetic effect as well as an individuality of "handwriting" (Pl. 70, p. 359; Pl. 85, p. 416; Fig. 595). Lichtenstein makes his "brushstrokes" into *things,* detached from descriptive or passionate function and formally isolated within the limits of his canvas. There is a mock insensitivity in the artist's self-restriction to a few commercial colors. He does have formal values in terms of the aesthetics of his paintings and enjoys the paradox between how real the image seems to the public and how unreal the contrast between its physical nature and the final rendering.

*opposite:* 470. ANDY WARHOL. *Campbell Soup Can.* 1962. Magna on canvas, 5′10″ × 4′6″. Leo Castelli Gallery, New York.

*above:* 471. ROY LICHTENSTEIN. *Yellow and Green Brushstrokes.* 1966. Oil and magna on canvas, 3′ × 5′8″. Collection Robert Fraser.

**The Use and Making of Objects** Throughout history, sculptors and artisans have made objects for a variety of practical purposes, utility and decoration included, to gratify the desires of their patrons. Traditionally these artists were responsible for the invention and execution of their objects, although assistants might have carried out some of the tedious craftsmanship. In this century artists have entered into new relationships with objects, either employing objects not of their own design and manufacture, hence made by others, or else creating things useless or impractical beyond their aesthetic or personally expressive content. The break with tradition came partly with the Cubists' collage: The introduction of a variety of materials, and sometimes objects, foreign to art media countered existing notions of purity (or homogeneity) of means and consistency of illusionism. Another determinant of this break occurred in 1913, when Duchamp mounted on a stool a bicycle wheel turned upside down (Fig. 472). For Duchamp this was a logical step after centuries of illusionistic painting of objects which had lead, he felt, to a senseless glorification of the artist's hand. Art was not to be found in manual execution. Duchamp developed expressive activity beyond existing artistic means by using *readymade* objects of commercial production, such as the bicycle wheel; he chose these on the basis of chance and indifference, not because of aesthetic appeal, and then displaced them from their normal environment or context. To the artist these readymades had

*far left:* 472. Marcel Duchamp. *Bicycle Wheel.* 1951, third version after lost original of 1913. Assemblage, metal wheel on paintedwood stool; height 4′2½″. Museum of Modern Art, New York (Sidney and Harriet Janis Collection).

*left:* 473. Joseph Cornell. *Medici Slot Machine.* 1942. Construction, 15½ × 12 × 4⅜″. Collection Mr. and Mrs. Bernard J. Reis, New York.

a mystique and were a metaphysical projection of invisible reality. Later artists did not always understand or share his metaphysics, but they appreciated his new premise that art was made in the mind of the artist and not by his hand. Selection replaced execution for many artists after 1913, and today there are artists who have extended Duchamp's premise to include the notion that art need not be visible but can exist on the level of ideas, communicated by words (Figs. 612, 613).

Perhaps the most sensitive manipulator of objects for the poetic associations they inspire has been the American Joseph Cornell (b. 1903), who since the late thirties has been staging private dramas in small glass-covered boxes. Their smallness of scale and undecipherable plots are constant, ensuring intimacy and meditation in the reaction of the beholder. His sets and actors are sometimes repertorial, since he has occasionally worked in series, but more often they change with the mood of the piece. *Medici Slot Machine* (Fig. 473) conjoins in title and form reveries on a long dead young prince and on the childish delight in the box of chance from an amusement parlor. Gunsight, compass, and map are used to deceive our sense of orientation, while strips of pictures of a painted portrait evoke the film medium and its now unfamiliar fairy-tale potential. Jacks and marbles and the numbers attached to the outside of the box also relate to play; they are appropriate to the aristocratic child, to the associations of the slot machine, and to Cornell's own gentle soliticitation to suspend disbelief and the rules of reason as the admission price to his theater. Surrealism of the thirties encouraged Cornell to collapse the differences between near and far, past and present, painting and sculpture, art and nonart, linear logic and absurdity. His soft-voiced modesty of expression and reluctance to talk about his work counter the public's image of the modern artist clamoring for public attention.

Similar in spirit to Duchamp, the Swiss artist Jean Tinguely (b. 1925) has created *assemblages* from metal scrap heaps, which are parodies of machines and witty commentaries on art and social values. They are usually designed to break down, be nonproductive, and underscore the "dumb" movement of the machine, thereby providing comic relief for a public accustomed to standing in awe of things mechanical. His Swiss nationality has lead to jokes that Tinguely is personally doing penance for the legendary dependability and precision of his country's timepieces. His scorn for all forms of virtuosity and the handmade led to his "meta-matics" (Fig. 474), mechanical contraptions that contrive to turn out thousands of abstract drawings, rebutting the inviolability of art by the machine

Further undermining the public's expectation that sculpture be serious as well as durable (hard) are the soft constructions (Fig. 475) of the Swedish-born artist Claes Oldenburg (b. 1929). Gravity is his collaborator, sewing his means of joining, canvas and kapok his materials, so that bathroom fixtures slump, electric fans wilt, typewriters slouch, auto engines melt, and telephones sag. Bigger than life, but often like their counterparts in commercial advertising, Oldenburg's objects shock or amuse. The blatant familiarity of his subjects obscures his intentions, which are to involve himself in the relation of hardness to softness, conditions of antithesis which express his experience of the world around him:

> I think the objects are more or less chosen as excuses that I can hang my expression of what it feels like to be alive on. Thus I would take a hard object like a telephone and make a soft version of it which would remind you of the hard version and kind of set you thinking or feeling about the contrast between hard and soft in nature.

To make art Oldenburg involves his body in an exchange with nature; similarly many artists of the last decade have permitted bodily as well as intellectual response to their

*bove:* Plate 65. GIORGIO DE CHIRICO. *Grand Metaphysical Interior.* 917. Oil on canvas, $37^3/_4 \times 28^3/_8$″. Collection James Thrall Soby, New Canaan, Conn. (See p. 343.)

*ight:* Plate 66. MARCEL DUCHAMP. *The Bride Stripped Bare by Her Bachelors, Even.* 1915–23. Oil and lead wire on glass, $9'1^1/_4$″ × $5'9^1/_8$″. Philadelphia Museum of Art (Louise and Walter Arensberg Collection). (See p. 343.)

*pposite:* Plate 67. JASPER JOHNS. *Target.* 1958. Encaustic and newsprint on canvas, with plaster casts and wood; 4′3″ × 3′8″. Collection Leo Castelli, New York. (See p. 344.)

*above:* Plate 63. Paul Cézanne. *Still Life with Compote.* 1879–82 Oil on canvas, $18\frac{1}{8} \times 21\frac{5}{8}''$. Louvre, Paris (formerly Collectio Auguste Pellerin). (See p. 340.)

*left:* Plate 64. Juan Gris. *Guitar and Flowers.* 1912. Oil o canvas, $44\frac{1}{8} \times 27\frac{5}{8}''$. Museum of Modern Art, New Yor (bequest of Anna Erickson Levene in memory of her husban Dr. Phoebus Aaron Theodor Levene). (See pp. 340, 341).

Plate 68. ROBERT RAUSCHENBERG. *Broadcast*. 1959. Combine painting, 5′2″ × 6′4″. Collection Ileana Sonnabend, Paris. (See p. 344.)

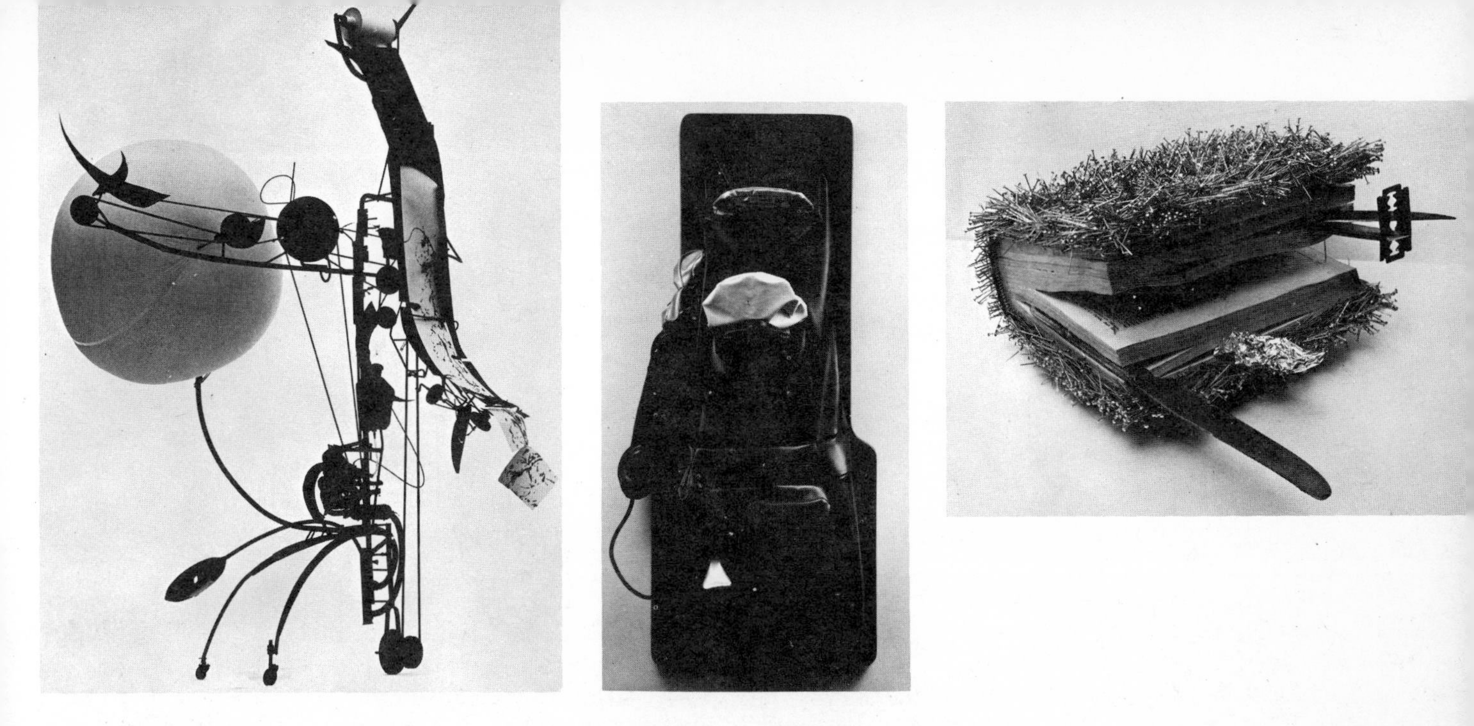

above left: 474. JEAN TINGUELY. *Meta-matic No. 17*. 1959. Iron, height 9′10″. Nationalmuseum, Stockholm.

above center: 475. CLAES OLDENBURG. *Soft Pay Telephone*. 1963. Vinyl filled with kapok, mounted on painted wood panel; $46^1/_2 \times 19 \times 12''$. Collection William Zierler, New York.

above right: 476. LUCAS SAMARAS. *Untitled*. 1962. Assemblage, partly-opened book with pins, razor blade, scissors, table knife, metal foil, piece of glass, and plastic rod; $5^1/_2 \times 8^1/_2 \times 11^7/_8''$. Museum of Modern Art, New York (gift of Philip Johnson).

environment. Sensual reaction to Oldenburg's *Telephone* or to a "book" (Fig. 476) devised by the Greek-born artist Lucas Samaras (b. 1936) would evoke thoughts of the tactile qualities of these familiar objects of communication. For Samaras all objects can induce erotic or occult associations. Samaras became an artist to have "something to do with meaning of things." Like prying open a book with sharp objects, making art is an erotic gesture, the creative act, one of narcissism or "making one's body into art." Samaras uses art as a form of self-dramatization, exposing through his objects obsessions about sex and violence and thereby realizing the self-liberation inherent in the artistic enterprise.

This introduction to the artist as a painter, sculptor, and manipulator of objects has suggested the scope of his performance, from imitator to creator to selector of objects; from fabricator of illusionistic familiar surroundings to inventor of new environments. He has ranged from playful deception through storytelling, personification, moralizing and philosophizing, metaphor and emblem making, aesthetic contemplation, and meaninglessness. The artists' involvement with objects reflects great changes both in style and in man's attitude toward his environment—whether it be one of fear, reverence, wonder, curiosity, pride, dependence, distaste, or pleasure.

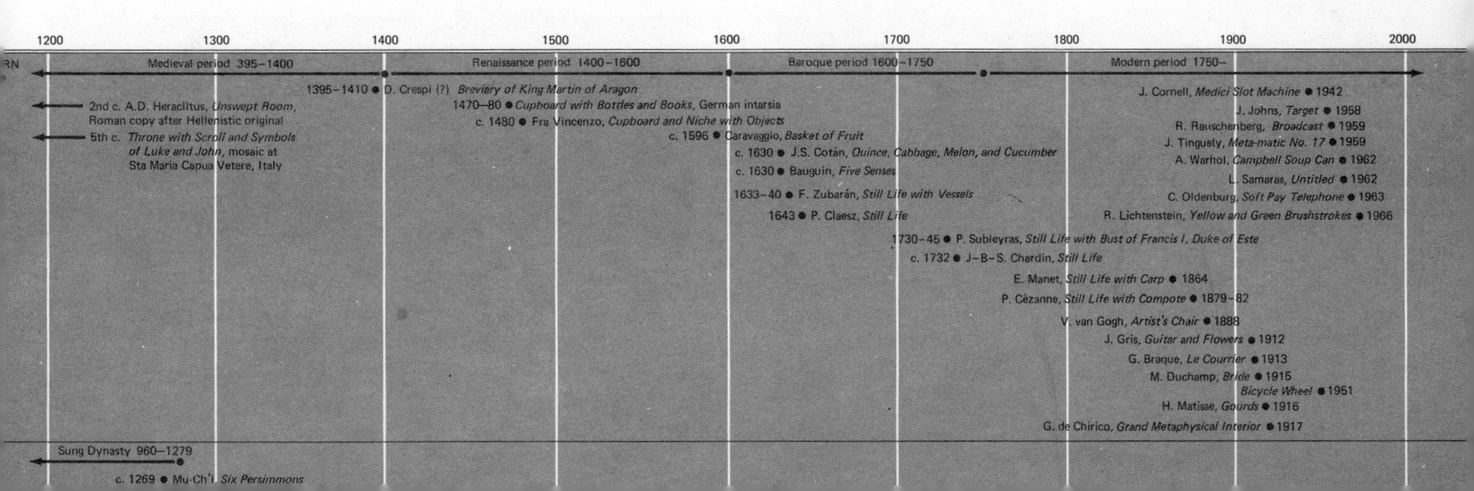

# 18

For centuries the artist was enjoined "to hold a mirror up to nature," and the mirror itself was a favored metaphor of truth and art. Every morning the mirror identifies who and where we are. The disquieting image created by René Magritte (1898–1967), *Portrait of Edward James Seen from the Back* (Fig. 477), betrays the role of the mirror and shocks us into remembering the importance of the face. Our language is riddled with clichés that by now unconsciously project the importance of this bodily feature: "to face the future," "to face up," "face to face," "face value," "on the face of it," "to put a good face on," "to lose" or "to save face," and so on. Courage, honesty, trust, deception, and dishonor are some of the connotations of these clichés, implying that character and judgment reside in the face. Before Magritte, the artist's task was to save a man's face for posterity, thereby gratifying the ego that resided behind it. The face is still our identity badge and insurance against anonymity, our calling card to social life, the politician's passport to success or failure. If one studies it closely enough, the back view of Edward James reveals his identity or individuality, as would his fingerprints or dentures. A man with no face, however, confronts as bleak a prospect as the featureless environment mirrored in Magritte's portrait. Only in this century would an artist either desire or be able to execute Magritte's enigmatic or dislocated portrait, for reasons that will come under consideration later, in relation to imaginative art (Fig. 572).

*left:* 477. RENÉ MAGRITTE. *La Reproduction Interdite (Portrait of Edward James Seen from the Back).* Oil on canvas, 37 × 25½". Reproduced by kind permission of the Edward James Foundation, West Dean, England.

**Problems and Possibilities for Portraitists** The face has presented the artist, whether chronicler or commentator, with an usual challenge. In the words of the German philosopher and sociologist Georg Simmel, "Within the perceptible world, there is no other structure like the human face which merges such a great variety of shapes and surfaces into an absolute unity of meaning." For the chronicler, or narrative artist, the problem was to unite a multiplicity of disparate elements. For the commentator, or interpretive artist—who could, in Leonardo's words, "mirror the motions" of his subject's mind—there was both the added difficulty of producing a lively interaction between these elements and the revelation that the smallest change in any feature altered the expression of the whole. Artists who worked from death masks in ancient Rome and in 15th-century Italy recognized that they had the materials for individuality, but not for facial liveliness; they could not achieve the expressiveness that separates the animated from the dead. Unless he desired an idealized face, the artist had to search for those irrational irregularities—the asymmetry of the right and left halves of the face—which he could use as protagonists in his facial drama, playing them against the

# THE PORTRAIT IN PAINTING AND SCULPTURE

general symmetry of the head. Beginning in the late 15th century, artists became concerned with facial animation and with the depiction of personality as well as individuality. As Simmel points out, Christianity in the West prescribed that a man's body be shown clothed, and consequently the face alone could project his personality. For almost 500 years artists have developed techniques based upon the acute observation and study of each other's work in order to catch the potential as well as actual mobility of the face as it responds to the spirit. Portraiture demonstrates how in Western society since the Renaissance the face has been the surrogate for the whole man.

It should surprise no one that the artist knows the face in subtle ways beyond our usual knowledge of it. He must be conscious of how it is made: how its cranial and muscular substructures press against the flesh; how features taper, swell, and merge; and how colors work up through the skin's surface. He must think in terms of distances and proportions. The eye affords him a "window to the soul"; how he shapes and focuses it, or otherwise supports the gaze, will influence the mood, personality, and character of his subject, his relation to the viewer and surroundings, and will divide or determine the space within the painting.

**Roman Portraits** Although modern psychology has taught us to be wary of physiognomic analysis in determining a person's character, the study of how an individual's features reflect his soul, spirit, or personality is an old concern of artists. Adherents of this "science" assume that the habitual set of the features, the angle at which the head is usually held, bodily posture, formation and gestures of the hands, and even clothing can be meaningful. The way a man sits or wears his coat has been an important consideration in artists' studies of personality or social status. In this century photography has preempted the portrait function, and many modern artists avoid portraiture because demands for likeness conflict with their personal aesthetic. Nonetheless, imitation has had an honorable history and inspired many powerful portraits without weakening their individuality of style.

The sculpture portraiture surviving from ancient Rome constitutes a significant record of that civilization, for no other people portrayed themselves so extensively in carved and painted works. The countless death masks and portraits made for Roman homes, tombs, palaces, and forums reflect ancestor worship and a healthy strain of egotism. The Republican portrait in Figure 478 displays the sunken cheeks and mouth of a dead man, and this marble image could well have been copied from a death mask. Except for official effigies of their leaders (Fig. 280), the Romans of the Republican period avoided self-flattery, preferring to portray the stark, harsh evidence that living left upon the face. Such is the candor of this art that the testimony of the many sur-

*left:* 478. *Portrait of a Roman.* Republican, 1st century B.C. Marble, height $14^{1}/_{2}$″. Vatican Museums, Rome.

*left:* 479. THÉODORE GÉRICAULT. *Portrait of a Kleptomaniac.* 1821–24. Oil on canvas, $23^1/_4 \times 19^5/_8$". Musée des Beaux-Arts, Ghent.

*opposite:* 480. RAPHAEL. *Baldassare Castiglione.* 1510. Oil on canvas, $32^3/_8 \times 26^1/_2$". Louvre, Paris.

viving portraits can be balanced against the weight the Romans placed on their values. These, in theory, were honesty and frugality, self-reliance, simplicity, firmness of purpose, gravity, and a sense of what was important. The Romans believed in toughness and discipline, in organization and a pragmatic approach to daily life. Their literature reveals many and spectacular exceptions, but the Roman conquest of the ancient world and the Pax Romana (see pp. 211–214) furnish much evidence that elevated standards did in fact prevail during the Republic and early Empire. The portrait here illustrated shows an honest and toughminded desire to represent the subject's individuality, from the dented skull to his sagging jowls. The simulation of flesh and bone is a compelling achievement. The natural discrepancies between the two sides of the man's face have been retained, and, even without the paint that originally defined the eyes, the shrewd gaze is consistent with the experience-worn features of the inner and outer man.

**Psychological Portraits** Throughout the Middle Ages, for almost a thousand years, the realistic likeness of a specific individual did not appear in European art (see Chap. 5). Its return in the 14th and 15th centuries coincided with the naturalism sponsored in secular art by royalty and a prosperous commercial class. No surviving antique paintings equal in anatomical exactness the faces painted in 15th-century Flanders (see Chap. 6). Eric Ambler has written:

> A man's features, the bone structure and the tissue which covers it, are the product of a biological process; but his face he creates for himself. It is a statement of his habitual emotional attitude; the attitude which his desires need for their fulfillment and which his fears demand for their protection from prying eyes. He wears it like a devil mask; a device to evoke in others the emotions complementary to his own. If he is afraid, then he must be feared; if he desires, then he must be desired. It is a screen to his mind's nakedness. Only a few men, painters, have been able to see the mind through the face.

Four centuries after Jan van Eyck brought such coincidence of virtuosity and powerful observation to his portrait of Giovanni Arnolfini and his bride (Pl. 73, p. 362), the French artist Théodore Géricault painted in oil a number of insane patients of his friend Doctor Georget, who believed that insanity proceeded from physiological rather than psychological causes, and that a close study of the face would produce pathological evidence. For clinical purposes, therefore, Géricault approached his deranged sitters (Fig. 479) with the same discerning scrutiny that Van Eyck had employed for his aristocratic subjects. With the patients' knowledge he was painting them but making no reference—in background, dress, or general pose—to their hospital environment, Géricault set about to study and record the mask into which each face had set, and also to mirror the grinding impulses behind it. In the portrait of a man afflicted with a monomania for theft, Géricault brought to bear all his sensibility for subtle color and surface inflections, thereby attaining considerable aesthetic as well as psychological value. The most obvious symptoms of the man's malady lie in his eyes and in the tention of the facial muscles.

Géricault's style, temperament, and interests were suited for this project. Often he focused on subjects without external anchorage, figures who by force of circumstance were thrown back upon their own resources (Fig. 405)—men portrayed in action or in a state of tense inaction, an oscillation at one with the severe sociopolitical changes occurring after Napoleon's fall.

**Ethical Portraits** Géricault painted portraits of those who were, in a sense, victims of modern society; the Renaissance artist Raphael painted portraits of those fortunates comprising the elite society that flourished in the early 16th century. Raphael was himself admitted into this society, an interesting commentary on the artist's increased social stature at that time. The portrait that best epitomizes the Renaissance social ideal both in style and subject is that of Baldassare Castiglione

(Fig. 480). In a manner of speaking, the picture was made before Raphael took up his brush. The pose, which largely determined the composition, was probably a joint decision of the sitter and the painter. Castiglione's treatise *The Courtier* set forth the requirements for the ideal Renaissance man—his skills, conduct, and objectives. Castiglione could have served as a model for his own book, since he was a poet, a brilliant scholar, and an outstanding ambassador and courtier. He commented thus on his ideal: "Besides nobleness of birth, I would that he have not only a wit, and a comely shape of person and countenance, but also a certain grace which shall make him at first sight acceptable and loving unto whosoever beholdeth him." The perfect courtier was also expected to be capable in arms and hardihood, to have ingenuity and loyalty, to be pleasant to all, forever witty and discreet, and to accomplish everything with grace. On clothing, Castiglione wrote:

> A black color has a better grace in garment than any other color . . . and this I mean for his ordinary apparel. . . . He ought to determine with himself what he will appear to be and so to apparel himself, and make his garments help him to be counted such a one, even of them that hear him not speak, nor see him do any manner of thing. . . . Our Courtier ought not to profess to be a glutton nor drunkard, nor riotous and inordinate in any ill condition, nor filthy and unclean in his living.

Not only did Raphael faithfully record Castiglione's appearance and manner, but he also enhanced the man's grace and bearing by subtle plays of shadow and light. The pyramidal shape formed by the figure and locked within the frame ensures its stability. The figure's advancing left arm forms a gentle barrier between him and the viewer, while the more frontal face promotes a certain impression of cordiality without excessive intimacy. The careful, yet easy and unostentatious placement of the hands further exteriorizes the man's inner grace—a matter of mind as well as of physique.

One of the great painters of 16th-century courtly life was Agnolo Bronzino (1503–72), whose style, like that of Jean Clouet in France (Pl. 38, p. 217), was perfectly attuned to the tastes of his aristocratic Florentine clientele. His *Portrait of a Young Man* (Pl. 69, p. 359) is the refined embodiment of Castiglione's ideal courtier, a comely man, discreetly elegant in dress, superbly in control of his body and feelings, and a gentleman of letters whose learning included art and architecture. In comparison with Castiglione's portrait, Bronzino's youth has a decidedly cool and more detached air, which seems to indicate the premium placed upon the social remoteness and exalted self-imagery of his elite group. Full comprehension of this portrait at the time of its creation presupposed as sophisticated a beholder as the subject himself.

The three-quarter format allowed more ample display of a manly figure and at the same time established the viewer at a greater distance than would have a bust-length portrait. It also permitted Bronzino to contrive a striking design involving the body, accessories, and architecture. The architectural backdrop underscores the youth's erectness, and its olive tones complement those of the flesh and costume. The purple tones of the table and chair, like those of the wall behind, are unnatural accents that reflect a taste for artifice. The entire painting is an ultrarefined study in contrasts, indicative of the fact that there is more than meets the untrained eye. The youth's body is treated like an abstraction, its contours alternately smooth and irregular, the spine rigid and the wrists supple. The aristocratic attitude of the elbow posture has had added to it an affected spread of the fingers against the hip. The complex, even perverse interests of this society are suggested by the contrasts between the perfectly formed beauty of the subject's face and the grotesque carved heads of the table and chair arm. That such extremes of beauty and ugliness could derive from the same imagination intrigued Bronzino and his clients. An austere or ascetic appearance often masked highly sophisticated erotic imagination and indulgence in Florentine courts. The youth's costume, for example, has a tight-fitting, constricting cut to the coat and an exaggerated codpiece.

A totally different ethic of manliness and painting produced the 17th-century Dutch *Portrait of a Man* (Pl. 70, p. 359) by Frans Hals (c. 1581–1666). Quiet reserve is superseded by frank affability and a shared intimacy between viewer and subject, calculated composure by the appearance of good-natured spontaneity. The Dutchman's unkempt state, casual

pose, and drinker's ruddiness make him the ideal male companion of his time and place, if not the ideal courtier.

Raphael's and Bronzino's smooth, immaculate picture surfaces, so in keeping with their subjects, have analogies only in the underpainting of Hals' portrait style. After painstakingly detailing his subject in a relatively tight surface treatment, Hals rapidly painted over the entire work in slashing strokes and ragged patches of color. Moreover, it is possible that by this late stage in his career Hals had dispensed with the underpainting. Raphael may be judged a superb picture-maker, Hals a consummate painter. In contributing to the total effect, the material substance of Hals' pigment is as vivid as are the man's physical qualities themselves. The painter's gusto is apparent in the way he has avoided the formal, contained posture used by Raphael and, instead, has twisted the hat, face, and body into angles opposed to those of the frame. Raphael's composition directly relates Castiglione to an impersonal ethical coordinate system; Hals' sitter has his own moral and aesthetic axis.

**Modern Informal Portraits** In the 19th century, portraitists loosened the conventions of the genre and permitted their subjects to assume more personal poses. The portraits of Jean-Auguste-Dominique Ingres demonstrate how a seated pose can be made to distinguish the complex of characteristics in a fully mature, highly individual personality (Fig. 481). Ingres had struggled unsuccessfully through many sittings to find the right pose to manifest the strong character of Louis-François Bertin, a newspaper owner. During a conversation with a friend, Bertin unconsciously assumed an attitude that caught the painter's eye, and even before a single stroke had been painted Ingres informed his client that the portrait "was done." The resulting portrait has the suggestion of some great predatory bird. The disarrayed hair, the attenuated nose, and the talonlike hands are not disguised but, rather, are accentuated. The man's ample girth is stressed, and Bertin quite overwhelms his chair. Even the wrinkled suit magnifies his energy. Ingres was at his painterly best not in the mythological or narrative scenes favored at the time (Figs. 406, 414), but rather in portraits, inspired by a unique and strong-willed human being.

**Private Portraiture in a Public Place** Ostensibly, *Place de la Concorde* (Fig. 482) by Edgar Degas depicts a small group of strollers, strangers to each other but united in their location on the pedestrian island of that great Paris square (Figs. 391, 392). Although not the first to employ this idea, Degas set up a portrait situation in which the Vicomte Lepic, his daughters Janine and Eylau, and their dog are shown not in the familiar intimacy of their home but in the most public place in Paris. This relocation of the portrait enabled Degas to portray the momentary mental estrangement of a family, perhaps while they were pacing and waiting for public transport; he thus avoided the sentimental gestures and poses of mutuality expected in family portraits. All of the familiar devices for pictorial coherence, such as reciprocal gesture and gaze, are ignored or pulled apart. The psychological fragmentation of the main figures, as well as the fragmentation of their forms and

*above:* 481. JEAN-AUGUSTE-DOMINIQUE INGRES. *Monsieur Louis Bertin.* 1832. Oil on canvas, 3′10″ × 3′1½″. Louvre, Paris.

*left:* 482. EDGAR DEGAS. *Place de la Concorde, Paris.* 1873–74. Oil on canvas, 31¾ × 47⅜″. Formerly Gerstenberg Collection, Berlin.

that of the bystander, is compounded by the picture's borders, which equate the field of vision with that of the viewer. Rare in the history of art are paintings in which the center is empty and the principal figures are about to walk out of the scene. Degas' view of his subjects' expression is extended to the way a hat is worn, the angle of a cigar clenched in the teeth, an umbrella gripped beneath the arm, and a hand tucked in the tail of a coat. Degas reminds us that portraits may be of momentary existence and not necessarily of a figure posed as if for eternity (Figs. 416–418).

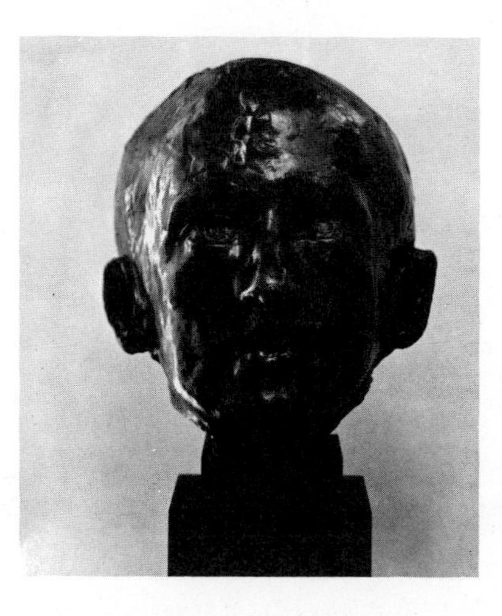

*left:* 483. AUGUSTE RODIN. *Head of Baudelaire.* 1892. Bronze, height 8″. Indiana University and Museum, Bloomington (gift of Mrs. Julian Bobbs).

*right:* 484. ALBERTO GIACOMETTI. *Diego.* c. 1955. Bronze, height 15½″. Walker Art Center, Minneapolis.

**Fixing the Fugitive in Sculpture** For the great French sculptor Auguste Rodin, the making of a portrait demanded an all-encompassing knowledge of his subject. Every inflection of the head had to be searched out, felt as well as seen. He began his work, by making an exhaustive study of every view of the head, even as seen from above. When these successive views were joined, he had an accurate physical resemblance. But what gives Rodin's superb modeling its final power is the revelation of character. In his head of the poet Baudelaire (Fig. 483) there is more than just a precise rendition of skin and skull; there is an unbearable intensity of expression in the taut mouth and transfixed eyes. The unformed lumps on the forehead were a final, sculptural touch, unrelated to real anatomy, yet crucial in bringing the effigy to life. Unusual in the history of portraiture is the deliberate severance of the head from both the neck and the chest; in so doing Rodin sought to create a portrait of a poet who lived completely the life of the intellect. The head is tilted upward as if the poet's gaze were directed toward some invisible horizon of his own thought. Paradoxically, Rodin, who could only model from living examples (Figs. 3, 491, 493, 497, 499, 502, 523), made a compelling spiritual portrait of a man he had never seen and who had been dead for some thirty years. He had found a young artist who resembled Baudelaire and had resorted to photographs of the poet for guidance. But Rodin also knew the poet's life and work by heart, which gave him insight into his subject's complex personality. His description of the portrait reflects a strongly psychological interpretation of facial features:

> It is not Baudelaire . . . but it is a head that resembles Baudelaire. There are a series of characteristics that . . . preserve the cerebral conformation that one calls the type; this bust is of a draftsman named Malteste who shows all the characteristics of the Baudelairean mask. See the enormous forehead, swollen at the temples, dented, tormented, handsome nevertheless, the face described at length by Claudel; the eyes have the look of disdain; the mouth is sarcastic, bitter in its sinuous line, but the swelling of the muscles, a little fat, announces the voluptuous appetites. In short, it is Baudelaire.

The rare fine portraiture in 20th-century art typically has been intimate, probing studies of unstable individuals. Offended by the demands of fidelity in portraiture, modern artists have preferred subjects and areas closer to their personal notions of what art should be. An exception was the Swiss-born artist Alberto Giacometti (1901–66), who found in portraiture the realization of his particular artistic goals. From his earliest works, he carefully studied the human face, almost exclusively that of his younger brother Diego (Fig. 484):

> Sculpture, painting, and drawing have always been for me the means by which I render to myself an account of my vision of the outer world and particularly of the face.... It is utterly impossible for me to model, paint, or draw a head... as I see it, and still, this is the only thing I am attempting to do. All that I will be able to make will be only a pale image of what I see.

From this we learn that his art was meant to satisfy Giacometti alone (Figs. 515, 516, 524). His dilemma and inspiration lay in a fascination with his elusive vision of the external. He was not trying to penetrate the surface and to reveal a man's character. For Giacometti, the problem was that when he focused on a detail, he tended to lose sight of the whole, and when he looked away from the live model to the clay he was shaping, he struggled to remember what he had seen. Given his portrait of Diego, the complexity and precariousness of Giacometti's art is manifest. *Diego* has an almost Egyptian remoteness, like an order of being unto itself. The fixity of this state is paradoxically achieved through an inconstant surface; the more closely we examine the head, the more remote it seems to become, for no part is a literal match for the surface or features of the actual face portrayed. For Giacometti, each face has a dual existence: the first is the face he observes; the second is the face which he sees in his imagination and which constantly eludes him. Therefore, to him, the finished sculpture is invariably an unhappy compromise.

485. PIERO POLLAIUOLO. *Portrait of a Young Lady*. c. 1475. Tempera on panel, $19^{1}/_{4} \times 13^{7}/_{8}$". Metropolitan Museum of Art, New York (bequest of Edward S. Harkness, 1950).

## PORTRAITS OF WOMEN

Until the last quarter of the 15th century, Italian portraits of men and women tended to be in profile, because the nobility of that era preferred to have only half the face committed to posterity. This preference was influenced by ancient coins and medallions that bore profile effigies of rulers. The significance of antiquity's attraction for Renaissance society is shrewdly put by Johan Huizinga in his book *Homo Ludens: A Study of the Play Element in Culture* (see pp. 24, 27):

> If ever an elite, fully conscious of its own merits, sought to segregate itself from the vulgar herd and live as a game of artistic perfection, that elite was the circle of choice Renaissance spirits.... The game of living in imitation of Antiquity was pursued in holy earnest.... The whole mental attitude of the Renaissance was one of play.... This striving ... for beauty and nobility of form is an instance of culture at play. The splendours of the Renaissance are nothing but a gorgeous and solemn masquerade in the accoutrements of an idealized past.

This elite segregation and search for beauty and nobility of form is manifest in the design of 15th-century Florentine palaces as well as in profile portraits. Renaissance palace designs were inaccurate attempts to revive the principles of ancient Roman palaces. In both instances the art forms may be conceived of as the public, social façades of their owners. Neither encourages a feeling of intimacy with the viewer. The relevance of such a comparison is apparent in Alberti's Palazzo Rucellai (Fig. 325) and the *Portrait of a Young Lady* by Piero Pollaiuolo (Fig. 485). In the profile portrait the sitter is caught in an attitude that is permanently aloof and detached. A background of blue sky serves to elevate the figure beyond earthly reference. The careful setting of the head within the picture area and the broad-based tapering form created by the pose add to the stability and dignity desired by the patron. While the profile pose eliminates the possibilities of a searching psychological study of the face, it encourages a stress on the aesthetic grace of the subject. Renaissance costumes and tastes share a certain cool, reserved surface elegance. The woman's tight-fitting bodice, upswept hairdo, and plucked eyebrows create a pronounced rhythmic sequence and a continuous graceful silhouette. There is no strong accent, modeling, or coloring of the face within its contours, so that emphasis remains upon the edges. The fashion favored an artificiality that disguised the natural potential of the flesh. In the grooming and costume the woman has herself altered nature, and it might be said that the artist continues in this spirit.

*above:* Plate 69. AGNOLO BRONZINO. *Portrait of a Young Man.* c. 1535–40. Oil on panel, $37^{5}/_{8} \times 29^{1}/_{2}''$. Metropolitan Museum of Art, New York (H. O. Havemeyer Collection). (See p. 355.)

*left:* Plate 70. FRANS HALS. *Portrait of a Man.* c. 1661–64. Oil on canvas, $31^{1}/_{8} \times 25^{5}/_{8}''$. Staatliche Kunstsammlungen, Kassel. (See pp. 355, 356.)

*opposite:* Plate 71. PETER PAUL RUBENS. *Susanna Fourment*. 1620. Oil on panel, $31 \times 21^{1}/_{2}''$. National Gallery, London (reproduced by courtesy of the Trustees). (See p. 363.)

*above:* Plate 72. HENRI MATISSE. *Woman with the Hat*. 1905. Oil on canvas, $32 \times 23^{1}/_{2}''$. Collection Mr. and Mrs. Walter A. Haas, San Francisco. (See p. 363.)

*left:* Plate 73. JAN VAN EYCK. *Giovanni Arnolfini and His Bride*. 1434. Oil on panel, $32^1/_4 \times 23^1/_2$″. National Gallery, London (reproduced by courtesy of the Trustees). (See p. 364.)

*below:* Plate 74. OSKAR KOKOSCHKA. *Hans Tietze and Erica Tietze-Conrat*. 1909. Oil on canvas, $2'6^1/_8'' \times 4'5^5/_8''$. Museum of Modern Art, New York (Abby Aldrich Rockefeller Fund). (See p. 365.)

The ideal woman of Peter Paul Rubens, as seen in Plate 71 (p. 360), the portrait of Susanna Fourment, enhanced her natural endowments with graceful and revealing clothes whose sensual textures flattered those of her flesh. She neither affected an imitative role nor held herself aloof, but was desirable in personality and body. To give fullest expression to the charms that delighted his eye, Rubens used a three-quarter frontal pose, which was at once modest and alluring. The vitality of the woman and her outgoing personality are set off by a turbulent sky and a splendid hat, which was perhaps a flattering recollection of the umbrellas or canopies under which royalty was accustomed to stand (Pl. 39, p. 217; Figs. 290, 297). It is possible for the viewer to enter into a private dialogue with Rubens' sitter. This, unlike Pollaiuolo's portrait, was a very personal painting, portraying a close friend whose younger sister Rubens was later to marry.

Rubens formed his subject of rich color, tempered or heightened by soft shadows and brilliant highlights. The astonishing range of his brushwork is revealed in the broad treatment of the sky and large areas of the sleeves, the more tightly executed forms of the feathers and hair, the subtly graded strokes in the flesh, and the deft touches that created highlights in the earrings and eyes. Both the outpouring and restraint of feeling in the completed painting would seem to reflect the mood of the woman portrayed.

486. PAUL CÉZANNE. *Madame Cézanne in the Conservatory*. c. 1890. Oil on canvas, 36¼ × 28¾". Metropolitan Museum of Art, New York (bequest of Stephen C. Clark, 1960).

Paul Cézanne executed a portrait of his wife (Fig. 486) which seems at first to lack the outgoing qualities and warmth of Rubens' portrayal of Susanna Fourment. Many have compared, unfavorably, his depiction of women to his painting of bottles (Pl. 63, p. 347), saying that he displayed no more feeling for the one than for the other. Cézanne was not without feeling toward his human subjects, however. In portraits he presents them as introverted, passive types, seemingly with infinite patience, for the endless hours they were required to sit for the artist would have required great forbearance. Accurate or flattering likeness was not enough for the painter, and he struggled with adjusting his figure to her surroundings. The tilt of the head and broad directions of Madame Cézanne's body are picked up in the tree and wall behind her, thus effecting a total harmony of the woman and her place. In this unfinished painting, the stages of its construction are still evident; the artist proceeded from a sketchy outlining and thin filling of color areas to a deepening and saturation of color as seen in the shoulders. Even the angles of the brushstrokes reiterate the major axes of the body.

The joyous hedonism of Rubens was shared by Henri Matisse, as attested in a portrait of Madame Matisse, commonly known as *Woman with the Hat* (Pl. 72, p. 361). Like Susanna Fourment, Madame Matisse wears a glorious hat piled high with flowers. Matisse did not insist upon a climactic facial focus, as did Rubens. It is not the flesh nor a mood of enticement that Matisse celebrates in this painting of his wife. He has painted her as a warm aesthetic delight. Her face is handsome and sympathetic, a strong, quiet foil for the riot of color and movement around her. Matisse painted ecstatically and unfettered color from previous obligations to modeling and texture (Pl. 89, p. 434; Figs. 580, 581). Rubens accentuated and modulated his bright colors by placing them next to subdued hues or by setting them in partial shadow. The flat areas of bright color in *Woman with the Hat* are modulated only by degrees of saturation; they range from pastel greens and pinks to full-bodied orange-reds and purples. The large color patches of the background complement others within the figure and serve as blocks to stabilize the form within the frame. Setting aside the finesse of brushwork of which he was capable, Matisse applied his paint with a raw haste, scrubbing and striping to effect the immediate release of his exuberant feelings. He dispersed his color accents according to the needs of aesthetic structure—thus making the painting, like Madame Matisse's hat, a beautiful bouquet of color sensations.

Sculpture as well as painting has recorded many faces of women, with some of the finest examples dating from as early as Egyptian times. A sculptural portrait of striking immediacy

*far left:* 487. GIANLORENZO BERNINI. *Costanza Buonarelli.* 1636–39. Marble, life-size. Museo Nazionale, Florence.

*left:* 488. CONSTANTIN BRANCUSI. *Mademoiselle Pogany.* 1913. Bronze, height 17¼″. Museum of Modern Art, New York (Lillie P. Bliss Bequest).

is that made in the 17th century by Gianlorenzo Bernini of his mistress Costanza Buonarelli (Fig. 487). She is rendered in movement, as if on the verge of speaking. Bernini re-created her as an impressionable, vital person. In removing the extraneous stone, he also lifted off all that masks the private, unguarded, and impulsive facets of woman's conduct. The intimate emotional nature of the relationship between the sculptor and the woman is hinted in her rather disheveled garment and hair, which seem to be extensions of an internal excitement. As a sculptural form, the bust knows no symmetrical blocklike confines but boldly twists into the space about it. The silhouette is irregular and agitated yet carefully controlled to return the eye to what lies within it. The iris of the eye is incised to complete the surface reception of light. Bernini's figures presuppose presence outside themselves to receive the outpouring of their feeling and action.

Constantin Brancusi worked through what he considered layers of superficial appearance in order to find essential, seminal forms, such as the ovoid of the egg, by which to prove his private belief in the underlying unity of living forms and to realize an absolute beauty characterized by simplicity, purity, and equity of existence (Fig. 501). He used reduction in facial detail and arbitrary redesigning of the features in his bronze portrait of Mlle. Pogany (Fig. 488). He stripped away those very characteristics and idiosyncrasies of the woman's face which so delighted Bernini; and by rearranging his subject, he created an impeccable clarity and continuity of rhythm and shape. The head has been contracted into a simple egg shape. Trained in a Budapest art academy, Brancusi abjured its surface virtuosity and naturalistic fidelity that produced what he called "beefsteak" art. He insisted upon the hard, smooth, closed, reflective surface inherent in metal, a concept alienating to the Baroque ideal of intermingling art and visible reality.

The expressiveness of the head lies not in animation of the features and flesh but in its total gesture, in the constantly changing reflections on the polished bronze surface, and in the evocative power of the design. The self-containment of the composition accords with the woman's introspective withdrawal. The sculpture retains a quality of "likeness," but its measure has become that of the work of art against the spirit of the woman and Brancusi's personal ideal of beauty.

## MARRIAGE PORTRAITS

The double portrait, already known in Egyptian and Roman times, has occurred quite often since the 14th century. A type of double portrait has marriage as its subject.

*Giovanni Arnolfini and His Bride* (Pl. 73, p. 362) was painted in 1434 by Jan van Eyck. The painting depicts a private wedding ceremony that took place in the bedroom of the bride of a wealthy Italian banker living in Flanders. The presence of witnesses is inferred, one of whom was the painter himself, indicated by the inscription above the mirror, "Jan van Eyck was here." Until the 16th century, two people by mutual consent could contract a legitimate marriage outside the rites of the Church. Van Eyck's painting is more than a superficial document of the occasion; quite literally, there is more than meets the eye in this portrait. It exteriorizes all the implications of the union of man and woman; in order to accomplish this, Van Eyck used a setting filled with objects whose symbolic connotations were well known to members of his society.

The bride and groom are shown full-length, standing in the center of the room with hands joined. To show the entire figure in a portrait requires a greater interval between viewer and subject; consequently, less area is devoted to the face. Despite this diminished area, the facial characterizations are strong.

It is as if Van Eyck believed that the accumulation of an infinite number of details would provide the circumstantial evidence to identify the character as well as the physical aspect of his subject (Pl. 18, p. 115; Figs. 149, 150). He did not attempt to flatter the groom, whose morbid sensuality and equine resemblance come through forcefully. The man is shown as the dominating figure by his frontal pose and solemnity, while the bride turns toward him in deference. Some have mistaken the proportions of the bride for signs of pregnancy, but in actuality she is holding the folds of her voluminous long skirt up to her waist.

The choice of the bedroom as the setting for the event and the painting was symbolic, for it was sanctioned by a long religious tradition as a nuptial chamber. Northern medieval painting usually showed the Annunciation to Mary as occurring in her bedroom. The lighted candle in the chandelier relates not only to a masculine symbol but also to its use in marriage rites and its implications of divine light. The dog is a sign of fidelity and, possibly, of passion; its inclusion might also relate to medieval tombs, on which a dog was placed at the feet of its master to serve him in death. The light filtering through the window may have alluded to the purity of the bride. The mirror directly above the joined hands of the newlyweds was a symbol of the all-seeing eye of God, its presence like a celestial notary seal, reflecting in miniature more of the contents of the room than are evident in the rest of the painting. Its spotless image of reality made the mirror a symbol of truth. This use of the reflected objects permitted a second wedding, that of the visible with the invisible. Poetic extensions of the figures themselves, the objects serve to identify the locale and to symbolize the hidden spiritual and sexual relationships.

Early in this century, Oskar Kokoschka (b. 1886) painted a portrait of the newly wed Hans Tietze and his bride Erica (Pl. 74, p. 362); it does not, however, depend upon elaborate symbols, setting, witnesses, or prescribed gestures to show the bond that exists between man and wife. The picture is given no specific locale; the figures are seen as if in terms of their self-awareness. The painter's intuitive expression of their feelings resulted in the absorbent, measureless space around them, the warm ephemeral colors, and the wiry lines etched into the paint surface about the figures by the hard end of his brush.

The hand gestures suggest a bridge between the man and woman, but it is an incomplete span, since, significantly, the hands do not touch. Kokoschka seems to have sensed an unbreachable gulf between the two, their essential isolation. In contrast to Giovanni Arnolfini, Hans Tietze is the more dependent member of the couple. His profile pose, slightly shorter height, lack of his wife's relative self-containment, all seem to bring to the surface certain private weaknesses. This was not a posed portrait; Kokoschka studied the movements and character of his subjects, as he searched for the moment that permitted him to pierce the social veneer. He valued the awkward gestures impelled by inner forces, as tangible surface evidence of the existence and power of the subconscious. What he presents is even more private and less decipherable than what would find outlet in his subjects' diaries. Kokoschka suggested, but never circumscribed, the ultimate complex depths within individuals in their relation to themselves and to others. Working in Vienna while Freud was teaching there, Kokoschka's findings were made in his own, visual terms and furnished yet another instance of modern artists' attainments in the study of man, independent of contemporary science.

Portraits fulfill myriad functions. The human face in painting and sculpture has been linked with religion and the need of the living to secure ties with their dead, as in Roman and certain primitive cultures. Status in a political or social sphere could claim the right to portraiture in many societies. The likeness and pose of an important figure could serve to perpetuate an ethic of ideal conduct. Concepts of manliness and femininity found interpretation in Renaissance and Baroque portraits. Inquiry into human nature as expressed through the physiognomic traits and psychological evidence of the face was another function of portraiture. The desire to convey intimate personal sentiments motivated many artists, whereas the problem of finding a mystical human essence joined with the quest for personal absolutes of beauty and perfection attracted others. A major function of portraiture was thus that of building a bridge between the artist and his natural and human environment.

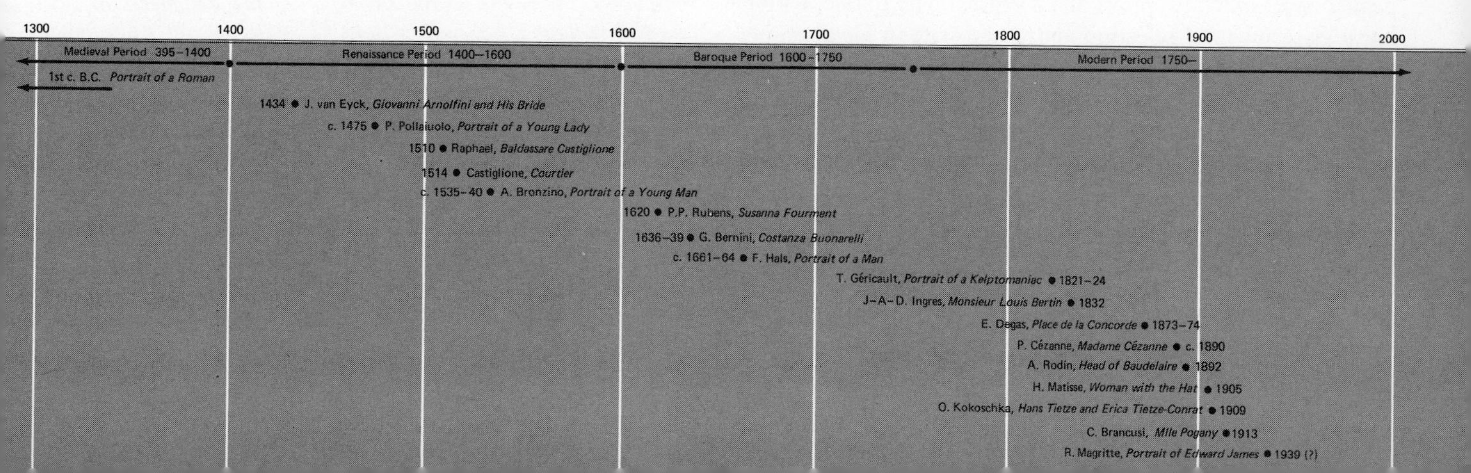

# 19

The persistance of the human form in sculpture from prehistoric to present times argues for man's need to re-create himself. Fidelity to ideology rather than biology helps to account for the fact that throughout its history sculpture has granted to the human body an infinite variety of interpretations. Until recently, not man as he *is*, but man as he *should be* has been the sculptor's model—along with statues made by his predecessors. The human form in sculpture has been as flexible as man's imagination and taste, and history does not support absolute and eternal standards of the good, the true, and the beautiful.

In Western art the great tradition of monumental sculpture—sponsored by rulers and institutions, destined for public display, and made by sculptors willing to interpret the values of their patrons—came to an end in the last century. We can recognize the success of this tradition and its aftermath by the fact that no modern sculpture has influenced as widely or become such a national symbol as Bartholdi's *Statue of Liberty,* completed less than a century ago. (Most recently, it has been used as a symbol for Women's Liberation.) This chapter considers the dream and the dilemma of modern sculptors who have chosen to make their own art and to create the need for it. Not only did they choose to make art from values private to themselves; they also had to persuade the public to believe in their achievement.

**The Pathetic Hero** Auguste Rodin (1840–1917) is the link between the grand tradition of public statuary and the modern period in which the most important sculpture develops independently of official support and a sympathetic public. Rodin knew governmental rejection and acceptance in his attempts to make sculptures with the power and appeal of Rude's *Departure of the Volunteers of 1792* on the Arc de Triomphe (Fig. 489). Rude's sculpture epitomized Rodin's conservative view that public art should first educate, then elevate, and finally delight his fellow citizens. Rude created heroic art at a time when France could still believe in heroism, as displayed by robust civilian volunteers who march off to war with the roll of drums at the call of Marianne, the symbol of France. Like "La Marseillaise," the national anthem, Rude's sculpture spoke to Frenchmen in stirring tones of duty, honor, and

*above:* 489. FRANÇOIS RUDE. *Departure of the Volunteers of 1792 (La Marseillaise)*. 1833–36. About 42 × 26′. Right stone relief, Arc de Triomphe de l'Etoile (Figs. 394, 395), Paris.

*opposite left:* 490. AUGUSTE RODIN. Study for *The Call to Arms (La Défense)*. 1878. Bronze, height 45″. Courtesy Paul Rosenberg & Co., New York.

*opposite centre:* 491. AUGUSTE RODIN. *Age of Bronze* (originally *The Vanquished*). 1876. Bronze, height 6′. Minneapolis Institute of Arts (John R. Van Derlip Fund).

*opposite right:* 492. POLYCLITUS. *Doryphorus (Spear Bearer)*. Roman copy of Greek original of c. 450–440 B.C. Marble, height 6′6″. National Museum, Naples.

self-sacrifice for one's country. It educated men by exhorting them to train and develop their bodies; it elevated their minds and spirits by the example of unflinching patriotic allegiance to France. Rude's relief narrative delighted the French taste for strong, clear form and logic of storytelling with an exalted purpose. Rodin read this sculpture as theater, the relief as a play in three acts. So compelling were Rude's design and interpretation of Marianne leading the people that Rodin eagerly paraphrased the winged figure in his own project for a national monument, *La Défense* (Fig. 490), which his government rejected in 1878. Incomprehensible as it may seem to us today, for more than thirty years France encouraged her best sculptors to create monuments celebrating that nation's glory and heroism after the most humiliating defeat in its history at the hands of Germany in 1870. Rodin's wounded warrior, roused almost from the grave by an angrily defiant Marianne, may reflect the sculptor's idea that the battered nation must rally to the call of duty, and he was probably also expressing his countrymen's sentiments that Germany must be fought again! His own government's rejection of *La Défense* may have derived from Rodin's too vivid characterization of the powerfully muscled but grievously wounded male figure. With Rodin, the pathetic hero had entered into sculpture.

A year earlier, in 1877, Rodin exhibited *The Vanquished,* later retitled *The Age of Bronze* (Fig. 491). Young French artists were delighted with the freshness and honesty of Rodin's re-creation of the human body; critics were dismayed by the ambiguity of its meaning and unsuitabilily as a model of physical culture or as an exemplar of a sound mind in a healthy body. The critical ideal Rodin was contradicting had been largely built upon ancient Greek Classical statuary, exemplified by *The Spear Carrier* (Fig. 492) of Polyclitus. Comparing *The Spear Carrier* with *The Age of Bronze*, we can see the beginning and the end, not of quality, but of the concept of the ideal in public statuary. A messenger of the gods, a soldier, a hero of the gymnasium—the specific identity of the Greek sculptor's subject is lost to us. Probably he was a politican, a man who, as ideal citizen educated in the

democratic tradition of the Athenian city-state or *polis*, could have been elected a general for one war and served as a spear carrier in the next. He represents the cultured person of 5th-century B.C. Athens, competent to function alternately as judge or legislator, an athelete whose musical and gymnastic training prepared him for both war and worship of the gods—in short, the Classical Greek ideal of the whole man in whom was achieved *virtue*. Here can be found the commencement of the tradition of the "Athlete of Virtue," the all-around individual of grace and strength, living, like the later medieval knight or churchman, a life of continence and fortitude, always exhibiting moral courage. *The Spear Carrier*'s step is confident. It speaks to us of the Greeks' self-image, of their desire to overcome the duality between man and the world, to affirm self-mastery, and to civilize nature. The unself-conscious attitude of the man who displays a body given him by nature but perfected by culture exemplifies the bold extension of the human ego into art, the affirmation of the here and now, unconcerned with death.

The Classical nude reflects a world in which man is the focus and measure of all things. Who, then, is *The Vanquished*? What ideal does he stand for? What does he offer to emulate? Rodin never said, and we cannot as easily reconstruct his identity and symbolism from the artist's culture as we can in the case of *The Spear Carrier*. Originally, Rodin had his figure holding, for support, the tip of a spear with his left hand, but he later removed the weapon and presumably its role as an identifying attribute because of its interference with an all-around view of the sculpture. Literally and figuratively he knocked the props out from under traditional meaning and purpose in statuary. No doubt Rodin was symbolizing the disillusioned youth of his age, groping in a world without certainty, man thrown back upon himself. The step is hesitant, the gestures despairing. All that is sure in the sculpture is Rodin's modeling. He admired Greek art but not its mathematical formulas for proportion, standards that began with Polyclitus (Fig. 492). He loved the Greeks' penchant for modeling from all the profiles of the figure, but he could not bring himself to idealize by improving on the physique of his model. Rodin was an empiricist, a passionate reporter of the language of living bodies, not a mimic of rules and counterfeit attitudes. Polyclitus' nude was "clothed" in cultural attributes, philosophical ideals, and scientific discoveries in the field of anatomy. Rodin had begun to strip his figure of centuries of conventions and literary associations, habits of the hand and mind. The hipshot stance of *The Vanquished* still pays homage to the Greek "beauty pose," with its balance of perfect energy and perfect repose, the countering of movements in different directions, and the expressive pathetic gesture of Michelangelo's *Bound Slave* (Fig. 197). What Rodin had discovered and displayed in his sculpture was "pure modeling," the joy of observing and creating a beautifully made surface that at

once could express body and spirit—the life of the flesh. Rodin brought to European sculpture an admiration for the beauty and expressiveness of the body, a compassion for the anguish of the spirit, and a passion for modeling more after nature than art.

**Rodin's Sculptural Alchemy** The heroes that inspired Rodin's most convincing but offically unacceptable sculptures were not abstractions but modern-day athletes of virtue, gymnasts of the mind and spirit, such as Honoré de Balzac, whose *Comédie Humaine* was an earlier literary counterpart to the *Gates of Hell* (Fig. 423). But when Rodin showed his model for a Balzac monument (Fig. 493) to a sponsoring committee in 1893, it was rejected as blasphemous. The problem Rodin had tackled was that of bringing to life in a heroic public statue a national hero idolized for feats of the pen, who was at the same time physically short, fat, and ugly. In life, Balzac's voice could transform his image among his listeners, so he could claim conquest of the most beautiful women of his time. Using different models for the body and head of the long-dead author,

*opposite:* 493. AUGUSTE RODIN. *Naked Balzac.* 1895. Bronze, height 30″. Courtesy Galerie Claude Bernard, Paris.

*right:* 494. WILHELM LEHMBRUCK. *Standing Youth.* 1913. Cast stone, height 7′8″. Museum of Modern Art, New York (gift of Abby Aldrich Rockefeller).

*far right:* 495. TILMAN RIEMENSCHNEIDER. *Adam.* 1493. Sandstone, height 6′2″. Mainfränkisches Museum, Würzburg.

Rodin's sculpture of body language faithfully re-created not only the hedonistic self-indulgence that corrupted an originally imperfect body, but also the defiant pride and genius that caused Balzac to speak of carrying a world in his head. Disguising nothing and employing an inspired idea for the pose, Rodin turned the short-legged, swollen-paunched, flabby-chested figure into a fork-stanced, battering ram, and citadel-like monument to Balzac's ego. For Rodin there was no ugly subject, only bad sculpture. He could transform anatomical lead into artistic gold.

## THE EXEMPLARY FIGURE BEFORE WORLD WAR I: IN PRAISE OF YOUTH

Between 1900 and World War I many of the most venturesome young sculptors, with no hope or desire for official patronage, continued to make exemplary figure sculptures invested with their views of modern man expressed without recourse to the revival of past styles. The German sculptor Wilhelm Lehmbruck (1881–1919) wrote: "Sculpture like all art is the highest expression of the age." He was optimistic that he and others would achieve a great monumental art in a contemporary heroic style. Lehmbruck's *Standing Youth* (Fig. 494), made on the eve of the war disastrous to all combatants—which led to his own suicide—is an inspired homage to an entire generation and to the powers of the self. By his sculpture Lehmbruck tells us that it is the artist who is the measure of man. Through the language of the inclined head, self-directed gestures, and stationary but not permanently static body, he optimistically evokes the inner moral and intellectual strength to overcome life's obstacles. Here again is the "Athlete of Virtue," expressed not through a Classically proportioned, gymnasium-honed body, but through the suggestion of spiritual striving. The lean attenuation and angularity of the sparse frame and the avoidance of lithesome coordination are reminiscent of medieval German sculpture, of the *Adam* (Fig. 495) by Tilman Riemenschneider (c. 1460–1531), for example, who takes no pride in his sinful body. Lehmbruck, unlike his forebear, knew the Classical tradition of body culture, but he suppressed this

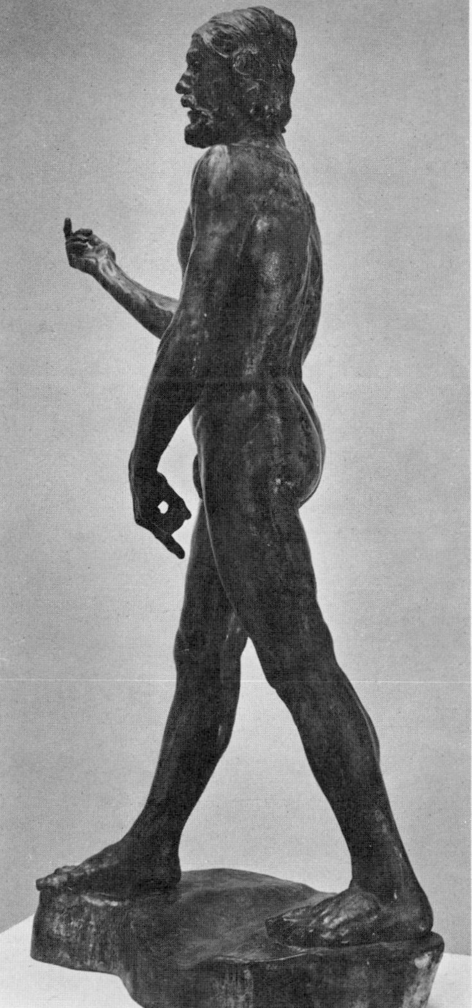

*far left:* 496. *Isaiah,* on the west portal of the Benedictine Abbey of Souillac. c. 1110–30.

*left:* 497. AUGUSTE RODIN. *St. John the Baptist.* 1878. Bronze, height 6′6³/₄″. Museum of Modern Art, New York (Mrs. Simon Guggenheim Fund).

inheritance in favor of a more northern, Germanic legacy that favored expressive rather than beautiful movements. From Rodin, Lehmbruck learned the pathos of posture, of finding instinctive self-revealing movements of the limbs, as well as the power of proportion and silhouette. The former is meticulously measured not from Polyclitus or an actual model but from the artist's ascetic vision of youth's virtue. The rugged silhouette is like the coarse track of the life youth must inevitably run.

We can see how personal yet how modern Lehmbruck's vision was by comparing it with a paradigmatic sculpture from the past, made about two centuries after the revival of large-scale stone sculpture in Europe. Carved in relief on the portal of the southern French abbey church of Souillac is the Old Testament prophet *Isaiah* (Fig. 496). It was probably inspired as much from manuscript painting as from relief sculpture, but not by a living model. Isaiah is presented in what appears to be a kind of ecstatic dance, but at the time the crossed legs may have been a posture reserved for dignitaries, a kind of status sign, or, else, the artist may have been suggesting the walking entailed in his ministry. The extended proportions related not to the sculptor's taste but to the prophet's exalted rank. The angular movements betray the sculptor's unawareness of Greek anatomical science and muscular coordination, and also the fact that he used an abstract linear armature in organizing his figures. This early medieval Christian hero testifies to the existence and superiority of a spiritual world transcending that of the mundane viewer. The gesture and proportion of the *Isaiah* were not intended to be confirmed by what the human eye could match it against, but were directed to the Church-educated mind. Despite the serene face of the prophet, the artist has endowed the pose with energy and excitement and created a total gesture of the figure that mirrors his spiritual intensity. Descended theologically from the virtuous Greek athlete, the medieval *Isaiah,* by his exemplary dedication to Christian virtue, is the remote ancestor of Lehmbruck's modern hero. Unlike the latter, however, *Isaiah* holds an identifying attribute, the scroll of his prophecy, which suggests his relatedness to elements outside himself and his existence within a stratified universal hierarchy.

**The Demise of Sculptural Rhetoric** In this century the rapidity of changing values and popular skepticism about the worthiness of individuals for celebration in monuments, though a broad generalization, may help to explain the decline of public statuary made by society's greatest artists. But sculpture itself was changing long before World War I. Rodin and then Lehmbruck broke with the self-evident, declamatory gesture, theretofore vital to public art, in favor of expressive gestures, movements of the body that were instinctive, credible, and touching but unparaphrasable in words. Their gestures were not conducive to enunciating eternal verities to inspire men. Still another change that irrevocably damaged the tradition of public didactic art was the renunciation of gesture and facial expression altogether as being too literary and contrary to the growing ideal of making sculpture more psychologically and formally self-sufficient. The stress was shifted from what the figure does to what the artist did. In 1908 Henri Matisse wrote: "What I am after, above all, is expression. . . [which] does not consist of the passion mirrored upon a human face or betrayed by a violent gesture. The whole arrangement of my picture is expressive." Matisse, who was a sculptor as well as a painter (Pl. 72, p. 361), could have substituted the word *sculpture* for *picture*.

Twenty years apart, the same model, Pignatelli, posed for Rodin's *St. John the Baptist* (Fig. 497) and Matisse's *The Serf* (Fig. 498). Matisse created this work to stake out his views on sculpture and his differences from Rodin, about whose method of work their common model had informed him. Rodin loved the freshness and vitality of the unprofessional model and saw in the young Pignatelli's animallike energy and bodily eloquence the means of completing a sculpture that would interpret the Biblical prophet, for which he had previously made only a torso. Matisse preferred experienced studio models and stock academic poses. He was not interested in building sculptures from previously made parts or in finishing details. He sought to achieve the overall effect of the figure from the outset, by its total arrangement. Rodin incorporated the traditional gestures of the saint pointing to Heaven and earth and then added his own ideas about how sculpture could be truer than photography in showing successive movements of the body. One is to read his *St. John* as a continuous flow, starting with the back foot and working forward, following the changing disposition of bodily weight as the figure moves into stride and brings the weight down upon the front foot. Matisse felt that sculpture was static and should not contravene its nature by simulating movement in a freestanding figure, and so he planted the body firmly. One reads Rodin's surfaces as marvels of finesse and observation in the contour mapping of the dense elevations and depressions offered by the flesh. Matisse did not want explanatory details but rather an expressive surface, one whose cutting and modeling would go further than Rodin's facture in richness, controlled response to light, and emphasis upon the body's directions. Thus, the muted expression of the serf's face is intentional and unclimactic. Overall, Matisse wanted the effect of stolid durability as well as a figure that seemed more perfectly and interestingly put together than the actual human form. Rodin sought a work larger than life, not just in size but in vitality. Matisse wanted us to be aware of the intervention of art, his intelligence, feelings, and sensibility—in fact their imposition on nature. Matisse's model superseded Pignatelli to become a distillation of his own sensation inspired by the repeated sight of the model and the emerging sculpture.

**The Partial Figure** *The Serf* lacks arms because Matisse removed them before casting, feeling perhaps that their rhetorical presence was distracting or, like Rodin in *The Vanquished,* to liberate expressive silhouettes. The arms were also irrelevant to his ideas of expression. But Matisse's action was made possible by Rodin's own pioneering of the *partial figure,* dramatized for the art world in 1900 by his exhibition of the

498. HENRI MATISSE. *The Serf.* 1900–03. Bronze, height $36^{1}/_{4}''$. Courtesy M. Knoedler & Co., New York.

headless and armless *Walking Man* (Fig. 499), which had originally served him in the building of his *St. John*. With the partial figure Rodin proclaimed that a finished sculpture need not presuppose the body intact. He was the first sculptor in history to make the partial figure important and consistent in his art, not as an imitation of a ruin, symbol of a god, or decorative figure, but as a self-sufficient artistic entity. Cutting off arms and heads severed Rodin's partial figures from the great rhetorical traditions of sculpture and the ideals of proportion based on the whole body, as well as from ideas about what constituted a complete work of art. He wanted to draw greater attention to his modeling and to give the body the expressiveness of the human face. His *Walking Man* celebrates not a historical or Biblical personage or event, but the human spirit that drives and animates biological man.

*below:* 499. AUGUSTE RODIN. *The Walking Man*. 1878–80. Bronze, height 33¹/₆″. National Gallery of Art, Washington D.C. (gift of Mrs. John W. Simpson).

*right:* 500. RAYMOND DUCHAMP-VILLON. *Torso of a Youth*. 1910. Bronze, height 1′9¹/₄″. Stanford University Museum of Art, Calif. (gift of the Committee for Art at Stanford).

**The Certainty of Sculpture in a Time of Flux** Many young sculptors at the turn of the century disliked Rodin for one reason or another, but they were still influenced by his ideas at crucial phases of their careers, and most contemporary figure sculptors have used the partial figure concept. Raymond Duchamp-Villon (1876–1918), the first self-trained professional sculptor of our time, objected to Rodin's modeling, which he felt was too emotional, anecdotal, and prey to accidental lighting effects. However, his *Torso of a Youth* of 1910 (Fig. 500), quite probably under the influence of the *Walking Man*, was cut down from a full figure of Adam when the arms and legs of the latter seemed to inhibit the figure's force and clarity. Duchamp-Villon consciously sought a modern relevance and aesthetic to counter that of business (as he said), by "clothing" his sculptures in the "virtues of simplicity and austerity." To achieve this aim, he felt that the body had to be remade so that it would present a harmony of "lines, planes and volumes seen at a distance." Guiding this reformation was Duchamp-Villon's interest in mathematics and his fascination with the surveyer's plumb line, which he felt makes "tangible for man a point in the infinite." His *Torso of a Youth* links thematically with Lehmbruck's optimism, although Duchamp-Villon's figure has a life more active than contemplative. In the stripped down, hard, cool surfaces of the striding figure there is the enactment of the sculptural ideal of *certitude*,

*left:* 501. CONSTANTIN BRANCUSI. *Torso of a Youth.* 1922. Maple, height 19″; limestone base, height 7″. Philadelphia Museum of Art (Louise and Walter Arensberg Collection).

*center:* 502. AUGUSTE RODIN. *Torso*, study for *The Walking Man* (Fig. 499). 1877–78. Bronze, height 20⅞″. Petit Palais, Paris.

*right:* 503. UMBERTO BOCCIONI. *Unique Forms of Continuity in Space.* 1913. Bronze, height 43½″. Museum of Modern Art, New York (acquired through the Lillie P. Bliss Bequest).

providing modern man in a time of flux with an image of something sure and unshakable, like an absolute truth.

**Figural Sculpture and the Art of Simple Forms** For Duchamp-Villon and Constantin Brancusi (1876–1957) modern figural sculpture had been afflicted by the disease of emotional insincerity, the trivial detail, and excessive facility of the hand. Their antidotes were to use the intellect to uncomplicate art and to rebuild with an art of simple forms. Brancusi's *Torso of a Youth* (Fig. 501) and his later *Bird in Space* (Fig. 445) exemplified his quest for "the sense of things," the essential in life and art, through purification of form. Compared with Rodin's *Torso* (Fig. 502), which was the starting point of *The Walking Man* and *St. John the Baptist,* Brancusi's image seems like a schematic, geometric rendering of the lower torso or a conjunction of tubes in a configuration that seems, but is not, invertible. Brancusi had earlier renounced anatomical fidelity and fleshy paraphrase in favor of a deeply personal and mystic vision of life and art (Fig. 488), a vision that had been influenced by African sculpture. Rodin's partial figures may have helped Brancusi evolve his focus on bodily fragments, but his own reduction of detail led him to discover how the purified human form has analogies in nature—such as the fork of a tree from which the sculpture was finally cut—and that one simplified part of the body reaches a point where it can be compared with another. The total configuration of *Torso* (Fig. 501), which lacks genitals, suggests the missing male sexual member. As we shall see, the partial figure was important in the development of a new sexual candor in modern sculpture.

**The Future Superman** Brancusi's meditations on sculpture resulted in quiet, beautiful forms whose effect depends on a reduced illusionism and concomitant physical assertiveness, discrete symbolic suggestion, and effacement of the hand in favor of individuality of vision. More militant and more obviously an exemplary figure—entering modern sculpture as a surrogate heroic public image—was the *Unique Forms of Continuity in Space* (Fig. 503) of Umberto Boccioni (1882–1916). It was a 20th-century answer to his Italian country-

*far left:* 504. *Victory of Samothrace.* c. 200–190 B.C. Marble, height 8′. Louvre, Paris.

*left:* 505. GIANLORENZO BERNINI. *David.* 1622–24. Marble, life-size. Galleria Borghese, Rome.

*opposite left:* 506. ELIE NADELMAN. *Man in the Open Air.* c. 1915. Bronze, height 4′6½″. Museum of Modern Art, New York (gift of William S. Paley).

*opposite center:* 507. PRAXITELES. *Apollo Sauroktonos (Lizard Slayer).* Roman copy of Greek original of c. 340 B.C. Marble, height 4′10⅜″. Louvre, Paris.

*opposite right:* 508. JACQUES LIPCHITZ. *Man with a Guitar.* 1915. Stone, height 38¼″. Museum of Modern Art, New York (Mrs. Simon Guggenheim Fund).

men's worship of the past and such ancient works as the *Victory of Samothrace* (Fig. 504), whose spread-legged stance, braced against a ship's prow, he may have paraphrased along with the interaction of figure and wind. Boccioni's aggressively striding figure was also in competition with Rodin's *Walking Man,* to which it owed its armless state:

> We proclaim that the whole visible world must fall in upon us, merging with us and creating a harmony measurable only by the creative imagination; that a leg, an arm . . . having no importance except as elements of plastic [sculptural] rhythm, can be abolished, not in order to imitate a Greek or Roman fragment, but to conform to the harmony the artist wishes to create. A sculptural entity . . . can only resemble itself, for in art the human figure . . . must exist apart from the logic of physiognomy.

What Boccioni celebrated in his sculpture was the superman of the future. Previous artists, such as Gianlorenzo Bernini (1598–1680), had memorialized Biblical supermen like *David* (Fig. 505). Bernini's coiled, muscular figure shows movement with a purpose underscored by the tensed lips and rock-filled sling. Boccioni's figure symbolizes his evolutionary vision of how modern man's body will be reshaped by his dynamic, high-speed interaction with his environment. Accordingly, he began to rip open the body's closure while aggravating the body's outward thrust against space. Unlike Bernini's form, the solid portions of the body that interact with space are not shown as taut muscles in a fixed position; to indicate the path of their motion through space they acquire an undulating, molten flow that also serves to fuse the silhouette with its environment.

**A Modern Dandy** For all his bravado in rejecting ancient art, its gods, and all previous sculpture, Boccioni's art was still informed by muscle power and figural syntax. The Polish-born sculptor Elie Nadelman (1885–1946) was more candid about his indebtedness to the ancient Greeks, in fact openly modernizing the Classical ideal. His *Man in the Open Air* (Fig. 506), made in New York City, was a transparent paraphrase of Praxiteles' *Apollo Sauroktonos* (Fig. 507). Nadelman gave us neither a superman nor a classless symbol of an age group, but instead the very model of a modern gentleman in bowler and bow-tied elegance. Apollo's posture of repose became Nadelman's gesture of nonchalance. Seurat's expressive purified silhouettes (Pl. 48, p. 297) intervened between the profiles of Praxiteles and Nadelman. Although in his earlier art the stylized nude served as a paragon of feminine beauty, Nadelman's 1915 image of the modern dandy effected a skin-tight fusion of body and contemporary fashion.

**Evoking the Figure** The exemplary figures of the artists previously discussed conveyed ideals, admittedly personal ones, that in different ways related to human conduct. The Cubist sculpture *Man with a Guitar* (Fig. 508) by Jacques Lipchitz (b. 1891) may be construed thematically as the enjoyment of art, but his important message concerned the new rights of the sculptor, which moved him even farther from traditional public statuary. Rodin had demonstrated the dispensability of parts of the body for finished sculpture; Lipchitz dispensed with sculpture's resemblance to the body's external appearance, thereby reducing its legibility. Lipchitz' model was not Rodin's imitation of nature, but rather sculptural invention. "We Cubists chose a man-made language rather than a naturalistic one, for we wanted to find a new language to adequately fit our feeling. Cubism is less attached to Mother Nature, it is more a pure invention of the human imagination." The human body has not been *de*formed but *re*-formed by the artist's intellect and aesthetic intuition. Anatomy and body language have given way to a new artistic sign language that *evokes* rather than imitates the human form. Although not working directly from a living model, Lipchitz held a mental image of the body as he assembled his flat, angular planes. That this internal body image of the artist had been influenced by Rodin's partial figure, the artist has acknowledged. He did not need to find sculptural equivalents for all parts of the body. In arriving at this type of crystalline art, Lipchitz did no violence to hallowed subjects, such as saints and statesmen, for his figures are anonymous. The revolution in early modern sculpture was not in subject but in form and in the concept of what sculpture could be.

**The Credibility Gap** By 1914, the beginning of World War I, the most important figural sculptures of the most daring artists could not be considered calls to patriotism, duty, and honor. They were injunctions to self-contemplation, pure action, aesthetic distraction, and good grooming. A Europe bent on self-destruction and an America determined on isolation could not rally behind these ideals. Sculptors not committed to past styles and government favor disowned the roles of illustrator, biographer, guardian of the public taste, and image-maker for a nation. The war did not inspire the best sculptors to memorialize generals, politicians, or victory. Lehmbruck did produce some moving sculptures of disillusion and dying, one of which found a home in a German military cemetery. Ironically, it was Rodin's *La Défense* (Fig. 490), enlarged and paid for by the Belgian nation in gratitude to France, that was set up near the terrible battlefield at Verdun after the artist's death. Modern sculptors and public values had encountered mutual disbelief. When important sculpture would again take its place in public, it would be on the artist's terms.

## THE SENSUOUS WOMAN AND PASSIONATE SCULPTORS

**A New Calm** The thematic revolution in modern sculpture took place between the two world wars, and its outlines can be traced in sculptures of women who preoccupied the leading sculptors far more than men. Before 1914, Aristide Maillol (1861–1944) had determined that he preferred the beauty of women to the dramatic possibilities of men. His *Young Girl Walking in Water* (Fig. 509) illustrates the new calm he brought to sculpture after Rodin's psychological and emotional excitement. The walking torso may have been his response to Rodin's *Walking Man* (Fig. 499). Capable of modeling impressive full figures, Maillol preferred the torso, for he hated the making of arms and legs. ("Arms are my Calvary," he complained.) Rodin's introduction of the partial figure liberated sculptors from private difficulties about making certain parts of the body. The arched, erect torso exemplifies Maillol's personal preference for a healthy, generously proportioned body whose surface has the still beauty of sunlight falling on a Mediterranean whitewashed wall. The resemblance of his sculpture to ancient Classical art is fortuitous, not derivative. Maillol dreamed of making sculpture as if it had never been made before, and its purpose was to give joy.

**The Ideal of Invention** Alexander Archipenko (1887–1964) was the first modern sculptor after Rodin to make a partial figure that was not and did not have the look of being the result of subtraction. *Bending* of 1910 (Fig. 510) was never intended to have arms. The clean continuity of the silhouette allowed him to shape space and form. Even before Lipchitz and the Cubists, Archipenko placed invention above imitation and drastically departed from bodily detail in favor of simple quasi-geometric and fluid shapes that imparted grace to the feminine image. Before Brancusi, he explored the highly polished, continuous surface that uniformly reflected light, and he was the first to integrate the base with the form of the sculpture. While he spoke vaguely of producing "sculptural signs to lead the masses" (not indicating where), Archipenko's sculpture was important to other artists before World War I for its formal audacity.

**The New Sexual Candor** Gaston Lachaise (1882–1935) produced in the late twenties and thirties some of the most candidly

*left:* 509. ARISTIDE MAILLOL. *Young Girl Walking in Water* (torso of *L'Ile-de-France*). 1921. Bronze, $47\frac{1}{2} \times 20''$. Courtesy Paul Rosenberg & Co., New York.

*center:* 510. ALEXANDER ARCHIPENKO. *Bending*. 1911–12. Chrome plated bronze, $11\frac{7}{8} \times 6\frac{1}{2} \times 2\frac{5}{8}''$. Collection Frances Archipenko Gray, New York.

*right:* 511. GASTON LACHAISE. *Torso*. 1932 (cast 1963). Bronze, height $9\frac{1}{2}''$. Estate of Isabel Lachaise (courtesy Felix Landau Gallery, Los Angeles, and Robert Schoelkopf Gallery, New York).

erotic fantasies (based on his wife's body) in modern sculpture (Fig. 511). The partial figure allowed this sexual focus, which in turn engendered the amazing reproportioning and contracting of the reproductive areas of the body. Lachaise's private fertility images recall those of prehistoric sculpture (Fig. 25) and the collective ideal of Indian art, which produced the ripe tree goddess on a gate of the Great Stūpa at Sānchi (Fig. 512). Unlike Lachaise's motionless figures, the sexuality of the Indian figure depends upon her subtle and provocative movement. No apparent internal skeleton inhibits the suggestive torsion of her inflated "Subtle Body." The Indian sculpture had its foundation or symbolic function in both Buddhism and Hinduism, which in their teachings and art convert the human erotic instinct to higher purposes, rather than merely being an end in itself (see pp. 40–46). The exaggeration of the Yakshi's sexual parts had a religious motivation and was intended to arouse those who looked upon her to initiate spiritual communion with the gods.

**The Search for Strange Meaning** Before the 20th century many cultures saw nature in terms of the human form. More recently, sculptors such as Jean Arp (Fig. 446) and Henry Moore (b. 1898) have interpreted the human form in terms of nature. A reclining human form signified a sea god to the Greeks, a river god to the Romans, times of day to Michelangelo (Fig. 199), a rain god to the ancient Mexicans (Fig. 514). Henry Moore's long series of reclining figures, begun in the 1930s, has no comparable culturally based and verifiable symbolism. The figures contain structures congruent with what he sees in the landscape, in rocks, caves, and mountains. Sculpture is Moore's personal mediation between the mystery and power of nature and his own being. The reclining feminine form (Fig. 513) is the motif that has most frequently been the occasion for giving form to his reflections on the analogies between hills and breasts, caves and body cavities, stone and bone. The parentage of his art is a mixture of Mediterranean

*left:* 512. *Yakshi* (Indian tree goddess), from the East Gate of the Great Stūpa, Sānchi. Early Andhra Period, 1st century B.C. Bracket figure.

*right:* 513. HENRY MOORE. *Reclining Figure.* 1939. Elm wood, 3′3″ × 6′7″ × 2′6″. Detroit Institute of Arts (gift of Dexter M. Ferry, Jr., Trustee Corporation).

*left:* 514. *Chac-Mool,* Mayan-Toltec rain god, from Chichén-Itzá, Mexico. Pre-Columbian, 10th–11th century. Stone, 3′5½″ × 4′10¼″. National Museum, Mexico City.

*below:* 515. ALBERTO GIACOMETTI. *Woman with Her Throat Cut.* 1932 (cast 1949). Bronze, length 34½″. Museum of Modern Art, New York (purchase).

*opposite left:* 516. ALBERTO GIACOMETTI. *The Invisible Object (Hands Holding the Void).* 1934–35. Bronze, height 5′1″. Courtesy Marlborough Gallery, New York.

*opposite right:* 517. JACQUES LIPCHITZ. *Figure.* 1926–31. Bronze, height 7′1¼″. Museum of Modern Art, New York (Van Gogh Purchase Fund).

and Mexican sculpture, Classical reclining figures from the Parthenon (Figs. 92, 93, 531), Michelangelo's Medici Tomb figures (Fig. 199), the Mayan-Toltec Chac-mool (Fig. 514), and modern sources in Picasso, Brancusi, and Arp. From stone- and wood-carving cultures came the paradigm of sculpture as a world language, predicated on a few elementary postures, formal hardness, and simplicity. Out of his own time he took the incentive to work from direct and strong personal feeling and intuition, and not, above all, "for harmony and beauty but rather for strange meaning." Moore's passion for art has conditioned his vision of nature. His recumbent women are not available, seductive sirens, even though their re-formation leads to sensual surfaces curled about openings in the block. They have dignity and energy even in repose. Their surfaces seem at once eroded by natural forces and also built up from internal pressure like the knuckle pushing against the flesh of a clenched fist. Woman has become in Moore's sculpture a metaphor for our awareness of the inside and outside of man and nature and our intimate relatedness to the earth. Moore reminds us that art is nature added to man.

**The Sculptor as Murderer and Visionary** Cubism had been an important breach in the historical tradition of making figural sculpture from a norm of the body's external appearance. Alberto Giacometti (1901–66) literally and figuratively took woman off the pedestal and internalized sculptural body imagery in *Woman with Her Throat Cut* (Fig. 515). For the first time in a partial figure, mutilation was a motif rather than a means. By his own account, Giacometti's sculpture, which was intended to be set on the floor, was a private vision of how a woman he met would look if brutally murdered. The fantasy incorporated elements of the skeletal armature, and the missing equivalent of the head was part of the imagined assault. The sculpture was worked out in the artist's imagination and then quickly executed, by contrast with Henry Moore's slow and loving dialogue with his materials and tools. For personal reasons, during the years 1925 to 1935 Giacometti found he could not work directly from the figure, but only in a visionary way. His enigmatic sculptures also included *The Invisible Object* (Fig. 516), another offspring of the artist's self. Framed and supported by a curious high-backed chair, her legs blocked by an upturned panel, the idol-like woman, whose eyes resemble bullet-pierced windows, cradles or caresses or circumscribes the "invisible object." She is like the imagined priestess of a legendary mystical sect, and

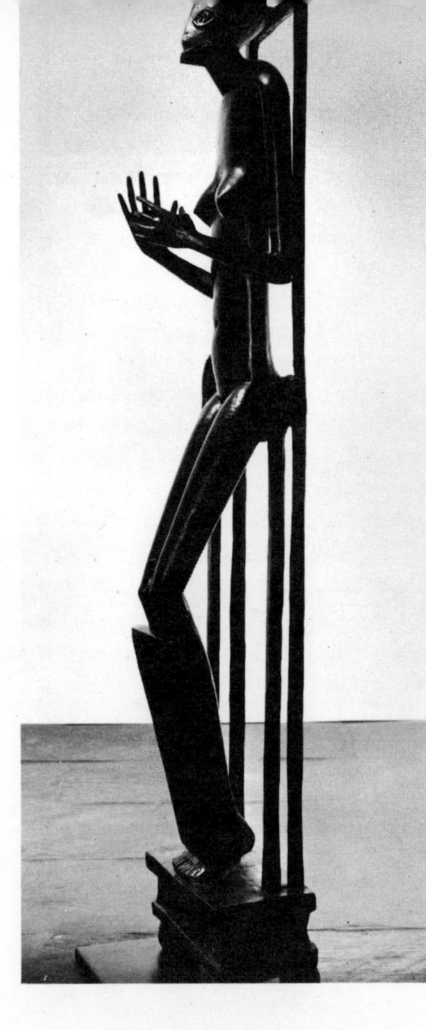

perhaps Giacometti's art was responding to the fascination with myth and the subconscious among avant-garde artists in Paris at the time. The immobility, symmetry, fixed gaze, and simple, tubular forms also suggest the influence of tribal and ancient art, both in form and in magical purpose. Modern organized religion and rationalism did not satisfy many artists between and after the two world wars. They sought to find the secret history and to take the mystical temperature of their times. Their search of the subconscious and religious art of early and tribal cultures often led to surrogate idols for invisible congregations, ambiguous but provocative figural evocations that emanated powerful presences.

**The Disturbing Presence** Important in this evolution was Lipchitz' *Figure* (Fig. 517), on which he worked for five years. The sculpture was initially inspired by encounters with stones on a beach and then nurtured by recollection of African masks having transfixed gazes. The resulting work is in part chainlike (at one point Lipchitz thought of it as two entwined figures), and is surmounted by a concave oval bearing two protruding cylinders. The vertical creases in the frontal links are references to feminine sexual organs. The immobility of the figure is paradoxically the result of the irresolvable antagonistic pulls of the chain, suggesting a metaphor of internal human tension, just as the inverted area of the head evokes its interior life. The woman who commissioned the sculpture for her home returned it to the artist as being "unbearable" to live with. Lipchitz had succeeded in making a disturbing, poetic, but almost inhuman presence, an inspired intuition about life, one of what Robert Goldwater called "the crucial symbols of human experience." But it could not and did not serve the modern public's ideal of exemplary sculpture.

**The Medium Is Not the Message** Just as damaging to the understanding of what serious modern sculptors like Giacometti and Lipchitz have done is the sympathetic writing on modern sculpture by those who stress only formal contributions and insist upon emphasizing the artist's methods and materials. The sculptors here discussed have had something to say. Matisse wanted his work to appear effortless, like a bird's song. Lipchitz never wanted to be a slave to his materials any more than Moore thinks only of sensual physical pleasures in cutting stone. Materials and methods are means to a more important end—art. What counted and still is paramount for

*left:* 518. Julio González. *Woman Combing Her Hair*. 1936. Wrought iron, height 4′4″. Museum of Modern Art, New York (Mrs. Simon Guggenheim Fund).

*below:* 519. Julio González. *Montserrat*. 1936–37. Iron, height 5′4½″. Stedelijk Museum, Amsterdam.

these sculptors is the fusion of form and meaning in the finished work. Craft is at the service of artistic vision. As for the public's resistance to what these sculptors had to offer, Julio González (1876–1942) had the answer: "Why demand everything of the artist? Why not also demand of the spectators that each one, according to his capabilities, try and elevate himself to the work of art? If they don't succeed at the first try, let them persist, even several times. I have often done this."

**Private Fantasy and Public Memorial** The sculpture of González in the 1930s and his work with Picasso in the late 1920s established iron, welding, the joining of disparate shapes in unorthodox balance, and "drawing in space" as valid and viable for modern sculpture. González had been an ironworker as well as a painter and sculptor, and what separated him as an artist from being an artisan, his art from craft, is, in the admiring words of David Smith, that his "art lies in the concept, not the technique." González' technique was at the service of a concept that started with the premise that, while iron had been used for centuries, "It is time this metal ceased to be a murderer." This was said in the thirties, when plowshares were being beaten into swords all over Europe. The paradigms for his new art were cathedral spires, "a point in the sky where our soul is suspended. . . points in the infinite which are precursors of the new art: *To draw in space*. . . by the marriage of material and space, a union of real forms with imaginary forms, obtained and suggested by established points, or by perforation. . . to mingle them and make them inseparable. . . as are the body and spirit." González' *Woman Combing Her Hair* (Fig. 518) exemplifies his thrust to restore to sculpture "a mysterious, fantastic, indeed diabolical aspect." This is no armature for a sculpture, no predictable paraphrase of any of the body's systems. Rather, it is an inspired configuration whose gestures and shapes eventually conjure what the title meant to the sculptor. But González also felt a deep obligation to the Spanish people beset by a civil war, and while continuing his art of fantasy, he made a more intelligible memorial to the Spanish resistance to fascism. It was named after the sacred mountain in the Basque country, Montserrat (Fig. 519), for Lachaise, Arp, Moore, and González all thought of mountains in feminine terms. González used the most sophisticated metalworking technique to arrive at two human forms of the utmost formal simplicity, thereby to celebrate the earthiness and spirit of the people. If the Loyalists and not Franco had won, González' *Montserrat* might perhaps have been given honor in Spain instead of permanent residence in the Stedelijk Museum in Amsterdam.

## POST-WORLD WAR II FIGURAL SCULPTURE

**Metaphors of the Hero** During the post-World War II period the human form has been moved further into metaphorical imagery but at the same time was brought closer to the artist's actual perception, and so it achieved simultaneously a new literalness and an alliance with its physical environment. Although a few sculptors continue to enact visions of the heroic, many have rejected the idea of man as he might be in favor of what he is, and some have been moved by the image of man made less than human by society's indifference.

*Sentinel* (Fig. 520) by Seymour Lipton (b. 1903) remains one of the most powerful sculptures based on the human form made anywhere since 1945, and it merits comparison with Donatello's sculpture of *St. George* (Fig. 521), carved for the armorers' guild in Florence early in the 15th century. Donatello's figure is descendant from medieval sculptures of knights, Christian Athletes of Virtue; it serves as both a serious advertisement of the products of his patrons (originally it was capped with a bronze helmet and in the right hand held a bronze sword) and as an exemplar of courage in times of adversity well known to Florentines of that violent age. *Sentinel* was made in New York City at the artist's initiative and took its form from Lipton's admiration for medieval armor and his desire to make sculpture that articulated the mysterious and heroic elements in man's private nature which have allowed him to survive. It makes an unintentional but ironic model for a New Yorker whose dangers lie within the city. *Sentinel's* almost calligraphic metaphor fuses ideas about spears, helmets, battlements, battering rams, and vertical coffins split open with a feeling for the human form. Donatello's sculpture relies in its force upon his understanding of body language—the

*left:* 520. SEYMOUR LIPTON. *Sentinel.* 1959. Monel metal, height 8′6″. Yale University Art Gallery, New Haven, Conn.

*right:* 521. DONATELLO. *St. George*. c. 1417. Marble, height 6′8¼″. Museo Nazionale, Florence.

right: 522. HENRY MOORE. *Three-Way Piece (Archer)*. 1964 (large version). Bronze, 10′8″ × 11′2″. Courtesy Marlborough Fine Art, Ltd., London.

below: 523. AUGUSTE RODIN. *The Burghers of Calais*. 1884–86. Bronze, 7′1″ × 8′2$^{1}/_{8}$″ × 6′6″. Joseph H. Hirshhorn Collection, New York.

alternately relaxed and tensed hands, the facial expression of alertness and concerned concentration, and the gravity-defying erect stance and pressure of the body against the ground. It is a posture that enforces privacy and not approachability. Lipton draws upon the language of our inherited and accumulated associations with shapes derived from objects and anatomy, signs, emblems, and surfaces identified with violence. The figure in sculpture, like the human body, can have its special psychological space. Both sculptures emanate a convincing, even intimidating presence, such that the beholder has no immediate inclination to invade the sculpture's personal space any more than if these were living personages. To

his contemporaries Donatello's greatness was that he brought new credibility and dignity to the human figure by rejecting medieval formulas in favor of merging fresh observations from life with a strong sense of design supporting the nobility of theme. More than five centuries later, Lipton's view was that once modern artists had departed from the ideal of imitating the external appearance of the body, they should begin to explore man's inner life and develop imaginative metaphors to suggest his heretofore unvoiced links with his environment. Unfortunately for Lipton, he does not live in a culture that, like 15th-century Florence, has looked to sculptors for a civic self-image. That role has been diffused among souvenir post cards, sporting teams, newspapers, and architecture, to name a few such image-makers.

**Public Art on the Artist's Terms** Thematically, Henry Moore's *Archer* (Fig. 522) is related to such a metaphorical statement and has even been proposed by others as a national emblem for Canada, as well as for the city of West Berlin. He did not begin the piece with either a political emblem or the title in mind. The latter came to him as he worked and saw in the emerging form the archer motif. Moore's sculpture is today to be found in public places all over the world, but it has been made on the artist's own terms. For many years Moore has refused to interpret someone else's idea, whether of an institution or a country. He prefers to make sculptures that, first of all, satisfy himself and that have many possible interpretations.

> I like the incentive to work for myself. I can't work for communication. . . . If it gives me a deep satisfaction, I am confident

that others now or later will have a similar sympathy or conditioning towards it. . . . It is important that there be continued interpretations. . . . People have an intrinsic interest in shapes. . . . It should have relevance in the public's opinion. If it has an immediate explanation as to why it is there, the average person will see this, go away and lose interest. It is better if the sculpture should be of some challenge or of a mystery.

In Moore's more recent sculpture (Fig. 522), unlike his reclining figures of the thirties (Fig. 513), "the human and animal are more fully mixed. . . . I now make sculpture that doesn't have any one basic plot." *Archer* still presupposes the partial figure: "A torso fragment has a condensed meaning. It can stand for an entire figure." From certain angles it suggests an arm thrust outward with a bow. Moore rejoices in the condition of art today that allows him to carry the form as far as possible without having to define its significance. He sees the purpose of his sculpture as comparable to that of older religious art in lifting its audience above the ordinary and the commonplace and making life seem more significant or mysterious.

**Figures in the City** In 1895, Rodin's *Burghers of Calais* (Fig. 523) was a great disappointment to that city, because the six medieval citizens who offered themselves as hostages to the King of England in order to spare their city were re-created by the sculptor as men with mortal feelings. Rodin had failed to perform the function of sculpture and religious art that Moore speaks of. For Rodin, the heroism of the six depended upon their demonstration of the anger, resignation, sorrow, despair, anguish, and incredulity that men have felt in the presence of death. Calais wanted saints, not pathetic heroes to rub elbows with in the marketplace, where Rodin would have sited the sculpture on the paving stones. Instead, they were placed on a pedestal and fenced off in an area closer to the sea. Ironically, the English honored the heroes and the artist by erecting the sculpture next to the Houses of Parliament. It is no distortion to say that, in terms of recognition, Rodin became a great artist in spite of France.

Rodin envisioned a modern monument to medieval heroism as a reminder to the middle class of the virtue they had lost by prosperity and self-satisfaction. The commission gave him the greatest opportunity of his life to work with body language, to search out gestures that conveyed the whole attitude of the figure, to link by formal rhyme figures isolated by grief, to depict how sackcloth hangs from a forlorn frame, even the way a man walks at the end of his life and the way his feet grip the ground as he resists the grave's authority. The almost dance-like semicircular composition may have been a half-recollected medieval Dance of Death; perhaps it symbolized eternal sacrifice. Because of its public location, he treated his figures like actors on a stage, whose gestures and expressions must be exaggerated in order to be credible as well as readable. He orchestrated his surfaces so that all lighting conditions, deep shadows as well as shimmering light, would evoke the polarities of life and death. This was the last great public monument in which sculpture successfully rivaled theater and literature.

Giacometti's *City Square* (Fig. 524) had none of these ambitions and reflects a more contemporary distrust of emotional display by sculptural figures or the reenactment of historical drama. Giacometti shows us anonymous figures conjoined for a fleeting instant on an urban street, as seen by himself from a distance. From the 1940s, Giacometti renounced his visionary art (Figs. 515, 516) in favor of vision. Previous figural art presupposed an ideal viewer anywhere from 6 to 12 feet away, and, as in Rodin's case, the details of the figure remained in focus as one came closer. Giacometti was fascinated by the problem of seeing the figure in part or as a whole and then remembering it as he turned to note his observations in clay. Memory intervenes between seeing and making. Giacometti realized that from certain distances figures lose volume and detail. Their size is reduced to inches. Sex and clothing become blurred. The point at which they separate from the surrounding space becomes ambiguous. His sculptures are residues of this vision, distillations from memory, thought, and the action of his fingers (Fig. 484). Giacometti gave new meaning to the idea of the artist as the measure of man. When asked if he was interested in the psychology of his subjects, Giacometti replied that he had enough trouble capturing their outer form. Although his art was eagerly adopted by existentialists in the 1950s as illustrative of their life attitude, Giacometti insisted on the nature of the perceptual problem as his motivation.

**The Sculpture of Ingenuity and Opportunism** Ernest Trova (b. 1927) is a rare modern sculptor who has deliberately sought a universally recognizable figural symbol—one that in his

*right:* 524. ALBERTO GIACOMETTI. *City Square*. 1948–49. Bronze; base 25 × 17″, height of tallest figure 8″. Courtesy Pierre Matisse Gallery, New York.

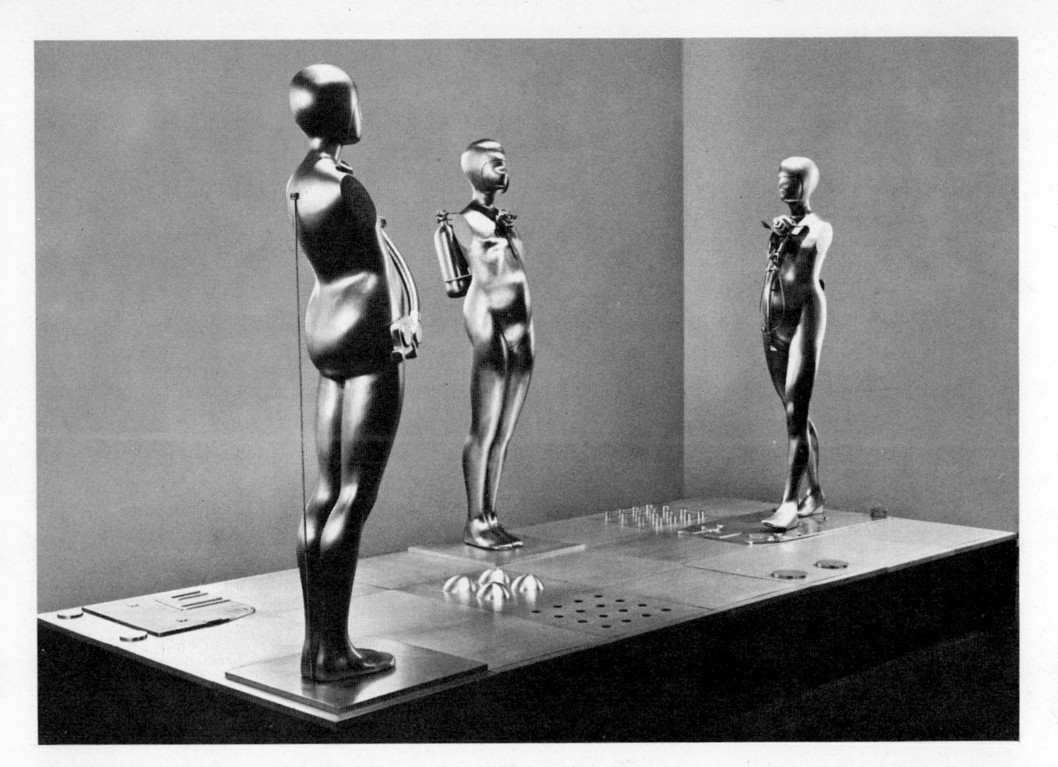

525. Ernest Trova. *Study: Falling Man, Venice Landscape.* 1965–66. Satin finish silicon bronze, 7′6″ × 14′ × 6′. Courtesy Pace Gallery, New York.

estimation has the world-wide recognition of Mickey Mouse—and who has tried to emulate Walt Disney's use of art and technology. Unlike Giacometti, Trova intentionally comments on the human condition. His armless, slack-stanced, sexless, mannequinlike figures are personal equivalents of Leonardo's model of the ideally proportioned man (Fig. 585) and are intended by Trova as surrogates for man, who is flawed, imperfect, and hence *fallen.* By attaching prosthetic equipment or servomechanisms to their bodies, as in this variant on *The Falling Man* series (Fig. 525), Trova refers to modern man's dependence upon technology as an amputee relies upon an artificial limb. Whether by himself or in groups confronting various psychologically challenging environments, Trova's *Falling Man* carries the message to his fellowman to relax. By reason, discipline, and calm we will muddle through whatever the future and technology may hold for us. Having found his exemplary figure, Trova is content to see its replication in a variety of scales and materials, including watch faces and kaleidoscopes. In effect, he lets technology work for him. For Trova, art involves opportunism and ingenuity in using the products of culture to interpret and criticize his society.

**The Sculptural Tableau as Cultural Mirror** Turning the products of culture back on themselves can result in a very different effect from that of sleek, chrome-plated mannequins in a science-fiction environment. Edward Kienholz (b. 1927) puts together what he calls *tableaus,* life-size environments made from discarded furniture and objects of bygone eras that somehow are still relevant to the moment, allowing us to live with more understanding of the present by means of the recent past. Kienholz' written intentions for *The State Hospital* (Fig. 526) best describe what he has done:

> This is a tableau about an old man who is a patient in a state mental hospital. He is in an arm restraint on a bed in a bare room. (The piece will have to include an actual room consisting of walls, ceiling, floor, barred door, etc.) There will be only a bedpan and a hospital table (just out of reach). The man is naked. He hurts. He has been beaten on the stomach with a bar of soap wrapped in a towel (to hide tell-tale bruises). His head is a lighted fish bowl with water that contains two live black fish. He lies very still on his side. There is no sound in the room. Above the old man in the bed is his exact duplicate, including the bed (beds will be stacked like bunks). The upper figure will also have the fish bowl head, two black fish, etc. But, additionally, it will be encased in some kind of lucite or plastic bubble (perhaps similar to a cartoon balloon), representing the old man's thoughts. His mind can't think for him past the present moment. He is committed there for the rest of his life. [From the descriptive portion of the "Concept Tableau" entitled "The State Hospital," 1964–67, reprinted in *American Sculpture of the Sixties,* edited by Maurice Tuchman.]

Kienholz' talents as an artist include not only his abilities as a carpenter, electrician, and scavenger of provocative junk ("all the little tragedies are evident in junk"), but also inventiveness in upsetting expectations established by his literal contexts, as in the treatment of the heads of his figures. His tableaus are set apart from those in wax museums by rich inventiveness and by the fact that the artist is not dealing with villains and heroes, pathetic or otherwise, but with victims of cities like Los Angeles, which he feels lack the dimensions of time, where there is no past and future, "only an eternal dizzying present." Like Rodin, Kienholz challenges theater and the novel as the image-makers of his time. His bodies are those of any man and the setting could be in any state.

The tableaus of George Segal (b. 1924) lack the bitterness, tragedy, and biting wit of Kienholz. They generally convey a more gentle commentary on human isolation in banal situations—a woman shaving her leg, sitting in a bus, emerging from a shower, or standing in a doorway. Segal's art results from "the everchanging aspects of three-dimensional encounters," and he sees his problem as lying in "the emotional choice of the most moving or the most revelatory series of experiences." His pecular gift is comparable to Rodin's—that of seeing and seizing his subject's self-revealing gestures, gestures that include the whole body: "People have attitudes locked up in their bodies, and you have to catch them." Segal literally takes plaster casts from his figures once he has decided on a revealing pose that the subject can hold for the twenty minutes required to reproduce one section of the body. His *Man Walking* (Fig. 527) was cast in sections, and the truest impression of the model is inside the sculpture. The outside is rough, every square inch has been reworked, details added and subtracted, and creases and angles help create a flow or break up an area. Segal's plaster figures are set among or against actual objects, such as an elevator gate, and remain unpainted. "The whiteness intrigues me for all its special connotations of disembodied spirit, inseparable from the fleshy corporeal details of the figure." Segal's thinking must include what is around the sculpture. "The peculiar shape and qualities of the empty air surrounding the volumes become an important part of the expressiveness of the whole piece. The distance between figure and another object becomes crucial. My pieces don't end at their physical boundaries."

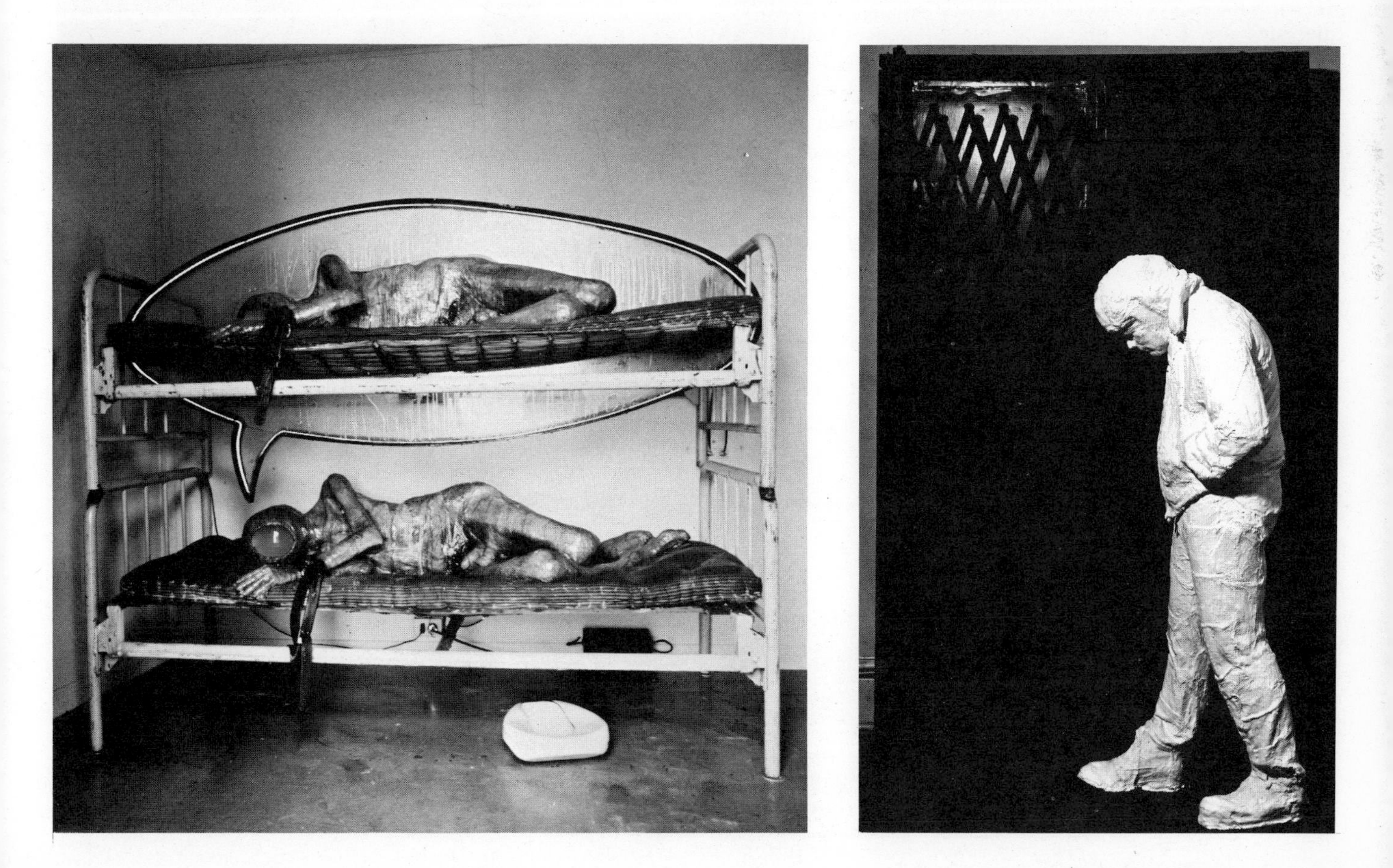

*left:* 526. EDWARD KIENHOLZ. *The State Hospital.* 1966. Mixed media, 8 × 12 × 10′. Moderna Museet, Stockholm.

*right:* 527. GEORGE SEGAL. *Man Walking.* 1966. Plaster, painted metal, and wood; 7′1″ × 4′10″ × 2′10″. Collection Norman B. Champ, St. Louis.

Rodin made *The Walking Man* (Fig. 499) to refute the charge that, like unscrupulous artists of his time, he took casts from life. Segal openly uses the life cast for his *Man Walking,* but this is merely a point of departure, and its final form is far less literal than the objects of the setting. Rodin wanted to bring art closer to life through the expression of genuine feeling and authentic gestures. Segal's goals are the same but extended into the tableau format that Rodin approached only when he dreamed of placing his *Burghers* in Calais' medieval square near the site of the gate through which the hostages had been forced to walk. By taking sculpture off the pedestal, Rodin contributed to Segal's placement of sculpture in our own environment. Rodin's contribution of the partial figure, only recently employed by Segal, has realized its most spectacular culmination in the fantasy of another artist, who uses it to revitalize the discredited idea of the monument.

**Monuments for the Imagination** *London Knees* (Fig. 528) by Claes Oldenburg (b. 1929) is one of this artist's wittiest projects for a modern monument, and clearly establishes the sculptor's point of view. Reproduced in plastic in a large edition, and packaged in a suitcaselike container, *Knees* shows Oldenburg's interest in modern materials and production techniques at the service of his way of looking at things. "Fragments have always interested me. I think one of the big differences between an artist's vision and a normal person's vision is that the artists tend to see in fragments . . . they tend to be very partial in their looking. . . . If I walked down the street I would only see certain things and I wanted to be true to that vision." In a drawing (Fig. 529), Oldenburg has set down his idea for a London monument consisting of "Colossal Knees on the Victoria Embankment," placed in that spot "to echo the four chimneys of the Battersea power plant." Why this subject for this location? "The object is chosen because in some ways it fits the shape, the conditions and the associations of the site." In addition, the artist remembers that in 1966 knees were very much on his mind. "I use my body to feel and come to know a city. In London, I constantly felt cold in my knees, they always ached. . . . 1966 was also the time of knee exhibitionism because of the mini-skirt, especially when framed by boots."

As Oldenburg puts it, "What are the symbols available for our time? The old symbol of the hero has disappeared." He feels that the artist should impose his reverie on nature, and

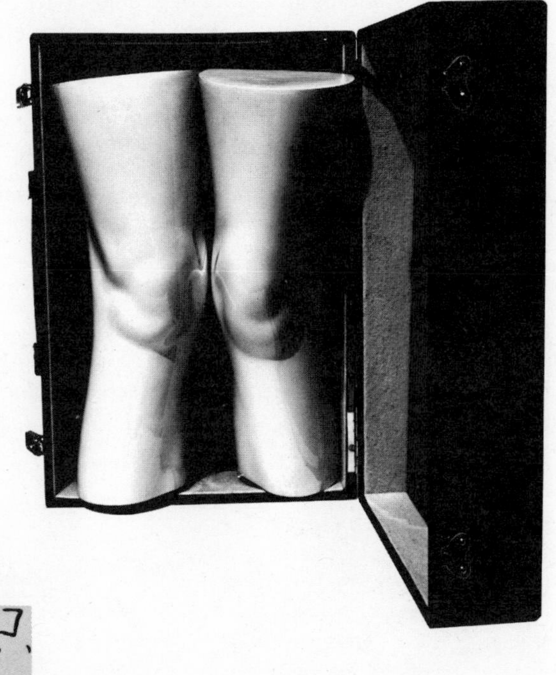

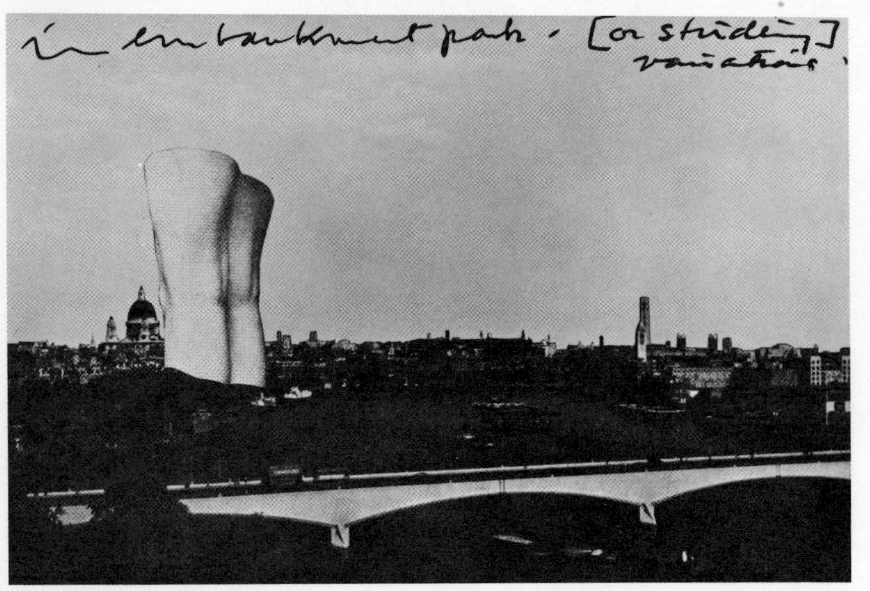

*above:* 528. CLAES OLDENBURG. *London Knees*. 1966. Plastic with suitcase, height 17″. Editions Alecto, London.

*left:* 529. CLAES OLDENBURG. *Proposed Colossal Monument, Victoria Embankment, London: Knees*. 1966. Clipping on postcard, 10 × $15^{3}/_{4}$″. Part of the multiple *London Knees 1966*, published by Editions Alecto, London, 1968.

*above:* 530. SAUL STEINBERG. *Monuments.* Drawing, from *The Labyrinth.* © 1958 Saul Steinberg (published in *The New Yorker*, then by Harper & Row, 1960).

that "absurd fact" is the best kind of all (Fig. 475). In 1966 he thought that "monuments should exist in the imagination." Since then, Oldenburg has begun to change his mind, for money, materials, and means have been forthcoming to realize on a large scale some of his reveries, such as a giant lipstick and an icebag. Still to be realized are his fantasies of substituting a gigantic electric fan for *The Statue of Liberty* and of inverting the old tradition of monuments that provide some public service with a monument that is an obstacle or obstruction, such as a gigantic concrete block set down at the busiest street intersection. So far, Oldenburg's projects for civic monuments have remained on paper, where they enjoy the advantage of aesthetically holding their scale as well as their surprise and humor. Much of the pleasure they induce is in our conjecture of what they would look like if built. Rare is the tradition that ends in laughter.

**The End?** Saul Steinberg (b. 1914) has wittily summarized the history of Western civilization and its monuments from medieval times to the present (Fig. 530). The hero of one period is overthrown in the next, until finally, in our own time, the common man stands with one foot on his own head. Appropriately enough to the history of sculpture, Steinberg has ended with a partial figure, and the delightful image also suggests man mastering himself but losing his head in the process.

With few exceptions, such as those cited at the end of this chapter, figural sculpture is not presently benefiting from the most venturesome ideas and youthful talents. The antihero is strong in literature and films and seems to have public endorsement. Most sculptors continue to feel that public values like patriotism and virtue are not worth celebrating, and thus they prefer abstraction. Collaboration with technology and with vernacular materials that resist being termed sculpture and are nonfigural—in this can be found the continuity of the artist's need to re-create what is human in himself rather than in others. An increasing number of young artists do not feel that sculpture can be continued, because either its options have been exhausted or more interesting alternatives are now available. Unless there are drastic changes in the near future, we may be witnessing the last phase of monumental art and of the great tradition of figural sculpture. It may not be coincidental that this is happening at a time when, for many, life and art are thought of as one. The rediscovery of the body, its culture, beautification, and celebration, has encouraged the revolution in dress and undress, enforcing the idea that everyman is an artist and what he does with his own body can be art.

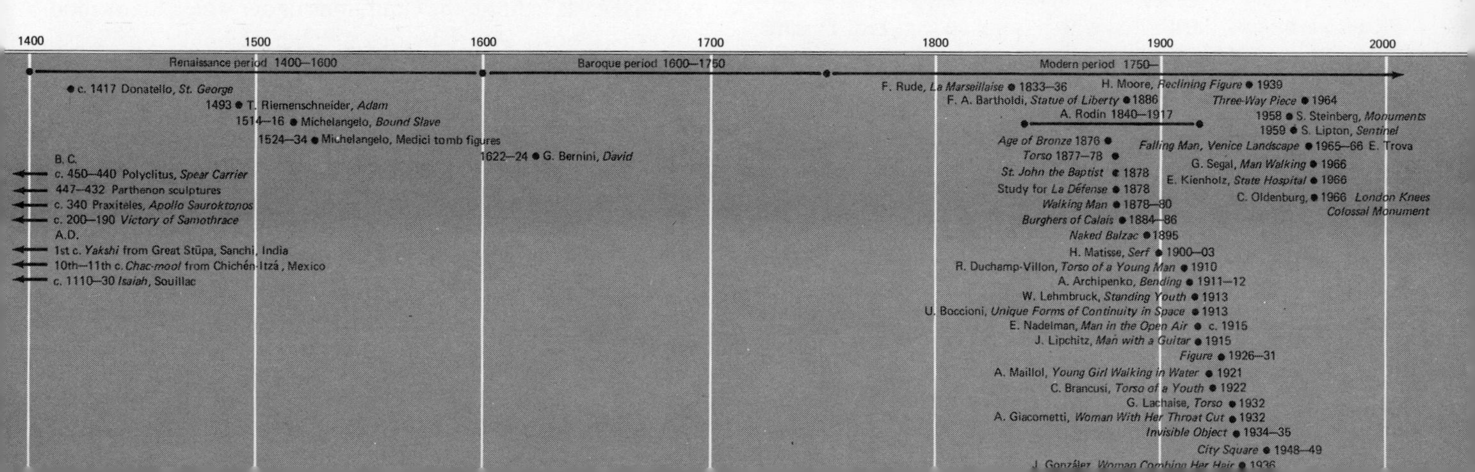

# 20

More than any other artist, Pablo Picasso symbolizes to the general public the revolutionary aspect in modern art. The American Civil Service Commission, for example, considers him to be subversive because he holds radical political views and often expresses them in his art. A census of his subjects, however, reveals that for the most part Picasso's subjects conform to those of older art—portraits, self-portraits, still lifes, landscapes, animals, the studio, mothers and children, lovers, illustrations of literature and myth, war and combat between men and animals, themes of pleasure and suffering, and the reinterpretation of past works of art. The extent and variety of subjects demonstrate the artist's tremendous range of interests and his sensibility to the aesthetic, social, psychological, emotional, and physical makeup of life.

Over the years Picasso has reflected on his own views concerning style and change:

> Every man is a colony.... One is constantly changing.... I have a curious restless quality that does not reflect self-doubt... but the creative spirit of a man sure of himself.... I have no preestablished aesthetic basis on which to make a choice.... If the subjects have suggested different ways of expression I have never hesitated to adopt them.... God is really only another artist. He invented the giraffe, elephant, cat. He has no real style. He keeps on trying other things. The same with the sculptor.... I am fundamentally an original artist in tune with the cultural discontents and attitudes of our age, but I often show a decided tendency to break away from the proved mold of modern society.

Picasso is one modern artist who has not specialized. This may be explained by his attitude toward what the artist is:

> The artist is a receptacle for emotions that come from all over the place: from the sky, from the earth, from a scrap of paper, from a passing shape, from a spider's web.... Where things are concerned there is no class distinction. We must pick out what is good for us where we can find it [1935].

Despite Picasso's seemingly encyclopedic interests, with but few exceptions he has not concerned himself with religious problems and Biblical themes. Picasso is close to Rembrandt (see Chap. 11) in his spiritual concern with man as he exists outside the organized church and its laws. Unlike Rembrandt, however, Picasso does not attach a deep philosophical importance to flesh, light, and pigment, though his strength lies in the way he has been able to interpret the human body.

Accompanying the variety of Picasso's subject matter is an equally diversified series of styles, sometimes utilized in the same period. Again the artist's own words are relevant:

> If the subjects I have wanted to express have suggested different ways of expression, I have never hesitated to adopt them.... This does not imply either evolution or progress, but an adaptation of the idea one wants to express and the means to express that idea [1923].

There is an ethical basis, then, for Picasso's modal system and his recourse to such diversified media as painting, graphics, drawing, and sculpture.

Throughout his life Picasso has returned to certain basic themes and problems, feeling that in growing older he has brought new insights to bear, as well as superior means of realization. With his pride in craft and concern with its problems and potential, there coexists a humanistic sense of inquiry and sympathy.

Merely outlining the statistics of Picasso's personal history, his travels, outstanding projects, and the people who have influenced him would take up an entire chapter. It should be noted, however, that there were no important and famous teachers in his youth, no sponsors of Renaissance stature—a fact that casts light on the conditions under which many modern artists work. A prodigious number of books on Picasso make his fascinating biography easily accessible. Let it suffice here to say that Picasso was born in 1881 in Málaga, Spain, the son of an art teacher, whose assistance enabled him to pass with distinction and amazing speed the entrance examinations for two Barcelona academies in 1895 and 1897.

The uneasiness that much of the public still has about Picasso's ability to draw accurately from a subject stems from an unfamiliarity with his naturalistic student drawings, such as a Conté crayon rendering made from a plaster cast of a reclining figure from the Parthenon, which was given as a

# PICASSO

problem to the Barcelona art students (Fig. 531). This early exposure to making art from art deeply influenced Picasso, and years later he was to continue making drawings and paintings in which his version of ancient sculpture and its fragments would be the subject or basis of his style (Pl. 75, p. 395). What the exercise demonstrates is the precocious control the young Picasso had over drawing as an instrument and the acuteness of his vision in preserving the proportions as well as the profile of the motif before his eyes. Picasso feels that as a child he could draw like Raphael; as an adult he consciously tries on occasion to recapture the open, naïve vision of the child. In Barcelona he came in contact with an important group of artists and intellectuals and with advanced European art of the day. By the time of his third trip to Paris in 1904, he had decided to settle in that city, where critical success was beginning to come to his work after initial neglect and privation.

Picasso's art before 1905 was filled with images of poverty, which were a sincere expression of his own economic plight and that of his Spanish and Parisian friends. His subjects were bohemians, artists, personal acquaintances, the part of society forced to live a difficult marginal existence. *The Frugal Repast* (Fig. 532) is one of Picasso's first prints, a virtuoso performance both in its technique and in its demonstration of the artist's ability to wed modes of drawing to the mood of his subjects. The seated figures, one of whom may be a self-portrait, reflect Picasso's early search for pathos in postures. Joined by the arrangement of their limbs, the bodies make a stable, closed composition that contrasts with the apparent instability and divergence of their attention and personalities. Their bony attenuation is an expressive device that at the same time conveys privation and permits extreme and elegant figure distortion. The greys and blacks of the etching are appropriate to the morbid subject. At this time Picasso was exploring the overall

*left:* 531. PABLO PICASSO. *Drawing from a Cast of the Figure of Dionysus* (east pediment of the Parthenon). 1893–94. Conté crayon. Private collection.

*above:* 532. PABLO PICASSO. *The Frugal Repast.* 1904. Etching, 18¼ × 14¾". Metropolitan Museum of Art, New York (Dick Fund, 1923).

use of single tonalities (such as blue or green), with wide latitude of nuance, to set the mood of an entire work.

Two years after *The Frugal Repast,* Picasso painted a vigorous self-portrait (Fig. 533) that reveals his changed attitude toward the human body and art. Elimination of pathos and social consciousness seems to have coincided with Picasso's improved financial status and artistic success. Throughout his work, the painter's life and his art intermingle in confessional, playful, or boastful tones. In this portrait Picasso avowed a new willfulness, which joined altered conceptions of what was manly and what was art. There is no melodrama or plea for sympathy. Instead, the portrait exudes frank self-confidence; Picasso keeps no secrets. His power comes from his will, eye, and hand and from the colors of the palette. Years later, Picasso was to remark that it was above all the hand that determined the painting. In this self-portrait, Picasso stripped away those details that might mitigate or be extraneous to the concentrated and immediate effect he desired. He had become aware that expression resides in the way the means of art are used, means reflecting the urgent feelings and the intelligence of the artist. Picasso here reduced his technique drastically from the manner of the etching. A contrast of the eyes and ears of the men in the two works is revealing, but comparing their right arms is an even more effective gauge. The right arm of the man in *The Frugal Repast* is one of the most beautiful in Picasso's art, born of a thousand tiny openings incised in the metal plate. In the painting, two major strokes establish the arm's shape, weight, direction, and robust strength. Picasso sought a forceful reduction of means, not necessarily simplification.

Picasso admired the intensity of expression in primitive masks, but he respected more the asymmetrical constructions of symmetrical human features and objects in Cézanne's art (Fig. 486; Pl. 63, p. 347). Also from Cézanne, Picasso received the idea of creating continuities in art where in nature there were discontinuities, and vice versa. The palette, for instance, is locked into place in the self-portrait by its close coincidence with the sleeve and bottom of the shirt. Cézanne's reduction of myriad shapes to multiples of each other found comprehension in Picasso's conjugation of ovoid forms in the head and the neckline of the shirt and the multiplicity of arcs within the same area. The young artist was learning to recognize and manipulate the emotive power of certain shapes in varied combination, and in his self-portrait he made of himself more an object of aesthetic rather than psychological study.

For some reason, Picasso removed the brush from his hand in the painting, and the heaviness of the pigment's application suggests that he might just as well have worked the paint with his fingers. In these years Picasso was searching for a new feeling of what the primal nature of art was and could be. Preserving a certain rawness of means, he gave the completed work a rugged, handmade look. Picasso had even eliminated the customary use of a mirror, as shown by the placement of his right arm on the left side of the painting.

*Les Demoiselles d'Avignon* (Pl. 75, p. 395) is one of Picasso's most notorious, but by no means most aesthetically successful, paintings. The ideas and energies unleashed in its creation, as well as its failures, make it important in the history of Picasso's art. The largest painting undertaken by Picasso until that time, it was destined to incompletion and inconsistency because of the rapidity and excitement with which his art was changing

*left:* 533. PABLO PICASSO. *Self-Portrait.* 1906. Oil on canvas, $36^1/_4 \times 28^3/_4$". Philadelphia Museum of Art (A. E. Gallatin Collection).

*right:* 534. PABLO PICASSO. *Head, Apple, and Box.* c. 1907. Drawing. Collection Douglas Cooper.

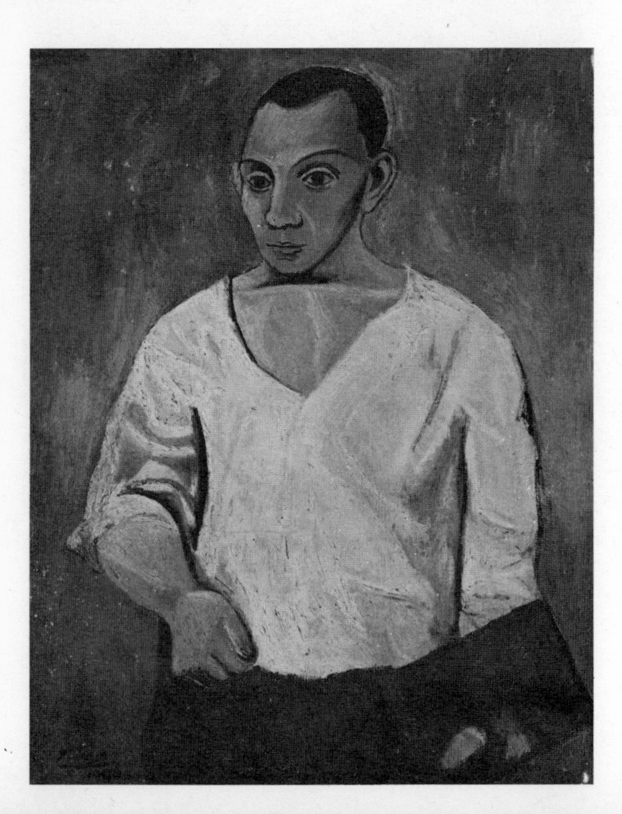

from month to month and from painting to painting. Thus, in 1906 and 1907, both emotionally and aesthetically, Picasso was incapable of producing a large, complex, and homogeneous canvas. In a single year of this phase his production of drawings and paintings equaled or exceeded the lifetime output of many artists of the past. Here was not only energy but also Picasso's compulsion to work out every idea and impulse in a flood of drawings and paintings, all interrelated and not to be taken in isolation at their point of entry into his artistic development.

*Les Demoiselles d'Avignon* was both a battleground and a nursery for Picasso's art. On its surface he seemed to wage war with the accumulated traditions of Western painting, accepting solely the demands of pictorial order. The tearing down accomplished in this work was partially balanced by what it presented as new and fruitful alternatives, for it was to take Picasso additional thousands of drawings, canvases, and sculptures—in fact, a lifetime—to realize and fulfill all that was begun or hinted at in this one painting. The painting's theme began in sketches as an allegory: "The wages of sin is death." Prostitutes in a brothel paraded before a sailor and, in one instance, a death's head. Accompanying the departure of the skull and sailor from the successive designs was also the moralizing intent. The painting passed through numerous stages until it lost any programmatic meaning and would then have been awkward to fit into the traditional category of genre. What Picasso approached at this time was painting primarily as an aesthetic object intended to move and delight the beholder. This meant stripping away the conventional sentiment of the female nude as well as other conventions of drawing, color, and composition. Brutal as its conception and execution may be, *Les Demoiselles d'Avignon* descends nonetheless from a long line of robust paintings of nudes. In retrospect, it seems almost a parody of sensuous nude studies by such Baroque painters as Rubens (Fig. 228). Picasso's nude females elbow against the nymphs, goddesses, and innocent bathers who for generations symbolized concord with nature and sinless fertility.

Picasso seemed undecided whether to stage the women indoors or out; the figure at the left seems to have a farm woman's tan, unlike the pink complexion of the woman next to her. Picasso's women are objects of display transformed by the instincts of the artist, which enter freely onto the canvas. The prostitutes are given a mixed ethnological background, reflecting Picasso's new-found excitement with ancient art (the central two figures) and with African tribal art (those on the sides). Picasso's primitivizing tendency adopted certain models of distortion and what he may have felt was the sexual intensity of African sculpture. These were grafted onto the Greek Classical beauty pose in the center, the rigid vertical Egyptian stance at the left, and the seated studio model at the right. The profile figure at the left has the Egyptian frontal eye, while in the two adjacent figures a profile nose appears on a frontal face.

The green-striped face of the woman at the upper right may have derived from primitive masks showing scarification, a process echoed in Picasso's brushwork. Each figure is either an ethnic or an aesthetic hybrid, and only the still life is finished and consistent. Left with too many fragments and ideas, the artist suspended his growth to complete the whole.

Within the frame of the painting, traces of Picasso's struggles to destroy and reconstruct are plainly visible, even notations such as the rough blue outline superimposed on the leg at the lower left. Picasso had set aside traditional means of uniting a group of figures: common focus, activity, moods, viewpoint, setting, light and shade, or coordinated limb arrangement no longer met his needs. To give his canvas its own autonomy, the figures and setting had to relinquish theirs. The body contours were broken into, and parts were made almost interchangeable by their reduction to such basic shapes as the V repeated in crotch, breast, elbow, and jagged background forms. Cohesion and expressiveness of surface demanded flat rather than voluminous bodies, the obscuring of the figure's means of support, making space relationships inconsistent, and, to intervals between figures, the assigning of accents and visual importance that rivaled the bodies themselves. The rhythms and force set by the restructuring of the bodies spill over into the indeterminate background.

The painting's pinks, blues, whites, browns, and blacks are a tonal recapitulation of all Picasso's previous periods. The blue between the central and right figures is glacial and sharply attractive to the eye. Picasso's conflicting impulses led him to mix outline and edge, modeled and flat surfaces, and black, white, and blue silhouettes. He could not resolve so much color and so many modes into a single dominant harmony of contrasts; yet ironically, much of the painting's initial appeal derives from this very freshness of color and raw juxtapositions. Picasso probably intended a painting with shock value, to stab directly at the senses or the emotions rather than at the intellect. With Matisse and others of the time, Picasso shared an ethic of the primacy of feeling in art as well as in life. His dilemma as a painter lay in possessing the instinct for lucid control and linear organization; ultimately, he was unable to liberate both color and drawing, as could Matisse (Pl. 72, p. 361).

Picasso's development was rapid and extremely varied. There was no simple continuous progression toward his completely Cubist paintings, but we shall try, briefly, to illustrate this latter direction. *Head, Apple, and Box* (Fig. 534) shows more consistency in style than does *Les Demoiselles d'Avignon*. It illustrates the artist's extension of the Cubist mode to objects as well as to the human form. The head's anatomical structure and the shapes of the objects do not predict the premises of Picasso's drawing. His design does not follow, say, the musculature of the face, the natural curves of the features, or the proportions and planes of the box as generally perceived. He increased the complexity and expressiveness of the face

*left:* 535. Pablo Picasso. *Mandolin.* 1914. Construction in wood, height 23⅝″. Collection the artist.

through new angles and facets. Though passive in mood, the woman's face is activated by the energized drawing in such inventions as the peaked eyes and the arbitrary placement and increased degree of shadow. There is no dominant symmetrical vertical axis in any of the forms; the artist clearly preferred disconnected sequences. The box, with its inverted perspective and multiplication of planes, becomes a crystal form of increased weight and stability. At this stage of Cubism, Picasso was still interested in light and shadow, mass and volume, and the sensual swelling of flesh.

*Ma Jolie* (Pl. 76, p. 396) was a painting of Marcelle Humbert, with whom Picasso was deeply in love and who died during World War I. "Ma Jolie" was both the epithet he gave to her and the title of a popular song. In line with his ideas of the years 1911 to 1912, Picasso could not paint her in the traditional portrait manner. In part he "inscribed" his love, as he put it, on the canvases devoted to her, with the words "J'aime Eva" and "Ma Jolie." Such sentiments had never before been so literally a part of the work of art. The fact that Picasso accomplished this without disrupting the integrity or logic of the painting is in itself a sign of Cubism's radical break with the past. From the Renaissance through the 19th century, art consisted in imitating the physical appearance of nature. With the development of Cubism, empirical verification was to be found only in the terms of the painting itself. The similitude to be appreciated became that of the final painting to the emotions of the artist who produced it. Expressed in another way, Picasso in *Ma Jolie* did not deal directly with the world of appearances, with respect for its distinctions and logic. His drawing and color were meant as visual equivalences of his love for Eva in the same way that the words "Ma Jolie" could be equivalences of a song and a woman without really looking or sounding like either. In a sense, the pulse of warm and cool color alternation and the shimmer of countless touches of thin brush give a palpable presence to the "vibrations" of Eva's life as Picasso felt them. The diagonals and vertical massing of the planes are vestiges of the seated human figure. Still, Picasso wanted the literal appearance not of a woman but of a painting, a unified, moving, and beautiful object. On the wooden stretcher of the canvas, Picasso wrote, "Woman with a Zither," probably the original title. Part of a hand seen at the lower right is properly in position to hold the instrument. The zither's design has analogies to the painting's vocabulary of forms. While music did not supply the theory or model for Cubist painting, it was a bond by which the artist and, in this case, the woman Picasso loved were joined. Though the resulting order of the painting reflects intellectual precision, the whole was done with genuine passion. The drawing and painting of *Ma Jolie* are disciplined and of great beauty.

Some of Picasso's own statements about Cubism, made in 1923, are important in understanding the artist's conception of its nature and its relation to the past:

> Cubism is . . . an art dealing primarily with forms, and when a form is realized, it is there to live its own life. . . . Drawing, design and color are understood and practiced in Cubism in the same spirit and manner that they are understood and practiced in all other schools. . . . We have kept our eyes open to our surroundings and also our brains. We give to form and color all their individual significance. . . . The fact that for a long time Cubism has not been understood . . . means nothing. I do not read an English book that is a blank book to me. This does not mean that the English language does not exist, and why should I blame anybody else but myself if I cannot understand what I know nothing about.

Picasso's inexhaustible creative energy and the fertile ideas of Cubism led him to work in sculpture in a manner as unprecedented as his painting. One of Picasso's most influential works is the wooden construction *Mandolin* (Fig. 535). Its fabrication and appearance appear to resist the label of sculpture, for it has not been cast, modeled, or carved; it does not sit upon a base, and its subject is a musical instrument. In Picasso's words: "What is sculpture? What is painting? Everyone clings to old fashioned ideas and outworn definitions, as if it were not precisely the role of the artist to provide new ones." For his materials Picasso here used scraps of wood from boxes and canvas stretchers, discards that lay about his study. The wood had been processed and shaped to fulfill utilitarian functions before being put to his purely aesthetic purposes. His selection of these scraps was not haphazard, for he was attracted initially by the grain, size, and shapes. Some pieces may have been used without reworking; in these, the "found object" is preserved intact in the sculpture. Most of the scraps had something done to them, however, by painting or by sawing. The curved white piece, like the planes in Cubist paintings, reveals the rough marks of its formation, for none of the forms was sanded. The rude finishing is essential to Picasso's ethic and aesthetic sense. The sculpture has been assembled, constructed, literally manipulated; this method of joining, along with the expanded tolerance of artistic materials, was to have a strong effect on subsequent modern sculpture.

Picasso, like other advanced artists of the time, was rebelling against the academic conception of "noble media," such as marble and bronze, and "noble subjects," such as the human figure in heroic action. Whatever heroism is present in the *Mandolin* resides in the courage and daring of the artist's defiance of tradition; literally and figuratively, Picasso helped to remove sculpture from the pedestal of tradition. His is not relief sculpture in the old sense, for it has no rectangular frame to contain the sculpture or to balance and coordinate the shapes within. The absence of the frame also introduces the possibility of a play of irregular shadows cast onto the wall by the projecting parts, and these shadows give added depth and vibrancy to the work. There is no consistent or uniform rear plane to which successive relief planes can be referred. Even more than in Cubist painting, the planes of this sculpture advance into the space of the beholder, and yet they display an inconsistent overlapping that maintains an ambivalence of inward and outward movement. Picasso painted some of the construction, reversing the trend begun with Michelangelo (see Chap. 8), one of the first major sculptors to give up painting his figures.

As an artist, Picasso has frequently indulged in playful activity, making his seriousness of purpose suspect to some. When, for example, he made the *Head of a Bull* (Fig. 536) by juxtaposing a bicycle seat and handlebars and hanging them on a wall, he was creating art from a child's toy. His earlier construction *Mandolin* had taught him the possibilities of transposing and manipulating materials and already existing objects, to which his eye and mind gave a second life.

Picasso looks upon every object as a potential metaphor and delights in rehabilitating old metaphors as well as object discards. The *Head of a Bull* exemplifies his idea of a "reversible" sculpture: "I find a bicycle seat and handlebars in the street, and I say, 'Well, there's a bull,' until a cyclist comes along and says, 'Well, there's a bicycle seat' and he makes a seat and a pair of handlebars out of it again. And that can go on back and forth, for an eternity, according to the needs of the mind and body."

Much of today's sculpture involving the rehabilitation of discarded objects, which derives its artistic value from the witty and imaginative visual plays of the sculptor rather than from manual reforming, owes a great deal to such earlier works as *Head of a Bull.* Picasso has never claimed that such playful activities as this constitute great art. He would be the first to remind us that what he has done in such works is not unlike what occurs to youthful imagination that is too soon lost as we become adults. As is true of much modern literary criticism, that of art is too often obsessed by false absolutes of greatness, which may cause both critic and audience to forfeit enjoyment of much that is good or interesting.

**The Artist and Model Series** Like Rembrandt, Picasso returned repeatedly to the theme of the making of art or the artist and model in the studio. Different versions of this theme reveal Picasso's ability to work in different modes. The etching *Painter with Model Knitting* (Fig. 537), an illustration for

*left:* 536. PABLO PICASSO. *Head of a Bull.* 1943. Handlebars and bicycle seat, height $16^1/_8$″. Collection the artist.

*right:* 537. PABLO PICASSO. *Painter with Model Knitting.* 1928. Etching, $7^5/_8 \times 11^3/_8$″. Museum of Modern Art, New York (gift of Henri Church).

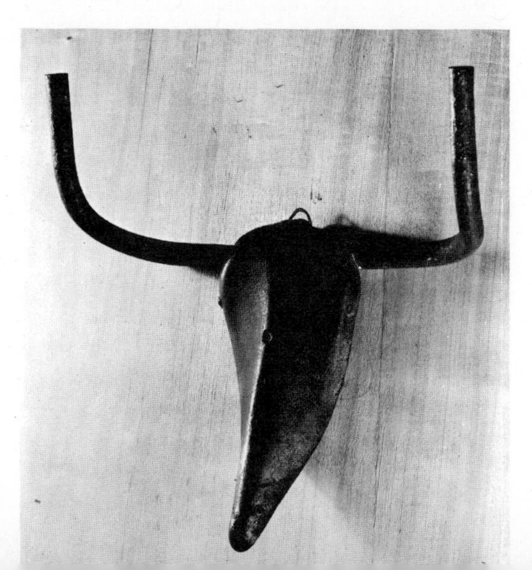

*left:* 538. PABLO PICASSO. *The Painter and His Model.* 1927. Oil on canvas, 7′1/4″ × 6′6 3/4″. Collection Mr. and Mrs. Sidney Janis.

*above:* 539. PABLO PICASSO. *The Painter and His Model.* 1928. Oil on canvas, 4′3 5/8″ × 5′3 7/8″. Museum of Modern Art, New York (gift of Mr. and Mrs. Sidney Janis.)

Balzac's *The Unknown Masterpiece,* has a subject that reveals the way Picasso worked. The short story is concerned with one Frenhofer, a 17th-century painter who devoted his life to achieving a perfect balance, within a single painting, of drawing and color. Poussin (Pl. 53, p. 309) and Rubens (Pl. 29, p. 162) were considered rivals championing, respectively, drawing and color. The artist's final masterpiece is a chaos of the two principles, producing a small but superb woman's foot. The old artist, recognizing his failure, destroys himself and his art.

In the etching, the artist's design bears no resemblance to the external appearance of the woman, but it does catch the spirit of Frenhofer's dictum that in drawing a hand it is not enough to show its attachment to the body, but it must also be shown as a continuation or extension of thought and feeling. The drawing on the canvas is a form of knitting, in which the woman is translated into a series of interwoven rhythmic configurations. Unlike the painting in progress in Vermeer's *The Artist in His Studio* (Pl. 34, p. 182), the outcome of the drawing is unforeseeable on the basis of the model. In 1935, Picasso said, "A picture is not thought out and settled beforehand. While it is being done, it changes as one's thoughts change. And when it is finished it still goes on changing according to the state of mind of whoever is looking at it."

It is unwise to try to label Picasso's modes or to call the drawing of the model in his illustration "abstract." On the use of this word, Picasso said in 1935:

> There is no abstract art. You must always start with something. Afterward you can remove all traces of reality. There's no danger then, anyway, because the idea of the object will have left an indelible mark. It is what started the artist off, excited his ideas, and stirred up his emotions [that] will in the end be prisoners in his work. . . . They form an integral part of it even when their presence is no longer discernible. Whether he likes it or not, man is the instrument of nature. It forces on him its character and appearance.

In 1927 Picasso also did a painting, *The Painter and His Model* (Fig. 538), in which the artist was remade into an angular linear frame and the woman became a hybrid entity, with drastic relocation of bodily features. The period of the late 1920s was one of Picasso's most fertile in terms of body imagery and imaginative nourishment of his art. Fantasies on the body took diverse forms, and in this particular painting the model has been brutally reduced to an animallike and precariously balanced shape. Strong sexual feeling freely entered Picasso's work at all times and inspired new inventions such as those used here for distinguishing the man and woman. What liberated Picasso's imagination still further after Cubism was the conviction that external appearances could be dispensed within painting and that there were alternative means originating in strong feeling by which to preserve reference to human subjects. Such independence from

Plate 75. Pablo Picasso. *Les Demoiselles d'Avignon*. 1907. Oil on canvas, 8′ × 7′8″. Museum of Modern Art, New York (Lillie P. Bliss Bequest). (See pp. 390, 391.)

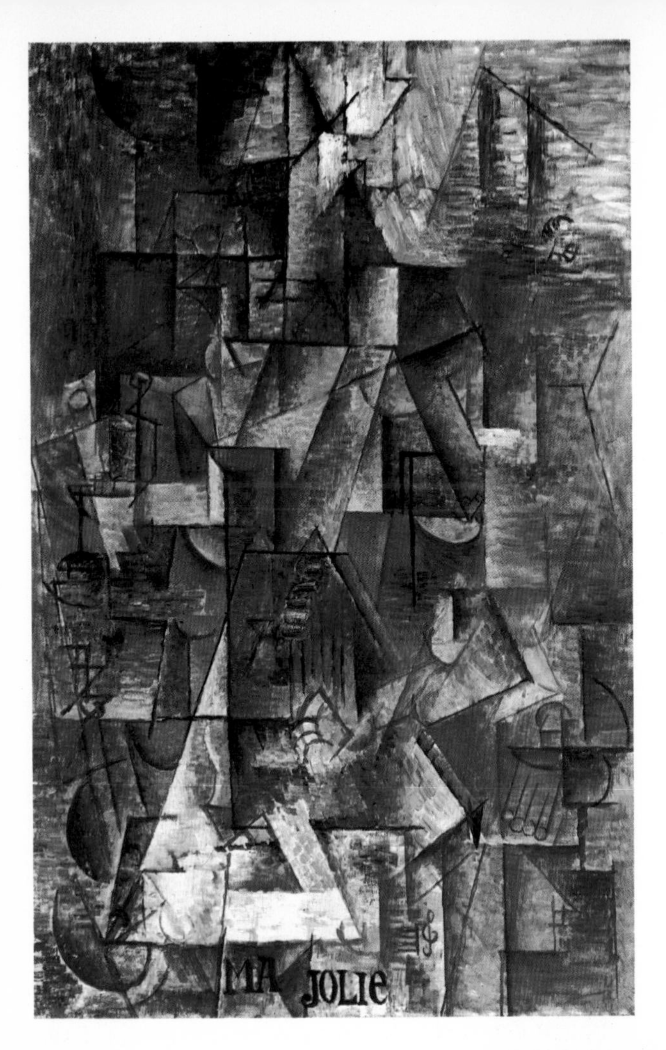

*left:* Plate 76. Pablo Picasso. *Ma Jolie*. 1911–12. Oil on canvas, $39^{3}/_{8} \times 25^{3}/_{4}''$. Museum of Modern Art, New York (Lillie P. Bliss Bequest). (See p. 392.)

*above:* Plate 77. Pablo Picasso. *Ram's Head*. 1924. Oil on canvas, $32^{1}/_{8} \times 39^{1}/_{2}''$. Private collection, New York. (See p. 398.)

Plate 78. Pablo Picasso. *Crucifixion*. February 7, 1930. Oil on wood, $20 \times 26''$. Collection the artist. (See p. 400.)

likeness and conventional modeling of the figure in painting was accompanied in this work by Picasso's separation of color from the limits of drawn contours, so that it is disposed in amorphous areas cutting across several of the drawn motifs.

In 1928 when Picasso again took up the theme *The Painter and his Model* (Fig. 539), color became wedded to the rigid compositional skeleton, itself a logical outgrowth of the earlier Cubist weblike structure. The entire painting surface has a continuous interlocking of distinct flat shapes that affirm the flatness of surface and the nonillusionistic, artificial character of Picasso's creation. Both painter and model have only token reference to actual physiognomy, and even these are rearranged to accord with the overall surface emphasis. The surprising element in the painting is the handsome naturalistic profile that the artist has heavily outlined upon his canvas, a reminder that for Picasso art can slip easily from the fantastic into the naturalistic.

In 1933 Picasso did a series of etchings for the dealer Ambroise Vollard that contain a rich assortment of themes and stylistic modes. Many of these plates were devoted to the theme of the sculptor in his studio. Despite their obvious reference to ancient sculpture, Picasso's own interest in this medium during these years makes the prints another kind of self-portrait. He shows the bearded sculptor, for example, reclining and contemplating a finished sculpture, whose model reclines next to him with a mask raised above her face (Fig. 540). In a departure from the previous works, Picasso drew the artist, model, and work of art in the same style, which was his personal version of classical drawing, inspired to a large extent by that of Matisse. The clean purity and assured lining of contours in this print presuppose Picasso's academic training and consummate knowledge of the body. The strong suggestion of the body's roundness conveyed by the character of the line made shading unnecessary, thereby conserving the surface unity as well. The print is also Picasso's personal ideal of the tranquillity necessary for a creative life. He recently wrote, "I have an unquestioning faith in the expressive power of the human body, untiring devotion to the glories of the nude."

It was natural for Picasso, when he worked with etchings, to think of Rembrandt. Not only was he fascinated by the older artist's etched gradations of black, but Picasso also did several prints of Rembrandt based on the latter's self-portraits in which he dressed himself in a fur-trimmed robe and soft cap and hung a gold chain across his ample chest. In 1934 he etched Rembrandt (Fig. 541), with his "elephant-like eyes," as Picasso called them, contemplating a beautiful bare-chested model, appropriate in view of Rembrandt's teachings and works on the subject of life drawing. Picasso evolved his own mode of involuted lines and their dense grouping to interpret the picturesque and richly detailed self-portraits of the old master. He could not resist framing one of his own women's heads in the pendant worn by Rembrandt, and the model could only be Picasso's creation. What unites the two artists, besides their prolific artistic production, is their abjuring of systematic theories and their commitment to working from art and life, which is most graphically presented in the studio portrait situation.

New styles can give new life to old themes, as we well know from popular musical arrangements. If the artist is truly the source of creation for art, how plausible then that Picasso should have made the artist himself the inspiration for imaginative painting.

*left:* 540. Pablo Picasso. *Sculptor at Work*. March 27, 1933. Etching, $10^1/_2 \times 7^5/_8$″. Museum of Modern Art, New York (purchase).

*below:* 541. Pablo Picasso. *Rembrandt with a Young Woman*. February 18, 1934. Etching, $5^1/_2 \times 8^1/_4$″.

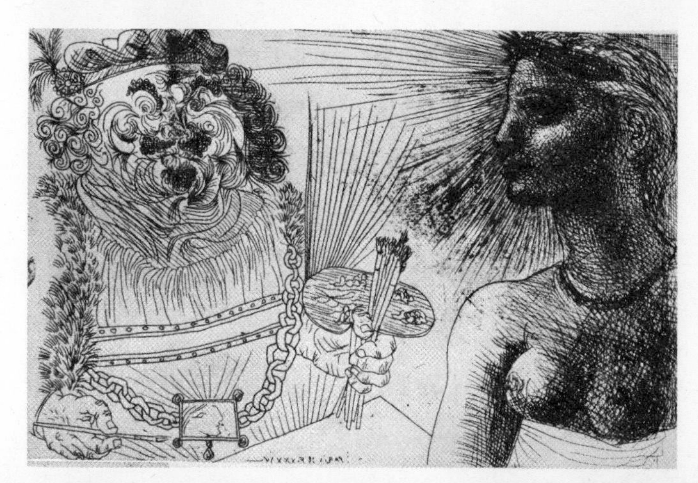

**Work Leading to Guernica** Although Picasso's painting of the bombing of Guernica was not accomplished until 1937, its sources within his own art go back many years and can be found among such seemingly unrelated subjects of the 1920s as still lifes, dancing figures, bathers, and, during the 1930s, his interpretation of the Crucifixion themes, bullfights, and Greek mythology.

The still life of the *Ram's Head* (Pl. 77, p. 396) testifies to the viability of the Cubist style and to Picasso's alertness to new subject matter. There is far less decomposition of objects than in *Ma Jolie* (Pl. 76, p. 396), and familiar textures and shapes facilitate reading the contents. What is new and unfamiliar in Picasso's art is the range of unpleasant sensations the objects inspire. The objects are foods in a raw inedible state, unlike the more ingratiating contents of earlier Cubist still lifes (Pl. 64, p. 347), with their sociable connotations and appeal to the touch. Picasso contrasted the horn and hair of the ram, fish scales, and shells with sharp edges against moist, pulpy substances like the squid at the lower left. Violence is to be seen in the subjects themselves—in the severed head of the ram and the arsenal of teeth in the gaping fish mouth—consonant with the abrupt conjunctions of textures. The yellow of the blue-veined lemon to the left of the ram's head, a rectangular patch cut by the circular lemon, adds a conspicuous note of color to the dominant blues, whites, and browns of the painting. The black linear scaffolding of *Ma Jolie* has disappeared; the composition includes large free-swinging curved lines and planes that alternate and join with rectilinear passages in tight cohesion. The colors and textures lie flat upon the surface, affirming its two-dimensionality. The objects are tautly grouped and held within the frame by such inventive drawing as the free repeat of the serrated edge under the ram's head and in the spine of the fish.

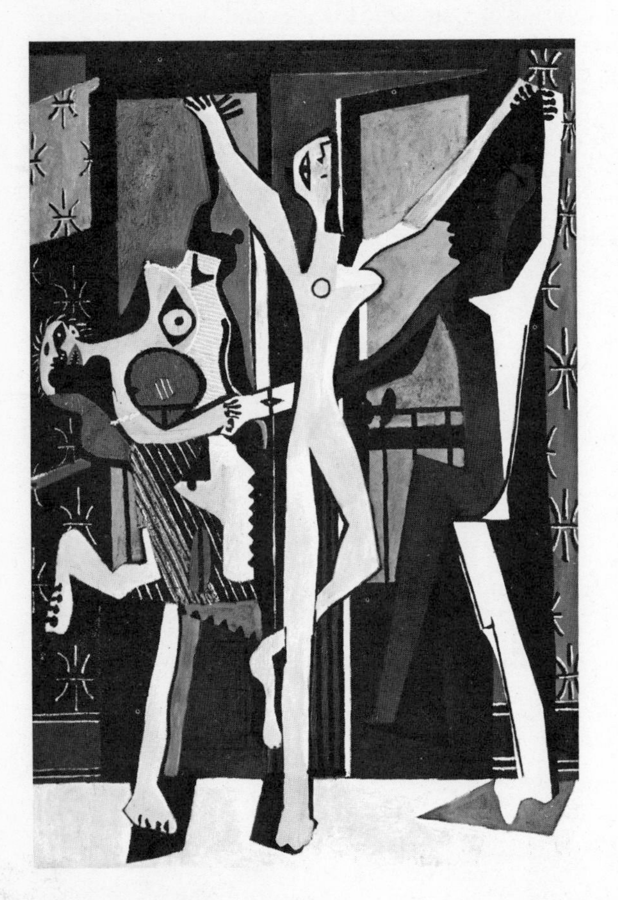

*left:* 542. Pablo Picasso. *Three Dancers.* 1925. Oil on canvas, 7′5/8″ × 4′8¼″. Tate Gallery, London.

*above:* 543. Pablo Picasso. *Seated Bather.* 1930. Oil on canvas, 5′4½″ × 4′3″. Museum of Modern Art, New York (Mrs. Simon Guggenheim Fund).

Another area of sensation into which Picasso's sensibilities forcefully expanded in the mid-1920s was that of internal body imagery, seen in *Three Dancers* (Fig. 542). Traditionally, naked figures in an interior meant that the artist was studying anatomy and poses. By 1925, Picasso had become interested in the art of fantasy as exhibited by Miró (Pl. 82, p. 414) and Arp. He was fascinated by their bold incursions into the irrational and the unlocking of inhibitions with respect to form and content. Rather than having created a studio study of the way three naked models might look to someone else,

Picasso seems to have imagined their own inner sensations as their bodies are given over to the abandon of a frenzied dance. Each dancer possesses a phantom double, a second and even a third self. This is made apparent in the black areas, which are not literal projected shadows but poetic extensions of each figure's consciousness of the body area in which the strongest feelings are localized. The figure at the left is given an extra breast, that to the right a second and larger head of different silhouette and expression. In an unclinical, intuitive way, Picasso showed how, in moments of great physical exertion and erotic stimulation, a new self-consciousness may come into being. Affected by these conditions may be the emphasis, size, weight, color, shape, location, and even orientation of the body parts. All the figures seem to be boneless, for example, and much of the distortion occurs in the most fleshy areas. Cubism's breakdown of the body as a continuous closed vessel was the foundation for this new imagery in Picasso's art. Picasso and other artists could now extend their most intimate sentiments to the complete internal as well as external reconstruction of the body in art. Picasso gave his figures a fictive transparency, so that we see simultaneously the pink of the flesh and the suggestions of internal organs.

In *Seated Bather* (Fig. 543), painted in 1930, Picasso was making a reconnaissance of an idea for a huge sculpture to be located on the Mediterranean coast. The solidity of the body was broken up, and there is an intriguing fusion of bone and flesh forms. The head of the "bather" has an astonishing and ominous viselike substitution for the jaws. The transparency of the sculpture derives from Picasso's transparent-metal sculpture-constructions of two years before, which themselves grew out of his pictorial armatures. The "cross-pollinating" of Picasso's work in different media has always been strong, and this tendency augments his seemingly inexhaustible ideas for metamorphosing the body. The artist had the impulse to make heroically scaled sculptures, feeling that there were certain artistic traditions which should not die and to which his viable art could give new life.

Thematically, some of Picasso's most personal images are his passionate portrayals of his mistress of the early 1930s, Marie-Thérèse Walter. She so inspired Picasso with sexual fantasies that they flowed equally into painting and sculpture. In the boldest and most imaginative artistic homage of a lover to his mistress, Picasso modeled a large woman's head whose features resembled male and female genitalia (Fig. 544). Picasso's aggressive procreative desires, coupled with his instinct for analogizing forms, were thus candidly transformed into a work that was both a portrait and image of sexual union. He had transferred to the human head activities of the male and female body. His strong carnal feeling, tempered with amazing insight into human body imagery, likewise produced the *Girl Before a Mirror* (Fig. 545), in which the young woman, inspired by Marie-Thérèse, contemplates herself in different ways. Picasso has shown, by the three

*right:* 544. PABLO PICASSO. *Woman's Head.* 1932. Bronze, $33\frac{1}{2} \times 14\frac{1}{2} \times 17\frac{7}{8}$″. Collection the artist.

*far right:* 545. PABLO PICASSO. *Girl Before a Mirror.* 1932. $5'3\frac{3}{4}'' \times 4'3\frac{1}{8}''$. Museum of Modern Art, New York (gift of Mrs. Simon Guggenheim).

*above:* 546. PABLO PICASSO. *Minotauromachia.* 1935. Etching, $19^1/_2 \times 27^3/_8$". Philadelphia Museum of Art (gift of Henry R. McIlhenny).

*right:* 547. PABLO PICASSO. *Weeping Head,* study for *Guernica* (Fig. 548). May 24, 1937. Pencil and wash on paper, $11^3/_8 \times 9$". Collection the artist, on extended loan to the Museum of Modern Art, New York.

views of the same woman's face and by the contrasting configurations of her body and its reflection, multiple modes of experience. Meyer Schapiro reads this work as Picasso painting "the body contemplated, loved and self-contemplating." It is a poetic evocation of the way a girl imagines she appears to others and is aroused by the sight of her naked body. Here, again, the artist has made use of analogies with the procreative portions of the human body; the brilliant color echoes the vitality of the woman and of the artist.

**Crucifixion and Guernica** The impulse to revitalize artistic traditions even when they seem to run counter to his own work is illustrated by Picasso's investigation of secular and religious themes that had been overworked and demeaned by insincere and uninspired handling.

The first painting in which he treated a theme of explicit violence, as contrasted with his own artistic violence in painting passive subjects, is a small picture done in 1930, after many drawings, entitled *Crucifixion* (Pl. 78, p. 396). This is an unusual painting for Picasso in many ways. It was the first time he had interpreted a subject drawn from literature, or the Bible, and it was a work not intended for a church or the public. We do not know what caused him to take up this theme, and its relation to his personal life or his possible reaction to a painting on the subject can only be conjectured. What seems to have initially attracted him to the subject of the Crucifixion, judging by the preliminary drawings, was not Christ's agonies on the Cross but rather the passionate sufferings of Mary Magdalen and the complex and expressive interweaving of limbs and faces. Owing to his own breakthrough in body imagery of the late 1920s, whereby the emotional state of the subject could be exteriorized by drastic changes in the appearance of the body, Picasso could reinterpret in a personal and subjective way one of the great themes of art, but one given up by most modern artists. Unlike the symbolic objects in *The Breviary of King Martin of Aragon* (Fig. 459), Picasso's painting does not permit us easily to interpret and relate all its parts. It is possible to identify the crucified Christ and the figure on a ladder nailing a hand to the Cross, the soldiers gambling for Christ's cloak, the mounted centurion who lances Christ's side, and at the far right the draped Magdalen figure with outstretched arms. The fantastic heads with gaping jaws seen in different parts of the painting, which spring from Picasso's previous secular imagery (Fig. 543), may have been introduced to symbolize the animallike brutality of the event; the creature to the left may be a crowing cock to illustrate the episode of Peter. The painting's intensity within such a small format results from its hot red and yellow colors, which, like the shapes, are crowded into a restricted space. As much as the drawing, these colors convey Picasso's passionate feeling and, rather than being decorative, add to the emotional dissonance of the conception.

During the 1930s Picasso was strongly attracted to ancient Greek mythology, partly as a reaction to the futility of rational conduct in the face of the rise of fascism. There resulted in Picasso's art, notably in his etching *Minotauromachia* (Fig. 546), the formation of private myths, rather than literal interpretations of such Greek legends as Theseus and the Minotaur. In many drawings, prints, and paintings preceding this etching, Picasso had created fantasies based upon the Minotaur, the bull, and the bullfight. These, coupled with prior themes in his art, were brought together in the *Minotauromachia* with no rational plan or discernible narrative. The whole is a model of the illusionistic Surrealist image built upon instinctive creation (see Chap. 21). The artist responded to obsessive themes mingling the bizarre, the erotic, the violent, and the innocent in free association.

Both in his previous interpretations and in the *Minotauromachia,* Picasso deviated from the original story of the Minotaur. In antiquity, the Minotaur was a destructive being to whom young girls were sacrificed. In Picasso's art the Minotaur has been severally shown as a pathetic victim, as a tender abductor or object of love, and as confounded with the person of Theseus. In the *Minotauromachia* the Minotaur is not a menacing figure but is shown reaching for the light held by the young girl. Just to the left of the Minotaur's legs is a white sail, instead of the black sail that in the Theseus myth was erroneously kept, resulting in the suicide of Aegeus. The horse and the woman toreador emerge from the earlier bullfight series; and as before, the woman shows evidence of violation. In her dreamlike state she menaces with the sword the gored horse rather than the Minotaur, who also has been fused with the bull in the bullfight series. The figure ascending the ladder at the left, who looks over his shoulder in the direction of the light, is Christ. The theme of Christ mounting to his death is an old one in Spanish art. Above the scene, in the niche of a blockhouse, are two young girls, who are seemingly witnesses to the scene but whose attention is upon two doves. These witness figures also derive from earlier studies of arena combat. The two birds standing before a niche occur in a painting done by Picasso's father before 1900. Rich and fascinating are the etching's myriad references and ambiguous interrelationships of time, place, and action.

In May, 1937, Picasso began work on studies for a large canvas to commemorate the bombing on April 26 of the Spanish Basque town of Guernica by Franco's German dive bombers. This was his first painting directly inspired by a specific historical event. Nevertheless, the studies and the completed painting were a logical outlet and summation of his imagery of the late 1920s and 1930s that had dealt with brutality and fantasies upon the body. One brilliant sketch (Fig. 547) shows how Picasso became deeply engrossed in the nonpolitical aspects of the project—notably the theme of the human deranged by pain. The woman's head has been completely detached from the body, and each feature's response to pain is shown separately. Even the normally neutral areas of eyelashes, brows, and hair participate aggressively. The eyebrows do not lie passively on the forehead but cut into it like deep scars. The hair pulls away from the head, resembling rawly exposed nerves such as are also suggested in the lines from the right eye running down the cheek. The eyes have been pulled apart and transposed into teardrop forms filled with and surrounded by splintering shapes. A large dark patch between the eyes localizes another area of intense aggravation. The nostrils, one almost detached from the nose, are swollen and flared. The entire head seems divested of its cranial skeleton as it is twisted into soft and angular contortions. The climactic feature is the mouth burst open in a scream, the lips peeled back to reveal the irregular and precariously rooted teeth, the lining of the palate, the black cavity of the throat, and the rigidification of the tongue into a sharp cutting instrument.

Grünewald's *Isenheim Altarpiece* (Pl. 7, p. 77) was a source of this drawing. From children's art, Picasso took the use of crayon, and deceptively childish scribbling within the facial contours achieved a graduated series of vaguely defined irritated spots. The drawing betrays the fierce pressure with which the crayon was dug into the paper, particularly in the brow and hair. Picasso's sadism, extended to his means as well as to his subject, is frankly manifest.

In the final painting of *Guernica* (Fig. 548), Picasso avoided specific or unmistakable political reference to the locale of

*below:* 548. PABLO PICASSO. *Guernica*. 1937. Oil on canvas, 11′5½″ × 25′8¾″. Collection the artist, on extended loan to the Museum of Modern Art, New York.

*below:* 549. Georg Lebrecht. *Dive Bombers over England.* 1941. Present whereabouts unknown.

*right:* 550. Pablo Picasso. *Horse's Head,* study for *Guernica* (Fig. 548). May 2, 1937. Oil on canvas, $25^1/_2 \times 36^1/_4''$. Collection the artist, on extended loan to the Museum of Modern Art, New York.

the tragedy, to the fascist aggressor, or to modern warfare, focusing his attention upon the agonies of the noncombatants. No cipherable links between the figures and groups exist, and while Picasso may have had private symbols in mind, he has consistently refused to spell out his intent. At various times in Picasso's art, the bull, like the horse and the dove, has signified Franco and the Spanish people. To assign to the bull at the left the role of aggressor is to overlook clear indications that the bull is also a victim. "The bull is a bull and the horse is a horse. They are animals, massacred animals. That is all, so far as I am concerned." In the center is the distended head of the dying horse, with its body pierced by a spear, recalling Christ's death on the cross. (The pathetic horse replaces Christ as the main focal point of a symbolic dream scene in another work by Picasso.) Beneath the horse are segments of a man whose arm clutches a broken sword and a flower. In older art, the figure fallen under a galloping horse was a victory symbol, but this tradition ended with *Guernica.* The hard lifeless head recalls the plaster figures that had been the subjects of Picasso's drawing since his student days in Barcelona (Fig. 531) and that in the 1920s began to appear in the artist's still lifes. The figure running in from the right is a descendant of earlier paintings of gigantesque nudes racing along a beach, but now the woman's form is swollen and constricted in exaggerated exteriorization of her internal distress.

Other reminiscences of earlier work are the mother and child, and the woman who leans from the window holding the lamp, providing vague connotations of justice. Within Picasso's art she is a descendant of the young girl who with a lamp suggests innocence (Fig. 546). Her gesture and expressive face relate her to older French images of Liberty and Justice, which Picasso had before his eyes in Paris (Pl. 43, p. 285; Fig. 489). There is ambiguity regarding the interior or exterior locus of the action (the people of Guernica died both indoors and outdoors) and a puzzling redundancy of light sources. *Guernica* is in part a study in panic; the two women at the right, deprived of all reason, are inexplicably drawn to rather than repelled by the center of the disaster.

The great scale of the *Guernica* was new for Picasso, and he made many drawings for the composition and ended by reducing the number of textures and colors. The use of blacks, greys, and whites not only eliminated certain color problems, but it also created suitable and dramatic accompaniment to the nightmarish theme. The stippled texture in the horse and the overall black and white, furthermore, resemble the qualities of newsprint and journalistic photos of violence during the turbulent period in which the painting was done. Quite apart from the fact that he did not work from literal photographic images, Picasso's recourse to the Classical pyramidal composition is not out of character, for he had taken many motifs and devices from Classical art in previous years. He could not, however, accept the Classical insistence upon the pyramid's centrality, symmetry, and stability, and the climax of the pyramid is not an idealized human but a terrorized beast. Picasso was also clearly familiar with the great paintings of war and disaster by Baron Gros, Géricault, and Delacroix in the Louvre (Pl. 40, p.218; Fig. 405; Pl. 43, p. 285). The pyramid is interlocked with the flanking areas through continuities and discontinuities of colors and shapes. The part thus tends to predict the whole, since no single figure is shown in the same tone, nor can its shape be detached from that to which it is adjacent.

In the *Guernica* Picasso demonstrated how Cubism could be a successful carrier of pathos. Figural fragmentation relates to brutal mutilation as well as to formal expression. The durability of *Guernica* as protest art is seen in the excerpting of its lower left-hand corner, showing the arm and head of the dead warrior, for use as an anti-Vietnam War poster in the United States. Picasso's conversion to Communism derived entirely from sympathy for Communist support of the Republican forces during the Spanish Civil War.

It is interesting to compare Picasso's commentary on war with a painting by a Nazi artist, *Dive Bombers over England* (Fig. 549). At first, this looks like a painting of a bright cloud-filled sky over a city, but then the bombers can be seen diving out of the sun toward the brown ruins below. Concern with aerial tactics rather than with human suffering guided the Nazi painter, whose style, ironically, has some indebtedness to French Impressionism, perhaps the most pacifistic art in history. For those people who feel that a democratic, humane art must have complete legibility, Nazi paintings should give pause.

So many ideas emerged in the process of painting the *Guernica,* as evidenced by changes in the final work, that their momentum was carried over to additional studies that Picasso undertook even after the painting was exhibited. One such postscript is a painting of the head of an agonized horse (Fig. 550). Here Picasso continued to build upon the insights generated by the internal experiences of pain. In the painting he has simulated the texture of the animal's hairy and smooth flesh and of the roof of the mouth. This single form set against a black ground is like a summation of the total anguish of the larger *Guernica.*

Since *Guernica*, Picasso seems to have found contentment in cultivating his own garden. Few of his later works match his earlier profundity and sustained inventiveness. He has been more playful and recreative, less self-critical. He has chosen to rework his own earlier themes and the art of the old masters and modes, particularly as they relate to his love of his children, women, and animals.

His *Seated Woman* (Fig. 551) shows how, late in life, Picasso could still conceive vigorously and paint uningratiating subjects in a strong style. The angularity of design and hairy armpits are a disenchanting but amusingly frank acknowledgment that this is a studio model. Within his own art, he continually reacts against his concocted delightful mythological figures and beautiful women by now and then reintroducing an earthy type. Picasso has described his own work as, "whimsical, tender, biting, garrulous, I often look at the world as a satirist. . . ." But he added, "I often record life with profound compassion and exalt the greatness and anguish of the human situation. . . ." [1964].

This is an apt commentary on one of Picasso's finest sculptures. Always exhibiting an awareness of his great facility, Picasso's *Man with a Lamb* (Fig. 552) is in part a suppression of this gift in order to create a sculpture that moves us not by virtuosity and surface appeal but by the simplicity and depth of its theme. Like many of his works, it was preceded by drawings and long meditation. Execution in clay was done in a single day during World War II. The shepherd's gentle cradling of the lamb is as much a part of Picasso's feelings for animals as those drawings and paintings in which they are

*right:* 551. PABLO PICASSO. *Seated Woman.* 1959. Oil on canvas, 4′9½″ × 3′9″. Collection Mr. and Mrs. Victor W. Ganz, New York.

used to destroy or are themselves destroyed. During the war a plaster cast of this work greeted those who came to the artist's Paris studio. Today a bronze cast stands in the southern French village of Vallauris where Picasso has worked for many years. Both locations indicate the strong feeling of the artist about how art images the artist and can still take its place in public to unite the community. The theme of the man with the lamb goes back to Egypt and ancient Greece (Fig. 63), where, indicating animal sacrifice, it was a votive gift to a god. Picasso once again revives and transforms an old idea, giving it relevance to himself and to his age. It is Picasso's personal peace offering. This aspect of Picasso's involvement with history and his motivation to continue painting and making sculpture helps explain what he meant when he said, "My whole life as an artist has been nothing more than a struggle against reaction and the death of art" [1937].

**Picasso's Goat : Invention, Economy, and Surprise** Picasso is now recognized as one of the major sculptors in modern art, and since *Guernica* his substantial work in this medium has been perhaps the strongest expression of his premises: "We mustn't be afraid to invent anything. . . . You must always work with economy in mind. . . I'm out to fool the mind, not the eye." Invention, economy, and surprise are conditions of Picasso's mind and habits of work that have overlapped and reinforced each other for the last sixty-five years of his life as an artist. They are brilliantly summarized in his sculpture entitled *Goat* (Fig. 553), often installed by prudish curators so as to conceal its most interesting view. Finding a palm branch on a sidewalk triggered the realization of an old desire to make a sculpture of a goat. The branch became the animal's spine, and a section of it also served as its forehead. A wicker basket made the frame for the stomach, terracotta milk jars the udder, angular tree branches the legs, copper wire the tail and whiskers, and a piece of metal pipe and a folded tin can lid the anus and vagina. All were overlaid with plaster and then cast in bronze for durability. The goat's form resulted from sources as heterogeneous as its proverbial diet. Picasso made no attempt to imitate the hair of the goat, but because of his inventive textures, the mind accepts the surface of the sculpture as analogous to that of a goat. The humble sources that served Picasso's inspiration recall his statement, "Painters beget pictures as princes beget children, not with princesses, but with country girls."

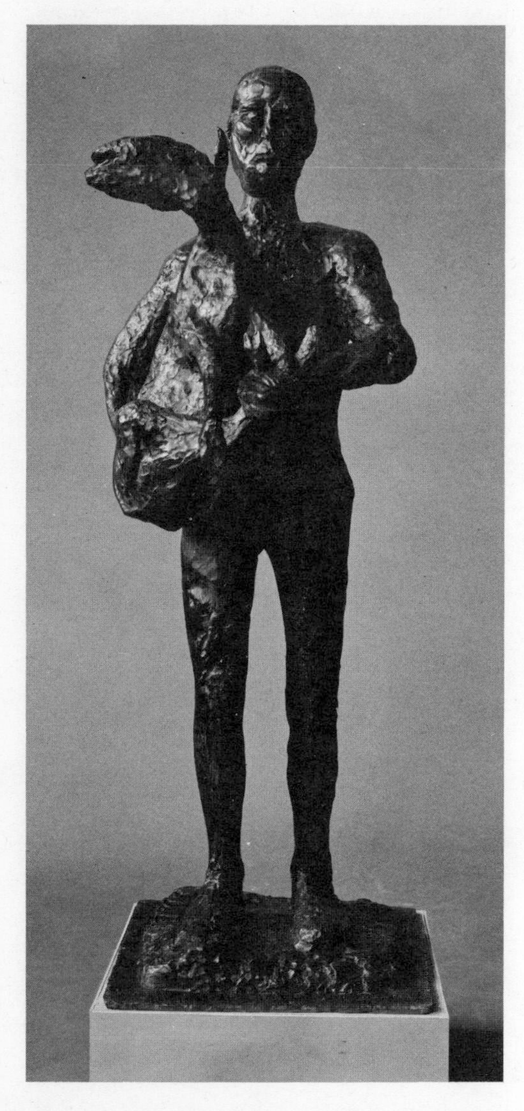

*left:* 552. Pablo Picasso. *Man with a Lamb*. 1944. Bronze, height 7′4″. Philadelphia Museum of Art (given by Mr. and Mrs. R. Sturgia Ingersoll).

*right:* 553. Pablo Picasso. *Goat*. 1950. Bronze, 3′11⁵/₈″ × 28³/₄″ × 4′7″. Collection the artist.

*right:* 554. PABLO PICASSO. *Head of a Woman (Chicago Picasso).* 1967. Steel, height 50′. Civic Center Plaza, Chicago.

**Monumental Sculpture** Picasso's dream of monumental sculpture has been realized in recent years with the aid of commissions, technology, and assistants, who oversee the enlargement of models he has made, such as the project for the Chicago Civic Center. Although physically dwarfed by the surrounding buildings, Picasso's *Head of a Woman* (Fig. 554), made of rusted Cor Ten steel, is so strong in form and so powerful as an image that it magnetizes one's gaze away from the buildings. Looking back at such works as the 1928 *Painter and His Model* (Fig. 539), one can see how the ideas for the Chicago head, such as the eyes piled atop the nose, were first conceived almost thirty-five years earlier. Brilliant in the inventiveness of its construction, it is nevertheless brutal in thematic conception, which Picasso may have considered appropriate to the city that now gives the work home. Since its completion the head has looked down on peaceful assemblies, puzzled tourists, and violent demonstrations. Not intended as a portrait, the sculpture is a fantasy on the idea of a head and not intended to be beautiful. "What is beauty anyway? There is no such thing. I never appreciate any more than I like. I love or I hate. . . ." These sentiments by Picasso accompanied an explanation of what art was all about for him. According to Picasso, art like African sculpture, is a kind of magical mediation between "this strange hostile world and us."

Since 1950 Picasso has exerted less influence on younger painters, for problems and possibilities different from those that intrigue him have been introduced into art. Many important developments occurred in the early art of this century for which Picasso was not responsible. Abstract art, for example, held peripheral interest for Picasso, whose thinking was mainly centered on the human form. The notoriety of his highly publicized private life and carefree ageless appearance, due perhaps to revitalization by incessant creation, make it difficult to arrive at a serious appraisal of his recent work. But few can disagree that before 1940 Picasso's protean energies, intelligence, attention to feeling, and sheer technical skill produced art of the highest quality in astonishing abundance. Not the least inspiration to Picasso, throughout all his years of living and of making art, has been his curiosity, concern, and delight with the faces of art and humanity.

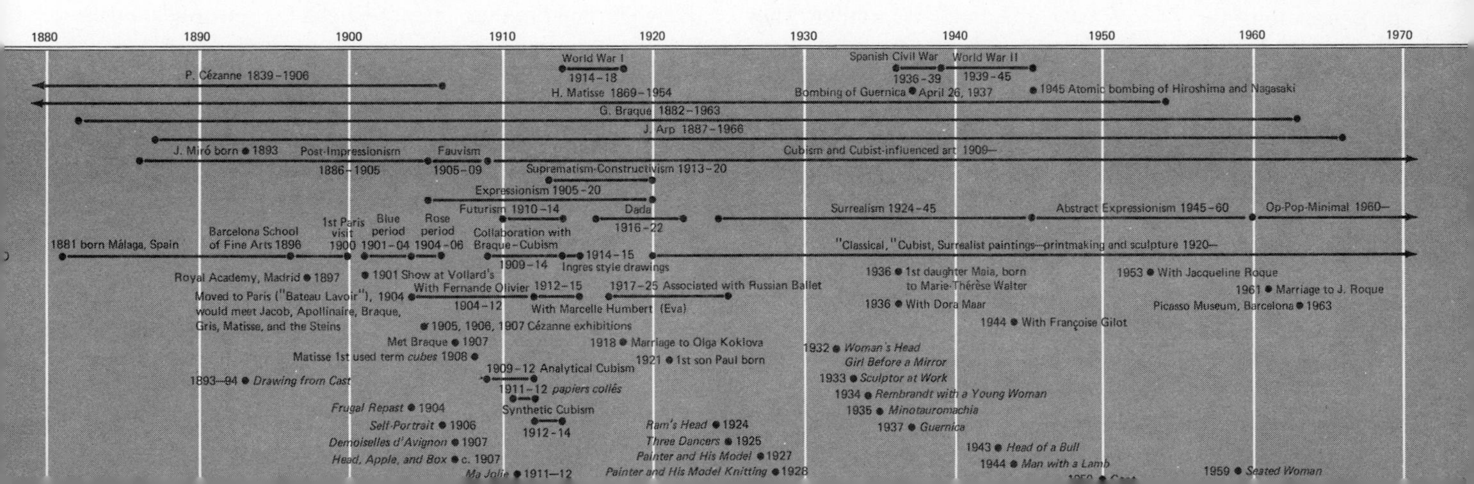

# 21

As presented so far, the history of art must seem to have been largely a continuous tribute to man's reason. We have seen how art performed loyal service to church, state, and society as a whole, and how it was frequently dedicated to practical purposes. Men and gods have been respectfully and reverently depicted. Our museums and art survey books usually focus selectively upon the good and beautiful. However, art, and therefore its history, also encompasses the ugly, the irreverent, and the disrespectful. The night world of dreams and demons has seen the light of day in painting, sculpture, prints, and drawings from antiquity to the present. Under the heading of *imaginative art* this chapter is concerned with art that derives from sources other than the imitation of the waking, visible world. These other sources include visions, revelations, dreams, reverie, fancy, hallucination, the realm of the bizarre, the grotesque, and the fantastic. Art produced from these origins tells us much about the social and moral histories and tastes of various cultures as well as the individual artists. The history of these subjects is still another way of clarifying for us the changes and departures from past traditions that have taken place in the art produced during the last one hundred years.

What may seem fantastic to us in older art, because it does not accord with our present frames of logical reference or with our concepts of what is rational, could originally have made sense and been intelligible to the artist and to the public of his time. Thus, ferocious African or Polynesian masks are not pure creations of their artists' imaginations; rather, they depend largely upon previous masks and upon the full cultural complex of tribal customs and beliefs reflecting a life view that we are only now beginning to understand even in small measure. For many years scholarship has been unraveling pictorial riddles in Western art, with the result that today we must be more cautious about using the word *fantastic*. We must discern and describe different manifestations of the imaginative in art. It is not always easy to separate what was genuinely the result of a dream experience from a symbol the artist may have appropriated from a predecessor. Freudian psychology has been a valuable but risky tool of research and has led to much unhistorical interpretation of artists of the past, and to conclusions drawn without sufficient reference to case histories or knowledge of the art and social context out of which the artists' work grew. Evidence that an artist of the past was not completely creative or entirely inventive in the formation of his symbols does not in itself detract from the potential importance of that artist, for he may have sought to preserve a sign language that was familiar to his audience while demonstrating considerable skill and imagination in reinterpreting his acquired symbol. By the same token, the fact that an artist has originated a symbol or created it purely out of his own fantasy has not been a guarantee of excellence in art. For the reader discomfited by the imaginative art he sees being created around him today, the first part of this chapter, concerning a protest written eight centuries ago against the meaninglessness of imaginative art, may be welcome.

## LITERARY AND ARTISTIC SOURCES

The great Western tradition of fantastic art has its roots in antiquity, but the subsequent Middle Ages experienced a more significant and influential expansion and development of painting and sculpture concerned with the demonic, the infernal, the unnatural, and the bizarre. From the 12th through the 15th centuries, in manuscripts and the sculptural decoration of architecture, this type of art remained literally and figuratively marginal to the central focus of the religious imagery of Christ, the saints, and the Bible. In Chapter 5, "The Sacred Book," it was pointed out that in initials and margins of medieval manuscripts, artists introduced monsters and hybrids of humans and of animals unrelated to the text itself (Fig. 555). On the great cathedrals and in the cloisters, sculptors imaginatively adorned column capitals, water spouts or gargoyles, the underside of choir seats, and many other places of importance secondary to the location of significant religious subjects, such as the framing areas of the great western portals. When the medieval artist was called upon to give a presence to the Devil or to Hell, or to moralize about vices, he

# IMAGINATIVE ART

had license to indulge his imagination as well as to reinterpret earlier art that dealt with the same subjects. Medieval imaginative art is largely related to the war of the Church on sin and the propagation of its views on the hereafter. As with the making of religious painting and sculpture of a beatific character, the conception of the monstrous and grotesque was tied to prototypes in art. The mouth of Hell, seen as a leviathan's open jaws in a 12th-century manuscript (Fig. 556), has precedents in medieval sculptural renderings of the Last Judgment (Figs. 69, 70). But to conclude that all of medieval fantastic art located in religious buildings was intelligible to and rationally justified by those who looked upon it is to ignore a most important witness against such argument. In the 12th century a great churchman, St. Bernard of Clairvaux, who devoted his life to ecclesiastical reform, wrote a letter to an abbot in which he complained about what he saw in the cloisters:

But in the cloister, under the eyes of the Brethren who read there, what profit is there in those ridiculous monsters, in that marvelous and deformed comeliness, that comely deformity? To what purpose are those unclean apes, those fierce lions, those monstrous centaurs, those half men, those striped tigers, those fighting knights, those hunters winding their horns? Many bodies are there seen under one head, or again, many heads to a single body. Here is a four-footed beast with a serpent's tail; there a fish with a beast's head. Here again the forepart of a horse trails half a goat behind it, or a horned beast bears the hinder quarters of a horse. In short, so many and so marvelous are the varieties of divers shapes on every hand, that we are more tempted to read

*left :* 555. "Drolleries," from *Les Heures et Recueil de Prières*. c. 1360. Manuscript illumination. Bibliothèque Nationale, Paris.

*right :* 556. *Mouth of Hell,* from *The Psalter of Winchester*. Before 1161. Manuscript illumination. British Museum, London.

*above :* 557. Capital, from the crypt of the Church of St-Eutrope, Saintes, France. 1081–96.

*right :* 558. HIERONYMUS BOSCH. *Hell,* side panel from *The Garden of Earthly Delights.* c. 1505–10. Oil on panel, height 6′5″. Prado, Madrid.

> in the marble than in our books, and to spend the whole day in wondering at these things rather than in meditating the law of God. For God's sake, if men are not ashamed of these follies, why at least do they not shrink from the expense.

Although we do not know exactly which sculptures St. Bernard had looked upon, a sufficient number of examples have survived to give us an idea of their appearance (Fig. 557). But, ironically, St. Bernard, who protests their existence, gives us a marvelously vivid and exact description of these sculptures, showing how long he had observed so many, and making convincing his closing lament about distraction. It is also evident that the artists and the patrons who commissioned them were not ashamed of "follies." The sources for the sculptures that St. Bernard described are to be found in both the sculpture and the painting of a much earlier time, some of which survived from antiquity in *bestiaries,* or books on animals.

**The Hell of Hieronymus Bosch** The belief that the terrible underworld of Hell was a near reality and that living man was surrounded by numberless demons persisted into the 15th and 16th centuries. Demonographers since the 12th and 13th centuries had catalogued the types and symbols of demons, and the 16th century saw ingenious census-taking of the Devil's agents as well as estimates of Hell's physical dimensions. The artist who first made demons and Hell the consistent central focus of high painting was the Netherlandish painter Hieronymus Bosch. His rendering of *Hell*, reproduced as Figure 558, from a three-panel painting entitled *The Garden of Earthly Delights*, has impressed many as being a premonition of modern fantastic art. No rational explanation or analogies to modern life are available to the viewer today to permit him to "read" the meaning of Bosch's *Hell*, hence the conclusion that this was a work of pure fantasy or dream experienced by the artist. Serious study by many art historians has shown, however, that Bosch drew heavily upon literary and pictorial sources in his inspired work, and that it is possible to compile an encyclopedia of meanings for his various symbols. During Bosch's lifetime, and long before, the Church taught men that all one saw in the world was symbolic of the invisible, whether godly or demonic. Bosch drew from the rich sources on this subject found in folklore, popular sayings, allegorical treatises, and Christian and Jewish religious literature, including medieval encyclopedias, as well as from astrology and writings on alchemy. Despite his preoccupation with sin and his belief that one could attain divine truth through sincere and deep prayer and contemplation, Bosch did not work in the service of the Church. He seems to have been a skeptic in his attitude toward both reason and the divine saving grace promised by the Church. Like many pessimists of his time, Bosch viewed the preponderance of immoral activity and folly about him as positive proof that the Devil had conquered the earth. His painting had a moralizing function—the exposure of man's susceptibility to vice and the Devil's temptations—and gave visible form to the nature of evil. Bosch's hero was St. Anthony, whose strength of soul alone permitted him to triumph over evil.

While Bosch had before him the achievements of advanced Flemish painting of the 15th century, such as perspective, he seems to have consciously chosen an archaic, or pre-Van Eyck style, as more appropriate to his purposes (see Chap. 6). Thus in his panel of *Hell,* the elevated viewpoint permits him to lay out in a vertical format a vast cross section of Hell, climaxed at the top by the vision of burning cities. Bruegel was later to take many pictorial and symbolic ideas from Bosch, such as the burning cities he appropriated for his *Triumph of Death* (Fig. 229). He did not, however, adopt Bosch's moralizing tone, his pessimism, or his view of folly as evil. While historians cannot unanimously agree on the exact meaning or implication of each symbol and allegorical image of the various episodes shown in *Hell,* they can re-create the intellectual atmosphere of Bosch's time, which inspired his choice of imagery. Prominent in Bosch's *Hell* is the compound heretical symbol made up of a human-headed, eggshell-bodied, and barren-tree-stump-legged figure. Within the shell, alchemists (who used eggshells in their recipes), wizards, or intellectuals are served by satanic innkeepers. The bagpipe on a platter above the head signified carnal love and obscenity, thus making a type of signboard for this infernal inn. The figures crucified on or tied to the harp and lute represent remorse, for these musical instruments were identified with praise of the Lord. Sexual references abound, presumably in the form of the knife, key, vases, and lanterns. The severed ears may derive from the Biblical reference to those who do not hear the word of the Lord. The rabbit devouring a man may have related to both sins of excess and the fear of death.

Charles De Tolnay, whose major study of Bosch has made this painter's work more intelligible to us, believes that the figure of a man leaning over the sides of the great broken eggshell is Bosch himself, and that the artist has shown himself daydreaming as if the scene before us originated or was contained within his mind. This would not be the first time that in art we have seen the dreamer and the dreamed, for Hugo van der Goes earlier depicted the vision of the descending Christ available only to the dead Virgin and not to the disciples (Fig. 154).

**Dream in Dürer's Art** In contrast to Bosch's daydream of the night world of Hell, the great German artist Albrecht Dürer in 1525 had a genuine sleeping dream so immanent that he gave it formal representation in a watercolor (Fig. 559). Probably it is the oldest example we have of an artist's attempt to transcribe such a personal experience. When Dürer painted the dream he also wrote below it a lengthy description:

559. ALBRECHT DÜRER. *Landscape Flooded with Waters from Heaven (Dream Vision)*. 1525. Pen and watercolor, $17\frac{7}{8} \times 9''$. Kunsthistorisches Museum, Vienna.

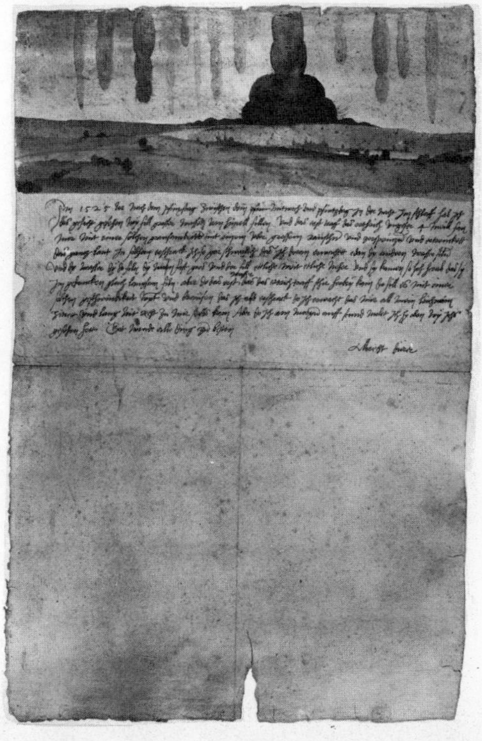

> In the night between Wednesday and Thursday after Whitsunday, I saw this appearance in my sleep—how many great waters fell from heaven. The first struck the earth about four miles away from me with terrific force and tremendous noise, and it broke up and drowned the whole land. I was so sore afraid that I awoke from it. Then the other waters fell, and as they fell they were very powerful and there were many of them, some further away, some nearer. And they came down from so great a height that they all seemed to fall with an equal slowness. But when the first water that touched the earth had very nearly reached it, it fell with such swiftness, with wind and roaring, and I was so sore afraid that when I awoke my whole body trembled and for a long while I could not recover myself. So when I arose in the morning I painted it above here as I saw it. God turned all things to the best.

What interests us about Dürer's dream is that, first, he painted it, but he also felt compelled to write about the vision, immediately translating his irrational experience into a rational and public language. Proceeding with the same intensity of empirical curiosity that he brought to his studies in the psychology of the artistic temperament (Fig. 13), in nature (Fig. 440), and in the phenomena of visual perception (Fig. 577), Dürer was careful to comment on such things as distances and velocities and to record his own thoughtful, waking observations of the "natural" scene. Early in the history of the revival of nature painting in Europe, Dürer visualized the earth as a landscape and introduced trees and houses to give scale to his nightmare.

560. MARTIN SCHONGAUER. *The Temptation of St. Anthony.* c. 1480–90. Engraving, $12^3/_8 \times 9^1/_8$″. National Gallery of Art, Washington, D.C. (Rosenwald Collection).

**The Temptation of St. Anthony** From the Middle Ages to the 17th century the Church encouraged the grotesque and the bizarre in its concern for the horrors that the Devil could work upon the Christian faithful. In art this often found demonstration in the "temptation" theme, not just of Christ but of the saints, such as St. Anthony in an engraving (Fig. 560) by the brilliant German printmaker Martin Schongauer (c. 1450–91). In medieval Christianity beauty was equated with God, ugliness with the Devil, and thus Schongauer dwelt at length on the pointed and prickly, endowing the demons with a large arsenal of dangerous weapons and repulsive bodies. Fortified by the great developments in naturalism in the 15th century, Schongauer was able to engrave an inventory of the unattractive properties of monsters, and his gift was to make this unnatural event, an aerial kidnaping, plausible to his audience, such that if his monsters could actually be seen to walk or fly, they would have the necessary anatomy or equipment to do so. Contrasting with the pugnaciousness and stupidity of his tormentors is St. Anthony, the quietude of his face expressive of stoic resignation and inner strength.

Perhaps the most inspired and persuasive of the temptations of St. Anthony was that of Matthias Grünewald (Fig. 561). His painting is one of the panels of the *Isenheim Altarpiece* (Pl. 7, p. 77), whose *Crucifixion* panel was discussed in Chapter 3, "Images of Gods." Grünewald showed St. Anthony crying out against the attacks of the demons. On a piece of paper in the lower right-hand corner, Grünewald wrote: "Where are you, good Jesus, where were you? And why did you not come and dress my wounds?" This plaint could well be that of the beleaguered saint, but also that of the rotting human corpse in the lower left-hand corner. Dermatologists have identified its sores as syphilitic, a diagnosis that relates the content of this picture to the skin afflictions of the patients who were brought to the altar painting to begin their therapy. Grünewald went beyond Bosch and Schongauer in depicting the surfaces of his monsters as symptoms of their various forms of corruption. Not content with showing the lurid, scaly, feathered, or fleshy covering of the foreground demons, he carried over into the ruined house of the hermit saint the jagged silhouettes and elusive forms of the Devil's legion. Unperceived by the hermit, but apparent to the patient apprehending the painting for the first time, the Lord can be seen looking down on the trials of the saint. Emerging from the radiance about the Lord's throne are luminous armed angels who will disperse the devils of darkness. With the resources of painting, Grünewald was inspired to re-create the transparencies of heavenly light and gangrenous flesh, the opaqueness of dark, demonic bodies, the shine of reptilian scales, and mucous dripping. Many things in Grünewald's painting and Schongauer's engraving are partially traceable both to previous art and to the written text of the "Life of St. Anthony" in Jacobus de Voragine's *Golden Legend,* which dates from the 13th century:

. . . he went into a hole or cave to hide himself, and anon he found there a great multitude of devils, that so much beat him that his servant bore him upon his shoulders into his house as if he had been dead. When the other hermits were assembled and wept his death, and would have done his service, suddenly St. Anthony revived and made his servants to bear him into the pit again where the devils had so evil beaten him, and began to summon the devils again. . . to battles. And they came in forms of diverse beasts wild and savage, of whom that one howled, another sniffled, and another cried, and another brayed and assailed St. Anthony, that one with the horns, the others with their teeth, and the others with their paws and claws, and . . . to rent his body that he supposed well to die. Then came a clear brightness and all the beasts fled away.

The great 17th-century French artist Jacques Callot (1592–1635), shortly before the death he knew was coming, made a drawing for a *Temptation of St. Anthony* which was engraved by Israel in 1635 (Fig. 562). Here the temptation theme was completely recast in terms of its focus, setting, and characters. Probably inspired by Italian popular theater and the theatrical productions put on in the courts of the Florentine nobility, Callot staged the temptation on an epic scale. Literally stagelike is the device of the framing of the scene by rocky cliffs on either side, the ruins of a tall arcaded stone building at the right, and the cast of thousands that sweeps onto the broad plain of the stage. Overhead the enormous figure of the Devil, chained to the rocks, spews demons and fire into what is now a scene in Hell. Callot joined together infernal scenes with those of the temptation, but the effect is more comic than frightening. The devils make war on themselves more than on the saint who is seen at the right, ringed by other devils, a naked woman, and a fire-belching monster. Perhaps caricaturing the extravagant weapons of war sponsored by the nobility, Callot transformed monsters into canons, or the reverse. An irreverent religious service is conducted just above St. Anthony, and throughout the print obscene "services" are rendered by the demons to one another. By the 17th century there often was a recession of the heroic or saintly focus (see Chap. 10), and Callot seems to have taken the trials of St. Anthony as the occasion for delivering a commentary, obscure as it may be to us today, on worldly institutions and human practices.

*left :* 561. MATTHIAS GRÜNEWALD. *The Temptation of St. Anthony,* from *The Isenheim Altarpiece* (Pl. 7, p. 77). 1512–15. Oil on panel, 8′8³/₈″ × 4′6³/₄″. Musée d'Unterlinden, Colmar.

*below :* 562. JACQUES CALLOT. *The Temptation of St. Anthony.* 1635. Etching (by Israel), 14 × 18¹/₄″. Indiana University, Art Museum, Bloomington.

**Arcimboldo and Double Imagery** The art of the Middle Ages and that of the 16th century provide abundant evidence that religious and secular fantasies could coexist in art. In 1563, the same year that the Council of Trent was preparing a statement on art as part of its war on the Reformation and secularism, an Italian artist, Giuseppe Arcimboldo (c. 1530–93), painted a series of heads composed entirely of nonhuman subjects. In the painting illustrated (Pl. 79, p. 413) we can see with what ingenuity Arcimboldo found a form of marine life that in a certain position and context, and from a distance, evoked some aspect of the human head and shoulders. Without repeating himself, the painter was able to assemble an astonishing repertory of crustacean and invertebrate forms, so that the head dissects into a shark, a ray, a starfish, eels, a walrus, and so on. It is a far-from-pleasant assemblage, and at first it suggests a nightmarish experience or aggressive gesture toward human dignity. But Arcimboldo was a famous court painter who did this and other pictures for the Emperor Maximilian II in Vienna. There he served not only as a painter but also as a decorator for pageants and set designer for the theater. The first Italian painter to make the grotesque more than a marginal or decorative element, without the sin-consciousness of Bosch, Arcimboldo focused his entire image upon the bizarre. There is a rational explanation for what he did, which does not detract from the artist's skill and cleverness in the way he painted this work. The title *Water* relates to his series on the elements, and identifies the source from which Arcimboldo drew all of his motifs. The precedent for relating nonhuman life to the human body existed in literature, notably philosophical and scientific speculation on the relation of man to nature, and nature to man. The comparison of the earth to a great organism had been made in the previous century and was known to Bruegel, which was pointed out in Chapter 16, "Art and Nature." Man was looked upon by many European intellectuals in the 16th century as the world in miniature, "Man—the little world." Cartographers equated land forms with figure types. Previously, artists had used human forms to symbolize nature and its seasons. Arcimboldo was using natural forms to symbolize man and, at the same time, was catering to his society's taste for metamorphosis. The 16th century produced a curious blending of science and myth; there was inquiry into facts but also tolerance of fantasy. It was a time of "half-science." Particularly in the courts, among intellectuals, the medieval taste for allegories, or symbols of all aspects of knowledge, persisted. The accuracy of Arcimboldo's rendering of water denizens, coupled with their substitution for facial features, thus epitomized the duality of thought in his own age.

**The Importance of the Self in Modern Imaginative Art** After Callot, the next major artist to devote a considerable number of drawings, prints, and paintings to the imaginative was the great Spanish court painter Francisco Goya. In 1799 Goya published a series of prints entitled *Los Caprichos* (Figs. 563, 564), which, though not in separate sequences, divided roughly into areas of subject matter: examples of human folly, or stupidity, and dishonesty; donkeys enacting the roles of humans; witchcraft and markedly fantastic beings. Unusual

*right:* 563. FRANCISCO GOYA. *The Sleep of Reason Produces Monsters,* from *Los Caprichos.* 1796–98. Etching, 8½ × 6″. Metropolitan Museum of Art, New York (gift of M. Knoedler & Co., 1918).

*far right:* 564. FRANCISCO GOYA. *They Make Their Toilet,* from *Los Caprichos.* 1797. Etching, 8½ × 6″. Metropolitan Museum of Art, New York (Rogers Fund, 1918).

*above:* Plate 79. GIUSEPPE ARCIMBOLDO. *Water*. 1563. Oil on canvas, $26^3/_8 \times 20^3/_8''$. Kunsthistorisches Museum, Vienna. (See p. 412.)

*right:* Plate 80. MARC CHAGALL. *I and the Village*. 1911. Oil on canvas, $6'3^1/_2'' \times 4'11^1/_2''$. Museum of Modern Art, New York (Mrs. Simon Guggenheim Fund). (See p. 420.)

*left:* Plate 81. JOAN MIRÓ. *The Farm.* 1921–22. Oil on canvas, $4'{}^{1}/_{2}'' \times 4'7{}^{1}/_{4}''$. Collection Mrs. Ernest Hemingway, New York. (See p. 426.)

*below:* Plate 82. JOAN MIRÓ. *The Hunter (Catalan Landscape).* 1923–24. Oil on canvas, $25{}^{1}/_{2} \times 39{}^{1}/_{2}''$. Museum of Modern Art, New York (purchase). (See pp. 426, 427.)

Plate 83. ARSHILLE GORKY. *The Liver Is the Cock's Comb*. 1944. Oil on canvas, 6′ × 8′2″. Albright-Knox Art Gallery, Buffalo, N. Y. (gift of Seymour H. Knox). (See p. 427.)

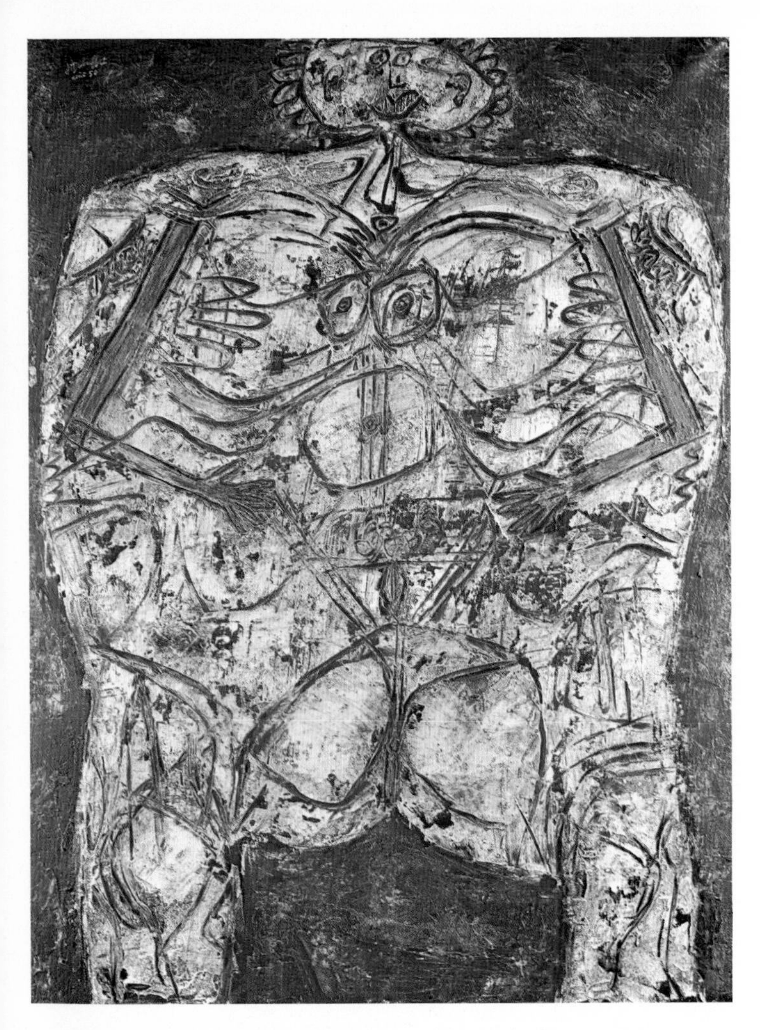

*above:* Plate 84. JEAN DUBUFFET. *Corps de Dame, Sanguine et Grenat*. 1950. Oil on canvas, $45^{5}/_{8} \times 35''$. Collection Alfonso A. Ossorio, East Hampton, N.Y. (See p. 427.)

*right:* Plate 85. WILLEM DE KOONING. *Woman and Bicycle*. 1952–53. Oil on canvas, $6'4^{1}/_{2}'' \times 4'1''$. Whitney Museum of American Art, New York. (See p. 428.)

in *Los Caprichos*—which means caprices, fantastic notions, fancy, or whim—is that the titles of the etchings and their inscriptions were added after the works were finished; they do not predate the artist's conceptions. In the work of Bosch, Dürer, Grünewald, and Callot, the title or subject existed before the work of art, which was its illustration. Goya's conceptions often first appeared in his own art, and then seem to have suggested associations with, for example, popular sayings. The artist was very much aware of folklore and demonology, and scholars of Spanish art and culture like Professor José López-Rey believe that there are many veiled references to individuals, customs, and institutions in *Los Caprichos,* which time has obscured for the modern audience. Fortunately, Goya published in a newspaper article on February 6, 1799, an announcement of his series of etchings that was accompanied by a statement of purpose:

> A Collection of Prints of Capricious Subjects, Invented and Etched by Don Francisco Goya. Since the artist is convinced that the censure of human errors and vices (though they may seem to be the province of Eloquence and Poetry) may also be the object of Painting, he has chosen as subjects adequate for his work, from the multitude of follies and blunders common in every civil society, as well as from the vulgar prejudices and lies authorized by custom, ignorance, or interest, those that he has thought most suitable for ridicule as well as for exercising the artificer's fancy.
>
> Since the majority of the objects represented in this work are ideal, it may not be too daring to expect that their defects will perhaps meet with forgiveness on the part of the connoisseurs as they will realize that the artist has neither followed the examples of others, nor been able to copy from nature. And if imitating Nature is as difficult as it is admirable when one succeeds in doing so, some esteem must be shown toward him who, holding aloof from her, has had to put before the eyes forms and attitudes that so far have existed only in the human mind, obscured and confused by lack of illustration, or excited by the unruliness of passion.
>
> One would be assuming too much ignorance of the fine arts, if one were to warn the public that in none of the compositions which form this series has the artist had in mind any one individual, in order to ridicule particular defects. For truly, to say so would mean narrowing overmuch the boundaries of talent, and mistaking the methods used by the arts of imitation in producing perfect works.
>
> Painting (like Poetry) chooses from the universal what it considers suitable to its own ends: it reunites in a single fantastic personage circumstances and characteristics that nature has divided among many. From such a combination, ingeniously arranged, results the kind of successful imitation for which a good artificer deserves the title of inventor and not that of a servile copyist. [*Diario de Madrid,* translation © by Professor José Lopez-Rey.]

For many reasons, this statement is interesting, and in the context of the imaginative art it is important because the artist disclaims recourse to the art of others and claims for himself the gift of invention. Living in the Age of Enlightenment, he professes to expose the night world of human conduct and imagination to the clear light of reason. One of the most famous of the plates in the series is that in which the artist has shown himself sleeping at his writing table (Fig. 563). Behind and from out of the darkness, presumably of his subconscious, comes a flight of owls and bats. Written on the desk is, "The sleep of reason produces monsters." In the ink drawing for this etching Goya wrote: "Universal Language. Drawn and Etched by Francisco de Goya. Year 1797." The word "Dream" was also written on the upper part, and below the drawing was added: "The artist dreaming. His only purpose is to banish harmful, vulgar beliefs, and to perpetuate in this work of caprices the solid testimony of truth." Beneath the etching Goya noted: "Imagination deserted by reason, begets impossible monsters. United with reason, she is the mother of all arts, and the source of their wonders." Despite these writings by the artist, the intention of *Los Caprichos* is still open to conjecture. The great number, strength, and inventiveness of these many etchings show not only the artist's fascination but also his obsession with the power of dreams, hallucinations, and visions of superstition, with human subservience to passions, response to impulses, and indulgence in folly (Fig. 405). Goya was tormented by deafness and concern over his own mental equilibrium, and we can only speculate on how much of *Los Caprichos* is personal fantasy. His own mind may have been at times disordered by sickness and anxiety.

The choice of etching, a medium of blacks, greys, and whites, was appropriate for this invisible world. When Goya showed humans, they often acted like monsters. In his etching *They Make Their Toilet* (Fig. 564), monsters act with the vanity of humans. The grim and the ludicrous intermingle in this conception of foul creatures preoccupied with what may strike us as hygiene; the inscription reads, "Long nails are so harmful that they are forbidden even among the witches." Goya's *hybrids,* beings that are part human, part animal, and part bird, lack the decipherability into intelligible symbols of those in the work of such an artist as Bosch. The vague separation between human and animal in the faces of the witches reflects the artist's interest in the old studies of correspondences between certain types of human and animal physiognomy, and the belief that physical ugliness was proof of the soul's corruption. Goya's etchings were based on his own drawings, but often the print is stronger in taking a motif, such as the witch's nail that is about to be cut, and using it as a menacing shape elsewhere, as in the scissors and wings. The many textural gradients he extracted from the etching process made possible the evocation of convincing textures for wings and flesh, as

*far left:* 565. Odilon Redon. *The Light of Day,* from *The Dream Series.* 1891. Lithograph, $8^1/_4 \times 6^1/_8$". Bibliothèque Nationale, Paris.

*left:* 566. Odilon Redon. *Swamp Flower, a Sad and Human Face,* from *Hommage à Goya.* 1885. Lithograph, $10^3/_8 \times 8$". Bibliothèque Nationale, Paris.

well as the dark mysterious depths and spaces in which these monsters thrived. Whether or not he was in the grip of a vision when he did these drawings and prints, we don't know. Their careful working and reworking in large and small areas shows the artist's persistent consciousness of the necessity of converting the conception into a work of art.

**Redon and the Logic of the Invisible** After his death Goya was greatly admired in France during the 19th century, but only in the work of one artist were there comparably imaginative prints. Odilon Redon (1840–1916), though less well known today than such of his contemporaries as Monet, Seurat, and Gauguin, was the great 19th-century French artist of fantasy. His reputation is based on the many charcoal drawings, lithographs, and pastels that he did, works that have no resemblance to the art of the 19th century discussed in Chapter 15. From the late 1860s through the first part of the 20th century, Redon refused to direct his vision toward the external world and the production of pleasing subjects after the manner of the Impressionists. He wrote in 1868 that the concerns of Manet and the Impressionists constituted a restricted and paltry research and that while true artists

> . . . recognize the necessity for a basis of *seen* reality, to them true art lies in a reality that is *felt*. . . . We must remember that we have other things than the eyes to satisfy, that we carry in ourselves . . . troubles, joys, or pains to which the great artist knows how to address himself.

One can understand Redon's imaginative alternatives to Impressionism by comparing his lithograph which shows a window (Fig. 565) with any of the 19th-century window views in Chapters 15 and 22. For Monet, Pissarro, Caillebotte, or Bonnard, the window looked out upon the real world of the city. In Gustave Caillebotte's painting, which shows a street view framed by a window in a room (Fig. 579), what lies on this side of the window is of the same order of reality as what is seen without. Redon shows us a segment of brightly illuminated tree through his window. But as we focus on our side of the window, we see that this is no ordinary room, and that vague, softly luminous shapes hover in the darkness. It is as if Redon were metaphorically showing us the mysterious dark world that exists behind the human eye. What we see through the window we can describe, but what lies in front of it has been only *suggested,* not defined, and this is the goal of his poetic thought. Of his drawings he wrote that they "inspire yet cannot be defined. They do not determine anything. Like music, they transport us into the ambiguous world of the undetermined."

Redon deliberately cultivated his subconscious as a source for his imagery; he also relied upon the stimulation he received from working in charcoal and lithography. In a letter of 1898, describing how he worked, Redon confessed:

> A sheet of white paper horrifies me. It impresses me disagreeably to the point of making me sterile, of depriving me of the taste for work. . . . I am forced as soon as it is on an easel, to scrawl on it with charcoal, with crayon or any other

> material, and this operation brings it to life. I believe that suggestive art owes much to the stimulus which the material itself exerts on the artist. . . .

Redon went on to describe how he abandoned himself to fantasy:

> Fantasy is also the messenger of the "unconscious" . . . nothing in art is achieved by will alone. Everything is done by docilely submitting to the arrival of the "unconcious." The analytical spirit must be quick when it appears, but afterwards it is of little importance to remember it. . . .

The fantastic world created by Redon was not intended, as Goya's probably was, to make comment on the people and behavior of his time. It is a private world of immeasurable spaces, and, often, of infinitesimal beings. Of great influence on Redon was the work of a gifted French biologist named Armand Clavaud, who introduced the artist to the world of the microscope, of natural history, and, especially, of botany. Redon was obsessed throughout his life with finding a logical structure for his imaginary beings that would parallel the newly discovered laws of biological life. His *Swamp Flower, a Sad and Human Face* (Fig. 566) was part of a series of lithographs that he dedicated to Goya. Rising from an endless expanse of water, beneath an infinite black sky, is Redon's imaginary growth, which blossoms into a radiant but lugubrious head, whose likes cannot be found in the work of any other artist.

Of great importance for artists who followed him in spirit, among them André Masson (Fig. 574), were such statements by Redon as, "My originality consists in bringing to life, in a human way, improbable beings and making them live according to the laws of probability, but putting—as far as possible—the logic of the visible at the service of the invisible." Writing at a time in 1880 when Monet and his contemporaries were intent on capturing the painterly equivalences of natural light and on abandoning the human-figure landscape, Redon wrote prophetically of himself, as well as many others to follow: "Man is a thinking being. Man will always be there; whatever the role played by light, it won't be able to turn him aside. To the contrary, the future belongs to the subjective world."

**De Chirico and Enigma** Down to the 20th century, much of fantastic art was obviously involved with the creation of the monstrous, in the form of unnatural hybrids, and of strange inaccessible places existing only in the imagination. While this continued in the work of certain modern artists, the sources and character of fantastic art have changed considerably in our time. More and more after 1900, artists followed the precedent of Redon, whether consciously or not, and departed from literature, previous art, and moralizing as a source for their imagery. Chapter 17, "Art, Objects, and the Object of Art," provided an introduction to Giorgio de Chirico's imaginative handling of objects (Pl. 65, p. 348). In his *Mystery and Melancholy of a Street* (Fig. 567), we again meet this new type of imaginative art in terms of a person and a place. Everything in the painting is recognizable or familiar—the arcades, the open, old-fashioned railroad van, the child rolling a hoop, the projecting shadows. What gives to De Chirico's painting the quality of the uncanny is his intentional divorce of such things as light, shadow, space, and silence from their previous rational associations in pictorial construction. They are transformed into enigmas, or unexpected inversions of what they ought to be. As if through a window or from a balcony, we look down on a scene that is unfolding before us. Things are not as they first seem. Perspective lines of the buildings do not recede to a common vanishing point; the angles of the shadows are inconsistent with a single light source; the sky is green. In the painting's context we tend to read the child against the van, which while open is so stationed as to conceal part of its interior. De Chirico is a painter who poses but does not answer

*right* : 567. GIORGIO DE CHIRICO. *The Mystery and Melancholy of a Street*. 1914. Oil on canvas, $34^3/_8 \times 28^1/_2$″. Collection Mr. and Mrs. Stanley R. Resor, New Canaan, Conn.

questions. He gives us no program notes or literary sources to transcribe his image. His poetic gift is to be haunted by irrational situations, and when he paints these images he does not eradicate but preserves their irrationality. The spaces of Dürer, Grünewald, Callot, and Goya are still formed according to perspective devices employed by them in the depiction of rational subjects. De Chirico's illusionistic world is constructed on the basis of an intuitive or irrational use of devices originally evolved for the rationalization of sight. In his memory De Chirico distilled certain physical, cultural characteristics of his native Italy, and while living in Paris between 1911 and 1914, he painted not a world remembered literally, but one that became a backdrop for mysterious relationships and unexpected encounters. Silence for De Chirico, which he sought to evoke in painting, had different characteristics, depending upon whether, for example, it existed before or after a catastrophe. Except for Redon, in the previous art of fantasy noise was assumed or suggested. A personal art became for De Chirico a refuge or alternative to the waking world of reality, an art of great personal consolation despite its disturbing qualities. In the same year he did the painting illustrated De Chirico wrote:

> To become truly immortal a work of art must escape all human limits: logic and common sense will only interfere. But once these barriers are broken, it will enter the regions of childhood vision and dream. Profound statements must be drawn by the artist from the most secret recesses of his being. . . . What I hear is valueless; only what I see is living, and when I close my eyes my vision is even more powerful. It is more important that we should rid art of all that it has contained of recognizable material to date; all familiar subjects, all traditional ideas, all popular symbols must be banished forthwith. . . . We must hold enormous faith in ourselves; it is essential that the revelation we receive . . . which has no sense in itself, which has not subject, which means *absolutely nothing* from the logical point of view. . . .

How personal was this world and how reflective of his temperament can be seen when the foregoing painting is compared with one done by a Russian-born artist working in Paris at the same time.

**Chagall and the Reality of the Interior World** The imaginative, private world of Marc Chagall (b. 1889), which he painted in *I and the Village* (Pl. 80, p. 413) while living in Paris in 1911, differs from that of De Chirico by its abundant qualities of joyfulness, warm sensuality, fragrance, and delightful vertigo. In his private souvenir of a childhood in Vitebsk, Chagall painted a green-faced boy holding a sprig of blossoms and confronted by the transparent head of a donkey. Surface and depth, right side up and upside down freely interchange, as Chagall's picture of loving, pleasurable memories resists translation into the normal language and syntax of rational painting. Both Chagall and De Chirico bring to modern painting the practice of free association whereby the selection and conjunction of objects or motifs are irrationally suggested to the artist during his conception or execution of the work. Chagall felt, however, that these associations had also to work in terms of the structural needs of his painting. The circle and X forms in the lower center of the painting may have had some private symbolism for the artist, but they also serve to unite disparate formal motifs on a common surface. De Chirico restored to painting the dramatic power of deep, clear space, whereas Chagall created an immeasurable, untraversable environment in which one cannot write of solids and voids, or the consistent diminution of size related to a fixed viewpoint. Scale, color, and solidity, or transparency, of figures and houses are not the function of a detached or objective observer from whose physical vantage point the scene is constructed. Rather, these properties reflect the weight and impulse of feeling and fantasy in the painter. Older artists interpreted another person's vision in pictorial terms that, like the literature in which dream experiences were recorded, served to codify the means of dealing with the irrational. Chagall, De Chirico, and the artists that follow their example fight codification or intelligibility on a public level. Years after *I and the Village* Chagall wrote:

> There is nothing anecdotal in my picture—no fairy tales—no literature in the sense of folk legend associations. . . . For me a picture is a plane surface covered with representations of objects—beasts, birds, or humans—in a certain order in which anecdotal illustrational logic has no importance. The visual effectiveness of the painted composition comes first. . . . I am against the terms "fantasy" and "symbolism" in themselves. All our interior world is reality . . . perhaps more so than our apparent world. To call everything that appears illogical, "fantasy," fairy tale, or chimera would he practically to admit not understanding nature. . . . The fact that I made use of cows, milkmaids, roosters and provincial Russian architecture as my source forms is because they are part of the environment from which I spring and which undoubtedly left the deepest impression on my visual memory of any experiences I have known. Every painter is born somewhere . . . a certain essence—a certain "aroma" of his birthplace clings to his work. But do not misunderstand me: the important thing here is not "subject" in the sense pictorial "subjects" were painted by the old academicians. The vital mark these early influences leave is, as it were, on the handwriting of the artist.

Both De Chirico and Chagall would have been very different and less effective painters if they had not come to Paris while still very young. At the turn of this century the exciting art environment of Paris acted as a liberating force on the imagination as well as on the styles of many young painters (see pp. 340–43, 389–91). Cubism, for example, was the artist's declaration of independence from the world of appearances. Both De Chirico and Chagall were influenced by it, despite

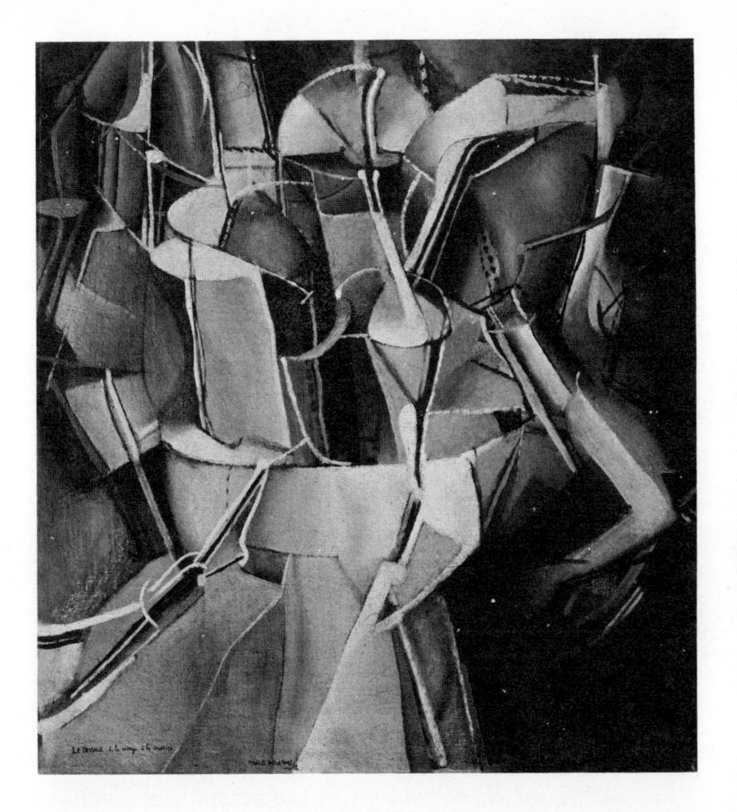

*left:* 568. MARCEL DUCHAMP. *The Bride (Le Passage de la Vierge à la Mariée)*. 1912. Oil on canvas, $23^3/_8 \times 21^1/_4$″. Museum of Modern Art, New York (purchase).

the fact that they could not content themselves with imitating the forms of Picasso and Braque, nor be wholly satisfied with its dark colors and conventional subjects of still life and the figure. When the Cubists broke up the closed character of objects and destroyed rational, measurable space, this was a crucial breakthrough of old boundaries for painters who by inclination believed that the world one sees with the eyes closed should preserve its imaginative qualities in painting.

It is in the 20th century, beginning with such artists as Chagall, that *originality* becomes a conscious aim for the artist. Following the Middle Ages artists sought individuality, but Chagall wanted an art which did not look like anything that had come before or that could be seen at the time. Goya claimed for himself the title of inventor, but his drawings and prints are at times closer in spirit or form to those of Rembrandt (see Chap. 11) and Callot than are Chagall's paintings to the work of any other artist. This imperative of originality derives largely from the 19th-century ethic of faithfulness to one's own experience in a style personally acquired.

**Inside THE BRIDE** In the same years before World War I during which there were so many formal and psychological breakthroughs in modern art, one of the most important innovations was that of the artist imaginatively interpreting the internal nature of the human body by denying its surface appearance. More famous for his *Nude Descending a Staircase* of the same year, French-born Marcel Duchamp painted in 1912 *The Bride* (Fig. 568). The former painting was described somewhat pejoratively by President Theodore Roosevelt as resembling "an explosion in a shingle factory." *The Bride* in turn avoids all that is sentimentally associated with the title—something old, something new, something borrowed, and something blue—in favor of showing woman as consisting of a complicated pumping and filter plant. The painting is at once an imaginative dissection of both the body and public taste. With the detached attitude of an anatomist, Duchamp ironically reconstructs the inner organs in terms of mechanical and quasiorganic forms, a network of pipes and filters, painted in a brownish color, with a slick, even slippery, type of surface that, more than the individual objects, conveys a visceral quality to the whole. In Chapter 17 (pp. 343, 344) Duchamp's *Bride Stripped Bare by Her Bachelors, Even* of 1923 (Pl. 66, p. 348) was discussed, and in the earlier work, *The Bride* (Fig. 568), we can see the beginnings of this artist's fantasies upon sex and science. Unlike the moralizing of Hieronymus Bosch, whose cynical views of man led him to receive and invent human-animal-mechanical hybrids, Duchamp's conception is divorced from this larger frame of reference and derives from personal reflections on the nature and purposes of art. He later wrote, "A painting that doesn't shock isn't worth painting."

**Max Ernst and "No-sense" Art** During and after World War I, artists of many nationalities continued to explore the possibilities of art based upon free association, intuition, or the logic of the illogical. Between about 1915 and 1922 there was a loose international confederation of artists who called themselves *Dadaists,* the French word *Dada,* meaning "hobby-horse," supposedly having been picked by chance from a Larousse dictionary. It was a movement dedicated to art that made no sense, one that championed irreverence and irrationality and disclaimed all system or aesthetic pretentions (which in itself required a system). It was the first movement in art history openly to seek originality and a complete break with the past. Painterly technique and questions of style were damned by most of the group, who sought a directness in their imaginative images, thereby opposing what they felt was the cult of painterly virtuosity or individuality. Their appeal to the public was intended to be on the instinctive rather than conscious or verbal level. Dada believed that the unexpected was as much a part of life as was the predictable, and infinitely more stimulating to creativity and audience response. One of the most imaginative and productive of the Dadaists was the German-born Max Ernst (b. 1891). In his desire to move away

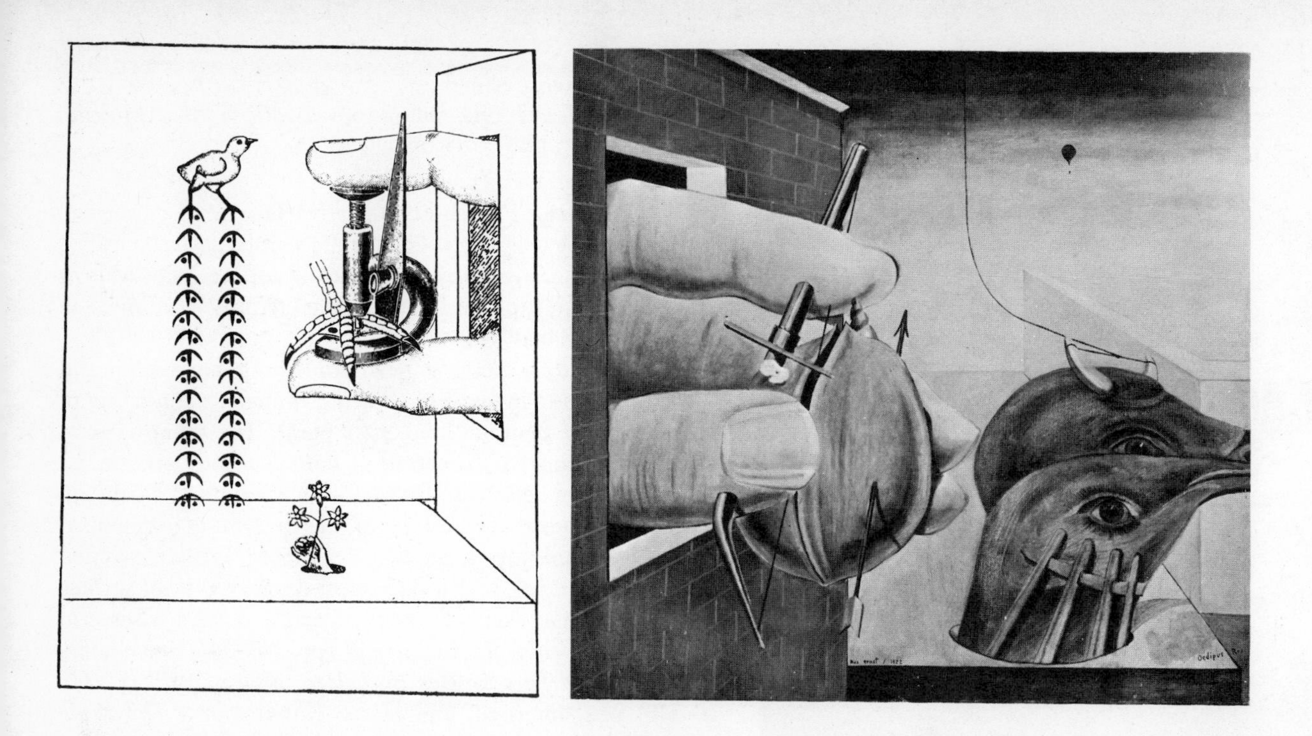

*above left :* 569. MAX ERNST. *The Invention,* from Paul Eluard. *Répétitions.* 1922. Collage.

*above right :* 570. MAX ERNST. *Oedipus Rex.* 1922. Oil on canvas, 35 × 45¾″. Collection Claude Hersaint, Paris.

from Western technical traditions, he developed the collage beyond what the Cubists had done and elevated it from a means to a principle of organization, composition being the one rule from the past observed by the Dadaists. In his collage *The Invention* (Fig. 569), Ernst cut out 19th-century wood engravings of objects and pasted them into a new context. The title may refer to the process of assembling the picture, for Ernst captioned his works after they were done according to the ideas suggested to him by the finished pieces. He transferred to painting the principle of irrational juxtaposition of familiar objects in unexpected situations or locations. Ernst liked to repeat a phrase by the 19th-century poet Isadore Ducasse (known as the Comte de Lautréamont): "Beautiful, like the chance meeting on a dissecting table of an umbrella and sewing machine." Ernst's painting *Oedipus Rex* (Fig. 570) seems to have been based upon *The Invention,* but now the artist added a new and unpleasant simulation—while extended through the window the fingers are penetrated by the object they hold. More than the collage, the painting was done with methods that were almost academic or reactionary in their rendering of objects and space. This reflects Ernst's reaction against the earlier revolutionary styles of Cubism and was his appeal to the good taste of such artists as Matisse. By these reactionary means Ernst was able to achieve the total illusion of his subject without imposing on the spectator's consciousness evidence of his hand and brush. In this alone is Ernst like Bosch, for the Dadaists did not set good against evil. The absurd was a fact of life for them, and art was to accept this condition and act accordingly.

**Dali's Hallucinations** Since the 1920s imaginative art has polarized around two essentially different modes of expression. One of these modes has, since the appearance of Ernst's *Oedipus Rex,* been expressed by artists creating illusionistic irrational images in paintings whose deep, three-dimensional space approximates, in many respects, that of older illusionistic art. The objects filling these spaces are often, either by themselves or in their components, based upon what is available to us in the external world. For the Surrealists and their satellites, from 1923, the aim of painting was to cull scientifically from the subconscious. The "inner world" was thought to be of a higher reality than the external world. They adopted the Dadaists' device of working from free association and with the unpredictable juxtaposition of the familiar.

The artist whose work epitomizes the illusionistic, imagistic, "hand-painted" dream picture of Surrealism is Salvador Dali (b. 1904). He created his most inspired and sincere works during the late twenties and early thirties. One of these, *The Persistence of Memory* (Fig. 571), contains subjective, obsessional features such as the rocky coast of Spain, the arid plain, and the startling confrontation of "melted" watches with a fetal form and a dead tree positioned on a blocklike object. Frequently Dali would paint a picture in parts, working on individual areas and objects as they appeared to him in hallucinations often induced by the austere act of staring at the blank canvas. The

*below :* 571. Salvador Dali. *The Persistence of Memory.* 1931. Oil on canvas, $9^1/_2 \times 13''$. Museum of Modern Art, New York.

*right :* 572. René Magritte. *The Six Elements.* 1928. Oil on canvas, $28^7/_8 \times 39^1/_2''$. Philadelphia Museum of Art (Louise and Walter Arensberg Collection).

limpid timepieces may have been punning references to the artist's conceit over bending time to his will, or perhaps to childhood regressions in which Dali compared the exposure of his soft tongue to the molten watches. The French word for watch is *montre,* as is the personal imperative of the verb *montrer* ("to show") used by a doctor asking a sick child to expose his tongue. Dali drew freely upon his own extraordinary and disturbed past for ideas that his mastery of academic drawing enabled him to render with dazzling precision.

The enactment of Dali's psychologically inspired dramas usually takes place in a profound, lucid space. The paradox he loved was this exact transcription of what seemed to make no sense: the juxtaposition or fusion of unrelated objects; inversions of the familiar or of expected properties of the animate and inanimate; double images like those of his own head, but images that resist the programmatic translation of those in Arcimboldo's work (Pl. 79); the mingling of animal, vegetable, and mineral motifs into a molten hybrid.

Many Surrealists did not look upon their work as art but as scientific documents in the systematic exploration of their own subconsciousness. They sought to liberate creativity from mechanistic materialism; but, paradoxically, instead of freeing the mind, they established new and strict limits for creativity. Reason was denied any function (which disqualified the Surrealists as scientists), and, in the words of Herbert Muller, "the studio in the psyche became an underground dungeon."

Like many movements in modern art, Surrealism was not homogeneous, and there were many artists who accepted only certain aspects of its program. Its great value was in demonstrating the possibilities of instinctive creation and in opening up new sources of imagery, thereby widening to a generous new dimension the *possibilities* available to artists.

**Magritte's Dislocations** The difficulty with a word like *Surrealism*, as with many art labels, is that it does not describe, illustrate, or explain what the artists identified with it have done. There is little agreement in style, subject, or intent among the various Surrealists, beyond what they will *not* show—the external world in terms of its familiar logic of appearance. The Belgian artist René Magritte (1898–1967) gives us paintings that are exact transcriptions of what he sees as the "unexpected" in the visible world. His *Six Elements* (Fig. 572), for example, shows six framed segments of subjects that in themselves are describable, but once we have made this simple, rational observation, it is possible to go no further in explaining why these subjects and scenes are where they are. Magritte used the device of a window frame (or picture frame), with which we normally associate views of the familiar, external world. But in imaginative painting of the 20th century, and that dating back to Redon, the window is no longer associated with conscious experience. Even Magritte's framing device is out of joint, inflected or bent in a way that is comparable to the dislocation he has made in the expected sequence of his subjects. Writing about his intentions, Magritte has said:

> The art of painting, as I conceive of it, consists in representing through pictorial technique the *unforeseen* images that might appear to me at certain moments whether my eyes are open or shut. . . . I readily avoid explaining the things I love . . . we get no enrichment from a thing explained. In effect, the thing explained drops out of sight in favor of the practical explanation itself or a more or less intelligent hypothesis. . . .

Magritte thus plays against our natural inclination to rationalize what we see. He wants to evoke the mysterious and the unpredictable in the commonplace subjects that we accept every day without second thought (Fig. 477). *What* he paints is paramount, but Magritte takes little pleasure from the act of painting. Because for this artist painting is the most effective instrument for realizing his revelations, he does not want his work to be viewed primarily for its aesthetic quality.

At the same time, the possibilities of painting private fantasies have attracted men who feel passionately about painting itself and who pride themselves on the inventiveness of their forms and color, and on the power of their art to move the viewer aesthetically as well as through thought and feeling. Such an artist was Max Beckmann, whose paintings, while not Surrealist, reveal his involvement with some of the major problems confronting the modern artist committed to the exploration and use of his own imagination for new and experimental artistic purposes.

**Beckmann's DEPARTURE** By adhering to the morality of being true to one's own experiences and needs, many of the most creative artists of this century have, without question, produced works that are largely unintelligible to the general public. Frequently, when the artist has wanted to express something of importance to mankind, the very nature of his meaning, which like his form is partly derived from intuition, has been incompletely or inconsistently understood by the layman. It is not at all unusual for the meaning of a complex painting to change for the artist while he works on it, and even subsequent to the work's completion. One of the most powerful personal statements by a modern painter, expressing the complex of his responses to himself, to his times, and to the history of the human race is the three-panel painting by Max Beckmann entitled *Departure* (Fig. 573). It was painted in Berlin in 1932 and 1933, following Beckmann's dismissal by the Nazis from his directorship of an art school. Fearing confiscation of his painting, the artist wrote on the back of the canvas, "Scenes from Shakespeare's Tempest." The panels were not, however, the illustration of a literary source. Beckmann's hope was that

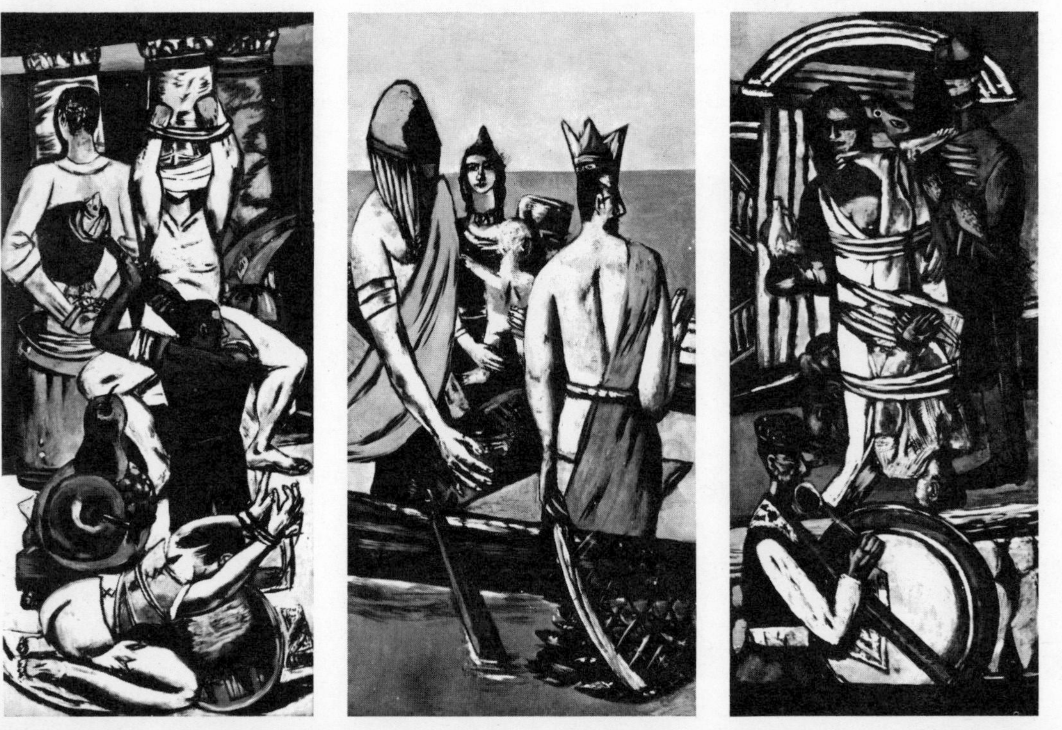

573. MAX BECKMANN, *Departure*. 1932–33. Oil on canvas; center 7′3/4″ × 3′9 3/8″, sides 7′3/4″ × 3′3 1/4″. Museum of Modern Art, New York.

the sympathetic viewer would meditate upon all three panels at once. He felt that their visual interrelationship would reveal his intentions. Historically, such three-panel paintings had precedents in Christian altarpieces, and it is possible that Beckmann intentionally revived this format, with its religious connotations, as the vehicle for his reflections on human spiritual history. The two flanking panels are narrower, darker, and more congested than the central one, and both are filled with unpleasant images of torture, noise, and nightmarish situations. By its greater size, its bright spaciousness, and the freedom of movement available to its characters, the center panel immediately establishes a different, more hopeful, but solemn mood and implication. Thus, even before we examine individual figures or speculate on the significance of gestures, we can sense the importance of these fundamental and readily apparent major contrasts, just as T. S. Eliot believed that an artist begins to communicate before he is understood. Like the work of other modern artists who attach symbolic significance to objects and gestures, Beckmann's previous art does not give us the basis for interpreting his imagery, for the German painter has not been consistent from painting to painting in the associations or values assigned to the same contents. Each object must be related to its particular context. The brutality in the left panel may possibly relate to Nazi tortures, of which Beckmann was all too well aware. This, however, is not made explicit, and the artist would have considered a more direct statement a limit to the scope of this painting's potential reference. While inventorying the indignities and violence to which the human body has been subjected, not unlike Goya in *May 3, 1808* (Fig. 404) and *Los Caprichos,* Beckmann surprises us by not introducing a plausible weapon or instrument for violence. We cannot even be sure that the stripe-shirted figure is an executioner. The settings of the framing panels are a curious mixture of references to a columned room and a stage. They are of an ambiguity that makes it impossible to localize the action. There is also an intriguing mixture of clothing that ranges from the uniform of a bellhop and the drummer's ermine collar to the ancient draperies and crown of the central figures. This should remind us that Beckmann does not want to specify the who, when, where, what, and why of *Departure*. In a letter to a friend he set down his thoughts on the painting:

> The center is the end of the tragedy, but the meaning can only be understood by the three parts together. Life is what you see right and left. Life is torture, pain of every kind—physical and mental—men and women are subjected to it equally. On the right wing you can see yourself trying to find your way in the darkness, lighting the halls and stair-cases with a miserable lamp, dragging along tied to you as a part of yourself, the corpse of your memories, of your wrongs and failures, the murder everyone commits at some time of his life—you can never free yourself of your past, you have to carry that corpse while life plays the drum. In the center, the King and Queen have freed themselves, freed themselves of the tortures of life. They have overcome them. The Queen carries the greatest treasure—Freedom—as her child on her lap. Freedom is the one thing that matters—it is the departure, the new start.

On another occasion Beckmann said, "Departure, yes departure, from the illusion of life toward the essential realities that lie hidden beyond." It is as if he is commenting on the timelessness of oppression, but also on the capacity of the human spirit to overstride evil and to renew itself. But it is tribute to the poetic power of Beckmann's painting that once he has described so eloquently what he feels about its meaning, we can return to the work with still more questions, or the feeling that its ramifications are even deeper and more complex. Where Beckmann's *Departure* and Picasso's *Guernica* (Fig. 548) share a common ground is in their mingling of violent myth with the contemporaneous fascist movement of the 1930s. It is in the artists' interpretation of a subject that was topical yet timeless, in the reaction they both felt against the forces of inhumanity and for the survival of the spirit.

## AUTOMATISM AND IMAGINATIVE PAINTING

So far in this chapter all the imaginative art illustrated has had an illusionistic character, its subjects exhibited as if in a three-dimensional world existing behind the surface of the painting or print. Further, it has been possible to relate and identify objects and figures, entities physically complete despite their often hybrid makeup. Shortly after World War I, at about the time the work of the Alsatian artist Hans Arp began to appear, and during the early 1920s, there evolved an immensely fruitful and influential device for the creation of works of art, one that was employed by artists expressing a wide range of temperaments and styles. This was the device known as *automatism,* and it has been adopted in a nonillusionistic context emphasizing the surfaceness of the drawing or painting by such artists as Masson, Miró, Gorky, and Pollock (Pl. 57, p. 327), who have produced much of the best art to appear between the two wars. Automatism has had continued, widespread use since 1945, and it is the second of the two major modes that have engaged the interest of artists whose works explore the imagination.

The earliest and most important definition of automatism was given by the French writer André Breton, who became the leader, high priest, and chief impresario of Surrealism. Writing in the *First Surrealist Manifesto* of 1924, Breton said: "SURREALISM. Pure psychic automatism by which one seeks to express, be it verbally, in writing or in any other manner, the real workings of the mind. Dictated by the unconscious, in the absence of any control exercised by reason and free from

574. ANDRÉ MASSON. *Battle of Fishes*. 1927. Pencil, oil, and sand on canvas; 14¹/₄ × 28³/₄". Museum of Modern Art, New York (purchase).

aesthetic or moral preoccupations." The use of the principle of automatism in literature and music would be what was known as "stream of consciousness" and jazz improvisation. For the layman, automatism is practiced in "doodling "or saying the first thing that comes into one's head. Many of the artists employing automatism did not live up to its literal definition or to Breton's injunction not to let reason enter into the creative process at all. The artists' previous training and commitment to composition, as well as their taste, undoubtedly played some part in what they did. The historical emergence of automatism was related to the concern of many artists with the problem of how to be truly creative in a mechanistic world, and the belief that reason did not tap all of the potential source of important imagery in an artist's makeup. Automatism was thought to be essential to the "liberation" of the subconscious.

The automatist drawings and sand paintings produced by André Masson (b. 1896) between 1924 and 1929 illustrate perhaps the purest utilization of this artistic device. He approached the sheet of paper or canvas with no preconceived image in mind. To stimulate or irritate his imagination he sometimes fixed sand to the canvas but, again, with no predetermined or definite configuration (Fig. 574). As if in a trance, Masson let his pen or brush move across the surface until he began to see possible images emerging. Thus, his "painting" began abstractly and then, with the introduction of certain instantaneous judgments, moved in the direction of a human configuration.

> I begin without an image or plan in mind, but just draw or paint rapidly according to my impulses. Gradually, in the marks I make, I see suggestions of figures or objects. I encourage these to emerge, trying to bring out their implications even as I consciously try to give order to the composition.

These decisions did not interrupt the continual movement of his hand, however. When the possibilities of a certain image became apparent, Masson made them more articulate, but he never took his drawing or painting to the stage that it became literal. During the process of evoking the final configuration, the artist was both creator and spectator, observing what resulted from his unconsciously controlled hand movements. Masson and other artists in the mid-1920s considered what they were doing to be "beyond painting," but they were not antiart. Like much that has happened in this century, the history of Masson's work is that after it was made the word *art* was stretched to encompass it. (*Art* is probably the most elastic word ever invented by man.)

A second artist who, like Masson, produced many of his most important paintings in the 1920s and worked "automatically," was the Spaniard Joan Miró (b. 1893). We can see the consequences of Miró's assimilation of the automatic method and how it radically altered the look and meaning of his art in two paintings. The first, entitled *The Farm* (Pl. 81, p. 414), was done in 1921–22, while the artist was at his home in Montroig, Spain, and then in Paris. For the picture he used souvenirs of his beloved homeland. The intense particularization of all objects in an airless space contributes to their charm and eventual ambiguity. Simultaneously, we are given the diversity and unity of a staggering number of objects, so that we become aware of a conjugated series, of visual puns based on holes and circular patches, scalloped and peaked shapes, radial spoke forms in the trees and grass, parallel diagonals and horizontals in roof and earth. The vivid interest of the painting comes from the even distribution and the avoidance of overlap in a wide range of shapes, from the tiny pebbles through the buildings and trees to the infinity of the sky.

The fantasy incipient in *The Farm* was unchecked in Miró's *The Hunter (Catalan Landscape)*, reproduced as Plate 82 (p. 414). Suspended upon a flat surface of yellow above and pink below is an aggregate of lines and shapes derived from the earlier painting. Now, however, the drawing has suggested the object, so that the undulating line lives a ubiquitous life as a mustache, the horizon, an animal body, waves, and birds. Certain shapes and lines obsessive to Miró are now disassociated from the objects that generated them. There is a playful mocking of geometry in the use of the ruled line and the triangle. First, the triangle appears in its more familiar state at the lower left, but then it becomes part of the rabbit's tail just to the right and, above, the hunter's head. The pipe-smoking hunter has a large ear, not inappropriate for the chase, an exposed heart, and a scraggly beard whose mossy shapes appear on the wall of the farmhouse in the earlier painting. The dotted trail that he follows meanders playfully against the lines of his body and arms. Influenced by his contact with Cubism, Miró detached a large eye from a head and introduced the letters S A R D, perhaps from the Spanish word *sardana,* a Catalan folk dance. The earlier disposition of elements has become more random and whimsical. The range from minute to large is retained from the earlier work, but here Miró has magnified and reconstituted certain objects, such as the rabbit and insect forms, in a much more arbitrary way, according to the weight of the objects in his general awareness of them and the dictates of fantasy. While vestiges of a scene or a subject remain, they are accompanied by less decipherable elements, and the painting's poetry is more obvious in its rhymes, more arcane in its meaning. There is no longer the intent to follow the logic of nature's appearance. Miró's creatures live only on the surface of the painting. The artist's full conversion to an art based not upon the restraint of reason but upon the encouraged, instinctive, or automatic outpouring of fantasy was a complete and moral one.

The great stylistic divergence possible in art induced partly by the practice of automatism can be seen in a comparison of Miró's painting with one by the Armenian-born American artist Arshile Gorky (1904–48), entitled *The Liver Is the Cock's Comb* (Pl. 83, p. 415). Miró's motifs are cleanly drawn, and they float in an airless, imaginary, and seemingly limited space or on the painting's surface. Gorky's configurations are still more illegible and difficult to decipher, being tortured twistings that fuse or separate from one another in an intensely congested environment. Color ranges from deep earth tones to hot patches, and none of the color is related to the linear outlines. The artist's technical range in manipulating his paint is far greater and more subtle than Miró's. Gorky derived his imaginative composition from a drawing, or, as he thought of it, a blueprint, where he mingled fantasies upon things directly observed in nature, visions of internal human organs, recollections of art he had seen, and a consciousness of the need for composing his creations so that they made sense in terms of the painting's form. The title of the work is in no way related to the painting's inception and provides no clue to its interpretation. Often Gorky's titles were suggested, at his invitation, by friends. He was not the first artist to rebel against the "tyranny of the title." Gorky demanded an audience that would pay continued attention to his painting, not to the words by which it was labeled. With Surrealism, as Gorky's biographer Ethel Schwabacher has written, "art entered into man," which implies that artists were exteriorizing through art, as directly as possible, the inner world of their own feelings and imagination. Gorky, in turn, wanted his painting to enter, through sympathetic eyes, into the consciousness and subconsciousness of his audience. With time, one becomes aware not only of the implied violence of the motifs and strong sexual references, but also of the beauty of the drawing, the painter's intimate handwriting, with its delicate or vehement passages, the careful adjustment of colors to each other, and the shape they share with the linear fabric of the composition. To content oneself with a game of hide-and-seek, or a few conclusions about a specific passage, is to deny the occasion for seeing and feeling the conception of a Gorky painting as a whole, with its abundance of interrelationships that resist exhaustion throughout a long and continuous association.

It is indeed true that much of modern imaginative art deals with the unpleasant, and that for many people its form poses a parallel problem in being contrary to conventional taste. But even our synoptic sampling of older art derived from irrational experience has shown us that there is a precedent for art's contradiction of the polite, the prudish, and the pleasing. Tradition and familiarity make Goya and Bosch acceptable to those who rankle at Gorky or the French artist Jean Dubuffet (b. 1901). One cannot guess how many times, during exhibitions, the images in Dubuffet's *Corps de Dame* series (Pl. 84, p. 416) have been likened to a naked woman run over by a steam roller on a newly paved street. Second in frequency might be the comment that it looks like something scrawled on a wall in a public rest room. While Gorky paid homage to the "cookery" of brush painting, Dubuffet literally concocted his own recipes for paint and other substances in order to achieve a medium that in itself would stimulate his imagination. By incising his lines with the end of a paintbrush or a stick, he has invited comparison with defacement of walls; in fact, Dubuffet, a middle-class former wine merchant, has spent many years in the study of *l'art brut*—the "raw art" or "unschooled, unadulterated art" made by psychotics, children, and the "self-taught" draftsmen who leave their mark in public places. What he finds interesting is the direct, frank character of this type of art, its expression of another, invisible, or repressed side of men and women.

The *Corps de Dame* series (which Dubuffet followed with a comparable treatment of men) submitted the body to brutal handling, not by someone in the painting, as in paintings of anatomy dissections or martyrdoms (Figs. 225, 266), but by the artist himself. Ugly women are to be found in Leonardo's drawings from deformed subjects, in Goya's *Los Caprichos* as symbols of vanity and evil, and in countless caricatures, but Dubuffet's predecessors in Western, post-Renaissance painting located their gruesome subjects in a world of space and light and sought to make them appear as lifelike as possible. Dubuffet has said that in doing the series he was working with "a general concept," which prevents our assuming he intended moralizing caricature or scientific investigation. Dubuffet has said his women exist in "a state of immateriality"; they are made of and live in the substance of the medium used. One can only conjecture whether Dubuffet's conception is a personal antidote to the popular notion of "woman" created in France by the mass media.

In the same year that Dubuffet was doing his *Corps de Dame* pictures in Paris, the Dutch-born American Willem de Kooning (b. 1904) began in New York a series called *Woman,* which continued for the next three years and intermittently thereafter to the present time (Pl. 85, p. 416). Despite the coincidence of dates, no conscious influence occurred between the two. De Kooning's *Woman* series grew out of paintings he had done in the 1940s involving both the subject of the feminine form and abstraction. Sometimes referred to as *Abstract Surrealism,* De Kooning's work depends in part upon automatism and the spontaneous release of ideas. In it, however, the ideas are continually subjected to destruction and reconstruction during vigorous painting operations, so that there is no point at which the image is completely or irrevocably finished. The painting grows or fades according to the artist's life at the moment he confronts it or is involved with it. His series and subsequent abstractions are really one continuous painting tied to his own changing moods, like a personal diary of partially eradicated entries. As with Dubuffet, the violence of De Kooning's art lies not in any action depicted, but in the action of making and remaking the painting by means of assaults on the canvas. In *Woman and Bicycle* (Pl. 85, p. 416), the subject seems all eyes, teeth, and breasts, standing passively by her conveyance. Her form materializes from and is threatened by the painter's slashing applications of paint to the surface. She does not intentionally symbolize, allegorize, or allude specifically to any one person or public concept. She belongs to the reality of a painted surface and is a recurring hallucination for the painter. The artist has described his obsessional image and suggested the intervention of his inner feelings and subconscious during its realization: "I always started out with the idea of a young person, a beautiful woman. I noticed them change. Somebody would step out—a middle-aged woman. I didn't mean to make them such monsters." On another occasion he said: "Women irritate me sometimes. I painted that irritation in the *Woman* series, that's all." De Kooning is a reactive artist, potentially irritated by a wide variety of sensations and visual suggestions from all over. In one sense his painting is antidotal to the disease of emotional insincerity in society and its public glorification of women within the context of cleanliness, motherhood, happiness, youthfulness, and sex. De Kooning's method of working on *Woman and Bicycle,* and the other pictures in the series, was to build up an unpremeditated image from scrap of his earlier drawings, cutouts from newspapers or photographs, freehand drawings of letters, and the dictates of emotion, lacing it all with technical preoccupations relating to his craft. Like Frankenstein's monster, *Woman and Bicycle* is a synthetic concoction of used parts. "Whatever I see becomes my shapes and my condition. The recognizable form people sometimes see in the pictures after they are painted I see myself, but whether they got there accidentally or not, who knows?"

## THE LIMITS OF REASON

Although he died in 1940, it is fitting to conclude this chapter with a work by Paul Klee, the most gifted and consistently excellent creator of imaginative art in this century. In Chapter 16, "Art, Objects, and the Object of Art," the reader was introduced to some of Klee's ideas regarding creation (Pl. 55, p. 310). An artist endowed with both whimsy and wisdom, who worked with facts, fables, and fantasy, Klee devoted his art to the rendering of the world seen with closed eyes. His hundreds of paintings reveal how he could preserve the special qualities of images of the mind. Klee invented his own modes of drawing, charted new spaces, and enacted fresh artistic laws for light and gravity. In his contacts with the external world, with what he saw, heard, and read, Klee con-

*opposite :* 575. PAUL KLEE. *The Limits of Reason.* 1927. Oil and watercolor, $21^{5}/_{8} \times 16^{1}/_{8}''$. Private collection, Munich.

*above:* 576. E. J. SULLIVAN. *Sartor Resartus.* 1898. Wood engraving.

tinually and consistently nourished the sources of his imagination. Science, philosophy, and art fuse in his images. Klee could reinterpret an old idea, one that had a verbal or established visual history, and give it new dimensions marked with his personal touch. Consider his *Limits of Reason* (Fig. 575) and a late 19th-century wood engraving by E. J. Sullivan from Thomas Carlyle's *Sartor Resartus* (Fig. 576). Sullivan shows that man ascends the heights of knowledge on a mountain of books. The path to enlightenment is paved with the written word. One could read this description and in the absence of Sullivan's print still conjure the image in one's mind. But how difficult to evoke through words Klee's conception! The linear contraption at the bottom of his picture broadly suggests modern technological inventions, the means by which man aspires to reach what Klee shows to be ultimately unattainable via the ladders of reason. In Bruegel's time, and even earlier in the Middle Ages, the analogous commentary on folly was the depiction of the building of the Tower of Babel. Made in 1927, Klee's conception prophesied present-day devices by which we seek to explore the unknown spaces of the universe.

In the study of art, it is one thing to become aware of its possibilities and another its impossibilities. This book has been very much concerned for the former. With regard to imaginative art, we can learn that it is impossible for us to understand completely the meaning and intention of paintings by Redon, De Chirico, Magritte, and Beckmann, for example. Just as there is no objective way to prove good and bad values for art, so is it in many cases impossible even for the artist to verify the meaning of his work. Meyer Schapiro admirably summed up the situation for many modern painters when he wrote:

> The artist does not wish to create a work in which he transmits an already prepared and complete message to a relatively indifferent and impersonal receiver. The painter aims rather at such a quality of the whole that, unless you achieve the proper set of mind and feeling towards it, you will not experience anything of it at all.

Max Beckmann realized that there were many in his audience who could not understand his work. He hoped that viewers would employ their own inner "creative sympathy" when looking at his paintings: "I can only speak to people who, consciously or unconsciously, already carry within them a similar metaphysical code." Contrary to what the public and many art educators may wish, art is not for every man, just as every man is not for art. Both creating and communing with art involve the experience and training of imagination.

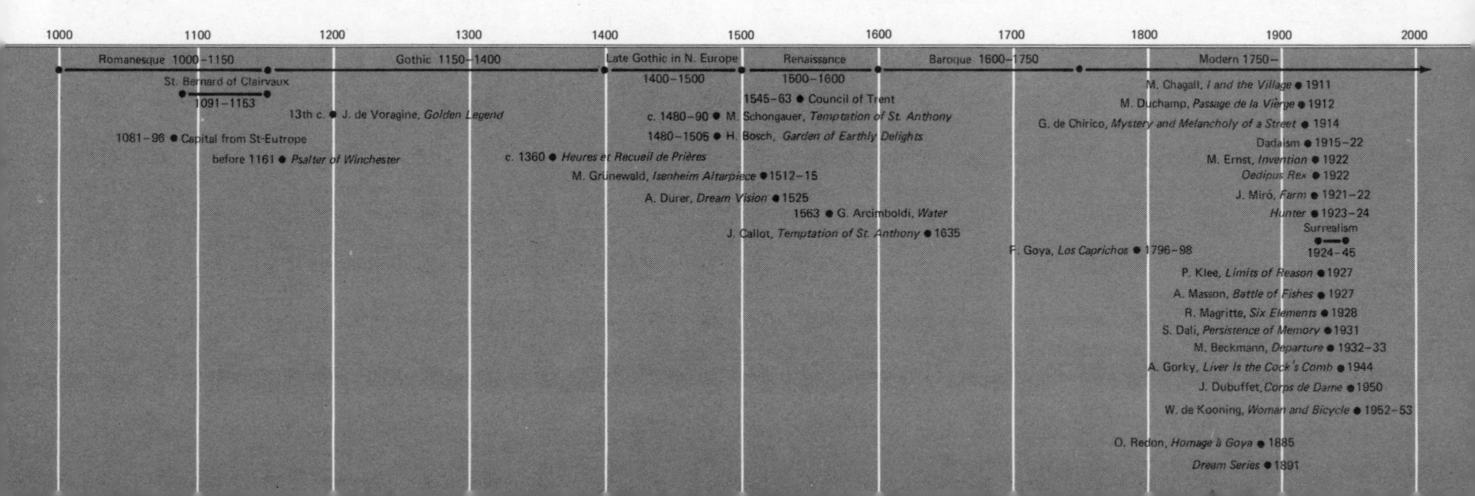

# 22

The emergence of abstract painting and sculpture after 1909 constituted one of the great revolutions in the history of art. The *picture window* concept of illusionistic painting, which came into being in the 15th century and thrived unchallenged for more than 500 years, was rejected by several artists before, during, and after World War I in favor of a nonillusionistic and in many cases nonrepresentational art. *Abstract* is not an adequate or correct word to describe this new art but, like the terms *Baroque* and *Gothic*, it is used for convenience. The reader will not generally be burdened with explanations of the terms applied to various movements or with attempts to fit paintings into tidy verbal compartments, for, in the succinct commentary of artist Harry Holtzman, "Hardening of the categories produces art disease."

The title of this chapter is *not* intended to apply to all art of the last sixty years, since many artists continue to work illusionistically; rather, it relates to those artists who since 1910 for ethical, philosophical, and aesthetic reasons have found illusionism or imitative art no longer meaningful. For these artists the seemingly transparent picture surface with its simulation of the three-dimensional visual world was dead. Independence from likeness in art did not come overnight or without its problems. The pioneer abstractionists moved into uncharted territory and were faced with creating their own shapes and

*above:* 577. ALBRECHT DÜRER. *Draftsman Drawing a Portrait.* 1525. Woodcut, 5¹/₈ × 6″. Metropolitan Museum of Art, New York (gift of Henry Walters, 1917).

*right:* 578. PIETER DE HOOCH. *Interior of a Dutch House.* 1658. Oil on canvas, 29 × 25″. National Gallery, London (reproduced by courtesy of the Trustees).

# ABSTRACTION
# Death of the Window and Life of the Square

composition to replace those provided by nature and tradition in art. This chapter outlines a few of the crucial steps taken toward abstraction, adopting the motif of the square to suggest the variety in nonrepresentational art and the way it has satisfied many artists of differing temperaments and tastes.

**The Window View of Art** *Draftsman Drawing a Portrait* (Fig. 577), a woodcut by Albrecht Dürer, an illustration for his treatise on perspective, helps us to understand the old window theory of illusionistic painting. Dürer has shown the artist stationed behind a table looking through an eyepiece set at a certain height, thereby giving a fixed viewpoint. Looking at the sight, the painter sees the seated model through a framed piece of glass that intercepts his line of vision. The pane of glass is like a window and is the actual surface on which he is painting. By painting what he sees upon the glass the artist thus transfers the model to a two-dimensional surface. Earlier in the 15th century, with regard to the painting's surface, Leon Battista Alberti had instructed the artist "to present the forms of the objects on this surface as if it were a transparent pane of glass" (see Chap. 7). Alberti's definition of painting is likewise illustrated in Dürer's print: "Painting, then, is nothing other than a cross section of a visual pyramid upon a certain surface, artificially represented with lines and color at a given distance, with a central stance established and lights arranged. . . ." How many painters actually employed Dürer's device would be hard to estimate, but the translation of the three-dimensional world onto the painted surface, regardless of the device used, was more than just a mechanical operation. It took centuries to develop an extensive repertory of illusionistic devices, such as modeling and atmospheric effects achieved by light and shadow, overlap, recession of lines, and diminishing scale of subjects. These techniques did not all vanish immediately from painting at the end of the 19th century, but as we saw in Chapter 15, they were gradually set aside as painters found new means to interpret a reality that was not confined to the visible world.

The Renaissance window theory of painting had implications that went beyond the making of pictures. In the Renaissance, systematic perspective was used to create an ideal world, the model of harmonious social and natural order. In the 17th century Pieter de Hooch composed *Interior of a Dutch House* (Fig. 578), a model of polite, genteel sociability which is set in an immaculate, comfortable interior illuminated by means of numerous windows. Like the glass in the windows, we look through the painting's surface, aided by the receding black and white tiled floor that also serves as a device by means of which we can measure our distance from all the figures and objects in the room. The rectangles of the rafters, the squared shapes of the map, painting, and fireplace, and the window frames and flooring establish a clear metrical shape and rhythmic order that would make an interesting painting without the figures. Within his spatial box the Dutch painter could maneuver his figures, adjusting them to the setting, but relying more on the fixed relationships of the latter than on those of the figures. The map, the architecture, and the tidiness of the room help us to understand how much the middle-class Dutch loved to see things put into order and well made. Because of its varied repetition and frequency of occurrence, to modern eyes conditioned by abstract art it is almost as if the artist is paying homage to the square. At the same time, while the 17th-century Dutch knew the principles of geometry, they could not conceive of painting denuded of people, places, and things. More than two centuries of naturalistic painting had to pass before a number of circumstances permitted artists to feel that the time was right for giving up illusionism.

**Closing the Window** The window approach to painting reached its culmination and denial in 19th-century Impressionism. A painting by Gustave Caillebotte (1848–94)—a friend of the Impressionists and a wealthy boat builder, art collector, and painter—of a man standing in front of an open window epitomizes the Impressionist approach to life and art (Fig. 579). The man is not restricted in his view by the mechanical sighting device of Dürer, but casually stands at an angle to the window, hands in his pockets, looking out on the scene below. An impressionable person, he is quietly enjoying the aesthetic moments of seeing the life of the street without himself being seen. Around the time of Caillebotte's painting, Edmond Duranty, a writer sympathetic to Impressionism, wrote an essay entitled *The New Painting,* in which he described the window as it is encountered in paintings such as those of Caillebotte, Monet, and, later, Pissarro:

> From within, it is through the window that we communicate with the outside; the window is still a frame which accompanies us without cease, lasting while we are in the house, and this time is considerable. The frame of the window, according to whether we are far from it or near it, whether we are seated or standing, cuts off the outside scene in the most unexpected, the most changing manner, procuring for us the eternal variety, the spontaneity which is one of the great zests of reality [1876].

Claude Monet's painting of *Rue Montorgueil, Fête Nationale du 30 Juin, 1878* (Pl. 45, p. 295), is a view from a window of the flag-bedecked street, and in some of his boulevard paintings Monet showed top-hatted figures leaning out of windows looking at the crowds below. Caillebotte, Pissarro, and Monet did not use the window as a framing device for a centralized focus upon a few figures in static situations; rather, they preserved the quality of traffic flow in and out of our frame of vision. The tilting of the street makes the picture's depth difficult to read and serves as a device for presenting the unarranged and ambiguous experiences of seeing the city from an elevated window.

Shortly before 1900, while in London, Monet painted *Leicester Square* seen on a rainy night (Pl. 86, p. 433). It is as if the artist were viewing the city not from an open window but through the rain-spattered glass, which caused the colors and lights to run together. In making us aware of the closed window, or semitransparency of the viewing surface, Monet also makes us more conscious of the painting's physical surface.

Henri Matisse is the modern painter who, along with Pablo Picasso, has been the most influential in preserving representation while denying traditional illusionism. Matisse's evolution toward a surface style after 1900 can be summarized by comparing two paintings of the same subject done about ten years apart. In the *Dinner Table* of 1897 (Fig. 580) Matisse was presenting to the public his masterpiece, showing in a large painting all that he had mastered up to that time. For Matisse, good living always met the requirements of art, and, characteristically, the subject here is an aesthetic one—the maid in arranging the flowers on the table is herself performing an artistic activity. In displaying his skill as a painter he showed the light source coming through a curtained window in the background, so that most of the picture is not seen in full or direct light. Yet, he caught the sparkle of light on the glassware. Having previously copied the old masters, Matisse knew the great tradition of table paintings, still lifes, and genre scenes, and with this work he was claiming his right to be compared with them. Alberti's requirements for painting, that it consist of circumscribing objects, their composition, and the showing of their reception of light, still obtain.

In 1908, Matisse again painted the subject of the dinner table, *Harmony in Red* (Fig. 581), which required that painting now be defined in terms of the harmonious and expressive arrangement of lines and colors upon a surface independent of the subject. There is no simulation of relief or the depth Alberti wanted to achieve by the use of geometry. Consonant with this new two-dimensional world was the absence of a natural or artificial light source, there being no air or space for light to pass through. The colors themselves give off luminosity and create depth. Color and drawing replace the subtle textural distinctions of earlier paintings as the means for separating objects. In place of the earlier transparent window, Matisse has placed on the wall what is either a window or a painting, the latter, of course, being comparably flat and arbitrary in color. Sensibility to distance and light, so important to De Hooch, is replaced by Matisse's sensibility to the interaction of color.

*left:* 579. GUSTAVE CAILLEBOTTE. *Man at a Window.* c. 1875. Oil on canvas, 46 × 32 1/2″. Private collection, Paris.

Plate 91. MARK ROTHKO. *Tan and Black on Red*. 1957. Oil on canvas, 5′9$^{3}/_{8}$″ × 4′5$^{3}/_{8}$″. Collection Mr. and Mrs. I. Donald Grossman, New York. (See p. 448.)

*above:* 580. HENRI MATISSE. *Dinner Table*. 1897. Oil on canvas, 3′3½″ × 4′3½″. Collection Stavros S. Niarchos, London.

*below:* 581. HENRI MATISSE. *Harmony in Red*. 1908–09. Oil on canvas, 5′9¾″ × 7′1⅞″. Hermitage, Leningrad (copyright Editions du Cercle d'Art, Paris).

Social or human relationships that dramatized Western painting since the Renaissance have given way to aesthetic relationships. Matisse, too, wanted his painting to evoke recollections of pleasurable experiences in the home, but on new terms that make of painting a decorative object. The viewer cannot mentally project himself into this painting .The artist imposes his vision by forcing us to absorb the effects of the painting as a whole, not to read it serially, as in the De Hooch. The disparate functions of windows, mirrors, and paintings seen in older art are leveled out in Matisse. Wallpaper has the same characteristics, or lack of them, as trees or the human figure.

As with Picasso's print of the *Painter with Model Knitting* (Fig. 537), there is no projection principle such as Dürer demonstrated by which we could predict what Matisse would have put on the surface of his painting. His decisions are governed by the need for colors to accord with the dominant tone he has chosen, and the shapes must animate the surface and ensure that the entire painting be equally expressive. He was painting to delight the eye, to surrender its total effect more fully and immediately than did the works in the style of 1897.

The eye, the window, the mirror, and the camera lens—all have been identified with reproduction of the visible world and what for most people is reality. By contrasting *View of Delft*

(Fig. 582) by Jan Vermeer with *The City* (Pl. 87, p. 433) by Fernand Léger (1881–1955), we can see how the same motif has been interpreted using all and none of these devices. The researches of scholars such as P.T.A. Swillens and Charles Seymour, Jr., have confirmed that when Vermeer depicted his native city he worked near a window in a darkened room of a house across the river from the main port of Delft. Professor Seymour has presented a good argument for Vermeer's having used a *camera obscura,* or boxlike viewing device much like the modern camera, similar to the one reproduced in an old print (Fig. 583). By means of this device, which contained a mirror to right the inverted lens image, Vermeer would have been able to see the city reflected onto a flat surface, thus facilitating its reproduction and merging of the refracted image with his painting surface. The crucial evidence for this argument lies in the tiny unfocused areas of light in the painting, which correspond to those produced by a camera lens that cannot quite correct or sharpen focus for highlighted areas. Vermeer was thus able to patiently reconstruct, detail by detail, the panorama of the city seen 400 feet away across the Schie River at about noon on a summer day when the wind was blowing from the southwest. The character of the architecture and the slow pace of the city's life lent themselves to sedentary contemplation. Delft's countless delightful prospects revealed themselves only to the unhurried, discriminating eye.

For Léger, the modern city was too big and too complex to be seen from a window or caught in a camera lens. He passionately loved the machines and the engineering that produced the new metropolis and could only condone a style that captured these new urban characteristics. He did not see himself as an eye reflecting the visual world, but as a painter-engineer who constructed his image with the same intellectual precision and multiplicity of viewpoints as city builders did their blueprints. Cubism provided Léger with a new syntax for presenting in a pictorially connected manner objects that appear to be disconnected. His colors, unlike those of Vermeer, are the strong, pure hues of commercial advertising, or those of metal and cement. The textured patterns were inspired by railings, iron stairways, the Eiffel Tower, segments of mass-produced, stenciled letters, and billboard figures—everything that might suggest the handmade or traditionally picturesque has been omitted. The smooth surfaces and hard edges were painted impersonally. Robotlike figures on stairs are the ideal inhabitants of Léger's mechanized metropolis. Natural light, so important in lending poetry to the urban painting of Vermeer and the Impressionists, plays no part in *The City*. As with the painting of Matisse, the shapes are self-illuminating, rarely tempered by shadings. They are always clear, clean, and hard, unnatural in their edges and juncture. Vermeer and Monet delighted in soft clouds; Léger mechanized smoke into a globular sequence above the stairway figures. For him smoke symbolized civilization, and, using hard lines, he gave it form as an affirmation of his own masculine command.

In giving up illusionism, however, Léger preserved some of its characteristics, notably the importance of contrasts. The visual spice of his painting comes from unpredictable contrasts

*left:* 582. Jan Vermeer. *View of Delft*. c. 1658. Oil on canvas, 38½ × 46″. Mauritshuis, The Hague.

*below:* 583. *Camera Obscura*. 17th century. Woodcut.

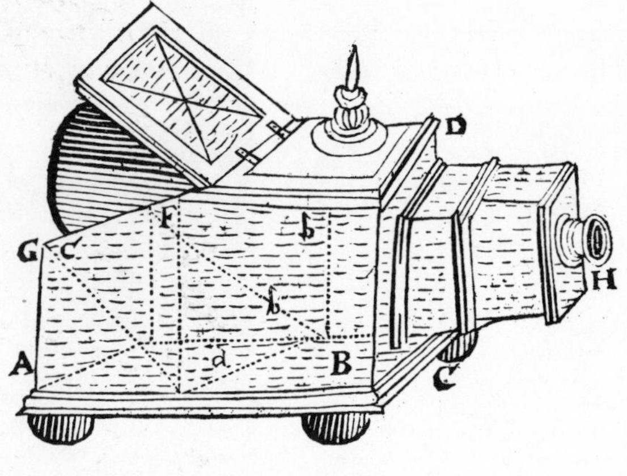

*right:* 584. ROBERT DELAUNAY. *The City.* 1910. Oil on canvas, 4′9½″ × 3′8″. Musée National d'Art Moderne, Paris.

such as bright and dull colors, a round column against flat shapes. Contrast of scale depends upon the single tall column that stands against so many medium and small shapes. In moving away from the natural, Léger's shapes tend toward the geometrically curved and angular. However, unlike the abstract artists to be discussed subsequently, he could not restrict himself solely to the rectilinear, since this would have contradicted his ideal of contrast as a life and artistic ethic. For Léger, faithfulness to perception, to the eye as a window, mirror, or camera lens, had to be replaced by art as a conception—resulting from the intellect and feeling.

The window as an imaginative rather than a rational frame for viewing the city became the subject of a series of paintings begun in 1910 by the Parisian painter Robert Delaunay (1885–1941), which culminated in 1915 in abstraction. In an early version of his *Fenêtre,* or *Window,* series (Fig. 584), Delaunay gives us a view from an imaginary curtain-framed window overlooking Paris in the direction of the Eiffel Tower, which can be made out at the top. Delaunay loved the Eiffel Tower and the knowledge and skill that were required for its construction. Like Léger, Delaunay wanted to bring to painting the inquisitiveness and objectivity of the scientist. Although lacking the systematic and consistent method of the latter, he sought to inquire into the possibilities of light and color and the dissolving effects of their interaction upon solid forms as perceived by the eye. He was also conscious of Cubism's liberation from likeness in these years and the possibilities of constructing painterly compositions that diminished emphasis upon illusionism and that stressed the components of painting, notably its color and surfaceness. In his 1910 *Fenêtre* he superimposed a checkerboard pattern of color over parts of the composition in order to link what seemed distant with the surface plane and to activate the contrasts of color throughout. In a 1911 version of his *Fenêtre* (Pl. 88, p. 433), reference to a window and distance beyond has been eliminated, as have distinct buildings. What has been preserved are certain segmented curves that recall perhaps the profile of the Eiffel Tower. Color is laid down in large patches that softly vibrate in the viewer's eye. It is as if color were seen through a prism. Delaunay was moving in the direction of making color interaction the sole subject of his work. As with Matisse, but more removed from the world of objects, Delaunay wanted formal relationships to be the purpose of his art and the source of its enjoyment. Unlike the physicist, who relies on science for his color studies, Delaunay depended finally upon taste or aesthetic sensibility in the selection and juxtaposition of colors, which include reds, blues, and oranges. Drawing, shading, perspective, textures, and strong value contrasts of light and dark, the prerequisites of illusionism, were no longer the basis for his painting. He extended his color contrasts beyond the canvas onto the border of the painting itself, thus denying even to the picture frame its traditional enhancement of illusion. We tend to take the picture frame for granted, and for many people it is a surprise to see abstract painting lacking frames or simply bordered with thin strips of wood. The Impressionists were the first, in the early 1880s, to frame their paintings in simple white borders, thereby reinforcing the intensity of their colors. Seurat painted inner frames with colors that were the complementaries of those in adjacent areas of the canvas to ensure the brilliance of the latter. The traditional black frame of the Dutch or the elaborate carved gold frames of the past, familiar in every museum, had been thought not only to establish the worth of the painting and dignify it but also to enforce its illusionism or window character. The death of illusionism in modern art was also the demise of the elaborate picture frame as the setting for the new painting. The absence of the frame emphasizes the nonprecious character of the art, adds to its concreteness as an object, and asserts that it is by the hand of the artist.

**More than Four Sides to the Square** Until abstraction evolved in the 20th century, shapes such as triangles, circles, and squares had a long history of symbolizing concepts and values. All three of these shapes, for example, have represented God. The Roman philosopher Philo compared God to an infinite circle whose center was everywhere and whose perimeter nowhere. The Chinese spoke of infinity as a square without angles. The circle has stood for eternity, resurrection, the earth and Heaven, the ideal city, perfection, and so on. Pythagoras referred to the triangle as symbolizing human knowledge. In Christianity the shape has stood for the Trinity, and it has signified hieratic social systems. Walt Whitman extolled God in his poem "Chanting the Square Deific." Egyptian priests symbolized man as a square. In a drawing reproduced as Figure 585, Leonardo da Vinci used a square and circle to illustrate how these shapes could contain a perfectly proportioned figure. Squares have been associated with talismans against plague, mystical architectural ground plans, games, and puzzles. The square has variously symbolized the four seasons, the elements, the points of the compass, the earth, and the sun. Our language has many idioms that utilize shapes like the square as metaphors to denote variously a social conservative, honesty, true relationships, or the straightening of accounts. Behind the symbolism of the square in history and in current vernacular language is the fact that its meanings had a public currency. None of the past public associations with the square, including those of the geometer, have been drawn upon by abstract artists, despite the fact that they intended their art to move the viewer with sympathy. Beginning in 1913, when the shape first appeared in modern art, each artist, like Walt Whitman, has found by reason, feeling, or intuition his own values in the square. The physical appearance of the square—its size, means of delineation and relative distinctiveness, color, weight, texture, disposition within the field of the painting, and relation to other shapes or the canvas edges—while unimportant to a geometer or to its previous symbolic effectiveness, has been paramount for many painters. Artists have given a changing face to the square similar to the change seen in the rendering of Christ through the history of art. The shape has been made a personal extension of the artist, so that we would not confuse a square by Mondrian (Fig. 594) with one by Rothko (Pl. 91, p. 436). In another sense, being closed or bounded by an edge, a square belongs to the broad class of objects. Its theme and variation in modern art are like those of the bottle, glass, or apple in the history of still-life painting. As with these objects, when set into the personal history and intentions of the artist, the square acquires new dimensions of meaning, but unlike previous meanings of objects, those for the square are often not discursive or verbal.

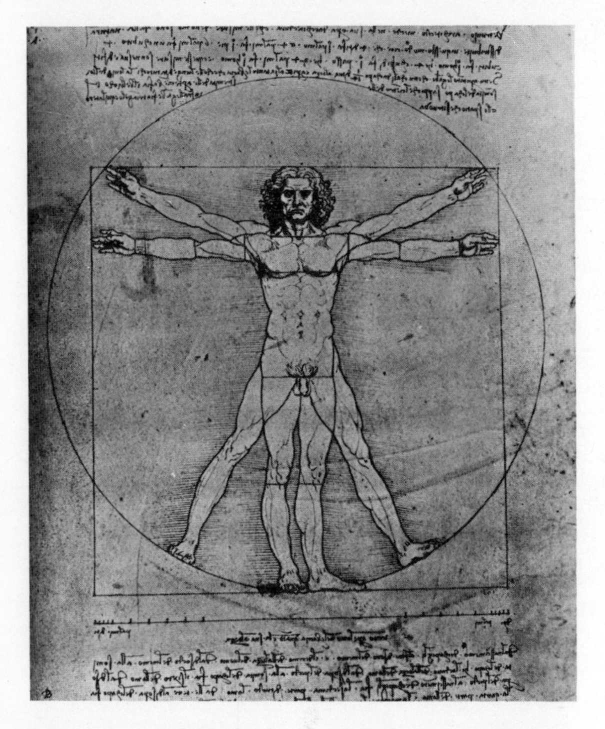

585. Leonardo da Vinci. *Study of Human Proportions According to Vitruvius.* c. 1485–90. Pen and ink, $13^1/_2 \times 9^3/_4$″. Accademia, Venice.

**The Life of the Square** The entrance of the square into modern art coincides with political upheaval and revolution in Europe. Naturalism and many pre-1914 avant-garde movements such as Cubism and Futurism came to be viewed in the eyes of political and artistic revolutionaries as the products of social systems responsible for the tragic catastrophe of World War I. In Russia, Holland, Switzerland, and Germany during and after the war abstraction took hold, and artists linked their efforts with the emergence of new social and political systems. Individuality was viewed by these revolutionaries as inimical to a new society founded upon collective cooperation among all men and upon maximum utilization of the new technology. In view of present-day Soviet Communism's criticism of abstract art and its insistence upon a socially conscious naturalism in painting and sculpture, it is hard for us to imagine that during and immediately after the Russian Revolution abstraction was looked upon as the true expression of the new Communist society. But by 1920 there were in fact more museums of modern art and abstract artists in Russia than in any other country. Kandinsky (Pl. 56, p. 310; Fig. 443) was the first of the Russian abstract artists. The second was Kazimir Malevich (1878–1935), who in 1913 began a series of pencil drawings that departed from his paintings of peasants and Cubist assemblages. One drawing in his abstract series was of a pair of black squares meticulously placed within the white of the paper (Fig. 586). In essays begun in 1915 and published in 1927, *The Non-Objective World,* Malevich reconstructed the circumstances in which he created an art of pure feeling, the feeling of "objectlessness":

When in the year 1913, in my desperate attempt to free art from the ballast of objectivity, I took refuge in the square form and exhibited a picture which consisted of nothing more than a black square on a white field, the critics and, along with them, the public sighed, "Everything which we loved is lost. We are in a desert. . . . Before us is nothing but a black square on a white background!" But this desert is filled with the spirit of non-objective sensation which pervades everything. Even I was gripped by a kind of timidity bordering on fear when it came to leaving "the world of will and idea," in which I had lived and worked, in the reality of which I believed. But a blissful sense of liberating non-objectivity drew me forth into the "desert" where nothing is real except feeling . . . and so feeling became the substance of my life. This was no "empty square" which I had exhibited but rather the feeling of non-objectivity. . . . The black square on the white field was the first form in which non-objective feeling came to be expressed. The square = feeling, the white field = the void beyond this feeling.

The moving life experiences that Malevich was referring to, in which we do not encounter objects and seem to confront infinity, include those on the sea, the desert, and in the air. Malevich wanted a mystical art that captured feeling induced by the absence of objects and what lay beyond sight. It was an art that did not imitate the appearance of nature, but that resulted from the inventiveness of the human mind: "Is it not my brain which is the true factory, from which the new iron-transformed world runs. . . . I wish to be the maker of the new signs of my inner movements. . . . I do not wish to copy and spoil the movement of an object and other varieties and forms of nature." In 1918 he did a painting which brought, it would seem, millenniums of art to a conclusion or dead end. In his *Suprematist Composition: White on White* (Fig. 587), a white square is seen against or within a white background. The artist wrote, "The blue color of clouds is overcome in the Suprematist system, ruptured and enters white as the true, real representation of infinity, and is therefore freed from the coloured background of the sky." This painting is historically the first one-color conception, achieving its only contrast, tension, or drama by the acute angle at which the inner square is set in relation to its field, as opposed to its symmetrical disposition in the 1913 drawing. Malevich gave up painting for a number of years after this work, and when he returned to it his style was no longer abstract. The power of the Russian army and desire of political leaders such as Stalin to placate this force brought an end to Communist support of abstraction such as that of Malevich. Ironically, present-day Communist art has taken its basic stylistic character from styles that were evolved during the 19th century in cultures condemned by institutional Communism as ideologically, economically, and socially decadent.

*left:* 586. KAZIMIR MALEVICH. *Suprematist Elements: Two Squares.* 1913. Pencil; ruled margins $6\frac{3}{4} \times 11\frac{1}{4}''$, sheet $9\frac{3}{4} \times 14\frac{1}{2}''$. Museum of Modern Art, New York.

*below:* 587. KAZIMIR MALEVICH. *Suprematist Composition: White on White.* c. 1918. Oil on canvas, $31\frac{1}{4}''$ square. Museum of Modern Art, New York.

In 1917, a small group of avant-garde artists led by Theo van Doesburg (1883–1931) and Piet Mondrian formed a movement in Holland called *De Stijl* ("The Style"). Similar to Malevich's Suprematist movement in Russia, De Stijl was intended as a positive, utopian alternative to previous artistic and social systems. Naturalism and individuality were to be sacrificed for the spiritual and artistic rehabilitation of art and society, and a new universal language of art, design, architecture, and poetry was to be formed. In addition to the publications of De Stijl, Van Doesburg toured Europe giving lectures on the aims of this art, using as illustration his aesthetic transformations of a cow (Figs. 588–592). The paintings of both Van Doesburg and Mondrian can here serve as a means of visualizing the aims of De Stijl. Sentiment or subjectivity and subject matter were to be eliminated. The curve signified the former, the cow the latter. The style of De Stijl meant rhythmical relationships of rectilinear conjunctions of lines and primary-colored rectangles seen against white. The task set by these artists was to make visible what they felt were the laws of nature. "The living beauty of nature cannot be copied: it can

588–592. THEO VAN DOESBURG. *left: The Cow.* Three studies from a series of eight drawings. Undated. *below right: Composition (The Cow).* 1916. Gouache, $15^5/_8 \times 23^3/_4$". *bottom right: Composition (The Cow).* 1916–17. Oil on canvas, $14^3/_4 \times 25$". All, Museum of Modern Art, New York (purchase).

only be expressed," wrote Mondrian (Figs. 441, 442). The reasoned structure of things, not their appearance, led the two artists to straight lines joining at right angles. To them, the right angle was the perfect objective expression of dynamic relationships in nature and the rectangle the resolution of all tensions.

Primary colors plus white and straight black lines were the necessary elementary means of expressing a content that the De Stijl artists felt had to be universal. Van Doesburg and Mondrian sought to "set the world right according to pure aesthetical principles with the aid of . . . discords and . . . consonants of color and form. . . . By being aesthetically affected by a purely visual work of art, the contemplator immediately sets himself right" [Van Doesburg, 1918]. Painting such as Van Doesburg's and Mondrian's was intended to present the public with a vision of true harmony and beauty otherwise unavailable to them, thereby bringing spiritual peace. It was performing a function analogous to that of De Hooch and 17th-century Dutch painters.

To the reader wondering about the subject matter in the transformations of the cow, Van Doesburg stated: "The modern work of art indeed lacks subject matter. But it does not lack a subject. This subject is of a pictorial nature, it is aesthetical balance, unity, harmony in a higher sense."

Van Doesburg characterized his work as "peripheric composition." This we can see in the later version of the cow.

> In the course of time the symmetrical composition (Christ, Mary, Cross, Guitar, Bottle, etc.) has "pressed" itself more and more towards the center . . . to such a degree, that the composition is entirely pivot-shaped and the periphery of the canvas remains blank and therefore gives an impression of emptiness. . . . Very important is the essential renewal of the method of composition. Gradual abolition of the center and all passive emptiness. The composition develops itself . . . instead of towards the center, towards the extreme periphery of the canvas, it even appears . . . to continue beyond it. . . .

By its pictorial transformations the cow lost its specific identity, but De Stijl artists argued that it thus became part of the universal form of nature. While the philosophy of De Stijl was not always shared by artists influenced by the movement, its emphasis upon the total expressive design of the painting and devaluation of a previously climactic area, such as the center, was of enormous consequence.

So strongly did Mondrian believe in the purity and rightness of the right angle as an expression of the individual's relation to the universe that when Van Doesburg introduced a diagonal into his art around 1925, the two men broke their friendship; Van Doesburg felt that the diagonal was a dynamic symbol, but Mondrian contended that it was a neutral form. Mondrian was the most imaginative and gifted artist of the De Stijl group, and he found innumerable ways to vary his compositions without compromising his basic beliefs. For

593. PIET MONDRIAN. *Composition with Blue*. 1926. Oil on canvas, 23½" square. Philadelphia Museum of Art (A. E. Gallatin Collection).

example, rather than introduce a diagonal into the field of his composition, he turned the painting 45 degrees so that its four sides made a diamond shape within which his lines remained vertical and horizontal in relation to the viewer. In his *Composition with Blue* (Fig. 593), with but two straight lines he created four shapes (three white and one blue) having at least one right angle but varying in scale and length of sides. Mondrian demonstrated how much could be achieved with so little, and his considerable influence on American painting since 1945 has derived from the belief that "less is more." His art has an elegance determined by the high ratio of output to input, or minimum means achieving maximum contrast.

Mondrian had also been an important pioneer in what is referred to as *relational painting*. His last completed work, *Broadway Boogie Woogie* (Fig. 594), depends upon our seeing and sensing the rightness of its relationships of color and the proportions of these colored areas to each other. Despite its impersonal appearance, the making of paintings such as this involved not mathematical calculations but endless hours of trial in which Mondrian judged each effect visually and intellectually. Although his art has the look and "feel" of geometry, its origin is based upon a balance of thought and intuition, and execution by hand, not by machine.

*Broadway Boogie Woogie* gave form to Mondrian's love of American music and the rhythms of New York, where he spent the last years of his life. The entire composition is made up of elementary units, variations upon a rectangle, orchestrated to achieve a maximum of richness and variety. Set against a white ground, the colors are pure tones of red, yellow, grey, and black. There is precision but also unpredictability in Mondrian's structural analogue of jazz, with its discipline and improvisation. His intentions were set forth in writing: "The art of the past established rhythm . . . veiled by subject matter and particular forms. . . . In our time, rhythm is more and more accentuated, not only in art, but in mechanized reality and in the whole life." The feel and visual concept of music were important to Mondrian, not the imaging of musicians, instruments, and dancers. Privately he admired the city's youth and the sensual manifestations of the city's vitality. His writings show that he conceived of the city as the basis for a new style:

> The genuinely modern artist sees the metropolis as abstract living converted into form: it is nearer to him than nature. . . . In the metropolis the natural has already been stiffened up, ordered by the human spirit. The proportion and the rhythm of patch and line in architecture will speak a more direct language to him than the capriciousness of nature. In the metropolis beauty expresses itself more mathematically.

The square and squared compositional armature appealed to many artists in the early days of abstraction as one of the first and most fruitful alternatives to representational art while conveying mystical, emotional, or philosophical associations. Unlike Klee's small paintings, which deal with the minute, and his inductive construction built upon individual elements (Pl. 55, p. 310; Fig. 575), Matisse's art often embraces a large scale, even when it alludes to a subject that is minute. In *The Snail* (Pl. 89, p. 434), one of his most abstract paintings, done a year before his death, Matisse assembled, cut, and pasted paper on a scale 9 × 9′. Allusion to the snail is restricted to the roughly spiral placement of diversely shaped rectangles. Paradoxically, none of the curving structure of the snail's shell is literally referred to. Not satisfied with commercial colored papers, Matisse mixed his own colors, painted sheets of paper, and then cut out his shapes with scissors. The colors are bright shades of red, blue, orange, green, and lavender, with the white of the paper showing through in large areas. His early development of self-luminosity of color, or color light, continues. He varied the transparency or density of his colors, but neutralized their surfaces with respect to texture and brush mark to facilitate the viewer's absorption of the whole. The fresh, cheerful combination of colors comes from a lifetime of taste and disciplined control of drawing and composing, as well as a conviction that colors should be decorative and "have also the inherent power of affecting the feelings of those who look at them. . . . A blue, for instance, accompanied by the shimmer of its complementaries, acts upon the inner sensibility like the sudden stroke of a gong. The same with red and yellow; the artist must be able to strike them when he needs to." Working in cut-out papers originated from Matisse's desire to get a quick idea of certain effects in planning large compositions. Illness, which limited the use of his hands, also led him to this medium. That this way of working still preserved his cherished values of draftsmanship and of realizing a work entirely in terms of color is supported by his statement: "Cutting colored papers permits me to draw in the color. For me it is a matter of simplification. Instead of establishing a contour, and then filling it with color—the one modifying the other—I draw directly in color. . . . This guarantees a precise union of the two processes; they become one."

All that Matisse and European art stood for were alien to the American painter Franz Kline (1910–62). Matisse never countenanced consistent abstraction, claiming that he always began with an object and moved toward the abstract. He wanted his color, shapes, and compositions to be referred to the world of objects and people. Kline's big black-and-white paintings of the early 1950s allude to nothing, and they have a rawness and tough strength remote from the grace, finesse, and ingratiating character of Matisse's work. The traces of Kline's creative gestures are explicit and emphatic. With a housepainter's brush he enlarged small sketches onto big sur-

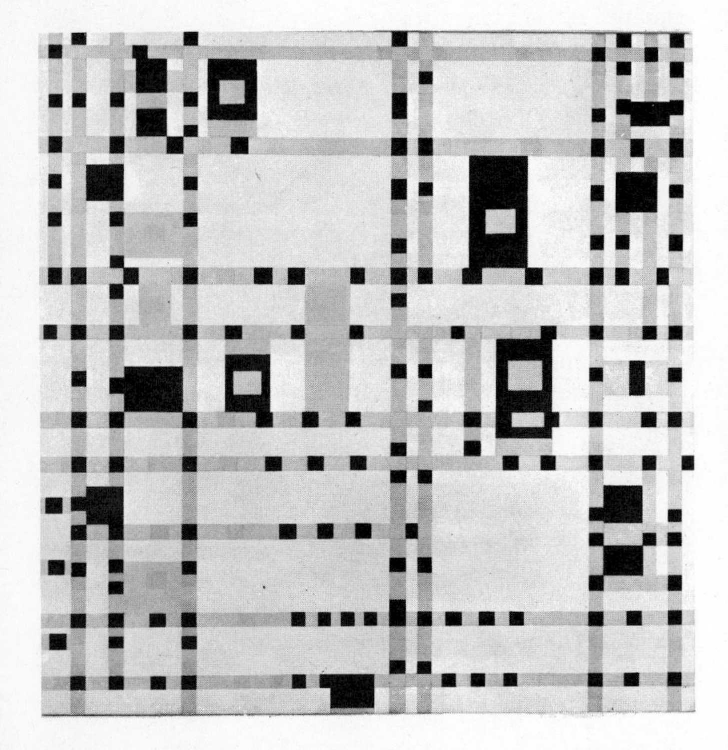

*left:* 594. PIET MONDRIAN. *Broadway Boogie Woogie*. 1942–43. Oil on canvas, 4′2″ square. Museum of Modern Art, New York.

*left:* Plate 92. JOSEF ALBERS. *Homage to the Square 'Curious.'* 1963. Oil on canvas, 30″ square. Collection R. Alistair McAlpine, London. (See p. 448.)

*below:* Plate 93. RICHARD ANUSZKIEWICZ. *Injured by Green.* 1963. Liquitex on board, 36″ square. Collection Mrs. Janet S. Fleisher, Elkins Park, Pa. (See p. 450.)

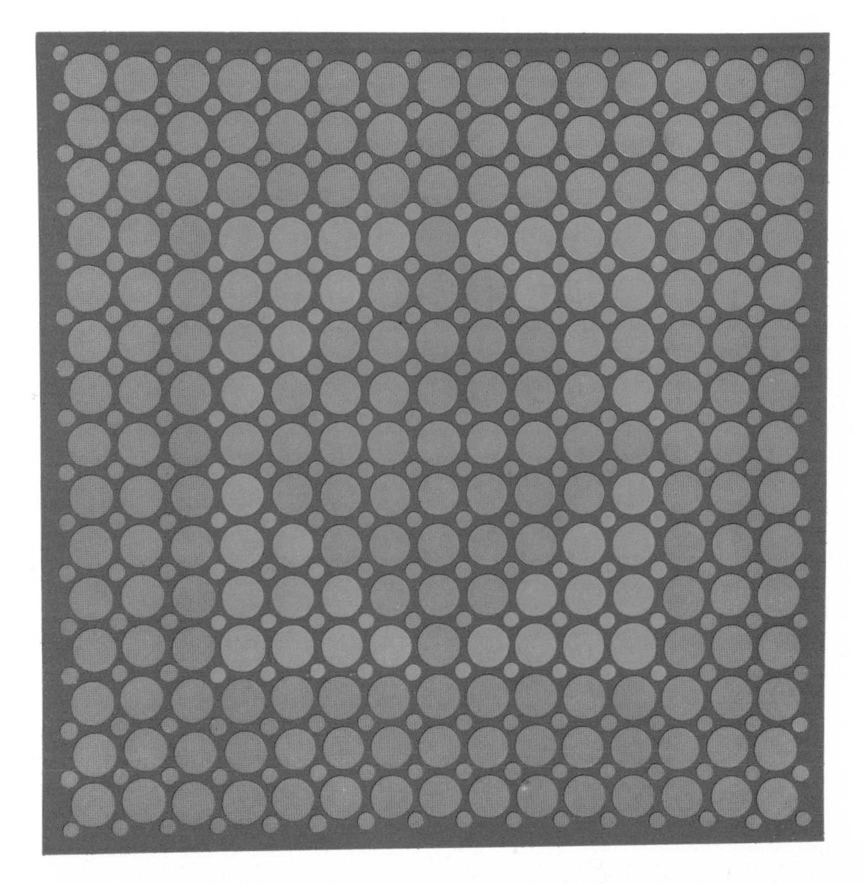

*below:* Plate 94. FRANK STELLA. *Port Tampa City*. 1962. Acrylic on canvas, 12′ square. Collection J. Frederic Byers, III, New York. (See p. 451.)

*above right:* Plate 95. DAVID SMITH. *Cubi XXVII*. 1965. Steel, height $9^{5}/_{8}''$. Solom R. Guggenheim Museum, New York. (See p. 452.)

*below:* Plate 96. DAN FLAVIN. *Untitled (to S. M.)*. 1969. Fluorescent light, corrid 9′6″ × 8′ × 64′. Shown installed for an exhibition at the National Gallery Canada, Ottawa. (See p. 454.)

faces, preserving or enhancing the tensions and competition of his blacks and whites, a renunciation of colors rare in European painting. Confident of his capacity to constantly create new configurations, Kline refused to draw upon a repertory of shapes. The square seen in *Painting Number 7* (Fig. 595) is unusual in his work. But his square has qualities we have not seen before. It is formed as if by pressures from within and without, and the white and black seem to eat into one another around the edges. The white is as important as the black, for Kline believed that the two should be seen and felt simultaneously. Absent in Kline's painterly gestures are the clean joining of the corners and the trued or faired edges of Mondrian's and Malevich's squares, as well as the sharp scissor cut of Matisse's cutouts. Kline's visual drama lies in blatant contrasts and the taut suspension of shapes against the edges of the painting.

For many years Kline was a representational painter committed to painting the specific characteristics of a given place. When he turned to abstraction in 1950 it was to free his art from description in favor of expressing strong feelings that resulted from a variety of visual experiences. Abstract painting became for Kline a more direct expression of what he felt was emotionally true. Kline's was arm painting, not the wrist painting of European art. To achieve the big black swaths across his canvas meant working with sweeping motions that involved the entire body. Analogies with oriental calligraphy have been made, but they are deceptive, for Kline's pictorial writing is his own, not imitated, and not intended to be deciphered.

Since the late 1940s one of the most significant developments in painting in the United States has been emphasis on the effects of color, surface, and scale. This focus has led to large-scale paintings in which one, two, or three colors spread out and occupy most if not all of the surface. While brush stroke is unobtrusive, it can be employed to create subtle directions. Usually, no attempt is made to call attention to textures or the physical substance of the medium, and there is no insistence upon arranging a number of different shapes. Color in the work of Barnett Newman (1905–70) and Mark Rothko (1903–70) occupies areas that roughly accord with the rectangular shape of the canvas. Scale is crucial to the painting's effect and is in large part a coefficient of the color chosen. In the past the scale of a painting might have been determined by a wall, subject, or conventions of public exhibitions and commerce. Newman, Rothko, and others, however, judged scale in relation to themselves—standing in front of the painting as it evolved. Newman's paintings often have a vertical or horizontal interval, a pause or tension, depending upon the individual painting, between rectangular areas of a single color (Pl. 90, p. 435). Geometry was not even thought of as governing the shape of the color area. According to Newman: "It is precisely this death image, the grip of geometry, that has to be confronted. . . . Unless we face up to it and discover a new

595. Franz Kline. *Painting Number 7*. 1952. Oil on canvas, 4′9½″ × 6′9¾″. Solomon R. Guggenheim Museum, New York.

image based on new principles, there is no hope of freedom. . . ." In his final painting, Newman worked out its size, measure between intervals, and the location of these intervals as he painted over the surface, responding to the energy of the color with which he worked and to his personal associations with it. While it is tempting to think of his large paintings as decorative, they are not intended as background music nor to be seen out of the corner of one's eye. Their scale, intensity, and phrasing can compel attention in those who will let the painting work on them. For Newman, color by itself as well as completed paintings convey strong feelings that have to do with earthly and sublime experiences. "The rich tones of orange to the lowest octave of dark brown," Newman wrote, can express "the majestic strength of our ties with the earth." He chose Biblical titles—*Adam* and *Genesis*—as well as heroic ones—*Ulysses* and *Prometheus*. They were not illustrative in the sense of older art but, rather, the artist's own associations with his paintings. With remarkable terseness Newman explained: "An artist paints so that he will have something to look at." More specifically, he saw the rectangle as "a living thing, a vehicle for an abstract thought-complex, a carrier of awesome feelings."

Mark Rothko's painting can be characterized as silent and almost immobile, and it might be described as art based on color sensation. Color and scale are the two basic ingredients of such canvases as *Tan and Black on Red* (Pl. 91, p. 436). The large size of Rothko's surfaces is necessary to the power of his color sensations. Used in a smaller area, tan, black, and red do not evoke the same emotional responses as they do on the large scale that Rothko employed. The great size allows the beholder to become absorbed in the painting. Rothko, like Newman, was not as dispassionate or liberal in selecting his colors as is Josef Albers (Pl. 92, p. 445). Rothko took over a color and made it his own, after the color proved right for his feeling. Rothko's paintings as a group seem less like color demonstrations or exercises than those of Albers, and they attain greater gravity. There are no allusive elements in the painting, only soft, vaporous-edged, rectangular patches hovering against and in front of one another. Color is unconstrained by drawn or hard boundaries; it breathes and finds its own shape. Often the colors are so close in value as to make their reproduction in black and white meaningless. Rothko soaked or stained the canvas in addition to brushing on the color, so that the final effect is not opaque color lying *upon* a surface, but rather the indefinite suspension of absorbent color. For Rothko, color was form and content, the sole carrier of his idea, which varied from painting to painting and which, to oversimplify, may be described as a mood, perhaps, of tragedy, exhilaration, or withdrawal. In the painter's words, he wanted "the elimination of all obstacles between the painter and the ideas, and between the idea and the observer." Objects, forms, marks of the artist's hand would be "obstacles." The variety and drama in Rothko's art comes from the way large color areas interact, so that, for example, redness and blackness induce anguish without being translated into a specific situation.

With much of modern painting, we can be assured of the artist's sincerity. The burden of sincerity often rests with the beholder and the way he chooses to receive the painting. There is an ethic to viewing a painting as well as to making it, and the observer must adapt himself to the new experiences this art affords. Like the artist, the viewer must also be open and adventurous; he must make decisions and take risks. Rothko expressed his feelings about the life of a painting: "A picture lives by companionship, expanding and quickening in the eyes of the sensitive observer. It dies by the same token." Thus, the paintings illustrated in this chapter require that the viewer achieve a communion with what is directly given to the eye.

When painters such as Newman, Rothko, and Ad Reinhardt (1913–67) have talked or written about their work, much of what they say concerns what their painting is not. This is to offset misinterpretation, but it also reflects how much of the history of art they have rejected in their work and how strongly and uncompromisingly they paint for themselves. Reinhardt epitomized the exclusivist or purist view, and he approached invisible painting: "The one thing to say about art is that it is one thing. Art is art-as-art and everything else is everything else." His is the best description of what he has done and not done:

> A clearly defined object, independent and separate from all other objects and circumstances, in which we cannot see whatever we choose or make of it anything we want, whose meaning is not detachable or translatable, where nothing can be added and nothing can be taken away. A free, unmanipulated and unmanipulatable, useless, unmarketable, irreducible, unphotographable, unreproducible, inexplicable icon. A non-entertainment, not for art-commerce or mass-art-publics, non-expressionist, not for oneself.

The difficulties of reproducing Reinhardt's *Abstract Painting* (Fig. 596) are apparent and derive from the fact it is all black; for this reason the artist himself discouraged its reproduction. When we read his statement of 1961 we are reminded of Zola's comment about Manet—looking at Reinhardt's painting with sympathy demands forgetting a thousand things about art. Like all of the artists in this last section, Reinhardt wanted the viewer to look *at*, not into, his painting.

> A square (neutral, shapeless) canvas, five feet wide, five feet high, as high as a man, as wide as a man's outstretched arms (not large, not small, sizeless) trisected (no composition), one horizontal form negating one vertical form (formless, no top, no bottom, directionless), three (more or less) dark (lightless) non-contrasting (colorless) colors, brushwork brushed out to remove brushwork, a man, flat, free hand painted surface (glossless, textureless, non-linear, no hard edge, no soft edge) which

*left:* 596. AD REINHARDT. *Abstract Painting*. 1960–61. Oil on canvas, 5′ square. Museum of Modern Art, New York (purchase).

does not reflect its surroundings—a pure, abstract, non-objective timeless, spaceless, changeless, relationless, disinterested painting—an object that is self-conscious (no consciousness) ideal, transcendant, aware of no thing but Art (absolutely no anti-art) [1961].

Unlike Malevich, Reinhardt did not give up painting, but after his own logic he continued to paint essentially the same black painting until he died. One of the jokes of the New York art world in the 1960s was that, with regard to painting, "Rothko pulled down the shades, Newman closed the doors, and Reinhardt turned out the light."

Long before the 20th century, painters such as Poussin (Pl. 53, p. 309) and Delacroix (Pl. 43, p. 285; Fig. 407) wrote and dreamed of an art whose sole purpose would be to delight the eye. Their painting, however, was always connected with literature and with ideas. It was not until this century, with art such as that of Matisse, that their vision of art was realized. Mondrian's relational painting was directed toward sensitive viewers whose aesthetic reaction to his work would bring them inner peace. The German-born artist Josef Albers (b. 1888), who taught at the Bauhaus with Klee and Kandinsky and who for many years has been an influential teacher at Yale University, fell in love with color and has devoted his life to its study. He has not established a system or rules in his teaching, but rather has encouraged serious students of art to study color, to learn its many properties and inexhaustible combinations. For more than fifteen years, in his series of over one hundred paintings called *Homage to the Square* (Pl. 92, p. 445), Albers has in a sense painted the same picture. He has found an ideal reproducible format by which to show endless color relationships. The paintings are approximately the same size, and the basic format is a series of concentric squares (which include the paintings's four edges) with the smallest and innermost square being generally located toward the bottom of the canvas. These squares have a common central axis, but they vary in proportion and size. The greatest variation in Albers' series is seen in his use of color. For him any combination of colors is possible. His preferred format allows him to make "colors do something they don't do by themselves" and to study the various properties of colors displayed when they interact and depend upon each other. Painting such as this allows us to see color in ways other than it appears in advertisements, for example, where the color is subordinate to the commercial message. Albers has written: "In visual perception a color is almost never seen as it really is—as it physically is. This fact makes color the most relative medium in art." Like the Impressionists and Seurat (Pl. 48, p. 297), Albers is aware that certain colors produce afterimages, or complementaries of their own color, so that to stare at violet and then to look upon white will suggest yellow to the viewer. In composing his color chords Albers takes this property along with many others into account. He seeks to demonstrate that there is no "ugly" color, and that it is possible for our normal prejudices against certain hues to be dissolved within the context of his use of colors.

**Perceptual Abstraction : Op Art** The basic premise of Perceptual Abstraction or *Op Art* is that it does not induce associations with the visual world or symbolize ideas independent of the painting itself. The artists' concern is with the way the eye and mind respond to certain visual phenomena achievable in art. The paintings are generally characterized by a tight uniform network, often symmetrical, of small and/or repeated units. There are usually no climactic shapes, single focus, or significant variations in the scale of shapes that permit us to isolate them with ease, as in Matisse's art. This is not painting that soothes; rather, it attacks the eye and the mind. Its effects depend upon induced or after images and our tendency to fuse what is separate. Instead of being depicted by the artist, movement occurs in the eye and mind of the viewer.

Much of Perceptual Abstraction has evolved from studies in optics, psychology, and design, thereby reuniting art and science. It should be remembered that Renaissance perspective and body imagery came from discoveries of Florentine mathematicians and from anatomical study, and that for centuries artists have taken ideas from a wide variety of sources both inside and outside the world of art.

The square has been a frequently used motif by Perceptual Abstractionists because it lends itself to repetition and coordination with the axes of the painting surface. In a composition known as *Straight Curve* (Fig. 597), the British artist Bridget Riley (b. 1931) worked from a single unit that she found susceptible to serial repetition. (It is of interest to note that this artist employs technicians to finish her works.) The unit used is a rectangle subdivided into two equal black-and-white triangles. The artist kept constant the subdivision as well as the four straight sides of the rectangle, but she varied the proportion of the height and width of the rectangles. In each vertical or horizontal stratum uniformity of these units is avoided. What created the illusion of curving lines, where there is not a single curved line in the entire composition, is the changing of proportions from one layer to the next. Unlike Mondrian's *Broadway Boogie Woogie* (Fig. 594), so densely grouped are the rectangles in *Straight Curve* that it is difficult to isolate them, and we are forced to look upon them in larger areas, which causes the shapes to seem blurred. Riley has varied different zones to give the composition a pulse or change of pace. This variation also helps to create the impression of lines curving back and forth in depth. To look at *Straight Curve* for a long time or to look at it at different times is to induce different responses in terms of the direction and character of movement. Our eyes are forced to move over the painting's surface because it is impossible to take in the whole all at once. To preserve the purity of the illusions created in the eye rather than by the painter on her surface, as in illusionistic art, texture and evidence of drawing have been eliminated. Another characteristic is the lack of distinction between the square and the background. The basic motif occupies the whole of the surface.

One reason that it is difficult to look at a Perceptual Abstraction painting for the first time is that colors having a maximum intensity are used repetitively. In his *Injured by Green* (Pl. 93, p. 445) Richard Anuszkiewicz (b. 1930), a former student of Albers, restricted his colors to red, green, and blue, with the last two consistently applied in circles seen against a uniform red background. Anuszkiewicz is aware that the eye tends to blend separate colors when they are seen simultaneously. The result is a compromise color: thus the same red appears different when seen against green and blue circles. The eye also tends to alter focal lengths when it is exposed to red, blue, and green. Without one straight line, the artist created the illusion of three squares, with the innermost green one appearing to be set at a 45-degree angle to the others. He thus achieved the suggestion of a shape by its antithesis:

> My work is of an experimental nature and has centered on an investigation into the effects of complementary colors of full intensity when juxtaposed and the optical changes that occur as a result. Also, a study of the dynamic effect of the whole under changing conditions of light, and the effect of light on the color.

The light effects that Anuszkiewicz refers to are those of the room in which his paintings hang, not simulated light in the painting itself, a characteristic of illusionistic painting. As the light becomes brighter or darker on the painting, the various interrelationships of the colors and of the suggested squares change.

Historically, Seurat is the pioneer whose lead Riley and Anuszkiewicz have followed. Seurat's systematic studies of color with respect to achieving the greatest intensity by placing complementary colors adjacent to each other, as well as his reliance upon systematic study of optical phenomena, make *Injured by Green* a descendant of *La Grande Jatte* (Pl. 48, p. 297). *La Grande Jatte,* in turn, depends upon the work of Impressionists such as Monet, who brought a new brilliance to painting, the equivalent of sunlight and flicker, by the use of small areas of pure colors. And Monet and the Impressionists had been influenced by Delacroix, among others, who was convinced of the emotive power of strong pure color. Delacroix in turn learned much from Rubens. We could keep tracing influences in this way back through the Renaissance, the Middle Ages, and into antiquity, with side excursions into Near Eastern and Far Eastern art. This is art history, and while Anuszkiewicz' *Injured by Green* may not look like any painting before it, it presupposes the history of art. Art is more than selection, it is also rejection, and all abstract painters made decisions, historical as well as personal, when they decided not to paint in a certain way.

*opposite:* 597. BRIDGET RILEY. *Straight Curve*. 1963. Emulsion on board, 28 × 24½″. Collection Victor Musgrove.

*right:* 598. FRANK STELLA. *Ileana Sonnabend*. 1963. Oil on canvas, 7′5″ × 10′7″. Courtesy Leo Castelli Gallery, New York.

**Uncomplicating Painting** Frank Stella's shaped canvases and one-color, symmetrical compositions, such as *Port Tampa City* (Pl. 94, p. 446), made him one of the most daring, controversial, and influential painters of the 1960s. To create an alternative to the painting of Rothko, Newman, Kline, and De Kooning, which dominated the interest of younger artists in the 1950s, Stella discarded the hallowed idea of painting as warfare—as an emotional struggle in which the artist constantly courted the risk of failure so as to bring into being a new image each time he confronted the canvas. Stella made peace with art by letting the shapes of his canvases dictate their internal design. For rhythm and contrast, he allowed the raw canvas to show through the colored bands laid on with flat, monochrome commercial paints. As in Perceptual Abstraction, the artist made no show of drawing with the brush and exhibited no interest in relational color. In *Ileana Sonnabend* (Fig. 598), named for a noted New York-Paris art dealer who supports certain young artists, Stella has made what looks like a rhomboidal picture frame. Whereas illusionistic painting simulated the enclosure of space, this work literally frames space. Imperceptible in reproduction is the reflecting action of the metallic paint and the delicately inconstant interval between the stripes.

Stella sought and gained *uncomplicated* painting. He was not interested in the earlier "geometries" of European and American painting, which he called "dreary." As arrogantly as he defied the convention of the rectangular canvas, so Stella confounded the art world by embracing symmetry, which had been equated in art with all that was dull and unimaginative. He wanted "the force of symmetry," and the center of his image became the center of his canvas. There was no honoring of the traditional balance of unlike elements—Stella was not "trying to jockey everything around." His "schemes" or images were tied to his consciousness of the flat surface to be painted and to the purity of his commercial colors while still in the can. He wanted to preserve the primary integrity of both the ground and the medium. There is no fussiness about the way the artist set down his schemes, no dazzling us with painterly handwriting. Stella still believes that once an artist has broken with traditions, he cannot go back. He uses deep stretches to hold his paintings well off from the wall, a device that he felt would also serve to emphasize the surface of the paintings, therefore their nature as painting. Unlike Rothko, Stella does not extend the painting around the edges. He wants us to see the whole idea without any confusion—a pleasurable visual sensation: "What you see is what you see." His model of effective simplicity is a major-league baseball player like Henry Aron hitting the ball out of the park. Stella continues the inquiry of earlier 20th-century artists into the minimum conditions necessary for making a successful picture. For some, this pursuit has only the historical value of demonstration, or it suggests the artist painting himself into a corner. But there is no evidence that his principle has been explored to the fullest. Certain young painters like Stella still find many untapped possibilities in radical simplicity. On the other hand, some artists feel that painting has run its course, that the options have been exhausted, and that now the development must be toward sculpture or toward entirely new forms of expression.

**Sculpture and the Art of Simple Forms** During the decade of the 1960s in the United States and England, a number of sculptors brought a new authority, intelligence, and sensibility to abstract sculpture. The artists in this last section share in common a preference for simple forms and uncomplicated structures, such as the cube. Like their counterparts in painting, who made the square the principal unit of their expression, the new sculptors have invested the simple cubic form with their artistic ideals, respective personalities, and vision. Their common cause has been a literal, formalistic art, devoid of symbol or metaphor, that forces the beholder to attend to such given physical characteristics as overall shape, scale, and proportion; axes and edges; surface; and occasionally depth. With the single exception of David Smith, these sculptors did not employ artificial bases, an omission comparable to the dismissal of frames in abstract painting. They preferred to posit their sculptures directly on the earth or floor, to bring their sculpture down to earth in a figurative and literal sense. The removal of the base helped separate these sculptures from illusionistic, heroic public art of the past, while reinforcing their concreteness as objects and as the personal conception of the artist. As with abstract painting, abstract sculpture teaches us that non-imitative signs, such as those enumerated above, can be carriers of form and expression.

In the minds of many young American sculptors, David Smith is still a heroic figure who, more than any sculptor to develop in the United States, successfully established, in his own words, "the full right for the function of pure esthetics." In the late fifties and sixties, Smith had moved away from explicitly metaphorical sculpture such as *Hudson River Landscape* (Fig. 447) into an art of simple shapes composed in purely formal relationships that were embued with his own belligerent vitality. *Cubi XXVII* (Pl. 95, p. 446), done shortly before he died in 1965, stands like a gateway, strong in stance, aggressively occupying and framing space. Its steel-jacketed Euclidian shapes rudely refuse axial alignment. Paradoxically, they still produce a simple overall form of seeming solidity. The precarious poise of the parts reflects Smith's life-long preoccupation with the structures in human and animal forms.

In common with friends of his generation, such as Kline and De Kooning, Smith did not completely prevision his sculptures. He preferred adjustments in the process of making, accommodating "intuitive accidents." The final form was decided upon only when the last shape had been fitted into place. Smith fought to avoid the predictable and the ingratiating by seeking "to push beauty to the very edge of rawness." Smith took pride in his personal toughness and shunned social polish, characteristics that could have been mirrored in his sculptures. Steel appealed to him for many reasons: ". . . its associations are primarily of this century. It is structure, movement, progress, suspension, cantilever, and at times destruction and brutality. . . its forms of geometry, planes, hard lines are all constant with my time." For exposure to the weather out of doors and reflection of colorful surroundings, steel was truly his best material. Its rough burnishing allowed both emphatic surface quality and depth, strong reflection and absorption of light that challenge the density and hardness of the steel. Above all, Smith wanted "a structure that can face the sun and hold its own."

Among the most important artists influenced by David Smith is the English sculptor Anthony Caro (b. 1924), whose conversion about 1960 from figural modeling to abstraction came after his contact with the American sculptor's work had convinced him of the rightness of abstraction. In *Homage to David Smith* (Fig. 559) Caro incorporated a reference to the door-window gate form of *Cubi XXVII* and also to Smith's use of industrial metals welded together in a deceptively improvisatory way. Caro's idiom distinguishes itself through the artist's disinterest in thick, closed, heavy shapes and through a lively concern with sculpture's "extent," its lateral movement in different directions along the ground. There is no center, no climactic focus in his art. It is not possible to take in all of his sculpture from any single viewpoint. Caro's small London studio does not permit the full erection of his works; they must be assembled outdoors in the mews where he works, which

*left:* 599. ANTHONY CARO. *Homage to David Smith.* 1966. Steel painted red, 4′6″ × 10′ × 5′4″. Collection Mrs. Mary Swift, Washington, D.C.

*opposite:* 600. ROBERT MORRIS. *Untitled.* 1966. Fiberglas, 3 × 3 × 2″. Collection Dwan Gallery, New York. Courtesy Leo Castelli Gallery, New York.

makes his own experience of the large pieces sequential. Whether initially conscious of it or not, Caro accepts the fact that it is impossible for a viewer to take in simultaneously all parts and their relationships in a large, complex work. He avoids making adjustments in a piece so as to facilitate instantaneous reading or simple scanning. This sort of sculpture has come to be called "nonrelational." It differs from Mondrian's grids, in which one feels the artist's intention was to have all axes function in consonance with one another at once. Caro usually has applied a single color uniformly to the whole of a sculpture, a color that seems peculiarly appropriate to its individual shapes and their scale. Such use of one hue serves both to unify all the disparate parts and to mute the "corporeality," or actual physical nature, of the material without destroying its substantiality. The additive method of joining similar but unlike shapes results from decisions made in the process of building the form. T-beams of varying lengths and widths and axial placement produce different effects. Caro, like David Smith, does not begin with a final form fixed in his mind, one that would determine his selection of units and their mutual interaction.

Recent abstract sculpture depends upon the world of taste, an admittedly circumscribed audience with the money, leisure, knowledge, and patience to follow closely the ideas and changes developed within the avant-garde community. The channels of communication in this tight culture are the art magazines, which make new concepts and sculptures available in a period of mere weeks to an audience of international range.

**The Ideal of Wholeness** A number of young sculptors have learned that modest scale and simple forms raise their expectations for achieving perfection, consistency, and completeness. By comparison with the sculpture of Robert Morris (b. 1931), the work of Smith and Caro seems prolix in its quantity of parts and surface events, and muscular in the way the pieces have been assembled. Morris and other sculptors sympathetic to his reasoning felt, in the second half of the 1960s, that a new literal basis for sculpture had to be established as an alternative to illusionism. This attitude meant reexamining the fundamental characteristics of sculpture and the realization of an undramatic form that was indivisible and dependent on the movements of the beholder. Simple forms did not mean simple experiences for Morris. If the viewers were to come to the piece reproduced in Figure 600 expecting craftsmanship, virtuoso handling, bright color, novel shapes, or exotic textures, they might well find the work monotonous. With unflinching literalness Morris insisted upon what for him were the concrete facts of sculpture: space, light, and materials that do not constitute themselves into an image of something other than what they are. Because of its neutrality, the color the artist chose does not call attention to itself but fuses with the shape, its configuration, and its surface texture. Morris used a simple polyhedron, a shape easily recognized and remembered, and for the artist one not "self-important." He expects the viewer to move around the four shapes. For the viewer each perspective change introduces new relationships among the forms and produces an intensified sense of his own scale. "One's awareness of one's self existing in the same space as the work is stronger than in previous work. . . . One is more aware than before that he himself is establishing relationships as he apprehends the object from various positions and under varying conditions of light and context." It is not imagination that Morris appeals to but to aesthetic consciousness.

As did American painters in the sixties—Stella (Pl. 94), Lichtenstein (Fig. 471), and Warhol (Fig. 470)—sculptors like Morris and Donald Judd (b. 1928) developed an idiom that contradicted the traditions of European art. Their objective was not to make an "American art," or "reductivist" sculpture, but rather to realize personal visions of what art could look like. "Art is something you look at," in the words of Judd. Behind Judd's preference for an art of simple forms is a rejection of what he feels to be the public's expectation that sculpture should look "old and heavy." His manipulations of cubes formed in a variety of industrial materials are intended to make them appear new and lighter than they are (Fig. 601). Composition resulting from a complexity of parts, their subtle integration, or asymmetrical order does not interest him. He prefers the box form because it does not look "like order or disorder" —it is neutral. He does not want his sparse sculpture to make extravagant claims on our imagination any more than he intends his means of ordering to symbolize a rationalistic philosophical order outside his work.

> A shape, a volume, a color, a surface is something itself. It shouldn't be concealed as part of a fairly different whole. The shapes and materials shouldn't be altered by their context. One or four box shapes in a row . . . is local order, just an arrangement, barely order at all. The series is mine . . . and clearly not

some larger order. It has nothing to do with either order or disorder in general. Both are matters of fact. The series of four or six doesn't change the galvanized iron or steel, or whatever the boxes are made of.

By daring to base their visual statement on a select few parts or just "one thing," these artists, unlike the Cubists, diminish the importance that the act of ordering can have for our experience.

Morris and Judd make drawings for their works and prepare specifications for designs that, with great precision, technicians execute in a variety of materials (Fig. 602). Morris has used the telephone to convey instructions to museum carpenters. This division of labor, between creator and executor, has many precedents in European sculpture. Traditionally, however, the technicians were artists, which permitted them some latitude for interpretation and gained for their skills the recognition of patron and public. By contrast, the carpenters and metalworkers who make boxes for Judd and Morris may have had no other experience with sculpture. Just as the validity of Stella's painting does not depend upon the tangibility of the painter's stroke or evidence of "making," the sculpture of Judd and Morris does not take its power from nuance or from the chance effect made by the hand.

**Image-Objects** There is no more fiercely individualist artist today than Dan Flavin (b. 1933), yet in his work one finds important symptoms of broader changes in contemporary art that are both negative and strongly positive in character. Since 1963 Flavin has been making what he terms "image-objects," using standard lengths of fluorescent tubing. He prizes the unhistorical look of his materials, resists categorizing his work into painting, sculpture, or "light" art, and rejects the commercial gallery system of the art business, which he sees as having made victims of artists. His arrangements depend upon ordinary electrical systems, which can be disassembled and, if need be, returned to the hardware store. Rather than participate in group shows, Flavin prefers to take over an entire

*above:* 601. DONALD JUDD. *Untitled.* 1966. Galvanized iron and aluminum, 3′4″ × 15′10″ × 3′4″. Pasadena Art Museum (gift of Mr. and Mrs. Robert A. Rowan).

*opposite:* 602. DONALD JUDD. *Drawing for Untitled, 1968, Stainless Steel.* 1968. Ink on yellow paper, 17 × 22″. Collection Mr. and Mrs. Michael Del Balso.

gallery and make a careful study of its dimensions and physical characteristics before installing his pieces.

What Flavin has accomplished is not a new symbolism or mystic conception of light, but rather a fruitful extension of formalism as it developed in the United States during the 1960s. The titles Flavin has given his compositions are sentimental gestures of gratitude to friends, not keys to supposedly hidden meanings in an arrangement of lights. Never concealed, the tubes and their metal boxes are emphatic elements in the serial organization, and the boxes themselves, along with walls, floors, and ceilings, serve as reflecting surfaces. In his *Untitled (to S.M.)* (Pl. 96, p. 446) red, yellow, pink, and blue fluorescent lights are fixed in four triangular units, which look like eight titled squares. Flavin wants art to shed its "vaunted mystery," and he favors keenly realized decoration. What may appear as restrictions to the layman—the uniformity of tube axes and lengths and the few fluorescent colors—has provided Flavin with a means of discovering an infinity of new ways for creating luminous environments. Sometimes the lights are turned away from the viewer; the colors may or may not be serially repeated; tubes have been deployed in arcs on the floors or walls, attached to corners of rooms, or centered on walls. In each situation the artist sets up, the admixture of colored light from various direct and reflected sources creates different effects, none of which encourages normal activity in the space they occupy. In a room prepared by Don Flavin, most viewers find themselves passive, in a state of meditative absorption.

After 1900, when certain artists gave up illusionism and representation, it would seem that they had left to them only the rectangular, white, flat surface of the canvas. All that

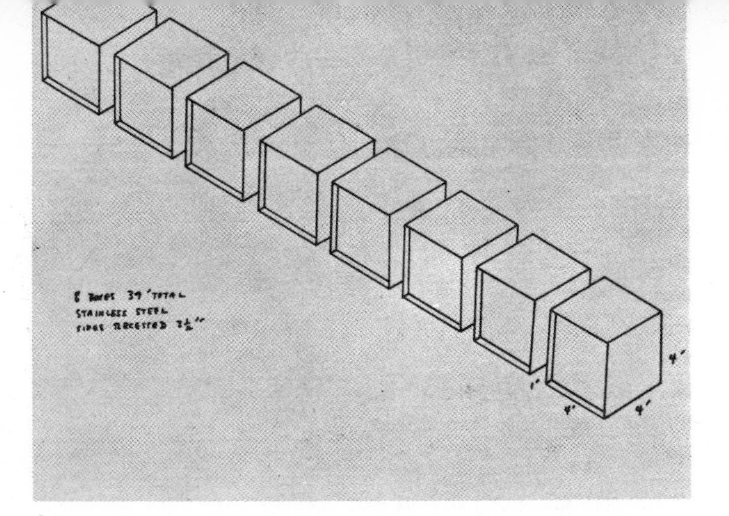


remained of the window was its shape. The only object was the sheet of paper or canvas itself stretched on a wooden frame. Not nature or previous art but the inventiveness of the artist could fill the new surface. In Chapter 16, "Art and Nature," we saw that artists like Mondrian, Kandinsky, and Pollock did not come unarmed to this task, but worked logically out of their early illusionistic and representational style. Habits of composition, derived from naturalistic painting, for example, could still manifest themselves in abstraction. In the work of almost all the artists in this last section there is a gradual development that prepares the dramatic situations or beginnings described above. The denial of illusionism did not come easily to any of the pioneer abstractionists, and many felt impelled to write thousands of words explaining the motives behind their decision. It was not photography, the exhaustion of the naturalistic tradition, or desire for novelty that caused these artists to evolve a new art. Positive attitudes toward what was reality, or the true nature of nature, and the purpose and character of art itself in this century gave the first generation of abstract artists the incentive, courage, and momentum to make this historic break. Artists encouraged as well as severely criticized each other. To the nonartist, the world of art is identified with museums, auctions, galleries, loft studios on 10th Street in New York, *New Yorker* cartoons, cocktail parties, critics, dealers, and crowded opening nights. To the serious artist, it is artists and all the art works ever made, the sense of the historical continuity of formal ideas, which he accepts or rejects, and moments of exhilaration and anguish when in his studio he has the chance to continue the history of art. Abstract art has a context with which we must familiarize ourselves if we are to view it with understanding, whether or not it pleases us. Abstract art, like religion, presupposes faith, and one either acquires it or one does not. To the layman, abstraction is always somehow less than what he wants. To see a painting with only a colored square in it makes many people feel that they have been cheated. Execution is favored over conception, possibly a symptom of the old gospel of labor. There is no tangible evidence of labor, no moral or symbol that can be seen or talked about, nothing with which the layman can identify or escape into as he can with television or illusionistic painting. He feels that the artist has given him too little or nothing. While this is possible, in some cases it is also highly probable that the layman has given nothing to the art and the artist in terms of sensitivity, exposure, and an open mind. Painting and sculpture, like music, poetry, or baseball, come to life for a knowledgeable, experienced, and sympathetic audience. Unlike Baroque painting, whose rich interpretations of figures at a table drew upon many experiences, abstraction provides its audience with experiences that are artistic in origin. That abstraction does not touch much that is important in our lives is readily acknowledged by the artists themselves. But since these artists have ethically defined what art is for them (and it is the artist today who decides what is art), it is not possible or desirable for them to do anything other than what they have done, that which is most important in their lives. As a whole, the staggering variety of painting and sculpture accomplished in this century does touch many aspects of our lives and a wide variety of tastes. To urge that artists make concessions in their art for the sake of communication would be to require a dilution of their freedom and individuality. In art as well as in civilization's history, freedom has been achieved only after a long struggle, and it is a precious right to preserve for the health of all society.

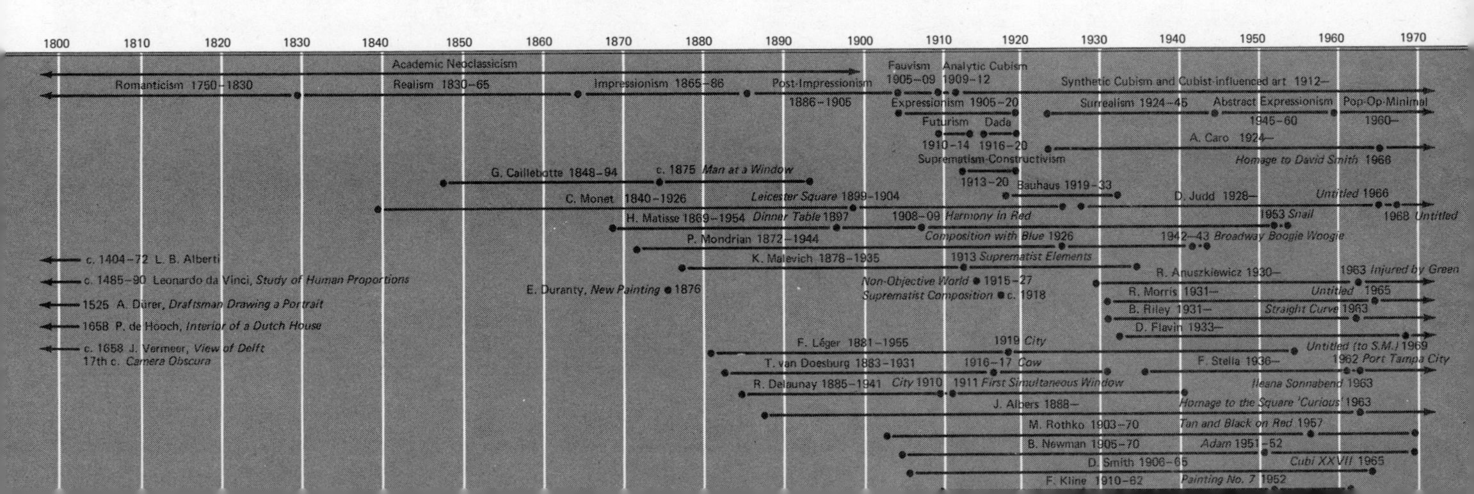

# 23

Until recent times the artist's role in his culture and in his service to his patron—whether tribal chief, bishop, prince, or town council—was clear, as Saul Steinberg wittily epitomized in his depiction of the statue's evolution (Fig. 530). Art was an instrument of political or religious rule and ritual, moralizing and myth-making, philosophizing and pageantry. It mediated between the visible and invisible forces that governed men's lives. The artist was expected to gratify his patron and to enhance the community by the celebration of its heroes and values, to educate the unlettered, delight the intellectual and connoisseur, and satisfy the financial speculator. At various times in history the artist has played the role of magician and scientist, propagandist and ambassador, decorator and entertainer, visionary and prophet. For the most part, until the 19th century the artist imaged the world as others would have it.

**The Self and Portraits of the Artists** One of the most important developments in the art of the last hundred years has been the effort of artists to bring art closer to its sources in the self, to affirm their identities and those of their means and materials. For example, a small iron sculpture, *The Self* (Fig. 603) by Isamu Noguchi (b. 1904), issued from meditations on "what sculpture was fundamentally about . . . its relations to people, space and uses in the past." Noguchi wanted to free sculpture from "its captivity by coterie points of view," in order to find "some larger, more noble and more essentially sculptural purpose to sculpture." His emblem for the self is subtly contradictory; at once symmetrical and asymmetrical, it reveals and conceals itself as the light fluctuates; it is made of iron, yet it suggests growth and change. The material and casting came from Noguchi's experience of ancient Japanese art, his form from 20th-century Western abstraction, and his

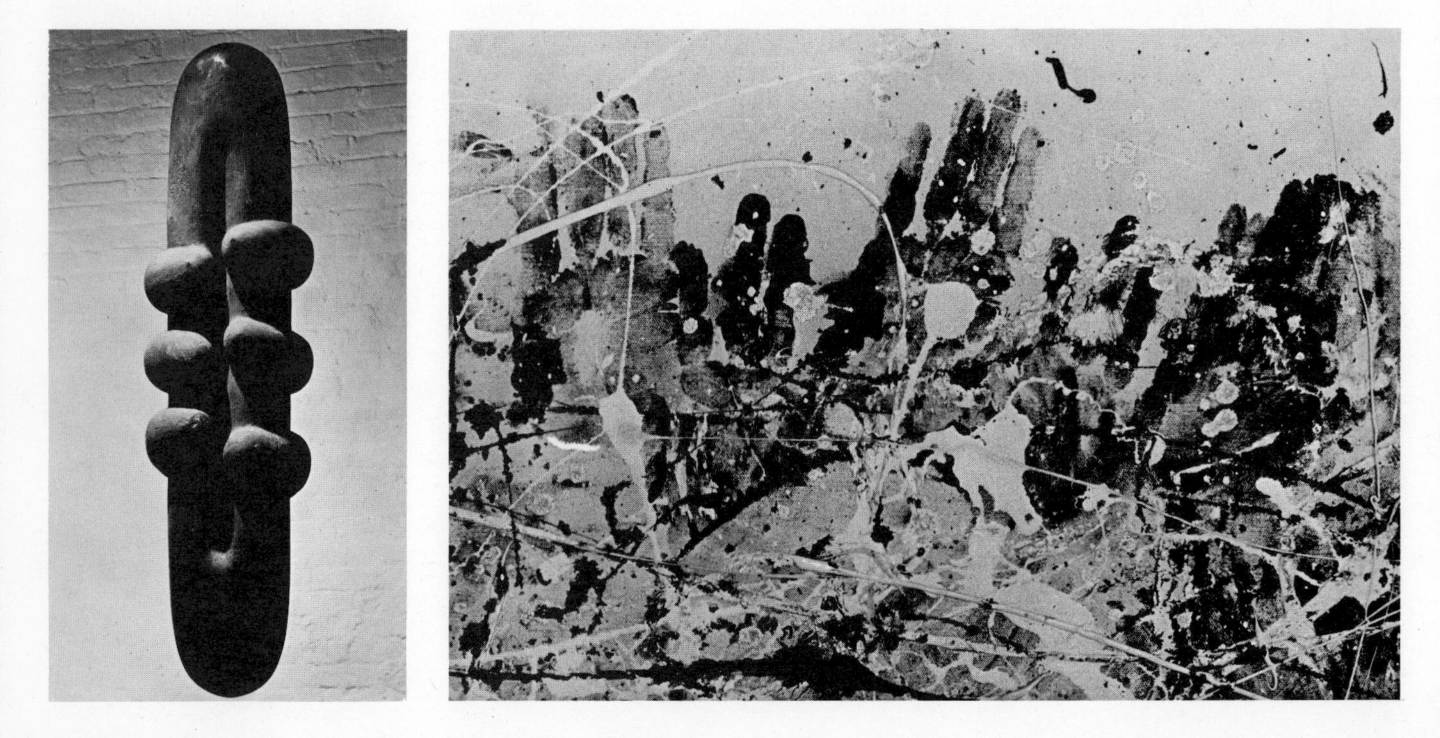

# CODA
# The Modern Artist

meaning from the exposure of a citizen of the world to its accumulated wisdom.

The long history of art also joins the anonymous hands at Altamira (Fig. 2) with that of Jackson Pollock (Fig. 604). For the latter to occur as it does in a painting has required that art evolve from service to the tribe, church, state, or society to a gratification of the self. The appearance of art has left behind collective public symbols and moved through phases of naturalism to complete abstraction and total permissiveness of means. How fitting that a painting—perhaps the only object of significant value a man can still make by hand in this technological age—should have been signed not with the traditional "Made by my hand," but with the artist's own handprint.

The process by which the modern artist has made his art a more intimate extension of the self often has demanded a radical transformation of the appearance and means of art. The self-portrait offers the most dramatic and candid revelation of this intimacy, as seen in a comparison of drawings by Leonardo da Vinci and Joan Miró (Figs. 605, 606). At sixty, Leonardo approached the drawing of his own countenance with the same curiosity and discernment that he brought to his observation of nature. In many respects, his drawing is an objective likeness, but Leonardo accentuated his eyes and made them the focal point of the work. The eye was an endlessly fascinating organism for Leonardo; he was amazed that within its small dimensions the whole external world could be perceived. In the drawing there is a graduated intensity of focus from the cursory outline of the top of the head and the broad, undulant treatment of the beard through the darkening and increased detail of the brows, mouth, and nose to the deeply recessed and shaded eyes. The head is a summary of studies of bone and muscle structure (Fig. 585), as well as of the opera-

*opposite left :* 603. ISAMU NOGUCHI. *The Self.* 1957. Cast iron, height 34 1/2". Collection Lillian H. Florsheim Foundation for Fine Arts, Chicago.

*opposite right :* 604. JACKSON POLLOCK. Detail of *Number 1* (Fig. 4). 1948.

*right :* 605. LEONARDO DA VINCI. *Self-Portrait.* 1510–13. Red chalk, 12 × 8 1/4". Bibliotèca Reale, Turin.

*far right :* 606. JOAN MIRÓ. *Self-Portrait.* 1937–38. Oil, crayon, and pencil on canvas; 4′9 1/2″ × 3′2 1/4″. Collection James Thrall Soby, New Canaan, Conn.

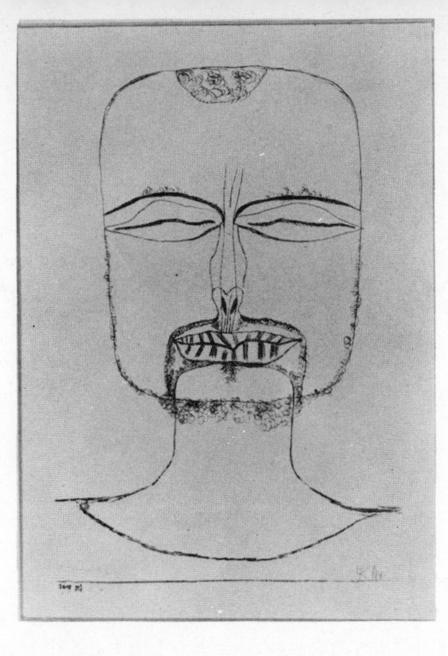

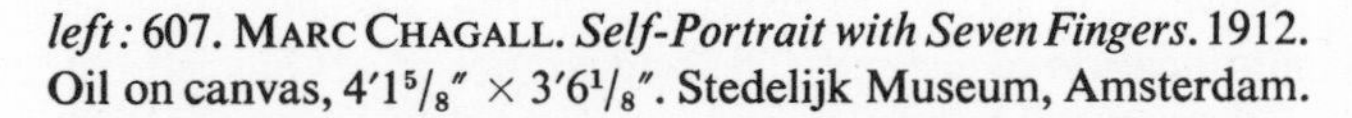

*left:* 607. Marc Chagall. *Self-Portrait with Seven Fingers.* 1912. Oil on canvas, $4'1\frac{5}{8}'' \times 3'6\frac{1}{8}''$. Stedelijk Museum, Amsterdam.

*above:* 608. Paul Klee. *Lost in Thought (Self-Portrait).* 1919. Lithograph, $9\frac{1}{4} \times 6\frac{1}{4}''$. Paul Klee Foundation, Museum of Fine Arts, Berne.

tion of the mind behind the face. The beard recalls the new modes of drawing Leonardo developed to capture the flow of water and the upheaval of dust clouds (Fig. 433). Just as he made painstaking studies of the action of weather on the earth's surface, so also Leonardo set down in closely matched sequences of thin parallel lines the effects of age upon his face. He made no attempt to elicit sympathy or to further a personal interchange between himself and the viewer. Omitting reference to his hands, he drew attention exclusively to the fountainhead of his extraordinary ideas and visions (Figs. 192, 219).

Miró's partly intuitive, partly mental self-image dates from a period when, because of poverty and hunger, he suffered hallucinations. Drawing from a reflection in a convex mirror, he allowed free play to the fantasies induced by irritability at the sight of his own features. Miró could not be neutral toward any part of the head, and he found in each feature of his face deeply personal and playful associations that could be expressed only in his unique pictorial language. He did not superpose his invented forms on the face but made them an integral part of its new structure. He exaggerated the asymmetry not only of the face, but of each pair of features. Weight, texture, shape, and tangibility have been consistently reworked, and the artist has deliberately inverted or parodied functions. He was drawn to openings in the head, such as the mouth, and so he accented their existence, at the same time suggesting their relatedness to other parts of the body. The head itself seems unable to hold the wealth of sensations and ideas induced there, and certain shapes encompass areas both within and outside the face. Miró and other 20th-century artists prophesied the recent studies, by psychologists such as Julius Fast, into body imagery and our claim to the intimate space around us as a personal extension.

Perhaps the most beautiful and imaginative narcissistic self-portrait in this century (Fig. 607) was done by Marc Chagall shortly after his arrival in Paris from Russia before World War I. The painting literally mingles the sights of Paris and memories of Vitebsk, and the whole is like a lover's bouquet. The artist, dressed as a gentleman, suggests his perfumed fragrance as well as his striking looks. Obsession with the miracles of art performed by his hand may have caused him to endow it with seven fingers. The painting on the easel, inspired by his homeland, alerts the beholder to the fact that Chagall painted with both his head and his heart (Pl. 80, p. 413). By contrast, Paul Klee executed a lithograph of himself, *Lost in Thought* (Fig. 608), which evokes the painful aspects of his gift. This artist, privy to secrets of soil and cosmos, shares with us the anguish of his creative effort, which, as in this portrait, called forth in each fresh revelation a new mode of drawing in order to be faithful to its character (Pl. 55, p. 310; Fig. 575). Experienced in the grinding impulses that drive the artist (Fig. 573), Max Beckmann chose to show himself in total control, stifling his innermost thoughts in order to produce a supremely cool and confident image—proud, tough, and with a touch of elegance (Pl. 97, p. 463). To continue the scanning of polarities of modern self-portraits, one could pair with Beckmann's detached self-study that of the English artist Francis Bacon (b. 1910), who relies upon violent involuntary movements of his brush to wrest from his own emerging image what instinct dictates. Bacon's self-portrait (Pl. 98, p. 463) seems willfully abusive in its distortions of anatomy and taste, but his concerns are with the power of art to achieve a more vehement sensation and feeling of life.

In recent years many artists, while preoccuppied with the self, have chosen to avoid dramatic displays of anguish, intimate confession, or revelations of the studio in the psyche, in favor of photographs and documentation. Robert Rauschenberg ironically continues the "breakthroughs" of modern imagery that have led artists to fantasize about the body's interior (Fig. 568); his own X rays, actual size, have been transferred by a silkscreen process into autobiographical assemblages (Fig. 609). This is a far cry from the morbid meditations of James Ensor on human mortality (Pl. 46, p. 295), which led to the baring of his own bones in the etching *Portrait of Myself in 1960* (Fig. 610).

Consonant with his commitment to systems or programmed art rather than aesthetics is Donald Burgy's *Selected Mental and Physical Characteristic of Donald Burgy, 1970*, in which, after an extensive medical checkup, he displayed the results of his having been processed by modern science. The work included:

Documentation of selected mental and physical characteristics of Donald Burgy from 1/20/69 to 1/20/69
Body measurements
Body photographs
Dermatology report
Electrocardiogram
Electroencephalogram
Family medical history
Laboratory reports
Minnesota Multiphasio Personality Inventory
Ophthalmology report and photographs
X rays

**Who Is an Artist?** One of the most dramatic developments in the recent history of art has been the questioning of the artist's identity. Who is an artist? The problem never would have occurred to anyone before 1900. With few exceptions, an artist's credentials for the profession were clear and traditional. They included his craft and art school training, the making of objects, and their exhibition where other artists also showed their work. In the 18th century Jean-Baptiste-Siméon Chardin

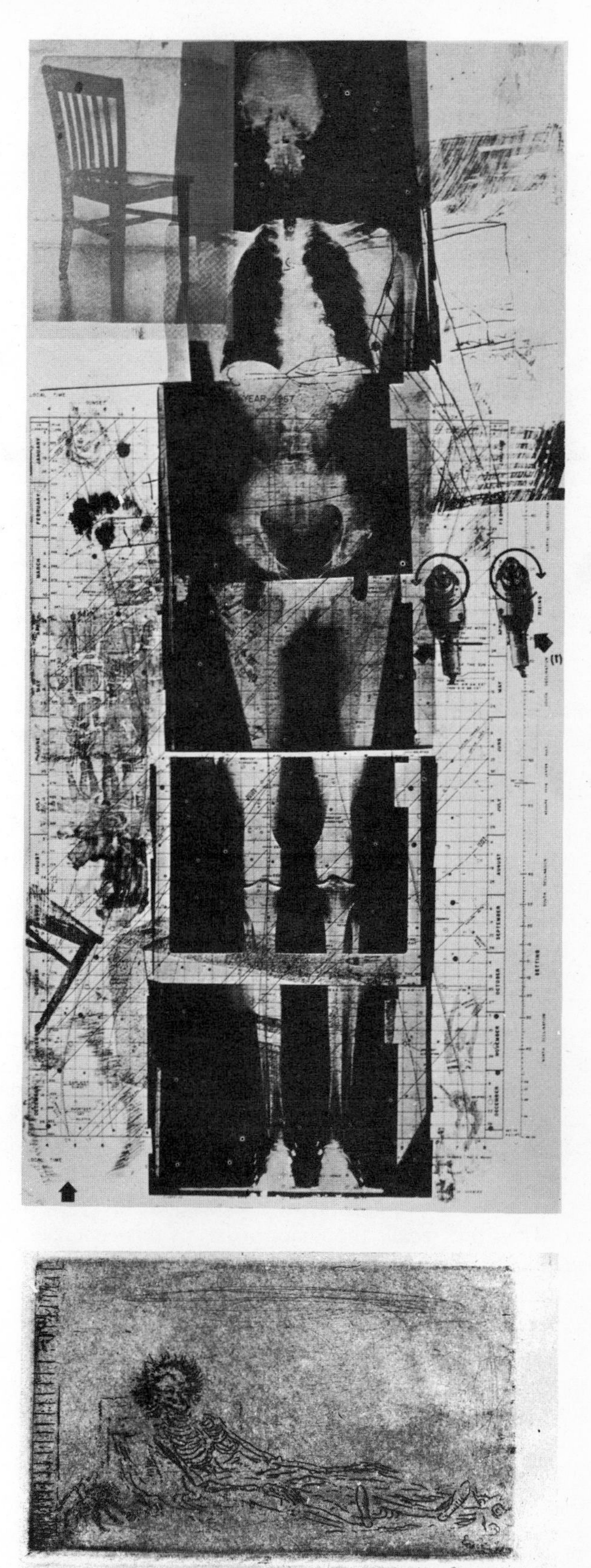

*above:* 609. ROBERT RAUSCHENBERG. *Booster*. 1967. Color lithograph and silkscreen, 6 × 3′. Courtesy Leo Castelli Gallery, New York.

*right:* 610. JAMES ENSOR. *Portrait of Myself in 1960*. 1888. Etching, 2³/₄ × 4³/₄″. Bibliothèque Royale Albert 1er, Brussels.

*left :* 611. JEAN-BAPTISTE-SIMÉON CHARDIN. *The Attributes of the Arts and the Regards which Are Accorded Them.* 1776. Oil on linen, $3'8^1/_2'' \times 4'9^1/_4''$. Minneapolis Institute of Arts (William Hood Dunwoody Fund).

(Pl. 61, 338) was able to paint his attributes (Fig. 611). To be sure, there was a long tradition—going back to ancient Rome—of *dilettantes,* talented amateurs who worked at art as an avocation. With the development of modern oil paints available in tubes and the Impressionists' scorn of drawing or work based on the imitation of older art, painting became physically and psychologically more accessible to amateurs such as Gauguin (Pl. 49, p. 298) and Caillebotte (Fig. 579). The collage (Fig. 468), which included photographs and vernacular material, reduced further the emphasis on drawing and imitative skills, and the use of "readymades" sanctioned by Duchamp struck blows against originality and the hand-fashioned (Fig. 472). All that has minimized craft and skill of execution in this century has encouraged untrained individuals to put their minds if not their hands to art. Since World War I, it is the individual who has determined whether or not he is an artist, and it has become his challenge, if he cared, to get others to agree that he was an artist and made art. For many this has meant a debasing of art and the artist's profession, an invitation to charlatans. For others it is a realistic adjustment to historical evolution and a necessary deflation of the accumulated mystique concerning who could make art and what it should look like. The question then becomes not who are the artists, but who are the good ones?

When one recalls the major artists of this century—men such as Picasso, Matisse, Klee, Mondrian, Kandinsky, Duchamp, Miró, Brancusi, Moore, Pollock, and Rothko—it is apparent that the new permissiveness of entrée into the profession has not yet produced artists of their stature. Those mentioned all experienced some art school training or instruction from artist-teachers and otherwise carried traditional credentials. At the turn of the century there were a few important artists, such as Gauguin and Duchamp-Villon (Fig. 500), who were self-taught. Although the idea was not new, it was Courbet (Figs. 22, 436, 437) who most dramatically proclaimed that art could not be taught either in art schools or by teachers. Earlier artists had argued that the art schools stifled genius, but reform within the educational system was usually the objective. Since the second half of the last century the most venturesome artists have felt that art schools could not provide inspiration. They prefer to study the art that interests them most on their own, in museums and galleries or from photographs. Cézanne (Pl. 54, p. 309; Pl. 63, p. 347; Fig. 486), who had formal training, and many artists influenced by him after 1900 saw themselves as the new "primitives," confronting art and nature in an unprejudiced way. In the last few years, many artists have become involved in technology and materials not previously deemed suitable for art, with the result that the general attitude has been to learn what one must learn on one's own to get the job done. There is no way to codify into curricula all that today's artist needs to know. For the artist who would educate himself, art exhibitions and periodicals, with their international circulation, serve as source books, replacing the prints, drawings, and plaster casts of the classical academies.

**What Is Art?** Before this century there were undoubtedly cultures and long periods of time in which the word *art* and the modern concept of art were not known or used. Repeatedly, civilizations have developed their own tacit or explicit definitions of *art*. Many tribal cultures recognized the beauty as well as the utility of objects that are now divided between art and anthropological museums. The great tradition of the crafts in the East and in the West produced countless useful objects made by men such as Pierre the Fleming (Fig. 159) who often fashioned not only skilled but inspired work that makes meaningless the distinctions drawn since the 18th century between the "fine" and the "applied" arts, between the worker and the artist. In our own century, for the first time, there has been a prolonged questioning by artists of what art is. Many individuals and groups have attempted either to push back its traditional limits or to go beyond them, while not claiming that what they have done is art. The 20th century has witnessed a drastic shrinkage of what is *not* art. In the decade of the 1960s artists began to build upon premises established by Duchamp (who questioned that anything man-made was not art), Picasso, the Dadaists, and Dubuffet, to name a few (see Chap. 21), with results that seem to have stripped the word *art* of all meaning. When painters set aside the picture frame and sculptors eschewed the pedestal and base so as to make their works more tangible or concrete as aesthetic objects, we saw the contravening of art's tradition of illusion and preciousness.

Many young artists today speak of "demythologizing" art, taking it out of the realm of "inspired genius" where it was put during the Renaissance, and renouncing "miracles" of the hand. We have defined *art* as the skillful interpretation of human experience in a man-made object capable of producing an aesthetic response. When an artist like Picasso (see Chap. 20) minimizes his skill, when a sculptor like Judd (Fig. 601) turns the execution of his work over to industrial metalworkers, it is evident that the viewer's enjoyment of skill or craft is not something the artist desires or anticipates. The interpretation of human experience, with its connotations of symbolism, metaphor, and analogy, has been increasingly set aside by many young artists who make "specific" objects to be taken literally and at face value. The desirability of inducing an aesthetic response or appealing to taste has also fallen before the onslaught of countless artists throughout the world, who see beauty as something "irrelevant," "elitist," and smacking of "class" or "establishment" snobbery. Beauty, to them, is less interesting than what they are doing. One can be interested or deeply moved by an artist's work even though it is not beautiful, as Picasso, Pollock, and De Kooning (Pl. 85, p. 416) have taught us. However, in the case of these three artists it could be argued that in their search for truth in art they have established a new aesthetic of the brutal or violent.

The work of art as an object that is permanent, negotiable, and precious because of uniqueness and the skill lavished on it no longer interests the artist preoccupied with motion, concepts, and the ephemeral. Artists who use technology to produce works that actually move or who employ machines and systems for their effects—works that plug into a wall socket like Flavin's (Pl. 96, p. 446) or depend on the postal service, medical checkups, and earth movers, for example—have no patience with the hard and fast. The premise that a work of art must be visible is rejected by conceptual artists like Stephen Kaltenbach (b. 1940) and Joseph Kosuth, both of whom believe that art comes into being in the artist's mind and that the intermediary with his audience can be a diagram or words (Figs. 612, 613). Artists who place more value on the making or the process of assembling vernacular materials that may or may not be keyed to a certain site set no store by a finished art object. After the artist has stopped or the show is over, the work is disassembled or destroyed. Order or composition leading to "good form," which was one of the last ties to traditional art, is scrupulously avoided by certain artists who refuse either to arrange their materials consciously or to repeat themselves, for the latter would imply the development of a style. Obviously, what has been described is usually unsalable, uncollectable, and even hard to document photographically. Art critics are experiencing their own crises, and when their work goes beyond reporting it is considered dispensable by some artists. Many young people are rebelling against the notion of art earning a profit for the owner rather than the artist. Instead, they seek fees or commissions as a means of sponsoring their artistic ephemera. Owning but not possessing is a condition that some patrons are learning to live with. About all that remains of the tradition of at least the last century of Western art is that, for

above : 612. Stephen Kaltenbach. "*Art Works*": *First Sidewalk Plaque*. 1958 (unfinished, to be completed when owner places in cement sidewalk). Brass, $5^1/_2 \times 7''$.

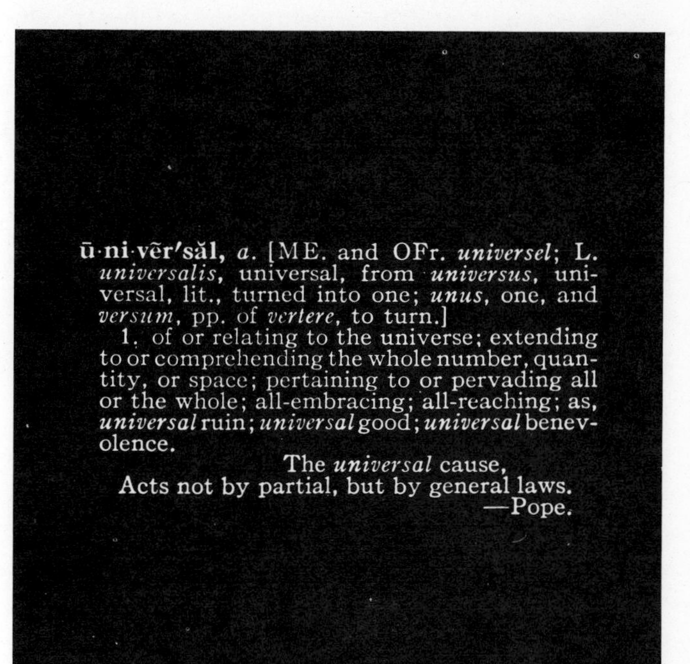


right: 613. Joseph Kosuth. "Titled *(Art as Idea as Idea)*." 1967. Enlargement of dictionary definition, 5′ square. Courtesy the artist.

many contemporary artists, art is an expressive activity in which the product or result is useless for any other purpose.

**The Dilemma of the Artist Militant** One of the most persistant concerns of the modern artist—relieved of the necessity to work within the institutions that traditionally sponsored art—has been to make his profession and his art responsive to the needs of his society. The ideal of bridging art and life, of fusing artist and worker to achieve a social utopia that would make art irrelevant or redundant has brought many artists to the realization that they were working for their own theoretical extinction. The artist's profession has in fact been threatened with extinction, many times, in many places, for many different reasons—internal and external, ideological and economic.

The idea of an avant-garde, an élite of artistic and cultural geniuses who would lead society to a better life, emerged in France during the 1830s. Artistic advances were to be compatible with the improvement of social and political conditions. Courbet (see pp. 282, 283), for example, honestly believed in the didactic and social purposes of art. Many avant-garde movements such as Art Nouveau, German Expressionism, Futurism, De Stijl in Holland, Constructivism in Russia, and the Bauhaus in Germany were dedicated to reforming society. Ironically, these movements for the most part were regressive with respect to the centuries-long evolution of the separation of artists and craftsmen; they sought a reunification of the two and elimination of the 18th-century ideal of "fine art." The artist should function as a worker or craftsman, an educator, a visionary dedicated to the good of society.

The artist militant has been more than just a formal revolutionary, but aside from the photographer and the cartoonist, his history has not been marked with success. Avant-garde artists and movements often have been unable to reconcile the claims of genius and art with the social and political needs of society. The Impressionist and Post-Impressionist groups included those who were anarchists in private life, but their art alone would not tell us this (Pl. 49, p. 298; Fig. 419). Since the 1930s there has been a great distrust of politically or socially didactic "message" art among the most venturesome artists. With the invention of photography early in the last century the arts were challenged, for the first time in history, in their exclusive claim to represent the visual world and the development of national self-imagery. Artists have often incorporated photography into their work, and many photographers have been creative artists. But it is primarily photography that has assumed the burden of visually recording and commenting upon events. For example, when the Art Workers Coalition in New York City prepared a poster depicting the My Lai massacre, it chose to reproduce in color a photograph of that atrocity (Fig. 614).

**Possibilities and Pressures** In the 1960s the phenomenon of the avant-garde died. The reasons for its demise included the great number of movements and the diversity of their direction, the increased mutual acceptance of artists and public, and the embracing of mass culture by Pop artists. Rebellion and risk-taking, so vital and exciting to the creative act for sculptors and painters of the 1950s, yielded to the premeditated, impersonal facture and "safe" format. In the last decade the artist has had to share his much-publicized alienation from society with a whole generation of young people and minority groups. The image of the suffering artist has paled before exposure in the mass media of the unspeakable anguish, privation, and dehumanization of millions of people afflicted by natural disasters, cruel wars, social injustice, poverty, and starvation. The consumer advocate, the poverty lawyer, the militant feminist, the engineer, and the ecologist have eclipsed the artist, for these seem to promise utopian visions to a society that seeks reform. What, then, are the incentives for becoming an artist?

The artist continues to be most successful as a rebel against art, yet, as before, what he now believes to be an assault on old bastions of taste and thought will be tomorrow's art school curriculum. The revolutionary quickly becomes evolutionary. In financial terms the profession continues as a poor risk. According to expert testimony, less than 3 percent of all artists live to see their work appreciate in value, and it is doubtful that as many can make a living exclusively from their art. Statistically art has been a dying profession since the 19th century, when academic art was at its numerical height. The desire for competition—a striving for critical or public recognition on the one hand and a private contest with the history of art on the other—may be an incentive, but it is probably not sufficient to launch a man or woman on a studio career. The one area in which artists continue to lead scientists—notably psychiatrists—is in recognizing the need to discover and enjoy the

*left:* 614. ART WORKERS COALITION and R. L. HAEBERLE. *Q. and Babies? A. and Babies.* 1970. Offset lithograph, 25 × 38″. Museum of Modern Art, New York.

*left:* Plate 97. MAX BECKMANN. *Self-Portrait in a Tuxedo*. 1927. Oil on canvas, 4′6½″ × 3′1¾″. Busch-Reisinger Museum, Harvard University, Cambridge, Mass. (See pp. 458, 459.)

*below:* Plate 98. FRANCIS BACON. Center panel from *3 Studies for a Self-Portrait*. 1967. Oil on panel, 14 × 12″. Courtesy Marlborough Fine Art, Ltd., London. (See p. 459.)

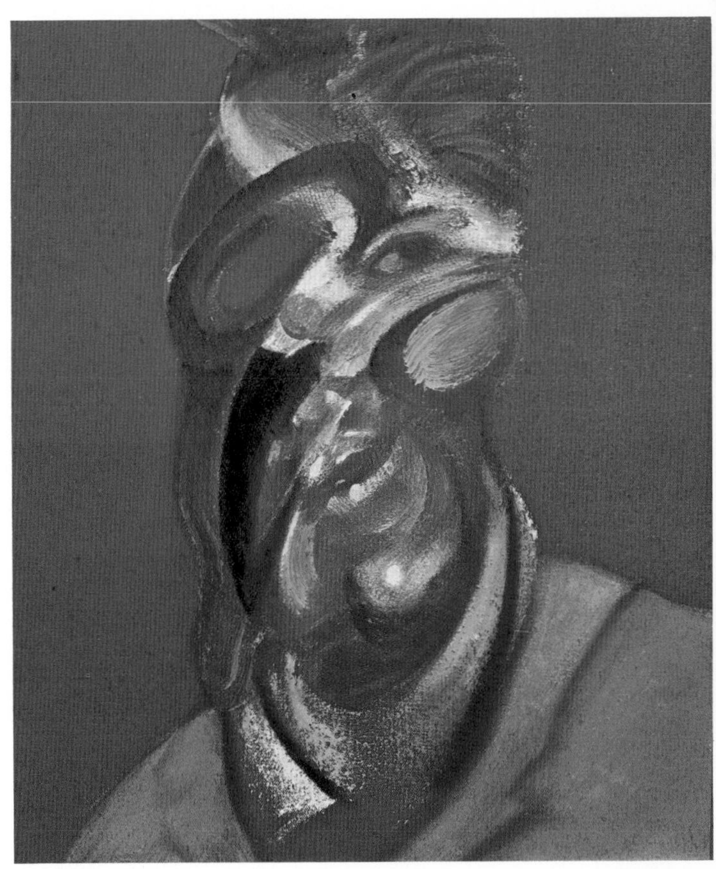

*below:* Plate 99. *The Wall of Dignity*, Detroit, Mich. (See p. 465.)

*left:* Plate 100. ROMARE BEARDEN. *Blue Interior, Morning*. 1968. Collage, 3′8″ × 4′8″. Collection Chase Manhattan Bank, New York. (See p. 466.)

*right :* 615. THE PULSA GROUP. *Television Sensorium.* 1971. Video projectors, television, cameras, strobe lights, plants, electronic control equipment, and speakers. Automation House, New York.

self, not the self trained by society, but the second, creative self that emerges in flashes of insight or inspiration. Being an artist means finding or inventing one's self. Since the 19th century and the bohemians, art, of all the professions, has been the most equatable with a life style in which the self can find fullest and most consistent expression.

The artist looks at the history of art and says, "What is missing is *me.*" As Carl André has stated, "Men climb mountains because they are there. Men make art because it isn't." In the past, society and a prosperous middle class created the need for art. Today, lacking a similar patronage or demand and in competition with other visual media, the artist must create the need for his work by making it so effective that it will be desired by others—that is, if he wants more than just self-gratification. The artist's profession still offers the satisfaction of making or doing something—a whole object for contemplation, an effect, or even intervention in an existing system—whose conception, if not execution, is still individual. Some young artists, such as the Pulsa Group at Yale (Fig. 615), even submerge individuality in favor of group identity to combine life and art style, thus making complex technology work for them instead of the reverse. A number of artists are working with science in the hope of civilizing technology and preventing its domination of our lives, not to mention our tastes.

The contemporary artist has been described as holding a poker hand in which all the cards are wild. In theory, he can make his move in any direction. Art of this century is omnidirectional, reactionary as well as radical. Frank Stella (Pl. 94, p. 446; Fig. 598) has argued that "you can never go back," others have opted to work with motifs, styles, and materials of other periods, in the belief that there is no such thing as progress or "modernity." In the last century a tacit imperative by which advanced art was judged demanded to know whether or not art was of its time (see Chap. 15). Now, the word *relevance* plays a similar but more vague role as the criterion of an art's validity. The relativity of this criterion has paradoxically ensured the artist's cherished freedom. For example, oil painting is irrelevant to the artist who uses acrylics, modeling is obsolete to the welder, physical objects are no longer valid to the artist working in light, artistic "engineering" is shunned by the earth worker who opts for vernacular materials or nature itself. "Process art" is a fraud for the conceptual artist, who is content with sketched or written "proposals." And, of course, all of the foregoing are evasions of serious artistic problems, charades, travesties, or reductions to absurdity in the view of the painter who lovingly brushes his oil paint on canvas into the form of a human face or still life in a way that Manet or Cézanne would recognize.

Relevancy and the possibilities and pressures of art have different meanings for hundreds of black artists, who do not consider what white artists have done or are doing to be important for them. Some Afro-American artists are now concerned with expressing their race, something no African artist aspired to do. The pressures for a black art and an expression of what it means to be black in a white-dominated society have come from within the black community, from its writers and political leaders in the 1960s, more perhaps than from the artists themselves. For some black artists this means racial subject matter: a *Wall of Dignity* or heroes in a Detroit ghetto (Pl. 99, p. 464), black artists celebrated on a Boston handball court, or a painting by Dana Chandler, Jr. (b. 1941), of the bullet-riddled door of Fred Hampton (Fig. 616), the Black Panther leader killed by Chicago police. When white critics point out that this is like American social protest art of the 1930s, an artistic throwback and cliché art, the blacks who paint these walls and memorials reply that their art is for the black urban community *now*, not the white art establishment that has practiced deliberate and unconscious discrimination against artists of their race. They want to establish racial pride through chronicle and commentary, daily reminders of heroism and injustice. In the minds of these artists, quality cannot be sensed by Caucasian critics tuned in only to "Whitey's tastes." In any case, it is a secondary consideration.

The drive to rediscover the African strain of their cultural heritage has led some black artists to include Benin bronzes (Fig. 277) in still-life oil paintings or, like Joe Overstreet (b. 1933), to make abstractions using colors found in African textiles (Fig. 617). But there are also many gifted black artists, such as Sam Gilliam (b. 1933) and Richard Hunt (b. 1935), who, while working privately for their race, try in their pro-

fession to make the best art possible (Figs. 618, 619). Although their art is abstract, they consider it to be an expression of their experience as black men in a predominately white culture.

There is no more a stereotyped black artist today than there is a white or an African one. The black sculptor Ed Wilson tells his students: "Malcolm X is my brother, Martin Luther King is my brother, Eldridge Cleaver is my brother! But Michelangelo is my grandfather!" The ancestry of the art produced by Romare Bearden (b. 1914) comprises African sculpture, Dutch 17th-century painting, abstraction, collage, and photographic documentaries. The spirit of his work traces back to his having lived in the South, Manhattan, and Paris. Bearden's work succeeds in fusing racial consciousness, compassion for humanity, and awareness of the possibilities open to modern artists. *Blue Interior, Morning* (Pl. 100, p. 464) speaks of "the life I know best, those things common to all cultures." It also carries his conviction that black culture in the United States "is perhaps the richest because it is the one life style that is talking about life and about the continuation of life. . . and through all of the anguish—the joy of life."

For all his freedoms, the contemporary artist must live with terrific pressures beyond those described. His profession is as competitive as that of business; whether he likes it or not, he is part of the art business and art history. Rare is the artist who wants no recognition and refuses to show, document, or sell his art, to grant interviews and be written about. In past centuries he competed for mastery in his guild, commissions at court, civic appointments, government prizes, and free entry into official annual salons. Today he still competes for exposure and for acceptance by periodicals, museums, galleries, and col-

*above left* : 616. DANA CHANDLER, JR., with *Fred Hampton's Door*. 1970. Acrylic on board, real bullet holes; 26 × 22″. Collection the artist.

*above right* : 617. JOE OVERSTREET, with *Indian Sun*. 1969. Diameter 12′. Courtesy Ankrum Gallery, Los Angeles.

618. SAM GILLIAM, with *Carrousel Change*. 1970. Acrylics with powdered aluminum on work canvas, 10 × 75′. Collection Darthea Speyer, Paris.

*above:* 619. Richard Hunt. *Minor Monument, Number 1.* 1963. Welded steel, height 4′ 2″. Collection Mr. and Mrs. B. C. Holland, Chicago.

*right:* 620. Ad Reinhardt in his studio. 1961. Courtesy Jewish Museum, New York.

lectors, for teaching positions and fellowships. These pressures are in all probability comparable in pleasure and pain to those suffered by artists in the past. But the contemporary artist experiences an even more serious threat to sustained recognition—and especially to his self-confidence—in the staggering number of his compatriots and the velocity of current artistic change. The artist may actually feel that he faces obsolescence. Leonardo complained that art was changing every ten years. Rembrandt came to know critical scorn and neglect in favor of younger, more typically Dutch painters (see Chap. 11). By age twenty-three James Ensor was renounced by the same critics who had exalted him, and he saw himself as Christ crucified by his detractors (Pl. 46, p. 295). At the end of the 19th century the velocities of change were felt roughly every five years. Between 1907 and 1914 they had accelerated into annual phenomena for a relatively small number of artists. In Russia between 1913 and 1917 they were almost monthly. Today they are at least seasonal for untold thousands. Each emerging wave from the art schools tries to sweep over its predecessors. Artists barely over thirty are given retrospectives of ten years' work or less, and then they often disappear from sight. Artists like Stella, Johns, and Lichtenstein, who have held their international reputations for a decade, are becoming rare. Andy Warhol, who has given up painting for filmmaking, foresees in the near future that "everyone will have fifteen minutes of fame." (Warhol is thinking of changing his name to John Doe.) It is not certain that this high speed of change is a threat to art; it is more unsettling to artists, in terms of the emotional and psychological pressures that build up as a young artist, still in his twenties, suddenly finds his work "dated" or "invalid."

What makes art worth the effort to the artist? Perhaps it is still the freedom to choose and pursue ideas, to discover the self by means of art. A great and superbly realized photograph of the late Ad Reinhardt (Fig. 620) calls to mind the phenomenon of the modern artist who carries within his mind the history of art but who, in order to extend it meaningfully, logically, and personally, must reject what has gone before. The photograph, which frames the artist against a window squared like his canvases (Fig. 596), shows him inactive but contemplative, reminding us of the importance of creative idleness. In moments like these the artist confronts his drawing or canvas and sees the field of his materials where he is born, lives, dies, and is reborn. Art remains like an act of love, a potent gesture of life, a fist clenched against death.

# Bibliography

The following books and articles were consulted in the preparation of the text. This bibliography is by no means an attempt to list all the material available on these subjects.


Suggested Readings in the History of Art

Clark, K. M., *Civilisation: A Personal View*. New York: Harper & Row, 1969.

Clark, K. M., *The Nude: A Study in Ideal Form*. New York: Pantheon Books, 1956.

Gombrich, E. H., *The Story of Art*. New York: Phaidon, 1958. One of the most lucid and intelligent general introductions to the chronology of art history; written for English high school students, but excellent for the layman.

Gombrich, E. H., *Art and Illusion: A Study in the Psychology of Pictorial Representation*. New York: Pantheon, 1960. An important and interesting treatment of the subject, beautifully illustrated and intelligible to the educated layman.

Hauser, A., *The Social History of Art*, 4 vols. New York: Vintage, 1957–58. An important sociological approach to the history of art.

Janson, H. W., *The History of Art*, rev. New York: Abrams, 1969. A beautifully illustrated and informed text covering the chronological history of art.

Lee, S., *A History of Far Eastern Art*. New York: Abrams, 1964. The best-written and -illustrated general history of the subject.

Millon, H. A., *Key Monuments of the History of Architecture*. New York: Abrams, 1964. A well-selected photographic history of architecture.

Panofsky, E., *Meaning in the Visual Arts*. Garden City, N.Y.: Anchor Books, 1955.

Pevsner, N., *An Outline of European Architecture*, Jubilee ed. Baltimore: Penguin, 1960.

Schapiro, M., "On Perfection, Coherence, and Unity of Form and Content," *Art and Philosophy* (ed. by S. Hook). New York: New York U. Press, 1966.

Wittkower, R. and M., *Born under Saturn*. New York: Random House, 1963. An excellent psychological study of artists from antiquity to the beginning of the 19th century.

The Artist

"The Academy" (ed. by T. Hess and J. Ashbery). *Art News Annual*. XXXIII, 1967.

Elsen, A. E., "Lively Art from a Dying Profession: The Role of the Modern Artist." *Journal of Aesthetics and Art Criticism*, 18: 446–455, 1960.

Haskell, F., *Patrons and Painters: A Study in the Relations between Italian Art and Society in the Age of the Baroque*. New York: Knopf, 1963.

Hauser, A., *The Social History of Art*, 4 vols. New York: Vintage, 1957–58.

Pelles, G., *Art, Artists and Society: Origins of a Modern Dilemma*. Englewood Cliffs, N. J.: Prentice-Hall, 1963.

Pevsner, N., *Academies of Art*. London: Cambridge, 1940.

Schapiro, M., "On Some Problems in the Semiotics of Visual Art: Field and Vehicle in Image-Signs," *Semiotica*, 223–242, 1969.

Schapiro, M., "Style," *Anthropology Today* (ed. by A. Kroeber). Chicago: U. of Chicago Press, 1953.

White, H. C. and A. C., *Canvases and Careers: Institutional Change in the French Painting World*. New York: Wiley, 1965.

Wittkower, R. and M., *Born under Saturn*. New York: Random House, 1963.

Art as a Matter of Life and Death

Adam, L., *Primitive Art*. Harmondsworth, Middlesex, Eng., 1949.

Disselhoff, H-D., and Linné, S., *Art of Ancient America*. New York: Crown, 1961.

Elisofon, E., W. Fagg, and R. Linton, *The Sculpture of Africa*. London: Thames & Hudson, 1958.

Fagg, W., *African Sculpture:* Loan Exhibition. Washington: International Exhibitions Foundation, 1970.

Fagg, W., *Nigerian Images*. London & New York: Praeger, 1963.

Frankfort, H., *Art and Architecture of the Ancient Orient*. Baltimore: Penguin, 1954.

Fraser, D., *Primitive Art*. New York: Doubleday, 1962.

Groenewegen-Frankfort, H. A., *Arrest and Movement*. New York: Humanities, 1951.

Guiart, J., *The Arts of the South Pacific*. New York: Golden Press, 1963.

Herskovits, M. J., *The Backgrounds of African Art*. Denver Art Museum, 1946.

Laming, A., *Lascaux*. Baltimore: Penguin, 1959.

Leuzinger, E., *Africa: The Art of the Negro Peoples*. New York: McGraw-Hill, 1960.

Lévi-Strauss, C., *The Savage Mind*. Chicago: U. of Chicago Press, 1968.

Lévi-Strauss, C., *Structural Anthropology*. Garden City, N.Y.: Anchor Books, 1967.

Miki, F., *Haniwa: The Clay Sculpture of Protohistoric Japan*. Rutland, Vt.: Tuttle, 1960.

Noma, S., *Haniwa*. New York: Abrams, 1963.

Schilder, P., *The Image and Appearance of the Human Body*. New York: International U. Press, 1950.

Sickman, L., and A. Soper, *The Art and Architecture of China*. Baltimore: Penguin, 1956.

Sieber, R., "Masks as Agents of Social Control." *African Studies Bulletin*, 5: 8–13, May, 1962.

Sieber, R., and Rubin, A., *Sculpture of Black Africa: The Paul Tishman Collection*. Los Angeles: Los Angeles County Museum of Art, 1968.

Sullivan, M., *An Introduction to Chinese Art*. Berkeley: U. of California Press, 1961.

Wingert, P., *Primitive Art*. New York: Oxford, 1962.

Images of Gods

*Apollo*

Guthrie, W. K. C., *The Greeks and Their Gods*. Boston: Beacon Press, 1955.

Hirmer, M., and R. Lullies, *Greek Sculpture* (tr. by M. Bullock). New York: Abrams, 1957.

Kitto, H. D. F., *The Greeks*. Baltimore: Penguin, 1951.

Malraux, A., *The Metamorphosis of the Gods* (tr. by S. Gilbert). New York: Doubleday, 1960.

Murray, G., *Five Stages of Greek Religion*. Boston: Beacon Press, 1952.

Richter, G. M. A., *The Sculpture and Sculptors of the Greeks*, rev. New Haven, Conn.: Yale U. Press, 1950.

*Buddha*

Bowie, T. (ed.), *The Arts of Thailand*. Bloomington: Indiana U. Press, 1961.

Bowie, T. (ed.), *East-West in Art: Patterns of Cultural and Aesthetic Relationships*. Bloomington: Indiana U. Press, 1966.

Coomaraswamy, A. K., *A History of Indian and Indonesian Art*. New York: Weyhe, 1927.

Coomaraswamy, A. K., *The Transformation of Nature in Art*. New York: Dover, 1957.

Kramrisch, S., *The Art of India through the Ages*. New York: Phaidon, 1954.

Lee, S., *A History of Far Eastern Art*. New York: Abrams, 1964.

Rowland, B., Jr., *The Art and Architecture of India*. Baltimore: Penguin, 1953.

Rowland, B., Jr., *Art in East and West*. Cambridge, Mass.: Harvard U. Press, 1955.

Rowland, B., Jr. (ed.), *The Evolution of the Buddha Image*. New York: Abrams, 1963.

*Christ*

Barr, A. J., Jr., *Matisse, His Art and His Public*. New York: Museum of Modern Art, 1952.

Grabar, A., *Byzantine Painting*. Geneva–New York: Skira, 1953.

Grabar, A., *Christian Iconography: A Study of Its Origins* (tr. by T. Grabar). Princeton, N.J.: Princeton U. Press, 1968.

Hauser, A., *The Social History of Art*, 4 vols. New York: Vintage, 1957–58.

Kayser, S. S., "Grünewald's Christianity." *Review of Religion*, 5: 3–35, November, 1940.

Mâle, E., *L'Art religieux du XII^e siècle en France*. Paris: Colin, 1953.

Malraux, A., *The Metamorphosis of the Gods* (tr. by S. Gilbert). New York: Doubleday, 1960.

Muller, H. J., *Uses of the Past*. New York: Oxford, 1957.

Pevsner, N., and M. Meier (eds.), *Grünewald*. New York: Abrams, 1958.

Schapiro, M., "The Romanesque Sculpture of Moissac," Parts I and II. *Art Bulletin*, 13: 248–351, 464–531, September–December, 1931.

Thoby, P., *Le Crucifix des origines au Concile de Trente*. Nantes: Bellanger, 1959.

Von Simson, O. G., *Sacred Fortress: Byzantine Art and Statecraft in Ravenna*. U. of Chicago Press, 1948.

Religious Architecture

*The Parthenon*

Berve, H., and G. Gruben, *Greek Temples, Theaters and Shrines*. New York: Abrams, 1963.

Carpenter, R., *The Architects of the Parthenon*. Baltimore: Penguin, 1970.

Dinsmoor, W. B., *The Architecture of Ancient Greece*. London: Batsford, 1950.
Lawrence, A. W., *Greek Architecture*. Baltimore: Penguin, 1957.
Muller, H. J., *Uses of the Past*. New York: Oxford, 1957.
Scranton, R. L., *Greek Architecture*. New York: Braziller, 1962.
Scully, V. J., *The Earth, the Temple and the Gods: Greek Sacred Architecture*. New Haven, Conn.: Yale U. Press, 1962.
Stevens, G. P., *Restorations of Classical Buildings*. Princeton, N.J.: American School of Classical Studies at Athens, 1958.
Yalouris, N., *Classical Greece: The Elgin Marbles*. New York Graphic Society, 1960.

*The Gothic Cathedrals*

Bowie, T. R. (ed.), *The Sketchbook of Villard de Honnencourt*. Bloomington: Indiana U. Press, 1959.
Branner, R., *Chartres Cathedral*. New York: Norton, 1969.
Branner, R., *Gothic Architecture*. New York: Braziller, 1961.
Crosby, S. M., Review of Von Simson's *The Gothic Cathedral*. *Art Bulletin*, 42: 149–60, 1960.
Dow, H. J., "The Rose Window." *Journal of the Warburg and Courtauld Institutes*, 20:248–97, July, 1957.
Frankl, P., *The Gothic*. Princeton, N. J.: Princeton U. Press, 1960.
Frankl, P., *Gothic Architecture*. Baltimore: Penguin, 1963.
Gilbert, K., and H. Kuhn, *A History of Esthetics*, rev. Bloomington: Indiana U. Press, 1953.
Gimpel, J., *The Cathedral Builders*. New York: Grove, 1961.
Harvey, J., *The Gothic World*. London: Batsford, 1950.
Henderson, G., *Chartres*. Harmondsworth, Eng.: Penguin, 1968.
Henderson, G., *Gothic*. Harmondsworth, Eng.: Penguin, 1967.
Holt, E. G. (ed.), *A Documentary History of Art*, Vol. 1: *The Middle Ages and the Renaissance*. New York: Anchor, 1957.
Horn, W., and E. Born, *The Aisled Medieval Timbered Hall: A Study of Its Origins, Development and Survival*. Berkeley: U. of California Press.
Hürliman, M., and J. Bony, *French Cathedrals*, rev. New York: Viking, 1961.
Jantzen, H., *High Gothic*. New York: Pantheon, 1962.
Johnson, J. R., *The Radiance of Chartres*. New York: Random House, 1965.
Katzenellenbogen, A., *The Sculptural Programs of Chartres Cathedral: Christ-Mary-Ecclesia*. Baltimore: Johns Hopkins Press, 1959.
Knoop, D., and G. P. Jones, *The Medieval Mason*. Manchester, Eng.: Manchester University Press, 1933.
Kraus, H., *The Living Theatre of Medieval Art*. Bloomington: Indiana U. Press, 1967.
Krautheimer, R., "Introduction to an 'Iconography of Medieval Architecture.'" *Journal of the Warburg and Courtauld Institutes*, 5: 1–33, January, 1942.
Muller, H. J., *Uses of the Past*. New York: Oxford, 1957.
Panofsky, E. (ed.), *Abbot Suger on the Abbey Church of St-Denis and Its Art Treasures*. Princeton, N. J.: Princeton U. Press, 1946.
Panofsky, E., *Gothic Architecture and Scholasticism*. New York: Meridian, 1957.
Smith, B., *Architectural Symbolism of Imperial Rome and the Middle Ages*. Princeton, N. J.: Princeton U. Press, 1956.
Smith, N., *Medieval Art: An Introduction to the Art and Architecture of Europe, A.D.300–A.D. 1300*. Dubuque, Iowa: W. C. Brown, 1967.
Temko, A., *Notre Dame of Paris*. New York: Viking, 1959.
Von Simson, O., *The Gothic Cathedral*. New York: Pantheon, 1956.

*Notre Dame du Haut, Ronchamp*

Le Corbusier, *The Chapel at Ronchamp* (tr. by J. Cullen). New York: Praeger, 1958.
Le Corbusier, *Towards a New Architecture* (tr. by Etchells). New York: Praeger, 1946.

The Sacred Book

Beckwith, J., *Early Medieval Art*. New York: Praeger, 1964.
*Early Medieval Illumination*. Introduction by H. Swarzenski. New York: Oxford, 1951.
Goldschmidt, A., *German Illumination*, 2 vols. New York: Harcourt, 1928.
Henderson, G., *Gothic*. Harmondsworth, Eng.: Penguin Books, 1967.
Hinks, R. P., *Carolingian Art*. London: Sidgwick & Jackson, 1935.
Metz, P., *The Golden Gospels of Echternach* (tr. by I. Schrier and P. Gorge). New York: Praeger, 1957.
Nordenfalk, C., and A. Grabar, *Early Medieval Painting* (tr. by S. Gilbert). Geneva–New York: Skira, 1957.
Nordenfalk, C., and A. Grabar, *Romanesque Painting* (tr. by S. Gilbert). Geneva–New York: Skira, 1958.
Porcher, J., *Medieval French Miniatures*. New York: Abrams, 1959.

The Synthesis of Heaven and Earth in 15th-Century Art

*Flemish Art*

Cuttler, C., *Northern Painting from Pucelle to Bruegel: 14th, 15th, and 16th Centuries*. New York: Holt, Rinehart, & Winston, 1968.
De Tolnay, C., *Hieronymous Bosch*. Bâle: Editions Holbein, 1937.
Elst, J. J. M. I. van der, *Last Flowering of the Middle Ages*. New York: Doubleday, 1944.
*Flanders in the Fifteenth Century: Art and Civilization*. Detroit Institute of Arts, 1960.
Freeman, M. B., "Iconography of the Mérode Altarpiece." *Bulletin of the Metropolitan Museum of Art*, 16: 130–39, December, 1957.
Friedländer, M. J., *From Van Eyck to Bruegel*. New York: Phaidon, 1956.
Gomez-Moreno, C., *Medieval Art from Private Collections*. New York: Metropolitan Museum of Art, 1969.
Held, J. S., Review of E. Panofsky's *Early Netherlandish Painting*. *Art Bulletin*, 37: 205–34, September, 1955.
Huizinga, J., *The Waning of the Middle Ages*. London: Edward Arnold & Co., 1937.
Meiss, M., "Light as Form and Symbol in Some Fifteenth Century Paintings." *Art Bulletin*, 27: 175–81, September, 1945.
Oman, C. C., *Medieval Silver Nefs*. Victoria & Albert Museum, Monograph No. 15. London: H. M. Stationery Office, 1963.
Panofsky, E., *Early Netherlandish Painting*, 2 vols. Cambridge, Mass.: Harvard U. Press, 1954.
Philip, L. B., "The Prado Epiphany by Jerome Bosch." *Art Bulletin*, 35: 267–93, December, 1953.
Rousseau, T., "Mérode Altarpiece." *Bulletin of the Metropolitan Museum of Art*, 16: 117–29, December, 1957.
Schapiro, M., "Muscipula Diaboli; The Symbolism of the Mérode Altarpiece by the Master of Flémalle." *Art Bulletin*, 27: 182–87, September, 1945.
Von Simson, O., "Compassion and Co-Redemption in Rogier vân der Weyden's *Descent from the Cross*." *Art Bulletin*, Vol. 35, March, 1953.
Wittkower, R. and M., *Born under Saturn*. New York: Random House, 1963.

*Italian Art*

Bellew, P., and A. Schutz (eds.), *Masaccio: Frescoes in Florence*. Introduction by P. Hendy. New York Graphic Society, 1957.
Clark, K., *Piero della Francesca*. New York: Phaidon, 1951.
Clark, K., *Leonardo da Vinci*. New York: Macmillan, 1939.
De Wald, E. T., *Italian Painting: 1200–1600*. New York: Holt, Rinehart & Winston, 1961.
Hartt, F., *History of Italian Renaissance Art: Painting, Sculpture, Architecture*. New York: Abrams, 1969.
Freedberg, S., *Painting of the High Renaissance in Rome and Florence*, 2 vols. Cambridge, Mass.: Harvard U. Press, 1961.
Horizon Magazine (eds.), *The Horizon Book of the Renaissance*. New York: American Heritage Publishing C., 1961.
Eisler, C., "The Athlete of Virtue: The Iconography of Aestheticism," *Essays in Honor of Erwin Panofsky*, 2 vols. New York: New York U. Press, 1961.
Janson, H. W., *The Sculpture of Donatello*, 2 vols. Princeton, N. J.: Princeton U. Press, 1957.
Krautheimer, R., and T. H. Krautheimer, *Lorenzo Ghiberti*. Princeton, N. J.: Princeton U. Press, 1956.
Lavin, M., "Piero Della Francesca's *Flagellation:* The Triumph of Christian Glory." *Art Bulletin*, 4: 321–42, December, 1968.
Levy, M., *Early Renaissance*. Harmondsworth, Eng.: Penguin, 1967.
Meiss, M., *Giovanni Bellini's St. Francis in the Frick Collection*. Princeton, N. J.: Princeton U. Press, 1964.
Muller, H. J., *Freedom in the Western World: From the Dark Ages to the Rise of Democracy*. New York: Harper & Row, 1963.

Offner, R., "Giotto, Non-Giotto." *Burlington Magazine,* 74: 258–69; 75: 96–109+, June, September, 1939.
Olschki, L., *The Genius of Italy.* Ithaca, N.Y.: Cornell U. Press, 1954.
Panofsky, E., *Renaissance and Renascenses in Western Art.* Stockholm: Imqvist & Wiksell, 1960.
Pope-Hennessy, J., *The Complete Work of Paolo Uccello.* New York: Phaidon, 1950.
Stubblebine, J., *Giotto: The Arena Chapel Frescoes.* New York: Norton, 1969.
Tietze-Conrat, E., *Mantegna.* New York: Phaidon, 1955.
White, J., *Art and Architecture in Italy, 1250–1400.* Harmondsworth, Eng.: Penguin, 1966.
White, J., *The Birth and Rebirth of Pictorial Space.* New York: T. Yoseloff, 1958.

Michelangelo

Ackerman, J. S., *The Architecture of Michelangelo,* 2 vols. New York: Viking, 1961.
Blunt, A., *Artistic Theory in Italy, 1450–1600.* New York: Oxford, 1962.
Clark, K. M., *The Nude: A Study in Ideal Form.* New York: Pantheon, 1956.
Condivi, A., *The Life of Michelangelo* (tr. by H. P. Horne). Boston: Merrymount Press, 1904.
De Tolnay, C., *Michelangelo,* 5 vols. Princeton, N.J.: Princeton U. Press, 1943–60.
De Tolnay, C., *The Art and Thought of Michelangelo.* New York: Pantheon, 1964.
Goldscheider, L. (ed.), *Michelangelo Drawings* (tr. by R. H. Boothroyd). New York: Phaidon, 1951.
Goldwater, R. J., and M. Treves (eds. and trs.), *Artists on Art.* New York: Pantheon, 1945.
Hartt, F., "The Meaning of Michelangelo's Medici Chapel." In O. Goetz (ed.), *Essays in Honor of Georg Swarzenski.* Chicago: Regnery, 1952.
Hartt, F., *Michelangelo.* New York: Abrams, 1965.
Hartt, F., *Michelangelo: The Complete Sculpture.* New York: Abrams, 1968.
Michelangelo, *Letters,* 2 vols. (ed. and tr. by E. H. Ramsden). Stanford, Calif.: Stanford U. Press, 1963.
Michelangelo, *Paintings* (ed. by F. Hartt). New York: Abrams, 1965.
Olschki, L., *The Genius of Italy.* Ithaca, N.Y.: Cornell U. Press, 1954.
Panofsky, E., *Studies in Iconology: Humanistic Themes in the Art of the Renaissance.* New York: Oxford, 1939.
Pope-Hennessy, J., *Introduction to Italian Sculpture.* Pt. 3: *Italian Higher Renaissance and Baroque Sculpture,* 3 pts. New York: Phaidon, 1963.
Steinberg, L.,"Michelangelo's Florentine *Pietà*: The Missing Leg," *Art Bulletin,* 4: 343–53, December, 1968.

The Synthesis of Heaven and Earth in 16th- and 17th-Century Art

*Art as Religious Propaganda*

Blunt, A., *Artistic Theory in Italy,* 1450–1600. New York: Oxford, 1962.
Bousquet, J., *Mannerism: The Painting and Style of the Late Renaissance* (tr. by S. W. Taylor). New York: Braziller, 1964.
Burckhardt, J., *Recollections of Rubens* (ed. by H. Gerson, tr. by M. Hottinger). New York: Phaidon, 1950.
De Tolnay, C., *Pieter Bruegel l'ancien.* Bruxelles: Nouvelle Société d'éditions, 1935.
Dvořák, M., "El Greco and Mannerism" (tr. by J. Coolidge). *Magazine of Art,* 46: 14–23, January, 1953.
Friedlaender, W. F., *Caravaggio Studies.* Princeton, N.J.: Princeton U. Press, 1955.
Hinks, R. P., *Michelangelo Merisi da Caravaggio.* New York: Beechhurst, 1954.
Holt, E. G. (ed.), *Documentary History of Art.* Vol. 2: *Michelangelo and the Mannerists, the Baroque, and the Eighteenth Century.* New York: Anchor, 1958.
*Le Siècle de Bruegel,* catalogue of an exhibition. Musées Royaux des Beaux-Arts de Belgique, 1965.
*Le Siècle de Rubens,* catalogue of an exhibition. Musées Royaux des Beaux-Arts de Belgique, 1965.
Mâle, E., *L'Art religieux de la fin du XVI*e *siècle, du XVII*e *siècle et du XVIII*e *siècle.* Paris: Colin, 1951.
Meier-Graefe, J. A., *The Spanish Journey* (tr. by J. H. Reece). New York: Harcourt, 1927.
Wethey, H. E., *El Greco and His School.* Princeton, N. J.: Princeton University Press, 1962.
Wittkower, R., *Gian Lorenzo Bernini.* New York: Phaidon, 1955.
Wittkower, R., "El Greco's Language of Gestures." *Art News,* 56: 44–49+, March, 1957.
Wittkower, R., *Art and Architecture in Italy, 1600–1750.* Baltimore: Penguin, 1958.
Wölfflin, H., *Principles of Art History* (tr. by M. D. Hottinger). New York: Dover, 1950.

*Figures at a Table in Baroque Secular Art*

Blunt, A., *Art and Architecture in France, 1500–1700.* Baltimore: Penguin, 1954.
Bousquet, J., *Mannerism: The Painting and Style of the Late Renaissance* (tr. by S. W. Taylor). New York: Braziller, 1964.
De Tolnay, C., "Vermeer's 'The Artist's Studio'." *Gazette des Beaux-Arts,* s 6, 41: 265–72, 292–94, April, 1953.
*Fêtes de la palette,* catalogue of an exhibition. New Orleans: Isaac Delgado Museum, 1963.
Friedländer, M. J., *Landscape, Portrait, Still Life* (tr. by R. F. C. Hull). Oxford, Eng.: Cassirer, 1949.
Furness, S. M. M., *Georges de la Tour of Lorraine,* London: Routledge & Kegan Paul, 1949.
Gilbert, C., *Figures at a Table,* catalogue of an exhibition. Saratoga, Fla.: John and Mable Ringling Museum of Art, 1960.
Held, J. S., *Flemish Painting.* New York: Abrams, 1953.
Highet, G., "Bruegel's Rustic Wedding." *Magazine of Art,* 38: 274–76, November, 1945.
López-Rey, J., *Velázquez.* London: Faber, 1963.
Puyvelde, L. van, *Jordaens.* Paris, New York: Elsevier, 1953.
Swillens, P. T. A., *Johannes Vermeer* (tr. by C. M. Breuning-Williams). Utrecht, Netherlands: Spectrum, 1950.
Thuillier, J., and A. Châtelet, *French Painting, from Le Nain to Fragonard.* Geneva–New York: Skira, 1964.

Rembrandt

Benesch, O., *Rembrandt* (tr. by J. Emmons). Geneva–New York: Skira, 1957.
Clark, K. M., *Rembrandt and the Italian Renaissance.* New York: New York U. Press, 1966.
De Tolnay, C., "The Syndics of the Drapers' Guild by Rembrandt: An Interpretation." *Gazette des Beaux-Arts,* s 6, 23: 31–38, January, 1943.
Fromentin, E., *Masters of Past Time* (tr. by A. Boyle). New York: Dutton, 1913.
Heckscher, W. S., "Rembrandt's Anatomy of Dr. Nicolaas Tulp." New York U. Press, 1958.
Held, J. S., "Rembrandt: The Self-Education of an Artist." *Art News,* 40: 10–19+, February 1, 1942.
Held, J. S., "Rembrandt's Polish Rider." *Art Bulletin,* 26: 246–65, December, 1944.
Held, J. S., "Debunking Rembrandt's Legend." *Art News,* 48: 20–24, February, 1950.
Held, J. S., *Rembrandt and the Book of Tobit.* Northampton, Mass.: Gehenna Press, 1964.
Hind, A. M., *Rembrandt.* Cambridge, Mass.: Harvard U. Press, 1932.
Münz, L., *Rembrandt.* New York: Abrams, 1954.
Rembrandt, H. van Rijn, *Selected Drawings,* by O. Benesch. New York: Phaidon, 1947.
Rembrandt, H. van Rijn, *Etchings* (ed. by L. Münz), 2 vols. New York: Phaidon, 1952.
Rosenberg, J., *Rembrandt.* New York: Phaidon, 1964.
Slive, S., *Rembrandt and His Critics, 1630–1730.* The Hague: Nijhoff, 1953.
White, C., *Rembrandt and His World.* London: Thames & Hudson, 1964.
White, C., *Rembrandt as an Etcher: A Study of the Artist at Work.* London: A. Zwemmer Ltd., 1969.

Images of Authority

Blunt, A., *Art and Architecture in France, 1500–1700.* Baltimore: Penguin, 1954.
Clark, K., *Piero della Francesca.* New York: Phaidon, 1951.
De Kooning, E., "Painting a Portrait of the President." *Art News,* Summer, 1964.
Frankfort, H., *Art and Architecture of the Ancient Orient.* Baltimore: Penguin, 1954.
Frankfort, H., *Kingship and the Gods: A Study of Ancient Near Eastern Religion as the Integration of Society and Nature.* University of Chicago Press, 1948.
Ghirshman, R., *Iran: Parthes et Sassanides.* Paris: Gallimard, 1962.
Grabar, A., *L'Empereur dans l'art byzantin.* Paris: Les Belles lettres, 1936.
Groenewegen-Frankfort, H. A., *Arrest and Movement.* New York: Humanities, 1951.
Hamberg, P. G., *Studies in Roman Imperial Art.* Copenhagen: Munksgaard, 1945.

Held, J., "*Le Roi à la chasse:* Van Dyck's Portrait of Charles I." *Art Bulletin*, 40: 139–49, June, 1958.
Jenkins, M. D., *The State Portrait. Art Bulletin* Monograph, 1947.
Lehmann-Haupt, H., *Art under a Dictatorship.* New York: Oxford, 1954.
Lewis, W. H., *The Splendid Century: Life in the France of Louis XIV.* New York: Anchor, 1957.
Lipman, J. H., "The Florentine Profile Portrait in the Quattrocento." *Art Bulletin*, 18: 54–102, March, 1956.
Liudprandus of Cremona, *Works.* London: Routledge, 1930.
Mattingly, Garrett, *The Armada.* Boston: Houghton Mifflin, 1959.
Strong, E., *Apotheosis and After Life.* London: Constable, 1915.
Titian, *Paintings and Drawings.* Introduction by H. Tietze. New York: Phaidon, 1937.
Wittkower, R., *Gian Lorenzo Bernini.* New York: Phaidon, 1955.
Yuzan, D. S., *The Beginner's Book of Bushido* (tr. by A. L. Sadler). Tokyo: Kokusai Bunka Shinkokai, 1941.

Architecture of Authority

Anderson, J., and R. P. Spiers, *The Architecture of Greece and Rome.* Vol. 2: *The Architecture of Ancient Rome* (revised and rewritten by T. Ashby). London: V. T. Batsford, 1927.
Blunt, A., *Art and Architecture in France, 1500–1700.* Baltimore: Penguin, 1954.
Brown, F. E., "Roman Architecture." *College Art Journal*, 17: 105–14, 1958.
Drexler, A., *The Architecture of Japan.* New York: Museum of Modern Art, 1955.
Evenson, N., *Chandigarh.* Berkeley: U. of California Press, 1966.
Frankfort, H., *Art and Architecture of the Ancient Orient.* Baltimore: Penguin, 1954.
Gropius, W., K. Tange, and Y. Ishimoto, *Katsura: Tradition and Creation in Japanese Architecture.* New Haven, Conn.: Yale U. Press, 1960.
Masson, G., *Italian Villas and Palaces.* London: Thames & Hudson, 1959.
Mylonas, G. E., *Ancient Mycenae, the Capital City of Agamemnon.* Princeton, N. J.: Princeton U. Press, 1957.
Pevsner, N., *An Outline of European Architecture*, Jubilee ed. Baltimore: Penguin, 1960.
Schapiro, M., "Taste," *Encyclopedia of the Social Sciences* (ed. by E. R. A. Seligmann), Vol. XIV, pp. 523–25. New York: Macmillan, 1934.
Smith, E. B., *Egyptian Architecture as Cultural Expression.* New York: Appleton-Century, 1938.
Wittkower, R., *Art and Architecture in Italy, 1600–1750.* Baltimore: Penguin, 1958.
Wölfflin, H., *Renaissance and Baroque* (tr. by K. Simon). New York: Collins, 1964.
Wright, F. L., *On Architecture; Selected Writings, 1894–1940* (ed. by F. Guttheim). New York: Grosset & Dunlop, 1959.
Wright, F. L., *Writings and Buildings* (sel. by E. Kaufmann and B. Raeburn). New York: Meridian, 1960.

The Life and Death of the City Square

Argan, G. C., *The Renaissance City* (Planning & Cities Series, ed. by G. R. Collins). New York: Braziller, 1969.
Carcopino, J., *Daily Life in Ancient Rome* (ed. by H. T. Rowell; tr. by E. O. Lorimer) New Haven: Yale U. Press, 1960.
Gutkind, E. A., *International History of City Development*, 5 vols. (See vol. 1, *Urban Development in Central Europe*; vol. 4, *Urban Development in Southern Europe: Italy and Greece.*) London: Collier-MacMillan, 1964–69.
Hardoy, J., *Urban Planning in Pre-Columbian America* (Planning & Cities Series). New York: Braziller, 1968.
Jacobs, J., *The Death and Life of Great American Cities.* New York: Vintage, 1961.
Lavedan, P., *Histoire de l'urbanisme, antiquité–moyen âge.* Paris: Laurens, 1926.
Leefe, J. M., "Ghirardelli Square," *Interiors*, October 1965.
MacDonald, W. L., *The Architecture of the Roman Empire.* New Haven: Yale U. Press, 1965.
Moholy-Nagy, S., *Matrix of Man: An Illustrated History of Urban Environment.* London: Pall Mall, 1968.
Moore, C., "Ghirardelli Square," *Architectural Forum*, June 1965.
Mumford, L., *The City in History, Its Origins, Its Transformation and Its Prospects.* New York: Harcourt, 1961.
Rudofsky, B., *Streets for People: A Primer For Americans.* Garden City: Doubleday, 1969.
Saalman, H., *Medieval Cities* (Planning & Cities Series, ed. by G. R. Collins). New York: Braziller, 1968.
Scully, V., *American Architecture and Urbanism: A Historical Essay.* New York: Praeger, 1969.
Sitte, C., *City Planning According to Artistic Principles* (tr. by G. R. Collins and C. C. Collins). New York: Random House, 1965.
Von Eckardt, W., *A Place to Live.* New York: Delta, 1969.
Von Eckardt, W., "A Daring Design That Paid Off" (Boston's new City Hall), *San Francisco Chronicle*, February 17, 1969.
Wittkower, R., *Art and Architecture in Italy, 1600–1750.* Maryland: Penguin, 1958.
Wycherly, R. E., *How the Greeks Built Cities.* New York: Anchor, 1969.
Zucker, P., *Town and Square: From the Agora to the Village Green.* New York: Columbia U. Press, 1966.

The Synthesis of Past and Present
in 19th-Century Art

Adhémar, J., *Daumier.* London: Zwemmer, 1954.
Benesch, O., *Edvard Munch* (tr. by J. Spencer). New York: Phaidon, 1960.
Boggs, J. S., *Portraits by Degas.* Berkeley: U. of California Press, 1962.
Cooper, D., *Toulouse-Lautrec.* New York: Abrams, 1956.
Deknatel, F. B., *Edvard Munch.* New York: Museum of Modern Art, 1950.
Elsen, A. E., *Rodin's Gates of Hell.* Minneapolis: U. of Minnesota Press, 1960.
Friedlaender, W. F., *David to Delacroix* (tr. by R. Goldwater). Cambridge, Mass.: Harvard U. Press, 1952.
Gauguin, P., *Gauguin* (ed. by R. Goldwater). New York: Abrams, 1957.
Hamilton, G. H., *Painting and Sculpture in Europe, 1880–1940.* Baltimore: Penguin, 1967.
Hoffmann, W., *The Earthly Paradise.* New York: Braziller, 1961.
Honour, H., *Neo-Classicism.* Harmondsworth, Eng.: Penguin, 1968.
Johnson, L., *Delacroix.* New York: Norton, 1963.
Lövgren, S., *The Genesis of Modernism.* Stockholm: Almqvist & Wiksell, 1959.
Meier-Graefe, J., *Modern Art* (tr. by F. Simmonds and G. W. Chrystal), 2 vols. New York: Putnam, 1908.
Rewald, J., *Pierre Bonnard.* New York: Museum of Modern Art, 1948.
Rewald, J., *Post-Impressionism from Van Gogh to Gauguin.* New York: Museum of Modern Art, 1958.
Rewald, J., *The History of Impressionism*, rev. New York: Museum of Modern Art, 1962.
Rewald, J., *Pissarro* (ed. by M. S. Fox). New York: Abrams, 1963.
Rich, D. C. (ed.), *Degas.* New York: Abrams, 1951.
Russell, J., *Seurat.* New York: Praeger, 1965.
Schapiro, M., "New Light on Seurat," *Art News*, 57: 22–24, April, 1958.
Schapiro, M., *Vincent Van Gogh.* New York: Abrams, 1950.
Seitz, W., *Monet.* New York: Abrams, 1960.
Tannenbaum, L., *James Ensor.* New York: Museum of Modern Art, 1951.
Wildenstein, G., *Ingres.* New York: Phaidon, 1954.

Art and Nature

Blunt, A., *Art and Architecture in France, 1500–1700.* Baltimore: Penguin, 1954.
Burnham, J., "Hans Haacke, Wind and Water Sculpture." *Tri-Quarterly Supplement*, No. 1, Spring 1967, Northwestern U. Press.
Burnham, J., "Real Time Systems." *ArtForum*, 49–55, September, 1969.
Celant, G., *Art Povera.* New York: Praeger, 1969.
Clark, K. M., *Leonardo da Vinci.* New York: Phaidon, 1955.
Collins, L. C., *Hercules Seghers.* U. of Chicago Press, 1953.
Elsen, A., "Seymour Lipton: Odyssey of the Unquiet Metaphor." *Art International*, 5: 39–44, February, 1961.
Friedländer, M. J., *Landscape, Portrait, Still Life* (tr. by R. F. C. Hull). Oxford, Eng.: Cassirer, 1949.
Geist, S., *Brancusi: A Study of the Sculpture.* New York: Grossman, 1968.
Giedion-Welcker, C., *Jean Arp.* London: Thames & Hudson, 1958.
Grohmann, W., *Paul Klee.* New York: Abrams, 1954.
Haftmann, W., *The Mind and Work of Paul Klee.* London: Faber, 1954.

Heizer, M., "The Art of Michael Heizer," *ArtForum*, VIII, 32–39, December, 1969.
Lee, S., *A History of Far Eastern Art*. New York: Abrams, 1964.
Leonardo da Vinci, *Notebooks* (ed. by E. MacCurdy). New York: Braziller, 1955.
Merleau-Ponty, M., "Cezanne's Doubt," *Sense and Non-Sense* (tr. by H. Dreyfus and P. Dreyfus). Evanston: Northwestern U. Press, 1964.
Panofsky, E., *The Life and Art of Albrecht Dürer*. Princeton, N. J.: Princeton University Press, 1955.
Robbin, A., "Smithson's Non-Sights," *Art News*, February, 1969.
Rowley, G., *Principles of Chinese Painting*. Princeton, N. J.: Princeton U. Press, 1947.
Rubin, W., *Matta*. New York: Museum of Modern Art, 1958.
Schapiro, M., *Vincent Van Gogh*. New York: Abrams, 1950.
Schapiro, M., *Paul Cézanne*. New York: Abrams, 1952.
Selz, P., *The Work of Jean Dubuffet*. New York: Museum of Modern Art, 1962.
Sickman, L., and A. Soper, *Art and Architecture of China*. Baltimore: Penguin, 1956.
Sirén, O., *Chinese Painting*. Pt. 1: Vol. 1. *Early Chinese Painting*; Vol. 2. *The Sung Period*. New York: Ronald, 1956.
Smithson, R., "A Sedimentation of the Mind: Earth Proposals," *ArtForum*, VII, 44–50, September, 1968.
Soper, A., "Early Chinese Landscape Painting." *Art Bulletin*, 23: 141–64, June, 1941.
Spear, A., *Brancusi's Birds*. New York: New York U. Press, for the College Art Association of America, 1969.
Stechow, W., *Dutch Landscape Painting of the Seventeenth Century*. London: Phaidon, 1966.
Sweeney, J., *Alexander Calder*. New York: Museum of Modern Art, 1943.
Turner, A. R., *The Vision of Landscape in Renaissance Italy*. Princeton, N. J.: Princeton U. Press, 1966.
Van Gogh, V., *Complete Letters* (tr. by J. van Gogh-Bouger and E. de Dood; re-ed. by Mrs. R. Amussen, et al.), 3 vols. New York Graphic Society, 1958.

## Art, Objects, and the Object of Art

Alloway, L., *Samaras: Selected Works 1960–66*. New York: The Pace Gallery, 1966.
Barr, A. H., Jr., *Matisse: His Art and His Public*. New York: Museum of Modern Art, 1951.
Bergstrom, I., *Dutch Still-Life Painting in the Seventeenth Century* (tr. by C. Hedstrom and G. Taylor). London: Faber & Faber, 1956.
*Fêtes de la palette*, catalogue of an exhibition. New Orleans: Isaac Delgado Museum, 1963.
Friedländer, M. J., *Landscape, Portrait, Still Life* (tr. by R. F. C. Hull). Oxford, Eng.: Cassirer, 1949.
Friedman, B. H. (ed.), *School of New York*. New York: Grove, 1959.
Hultén, K. G., *The Machine, As Seen at the End of the Mechanical Age*. New York: Museum of Modern Art, 1968.
Level, R., *Marcel Duchamp* (tr. by G. H. Hamilton). New York: Grove, 1959.
Robbins, D., *Recent Still Life*. Providence: Museum of Art, Rhode Island School of Design, 1966.
Rowley, G., *Principles of Chinese Painting*. Princeton, N. J.: Princeton U. Press, 1947.
*Roy Lichtenstein*. Exhibition organized by John Coplans. Pasadena: Pasadena, California Art Museum, 1967.
Rubin, W., *Dada, Surrealism, and Their Heritage*. New York: Museum of Modern Art, 1968.
Schapiro, Meyer, "The Apples of Cézanne: An Essay on the Meaning of Still-Life," in "The Avant-Garde," *Art News Annual*, XXXIV, 34–53, 1968.
Schapiro, M., *Vincent Van Gogh*. New York: Abrams, 1950.
Schapiro, M., *Paul Cézanne*. New York: Abrams, 1952.
Soby, J. T., *Giorgio de Chirico*. New York: Museum of Modern Art, 1955.
Solomon, A. R. (comp.), *Robert Rauschenberg*. New York: The Jewish Museum, 1964.
Soria, M. S. (ed.), *Francisco Zurbarán*. New York: Phaidon, 1953.
Steinberg, L., *Jasper Johns*. New York: Wittenborn, 1963.
Sterling, C., *Still Life Painting: From Antiquity to the Present Time* (tr. by J. Emmons), rev. ed. New York: Universe Books, 1959.

## The Portrait in Painting and Sculpture

Ambler, E., *A Coffin for Dimitrios*. New York: Dell, 1957.
Elsen, A., "Rodin's Portrait of Baudelaire." No. 25, *A Catalogue and Collection of Essays Honoring Henry Hope*. Bloomington: Indiana U. Press, 1966.
Friedländer, M. J., *Landscape, Portrait, Still Life* (tr. by R. F. C. Hull). Oxford, Eng.: Cassirer, 1949.
Geist, S., *Brancusi: A Study of the Sculpture*. New York: Grossman, 1968.
Held, J. (ed.), *Peter Paul Rubens*. New York: Abrams, 1953.
Hoffman, E., *Kokoschka: Life and Work*. London: Faber, 1947.
Lange, K., and M. Hirmer, *Egypt: Architecture, Sculpture, Painting in Three Thousand Years* (tr. by R. H. Boothroyd). New York: Phaidon, 1956.
Levey, M., "A Prince of Court Painters: Bronzino." *Apollo*, 76: 165–72, 1962.
Lipman, J. H., "The Florentine Profile Portrait in the Quattrocento." *Art Bulletin*, 18: 54–102, March, 1936.
Meiss, M., "Nicholas Albergati and the Chronology of Jan Van Eyck's Portraits." *Burlington Magazine*, 94: 137–46; 95: 27, May, 1952, January, 1953.
Miller, J., "On the Face of It," *The Sunday Times Magazine*, special issue on *The Human Face*, London, December 4, 1966.
Miller, M., "Géricault's Portraits of the Insane." *Journal of the Warburg and Courtauld Institutes*, 4: 151–63, April–July, 1940–41.
Panofsky, E., *Early Netherlandish Painting*, 2 vols, Cambridge, Mass.: Harvard U. Press, 1954.
Pope-Hennessy, J., *The Portrait in the Renaissance*. New York: Pantheon Books, 1966.
Schapiro, M., *Vincent Van Gogh*. New York: Abrams, 1950.
Schapiro, M., *Paul Cézanne*. New York: Abrams, 1952.
Simmel, G., "The Aesthetic Significance of the Face," *Essays on Sociology, Philosophy, and Aesthetics* (ed. by Kurt Wolff). New York: Harper Torchbooks, 1965.
Soby, J. T., *Joan Miró*. New York: Museum of Modern Art, 1959.
Sylvester, D., *Alberto Giacometti*. Exhibition, Arts Council Gallery. London: Arts Council of Great Britain, 1955.

## The Figure in Sculpture

### *The Figure in Older Sculpture*

Clark, K. M., *The Nude: A Study in Ideal Form*. New York: Pantheon, 1956.
Janson, H. W., *The Sculpture of Donatello*, 2 vols. Princeton, N. J.: Princeton U. Press, 1957.
Kramrisch, S., *The Art of India*. New York: Phaidon, 1954.
Panofsky, E., "The History of the Theory of Human Proportions as a Reflection of the History of Styles." In *Meaning in the Visual Arts*. New York: Anchor, 1955.
Schapiro, M., "The Sculptures of Souillac." In W. R. W. Koehler (ed.), *Medieval Studies in Memory of Arthur Kingsley Porter*. Cambridge, Mass.: Harvard U. Press, 1939.
Wittkower, R., *Gian Lorenzo Bernini*. New York: Phaidon, 1955.

### *Transformations of the Figure in Modern Sculpture*

Elsen, A. E., *The Partial Figure in Modern Sculpture: from Rodin to 1969*. Baltimore: Baltimore Museum of Art, 1969.
Elsen, A. E., *Rodin*. New York: Museum of Modern Art, 1963.
Elsen, A. E., *The Sculpture of Henri Matisse*. New York: Abrams, 1971.
Geist, S., *Brancusi: A Study of the Sculpture*. New York: Grossman, 1968.
Goldwater, R., *Lipchitz*. New York: Universe Books, 1959.
Goldwater, R., *What Is Modern Sculpture?* New York: Museum of Modern Art, 1969.
Grohmann, W., *The Art of Henry Moore*. New York: Abrams, 1960.
Nordland, G., *Gaston Lachaise: Sculpture and Drawings*. Los Angeles: Los Angeles County Museum of Art, 1963.
Ritchie, A. C., *Sculpture of the Twentieth Century*. New York: Museum of Modern Art, 1953.
Selz, P., *Alberto Giacometti*. Garden City, N.Y.: Doubleday, 1965.
Soby, J., *Jean Arp*. Garden City, N.Y.: Doubleday, 1958.
Steinberg, Leo, *Rodin*. New York: Slatkin Gallery, 1963.
Sylvester, D., *Alberto Giacometti*. Exhibition, Arts Council Gallery. London: Arts Council of Great Britain, 1955.
Sylvester, D., *Henry Moore*. London: Arts Council of Great Britain, 1968.

Picasso

Barr, A. H., Jr. (ed.), *Picasso: Forty Years of His Art*. New York: Museum of Modern Art, 1939.
Blunt, A., *Picasso's 'Guernica.'* London–New York: Oxford, 1969.
Blunt, A., and P. Pool, *Picasso, The Formative Years*. New York Graphic Society, 1962.
Boeck, W., and J. Sabartés, *Picasso*. New York: Abrams, 1955.
Elsen, A. E., "The Many Faces of Picasso's Sculpture," *Art International*, 24–34, Summer, 1969.
Elsen, A. E., "Surprise, Invention, Economy in the Sculpture of Picasso," *ArtForum*, VI, 17–23, November, 1967.
Gilot, F., and C. Lake, *Life with Picasso*. New York: Signet, 1965.
Greenberg, C., "Picasso at Seventy-five." In *Art and Culture: Critical Essays*. Boston: Beacon Press, 1961.
Kahnweiler, D. H., *The Sculptures of Picasso* (phot. by Brassaï; tr. by A. D. B. Sylvester). London: Rodney Phillips, 1949.
Penrose, R., *Picasso: His Life and Work*. New York: Harper, 1959.
Penrose, R., *The Sculpture of Picasso*. New York: Museum of Modern Art, 1967.
Rosenblum, R., *Cubism and Twentieth-Century Art*. New York: Abrams, 1961.
Rosenblum, R., "Picasso and the Anatomy of Eroticism." *Studies in Erotic Art* (ed. by T. Bowie and C. Christenson). New York: Basic Books, Inc., 1970.
Steinberg, L., "Sleep Watchers." *Life* (Special Double Issue on Picasso), December 27, 1968.

Imaginative Art

*General*

Baltrusaitis, J., *Réveils et prodiges: Le Gothique fantastique*. Paris: Colin, 1960.
Barr, A. H., Jr., *Fantastic Art, Dada, and Surrealism*. New York: Museum of Modern Art, 1936.
Bousquet, J., *Mannerism: The Painting and Style of the Late Renaissance* (tr. by S. W. Taylor). New York: Braziller, 1964.
Daniel, H., *Devils, Monsters and Nightmares*. New York: Abelard-Schuman, 1964.
Goldwater, R., and M. Treves (eds. and trs.), *Artists on Art*. New York: Pantheon, 1945.
Rubin, W., *Dada, Surrealism, and Their Heritage*. New York: Museum of Modern Art, 1968.

*Individual Artists*

Benesch, O., *The Art of the Renaissance in Northern Europe* (on Dürer). Hamden, Conn: Shoe String, 1964.
Combe, J., *Jerome Bosch*. Paris: Tisné, 1957.
Dali, S., *The Secret Life of Salvador Dali*. New York: Dial, 1942.
De Tolnay, C., *Hieronymous Bosch*. Bâle: Editions Holbein, 1937.
Grohmann, W., *Paul Klee*. New York: Abrams, 1954.
Harris, T., *Goya, Engravings and Lithographs*, 2 vols. Oxford, Eng.: Cassirer, 1964.
Hess, T. B., *Willem de Kooning*. New York: Braziller, 1959.
Lebel, R., *Marcel Duchamp* (tr. by G. H. Hamilton). New York: Grove, 1959.
Lieberman, W. S. (ed.), *Max Ernst*. New York: Museum of Modern Art, 1961.
López-Rey, J., *Goya's Caprichos*, 2 vols. Princeton, N.J.: Princeton U. Press, 1953.
Mellerio, A., *Odilon Redon*. New York: Da Capo Press, 1968.
Meyer, F. (ed.), *Marc Chagall; His Graphic Work*. New York: Abrams, 1957.
*Odilon Redon, Gustave Moreau, Rudolf Bresdin*, catalogue of an exhibition. New York: Museum of Modern Art, 1961.
Panofsky, E., *The Life and Art of Albrecht Dürer*. Princeton, N. J.: Princeton U. Press, 1955.
Schwabacher, E. K., *Arshile Gorky*. New York: Macmillan, 1957.
Seitz, W. C., *René Magritte*. New York: Museum of Modern Art, 1965.
Selz, P., *The Work of Jean Dubuffet*. New York: Museum of Modern Art, 1962.
Selz, P., and others, *Max Beckmann*. New York: Museum of Modern Art.
Soby, J. T., *Giorgio de Chirico*. New York: Museum of Modern Art, 1955.
Tzara, T., *Bizzarie di varie figure di Giovanbatista Bracelli, pittore fiorentino*. Paris: A. Brieux, 1963.

Death of the Window and Life of the Square: Abstraction

Albers, J., *Interaction of Color*. New Haven, Conn.: Yale U. Press, 1963.
Arp, H., *On My Way*. New York: Wittenborn, 1948.
Battcock, G., *Minimal Art: A Critical Anthology*. New York: E. P. Dutton, 1968.
Burnham, J., "A Dan Flavin Retrospective in Ottawa," *ArtForum*, VIII, 48–55, December, 1969.
De Kooning, E., in *Franz Kline Memorial Exhibition*. Washington D. C.: Gallery of Modern Art, 1962.
Fried, M., *Three American Painters: Kenneth Noland, Jules Olitski, Frank Stella*. Cambridge, Mass.: Harvard U. Press, 1965.
Goldwater, R. S., "Reflections on the Rothko Exhibition." *Arts*, 35: 42–45, March, 1961.
Gray, C., *David Smith by David Smith*. New York: Holt, Rinehart & Winston, 1968.
Haftmann, W., *The Mind and Work of Paul Klee*. London: Faber, 1954.
Hess, T. B., *Barnett Newman*. New York: Walker, 1969.
Jaffé, H. L. C., *De Stijl, 1917–1931; The Dutch Contribution to Modern Art*. Amsterdam: J. M. Meulenhoff, 1956.
Malevich, K. S., *The Non-Objective World* (tr. by H. Dearstyne). Chicago: Theobald, 1960.
Mondrian, P. C., *Plastic Art and Pure Plastic Art, 1937, and Other Essays, 1941–1943*. New York: Wittenborn, 1945.
Munari, B., *The Square*. New York: Wittenborn, 1966.
Reinhardt, A., statements in D. C. Miller (ed.), *Americans 1963*, catalogue of an exhibition. New York: Museum of Modern Art, 1963.
Rosenberg, H., "Barnett Newman: The Living Rectangle," *The Anxious Object*. New York: Horizon, 1964.
Rubin, W., *Frank Stella*. New York: Museum of Modern Art, 1970.
Schapiro, M., "The Liberating Quality of Avant Garde Art." *Art News*, 56: 36–42, June, 1957.
Schapiro, M., "On the Humanity of Abstract Painting" (Blashfield Address), *Proceedings of the American Academy of Arts and Letters and the National Institute of Arts and Letters*, Ser. 2, No. 10, pp. 316–23, 1960.
Seitz, W. C., *The Responsive Eye*. New York: Museum of Modern Art, 1965.
Soby, J. T., *René Magritte*. New York: Museum of Modern Art, 1966.
Wheeler, M., *The Last Works of Henri Matisse*. New York: Museum of Modern Art, 1961.

# Glossary

Indivisible as the aesthetic experience is and must become for the serious student of art, art in its complexity does have a number of parts, and over the years and centuries usage has provided a basic nomenclature for identifying in verbal discourse those components and their interrelationships. At this juncture, for the want of context and demonstration, the terms as they shall be introduced may seem somewhat arbitrary and abstract, definitions as one would expect to find them in a dictionary. But brief and rudimentary as the present explanations must be, they nonetheless can provide enough familiarity with a specialized language to permit the reader to begin with security in any part of the book—in portraits, in fantasy art, in figural sculpture, or in religious or secular architecture—according to his or her specific needs and interests. A wider range of terminology and a deeper understanding of its usage will come with the reader's thoughtful response to the art works reproduced in the book and to the discussions and analyses that accompany them.

The first part of the glossary has been prepared as a narrative essay designed to give a brief overview of those concepts and their related terms that help make coherent our verbal commentary on the visual arts, which themselves are a language capable of powerful communication. The reader may find it beneficial to follow this essay somewhat carefully at the outset of his study in the book and then refer to the remainder of the glossary, which is arranged in the standard format of lexicography, for definitions of other terms as these appear in the course of reading the text.

## THE ELEMENTS OF FORMAL EXPRESSION

Two broad and very important domains of equal importance within the total experience of the visual arts are *subject* and *form,* since no work of *visual* art, even that conceived and executed explicitly to have neither form nor subject, can be proved absolutely to exist without some sort of conceptual as well as physical structure. Subject matter is generally thought of as the identifiable objects, incidents, and situations *represented* in a painting or sculpture, or in architecture the evident function, public or private, that a building has been designed to perform. Subject matter can also be construed as experience not actually represented by images but implied or referred to by the visual evidence the artist has provided in his work. This is especially true of the more radical and advanced forms of modern abstract art. The most elementary physical factors that give the visual arts their *form* are *line, plane, color, shading, texture, shape, mass* or *volume, scale, space,* and *composition,* the latter being the organization that the artist, exploiting the possibilities of the materials and processes available to him, consciously has imposed upon his particular selection among all the other factors or elements for the creation of a unique work of art. In the fullness of their worth, form and subject fuse and function together to produce what could be called the *expressive content,* and it is this, an ultimately undefinable reality, that gives art its meaning and significance. Matured to a high level of consistency, in the work of an individual artist or of a group of artists, these qualities become *style*.

*Line*. The most commonplace definition of line is a mark left in its path by a moving point. It can also be seen as the edge of a flat shape, as the *contour* of a solid object, and as the implied *axis* of a shape or through a group of forms. The potential for expressiveness that line offers is immense, and by making his line continuous and even, modulated in thickness, meandering, or broken, emphatic, flowing, or crabbed, the artist can cause his work to seem mechanical, spontaneous, or virtuoso in its freedom and security. A line by itself provides the means to stress form and to create mood, whether lyric, tragic, or humorous, and it is especially potent as a device for suggesting direction and movement in all degrees of depth and dynamics, which in turn implies both time and space. The line in the work of a mature artist, especially in his drawings, reveals the training he had, the art to which he was exposed, what he knew about this subject, his perceptiveness, the way he made decisions, and whether or not he was willing to take risks. Used to interpret the human body or a landscape, a given line represents the arbitrary choice of the artist, for there are no lines in nature, only continuous surfaces. Line can serve as an alternative to these surfaces, and it is interesting to observe how a gifted artist has made this alternative plausible and used it to suggest the many properties of his subject. Wrought by a sensitive draftsman, a contour line following closely each inflection in the silhouette of the human body has the capacity to evoke memories of the skeleton and musculature as well as the body's surface hollows and swellings, even to project the personality of the subject and establish the artist's point of view toward it. In brief, lines create a sense of structure, movement, and character.

*Plane* could be said to be the extension in breadth of the element called *line*. It is a flat surface; that is, a surface defined as measurable in two dimensions. But like line, also a two-dimensional element, a plane can be made physically to move into depth, or the third dimension, and to give the illusion of having a function in the geometries of three-dimensional space. The *picture plane* is that which is assumed to be at the front surface of a painting.

*Color*. Sunlight, or "white" light, contains the elements of all colors, and because it contains them all, each is canceled. The component colors of the full visible spectrum can be obtained from white light by projecting it through a prism. An object has a certain color because it reflects those elements of white light that produce the color and absorbs the others. An apple, for instance, provides the sensation of red by permitting the reflection of the red element in the spectrum and by absorbing all remaining color elements.

The term *color* refers to a combination of *hue, saturation,* and *value*. *Hue* is the property of a color that gives it a name, that distinguishes one color from another as red, green, violet, etc. Expressed as a continuous circle, the visible spectrum can, in theory, be divided into twelve hues—three called *primary* and three *secondary*. In artists' colors (as opposed to light, which because of its purity creates a different set of conditions) the primary hues, or colors, are red, yellow, and blue. When mixed, these can, in theory, produce all other hues, including the secondaries, which are orange, green, and violet. The primaries mixed with their secondaries yield six additional colors. Arranged on a color wheel and read clockwise from the top, these twelve colors appear as yellow, yellow-green, green, blue-green, blue, blue-violet, violet, red-violet, red, red-orange, orange, and yellow-orange. Colors directly opposite each other in this circular arrangement are called *complementary colors* and have the property of dulling or canceling each other when mixed. This occurs because red, for example, represents the absorption of all hues other than red and because green, which falls directly opposite red on the color wheel, represents the reflection only of blue, green, and yellow and the absorption of all red; therefore, in a mixture of red and green all hues would be absorbed and none left to reflect. On the other hand, complementaries have the property of intensifying each other if placed side by side. Beginning with Turner and Delacroix and continuing with the Impressionists and Post-Impressionists, 19th-century painters increasingly found system in the juxtaposition of complementaries so as to attain maximum intensity in, for example, yellow by supporting it with an adjacent stroke of violet, in blue with orange, and in red with green.

*Saturation* refers to the purity, vividness, or intensity of a color. A brilliant red is said to be of high saturation, and a soft yellow to be of low saturation.

The technical term for *shading* is *value,* and this distinguishes the property of color that makes it seem light or dark. Only the values of colors are apparent in black-and-white reproductions of art works. Light colors are considered to be high in value, while dark colors are described as low in value. A *tint,* or very high value, of a color can be obtained by mixing the color with white, and a *shade,* or low-value color, derives from mixing a hue with black. While in theory white is held to be the total reflection of all potential hues, black is believed to reflect none at all.

Artists often orchestrate a wide range of color properties in order to convey specific ideas and feelings. If placed near a strong color, white or neutral grey will appear to reflect something of the color's complementary. This effect of simultaneous contrast can also occur in combinations of colors: red next to yellow can suggest yellow's complement, violet; and the yellow will appear to contain a touch of green, the complement of red. Because of our associations of certain colors with light and heat, the colors of yellow, red, orange, and sometimes violet are sensed to be *warm,* and those of green and blue to be *cool*. Warm colors often seem to make an object appear larger than its actual size, while the tendency of cool colors is to diminish the appearance of size. Warm colors produce the effect of advancing toward the viewer; cool colors seem to recede. However, given maximum saturation, a cool color can be made to come forward ahead of a warm color of low saturation. In countless ways, colors can be caused to mutually intensify, clash, or harmonize. *Local color* signifies the natural color of the subject, and *chroma* is synonymous with saturation and intensity.

*Texture* is the actual or implied tactile quality of surface: smooth or rough, slick or grainy, soft or hard. In painting, texture can be the actual, physical surface made by the paint substance or the surfaces represented by the artist using such visual devices as contrast in colors and in light and dark.

*Shape* and *mass* are forms thought to be characterized as having their existence in, respectively, two and three dimensions. A shape is an area or a plane with distinguishable boundaries, such as a square or a circle, and it can be formed whenever a line turns or meets, as in an S shape or a T shape. In three-dimensional forms, shape is defined by outline or silhouette. Mass may be construed as the actual or implied physical bulk, weight, and density of three-dimensional forms occupying real or suggested spatial depth. Although often used synonymously with mass, *volume* must in fact be distinguished as any three-dimensional quantity that is bounded or enclosed, whether solid or void. Thus, there can be said to exist both positive (solid) and negative (hollow) volumes.

*Size* refers to the physical magnitude of objects, elements, and quantities, but size has importance primarily in relation to expectations and to other things, which themselves have size. Relative or proportional size is termed *scale*. The principal unit of measure in human experience is man himself. With the human body as the basic module of measure, a cathedral could be seen as very large in scale, and the illuminated page of a medieval manuscript as very small in scale, although a decorative initial which covers the entire surface of a manuscript page would have very considerable scale in *proportion* to the surface space available to it. Dependent upon proportional sizes and relationships among its component elements, an art work with the dimensions of the human hand could have a *monumental* scale or indeed be miniature in scale. The student working with reproductions in a book like *Purposes of Art* must be especially alert to the significance of scale, for however much a designer may have been concerned to scale illustrations so as to respect the dimensions of subjects relative to each other as they appear on a page or on facing pages, all such illustrations have of necessity been scaled to the size of the book itself. To help diminish the difficulty of appreciating the actual size and scale of the art works and monuments reproduced in *Purposes of Art*, the dimensions for each are cited in the accompanying legends, except for objects that are inherently large or small, such as manuscript pages, drawings, prints, wall paintings, and architecture.

*Space* is as fundamental to the visual arts as color, and it is equal to color in its stubborn resistance to simple and clear explanations. Space can be seen as a hollow volume available for occupation by a form, but, like volume, space can be used positively as well as negatively. It is an extent, measurable or infinite, which can be understood as an area or a distance. Solid, three-dimensional objects, such as sculpture and architecture, exist in deep or three-dimensional space. The space of painting has been measured, traditionally, in the two dimensions of height and width. This type of space is "real" space, but even on a flat surface, the third dimension can be represented or simulated by all manner of *pictorial* techniques so as to achieve a sense of *perspective*.

These include the simple overlapping of forms and *modeling*, which is the depiction on a flat surface of three-dimensional forms by means of variations in the use of color properties. In painting, objects can be modeled to appear solid by representing receding planes, relative to a light source, in low values of local colors or in cool colors and the advancing planes in high values or in warm colors. Also principal among these techniques are the systems developed in Europe during the 15th century for attaining in two dimensions a convincing representation of solid, volumetric forms posed at varying intervals within an open space that appears to be a continuous extension into great depth and distance. In Italy, the scheme was quasi-mathematical and assumed that all parallel lines going in one direction meet at a single point on the horizon known as a *vanishing point*. Placed at intervals along the assumed parallels converging toward the vanishing point, objects were scaled in their sizes to diminish in relation to their distance from the picture. Called *linear perspective*, this was an aesthetic system intended to create an independent order of reality, a pictorial world that was an idealized equivalent of the real world. To obtain greater naturalism from the system, it was eventually modified to function with more than a single vanishing point. In its artificial way, linear perspective can be considered a successful means for making the picture space appear to be a continuation of the actual space in which the viewer stands. In northern Europe, a perspective system developed that revived pictorial techniques of spatial representation already used long before not only by the Romans but also by Chinese and Japanese painters. Called *atmospheric* or *aerial perspective*, the effects exploited by the system include the blurring of outlines, loss of detail, alternation of hues toward the cool colors, and the diminution of color saturation and value contrast. The greater the distance of the object from the viewer, the more pronounced the incidence of all these effects. Normally functioning within the perspective systems for the pictorial simulation of three-dimensionality is the technique of *foreshortening*. A painter can achieve this effect by adopting the principle of continuous diminution in size along the entire length of a form whose bulk is intended to recede into space. In *illusionistic* art the picture space that appears to extend back beyond the picture plane can have objects located on a *ground plane*, the surface represented as that on which figures seem to stand. The degree of apparent recession into the picture space can be described as *foreground, middle-ground,* and *background*.

*Illusionism* is the representation—that is, the depiction or illustration by the graphic means of the visual arts—of forms and images (human beings, flowers, the landscape, architecture, etc.) as the eye would perceive them physically to exist in the real, empirical world. In representational or illusionistic painting there often is relatively little problem in identifying subjects, although such identification may not in fact reveal the actual meaning of the works containing the subjects. The study and knowledge of the meanings to be attached to pictorial representations is known as *iconography*. *Figuration* indicates a preoccupation in painting and sculpture with the shapes of forms, whether human or abstract. *Abstraction* is the process of subordinating the real appearance of subjects to an aesthetic concept of form composed of shapes, lines, and colors. Abstraction is a matter of degree, and in some works the subjects, although highly *schematized*, are clearly apprehendable, while in others the subjects may be so thoroughly assimilated into a formal design as to seem to disappear altogether. *Nonrepresentational* art, however, makes no reference whatever to the world of persons, places, and the objects associated with them, and its formal existence is a subject unto itself.

*Composition* is the ordering or logical relationships of parts to each other and to the whole. Stated in another way, it is the imaginative disposition of all elements of subject and form—figures, objects, forms in nature, lines, planes, colors, values, textures, shapes, volumes, mass, scale, and space—so as to produce an intellectual and visual coherence. Like life, the order in art requires both unity and variety, and some of the devices for achieving unity and variety in the visual arts are the following: *Balance* is thought of as the equilibrium of opposing or self-completing forces. Balance can be developed in relation to the left and right sides of an actual or an implied axis, or it can radiate from an actual or an implied central point. Symmetrical balance has similar or identical elements arranged on either side of the axis. In asymmetrical balance an equilibrium is attained among elements dissimilar in size or shape. Repetition, or the relationship between similar or identical things, *analagous forms*, can serve to give the effect of unity. Variety can grow out of contrast. Unity and variety appear in gradation and climax, or the kind of step-by-step development that suggests direction and builds to a climax. And all these factors can be oriented in relation to the viewer, to the shape of the work at its edges, or to the volume in which it has been sited, to some stabilizing point established within the work, or yet to any one of countless points of reference that artists have succeeded in finding for the realization of their expressive purposes. An artist's search for expressiveness may in fact have caused him to exploit some one, group, or all of these means by the process of denial or conscious subversion. A harmonious composition is hardly the vehicle for expressing a troubled idea.

*Style* and *form, formal* and *stylistic analysis* —these terms are used interchangeably in commentary on the way an artist works. Form consists of the shapes, structure, and expressiveness, the total configuration of the work of art. Meyer Schapiro, an authority on style, has provided this definition: "Style is the constant form, qualities, and expression in the art of an individual or group." Both form and style are concerned with the quantitative or measurable and the qualitative or nonmeasurable aspects of art, their composition and resultant expressive effect. Form and style signify trained shaping and ordering of thoughts and feelings in the medium with which the artist is working. When we say that an artist has achieved form or a style, we recognize his mastery and individuality in art. Style can be a group as well as an individual phenomenon, and it may be revealing of the personality of one man or of an entire society. Finally, it is important to bear in mind that an artist can, through what he does with his form, create a beautiful work of art that is based on an ugly subject.

## CHARACTERISTICS, MATERIALS, AND TECHNICAL PROCESSES WITHIN THE VISUAL ARTS

Traditionally, the *pictorial* arts of *drawing, printmaking,* and *painting* have been considered the flat arts, that is, artists producing drawings, prints, and paintings have, in general, accepted the conventions of working within two dimensions, usually in a space shaped in a rectangular format. This has not, however, eliminated from their interests the very real presence of a third dimension. In fact, painters often have been preoccupied to the point of obsession with the fascinating problem of acknowledging three-dimensional space within the two dimensions of a flat surface. In modern art, the tendency has been to seek a spatial integrity that is uniquely suitable to art and to its expressive content, not to some other reality, such as nature. This has led to an increasing dramatization of the flatness inherent in the two-dimensional arts, with the third dimension construed more in terms of the picture plane and the shape of the support at its edges than to a point represented as recessed into deep space somewhere on a distant horizon or in relation to space occupied by the viewer.

*Drawing*. The surface upon which the two-dimensional arts are made is termed the *ground* or *support*. The material used to work upon the ground is known as the *medium*. The ground most often utilized for drawings is paper. The media of drawing include those which are dry —pencil (the "lead" actually made of graphite), silverpoint, charcoal, chalk, and crayon—and those that are liquid—ink and watercolor applied with pens and brushes.

The great value of a drawing is not only that it provides an exciting aesthetic experience but also that often it is the artist's most intimate expression, the most direct manifestation of his pictorial handwriting. Drawings permit us to retrace the artist's notations, experiments, and explorations. Artists usually make drawings primarily for themselves, and this private character of the drawing encourages the artist to be uninhibited and daring in ways not always followed in his painting or sculpture. An artist may stop drawing after setting down only a few strokes, for his idea may be so completely captured that further work would be superfluous. Drawings display a wealth of expressive qualities communicated by means of line, texture, shading, and composition.

Just as there is no one subject for drawings, so there is no single technique by which a perfect or beautiful drawing can be made. Although line is the most frequently used formal element in drawings, some draftsmen work in values only, and painters may wish to draw in color with a brush. The worth of drawings lies in what might be called the coding system through which the artist's feelings, knowledge, and interest in his subject are given aesthetic form.

Gesture and movement in drawing are not limited to the action of limbs. Gesture may describe the total of all movements in a drawing. Many artists drawing from a dimensional subject see it in terms of motion forward, into depth, or sideways. The human head can be schematically reduced to planes or surfaces working with or against each other—in terms of direction, outward, or away from the surface of the drawing. Also, a draftsman may seek equivalents in line and shadow for the weight associated with each part of the head.

When an artist draws a figure in movement, he may quickly and summarily indicate the general limits of the figure and the areas through which it has passed and not sharply define any one part of the figure. It is not unusual for artists trying to capture a feeling of displacement in a human figure to imagine the driving force within the body and then to establish a type of stable axis or core about which the body is seen to move.

*Printmaking*. A print is an art work realized by a duplicating process, but because in printmaking the artist works toward the print as the final expression of his idea, the resulting work has the status of an "original" art work, although it is a *multiple,* not a unique product of the artist's hand. Printmaking is a process in which the artist prepares an image upon a master plate and, using ink or similar substance as medium, causes the image to be transferred, usually by means of a mechanical press, to a ground, most often paper. An *edition* is thought of as the total number of prints made and approved by the artist. Different stages of a composition, once printed, are called *states*.

In the *relief* processes the image to be printed projects forward on the plate while the areas intended not to print are in recess. *Woodcut, wood engraving,* and *linoleum cut* are relief processes, and these plates or blocks print very much like a rubber stamp—the raised surface inked for transfer to another surface. In woodcut tones of grey and textures are simulated by the juxtaposition of black lines and white areas and by the grain, weathering, and knots of the wood. Woodcuts can be printed by a rubbing process called *burnishing*. Rice paper, the usual ground, is placed on the inked block and then rubbed firmly with the back of a wooden spoon. Pressure on the spoon controls the intensity of the blacks.

In the *intaglio* processes it is the recesses, not the projections, that are filled with ink for transfer to a surface. The techniques by which images can be sunk into a plate and then printed are *engraving, etching,* and *drypoint*. Engraving involves cutting an image into a metal plate, such as copper or zinc, with a graver or *burin,* a steel-pointed cutting tool. In this process, the image is produced from incised lines. While engraving is a medium best adapted to line, rich textures and tonalities can be obtained by interweaving and overlapping the line patterns. Engraving requires considerable control, but it is the most direct graphic technique for work on metal plates. The resistance of the metal demands that the artist exert physical force on his burin, always being careful that the metal is penetrated to just the proper depth. For printing, the plate is inked and then wiped so that the uncut areas are clean. Plate and paper pass through a press, and the paper is forced into the engraved areas, producing a slightly raised series of lines on the finished print. Drypoint, in principle, is like engraving. On a similar metal plate, the artist draws with a steel- or diamond-pointed needle. As the point cuts into the metal, it raises a furrow, or *burr*. The indentation in the metal is negligible. The rough burr holds the ink and gives the drypoint its distinguishing characteristic—its soft, modulated, velvety line. Drypoint is a tenuous medium as the burr begins to wear after successive printings. In etching, the image is cut into a metal plate by the corrosive action of acids. The image is usually drawn through acid-resistant grounds—hard ground, soft ground, wax, or stop-out varnish. The width of a line or expanse of exposed area plus the accumulated time of the plate's exposure to the acid determine the darkness and depth of line.

The *planographic* processes have plates that are completely flat; they have neither projections nor recesses. *Monotype* and *lithography* are two such processes, the latter one of the most often used in all of modern printmaking. It derives from the antipathy of grease and water, which permits an image to be drawn with a grease crayon or waxy ink upon a grained surface, such as limestone, for offset onto paper, once the stone or plate has been wetted and charged with ink. The resulting image, in its apparent freshness and immediacy of touch, is remarkably close to the original drawing on stone.

Of the *stencil* processes, the principal technique is *silkscreen,* often identified as *serigraphy*. It is a means through which a print can be realized by filling or covering the pores of silk fabric (stretched on a frame) so as to leave open areas in the form of a design, which can be transferred to paper from ink rolled over the screen and pressed through the open pores in the design areas.

*Painting*. Although color can be introduced into both the medium and the ground used for drawing and printmaking—and modern drawings and prints frequently are produced in brilliant color—it is painting that seems always to have had color as its most distinguishing characteristic. A dry powder called *pigment* is the coloring agent in artists' colors, and, depending on the binding agent or *binder* used (the substance which holds the color particles together and makes them adhere to a surface), pigments can produce such media of painting as *oil, tempera, watercolor, fresco,* encaustic, casein, and acrylic resin. These can be worked on such grounds or supports as paper, canvas, wood panel, and plaster. If the support has been given a preparatory coating, by priming and sizing, the surface thus formed is considered to be the ground, which intervenes between the painting and its support. Paints can be applied in a single layer *(alla prima)* or in many layers. In *watercolor,* transparent layers are *washes;* in oil they have the name *glazes. Scumbling* is the process of drawing opaque paint loosely over previously applied colors without obscuring them. The term for paint applied in richly textured quantities is *impasto.* Brushes, palette knives, and the artist's own fingers typically serve as the instruments fof applying paint to surfaces.

*Sculpture.* The most obvious difference between painting, for instance, and sculpture is that the latter has its existence in three dimensions; the third dimension in sculpture is a physical fact, not an illusion suggested by formal devices worked upon the flat surface of a canvas. And the complex spatial character of sculpture is such that the space surrounding its solids is an inseparable part of the total work, whether the forms and materials are dense, blocklike, and self-contained or open, sheer, transparent, perforated, and dynamically involved with space. Most sculptures either stand free or they project from a background. The former are called *freestanding,* the latter *relief.* Pronounced sculptural projection from a background is known as *high relief;* modest projection as low or *bas relief.* The aesthetic potential of bas relief is not totally dissimilar to that of the pictorial arts of painting, drawing, and printmaking.

Until the 20th century, techniques of sculpture could be characterized as *subtractive* or *additive.* Work in wood or stone involves subtracting extraneous material by means of hammers and mallets, saws, drills, chisels, gouges, files, and abrasives. For more than 2,500 years, stone sculptors have employed a point, an icepicklike tool, for cutting away the bulk of excess stone and revealing the subject's general outline. A claw chisel, shaped like a fork, is used to cut and shape the surface close to its final form, after which flat chisels and abrasives bring it to completion. Until the end of the 15th century, it was customary for painters or the sculptors themselves to cover the wood and stone with paint. Since that time, there has been a more constant admiration for the natural properties of wood and stone. The additive method of making sculpture is typified by *modeling* in clay or wax. This method is as old as stone carving, and modeled figurines have been found in prehistoric caves. The sculptor who models on a large scale constructs an *armature* of wire and pipes on which he builds up his form through countless small touches of clay. The modeling material is pliant and highly responsive to the touch and shaping action of fingers, knives, or loop-shaped instruments. When finished, the clay can also be fired in a kiln, becoming *terra-cotta,* or *cast* into plaster. From plaster molds, *bronze* casts can be made. Bronze casts are reproductions of clay, wax, or plaster originals; they are, like prints, a type of multiple. The bronze surface can be worked over, filed, and smoothed, and given a *patina,* or chemically induced color, and texture. Bronze casts have the advantages of durability, strength, and relative lightness.

Early in the 20th century, Picasso and other artists began to make sculptures involving several media. These works were fashioned by assembling and joining a wide variety of materials such as wood, cardboard, plastic, paper, and metal. This type of *construction* introduced the sculptor as a manipulator or constructor of materials and forms. Reused materials and manufactured objects have been employed by sculptors and painters (as in *collage*), thus linking the art object with the stuffs of which its environment consists. The junkyard has replaced the stone quarry for many modern sculptors. Unity and permanence can be imposed upon constructions by casting them in a single material, such as bronze. Components constructed to adhere loosely and move constitute a sculpture known as a *mobile.*

The single most important new technique of sculpture is that of welding, or cutting, metal with the oxyacetylene torch. First used in industry, the torch can create heat up to 6,000°F, which is sufficient to cut or melt many metals. Attached to gas tanks, the torch can be employed with a variety of tips, not unlike the range of brushes used by painters. With this equipment, the sculptor can cut, weld, melt, and braize one or more metals. Working with the torch permits the artist immediate and sustained involvement with his sculpture—almost as if he were drawing with pencil on paper—which enables him to make changes or corrections during the work's process and to experiment with the spatial effects made possible by metal's tensile strength.

*Architecture.* Traditionally, architecture was considered to be the art of building. Today, we are more inclined to define architecture as the art and science of enclosing space for human activity. With our modern concern for the physical and psychological well-being of a building's occupants, architecture is sometimes defined as the art, science, and social science of creating synthetic environments for human use and enjoyment. Architecture differs from engineering and ordinary buildings, such as a tool shed, in that it results from an intention to please aesthetically as well as to serve a useful purpose. Since antiquity, architecture has continued to be judged on the soundness of its construction, on usefulness matched against its purpose, and on the delight it affords those who look upon and use it.

The materials of architecture are the traditional ones of wood, clay brick, stone, and concrete, and, in modern times, steel, plastic, and reinforced concrete. The materials of architecture are used under *compression,* which is the sort of crushing strain that results when stone is placed upon stone, or under *tension,* which creates a strain that pulls materials apart, as in the cables of a suspension bridge. Most architecture takes its strength and stability from both compression and tension.

Three fundamental problems in architecture are the spanning of space, the supporting of structural members that span the space, and the enclosing of a space in such a way that the building can serve its intended purpose. Because it can both enclose space and support a roof span, the *wall* is a primary element in much architecture. An old and simple technique for supporting roofs and spanning spaces is the *post-and-lintel* method of construction, a combination of uprights supporting a crosspiece. A lintel extending beyond its supports is a *cantilever.* A lintel can be constructed as a *truss,* which, instead of solid stone or wood, is a light but strong framework made of small pieces joined so as to brace one another. The structural principle of the *arch* is such that it permits the spanning in stone or wood of a greater space between supporting members than could a lintel, due to the capacity of the curved form of the arch to divert the load—the compression of weight sustained—to the sides and downward toward the supporting uprights. The *buttress* is an upright structural element that can be made to supplement walls and posts in their support of the overhead load. The principle of the arch developed in antiquity into *vault* and *dome* construction. A *vault* is an arched roof fashioned of stone, brick, or concrete. The *tunnel* or *barrel vault* is an extension of the round arch, and to stay aloft it requires continuous buttressing along its two sides. The Romans made tunnel vaults intersect at right angles and thus realized a *groin vault,* so-called for the line at which the intersecting semicircular planes of the vaults join. Such *crossed vaults* are mutually supporting along the groins, which causes the groins to receive much of the stress of the load and carry it downward to the uprights at the four corners of the square formed by the intersecting tunnels. This in turn relieves the wall of enough of its load-bearing function to permit openings along the sides, leaving the corners solid as four legs bearing the focused weight of the vault, now divided into four sections *(quadripartite)* by the cross formed by the groins of the intersecting tunnel vaults. *Ribs* often have been used to strengthen and emphasize the groins, with the resulting arrangement called *ribbed groin vaults.* The square structural unit formed by the four corners of the crossed vaults is known as a *bay.* Altogether, the elements of the bay, once treated as a *modular* system, made possible the strong, stable, permanent, and exalted beauty of Romanesque and Gothic architecture, with its increasingly well-lighted and open interior spaces.

The *dome* is a hemispherical vault that transmits its weight evenly all along its circular base. In antiquity, the dome was supported by buttressed walls or carried by arches. Set on a square base, the dome poses the problem of joining a circular form to a round one. Two traditional solutions to the corner gaps were found in *pendentives* and *squinches.* Among modern solutions to architectural problems is the *geodesic dome,* which utilizes the geometry of the tetrahedron to create a light structure of enormous strength, one of almost infinite space-spanning potential.

It is possible to know the structural scheme of buildings through diagrams called *plans, elevations,* and *perspective views.* The plan reveals in two dimensions the arrangement and distribution of interior spaces and walls, as well as door and window openings. An elevation shows the side of a building without perspective distortion. Perspective views join elements of plan and elevation to reveal in a foreshortened rendering how a building would appear in three dimensions.

The *wall* is a form that responds with great sensitivity to the architect's expressive intent. The color, texture, and strength of the materials chosen for constructing and decorating a wall affect a building's attractiveness and its actual and apparent durability. The architect can emphasize the wall's physical substance or deny it by the use of painting, mosaic, and sculpture. Walls can also be made to play a symbolic role, as projection screens for the image and ideas the architect and his patrons wish to convey to the outside world. Such elements as *piers, columns,* and *pediments* are, for instance, status symbols of great power and dignity. In addition, the wall is a surface upon which doors, windows, and *arcades*—their size, scale, placement, and interrelationships—can be disposed so as to give architecture a distinctive quality and character, making it appear open and hospitable or closed and unreceptive. The wall permits the dramatization of its flatness or a rich *chiaroscuro* play of light over its textures and articulations. Before the age of glass walls, masonry offered architects rich expressive and design possibilities. A fundamental decision that an architect must make is whether to draw attention to the load and support functions of his elements; also whether to cause a building's exterior to reflect its interior horizontal and vertical divisions of space. The seemingly simple problem of integrating successive horizontal levels of a façade has produced countless formal solutions. The architect also makes specific choices about how to terminate walls at the top, to conceal or to reveal the roof, for instance.

Architecture offers many sensory experiences, sight and touch *and* sounds and smells, depending upon materials used and accoustical design. Before electricity and glass walls, architects orchestrated natural lighting in innumerable ways, even concealing windows from view in order to produce a luminous ambiance. Ground plans, like walls, remind us that of all the arts, architecture is historically the oldest and most consistent example of the artist's arbitrary imposition of order upon nature and human life. The plan reveals the architect's scheme for organizing space and for mobilizing the viewer. Internal architectural space is formed by the walls, floors, and roofing that enclose it. The distance between these frames affects our experience of space, as do the color, light, and texture of the container and the contained. Architecture, like Renaissance perspective, can involve us emotionally and psychologically with the experience of depth. By the rhythm of wall elements and colonnades, the architect can control the relative pace at which we instinctively seek to move through his spaces. Our experience of space becomes complex by perceiving it through and beyond walls and arcades, by the sense of limited or measureless space that a building gives. Stairways, interior and exterior, have provided some of the most dramatic encounters with space in the history of architecture.

Siting too affects our experience of architecture, whether it leads through footpaths and trees or begins abruptly with a close-range view of glass and masonry. Altogether, a sense of history helps put one in the frame of mind to appreciate moon-viewing platforms rather than electrical outlets, elegant stairways instead of elevators.

In the alphabetical section that follows, terms already defined in the essay are not redefined; for each of these a page number refers to the definition in the essay. In the essay, technical terms are set off by italic type. Within definitions, italicized terms are themselves defined in the glossary.

*abstraction*. See p. 475.
*additive sculpture*. See p. 477.
*aerial perspective*. See p. 475.
*aesthetic*. Having to do with the pleasurable and beautiful as distinguished from the useful, scientific, etc. The distinctive vocabulary of a given style. An *aesthetic response* is the perception and enjoyment of a work of art.
*aesthetics* is the branch of philosophy having to do with the nature of beauty and its relation to man.
*agora*. In ancient Greece, a market place of spiritual, legal, and commercial significance that in Roman times became the *forum*.
*aisle*. In *basilican* architecture, the longitudinal *spaces* situated parallel to the *nave* and formed by *walls, arcades,* and *colonnades*. The nave itself, having a similar form, is sometimes considered to be an aisle.
*altarpiece*. A painting, sculptural group, or *bas relief* prepared for and placed above and behind an *altar*.
*ambulatory*. Literally a place for walking, hence an *aisle* bent around the *apse* of a church allowing circulation behind the high *altar*.
*anthropomorphic*. Human characteristics attributed to nonhuman things.
*apotheosis*. Elevation to divine status; deification; glorification; exaltation; a glorified ideal.
*apse*. A semicircular *space, domed* or *vaulted,* extending the interior space of such architectural forms as Roman and Christian *basilicas;* in Western Europe most often found at the eastern end of the *nave* and serving to house the high altar.
*aquamanile*. A medieval pitcher or jug, often made in grotesque animal forms.
*arcade*. A series of *arches* supported by *piers* or *columns;* passageways with arched roofs.
*arch*. See p. 477.
*architectonic*. In *design* and *composition,* that which is *structural*.
*architecture*. See pp. 477, 478.
*architrave*. The *lintel* or lowest division of the *entablature* that in *post-and-lintel* architecture rests directly on the *capitals* of *columns*.
*archivolt*. The molding that frames an arch.
*armature*. See p. 477.
*atmospheric perspective*. See p. 475.
*atrium*. A Roman *form* that is an open court constructed within or in relation to a building.
*avant-garde*. A French term meaning "advanced guard," used to designate innovators whose experimental art challenges the values of the cultural establishment or even those of immediately preceding avant-garde *styles*.
*axis*. An imaginary *line* passing through a figure, building, or groups of *forms* about which component elements are organized, their direction and focus actually establishing the axis.
*background*. See p. 475.
*balance*. See p. 475.
*barrel vault*. See p. 477.
*basilica*. A rectangular *plan* building, with an *apse* at one or both ends, originating in Roman *secular* architecture and early adopted as the *form* most suited to the needs of Christian worship.
*bas-relief*. See p. 477.
*batter*. The inward tilt of a *wall* from the base upward.
*bay*. See p. 477.
*Bodhisattva*. In Mahayana Buddhism, an enlighted being who compassionately refrains from entering *nirvana* so as to save others. A potential *Buddha* and worshiped as a deity.
*bronze*. An alloy of copper and tin and the metal most frequently used in cast sculpture.
*the Buddha*. Gautama Buddha (563?–483 B.C.), the great religious teacher of Asia whose message was that suffering is inherent in life and that one can be best liberated from it by mental and moral self-purification. A major *subject* in Asian art.
*burin*. See p. 476.
*buttress*. See p. 477.
*calligraphy*. The art of beautiful writing, but, more broadly, any controlled, flowing, continuous use of *line* in painting, drawing, and sculpture; the character and quality of an artist's linear work; the *graphic* evidence of gesture in the visual arts.
*campanile*. In Italy, a bell tower, especially one that is *freestanding,* often next to but separate from a church building.
*canon*. A body of principles, rules, standards, or norms; a criterion for establishing measure, *scale,* and *proportion*.
*cantilever*. See p. 477.
*capital*. The upper member of a *column,* serving as transitions from *shaft* to *lintel* or *architrave*.
*cartoon*. A full-scale, preparatory drawing for a *pictorial composition,* usually a large one such as a wall painting or a tapestry. Also a humorous drawing or caricature.
*casting*. A process using plaster, clay, wax, or metal that, in a liquid form, is poured into a *mold*. When the liquid has solidified, the mold is removed, leaving a replica of the original work of art from which the mold was taken. See also p. 477.
*catacomb*. Associated with Early Christian Rome, an underground burial place consisting of *galleries* with recesses containing tombs.
*cathedral*. The official church of a bishop containing his "cathedra" or throne; a church that traditionally has been given *monumental* and magnificent architectural form.
*cella*. An enclosed chamber, the essential feature of a *Classical* temple, in which the cult statue usually stood.
*ceramics*. Objects made of clay that have been baked into a permanent *form;* often decorated with *glazes,* then fired to fuse the glazes to the clay body.

*chevet*. The *apse* or *choir* of a *basilican*-plan church surrounded by an *ambulatory* and a series of radiating chapels.

*chiaroscuro*. Literally "light-dark"; in art, the use of *value* contrasts to represent the effects of light and shadow.

*choir*. The complex at the east end of a *basilican*-plan church beyond the *crossing*, which could include *apse*, *ambulatory*, and radiating chapels. See *chevet*.

*chroma*. See *saturation;* also p. 475.

*civilization*. A *culture* in an advanced state of self-realization, thought to be characterized by marked efficiency and achievement in such realms as art, science, and letters, as well as in personal security and dignity.

*Classical*. The art of ancient Greece and Rome and subsequent stylistic imitations of Western antiquity. With a lower case "c," classic can mean established excellence, whatever the period, *style*, or *form*.

*clerestory*. A row of windows in the upper part of a *wall;* also, in church architecture, the upper portion of the interior walls pierced by windows for the admission of light.

*cloister*. In monastic architecture, a court bounded by covered walks that usually have *arcades* or *colonnades*.

*codex*. A manuscript prepared on leaves or pages and bound together like the modern book. It replaced the scroll form, or rotulus, of antiquity.

*coffer*. In architecture, a recessed panel in a ceiling. Coffering can lighten the weight of a massive-looking ceiling.

*collage*. From *papiers collés*, the French for "pasted papers"; a *composition* deriving from Cubism and made by pasting together on a flat surface such originally unrelated materials as bits of newspaper, wallpaper, cloth, cigarette packages, and printed photographs.

*colonnade*. A row of *columns*, usually spanned or connected by *lintels*.

*colonnette*. A small *column*, performing a decorative as well as a *structural* function.

*color*. See p. 474.

*column*. A cylindrical post or *support* which often has three distinct parts: *base*, *shaft*, and *capital*.

*complementary colors*. See p. 474.

*composition*. See p. 475.

*compression*. See p. 477.

*connoisseurship*. A discriminating knowledge of the qualities of art works and their *styles*.

*construction*. The process of making a sculpture by assembling and joining a wide variety of materials, such as wood, cardboard, plastic, paper, and metal. See also p. 477.

*content*. See p. 474.

*contour*. In the *pictorial arts*, an outline that forms the boundary of one *shape* and defines it in relation to other shapes and is expressively handled so as to suggest fullness and recession of *forms* and varieties in *texture*, such as those in bony structure and soft tissue. Contrasts with simple outline, which is no more than the boundary of a form defining a silhouette. See also p. 474.

*cool color*. See p. 474.

*Corinthian*. The most elaborate of the three *Classical orders* of temple architecture, characterized by slender *fluted columns* topped by highly carved, ornate *capitals* decorated with forms derived from the acanthus leaf. See also *Doric* and *Ionic*.

*cornice*. Any horizontal architectural member projecting from the top of a *wall;* in *Classical* architecture the crowning member of the *entablature*.

*Counter-Reformation*. A 17th-century movement within the Roman Catholic Church made in opposition to the Protestant Reformation of the 16th century.

*crossing*. In a *cruciform* church, the space formed by the intersection of the *nave* and the *transept*.

*cross vault*. See p. 477.

*cruciform*. Arranged or shaped like a cross.

*crypt*. A *vaulted* chamber, wholly or partly underground, that usually houses a chapel and is found in a church under the *choir*.

*culture*. The values and the system of their interrelationships that inform a society, motivate its behavior, and cause it to be functional to the general satisfaction of its members and to have a distinctive quality and character.

*design*. The patterned organization of a *composition*, usually seen in the arrangement of *lines* or the light-and-dark elements, rather than in *color*.

*dome*. See p. 477.

*Doric*. The oldest of the *Classical styles* of temple architecture, characterized by simple, sturdy *columns* that rise without a *base* to an unornamented, cushionlike *capital*. See *Ionic* and *Corinthian*.

*drawing*. See p. 476.

*drypoint*. See p. 476.

*earth work*. An intervention in open nature by the artist for no purpose other than the enactment of his own ideas of art.

*edition*. See p. 476.

*elevation*. See pp. 477, 478.

*empirical*. Based on experiment, observation, and practical experience without regard to science and theory.

*enamel*. Colored glass applied to metal in powder or paste form and fused by firing.

*engaged column*. A *columnlike form* projecting from a *wall* and articulating it visually.

*engraving*. See p. 476.

*entablature*. In architecture, that portion of a building between the *capitals* of the *columns* and the roof, including in *Classical* architecture the *architrave*, *frieze*, and *cornice*.

*entasis*. An almost imperceptible swelling in the *shaft* of a *column*.

*Epiphany*. January 6, the anniversary of the coming of the Wise Men to Christ at Bethlehem.

*etching*. See p. 476.

*eurythmy*. Harmonious proportion or movement.

*Evangelist*. One of the authors of the four Gospels in the Bible: Matthew, Mark, Luke, and John. Respectively their symbols are an angel, a lion, an ox, and an eagle, all derived from Revelations 4:6–10.

*fenestration*. The arrangement of windows, or all openings, in the *walls* of a building.

*figural, figuration*. In painting and sculpture, *subject* and *form* that have been derivated from the human or animal form. In contemporary *abstract* and *nonrepresentational* art, the term also signifies a general preoccupation with the *shapes* of *forms*.

*figure-ground*. In the *pictorial* arts, a phrase referring to an ambiguous, interdependent spatial relationship between forms and the backgrounds against which they have been placed.

*fluting*. Vertical channeling, roughly semicircular in section and used principally on *columns* and *pilasters*.

*flying buttress*. A *masonry* strut or segment of an *arch* that carries the *thrust* of a *vault* to a *buttress* positioned away from the main portion of the building; an important structural element in the architecture of Gothic cathedrals.

*foreground*. See p. 475.

*foreshortening*. See p. 475.

*form*. A *shape* or a *mass*, or, more comprehensively, the total configuration of the shapes, structure, and expressiveness that make an art work. See also pp. 474–476.

*formal analysis*. See pp. 475, 476.

*forum*. A precinct that as developed in ancient Roman cities provided for public assembly of a religious, commercial, judicial, and educational sort.

*freestanding*. See p. 477.

*fresco*. A process of painting on plaster, either dry or wet, wherein the *pigments* are mixed with water and become chemically bound to the plaster; a *medium* perfected during the Italian Renaissance.

*frieze*. The central portion of the *entablature* between the *architrave* and the *cornice;* any horizontal decorative or sculptural band.

*gallery*. A long and narrow room or passage, such as that in the *nave walls* above the *aisles* of a *basilican plan* church or that in a *catacomb*.

*genre*. In the *pictorial* arts and sculpture, the representations of everyday life and surroundings for their own sake.

*glaze*. In *oil painting*, a transparent film of paint laid over dried underpainting; in *ceramics*, a thin vitreous coating fused to a clay body by firing in a kiln.

*Gospels*. Ascribed to Matthew, Mark, Luke, and John, the four Biblical accounts of the birth, life, death, and resurrection of Jesus Christ.

*gouache*. *Watercolor* rendered opaque by the addition of a filler such as zinc white.

*graphic arts*. Vaguely related to the linear element, a term that identifies the visual arts of *drawing*, *printmaking*, typographic design, advertising design, and the technology of printing.

*graphic*. Demonstration and description by visual means.

*Greek cross*. A cross in which all the arms are the same length.

*groin vault*. See p. 477.

*ground*. See p. 476.

*ground plane*. In the *pictorial* arts, the surface *represented* as that on which figures seem to stand.

*hatching*. A *graphic* device by which a series of closely spaced parallel *lines* serve to indicate a *shaded* area.

*hieroglyphic*. A picture or a *symbol* of an object standing for a word, idea, or sound; developed by the ancient Egyptians into a system of writing.

*hue*. See p. 474.

*icon*. Greek for *image,* used to identify panel paintings made under Greek Orthodox influence that represented the image of a holy person—Christ, Mary, or a saint; such works often imbued with sanctity.
*iconography*. See p. 475.
*idealization*. The *representation* of objects, individuals, and events according to a *stylized,* perfected, preconceived model; a kind of *aesthetic* distortion of perceived reality.
*idol*. A *representation* or *symbol* of a deity used as an object of worship.
*illumination*. The medieval art of decorating the pages of manuscripts with ornamental initials, patterns, and illustrations, often in gold, silver, and bright color.
*illusionism*. The endeavor of the artist to *represent* as completely as his *formal* means may permit the visual phenomena of the real world.
*incising*. Cutting into a surface with a sharp instrument.
*Inquisition*. A former Roman Catholic tribunal established to discover and suppress heresy.
*intaglio*. See p. 476.
*intarsia*. Inlay work, primarily in wood and sometimes in mother-of-pearl, marble, etc.
*intercolumniation*. The space or the system of spacing between *columns* in a *colonnade*.
*Ionic*. One of the Greek *Classical* styles of temple architecture, which developed in Ionia in Asia Minor and is distinguished by slender *fluted columns* and by *capitals* decorated with volutes and scrolls. See also *Doric* and *Corinthian*.
*jamb*. The upright piece forming the side of a doorway or window frame; on the *portals* of Romanesque and Gothic church architecture, the locus of figural sculpture.
*keep*. The massive central tower and strongest part of a castle, used as a dwelling place and, in case of attack, as a final point of defense.
*keystone*. The topmost stone and the last to be placed in an *arch*.
*kiln*. An oven capable of controlled high temperatures in which clay objects are baked.
*labyrinth*. A place full of intricate passageways and blind alleys; a maze.
*landscape*. In the *pictorial* arts, the *representation* of scenery in nature.
*Latin cross*. A cross in which the vertical member is longer than the horizontal member, through whose midpoint it passes.
*line*. See p. 474.
*linear perspective*. See p. 475.
*lintel*. See p. 477.
*lithography*. See p. 476.
*liturgy*. A rite or body of rites prescribed for public worship.
*local color*. See p. 475.
*mahlstick*. A light, inflexible wooden rod, three or four feet long, which the painter uses as a support or rest to steady his brush or hand while executing particularly detailed and exacting work.
*masonry*. In architecture, stone- or brickwork.
*mass*. See p. 475.
*medium*. See p. 476.
*megaron*. In Minoan and Mycenaean times, a large, rectangular living hall with a hearth at the center and four columns supporting the roof, the space approached through a porch supported by two *columns* and a vestibule.
*memento mori*. Latin for "remember that you must die"; a reminder often symbolized by a skull.
*metope*. In the *frieze* of a *Doric entablature*, the panel between the *triglyphs*, often a surface decorated with *relief* sculptures.
*middle-ground*. See p. 475.
*miniature*. Broadly, any very small work of *pictorial* art, especially drawing and painting in an *illuminated* manuscript.
*Minotaur*. The issue of union between Pasiphaë, the wife of King Minos of Crete, and a sacrificial bull given to Minos by Poseidon, the Greek god of water; a monster with a bull's head and a man's body kept in the *Labyrinth* built on Crete by the architect Daedalus.
*mobile*. See p. 477.
*modeling*. See p. 477.
*module*. A basic unit of measure taken as a principle for determining the major divisions and *proportions* of an object, figure, building, or site.
*mold*. A hollow, or negative, container that produces a *cast* by giving its form to a substance placed within it and allowed to harden.
*monastery*. A dwelling place where monks live in community for spiritual purposes.
*monochrome*. A single *color* or the *value* variations of a single *hue*.
*montage*. A *composition* formed of pictures or portions of pictures previously photographed, painted, or drawn.
*monumental*. A work of art or architecture that is grand, noble, timeless, and essentially simple in *composition* and execution, whatever its *size*.
*mosaic*. An art medium requiring the use of small pieces of colored glass or stone *(tesserae)* fixed to or imbedded in a background material, such as cement or plaster.
*motif*. The *subject* or idea of an art work, such as *still life* or *landscape*, or an individual feature of a *subject* or *form*, usually one that recurs or predominates in the *composition*.
*mudra*. Any of a series of subtle hand gestures in the figural art and classical dancing of India, made to *represent* certain feelings.
*multiple*. See p. 476.
*mural*. A painting on a *wall*, usually large in *size*.
*mystical*. Having a spiritual meaning or reality that can be known only by intuition, insight, or similar subjective experience.
*myth*. A legend or story that seems to express the world view of a people or explain a practice.
*narthex*. A porch or vestibule of a church.
*nave*. The great central *space* in a church; in *basilican* plans the space extending from the entrance to the *apse*, or to the *crossing* or *choir* if these exist.
*nef*. A silver or gold table furnishing made in the form of a ship and intended to hold small quantities, such as salt, and utensils or simply to be decorative.
*nirvana*. The *Buddhist* idea of heavenly peace; the final beatitude that transcends suffering through the extinction of desire and individual consciousness.
*nonrepresentational*. See p. 475.
*oil painting*. The process of painting with a *medium* formed of ground colors held together with a binder of oil, usually linseed.
*order*. In *Classical* architecture, a style *represented* by a characteristic design of the *column* and its *entablature;* see *Doric*, *Ionic*, and *Corinthian*. Also the arrangement imposed upon all elements within a *composition;* in addition, a harmonious arrangement.
*painting*. See pp. 476, 477.
*patina*. See p. 477.
*pediment*. In *Classical* architecture, the triangular *space* (gable) at the end of a building, formed by the ends of the sloping roof and the *cornice;* also an ornamental feature having this shape.
*pendentive*. A concave, triangular piece of masonry (a triangular section of a hemisphere), four of which can be made to support a *dome* over a square *structure*.
*peripheral vision*. The ability to see to left and right so that objects outside the direct line of vision register on one's consciousness.
*perspective*. See p. 475.
*pictograph*. A prehistoric drawing or painting on a rock wall; a picture or image, usually *stylized*, that *represents* an idea; also writing using such means.
*pictorial*. See p. 476.
*picture plane*. See p. 474.
*pier*. A *mass* of *masonry* rising vertically to support an *arch, vault,* or other roofing member.
*pietà*. A devotional image of the sorrowing Virgin holding the dead Christ.
*pigment*. See p. 476.
*pilaster*. In architecture, a shallow, flat vertical member projecting from a *wall* surface and, like a *column*, articulated as a *base, shaft,* and *capital*. Usually more decorative than *structural*.
*pillar*. Any vertical architectural member—*pier, column,* or *pilaster*.
*plan*. See pp. 477, 478.
*plane*. See p. 474.
*planography*. See p. 476.
*polychrome*. Several *colors* rather than one *(monochrome)*.
*portcullis*. A strong gate or grating of iron made to slide up and down in grooves and used to close the gateway of a castle or fortress.
*portal*. An imposing door and the whole architectural *composition* surrounding it.
*portico*. A porch in the *Classical* manner, having a roof supported by *columns* and usually having an *entablature* and a *pediment*.
*post-and-lintel*. See p. 477.
*pottery*. See *ceramics*.
*primary colors*. See p. 474.
*printmaking*. See p. 476.
*proportion*. See p. 475.
*psalter*. A book of the Psalms found in the Bible.
*pylon*. The major entrance to an Egyptian temple, having in its developed form *battered* walls divided into twin towers capped with large cavetto moldings.
*reinforced concrete*. A building material composed of concrete with rods or webs of steel imbedded in it.
*relief*. See p. 476, 477.
*reliquary*. A small box, casket, or shrine for keeping sacred relics, usually made and decorated of precious materials.
*representation*. See p. 475.
*rhythm*. The regular repetition of a form.
*rib*. See p. 477.

*ribbed groin vault*. See p. 477.
*rustication*. The method of cutting and laying *masonry* so as to emphasize the joints and recesses between blocks.
*sanctuary*. A consecrated, sacred, or holy place; in Christian architecture, that part of the building where the altar is placed; also a refuge.
*sarcophagus*. A stone coffin.
*saturation*. See p. 474.
*scale*. See p. 475.
*schematize*. The process of reducing the identifying characteristics of a form—the human head, a plant, a building, etc.—to its diagrammatic essentials; a process of *abstraction*.
*scriptorium*. The workroom in a medieval monastery for the copying and the *illumination* of manuscripts.
*sculpture*. See p. 477.
*secondary colors*. See p. 474.
*section*. See p. 477, 478.
*secular*. Not religious, but relating to the wordly or temporal.
*serigraphy*. See p. 476.
*shading*. See p. 474.
*shaft*. The part of a *column* between the *capital* and the *base*.
*shape*. See p. 475.
*silkscreen*. See p. 476.
*Siva*. One of the Hindu triad of gods—Brahma, Vishnu, and Siva—who represents the principle of destruction and is worshiped as the gracious creator sustaining the world.
*size*. See p. 475.
*space*. See p. 475.
*squinch*. A *lintel* constructed to span the *space* between two *walls* that meet at right angles to form a corner, for the purpose of bridging the gap between the square *shape* of a building and a round *dome* that covers it. The squinch thus formed is often supported from below by a small *arch*.
*state*. See p. 476.
*statue*. A *freestanding figural* sculpture.
*stencil*. See p. 476.
*stigmata*. Marks resembling the wounds of the crucified Christ; in holy persons, such as St. Francis of Assisi, the physical manifestation of a deep mystical union with the suffering of Christ.
*still life*. In the *pictorial* arts, an arrangement of inanimate objects—fruit, flowers, pottery, etc.—taken as the *subject* or *motif* of a work of art.
*stoa*. In the *agoras* of ancient Greece, a building of one or two stories in the form of a *colonnade* or roofed portico providing space for a walkway and shops, offices, and storerooms.
*string course*. In architecture, a horizontal band or molding used as a decorative element on an exterior *wall*, usually reflecting interior *structure*.
*structure*. The *compositional* relationships in an art work; a building or other constructed architectural unit; the operative framework that supports a building.
*style, stylistic analysis*. See pp. 475, 476.
*stylize*. To simplify or generalize forms found in nature for the purpose of increasing their aesthetic and expressive effect.
*stylobate*. In Greek temple architecture, the upper step of the base that forms a platform for the *columns*.
*subject*. See p. 474.
*subtractive sculpture*. See p. 477.
*support*. See p. 476.
*symbol*. A *form*, image, sign, or *subject* standing for something else; in the visual arts, often a visible suggestion of something invisible.
*synoptic*. Affording a general, comprehensive, broad, or common view.
*synthesis*. The deduction of independent factors or entities into a compound that becomes a new, more complex whole.
*tabernacle*. A receptical for a holy or precious object; a container placed on the altar of a Catholic church to house the consecrated elements of the Eucharist.
*taste*. The evidence of preference having to do with enjoyment and appreciation.
*tempera*. A painting technique using as a *medium pigment* mixed with egg yolk, glue, or casein.
*tensile*. Capable of *tension*.
*tension*. See p. 477.
*terra-cotta*. Baked clay used in *ceramics*, sculpture, and architectural decoration; also a reddish-brown *color* similar to the color of baked clay.
*tesserae*. The bits of colored glass and stone used in *mosaic*.
*texture*. See p. 475.
*thermae*. Public bathing establishments in ancient Rome providing not only swimming facilities but also all the resources and opportunities of a superior social club.
*thrust*. A strong continued pressure, as in the force moving sideways from one part of a *structure* against another.
*tone*. The general coloristic quality of an art work; color gradations as these might be expressed in degrees of *saturation* and *value*.
*transept*. In a *cruciform* church, the whole arm set at right angles to the *nave*, which makes the *crossing*.
*triforium*. In church architecture, an *arcaded* area in the *nave wall* system that lies below the *clerestory* and above the *gallery*, if there is one, and the *nave arcade*. It can be open like a gallery or be sealed (blind).
*triglyph*. In the *frieze* of the *entablature* of the *Doric order*, the grooved vertical stone tablet that alternates with the metopes.
*trumeau*. An upright structural member placed in the center of a *portal* to support the *lintel* spanning the *space* between the two main lateral uprights; in medieval architecture often embellished with sculptural decoration.
*truss*. See p. 477.
*tunnel vault*. See p. 477.
*tympanum*. In medieval architecture, the surface enclosed by a *lintel* and an *arch* over a doorway; in *Classical* architecture, the recessed face of a *pediment*.
*value*. See p. 474.
*vanishing point*. See p. 475.
*vault*. See p. 477.
*vehicle*. The liquid in which *pigments* are dispersed to make paint.
*vellum*. Calfskin prepared as a *support* for writing or painting, especially in medieval manuscripts.
*verisimilitude*. The appearance of being true to the reality of the tangibly present world.
*void*. A hollow or empty *space*.
*volume*. See p. 475.
*votive*. Something offered in devotion, in supplication, or in fulfillment of a vow.
*wall*. See p. 478.
*warm colors*. See p. 474.
*wash*. See p. 477.
*watercolor*. *Pigments* mixed with water-soluble gum. Works executed in watercolor are characterized by the transparency of the *washes* possible in the *medium* and brilliance produced by the white paper showing through the transparent films of color. See also p. 477.
*woodcut*. See p. 476.
*Zeus*. The supreme god of the ancient Greek religion; the great father of gods and men who enforced the moral law and punished all who defied him.

# Index

References are to page numbers. Italic type identifies pages on which illustrations appear. (Pl.) following an italicized number indicates a color plate and the page where it can be found. The terms defined in the Glossary (pp. 474–481) have not been cited in the index.

# Photographic Sources

References are to figure numbers unless indicated Pl. (plate).

A.C.L., Brussels (479); A.C.L.–Art Reference Bureau, Ancram, N.Y. (149, 154, 161–163, 234–235, 321); Harry N. Abrams, Inc., New York (Pl. 78); Aero-films Ltd., London (317–318); Agraci–Art Reference Bureau, Ancram, N.Y. (22, 300, 409, 412, 416, 418, 465); Alinari–Art Reference Bureau, Ancram, N.Y. (11–13, 78, 133, 150, 153, 168, 171–172, 175–176, 182–184, 186, 188, 192–195, 197–202, 207, 209–211, 214–216, 219–220, 230–233, 238, 268, 293–294, 297, 307, 322–323, 326, 328, 330, 365–366, 371, 373, 386, 389, 396, 402, 405–406, 411, 414, 481, 487, 492); American School of Classical Studies, Athens, Agora Excavations (354); Anderson–Art Reference Bureau, Ancram, N.Y. (164–167, 169–170, 185, 187, 190–191, 203, 218, 229, 286, 296, 325, 369–370, 385, 404, 505); Archaeological Survey of India (55, 57); Archives Photographiques, Paris (21, 69–70, 98, 100, 144, 180, 251, 461, 480, 507); Art Forum, New York (612); Art Reference Bureau, Ancram, N.Y. (5–7, 15, 79–80, 145, 262, 276, 305, 426, 559, 565–566); Bailey, J. Edward, III, Detroit (Pl. 99); Baker, Oliver, New York (532); Barnes, Carl F., Jr., and Archives Photographiques, Paris (97); Beville, Henry, Alexandria, Va., and *Time* Magazine, New York (618); Boenzi, Neal, and *New York Times* (398); Boesch, Ferdinand, New York (525); Böhm–Art Reference Bureau, Ancram, N.Y. (378); Braun, Ernest, San Anselmo, Calif. (401); Brogi–Art Reference Bureau, Ancram, N.Y. (173–174, 324); Brown Brothers, New York (397); Bruckman–Art Reference Bureau, Ancram, N.Y. (16, 221–222, 228, 239, 252, 258, 431); Bruggmann, Werner, Winterthur, Switz. (41); Bulloz, Paris (502); Bulloz–Art Reference Bureau, Ancram, N.Y. (417, 489); Burckhardt, Rudolph, New York (476, 516); Burckhardt, Rudolph, New York, and Leo Castelli Gallery, New York (302, 471, 600); Cantor, Jay, New York (613); Leo Castelli Gallery, New York (Pl. 68); Chevojon Frères, Paris (536); Clements, Geoffrey, Staten Island, N.Y. (602); Clements, Geoffrey, Staten Island, N.Y., and Sidney Janis Gallery, New York (527); Courtauld Institute, London (420); Cserna, George, New York (337); Decker, Dr. Heinrich, and Umschau Verlag, Frankfurt-am-Main, W. Ger. (320); Durand-Ruel, Paris (482); Eastfoto, New York (Pl. 21); Editions du Cercle d'Art (copyright), Paris (581); Elisofon, Eliot, New York (512); Fleming, R. B., & Co., London (92–93, 265); Fogg Art Museum, Harvard Univ., Cambridge (58); Fotocielo, Rome (364, 372, 374–375, 384); Fototeca Unione, Rome (62, 204–205, 282, 309, 312, 355, 359); Fototeca Unione–Art Reference Bureau, Ancram, N.Y. (327, 458); Frantz, Alison, Princeton, N.J. (84); French Embassy Press and Information Division, New York (67, 95, 329); French Government Tourist Office, New York (102, 104, 393–395); French Institute of Indology (56); Fujisaki, Kazio, and Orion Press, Tokyo/Scala, New York (314); Futagawa, Y. (331); German Archaeological Institute, Istanbul (132); Giraudon, Paris (245, 248, 259, 287, 290, 298, 407, 504); Government of India Information Service (59, 345); Green, Ron, Portland, Ore. (400); Gross, John, and Stable Gallery, New York (603); Guerrero, Pedro E., New Canaan, Conn. (449); Solomon R. Guggenheim Museum, New York (473); Gundermann, Würzburg (495); Hammarskiold, Hans, and Tiofoto, Stockholm (474); Henrard, R. (392); Hervé, Lucien, Paris (82, 119); Hirmer Fotoarchiv, Munich (51, 64, 65, 74, 86, 127, 275, 281, 288, 303); Holton, George, Photo Researchers, Inc., New York (113); Horn, Prof. Walter W., Univ. of California, Berkeley (105); Houvet, E., Chartres (10); Howald, Gerhard, Berne, Switz. (Pl. 55); Italian State Tourist Office, New York [ENIT] (362, 390); Jackson, Errol, London (522); Sidney Janis Gallery, New York (Pl. 93); Jeiter, N., Aachen, W. Ger. (315); Jobert, Luc, Paris (493); Kasmin Limited, London (599); Kersting, A. F., London (316); King, John, New Canaan, Conn. (Pl. 67); Kleinhempel, Ralph, Hamburg, W. Ger. (Pl. 88); Kondas, Thomas R., Indianapolis (243); Koninklijk Museum voor Schone Kunsten, Antwerp (424, Pl. 46); Langenbach, Randolph, Cambridge, Mass. (338); Lauros-Giraudon, Paris (Pl. 45); Lazarus, Marvin, White Plains, N.Y. (620); Lerner, Frank, New York, and *Time* Magazine, New York (616–617); Loose, Louis, Brussels (Pl. 29); MAS, Barcelona (289, 455, Pl. 19); MAS–Art Reference Bureau, Ancram, N.Y. (558); Marburg–Art Reference Bureau, Ancram, N.Y. (106, 125, 142, 246, 264, 367, 496, 561); Marlborough Fine Art (London) Ltd. (Pl. 98); Marlborough Gallery Inc., New York (444); Pierre Matisse Gallery, Corp., New York (Pl. 81); Merkle, P. and E., Basel, Switz. (114); Metropolitan Museum of Art, New York (156); Meyer, K.G., Vienna (Pls. 32, 79); Moore, Peter, New York, and Intermedia Institute, New York (615); Morse, Ralph, *Life* Magazine, © Time, Inc., New York (Pl. 2); Museum of Modern Art, New York (538, 619, Pls. 65, 86, 91); National Gallery of Canada, Ottawa (Pl. 96); Nelson, O. E., New York, and Paul Rosenberg & Co., New York (Pl. 77); Nickel, Richard, Park Ridge, Ill. (Pl. 62); Nohr, Rosmarie, Munich (575); O'Sughrue, Claude, Montpellier, Fr. (436); Partridge, Rondal, Berkeley, Calif. (344); Powell, Josephine, Rome (71–72); Rabin, Nathan, New York (528, Pl. 94); Reed, John (Pl. 84); Rheinisches Bildarchiv, Cologne, W. Ger. (256); Rockefeller Center, New York, and Impact Photos Inc. (399); Rosenblum, Walter, New York (475); Rosenthal, Prof. Earl, Chicago, Ill. (196); Roubier, Jean, Paris (73); Saebens, Hans, Worpswede, W. Ger. (361); Scala, New York (Pls. 6, 20, 22–25, 27–28, 30, 50, 53, 59); Schiff, John D., New York (450, 511); Service de Documentation Photographique de la Réunion des Musées Nationaux, Paris (Pls. 42, 63); Sieber, Prof. Roy, Indiana Univ., Bloomington (30); Smith, G. E. Kidder, New York (115–116, 118); Sollars, E. A., Winchester, Eng. (138); Soprintendenza alle Gallerie, Florence (179, 217); Spanish National Tourist Office, New York (17); Steinkopf, Walter, Berlin (253, 435); Stoedtner-Prothmann Associates, Inc., Baldwin, N.Y. (311, 352); Studly, Adolph, New York (498); Sunami, Soichi, New York (517); Thomas, Frank J., Los Angeles (601); Trans World Airlines, New York (83, 308); Vaering, O.–Art Reference Bureau, Ancram, N.Y. (427); Vatican Photoarchives, Rome (280); Verkehrsverein, Tübingen (360); Viollet, Roger, Paris (313, 428); Von Matt, Leonard, Buochs, Switz. (61, 212); University Art Museum, Univ. of California, Berkeley (Pl. 100); Ward, William E., Cleveland (77); Webb, John, London (Pl. 58); Wildenstein & Co. Ltd., London (579); Wyatt, A. J., Philadelphia (3, 423, 445–446, 468, Pls. 66, 87).

Fig. 139 from *Dictionnaire des Miniatures du Moyen Age et de la Renaissance* by Erhard Aeschlimann (Milan: Ulrico Hoepli, 1949; reprinted Nendeln: Kraus-Hoepli, 1969). Fig. 353 redrawn from *Athenische Mitteilungen*, XXVII and XXIX. Fig. 343 from *Le Corbusier* 1910–1965, *the Complete Works*, edited by Willy Boeser and Hans Girsberger (Zürich: Verlag für Architektur Artemis, 1967). Fig. 356 redrawn from *Bolletino della commissione archeologica communale di Roma*, 61 (1933). Figs. 339–342, 346 from *Chandigarh*, by Norma Evenson (Berkeley: University of California Press, 1966). Figs. 107, 109 from *A History of Architecture on the Comparative Method* (17th ed.), by Banister Fletcher (New York: Charles Scribner's Sons, 1963). Fig. 123 from *Romanesque Painting* by André Grabar and Carl Nordenfalk (Geneva–New York: Skira Books, 1957). Fig. 358 from *The Architecture of the Roman Empire*, by William L. MacDonald (New Haven: Yale University Press, 1965). Fig. 376 from *The Art of Building Cities*, by Camillo Sitte, tr. by Charles T. Stewart (New York: Reinhold, 1945). Fig. 101 from *Architectural Symbolism of Imperial Rome and the Middle Ages*, by E. Baldwin Smith (copyright © 1956 by Princeton University Press). Fig. 363 from *Italy Builds* by G. E. Kidder Smith (New York: Reinhold, 1955). Figs. 332–336 from *Katsura: Tradition and Creation in Japanese Architecture* by Kenzo Tange (Tokyo: Zokeisha Publications Ltd.). Fig. 349 from *How the Greeks Built Cities*, by R. E. Wycherley (London: Macmillan & Co. Ltd., 1949). Fig. 387 from *Town and Square*, by Paul Zucker (New York: Columbia U. Press, 1966).